Torpedoes Away!

AT CLOSE QUARTERS

PT Boats in the
United States Navy

by

CAPTAIN ROBERT J. BULKLEY, Jr.

USNR (Retired)

with a Foreword by

PRESIDENT JOHN F. KENNEDY

and an Introduction by

REAR ADMIRAL ERNEST McNEILL ELLER, USN (Retired)

Director of Naval History

Naval Institute Press
Annapolis, Maryland

Naval Institute Press
291 Wood Road
Annapolis, MD 21402

Originally printed in 1962 by the Government Printing Office for the
Department of the Navy

First Naval Institute Press paperback edition, 2003

Library of Congress Cataloging-in-Publication Data
Bulkley, Robert J. (Robert Johns), 1911–1962.
       At close quarters: PT boats in the United States Navy / by Captain
Robert J. Bulkley, Jr.; with a foreword by President John F. Kennedy and an
introduction by Rear Admiral Ernest McNeill Eller.
       p. cm.
       Originally published: Washington, D.C.: U.S. Government Printing
Office, 1962.
Includes bibliographical references and index.
ISBN 1-59114-095-1 (alk. paper)
1. Torpedo boats—United States—History—20th century. 2. United States—
History, Naval—20th century. 3. World War, 1939–1945—Naval operations,
American. I. Title.
V833 .B85 2003
359.3'258'0973—dc21
                                                                2002041057

Printed in the United States of America on acid-free paper ∞
10 09 08 07 06 05 04 03   9 8 7 6 5 4 3 2 1

"PT boats filled an important need in World War II in shallow waters, complementing the achievements of greater ships in greater seas. This need for small, fast, versatile, strongly armed vessels does not wane."

—JOHN F. KENNEDY

FOREWORD

In the dark days of the American Revolution when the strongest
efforts on land seemed always frustrated by British seapower,
General Washington said,

"In any operation, and under all circumstances,
a decisive Naval superiority is to be considered as a
fundamental principle, and the basis upon which every
hope of success must ultimately depend."

The next year the French fleet defeated the British off the Virginia
Capes making possible the victory at Yorktown. Since that day the
destiny of our country has been inextricably interwoven with the sea.
This was never more true than in the giant World War II that involved
all seas and most of mankind. To fight the sea war we needed many
types of ships, large and small, from aircraft carriers and battleships
to PT boats.

Small though they were, the PT boats played a key role. Like
most naval ships, they could carry out numerous tasks with dispatch
and versatility. In narrow waters or in-fighting close to land they
could deliver a powerful punch with torpedo or gun. On occasion
they could lay mines or drop depth charges. They could speed
through reefs and shark infested waters to rescue downed pilots or

secretly close the shore to make contacts with coast watchers and guerrilla forces. PT boats were an embodiment of John Paul Jones' words:

"I wish to have no connection with any ship that does not sail fast for I intend to go in harms way."

Naval strength must function from shore to shore and on inland waters where the mobility and flexibility provided by ships can be employed to support land operations. PT boats filled an important need in World War II in shallow waters, complementing the achievements of greater ships in greater seas. This need for small, fast, versatile, strongly armed vessels does not wane. In fact it may increase in these troubled times when operations requiring just these capabilities are the most likely of those which may confront us.

The thorough and competent account herein of over-all PT boat operations in World War II, compiled by Captain Robert Bulkley, a distinguished PT boat commander, should therefore prove of wide interest. The widest use of the sea, integrated fully into our national strength, is as important to America in the age of nuclear power and space travel as in those stirring days of the birth of the Republic.

Introduction

"Histories" may or may not "make men wise." Certainly one of the hopes of the Navy Department in recording them in World War II and since has been that from the recorded facts men would learn for future leadership to serve our beloved nation.

Detailed action reports and war diaries were required from ships and higher commands in World War II. These were not only for clearer analysis that we might better fight the war but were to serve as source material for studies and histories in the future.

To supplement these fundamental building blocks of history, the Navy prepared in manuscript many command and administrative histories. For the most part the commands themselves prepared these histories. Some are outstanding, some are dreary; but all are akin in that they were prepared by participants who had just lived through the events recorded. The writers also had at hand the maximum amount of the command's file material likely ever to be available since most of the never ebbing tide of paperwork must be "given the deep six." Therefore they should have captured information on events which is not now discoverable.

These histories were prepared "for the record," not for publication. They have served their purpose admirably as a fount of irreplaceable information. We in the Navy turn to them constantly for "how it was done" in the Tenth Fleet, in the Mediterranean, in the Pacific, in the South Atlantic—in the many parts of the world where the complex, many faceted Navy serves America and freedom. Organization, procedures followed, lessons learned as in antisubmarine warfare—these we daily profit by in many parts of the Navy. The manuscripts have also been invaluable to serious civilian historians.

Some of the manuscript histories reached a quality of excellence that merited publication when the need and demand should arise. One of this select group appears in the following pages. This thorough and objective account of the operations of PT boats in the U.S. Navy in World War II was prepared in the year after V–J Day by an officer who served in them through most of the war in the far reaches of the Pacific.

He knew and loved these small, fast craft with hornet sting. They played their part with zest in the far reaching, powerful Navy team. He gave to the research into the records, into the memories of other participants, and to the writing itself the same zest. As a result he produced a shipshape manuscript.

Over the past 16 years a steady flow of researchers have gone to this manuscript for information, some for naval studies in the important area of close in fighting, some to write for publication. The number interested in it has grown measurably recently, hence publication seemed appropriate so that it will be readily available wherever needed.

Preparation for publication has included careful reading and some slight revision by Capt. F. Kent Loomis and Mr. Dean Allard of this office and by Captain Bulkley. Mr. Allard and his colleague, Mr. Bernard F. Cavalcante, also checked the manuscript for accuracy against the large body of records in our possession which now include captured ones not available to the author in 1945–46.

Captain Bulkley has also generously given his time in helping Comdr. D. V. Hickey and Lt. Comdr. Mary J. Linderman of the Curator Section of this office select the illustrations and in providing some not available in our large collection. Mr. Jesse B. Thomas has supervised the proofing, make-up, indexing, and other problems in voyaging from manuscript to finished book, assisted by Mr. Donald R. Martin.

This manuscript was prepared under the same overall "rules of the road" as the incomparable Samuel Eliot Morison series. That is to say, this office provided the source material, space and support in writing, checking of facts, review of manuscript and other aid helpful to a writer. The fabric of the story, its presentations and conclusions, however, are Captain Bulkley's.

It is really, of course, the book of the PT boat sailors. The Navy list in World War II included at the height some 7,000 ships of PT Boat-LCI size and up. Yet so vast were the duties throughout the world that ships were almost always in short supply for any task. Over 80 types of warships made up this global fleet. Sailors on mighty aircraft carriers and battleships or even minesweeps and LSTs called PT boats "spit kits," only partly in jest. Not so with most career officers in the Navy and especially not those who had long served America at sea—like Admiral Nimitz. He knew that the responsibilities of the fleet were great and the ships too few for far spreading tasks. He knew that PTs could not, of course, do the tasks of the mighty aircraft carriers, the battleships, cruisers, the workhorse destroyers, the silent submarines, or the many necessary special types like the amphibs, the net ships, the degaussers, the rocket ships. He knew the thousand and one duties that had to mesh in successful accomplishment to win the war—and that some of these could be accomplished best only by the small, daring PT boats.

This book tells how this particular type valiantly carried out necessary duties as their crews, mostly "citizen sailors," rose to the desperate challenge to freedom in the highest traditions of patriotism, skill and courage that have served America well at sea from her earliest struggles. It is hoped that readers will find in this book fuller appreciation of this stirring tradition of sacrifice and service without which our nation cannot endure as the leader of the hopes of men.

E. M. Eller,
Rear Admiral, USN (Retired),
Director of Naval History.

In Memoriam

Captain Robert J. Bulkley, Jr., Mid-Watch, 23 November 1962

Just as we received advance page proofs, and a few hours before he was to come to this office to assist us in putting the last touches on his fine history, soon after 0300, 23 November, Captain Bulkley sailed on to broader seas than those he cruised valiantly for America in World War II. Fittingly, his departure was in the last hour of the mid-watch—an hour that in many ships in many seas in World War II called American sailors to General Quarters as they prepared for dawn action. Many who read this book will know that in Captain Bulkley we have lost a gallant sailor, a true gentleman, and a fine American.

Preface

My involvement with PT boats began on a bright autumn day in 1941, when I cadged a ride on one of the new Elco 77-footers being fitted out for Squadron 2 at the New York Navy Yard. It was love at first sight. The deep-throated roar of the engines, the speed and maneuverability, the powerful armament, the obvious enthusiasm of the officers and crew would have been quite sufficient to win a convert, even without the proselytizing of Lt. Earl Caldwell, the squadron commander, who spoke with rapid intensity about the new "weapons of opportunity."

In June of 1942 I received orders to report to the Motor Torpedo Boat Squadrons Training Center at Melville, R.I. From then until the end of the war, except for a few months temporary duty in New York, I served in PT's, mostly in the Southwest Pacific—New Guinea and the Philippines. On V–J Day I was in Leyte Gulf. Soon thereafter a dispatch arrived from Washington asking if I would remain on active duty to write a history of motor torpedo boats. This book is the result.

The manuscript was delivered to the Navy Department at the end of 1946 as one of a number of manuscripts the Department had prepared on the Navy's widespread operations while these were fresh in participants' minds. Each became an important supplement to the source materials of the records.

Since the inauguration of President John F. Kennedy, when a PT boat was hauled down Pennsylvania Avenue in the inaugural parade as a reminder of Lieutenant Kennedy's wartime heroism, the public has shown renewed interest in PT's. Stories about the boats and the President's naval career have appeared in the public press, and several authors have published books on Lieutenant Kennedy and motor torpedo boat operations in the Solomons campaign.

People have been touched by these accounts, I believe, because they deal with basic and enduring qualities—courage, pertinacity, endurance, devotion. These qualities Lieutenant Kennedy possessed in high degree; they also were common property of officers and men of the PT service in every area of operations. It is appropriate that the record of their performance should now be published. PT's were indeed "weapons of opportunity" and the men who ran them seized opportunity aggressively, carrying the fight to the enemy in an astonishing variety of missions.

One of the few changes I have made in readying the manuscript for publication is its title. Originally I had called it *PT: A History of Motor Torpedo Boats in the United States Navy*. This was descriptive, but stodgy. The new title conveys the spirit better: PT's met the enemy at closer quarters (and with greater frequency) than any other type of surface craft. The crews of no other vessels experienced so high a degree of personal engagement with the enemy.

Also, the crews lived at close quarters. Two or three officers and 12 to 15 men on a small boat got to know each other very well and, of necessity, became a close-knit organization. The intimacy of close quarters, the fact that each man was individually important to his boat's success, together with the shared experience of close combat, made for an extraordinary esprit de corps.

I have tried to be conservative in dealing with claims of damage to the enemy. Damage to any major ship has been claimed only when it can be substantiated from enemy records. Some of the boats, particularly in the early days of the war, made claims of damage or sinking which cannot be substantiated. This is not surprising. The boats fought in the dark, usually under enemy fire. The boat captains and crews were eager to do damage and honestly thought they had done damage. There were heartbreaking cases like that of Lieutenant Kelly in the Philippines, who was certain he had torpedoed a Japanese cruiser. From Japanese sources we learn that he did, indeed, hit the cruiser, but the torpedo failed to explode.

Long as this book is, it involved selection and rejection. To those PT veterans whose exploits are unrecorded here, I apologize. More or less arbitrary pruning became necessary to keep the manuscript within reasonable bounds.

The faults of this book are my own; I had a completely free hand in writing it. If it has merit, it is because I have tried to set forth as simply as I know how the actions of brave men who fought at close quarters.

I should like to acknowledge my great indebtedness to my three commanding officers in the PT service, Captain John D. Bulkeley, USN; Rear Adm. Morton C. Mumma, Jr., USN (Retired); and Rear Adm. Selman S. Bowling, USN (Retired), all of whom have given generous assistance in preparation of this manuscript.

During my tour of duty in the Office of Naval History in 1946, my immediate superior was the late Capt. Archibald D. Turnbull, USNR (Retired), for whose kindness and encouragement I shall be forever grateful. At that time I received valuable help from Comdr. Walter M. Whitehill, USNR, and from the Misses Philibert, whose knowledge of Navy files and records was encyclopedic.

Lt. Frank A. Tredinnick, Jr., USNR, and Lt. Comdr. Harrison L. Bennett, USNR, prepared an administrative history of PT boats and gave me free access to their manuscript, their records, and their time. Much of Part II of this volume, covering development of PT boats, is based on their work.

Many PT officers passed through Washington in 1946, and I was able to review their action reports and other records with them. I have corresponded with many others. My thanks to all of them, in particular to Capt. Stanley M. Barnes; Comdr. James A. Danver, USNR (Retired); Comdr. Richard J. Dressling, USN (Retired); Lt. Comdr. Joseph R. Ellicott, USNR; Rear Adm. John Harllee, USN (Retired); Capt. Ronald K. Irving; Capt. Robert B. Kelly; Comdr. A. Murray Preston, USNR (Retired); Lt. Comdr. Weston C. Pullen, USNR (Retired); Capt. Hugh M. Robinson; the late Comdr. L. K. Scott, USN (Retired); Lt. Richard C. Simpson, USNR; Lt. Comdr. Henry S. Taylor, USNR; Lt. (jg.) Vance W. Torbert, USNR; Lt. George O. Walbridge II, USNR (Retired); Rear Adm. Thomas G. Warfield, USN (Retired); Lt. Comdr. Robert C. Wark, USNR; and Comdr. John K. Williams, USN (Retired).

I am indebted to John L. Page, RdM2c, USNR, who gave me the history of the destruction of PT 509. Since he was the sole survivor, the story was available from no other source.

I wish to express appreciation to Rear Adm. Ernest M. Eller, USN (Retired), Director of Naval History, and his assistant, Capt. F. Kent Loomis, USN (Retired), for bringing the manuscript to publication. Special thanks are due to Dean C. Allard, Jr., of the Naval History Division, for invaluable assistance in editing the manuscript and for a monumental job of checking it against original sources—including enemy records not available to me in 1946—to insure accuracy. Mr. Jesse B. Thomas of Naval History prepared the thorough index to this book and handled many other matters, while his associate, Mr. B. F. Cavalcante, assisted in preparation of charts and checking the manuscript.

Finally, to the officers and men of the PT service, my friends and former shipmates, this book is dedicated with affection, admiration, and respect.

ROBERT J. BULKLEY, Jr.,
Captain, USNR (Retired).

CHATHAM, PA., *June 2, 1962.*

Contents

Part IV. SOUTHWEST PACIFIC—*CONQUEST OF NEW GUINEA*

Part V. THE ALEUTIANS—*A BATTLE AGAINST WEATHER*

Illustrations

(Illustrations identified by numbers preceded by 80–G or 19–N are official U.S. Navy photos in USN collection in National Archives; those numbered with NR&L(MOD) prefixes are in the historical collection in U.S. Naval Photographic Center, Washington, D.C.)

PART I

Into Action—*Pearl Harbor and the Philippines*

Into Action—*Pearl Harbor and the Philippines*

1. THE LINEUP

WHEN JAPANESE planes attacked Pearl Harbor on the morning of December 7, 1941, there were three squadrons of PT's in the U.S. Navy. Motor Torpedo Boat Squadron 1, commanded by Lt. Comdr. William C. Specht,[1] had 12 boats based at Pearl Harbor, all of which opened fire on the attackers.

Motor Torpedo Boat Squadron 2, under Lt. Comdr. Earl S. Caldwell, was in the New York Navy Yard, completing the fitting out of 11 boats which, loaded on the aircraft ferry ships *Hammondsport* and *Kitty Hawk*, were to leave New York 10 days later to augment the defenses of the Panama Canal. These boats were not to meet the enemy until nearly a year later, when, with desperate optimism, they were to stand out night after night in the path of the mighty Tokyo Express at Guadalcanal.

Motor Torpedo Boat Squadron 3, six boats commanded by Lt. John D. Bulkeley, had arrived in Manila Bay on September 28. During the 4 dark months of the hopeless defense of the Philippines, the officers and men of Squadron 3 carried the fight to the enemy with determination and shining courage until the boats could fight no more.

Until war came, PT's in the U.S. Navy were an untried type. They had never met the test of action, and no standard doctrine for their employment had been established. But by the end of January, 1942, Rear Adm. Francis W. Rockwell, Commandant of the 16th Naval District, was able to write from Corregidor, "These boats are proving their worth in operations here, having sunk two ships of three to five thousand tons and three landing boats."

---

[1] Ranks and rates throughout this book are those held by the individuals at the time of the events described. Unless otherwise indicated, all ranks are USN.

These boats did prove their worth: the Navy built more of them. On December 7, 1941, there were 29 PT's; on December 7, 1943, there were more than 29 squadrons. PT's met the Tokyo Express at Guadalcanal. They cut enemy barge supply lines in the upper Solomons and along the New Guinea coast. They torpedoed German cargo lighters in the Mediterranean, and overcame E-boats in gunnery duels in the English Channel. They contributed to the rout of Japanese task forces in the Battle of Surigao Strait, and successfully countered vicious Kamikaze attacks at Mindoro. Under cover of darkness they freely landed agents, scouts, and reconnaissance parties throughout the Solomons, New Guinea, and the Philippines, and on the coasts of France and Italy. PT's were in more frequent contact with the enemy, and at closer range, than any other type of surface craft. They specialized in close-range, close-to-shore attack, and everywhere demonstrated that they could hurt the enemy with proportionately small damage to themselves.

2. "THEY LOOK LIKE JAPS"

On the morning of December 7, 1941, six PT's, the 20, 21, 22, 23, 24, and 25, were moored at the Pearl Harbor Submarine Base in three nests of two boats each, alongside and ahead of the YR–20, a covered barge which served, for lack of anything better, as tender for Squadron 1. Aboard the barge the boat crews were eating breakfast. The Squadron Duty Officer, Ens. N. E. Ball, USNR, was standing on the edge of the barge. Looking out across Kuahua Island, he saw planes in the sky, and watched them idly for a moment as they started to dive toward Battleship Row and Ford Island just beyond. Then four things happened, almost simultaneously. Ensign Ball recognized Japanese insignia on the wingtips; a chief petty officer at his elbow remarked, "They look like Japs"; the first bomb dropped, and Ensign Ball plunged into the messhall, shouting, "MAN THE GUNS!"

PT's in those days were lightly gunned—two pairs of .50-caliber machine-guns mounted in power-driven turrets, but in a matter of seconds all were firing. Joy Van Zyll de Jong, GM1c, and George B. Huffman, TM1c, who had been sitting on the deck of PT 23, got a slight head start on the men from the messhall. They vaulted into the 23 boat's turrets and claimed first blood with hits on a low-flying plane carrying one torpedo, which crashed in flames near Kuahua Island. They also hit a torpedo plane flying over Magazine Point. It burst into flames and fell near Halawa, behind the Submarine Base.

Across Southeast Loch from the Submarine Base, about halfway to Ford Island, the other six boats of the squadron were being loaded aboard the USS *Ramapo*, an oiler, for shipment to the Philippines. PT's 27, 29, 30, and 42 were in cradles resting on the *Ramapo's* deck. PT's 26 and 28 were in cradles on the dock beneath the huge hammerhead crane which had been about to hoist them aboard the oiler. To reduce fire hazard during shipment, the gasoline tanks of all six PT's had been blanketed with carbon dioxide. Consequently the crews could not start the gasoline engines to compress the air which in turn forced oil through cylinders to move the power turrets. The boat crews quickly cut the hydraulic lines, freeing the turrets from the brake of residual hydraulic pressure. Then each pair of .50-caliber machineguns went into action with a four-man crew: one man to fire the guns, two men to slew the turrets around by hand, and an officer to direct and coordinate the slewing and firing. The *Ramapo's* guns were firing, too. Though her starboard 3-inch guns were blanked off by the hammerhead crane on the dock, they managed to fire from time to time, to the acute discomfort of the crews of the PT's in cradles on the dock, whose decks were just high enough to catch the muzzle blast. One bomb struck near the port bow of the *Ramapo,* midway between the repair ship *Rigel* in the berth ahead and the heavy cruiser *New Orleans* opposite. The PT's, undamaged, poured out more than 4,000 rounds of .50 caliber. They appeared to be hitting Japanese planes, but so many ships were firing simultaneously that it would be futile to attempt to make specific claims.

3. MANILA BAY

The *Ramapo* was to have carried those six boats to Manila Bay, to be transferred to Squadron 3. But the Japanese descended so swiftly on the Philippines and with such concentrated force that shipping anything into Manila Bay was out of the question. The boats were put back into the water at Pearl Harbor, leaving Squadron 3 to do the best it could with its six boats, PT's 31, 32, 33, 34, 35, and 41.

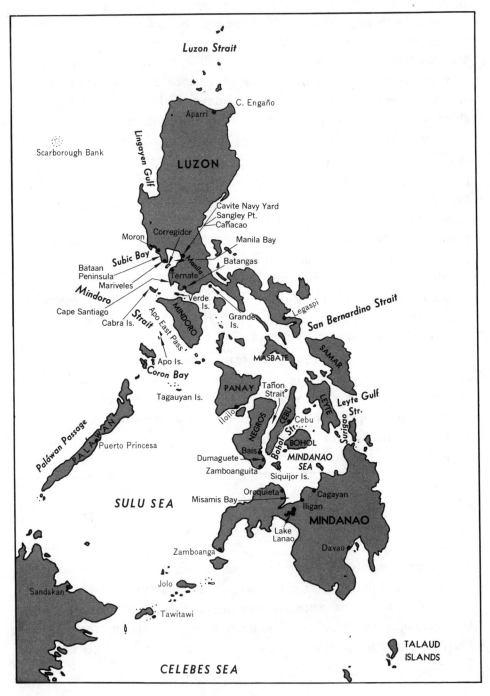

The Philippines.

The PT's of Squadron 3, based at the Cavite Navy Yard, went into action on December 10, when the Japanese made their first heavy air attack in the Manila Bay area. The air raid warning system was working well that day, giving the boats plenty of time to get underway into Manila Bay, where they could maneuver freely. The first planes started bombing Nichols Field at 1247.[2] A few minutes later a wave of some 35 started to work over shipping in Manila Bay. It was high-level bombing, 20,000 feet, well beyond the range of the PT's .50-caliber machineguns and the pair of .30-caliber Lewis guns which the Squadron 3 boats had installed in single mounts on the forward deck. Then five bombers peeled off deliberately and started to dive on the PT's. Theoretically, it was possible for a PT to wait until a diving plane reached its release point, and then, by putting the wheel hard over, to avoid the bomb. The boats proved the theory—not a bomb came close. Besides, PT 31 claimed to have shot down two planes and PT 35 one.

The first bomb fell on the Navy Yard at 1314. For more than an hour thereafter, 3 waves of 27 bombers each swept over, out of antiaircraft range, dropping their explosives at will. Practically every bomb fell within the Navy Yard limits, with direct hits on the powerplant, dispensary, torpedo repair shop, supply office, warehouse, signal station, commissary store, barracks, officers' quarters, and several ships, tugs, and barges along the waterfront. The entire yard and one-third of the city of Cavite were ablaze.

PT's could outmaneuver the planes; their spares and equipment could not. The only spares saved were nine engines which John Bulkeley had had the foresight to store in private garages in Manila. Of these, three were lost on January 2 when Manila was invaded. Of the other six, subsequently lightered to Corregidor, two were lost on January 9 when the Corregidor North Dock was bombed. The last four had to be left on Corregidor when the squadron departed in March. Nearly as serious as the loss of spares was the loss of thousands of drums of 100-octane gasoline.

The destruction of the Navy Yard was so complete that all remaining facilities had to be set up in new locations, well dispersed in anticipation of future air raids. Squadron 3 moved to Sisiman Bay, a little cove just east of Mariveles Harbor on the southern tip of the Bataan Peninsula, but not until after the boats had done yeoman service on the afternoon of December 10 transporting wounded from the Navy Yard to the hospital at Cañacao.

[2] Time is given according to the Navy 24-hour clock; e.g.: 0545 for 5:45 a.m., 1200 for noon, 1732 for 5:32 p.m.

4. THE FLEET WITHDRAWS

The first few weeks at Sisiman Bay were discouraging. The squadron took over a small fishing dock and a few native nipa huts ashore. Each morning John Bulkeley visited headquarters to receive orders for the night's operations. The boats made routine, nonproductive patrols of the Bataan coast north of Manila Bay, and along the Batangas Peninsula to the south, as far as Verde Island. Doctrine demanded that PT's patrol in two- or three-boat sections, so that if one boat should find itself in trouble, there would be another at hand to give assistance. But because there were so few boats, so few spares, so little gasoline, prudence had to make concessions. Seldom could more than one PT be spared for a patrol. Often one PT was accompanied by a YP, a small patrol vessel, either the *Maryanne,* the *Perry,* or the *Fisheries II,* or, until they departed from the area, one of two four-stack destroyers, the *Pillsbury* and the *Peary.* As the Japanese closed their net, nerves became tense and there were false reports of sightings along the Bataan coast. Many fruitless PT searches resulted.

PT's required constant maintenance. The only repair facilities available were the old submarine tender *Canopus,* anchored at Mariveles, which turned out miracles of improvisation for the boats, and the drydock *Dewey* which lifted each boat in turn. PT 32 had an accidental explosion in the engine-room. She was out of action for weeks.

During December most of the Asiatic Fleet moved south. The Japanese had command of the air and bombed Manila at will. Rear Admiral Rockwell moved his headquarters to Corregidor on December 21. Three days later he had a final conference with Adm. Thomas C. Hart, Commander in Chief Asiatic Fleet, at Admiral Hart's headquarters in the Marsman Building in Manila. During the conference the Marsman Building was bombed three times. Admiral Rockwell learned that Admiral Hart was moving south to be with the operating fleet, leaving Admiral Rockwell in command of all naval forces in the Manila area. On his return to Corregidor that evening, Admiral Rockwell found that Gen. Douglas MacArthur, President Manuel Quezon, and Francis B. Sayre, American High Commissioner to the Philippines, had also moved to the Rock.

On Christmas night Admiral Hart departed on the submarine *Shark.* Manila was about to be declared an open city, so Admiral Rockwell sent his aide, Lt. (jg.) M. M. Champlin, USNR, to arrange for destruction of gasoline and oil stores in the city. Lieutenant Champlin accomplished this with the help of oil company executives in Manila.

On December 26 Admiral Rockwell reported to General MacArthur for duty. During the day Japanese planes made determined efforts to sink gunboats, PT's, and especially the destroyers *Pillsbury* and *Peary*. Unwilling to risk the destroyers further, Admiral Rockwell ordered them south on the 27th. On December 28, the day Manila was declared an open city, Admiral Rockwell decided in conference with Capt. John Wilkes, Commander Submarines Asiatic Fleet, that "due to the increasing danger and difficulty of service in Mariveles, shortage and limitation of fuel and total lack of rest for personnel between patrols, as well as the likelihood of the Japanese blocking Manila Bay entrance," the basing of submarines in the area was no longer practicable. Captain Wilkes, his staff, and his submarines departed at the end of December, leaving behind the tender *Canopus* and the submarine rescue vessel *Pigeon* to serve as advance operating facilities for such submarines as might come into the Manila area.

Admiral Rockwell's forces, then, consisted of *Canopus* and *Pigeon;* three small, shallow-draft gunboats originally built to patrol Chinese rivers: *Mindanao, Luzon,* and *Oahu;* three old minesweepers: *Quail, Finch,* and *Tanager;* five tugs: *Genesee, Vaga, Napa, Trabajador,* and *Ranger;* three small patrol vessels: *Maryanne, Perry,* and *Fisheries II;* and the PT's of Motor Torpedo Boat Squadron 3.

On December 22 a convoy with 76 Japanese transports began to unload in Lingayen Gulf, about a hundred miles away.

The U.S. Army completed its withdrawal into Bataan Peninsula on December 31. On January 2 the Japanese Army entered Manila.

5. SS *"CORREGIDOR"*

On the night of December 17 there was a large explosion in Sisiman Cove. Looking out across the entrance to Manila Bay, the men of Squadron 3 could see many flashing lights on the water. Lieutenant Bulkeley immediately got PT's 32, 34, and 35 underway. At the edge of the minefield at the entrance of the bay they found the water thick with oil and dotted with survivors of the SS *Corregidor,* a Filipino ship carrying evacuees from Manila to Australia. Leaving the harbor on a faulty course, the *Corregidor* had struck a mine and gone down almost immediately.

The PT crews rigged ladders and lines over the side, and worked until they were exhausted hauling the wet and oily passengers aboard. Not until they put the survivors ashore at Corregidor and aboard the SS *Si-Kiang* at Mariveles were they able to count them. When they did, they could scarcely believe the total. The three boats had picked up 296 passengers, of whom all but 7 survived. PT 32, a 77-foot boat designed to carry 2 officers and 9 men, had taken aboard, in addition to its own crew, 196 passengers from the *Corregidor*.

6. "MOTOR TORPEDO BOATS ARE RAPIDLY DETERIORATING"

PT 33, patrolling south of Manila Bay with the *Pillsbury* on the night of December 24, went hard aground on a coral reef 5 miles north of Cape Santiago. On Christmas Day, PT's 31 and 41 made three attempts to pull the 33 boat off the reef, but could not move her. At 0830 December 26, after everything useful had been stripped from the boat, PT 33 was set afire to prevent her from falling into the hands of the enemy.

The War Diary of the Commandant 16th Naval District has a Christmas Day entry: "Motor Torpedo Boats are rapidly deteriorating due to lack of spare parts and bad gasoline. Because of emergency trips and patrol duties their crews are becoming exhausted and the boats are in poor operating condition.

"Due to the above facts and because one Motor Torpedo Boat ran aground during the night of 24–25 December it was decided to abandon the Verde Island patrol and Army authorities were advised of same. Remaining Motor Torpedo Boats are to be made available as despatch boats and for attack on enemy vessels in the immediate vicinity."

PT's kept patrolling the west coast of Bataan, however, frequently in pursuit of false sightings. Until relieved by Army-controlled Philippine "Q" boats, a type somewhat similar to PT's, the boats of Squadron 3 also made nightly patrols of Manila Bay.

Shortages of food contributed to the exhaustion of the men. On December 16 all naval personnel in the area were put on two meals a day. As time went on both quantity and quality of rations deteriorated.

Normal routine for all shore-based personnel was to call all hands at daybreak; turn to until breakfast at 0800; turn to until supper at 1600; turn to until dark. Men who went on night patrol could not follow this routine, but they worked many extra hours to make sure that their boats would be ready for action.

Bad gasoline was another problem. Lieutenant Bulkeley reported that much of his gasoline and oil had been sabotaged. "The former," he said, "was found to contain a soluble wax deposit in large quantities. This foreign substance clogged gas strainers and carburetor jets to such extent as to cause most unreliable operating, necessitating the cleaning of carburetors and strainers hourly. It was never known when a boat engine would stop. It eventually became necessary to open the gas tanks and thoroughly clean with the limited means available. The lubricating oil contained sand."

Gasoline was not only bad; it was becoming scarce. Much was lost in the bombing of the Navy Yard; much more when the stocks in Manila had to be destroyed. More was lost on December 19 when bombs destroyed most of the gasoline dispersed in drums on Sangley Point. Eight days later, 550 drums of gasoline which had survived bombing were destroyed to prevent capture. On December 29, one of the two large gasoline dumps on Corregidor received a direct hit and was completely destroyed.

7. VISIT TO BINANGA

When Lieutenant Bulkeley reported at headquarters on January 18, he received his orders in one concise paragraph, signed by Capt. Herbert J. Ray, Admiral Rockwell's Chief of Staff. They read: "Army reports four enemy ships in or lying off Binanga Bay (4 miles north of Moron). Force may include one destroyer, one large transport. Send two boats attack between dusk and dawn."

Lieutenant Bulkeley rode PT 34, temporarily commanded by Ens. Barron W. Chandler, USNR, in the absence of Lt. Robert B. Kelly, the squadron executive officer, who was in the Corregidor hospital with an infected finger. With the 34 was PT 31, Lt. Edward G. DeLong.

The two boats proceeded to the mouth of Subic Bay, at the northwestern end of the Bataan Peninsula. There, they separated in dead blackness, the 34 to creep up the western side of Subic and across to the entrance of Binanga Bay, a narrow finger of water indenting Bataan on the east side of Subic Bay. The 31 was to skirt the eastern side of Subic and rendezvous with the 34 at Binanga's entrance.

Entering Subic Bay half an hour after midnight, the 34 was challenged by a light on Biniptican Point, a mile on the port beam. The boat slowed from 18 knots to 10, and continued to sneak in. Then, on the starboard hand, a fieldpiece started firing from shore south of Binanga Bay. John Bulkeley thought it might have been firing at PT 31, on the other side of the bay. A little further on a small vessel flashed a light challenge. The 34 headed for this vessel, but could not see her clearly, so changed course to the east to meet the 31. Other lights flashed from Grande Island, a mile to the north, and from Ilinin Point, just south of Binanga Bay. Machine guns opened from Ilinin Point. The 31 was not at the rendezvous, so the 34 idled out into Subic Bay. Half an hour later the 31 was still not at the rendezvous. The 34 went in alone. Five hundred yards inside Binanga Bay a two-masted freighter loomed ahead. The ship challenged. PT 34 replied by firing two torpedoes. One stuck in the tube, a hot run, but the other cleared and exploded in less than a minute. Retiring at top speed, the crew of the 34 observed a fire, followed by two large flashes, in Port Binanga.

They could not stop to watch. Shore batteries had opened fire, and the crew had their hands full with the hot run on deck. With no water resistance to brake the propellers, the turbines of a torpedo build up such speed and heat that the turbines and casing may disintegrate. Then white-hot metal fragments fly out for yards around, fast and deadly as bullets. The only way to stop a hot run is to close a valve in the air line to the torpedo's combustion pot. This involves immediate contact with the roaring, hissing torpedo which may fly to pieces at any moment.

John Martino, CTM, knew what to do and did it. He stopped the hot run. But the torpedo was still hanging more than halfway out of the tube. The sea was choppy. Every time the bow of the boat went down, a wave washed over the torpedo's warhead, turning the blades of the impeller. With sufficient turns the warhead would be fully armed. Then a blow of 8-pound force or more would explode the torpedo—the boat—and the crew. Again Martino knew what to do and did it. He straddled the torpedo hanging out over the water and stuffed a wad of toilet paper into the impeller blades to stop them from turning. Four hours later the torpedo jolted harmlessly into the sea.

In the morning Lieutenant Bulkeley reported to Admiral Rockwell that he had scored a hit on a ship in Binanga Bay. Admiral Rockwell told him that Army observers, posted on Mariveles Mountain with 20-power binoculars, saw the ship sink. It was believed to have been a 5,000-ton merchant ship armed with 5.5-inch guns, which had been shelling Army positions in the

West Bataan sector. However, Japanese records captured after the war failed to confirm such a sinking.

Bulkeley also reported the 31 had not returned. Nothing had been heard from her crew.

8. END OF THE 31

The 31 had scarcely started its slow patrol along the eastern shore of Subic Bay before it was in trouble. The now familiar wax deposit clogged the strainers of both wing engines. Then the center-engine fresh water cooling system became airbound. Helpless, the 31 had drifted on a reef. Then a 3-inch gun near Ilinin Point started firing at the 31. Lieutenant DeLong walked out anchor and repeatedly attempted to back off. After 3 hours his reverse gears burned out and his boat was still aground. He gave the order to abandon ship.

The men removed the engine room canopy, lashed mattresses to it, and lowered it over the side. Ens. William H. Plant, USNR, the second officer, shoved off on the raft with the 11 men of the crew, while Lieutenant DeLong remained behind to destroy his boat. He chopped holes in the gasoline tanks, damaged the hull with hand grenades, and set the boat afire. Then he took to the water.

For an hour and a half, while his boat burned and exploded, Lieutenant DeLong tried to find the raft. At last he clambered across the reef to the beach. Shortly after dawn he found tracks in the sand half a mile to the south. He followed them to a clump of bushes where he found nine of his men. Ensign Plant, Rudolph Ballough, MM1c, and William R. Dean, QM3c, were missing: they were never seen again.

Just to the south, near the village of Moron, Japanese forces were attacking. Japanese planes were overhead.

"During the morning," Lieutenant DeLong reported, "the infantry fire discontinued and the artillery bursts drew further north and west, leading me to believe that the Japanese were retreating. If this continued I was determined to make a run for our own lines around the beach at about 1500, believing that our chances would be better during daylight. In the meantime I had planned as an alternate method, obtaining two or three bancas and making our way by night around into Bagac Bay to beach at dawn. From our vantage point I had already spotted one large banca about one-half mile toward Moron. We had obtained canvas for use as sail and had stripped barbed wire entanglements for rigging.

"Shortly before 1500 our artillery dropped back toward Moron and I abandoned any hope of making it around the beach. At about 1530 there being no planes in the air I sent two men out to investigate the bancas.

"At this time Japanese soldiers could be heard to the eastward and could be seen occasionally to the northward and along the beach in the vicinity of the mouth of the stream north of us. Four men were investigating a banca about a half mile north of us. My men were underarmed, having only six pistols and one rifle among the ten men, so I had ordered that unless we were rushed by superior numbers we were to allow any scouts to come in to the clump and then club them with the butt of a pistol or rifle.

"At about 1700 the two men returned and reported that the two bancas appeared to be in good condition but required out-rigging. At this time we sighted from our tree lookout what appeared to be two light armored cars or light tanks about one mile north heading down the trail toward the stream north of us. The bridge over this stream was partially broken down as I had been up there earlier in the afternoon looking unsuccessfully for water.

"At twilight we left our clump, took interval and made our way around to the bancas, rigged them and shoved off at 2000 with Japanese soldiers at this time within 200 yards of the beach.

"We had found two paddles, one board and two shovels for paddling plus the gear for rigging a sail if the wind was favorable. I also had obtained a tow line to tow the small banca.

"When we shoved off I wished to get well clear of the beach before attempting sailing. At about 2100 both bancas capsized and practically all equipment was lost. After righting the bancas we had two bailers and two paddles left between the two bancas. With this we managed to become more or less seaworthy and proceeded out well clear of Panibatujan Point then set course approximately southeast toward Napo Point with the small banca towing the larger one.

"At about 0130 I made the first attempt to round Napo Point but hit a very strong head wind. We continued to head around until about 0300 when my men were exhausted and we were barely holding our own so I decided to chance a landing at dark. We pulled in the lee and I picked the point for a landing.

"We landed at about 0330 in the vicinity of Napo Point, beached the bancas, crossed a barbed wire entanglement and found ourselves against a steep cliff. I kept my men right there until dawn when we were spotted by Philippine Army forces and identified ourselves. The spot I had picked for a landing was such that at high tide it was impossible to move along the beach and there was only one trail leading up over the cliff.

"We were taken to Captain Geo. H. Cockburn, 2nd Bn., 92nd Inf., 91st Div., U.S.A., who gave us food and water and arranged for transportation for us back to Mariveles, where we arrived at about 1730 on January 20, 1942."

9. GUNNERY ACTIONS

On the same night that PT's 34 and 31 visited Subic Bay, Ens. George E. Cox, Jr., USNR, took PT 41 to reconnoiter the south shore of Manila Bay near Ternate where the Japanese were reported to be placing heavy guns. Ensign Cox found no heavy guns, but 2 miles east of Ternate the 41 strafed several groups of Japanese soldiers on the beach. The Army reported later that 8 Japanese were dead and 14 or more wounded by the strafing.

Four nights later (January 22/23) Lieutenant Bulkeley again accompanied Ensign Chandler in the 34, this time on Bataan patrol. North of Cañas Point the 34 sank a 40-foot landing barge in the face of intense small-caliber return fire, which hit the PT boat 14 times. One .25 caliber bullet pierced the plywood and aluminum cockpit and both of Ensign Chandler's ankles.

The 34 could not return through the minefield until daylight. There was nothing to do but give Chandler first aid and continue on patrol. An attempt to search Bagac Bay to the north was frustrated by 3-inch and machinegun fire from our own Army forces ashore, who could not tell PT's from enemy landing craft. Heading south again, the 34 sighted another landing barge off Luzon Point. The PT closed the range, silenced the return fire, and pulled alongside. Bulkeley boarded the barge.

"All documents, despatch cases and equipment was removed by him for further examination," the official report stated. "Two wounded Japanese (including one officer) were taken prisoner after surrendering on their knees and were hoisted aboard the PT 34 as prisoners of war. A third Japanese already dead was left in the launch. The launch sank beneath the Squadron Commander, while he was rescuing the wounded men who were apparently too weak to swim."

Ensign Chandler was taken to the hospital on Corregidor, where he became a prisoner of war when the Rock fell on May 6, 1942. He was liberated after the return of U.S. forces to the Philippines nearly 2½ years later.

10. RETURN TO SUBIC

On the night of January 24 Bulkeley and DeLong returned to Subic Bay. Because of lack of fuel they took only one boat, George Cox's PT 41. Just to the west of the bay's entrance, in a cove near Sampaloc Point, they sighted what appeared to be an anchored transport, 4,000 to 6,000 tons, of new construction with streamlined bridge and comparatively small stack. With Cox on the wheel and DeLong at the torpedo director, the 41 closed to 800 yards and fired one torpedo. Under heavy fire from the transport, PT 41 held course for another 300 yards until DeLong let go a second torpedo. The tail of this one struck the deck on leaving the tube, but the first was seen to hit amidships. Everyone aboard saw and felt the explosion, and saw debris falling about the PT.

As the PT turned hard left, strafing the transport, a shore battery of four to six 3-inch guns opened fire. Shells splashed on both sides, astern and ahead. The 41 zigzagged out to sea at top speed, clearing by only 20 yards an obstruction net at the entrance of the cove that could have held the little boat like a fly in a web.

11. THE 32 IN ACTION

Maintenance of nightly patrols demanded that the 32 boat, with her hull held together by a jury rig of wires and braces, and top speed of 22 knots, take her regular turn. Her captain, Lt. (jg.) Vincent E. Schumacher, got the 32 underway on the night of February 1, with Lieutenant DeLong aboard as officer-in-tactical command, for Bataan coastal patrol in company with the *Maryanne*.

At 2130 a large ship, apparently a cruiser, was sighted 5,000 yards dead ahead, to the northward. It soon was apparent that 22 knots was insufficient to close the range. The cruiser pulled away steadily for half an hour in the direction of Subic Bay. Then it slowed and turned eastward, toward the Bataan shore.

The 32 then closed rapidly. At 5,000 yards the cruiser caught the 32 in its searchlight and lobbed a two-gun salvo. The shells, estimated by Schumacher as 6-inch, exploded in the water 500 yards ahead. The 32 fired its starboard torpedo. A second salvo landed 200 yards ahead; a third 200 yards astern. The PT fired its port torpedo and retired at top speed, about 25 knots now that the boat was rid of the weight of the torpedoes. For 2 minutes, during which two-gun salvos continued to drop around the PT, there was no apparent increase in range.

"At this time," Schumacher reported, "there was an explosion below the searchlight, definitely not gunfire, and debris came up into the searchlight beam. There was a pause in firing although the searchlight continued on and the ship apparently slowed as the range started opening. This was undoubtedly the second torpedo hitting as the PT 32 drew away indicating the ship had slowed to about 15 knots. Fire was resumed and was excellent continuing until the PT 32 succeeded in losing the searchlight about 2230 by a hard right turn."

It is impossible to state with certainty the results of this action. It appears definite that no Japanese ship was sunk. But Japanese records do show that on February 1 a Japanese minelayer, *Yaeyama,* suffered minor damage in Subic Bay. While this was attributed to shore fire, it is possible that the real cause was PT 32's attack.

12. SUBIC AGAIN

Squadron 3's last action in the Manila area came on the night of February 17, when John Bulkeley again entered Subic Bay, this time on PT 35, commanded by Ens. Anthony B. Akers, USNR. The 41 boat accompanied the 35 as far as the entrance to the bay, where it lay to. It was possible that an enemy destroyer might be lurking in the bay and would give chase to the 35. If this happened, Bulkeley wanted to be able to lead the destroyer past the 41's line of sight.

At the entrance, near Grande Island, the 35 fired a torpedo at a small vessel, probably a trawler of 200–400 tons. The torpedo appeared to pass under the ship without exploding. Further in the bay, near Olongapo Pier, another larger vessel was sighted. The 35 fired one torpedo at long range and retired immediately, strafing the beach on the way out in an attempt to reach the gun positions that had fired on the boats on their last visit to Subic Bay. However, no explosion of the torpedo was seen or heard.

13. THE GENERAL DEPARTS

General MacArthur informed Admiral Rockwell on March 4 that he had been instructed to leave Corregidor. He told the Admiral that a submarine had been placed at his disposal, and offered to take the admiral and several members of his staff with him. A few days later Admiral Rockwell received orders for himself and Captain Ray, his Chief of Staff, to accompany the General.

The original plan was to make the first leg of the journey by submarine, using PT's to assist in escort and disembarkation. The submarine, USS *Permit,* was to put into Corregidor, pick up the party and leave on the 14th.

Early in March, however, the radio press began broadcasting demands that General MacArthur be placed in command of all Allied Forces in Australia. On March 9 there was a sharp increase in activities of enemy craft, including minelayers, off Subic Bay. Surface patrols were reported off Corregidor. A destroyer division was sighted in the southern Philippines heading north at high speed. It was only too apparent that the Japanese Navy not only expected General MacArthur to attempt to leave Corregidor, but would do everything it could to intercept him. It was decided, therefore, not to wait for the *Permit* but to leave by PT as soon as preparations could be completed.

Admiral Rockwell gave Lieutenant Bulkeley his orders on March 10. Bulkeley, with PT 41, was to pick up his passengers, including General and Mrs. MacArthur and their son, and Maj. Gen. Richard K. Sutherland, General MacArthur's Chief of Staff, at the North Dock at Corregidor at 1930 the next day.

So that Japanese scouting planes might observe no unusual activity, Lieutenant Kelly, with PT 34, and Ensign Akers, with PT 35, were to wait at Sisiman Cove. Their passengers, including Admiral Rockwell and Captain Ray, who were to ride the 34, would be brought to them by launch from Corregidor. Lieutenant (jg.) Schumacher, with PT 32, was to pick up his passengers at Quarantine Dock, Mariveles, at 1915. All boats were to rendezvous at 2000 at the entrance to Manila Bay and proceed south in company, to arrive at Tagauayan Island, in the Cuyo Group, about 0730 March 12. Philippine "Q" boats were directed to stage a diversion off Subic Bay during the evening, to give the enemy the impression that PT's were still operating there.

Should any boat break down, she was to transfer her passengers to another boat and proceed independently, or if necessary, transfer all personnel and scuttle. All boats were to lie over in the lee of Tagauayan during the daylight hours, and get underway at 1700 March 12 for Cagayan on Mindanao, to arrive at 0700 March 13.

Boats were to evade the enemy if possible, but if discovered and attacked, the 41, with General MacArthur, was to turn away and attempt to escape while the others engaged the enemy. Alternate rendezvous points and hide-outs were prescribed in case any boat should not be able to reach Tagauayan or Cagayan on schedule. As a final precaution the *Permit* was directed to investigate Tagauayan Island at daylight March 13. If she should observe signals she was to prepare to take passengers aboard.

Just before the boats got underway a last-minute air reconnaissance report was received, stating that a destroyer had been sighted in Apo East Pass, just west of Mindoro, and a cruiser southwest of Mindoro.

The boats slipped out of Manila Bay on schedule, in column with the 41 leading. On the first leg, southwest toward Cabra Island, the flashing of many white lights ashore caused the boats to give the island a considerably wider berth than had been planned. Then, because of the reported sightings of a cruiser and a destroyer, the boats had to keep as far as possible to the west side of Mindoro Strait. A strong easterly wind made the going rough, with sheets of water rising over the bows and lashing the helmsmen's faces.

Almost from the outset the boats had difficulty keeping together. The 32 had never been satisfactorily repaired, and the other boats, after 3 months of steady operations without spares or adequate repairs, were something less than perfect. Kelly, in the 34, found himself dropping steadily behind the 41. He told his engineroom to tie down the throttles to give the boat all possible speed. In the meantime Bulkeley, in the 41, gave orders to slow down to permit the 34 to catch up. By the time Kelly could pass the word to the engineroom to untie the throttles, he had shot past the lead boat, to the astonishment of his senior passenger, Admiral Rockwell.

Before the night was over the boats became separated. PT 32 could use only two engines. The other boats had to stop from time to time to clean gasoline strainers. Just as dawn was breaking Schumacher saw what he believed to be a destroyer behind him. To increase speed he jettisoned his deckload of gasoline. He picked up a few knots, but the destroyer kept coming closer. He swung his boat around for a last-ditch torpedo attack—and realized that what he had taken for a destroyer was the PT 41, oddly magnified in the half light of dawn.

Kelly brought the 34 into Tagauayan at 0930, 2 hours late, but the first to arrive. He and his passengers passed an anxious day. It was not until late afternoon that PT 41 and PT 32 slid into the cove from other islands where they had hidden during the morning hours most likely to bring air attack. PT 35 was still missing.

The 32 obviously could not go on. The boats had to fuel at Tagauayan from the drums they carried on deck in order to reach Cagayan. The 32 had lost its deckload. Besides, only one of its three engines was working and the boat was leaking from loose struts. Passengers from the 32 were divided among the other boats. Schumacher was ordered to wait for the arrival of *Permit* and the 35, to give directions to their commanding officers, and then to make the best of his way to Iloilo, on the island of Panay, where he could obtain sufficient fuel to continue independently to Cagayan.

At 1800 the two remaining boats got underway, with PT 34 leading. "At 1900," Admiral Rockwell recalled later, "a Japanese cruiser was sighted to the northeastward, but we turned away and evidently he did not see us in the glare of the setting sun. At dark we headed to the eastward to cross the traffic lane, and then slipped along the coast line of Negros Island as close inshore as we thought was safe. Our navigation was pretty sketchy but we finally made a landfall on Silino Island at 0200 and laid our course for Cagayan. The weather was very bad from 0100 to daylight, with heavy seas and frequent rain squalls, but as we passed through the most likely patrol area during this time we were probably lucky at that."

Passengers and crews alike were drenched and exhausted when they reached the landing at Cagayan on the morning of March 13, but they had made a trip of 560 miles through Japanese-patrolled waters and had arrived precisely on time. And later that day, the third of the original four boats—the 35—also made it to Cagayan.

The B-17's, which were to carry the party from Mindanao to Australia, had not arrived. They did not arrive until 4 days later, and then there were only two, instead of the three that had been promised. It was decided that the two planes could carry all passengers if all baggage was left behind. Shortly after midnight on the 17th of March, the two planes, heavily overloaded, took off for Australia, where General MacArthur was to start building a force with which he eventually would return to liberate the Philippines.

14. THE 32

Lieutenant Bulkeley was directed to hide his boats in the vicinity of Cagayan until General MacArthur's departure. Then he was to attack enemy shipping as long as his boats would run.

Bulkeley's first concern was for the missing 32 boat. During his first week on Mindanao he flew over the coasts of Panay, Negros, and neighboring islands, but it was many weeks before he learned what happened to the 32.

By the time that *Permit* arrived at Tagauayan on the morning of March 13, Schumacher was convinced that the 32 was unseaworthy. The submarine took him and his crew aboard, and destroyed the PT by gunfire.

"When the vessel was abandoned and destroyed," Schumacher reported, "two engines were out of commission and the third unreliable due to sea water leakage into the engine room. The previously patched deck over the engine room was cracked and leaking badly from damage caused by a deck load of one thousand gallons of fuel in drums. The bolts holding the center shaft tail strut were sheared off, rendering the shaft out of commission and causing a leak into the after compartment. The only spare magneto available (an old one) had been used with unsatisfactory results. . . . Because of the unsafe condition of the vessel, the prevailing easterly wind, and the rough sea, and the probability of the third engine being flooded and put out of commission, the possibility of making a safe landing on the island of Panay was considered remote. Therefore, in order to safeguard the lives of the crew, assistance was requested from the U.S.S. *Permit* and the U.S.S. *PT* 32 was destroyed."

15. PRESIDENT QUEZON

Manuel Quezon, President of the Commonwealth of the Philippines, left Corregidor on February 20 in the submarine *Swordfish* with his wife, son and two daughters, and members of his staff. The Presidential party disembarked 2 days later on the lower coast of Panay. From there the President went to the neighboring island of Negros, but within a month the impending Japanese envelopment of the central Philippines made it imperative that he move again. The Army asked the PT's to bring the President and his family from Negros to Mindanao, whence they would be taken by plane to Australia.

Only the 35 and 41 were still in operating condition. Kelly's 34 had broken an anchor shackle and gone hard aground on coral, mangling shafts, struts, and propellers.

The 41, with Bulkeley and Cox, followed by Akers in the 35, left Cagayan at 1900 March 18, to meet the President and his party at Zamboanguita, on the southern tip of Negros. Though the run was comparatively short, only 100 miles, it might be perilous. Army aerial reconnaissance reported seven enemy destroyers patrolling the southern approaches to Negros. Near Apo Island, off Zamboanguita, the boats separated. The 41 went to Zamboanguita while the 35 patrolled 2 miles offshore to prevent possible surprise by enemy destroyers. Bulkeley waited for an hour at the dock—there was no one to meet him. Then Major Soriano, President Quezon's aide, arrived and requested that the PT's proceed to Dumaguete, 15 miles up the coast.

Only the 41 could go. The 35 had struck a submerged object, ripping a gaping hole in her bow. Akers kept patrolling, his men bailing with buckets, until the water got ahead of the buckets. Then he headed into Zamboanguita. The 41 took the 35's crew aboard, took the damaged boat in tow, got underway toward the beach, and cut the 35 loose, so that she beached herself.

The 41 went on to Dumaguete. Again, there was no sign of the Presidential party. Major Soriano took Bulkeley by automobile to Bais, another 25 miles up the coast. There they found the President. He had received a telegram from General Wainwright advising him that the trip was too dangerous to risk because of Japanese warships. He had decided not to go, but after questioning Bulkeley he changed his mind.

At 0320 the 41 left Dumaguete with a full load. Besides her own crew and the crew of the 35, she carried President and Mrs. Quezon and their two daughters, Vice President Sergio Osmeña, Maj. Gen. Basilio Valdes, Major Andres Soriano, nine members of the President's Cabinet, and a vast quantity of luggage for the entire party.

The trip from Dumaguete to Oroquieta, on Mindanao, was a short one, just over 60 miles, but the seas were vicious. Half an hour out, a heavy wave snapped the shear pins of the two after torpedoes, jolting the torpedoes halfway out of their tubes and starting hot runs. The electric firing circuits failed, probably shorted out by the sheets of water that came pounding over the bow. By the time the torpedomen, James D. Light, CTM, and John L. Houlihan, TM1c, could fire the torpedoes manually, a matter of no more than a minute, the afterbodies of the torpedoes were already glowing red hot.

The rest of the trip was uneventful. President Quezon and his party landed safely at Oroquieta at 0600 March 19.

16. ENGAGEMENT OFF CEBU

For a time PT 41 was the only operational boat in Squadron 3. Bulkeley returned in the 41 to Zamboanguita, put a patch on the 35 and towed her to Cebu City, where there was a marine railway. When he came back to Mindanao he found that Kelly had made emergency repairs to the 34 at a little machine shop in Inlug Cove, to the north of Cagayan. The 34 could make all of 12 knots without shaking herself to pieces. That was sufficient for the trip to Cebu, where further repairs could be made at the Opan Ship-building & Slipway Corp. This was a small yard whose 71-year-old pro-prietor, "Dad" Cleland, refused to worry about payment for his work. "You fight 'em and I'll fix 'em," he told Bulkeley.

While at Cebu the boat crews worked for 3 nights helping load two sub-marines with food and supplies for Corregidor. The submarines gave Bulkeley torpedoes to reload the 41's empty tubes.

The 34 went back in the water on the afternoon of April 8. On the same afternoon Bulkeley learned that Army planes had seen two enemy destroyers heading south through Tañon Strait, between Cebu and its western neighbor, Negros. The ships should clear the southern tip of Cebu about midnight.

Bulkeley, with Cox in the 41, followed by Kelly in the 34, slid down the eastern side of Cebu to meet the enemy force as it emerged from the strait. DeWitt L. Glover, CQM, on the 41, was the first to sight the enemy. "There she is!" he shouted. Then, as it dawned on him what he saw, "Jumping Jesus! There she is!"

What he saw, 5,000 yards ahead, gliding slowly eastward just 2 miles off the tip of Cebu, was not the expected destroyers, but a light cruiser, armed with 5.5- and 3-inch guns, bristling with smaller automatic weapons.

The 41 led the way, idling in on the cruiser's port side. At 500 yards Cox fired two torpedoes. They ran erratically, straddling the target bow and stern. The 41 increased speed, circled to the right, and Bulkeley fired her last two torpedoes. Both Bulkeley and Cox saw the torpedoes run true, one to the bow and the other beneath the bridge, but observed no explosion.

While the 41 was circling, Kelly brought the 34 in broad on the bow and fired two torpedoes at 500 yards. The cruiser's searchlight blazed a path through the night, sweeping the sky, then catching the 41 for a moment, finally settling on the 34. At the same time the cruiser opened fire and in-creased speed rapidly. Kelly saw his torpedoes miss astern.

The 41 circled to the starboard side of the cruiser to strafe her decks in an attempt to draw fire from the 34. But the cruiser held the 34 in the searchlight beam and directed automatic fire and salvos from its main battery at the PT. Kelly made a U-turn to the left, passing astern of the cruiser and coming up on the starboard quarter from almost dead astern. During the turn the 34 dropped back to about 2,500 yards. Kelly ordered his gunners to fire into the searchlight. Japanese shells were whistling over; one carried away the mast just aft of the cockpit. Willard J. Reynolds, CCStd, whose machineguns were the first to fire at the searchlight, was hit by shrapnel in the neck and shoulder.

"It was estimated," Kelly said, "that the cruiser was making 20–25 knots. Pursuit was maintained for about 5 or 10 minutes by which time the PT 34 was within 300 yards of the cruiser whose searchlight beam was depressed almost to the vertical in order to keep the PT 34 illuminated. Although this was considered a very poor position for firing torpedoes, the cruiser's automatic fire was coming so close that further delay was impossible. Two Mark XIV (45 knot) torpedoes were now fired with 6-foot depth setting in an overtaking shot from close on the cruiser's starboard quarter.

"The PT 34 now turned right at maximum speed to retire south only to be simultaneously taken under fire by a destroyer some 2,000 yards to starboard as well as being kept under fire and illumination by the cruiser. It looked like we were trapped. Our mast had been shot away and our topside was riddled with .50-caliber holes. The cruiser turned, apparently to follow us and prevent our escaping, the destroyer closing us to port. Just then two spouts of water some 20 feet high and 30 feet apart were seen by me through binoculars to appear amidships at the cruiser's waterline at 5-second intervals. My first reaction was that the cruiser had been hit by two rounds from the destroyer firing on me to starboard. However, Chief Torpedoman Martino had also seen the hits and reported them to me as torpedo hits. Apparently the cruiser had turned directly into the path of the torpedoes. All this occurred in less than a minute after firing. The cruiser's searchlight immediately began to fade as though there had been a power failure aboard. All its guns stopped firing and that was the last I ever saw of it."

The 34, able to make 38 knots now that her torpedoes were gone, then started maneuvering to evade the destroyer on her starboard hand. "By violent zigzagging and executing a series of right angle turns this was accomplished after about 10 minutes, without receiving further hits," Kelly said. "The PT 34 then headed northward for the entrance of Bohol Strait in order to return to Cebu City. Since there were no more torpedoes aboard, it was considered advisable to head back to the base before the Jap destroyers could cut us off.

"A few moments after setting a northeasterly course a destroyer was seen dead ahead bearing down on the 34 at high speed. Only by swerving to the left was a collision avoided and we passed down their starboard side close aboard without their firing a shot. They immediately turned and commenced pursuit illuminating us with their searchlight and taking us under fire with their main battery. They kept up the chase until about 0130 when we were some 5–6 miles to the north of them. Searchlights to the southward were observed by us until about 0200."

While the 34 was making its second attack and then maneuvering to shake the first destroyer, the 41 tried to create the illusion of many torpedo boats by firing machinegun bursts at different positions. The 41 then headed back toward the cruiser to ascertain its condition, but suddenly was illuminated by another destroyer which opened fire and gave chase. Heading east at top speed, the 41 found one enemy destroyer blocking its escape to the north, and two more to the east. The boat turned south and ran to Port Misamis, Mindanao, where the inlet was too shallow for destroyers to follow.

What were the results of the action? Kelly believed that the cruiser was of the 3,230-ton *Tenryu* class, because the center stack appeared to be wider than the other two. He is certain that his last two torpedoes hit. Eight days after the action, Kelly, having escaped through the Japanese lines on Cebu, reached Dumaguete, Negros. There he met a U.S. Army private who had been in an Army speedboat aground on Siquijor Island and had seen the action. The private told Kelly that he had seen a destroyer illuminate the cruiser and go alongside it half an hour after the engagement. He was sure that the cruiser had sunk later. Kelly also met at Dumaguete an American professor from the local university, who had watched the engagement from shore. He, too, believed the cruiser had sunk.

Bulkeley, on the 41, thought that the cruiser was of the 5,100-ton *Kuma* class, because of its widely flared stacks. He saw no explosions, but said that just after the 34's second attack, the cruiser was completely enveloped in a cloud of yellowish brown smoke. He also saw the searchlight dim gradually, then flicker out, as though from power failure. Finally, Bulkeley reported that the first destroyer swept past the cruiser and illuminated it briefly by searchlight. "It could be seen," he reported, "that the cruiser was sinking by the stern with her bow up in the air."

Japanese sources indicate that the *Kuma* was attacked by torpedo boats on this date, but that the *Kuma* took only one hit—a torpedo that failed to explode. Whatever the damage, or lack of it, the *Kuma* remained afloat until January 11, 1944, when she was sunk off Penang by a British submarine. And the magnitude of the damage, or lack of it, neither increases nor diminishes the courage of the officers and men who pressed home a close-range attack on a dangerous enemy 100 times their size.

17. "WE COULD NO LONGER FIGHT"

Kelly tried to take the 34 into Cebu City before daylight to get medical aid for Reynolds. But he had only a large-scale chart, useless for navigating the channel. He idled in, and just when his soundings told him that he was in 3 fathoms, his boat ground to a stop on a coral pinnacle. He sent his executive officer, Ens. Iliff D. Richardson, USNR, ashore in a dinghy to find a tug for the 34 and a doctor for Reynolds. By daylight Kelly was able to rock the boat free. His center propeller and strut were damaged, but he was able to proceed into the channel on two engines.

"Under ordinary conditions," he said, "it would have been considered suicidal to have been operating in this area after daylight. However, the Army authorities had assured us of air cover and given us the assigned radio frequencies of the planes. These planes were scheduled to arrive that morning from Australia to form an escort for coastal steamers due to leave Cebu the next day carrying food for Corregidor. The radio of the PT 34 had been rendered inoperable during the previous night's engagement. However, I had every confidence that the planes would be there having seen a copy of the dispatch concerning them the night before.

"Shortly after 0800 a bomb landed close off the PT 34's port bow. We had not heard any planes due to the noise of our engines. Four Jap float planes were seen to be diving on us out of the sun, the first already having dropped its bomb. The PT 34's amidship .50 cal. turrets were already manned and began firing immediately. The port bow .30 cal. Lewis machinegun was blown off its stand by the first bomb's blast. The starboard bow .30 caliber was manned immediately by the quartermaster and I took the wheel. During the next 15 minutes eight bombs were dropped on the PT 34. All were near misses (under 25 yards). The planes dove from about 500 feet altitude strafing as they came out of the sun. The first run killed the starboard .50 caliber gunner and disabled the gun. The next two runs knocked out the port .50 cal. turret. On the third run the quartermaster, Ross, hit one of the float planes causing it to smoke heavily. It was presumed to have crashed (although it was not seen to hit the water) since it was not seen during any subsequent attack. On the next run Ross was hit and his gun disabled.

"Since the PT 34 was in a narrow channel and only had two engines, maneuvering was extremely difficult. During the succeeding runs the boat was riddled with .30 cal. holes although it received no bomb hits. Chief Torpedoman Martino, who was acting as Executive Officer, rendered first aid to the crew and kept me informed of our damage. When I received word that the engine room was flooded with about 3 feet of water and the engines could not last much longer, it was decided to beach the boat since we could no longer fight."

Kelly beached his boat on Cauit Island and got his crew ashore. David W. Harris, TM2c, who had been in the starboard turret, was dead. Reynolds had been wounded again, this time fatally. Albert P. Ross, QM1c, who had hit the enemy plane; John Martino, CTM, and Velt F. Hunter, CMM, were wounded.

At 1230 the three planes returned while salvage operations were underway and bombed and strafed the 34 again. This time they set the boat afire, and it burned and exploded on the beach at Cauit Island, southern approach to Cebu City.

18. AND THEN THERE WERE NONE

Squadron 3 had fought its last action. The 35 was the next boat to go. Lt. (jg.) Henry J. Brantingham burned her in the slipway at Cebu on April 12, when the Japanese entered the city.

On Mindanao, Bulkeley reported the cruiser action to Brig. Gen. William F. Sharp, Commanding General, Mindanao Force, and told the General of his intention to return to Cebu to replace the 41's torpedoes. General Sharp informed him that the Japanese were already entering Cebu and that no torpedoes were available on Mindanao. The 41's career as a torpedo boat was ended.

Bulkeley's orders, which General Sutherland gave him before departing for Australia, concluded, "Upon completion of the offensive mission, due to destruction of material or lack of essential supplies, Lieutenant Bulkeley will proceed to Mindanao, reporting upon arrival to the Commanding General, Mindanao Force."

Bulkeley reported to General Sharp for duty. On April 13, under orders from General MacArthur, he was flown to Australia.

The Army intended to take the 41 to Lake Lanao, 15 miles inland, where she might be useful as a patrol boat to prevent Japanese floatplanes from landing on the lake. The boat was stripped at the dock at Iligan, and a valiant attempt was made to haul her up over the mountain road to Lake Lanao. Her engines actually reached the lake by truck, but it became necessary to destroy the 41 on the road when Japanese forces closed in.

19. END OF THE SQUADRON

The 83 officers and men of Squadron 3 were widely scattered. Five had been lost with the 31 and 34. Of the living, some were with the Mindanao Force, some with the Visayan Force on Cebu. Others were with the Inshore Patrol at Corregidor or the Naval Section Base at Mariveles.

Kelly, Cox, and Akers were flown to Australia at the end of April by order of General MacArthur. A few other officers and men were able to get out to Australia by submarine.

Of those who remained in the Philippines, some joined the guerrilla forces, among them Ensign Richardson, who became Colonel Kangleon's chief of staff on Leyte, with the rank of major; William F. Konko, RM3c, who worked as a radio technician for Colonel Fertig on Mindanao with rank of second lieutenant; Francis J. Napolillo, Jr., SC1c, who first operated a launch, then became a coding officer for Colonel Fertig; Paul A. Owen, CMM, who distilled alcohol from tuba to keep guerrilla engines operating; DeWitt L. Glover, CQM; John L. Tuggle, MM1c; and John H. Lewis, MM1c, who also joined Fertig's forces.

Thirty-eight officers and men, including most of those in the Manila Bay area, were taken prisoner. Most of these were removed in 1944 to prison camps in Japan or Manchuria. Nine died in prison camps; 29 were liberated. Squadron 3's total dead, including those dead or missing in the loss of PT's 31 and 34, is 3 officers, 15 enlisted men.

Lt. Comdr. John D. Bulkeley receives the Medal of Honor from President Franklin D. Roosevelt.

20. "TWO HUNDRED BOATS IF POSSIBLE"

When Lieutenant Bulkeley returned to the United States, he brought with him a verbal message from General MacArthur for delivery to the President of the United States, the Secretary of War, the Secretary of the Navy, the Commander in Chief U.S. Fleet and Chief of Naval Operations. He delivered it in this form:

Motor torpedo boats should be the basis of a separate branch of the service for specialists, and who must have confidence in their own weapons.

These boats can be used effectively for coastal defense 200 or 300 miles offshore, in the Philippine Islands, straits, narrows and potential blocks.

There is no other location such as the Philippine Islands and the islands south of the Philippines where they can be so effectively used.

With enough of this type of craft, hostile Japanese shipping could be kept from invading an island or continent, and kept 200 to 300 miles offshore.

I want 100 or more MTB's here of your type together with the improvements which have been developed since the outbreak of war. Two hundred boats if possible with the tenders, spare parts, and equipment necessary for them within 8 months.

It is not surprising that General MacArthur did not have 100 PT's, or even one-third of that number, within 8 months. The wonder is that before the end of the war 212 PT's, 11 tenders, and a string of PT bases were in operation throughout the Southwest Pacific area.

PART II

Development—*A New Type Emerges*

PART II

Development—*A New Type Emerges*

1. WHAT IS A PT?

DEAD IN THE water, a PT is squat and beamy. It was designed for speed, and in speed lies its beauty. As a PT gains momentum, its bow lifts clear of the water and it planes gracefully over the surface, throwing out a great wave from the chine on either side and a rooster tail of white water astern. The men who rode PT's cursed them for their pounding and discomfort, but loved them for the beauty that is born of their speed.

At first glance, it may seem paradoxical that high speed would not be used in a perfect torpedo attack. Ideally, a PT sneaks in slowly with muffled engines to firing range, launches its torpedoes, turns and idles silently away. This is seldom possible. Usually, by the time the torpedoes are launched, the enemy has been alerted and his guns are blazing away at the PT. Then speed, maneuverability, and a smokescreen are the PT's only protection. Speed also permits PT's to leave their base at dusk, thrust deep into enemy territory and return to base by dawn. It is imprudent to be out in daylight where the enemy controls the air. In a daylight contest between 1 or 2 PT's and 1 or 2 planes, the PT's have the advantage; but where 15 or 20 planes may attack 2 PT's, the advantage is the other way.

Good as it is, the speed of PT's frequently has been exaggerated. PT's do not make 70 knots—or even 60. They were designed to make better than 40 knots at full war load. And that, over the water, is fast—more than 45 land-miles per hour. With proper maintenance—a clean bottom, engines tuned, everything just right—a PT can be expected to turn up 40 knots without difficulty. But after long periods of operating in advanced areas, without proper maintenance and repair facilities, speed deteriorates. The men of the New Guinea squadrons sang a song which began:

> "Oh, some PT's do seventy-five,
>   And some do sixty-nine;
> When we get ours to run at all
>   We think we're doing fine . . ."

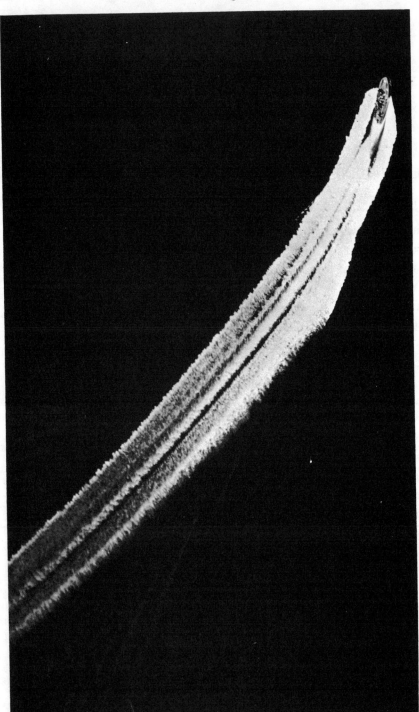

80—G—13091

The PT's wake was a thing of beauty.

The size of PT's varied somewhat. Of the first experimental boats, some were 58 feet overall, others 81 feet. The first satisfactory boats, copied from a British design, were 70 feet. These boats, built by the Elco Naval Division of the Electric Boat Co. at Bayonne, N.J., were designed to carry four 18-inch (diameter) torpedoes. While this was a standard British size, the United States had only a small stock of these torpedoes and had none in production. Accordingly, the size of the boat was increased to carry four of the heavier and longer 21-inch torpedoes, standard U.S. Navy size. So the next boats were the 77-foot Elco models which saw service at Pearl Harbor and in the Philippines. Finally, demands for heavier armament and better seakeeping qualities led to still larger boats; the 78-foot model built by Higgins Industries at New Orleans, and the Elco 80-footer. The Higgins 78-footer and the Elco 80 were of comparable size, both considerably larger boats, because of raised freeboard, than the Elco 77.

PT assembly line at Higgins Industries' City Park Plant, New Orleans, La.

At Elco's Bayonne, N.J., plant, PT construction was started with the boat upside down; when bottom and side planking was completed, the hull was turned over in a special sling.

These two boats became standard for the U.S. Navy. Including boats built for lend-lease, Elco turned out 320 and Higgins 205. While each type had its proponents, it is fair to say that the Elco boat had a slight edge in speed, and was drier. The Higgins had a tendency to nose under the waves, drenching the crew. The Higgins boat was considerably more maneuverable than the Elco, however, an extremely valuable feature in defense against air attack.

Except for a few of the early experimental boats, all U.S. PT's were powered by three 12-cylinder Packard marine engines. These engines, which burned 100-octane gasoline, were originally rated at 1,200 horsepower. As the boats grew in size and weight more power was needed, and the engine was modified to a 1,350- and finally to a 1,500-horsepower rating. The Packard engine, developed especially for PT use, was one of the most reliable items of PT equipment. Changing of engines for overhaul was prescribed after 600 hours of use, but spare engines were not always available. Many engines gave satisfactory performance after more than 1,200 hours. Sometimes boats were hit in combat and came limping home with several feet of water in the engineroom, the engines almost submerged but still running.

Although much plywood was used in PT construction, the hull itself was not plywood, but two layers of mahogany planking laid over laminated wood frames. A layer of airplane fabric, impregnated with marine glue, was ironed on between the two layers of planking. The result was a light, strong hull, resilient enough to stand up in heavy seas.

While each type had its own distinctive below-decks arrangement, both included engineroom, fuel tanks to carry 3,000 gallons of gasoline, fresh water tanks, charthouse (in which, besides a chart table, were the radio and

80—G—258667

PT's were surprisingly roomy below decks. The ship's cook had an adequate galley to feed a hungry crew. His problem: would the auxiliary generator hold out until the meal was cooked?

radar), separate living compartments for officers and men, and a galley equipped with electric range and refrigerator.

In relation to its size, the PT carried the heaviest armament of any naval vessel. The first boats carried only four torpedoes in tubes and two pairs of .50-caliber machineguns in turrets. Then a 20mm. cannon was added, useful against both airplanes and surface craft. Antibarge actions in the Solomons and New Guinea soon demonstrated the need for heavier guns. Early in 1943 experimental installation of single-shot 37mm. antitank guns were made in both theaters. Soon afterwards, automatic 37's were made available by the Army Air Corps. Mounted on the bow, the automatic 37 became a standard installation.

At first, the only torpedoes available for PT's were Mark VIII's of World War I vintage. Designed for use by destroyers, they had a range of 10,000 yards, a speed of 27 knots, and a 300-pound warhead. They were long and heavy, and had to be launched on an even keel, lest the gyro be upset. They were given to erratic runs, particularly at shallow depth setting. Their weight and slow speed were positive disadvantages; their long range was unnecessary because the boats' fire control was not sufficiently accurate to permit a long-range shot.

To avoid tumbling the gyro, it was necessary to launch the torpedo from a tube, a device which added still more weight to the boat. Tubes on the Elco boats employed a black powder charge for launching. This proved to be an additional hazard. In night actions the flash of the powder charge frequently disclosed the position of the PT to the enemy. Higgins Industries eliminated this hazard by developing a launching device which impelled the torpedo from the tube by compressed air.

Most of the difficulties were overcome when Mark XIII torpedoes became available. The Mark XIII, developed as an aircraft torpedo, was short range, but far smaller and lighter, and more reliable than the Mark VIII. It had a speed of 45 knots, carried a 600-pound warhead, and had a non-tumbling gyro. This made it possible to roll it into the water from a side-launching rack, which was much lighter than the torpedo tube.

With this double saving in weight—a lighter torpedo and a rack much lighter than the old tube—it was possible to carry a heavier gun than the 20mm. on the stern. Despite the fact that the Motor Torpedo Boat Squadrons Training Center at Melville, R.I., had turned in an unfavorable report on an experimental mounting of a 40-mm. cannon, Lt. Comdr. John Harllee,

80-G-17319

Loading a Mark VIII torpedo in its tube.

obtained authorization to mount 40's on four of his boats in Squadron 12, which arrived in New Guinea in August 1943.

This was the best antibarge gun the boats ever had, and eventually became standard armament on all boats. It was accurate, automatic, and sufficiently powerful to blast holes in the heaviest armored barge. With the addition of the 40 on the stern, the 20 was moved from the stern to the forecastle.

Three of the Solomons PT's were stripped of all original armament except the two twin-. 50-caliber gun mounts. Then two 40mm. cannon were installed, fore and aft, as well as four additional twin-. 50-caliber machineguns. These proved to be excellent gunboats, effective against the toughest Japanese barges.

In New Guinea, the PT's even experimented with 75mm. cannon in place of the 40 mm. Although the 75 was actually lighter than the 40, and carried a more powerful punch, it was discarded because the automatic 40 had a much higher rate of fire than the semiautomatic 75, and the 40 had tracer control—the gunner's eye could follow the flight of his shells—while the 75 did not.

Early in 1944 PT's both in the Mediterranean and in New Guinea made experimental installations of 4.5-inch barrage rocket projectors, one 12-

80—G—58547

A Mark XIII torpedo slides from its launching rack, propellers spinning and exhaust gases escaping from its tail. Compare with firing of Mark VIII torpedoes from tubes (Frontispiece).

round projector on each side of the deck, foward of the torpedo tubes. The rockets were tremendously destructive, but not accurate enough for effective use against surface targets. Consequently they were of little value in the Mediterranean, where radar-controlled shore batteries prevented PT's from coming within rocket range of shore objectives. In New Guinea, on the other hand, the boats could sneak close to land to bombard shore installations. Against shore targets, pinpoint accuracy was not essential, since a salvo of 24 rockets spread destruction over a wide area.

In 1945, boats in the Philippines received a new weapon of great promise— 5-inch spin-stabilized rockets. Far more potent than the 4.5-inch barrage rockets, these were roughly equivalent in power to the 5-inch shells of a destroyer—and they were accurate. This was such a late development, however, that there was little opportunity to test it in action.

Another weapon that should be mentioned is the so-called "Thunderbolt," developed by Elco. This was a power-driven mount containing four 20-mm. cannon. The first experimental Thunderbolt was mounted on PT 138, of Squadron 7, late in 1942. It was never entirely satisfactory in operation, and carried away in a heavy sea before it could be tested in action. Improved models were installed on four boats of Squadron 29 in 1944 for use in the Mediterranean, and on a few boats of Squadrons 10 and 21 early in 1945 in the Philippines. They were highly satisfactory in the few actions in which they were used.

ACME PHOTO

A depth charge explodes in the wake of a PT during training exercises in the Gulf of Panama.

Most PT's carried two depth charges, to be used in case a PT should cross the path of a submerging submarine. Inasmuch as no satisfactory sound gear was ever developed for PT's, they could never aspire to efficiency as antisubmarine vessels, but occasionally were able to harass, if not to damage, enemy underwater craft. During the early months of the war the boats of Squadron 1 were in constant demand for antisubmarine patrol duty at Pearl Harbor, as they were the only vessels available that could drop depth charges in the shallow restricted waters of the harbor and channel and get clear before the charges exploded. The squadron claimed credit for possible destruction of two submarines, but the claim is unconfirmed. On several occasions in New Guinea and the Solomons, PT's dropped depth charges on submerging submarines without demonstrable results.

Occasionally PT's used depth charges for another purpose, in a manner first developed by British boats in the English Channel. Sometimes, when a lugger or small cargo ship resisted destruction by gunfire, it was possible to break its back by dropping a depth charge close aboard.

The final item of ordnance equipment was purely defensive—a smoke-screen generator. Literally hundreds of times boats evaded enemy fire by running radical course changes behind adroitly laid puffs of smoke.

From the beginning, PT's were equipped with radio for communication with base or tender and with each other. Later a VHF (very high frequency) radio, with transmission limited to short distances, was added to give greater security to communications between boats and with cooperating planes.

The early boats had no radar. John Bulkeley had learned the need for it in the Philippines. He urgently requested, and received, 12 sets of aircraft radar for installation in the boats of his new Squadron 7. These sets suffered frequent breakdowns, and often failed to operate because of unreliable power supply, but they demonstrated clearly that radar was invaluable both for navigation and for locating the enemy. Within less than a year, practically all PT's were equipped with reliable radar especially developed for their use. Much of the subsequent success of PT's was directly attributable to this remarkable instrument, which gave them eyes to see in the dark.

2. ANCIENT HISTORY

At the time of World War II, the motor torpedo boat was less than 40 years old. In 1905, Yarrow, the British boatbuilder, launched an experimental torpedo boat powered by an Italian Napier engine. Only 15 feet long, the boat made 25 knots and carried two torpedoes. While Yarrow was experimenting with his model, another British builder, John I. Thornycroft, produced a larger motor torpedo boat, 40 feet overall, with a displacement of 4½ tons. This boat had a top speed of 18 knots and carried a single torpedo in a rack. Launching the torpedo was a precarious business, greatly endangering the stability of the boat.

There had been earlier torpedo boats, to be sure, but they were powered by steam. Builders saw in the internal combustion engine an opportunity to fulfill three requirements of torpedo boat design that had seemed mutually exclusive with steampower: high speed, economy, and a small target for the enemy to hit.

The lead of Yarrow and Thornycroft was quickly followed in other countries. The Italians developed a motor torpedo boat in 1906. By 1907, the French had built a steel-hulled boat, displacing a comparatively heavy 8 tons. In place of the torpedo rack which was a feature of the British models, this boat had a single torpedo tube built into the bow. Its trials produced such unexpectedly good results that the French Admiralty enthusiastically urged further experiments with the type.

The United States made its entry into the field in behalf of another power: Lewis Nixon designed, built, and sold to Russia 10 motor torpedo boats in 1908. These boats were powered by two 6-cylinder benzine-fueled engines. Nixon proved the seaworthiness of his design when one of his boats went without damage from New York to Sevastopol under its own power in a moderate sea.

In the same year that Nixon built his boats, the Assistant Secretary of the Navy recommended construction of a number of small motor torpedo boats to be used for coastal defense. The Navy's General Board felt that the funds could be better used for seagoing torpedo boats and no immediate action was taken. In 1909, however, Congress authorized the construction of two small torpedo boats. While these were never completed, the Navy did prepare tentative designs for a 150-foot and a 115-foot boat. Both carried a single 18-inch torpedo tube and two rapid-fire guns.

In 1912, the Navy gave serious consideration to an invention of Charles L. Burger of New York City which allowed small motorboats to be converted to fire torpedoes.

3. WORLD WAR I AND AFTER

Italy and Britain led the field in motor torpedo boat development in World
War I. By 1916 Italy had developed MAS boats (Motoscafi Anti-Sommer-
gibli) 50 to 69 feet long, carrying from 2 to 4 torpedoes, with a top speed
of about 33 knots. From the abbreviation, MAS, Gabriele d'Annunzio
formed a motto, "Memento Audare Sempre"—"Remember Always to
Dare"—good advice for motor torpedo boats of any nation.

The Italians carried out several successful raids against Austrian naval
units and shipping in Adriatic harbors, the most notable successes being the
sinking of the light cruiser *Wien* at Trieste on December 9, 1917, and the
sinking of the battleship *Szent Istvan* in the Straits of Otranto on June 8, 1918.

The first of the British CMB's (coastal motor boats) was built by Thornycroft in 1915. Tests of this 40-foot, 33.5-knot boat were satisfactory and the
Admiralty ordered a dozen. Thornycroft later designed a 55-footer, which
also was accepted by the Admiralty. By November of 1918 the Royal Navy
had commissioned 66 CMB's, and had designs for a 70-foot boat which could
have been put into production by the fall of 1919 had the war continued.

Like American PT's of World War II, the CMB's were not used exclusively
for torpedo attacks, but had a variety of functions, including minelaying,
antisubmarine patrol, laying of smokescreens, and rescue of aviators from
fallen planes. It is worth noting that what was probably the first air attack
on motor torpedo boats was made on August 10, 1918, when eight low-flying
German planes strafed six CMB's. All of the boats were put out of commission, though none was lost. Twenty-five years later the Japanese made
consistent efforts to combat PT's by air attack. Although the PT's were
heavier gunned than the CMB's, planes were still such a dangerous adver-
sary that it was tactically unsound to attempt to operate boats in daylight
where the enemy controlled the air.

The CMB's had their most spectacular success in a postwar operation,
a raid on Kronstadt in 1919 after the Russian Revolution, when they sank
the cruiser *Oleg* and damaged or disabled 2 capital ships and 2 destroyers
with the loss of only 1 CMB.

The U.S. Navy showed only slight interest in motor torpedo boats during
the war years, no doubt because of the geographical position of the country.
Motor torpedo boats were designed for strikes against enemy shipping and
fleet units within a short distance of a home base, and German seapower,

except for their U-boats, was incapable of making an assault on American shores.

Acting on recommendation of Rear Adm. Joseph Strauss, Chief of the Bureau of Ordnance, the Navy Department decided in 1915 to purchase a high-powered motorboat with which to conduct experiments to ascertain the value of the type. This project progressed only as far as acquisition of plans for a 50-foot boat to be built by the Greenport Basin & Construction Co., of Greenport, Long Island. This boat was designed for a maximum speed of 43 miles per hour and was to carry quick firing guns and a single torpedo tube.

In 1917 the Navy went a step further, testing a 40-foot boat which, though capable of 40 knots in smooth water, was unacceptable because of its rough action in a seaway. A year later a 27-foot craft known as W. Shearer's one-man torpedo boat was built and tested. The forward part of the boat was submersible; the torpedo was carried in a well, which when flooded permitted launching the torpedo under its own power. The trial board recommended construction of a flotilla of these boats for use against German bases, but the General Board quashed the recommendation, remarking, "It is thought labor and material for large numbers of such boats can be better employed to win the war in turning out destroyers, submarine chasers, submarines and aircraft."

In 1920, however, the General Board joined the Chief of the Bureau of Construction and Repair in recommending purchase of two of the Royal Navy's Thornycroft CMB's. The Navy acquired one of each type. Trials in 1922 revealed that the 40-footer could make 32.25 knots and the 55-footer 35.13 knots. No further experimental use was made of the 40-footer, which was used for torpedo recovery until 1928, when it was converted to a crashboat. It was condemned in 1934. Experiments with the 55-footer continued until 1930, when it was stricken from the Navy Register.

During the 1920's many other Thornycrofts appeared in sheltered coves and inlets along the east coast, brought to the United States under private sponsorship. These boats were employed in night operations designed to relieve the dryness of a thirsty nation. While the Navy remained relatively uninterested in development of fast motorboats, the rum trade carried on extensive experimentation, including the adaptation of the Liberty engine to marine use. One engineer whose experience and know-how were valuable to the World War II PT program was frequently known to preface his comments on perplexing technical problems with the remark, "Well, when I was a rummie, we . . ."

It would be interesting to know how many PT technicians had such a phrase flash through their minds but failed to utter it.

4. SCOTT-PAINE AND VOSPER

Hubert Scott-Paine, who was to make a lasting imprint on American PT design, completed plans in 1934 for a 60-foot boat which might be called the first modern motor torpedo boat. The Admiralty agreed to purchase two, then increased the order to six. Scott-Paine's British Power Boat Co. delivered the boats in 1936. The next year the boats proved their worth by running to Malta under their own power in heavy weather.

In 1938 another British company, Vosper, built a 68-foot boat designed to carry two torpedoes. This speculative enterprise paid off when the Admiralty ordered one boat, then increased the order to six. This was the prototype of the Vosper 70-footer which became standard for the British Coastal Forces during the war. Although this type was never adopted by the U.S. Navy, American yards built many of them for lend-lease to Britain and Russia.[3]

Early in 1939, Scott-Paine built his first 70-foot boat. It could carry two 21-inch or four 18-inch torpedoes, and machineguns in power-driven turrets. The boat was light, strong, fast, and maneuverable. On June 15, 1939, it crossed the English Channel and returned at an average speed of 42 knots. The British Power Boat Co. soon had orders for 50 boats from Britain and other major powers. Among them was an order for one boat from a private purchaser, which would have profound effect on the PT program in the United States.

---

[3] Vosper boats built in the United States for Britain and Russia were:

Builder	Britain	Russia	Total
Annapolis Yacht Yard, Annapolis, Md.	20	108	128
Herreshoff, Bristol, R.I.	8	20	28
R. Jacob, City Island, N.Y.	22	0	22
Harbor Boat Building Co., Terminal Island, Calif.	6	0	6
Total	56	128	184

Included in the totals for Russia are 38 boats built by the Annapolis Yacht Yard but never delivered.

5. RENEWED INTEREST

Foreign experimentation renewed interest in the United States. On December 5, 1936, Rear Adm. Emory S. Land, Chief of the Bureau of Construction and Repair, wrote to the Chief of Naval Operations, saying, "Developments since the War of the motor-torpedo-boat type, then known as Coastal Motor Boats, have been continuous and marked in most European Navies . . . The results being obtained in the foreign services are such as to indicate that vessels of considerable military effectiveness for the defense of local areas, are being built, the possibilities of which should not be allowed to go unexplored in our service. It is, of course, recognized that the general strategic situation in this country is entirely different from that in Europe, so that motor torpedo boats could not in all probability be used offensively by us. It appears very probable, however, that the type might very well be used to release for offensive service ships otherwise unavoidably assigned to guard important geographic points such as an advance base itself.

"If the department concurs, this Bureau suggests the inauguration of an experimental program of such boats and will endeavor to have included in its appropriations for experimental work, funds for the construction of two boats each year, preferably one by contract on designs of private naval architects and one from Departmental designs."

Admiral Land's recommendation was forwarded to the Secretary of the Navy, who in turn passed it to the General Board, with a request for the Board's recommendations. The General Board, while it agreed that "it is clearly evident that because of our strategic situation the type is of much less initial value to our Navy than to most, if not all, of the others," added, "future situations can occur under which it would be possible for such small craft to be used on directly offensive missions—as is no doubt contemplated in certain foreign navies."

The Board included among its recommendations "the inauguration of an experimental development program on a moderate scale." The Secretary of the Navy approved the Board's recommendations on May 7, 1937.

Just over a year later, Congress made the program possible by enacting Public Law 528, the Second Deficiency Bill for 1938, which included an appropriation of "the sum of $15,000,000 to be expended at the discretion of the President of the United States for the construction of experimental vessels, none of which shall exceed three thousand tons standard displacement."

6. THE DESIGN CONTEST

On July 11, 1938, the Navy publicly invited designers to submit plans for a 165-foot subchaser, a 110-foot subchaser, a 70-foot motor torpedo boat, and a 54-foot motor torpedo boat. A prize of $15,000 was offered for the winning design in each class, and prizes of $1,500 each to all entrants whose plans reached the final stage of competition.

Requirements for the larger motor torpedo boat included: an overall length of approximately 70 feet, not to exceed 80 feet; trial speed of 40 knots; minimum radius of 275 miles at top speed and 550 miles at cruising speed. Armament was to include at least two 21-inch torpedoes, four depth charges, and two .50-caliber machineguns.

The smaller boat was to be no more than 60 feet long, and was to have a hoisting weight of not more than 20 tons. The weight restriction and a specification that the hull structure "be of sufficient strength to permit of hoisting over side by means of slings under moderate weather conditions" were made with a view to easy oversea shipment and unloading. Such a boat would be within the boom capacity of many fleet auxiliaries and cargo ships. This boat also was to have a trial speed of 40 knots, but its radius need be only 120 miles at top speed and 240 miles at cruising speed. Armament specifications required only two torpedoes and depth charges, or an alternative armament of .50-caliber machineguns and smokescreen generator.

The preliminary design contest, which closed September 30, 1938, brought 24 designs from 21 contestants for the 54-foot boat, and 13 designs from 13 contestants for the 70-foot boat. Three designers in the 54-foot class and five in the 70-foot class were requested to submit detailed plans and specifications in the final design contest, which was to close on November 7, 1938. The Navy announced on March 21, 1939, that Sparkman and Stephens, naval architects previously known for their sailboat designs, had won the prize in the 70-foot class, and that Prof. George Crouch, who made his design for Henry B. Nevins, Inc., was the winner in the 54-foot class.

The first contract was let on May 25, 1939, to Higgins Industries, Inc., for PT's 5 and 6, the Sparkman and Stephens design, scaled to an overall length of 81 feet. On June 8, 1939, contracts were let to the Fogal Boat Yard, Inc., later known as the Miami Shipbuilding Co., of Miami, Fla., for PT's 1 and 2, and to the Fisher Boat Works, Detroit, Mich., for PT's 3 and 4. These four boats were essentially the Crouch design, modified in some details by the Bureau of Ships. At the same time the Philadelphia Navy Yard was authorized to start construction of PT's 7 and 8, 81-foot boats designed by the Bureau of Ships.

7. PT 9

As it turned out, the winning designs already were obsolete. Assistant Secretary of the Navy Charles Edison had been talking with Henry R. Sutphen, executive vice president of the Electric Boat Company. On January 13, 1939, Mr. Edison told the General Board that a 70-foot British motor torpedo boat was available. Adm. Thomas C. Hart, Chairman of the General Board, replied on January 16, "Inasmuch as said design is known to be the result of several years' development, the General Board considers it highly advisable that such craft be obtained as a check on our own development."

After preliminary conferences with Navy Department officials, Mr. Sutphen sailed for England on February 10, with Elco's chief designer, Irwin Chase. Mr. Sutphen made the trip at his own expense, and was to buy the boat at his own expense. He sailed, however, with the understanding that if he succeeded in purchasing a Scott-Paine boat, the Navy would buy it in accordance with the terms of a contract tentatively agreed upon by Elco and the Navy.

Mr. Sutphen was well known in British naval circles. During World War I his company had turned out 550 80-foot ML's (motor launches) for the Royal Navy in 488 days. Besides, he had had preliminary conversations with Scott-Paine's New York representative before sailing. While in England he and Mr. Chase also inspected the Thornycroft and Vosper boats, but were particularly impressed by the speed, maneuverability, and seaworthiness of the Scott-Paine. Mr. Sutphen concluded arrangements to purchase one boat and to obtain the American manufacturing rights, notifying the Navy Department of the purchase on March 17.

President Roosevelt, informed by the Secretary of the Navy of the proposed acquisition, scribbled his approval on the Secretary's letter: "O.K. if price is as low as the proposed American 70-footer."

As it turned out, engine development costs brought the average price of the American boats above the quoted price for the Scott-Paine boat. The Navy signed the purchase contract on June 1.

The Scott-Paine boat, by then designated PT 9, arrived in New York as deck cargo on the SS *President Roosevelt* on September 5, 1939, when World War II was 2 days old. Ironically, on the day of the British boat's arrival, President Roosevelt issued the neutrality proclamation required by the

The Navy's first PT boat, the Scott-Paine PT 9, is unloaded from SS President Roosevelt *in New York, September 5, 1939.*

Neutrality Act of 1937, clamping an immediate embargo on shipments of arms, munitions, and planes to all belligerents, including the United Kingdom.

PT 9 was lightered to the Electric Boat Co. plant at Groton, Conn., where Scott-Paine himself put the boat through its paces for a Navy trial board.

8. THE ELCO CONTRACT

War in Europe brought a note of urgency to the PT program. Only PT's 1 and 8 were actually under construction, and no one could say how the new boats might turn out.

Meanwhile, the Scott-Paine boat seemed acceptable. The difficult transition from drawing board to finished product had been made. Elco had the plans and the license to build. Furthermore, Elco's experience with British ML's in the last war was proof of the company's ability to produce.

On October 3, Mr. Edison, by then Acting Secretary of the Navy, informed the President that he wished to acquire additional boats of Scott-Paine design, using unexpended funds from the $15 million appropriation for construction of experimental vessels. The President indicated his approval on the face of the Secretary's letter, adding, "How many? How much?"

About $5 million remained of the original $15 million. Mr. Sutphen thought he might build 16 boats for this price, but after Mr. Edison pointed out that the Navy wished to operate the boats in squadrons of 12, he agreed to build 23 boats, which, with PT 9, would make 2 complete squadrons.*

Final decision was reserved until November 1, when PT 9 ran rough water trials. With Scott-Paine again at the wheel, the boat passed her test with flying colors. Comdr. Robert B. Carney, one of the inspecting officers, and later to become Chief of Naval Operations, reported to Mr. Edison:

> The weather conditions afforded an opportunity to see the boat in almost every condition of sea, and she was handled and maneuvered without reservation or without attempt to spare either boat or personnel and under all conditions of course, wind, sea, and speed, the boat performed amazingly well . . .
>
> As a sea boat PT 9 has my unqualified approval and I have such confidence in the boat after observing her in rough water that I would not hesitate to take her anywhere under any conditions . . .
>
> I started out on the trials frankly skeptical about the claims I have heard for this boat during the past year, and I asked for every condition which I thought might bring out weaknesses in the boat's performance; Mr. Scott-Paine was more than glad to go anywhere at any speed or on any course that I requested, and on the run from Watch Hill to Race Light he handled the boat much more roughly than was necessary to demonstrate the qualities of the boat.

On December 7, 1939, the Navy Department made an award to Elco for construction of 11 motor torpedo boats, PT's 10 to 20, and 12 motor boat submarine chasers, PTC's 1 to 12. The boats themselves were to be replicas of

---

* Mr. Sutphen has stated that his company lost $600,000 on this contract.

the Scott-Paine model. The only major deviation was the substitution of Packard engines for Rolls-Royce engines.

The Navy Department granted Elco a delay in delivering PT 9 until January 3, 1940, as an aid in building her sister craft. Company officials had a rude shock when they tried to work from the Scott-Paine plans. They discovered they had a hodgepodge of partial sets of blueprints for three separate boats, none of them exactly matching PT 9. They resolved the difficulty by using the PT 9 as a working model, measuring each and every part and making an entirely new set of blueprints from their measurements. Certain as this method was, it was necessarily slow. PT 9 was not delivered to the Navy until June 17, 1940. Even then it was the U.S. Navy's first PT.

9. THE SQUADRONS

With delivery of 32 boats in prospect, the Chief of Naval Operations in April 1940 established the organizational policy that was to continue unchanged throughout the war. The squadron was to be commissioned, while the individual boats were not to be commissioned, but placed in service in the squadron. This policy centralized administration, avoiding the unutterable confusion had each boat been a separate administrative unit.

At the same time the Chief of Naval Operations designated boats for the first squadrons: Motor Torpedo Boat Squadron 1 was to include PT's 1 to 8; Motor Torpedo Boat Squadron 2, PT's 9 to 20; and Motor Boat Submarine Chaser Squadron 1, PTC's 1 to 12.

Squadron 1 was commissioned July 24, 1940, with Lt. Earl S. Caldwell as Squadron Commander. It was then composed of PT's 3 and 4, which had been delivered to the Norfolk Navy Yard at the end of June, and PT 9, which it was to keep until the commissioning of Squadron 2.

Squadron 1 was a collection of experimental types. Its first boats, the 3 and 4, were the Fisher Boat Works 58-footers, powered by two Packard 1,200-horsepower engines. PT's 1 and 2, the Miami Shipbuilding Co.'s 58-footers, never joined the squadron. Their production was so delayed, waiting for installation of their 1,200-horsepower Vimalert engines, that by the time they were delivered in December 1941, they were obsolete and were reclassified as small boats.

Higgins Industries had considerable difficulty translating the Sparkman and Stephens design into a satisfactory boat. PT 5 was eventually placed in

The Scott-Paine PT 9 paces PT 3, the Fisher Boat Works' 58-foot boat.

service on March 17, 1941, but its performance was disappointing. The original PT 6 was never placed in service. It was sold to Finland in 1940. On his own initiative and with his own capital, Andrew Jackson Higgins decided to build a modified version. When it was delivered in February 1941, it was a Higgins design rather than a modified Sparkman and Stephens, and was accepted enthusiastically by operating personnel, many of whom considered it superior to any previous type, including the Scott-Paine.

The Philadelphia Navy Yard Government-designed boats, PT's 7 and 8, were delivered in October and November 1940. The 7 was powered by four Hall-Scott 900-horsepower engines. The 8, unique in that it had an aluminum hull, was powered by two Allison 2,000-horsepower engines (actually four V-engines mounted to form two X-engines) and one Hall-Scott 600-horsepower engine. These boats were sadly overweight when delivered, largely because the Navy Yard used heavy destroyer fittings and fixtures in their construction. PT 8 was further handicapped by its engine installation. The big Allison engines had no self-starters. It was necessary to build up a speed of 15 knots on the small Hall-Scott engines and then

19–N–25576

The aluminum hull PT 8, built by the Philadelphia Navy Yard.

drag in the Allisons. Nor did the Allisons have reverse gears. This made maneuvering close to a dock extremely difficult, dependent entirely on the small Hall-Scott engine.

With the delivery of PT 10, the first Elco boat, Motor Torpedo Boat Squadron 2 was commissioned November 8, 1940. Lieutenant Caldwell was commander of both squadrons until February 1941, when Lt. William C. Specht relieved him as commander of Squadron 1.

10. THE 77-FOOT BOAT

At the time that the first boats of Squadron 2 were being delivered, the Chief of the Bureau of Ordnance recommended an increase in the size of the boats to accommodate four 21-inch torpedo tubes. The General Board recommended that the new boat be approximately 80 feet overall, and suggested that the Navy acquire 24 with funds made available by a $50 million appropriation for small craft for the fiscal year beginning July 1, 1940. The Secretary of the Navy approved these recommendations, and on September 17, 1940, the Navy awarded a new contract to Elco for twenty-four 77-foot boats of modified Scott-Paine design. The earlier contract was modified so that PT 20, on which construction had not yet started, would be the first of the 77-footers.

11. SOUTHERN WATERS AND LEND-LEASE

Motor Torpedo Boat Squadrons 1 and 2 were ordered south for the winter. Squadron 2, completed with the delivery of her last boats on December 31, 1940, made the trip to Miami without undue difficulty. Squadron 1, then comprising only the PT's 3, 4, 7, and 8, was beset by engineering mishaps. In Florida the boats were joined by the first PT tender, USS *Niagara,* the former Manville yacht, *Hi-Esmaro.* Her repair facilities were limited, but she was the best available at the time, and the experience gained in operating with the *Niagara* was to prove valuable in planning later tenders.

All boats had been scheduled for shakedown cruises to Cuba, Puerto Rico, and the Virgin Islands, but the Squadron 1 boats were clearly so inadequate that Squadron 2 sailed alone for Cuba. Squadron 1 stayed in Florida, where it took delivery of the Higgins boats, PT's 5 and the second 6.

Squadron 2's cruise to Cienfuegos and return proved the Elco boats could stand punishment. The boats went through extremely heavy seas with remarkably little damage. Plans for further cruising in the West Indies were cut short at the end of March, when the squadrons were ordered to proceed to New York to transfer most of their boats to the British under lend-lease.

Of the Squadron 1 boats, only the Higgins-designed PT 6 was considered worth keeping for further tests; the British did not want the aluminum-hull PT 8, so PT's 3, 4, 5, and 7 were scheduled for transfer. The Squadron 2 boats were too small to carry four 21-inch torpedo tubes, and since the first 77-footers were due to be delivered in June, all could be turned over to the British, who desperately needed them in the Mediterranean. The Squadron 1 boats and PT's 9 to 15 were transferred in April. Thus PT 9, the original Scott-Paine boat, was returned to the British just over 2 years after Mr. Sutphen purchased it in England. Transfer of PT's 16 to 19 was delayed until July, so that those four boats, with PT's 6 and 8, could be sent to Newport, R.I., to assist in training new personnel pending delivery of the first 77-footers.

12. PTC's

Motor Boat Submarine Chaser Squadron 1 was placed in commission February 20, 1941, with Lt. (jg.) Edward G. De Long, as Squadron Commander. Its boats were identical with those of Squadron 2, except that they carried two dozen depth charges instead of four torpedoes. Equipped with racks from which depth charges could be dropped astern, and two Y-guns, which could throw four charges at a time, two on either side, the boats were able to lay down a good pattern for an underwater barrage.

While the squadron was still fitting out in New York, lend-lease cut it down to four boats. PTC's 5 to 12 were transferred to the British on April 4, for service in the Royal Navy as motor gunboats.

The remaining four boats, meanwhile, went to Key West, where each was fitted with a separate type of experimental sound gear. None worked. If the boat was underway the noise of its engines drowned out the echoes of the sound equipment. If the boat shut off its engines and lay to in anything but a dead calm, it developed such a short, sharp roll that it could not pick up the echoes. Although admirably armed against submarines, the PTC's had no way of locating them.

PTC's 1 to 4 returned to New York, where they were leased to the British on July 15, 1941. Two days later the squadron was decommissioned.

13. THE PLYWOOD DERBIES

The winter in Florida did provide experience. On May 19, 1941, Lieutenants Caldwell and Specht met with representatives of the Chief of Naval Operations, Bureau of Ships, Bureau of Inspection and Survey, and Interior Control Board, to discuss the future of PT's.

There was general agreement that all PT's had been defective either in military characteristics or construction, except for PT 20, which was still an unknown quantity. The conference recommended comparative service tests of PT's 6, 8, and 20; a new 76-foot boat designed and being constructed by Higgins Industries; and a new 72-foot boat designed by Frank Huckins, under construction at the Huckins Yacht Co., Jacksonville, Fla. They also recommended that no more boats of the PT 20 design be contracted for until the boats of this class should satisfactorily complete the tests.

Twelve days later Adm. Harold R. Stark, Chief of Naval Operations, wrote to the President of the Board of Inspection and Survey: "It is apparent that a considerable divergence of opinion exists among the various offices of the Navy Department and among officers of Motor Torpedo Boat Squadrons as to the suitability of various types of Motor Torpedo Boats which have been acquired, or are now being built. In order to crystallize as far as possible, opinion as to the suitability of these various types of Motor Boats and to establish criteria for future contracts, it is desired that the Board of Inspection and Survey conduct comparative service tests."

Accordingly, these boats were tested off New London, July 21 to 24, 1941:

1. PT 6: 81-foot Higgins; 3 Packard 1,200-hp engines.
2. PT 8: 81-foot Philadelphia Navy Yard; aluminum hull; 2 Allison 2,000-hp engines, 1 Hall-Scott 550-hp engine.
3. PT 20: 77-foot Elco; 3 Packard 1,200-hp engines; equipped with special propellers; special strengthening added to hull framing and deck.
4. PT's 26, 30, 31, 33: Same as PT 20, except with standard propellers and without special strengthening.
5. PT 69: 72-foot Huckins; 4 Packard 1,200-hp engines.
6. PT 70: 76-foot Higgins; 3 Packard 1,200-hp engines.
7. 70-foot boat built for British by Higgins; 3 Hall-Scott 900-hp engines.

The most important event on the program was an open-sea run of 190 miles at full throttle, forever after referred to by PT personnel as the "Plywood Derby." The course started at Sarah Ledge, led around the eastern end of Block Island, thence around Fire Island Lightship, with the finish line at Montauk Point Whistling Buoy. It was chosen to provide the

NR&L (MOD)—32475

PT 20, first of the Elco 77-footers, winner of the "Plywood Derby" in July 1941.

severest possible test under the prevailing weather conditions. The worst conditions encountered, however, turned out to be moderate swells with a cross-surface chop.

Since the Elco entries were the only boats with complete ordnance installations, the other boats were ballasted to the required weight.

PT 26 had developed cracks in the deck during preliminary trials on the 21st, and was unable to take part in the run. PT 33 developed similar cracks off Block Island, and withdrew from the race. PT 70 withdrew between Block Island and Montauk Point because of casualties to deck and frames. The Higgins-built British boat developed engine trouble within 5 minutes after crossing the starting line and had to retire. Elco's PT 30 suffered structural damage at the close of the race and was not considered to have completed this race satisfactorily.

The remaining Elco boats, PT's 20 and 31, easily led the rest of the field with average speeds for the 190-mile course of 39.72 knots and 37.01 knots, respectively. The Huckins entry, PT 69, was third, at 33.83 knots, and the Higgins PT 6 was fourth at 31.40 knots. The Philadelphia Navy Yard PT 8 was the slowest finisher, with a 30.73-knot average.

While the race was clearly an Elco victory, it demonstrated that the Elco hull required further strengthening. Strongbacks were later installed on all the Elco 77-footers to keep the decks from cracking.

The tests preceding the sea run also showed that the Elco boat was fastest over a measured mile. PT 20 ran the mile at 45.3 knots with light loading, and 44.1 knots heavy. The only other boats that exceeded 40 knots were the Huckins 69, with 43.8 knots light and 41.5 knots heavy, and the Higgins PT 70, with 41.2 knots light and 40.9 knots heavy.

In maneuverability tests, however, the Huckins PT 69, Higgins PT 6, and Navy Yard PT 8, in that order, proved to have smaller turning circles than the Elco PT 20. Turning circles of the Higgins PT 70 and the Higgins-built British boat were not observed.

Ballasting of the boats caused dissatisfaction with the Plywood Derby. Mr. Higgins contended, and the trial board conceded, that the ballast could not be disposed so as to give horizontal and vertical moments equal to the simulated loads, but had to be distributed in the best available stowage spaces on each boat. The board reported that the deck failure of PT 70 "was apparently due to the loading of weights on the deck in order to compensate for the armament which had not been installed on this design."

Because of this dissatisfaction, and to acquire more data for use in future design, a second Plywood Derby was scheduled for August 11 and 12, the earliest date that the boats could be put in repair.

Every effort was made to install actual ordnance weights. Of the boats participating in the second run, only the Higgins-built British boat had no ordnance and required ballasting.

By the time of the second Plywood Derby, PT 6 had been transferred to Britain under lend-lease. Besides the Higgins-built British boat, the entries were the Navy Yard PT 8, the Huckins PT 69, the Higgins PT 70, and PT 21, a 77-foot Elco boat. A second Elco 77-footer, PT 29, was assigned to pace PT 8, so that accelerometer readings could be taken to measure the comparative pounding of the two boats. In the first race PT 8 had been the easiest riding and the 77-foot Elcos the roughest.

The course was the same except that the starting line was moved to Race Rock, making it 5 miles shorter. Weather conditions were quite different, however, with heavy cross swells prevailing. West of Montauk the height of the swells was 6 to 8 feet, with occasional waves of 10 or 12 feet. In a confused sea south of Block Island and between Block Island and Montauk Point, the boats met short steep waves as high as 15 feet.

East of Block Island PT 69 suffered several fractured bilge stringers and withdrew. Elco again won the derby, with PT 21 setting an average speed of 27.5 knots, but this time the Higgins PT 70 was close behind, averaging 27.2 knots. PT 8 made 25.1 knots, with the Higgins-built British boat last at 24.8 knots. Some of PT 70's planking and deck fastenings pulled loose. PT 21 developed minor cracks in the deck though not to the extent of those suffered by the Elco boats in the earlier sea run.

The destroyer *Wilkes* was assigned to run the course with the PT's and was directed to be as nearly as possible at full power on crossing the starting line. The *Wilkes* ran the course in 6 hours 18 minutes, at an average speed of 29.8 knots. "This time," the Board reported, "was only 25 minutes better than that of PT 21, which required 6 hours 43 minutes to complete the run at an average speed of 27.5 knots. It appears, therefore, that for the assigned mission, modern destroyers possess no sensible advantage over the motor boats even under sea conditions highly unfavorable for the latter, and that in areas where limited visibility is not unusual the motor boats might readily prove much more adaptable than the larger vessels within the limitations of their operating ranges."

14. STANDARDIZATION

The comparative service tests made it possible to prescribe PT characteristics with more assurance. Representatives of the Chief of Naval Operations and Bureau of Ships, meeting in the fall of 1941, decided once again to increase the size of the boats. The Chief of Naval Operations requested the Bureau of Ships to prepare specifications for a new boat and to invite representatives of Elco, Higgins, and Huckins, the three contractors who had demonstrated their ability to build PT's, to a conference.

Capt. A. Loring Swasey and Mr. Sidney A. Peters, of the Bureau of Ships, worked day and night for 2 days to have the specifications ready for the conference on October 6. Mr. Sutphen, Mr. Higgins, and Mr. Huckins attended with their designers. Capt. E. L. Cochrane, of the Bureau of Ships, told them, "We are convinced that the boat isn't big enough to do the things we want it to do, and we need a heavier, more effective, more powerful boat."

Captain Cochrane gave the new specifications. Overall length was to be not less than 75 feet—the smallest that would permit the boat to fulfill performance requirements—and not more than 82 feet, the largest that could be transported easily. The boat was to be powered by three Packard engines, which were to be equipped with mufflers to permit silent approach. The boat was to make a trial speed of 40 knots, sustained for 1 hour, and have a cruising radius of 500 miles.

80-G-187331

PT 95, the first Huckins 78-foot boat.

80–G–88718

PT 84, one of the first of the Higgins 78-foot boats.

"The hull," the specifications stated, "shall be the hard chine stepless bottom type with lines formed with a view to minimizing stress on the hull and fatigue of crew under all conditions and to assure a suitable platform for torpedo and gun fire. The lines shall also be formed to insure easy maneuvering of the boat and a small turning circle at full speed and ability to change direction quickly. The sides shall flare outward from chine to gunwale."

The permanent influence of the Scott-Paine design may be seen in the requirements for a hard chine stepless bottom type hull, and the outward flare of the sides.

"The hull construction," the specifications added, "shall be of the lightest weight, consistent with adequate strength, stiffness and durability for the service intended, and with an eye to simplicity for mass production."

The three companies were invited to submit bids for boats in lots up to 32— the number for which funds were immediately available. As a result of the conference, Higgins received a contract for 24 boats, and Huckins for 8. Immediately after the entry of the United States into war, Elco was awarded a contract for 36 boats.

Elco, already geared to large-scale production, was the first to put the new boats in service, with Motor Torpedo Boat Squadron 5 (PT's 103–114),

80-G-256499

PT 601, one of the latest Elco 80-foot boats, built in 1945.

80-footers, commissioned in New York on June 16, 1942. Higgins followed with Squadron 13 (PT's 73–84), 78-footers, commissioned in New Orleans on September 18, 1942. The first of the Huckins 78-footers, PT's 95–97, went to Squadron 4 in July and August 1942, and PT's 98–102 were commissioned as Squadron 14 in Jacksonville on February 17, 1943. Huckins built only 10 more boats, commissioned as Squadron 26, and none of this type was used in combat. The Navy at last had standardized its PT's with the 80-foot Elco and the 78-foot Higgins.

15. RESHUFFLING THE SQUADRONS

Even-numbered boats of the Elco 77-footers were assigned to Squadron 2; odd-numbered boats to Squadron 1. Practically all were delivered during June and July 1941, permitting the lend-lease transfer of PT 6 and PT's 16–19. Most of the new boats as delivered were short of ordnance. Torpedo tubes were the most serious shortage—there had been many delays in getting the 21-inch tube in production. Thus, when early in August the Chief of Naval

Operations directed the formation of Squadron 3, six boats for immediate shipment to the Philippines, the new squadron received those boats that had complete ordnance equipment, PT's 31 to 35, and PT 41.

So also, when Squadron 1 was directed on August 13 to prepare for assignment to the Pacific Fleet, it was assigned the most nearly complete of the remaining boats, PT's 20 to 30, and PT 42. Squadron 2 was left to take the only other boats then contracted for, PT's 36 to 40 and PT's 43 to 48.

The beginning of the war and shipment of Squadron 2 to Panama in December brought immediate need for more boats to be used in training PT personnel in the United States. Elco's first 80-footers would be ready in June and would require trained officers and crews to operate them. Elco meanwhile had contracted to build under lend-lease for England 20 boats of the 77-foot class, PT's 49 to 68, which also carried the designation BPT's (British PT's) 1 to 20. It was agreed in December that the U.S. Navy should retain the second 10 of these boats.

Squadron 4, comprising PT's 59 to 68, was commissioned on January 13, with Lt. Comdr. Alan R. Montgomery as squadron commander. The squadron was assigned on completion of fitting out to the Motor Torpedo Boat Squadrons Training Center, Melville, R.I. There it remained throughout the war as the training squadron, though its boats changed from time to time to permit students to handle new types, and its personnel changed frequently to give combat veterans a breathing spell and to afford students the benefit of their battle experience.

16. THE TRAINING CENTER

The first attempt to establish an organized training program for new personnel was made in the late spring and summer of 1941. While Lieutenant Caldwell remained in New York to accept and fit out the new 77-foot Elcos, Lieutenant Specht took the boats that were in service to Newport with the *Niagara,* and established a familiarization school on the tender. This project came to a sudden end with the reshuffling of the squadrons in August.

After the designation of Squadron 4 as the training squadron, the Secretary of the Navy on February 17, 1942, directed the establishment of the Motor Torpedo Boat Squadrons Training Center at Melville, R.I., on Narragansett Bay just north of Newport. William C. Specht, who had been promoted to lieutenant commander, was relieved of command of Squadron 1 at Pearl Harbor in order to organize the training center, which inevitably came to be known as "Specht Tech." It began operations in the middle of March 1942.

From the beginning, it was the policy of the training center to use combat veterans as instructors. Among the first instructors were Lt. (jg.) Henry J. Brantingham and Ens. George E. Cox, Jr., who had been with Squadron 3 in the Philippines; Lt. John Harllee; Lt. H. M. S. Swift, USNR; Lt. (jg.) Leonard R. Hardy, USNR; Lt (jg.) Harold D. Howes, USNR; Ens. Edward I. Farley, USNR; and Ens. J. R. Thompson, USNR, who had been with Squadron 1 at Pearl Harbor. Among those who became boat captains in the training squadron were Ens. Anthony B. Akers, USNR, of Squadron 3, and Ens. Paul T. Rennell, USNR, and Ens. A. Murray Preston, USNR, of Squadron 1.

By the first week in April, 51 officers and 177 enlisted men were under instruction; the boats of Squadron 4 were available for training; 47 quonset huts were in various stages of completion, and a request had been submitted for the construction of 44 additional huts. Eventually the Training Center acquired 13 structures devoted to office space, 34 classrooms, 42 maintenance buildings, and 197 huts for living quarters. It was equipped to handle a normal load of 860 enlisted students and 90 student officers. Squadron 4 was gradually enlarged until at the end of 1944 it comprised 28 boats of 4 distinct types.

During the early days, before its own equipment was adequate, the Training Center made use of the superior facilities of the Naval Antiaircraft Training Center at Price's Neck, R.I.; the Naval Torpedo Station at Newport; the rifle range at the Naval Training Station, Newport; the Packard Engine School at Detroit; and the Elco plant at Bayonne, N.J.

In time the Training Center acquired a vast array of training devices. Well-equipped shops made possible not only the training of personnel but a large-scale experimental program. Development of a lightweight torpedo rack to replace the old tube is an outstanding example of the work accomplished under this program.

The period of training originally was 2 months. In 1943 a third month was added to the training period for officers and certain specialized enlisted rates. At first an attempt was made to give each man some training in all subjects, on the theory that in so small a crew each man should be able to pinch hit for any other man. It soon became apparent that the training period was too short for such a theory to be put into efficient practice. The men were apt to become jacks of all rates, with thorough grounding in

NR&L (MOD)—32490

PT 40, a battle-scarred veteran of Guadalcanal, returns to the MTB Squadrons Training Center in July 1944 to be used in training repair personnel.

Students of the Repair Training Unit at Melville put new planking on PT 40.

none. Thereafter more specialized training was given to each man in his own rate, with generally good results.

The Training Center became the personnel clearinghouse for the entire PT service. Officers and men returning from combat areas were ordered there for temporary duty, and the Bureau of Naval Personnel accepted the Training Center's recommendations for future assignment both of graduating students and experienced personnel returned from combat. In April 1944, the Training Center inaugurated a program of refresher courses, to bring returning personnel up to date on recent developments in PT operation and equipment.

The Repair Training Unit was established at the Training Center in March 1944 to give specialized instruction to personnel for PT bases and tenders. Many of the repair and maintenance problems of the first squadrons might have been avoided had such a unit been formed earlier. All too many bases and tenders were handicapped by inexperienced personnel who had to learn about PT's the hard way after they reached the operating areas.

80–G–40538

PT's in Panama: A sailor looks out at Taboga harbor from the U.S. Naval Station recreation hall, which before the war was a fashionable gambling casino.

In November 1944, a special command course was established for prospective squadron commanders and executive officers.

By the time of its third anniversary, March 16, 1945, the Training Center had trained 1,797 officers and 11,668 enlisted men.

17. TABOGA

U.S. Naval Station Taboga was established in August 1942, with Lt. Comdr. H. S. Cooper, USNR, as commanding officer. It was to support the PT squadron assigned as part of the naval defenses of the Panama Canal, and

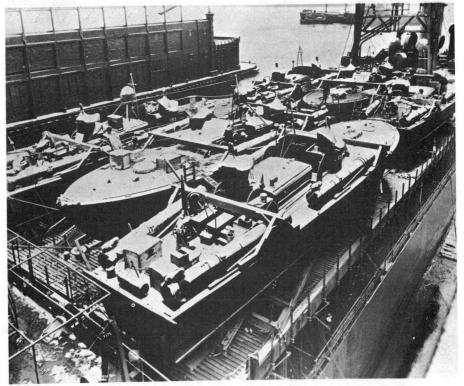

80–G–184393

A light snowfall whitens boats of Squadron 9, loaded three abreast on SS White Plains *in New York in December 1942 for shipment to Panama.*

80-G-31686

Squadron 5 boats, in a training run from Taboga to the Galapagos Islands in November 1942, fueled at sea from seaplane tender Pocomoke.

was to serve as a temporary training base for squadrons awaiting shipment to Pacific areas. The base was pleasantly situated on the small, mountainous island of Taboga just off the Pacific entrance to the Panama Canal. The site, leased from the Panamanian Government, included a gambling casino of modern masonry construction which (though the gambling devices were removed) made a splendid recreation hall. The Navy installed many facilties, including piers, concrete aprons for hauling boats, torpedo shops and storehouses, engineering shops, powerplant, radio station, gasoline storage tanks, magazines, and living and messing facilities for 125 officers and 700 enlisted men.

This was the base for Squadron 2, then for Squadron 5, which relieved Squadron 2 in September 1942, and finally for Squadron 14, which in turn relieved Squadron 5 early in 1943. It was also the temporary training and shakedown base for most squadrons en route to the Pacific. Early Elco squadrons were shipped to Panama from New York or Norfolk. Higgins squadrons and later Elco squadrons made the run through the Caribbean to Taboga on their own bottoms.

The first squadrons conducted their own training exercises. Later, under command of Lt. Comdr. Van L. Wanselow, USNR, the base developed an extensive training program. The base commander was designated Commander Motor Torpedo Boat Squadrons Panama Sea Frontier, and all squadrons were directed to report to him for operational control during their stay in the area.

Climatic and sea conditions were ideal for all phases of advanced training. Torpedo firing, barge hunting practice, gunnery practice, navigational cruises, and joint maneuvers with aircraft could be conducted throughout the year. The many small islands in the Gulf of Panama offered unlimited opportunities for exercises in barge hunting and radar tracking.

18. SHAKEDOWN

Shakedown training was essential to new squadrons. Most of the personnel had had only brief training at Melville and needed to learn to work together as a team. The Elco squadrons began sending their boats to Melville for shakedown, and most of them had an opportunity for further advanced training at Taboga.

For the Higgins boats, such a procedure was impractical because of the great distance between New Orleans and Melville. In April 1943, the PT shakedown detail was established as an adjunct of the Submarine Chaser Training Center at Miami, Fla. Lt. Comdr. Alan R. Montgomery, who had taken the second Squadron 3 to Guadalcanal, was first commanding officer of the new unit.

Montgomery worked out an intensive 14-day training program, later expanded to 3 weeks, which soon became standard for shakedown both at Melville and Miami. Severe winter weather conditions at Melville led to the decision to conduct all shakedown operations at Miami, for Elco as well as Higgins boats, starting in December 1943.

The shakedown detail also conducted a large amount of experimental work, often in conjunction with the experimental program at Melville. The two commands were entirely separate, but maintained close liaison in both their training and experimental programs.

19. COMMISSIONING DETAILS

To expedite the fitting out of squadrons, PT commissioning details were established in New York and New Orleans in June and August of 1942, respectively. Lt. R. J. Dressling organized and was first officer-in-charge of each unit.

The principal function of the commissioning details was to assist the squadrons in procuring the equipment that they would need in the operating areas: spare parts, tools, charts, paint, raincoats and salt water soap, generators and chain hoists, scrubbing brushes and office equipment, and a thousand other items. The commissioning details knew when boats were scheduled for delivery to squadrons. They could plan ahead and place orders for equipment well in advance, so that it would be ready for delivery when the squadron was organized. If material could not be delivered before a squad-

NR&L (MOD)—32477

Commissioning ceremonies of MTB Squadron 23 at Higgins Industrial Canal Plant, New Orleans, June 28, 1943.

ron's departure, the commissioning detail followed through on the order, and saw that it was shipped to the squadron's destination. These units lifted a tremendous burden from the squadron commanders, and greatly accelerated the fitting-out period.

20. FERRYING COMMAND

Squadron 43, a Higgins squadron commissioned in December 1944, was ordered to decommission in New Orleans in March 1945, so that its boats might be transferred to the Russian Navy. At the same time 36 other new Higgins PT's, not yet delivered, were designated for transfer to the Russians. To accomplish delivery of these boats, the Chief of Naval Operations established the PT Ferrying Command, with Lt. George C. Miller, USNR, as commanding officer. PT's were sent from New Orleans to Seattle loaded on LST's, four to a ship. The Ferrying Command provided a crew for each PT. Boat lashings were arranged for immediate release of the PT's; if the LST should be sunk, the boats could float free and their crews could run them to the nearest port under their own power. As it turned out, no LST was ever sunk on one of these ferrying runs.

At the end of the each LST run, the crews turned the boats over to Russian Navy representatives in Seattle and returned to New Orleans for more boats.

The Ferrying Command also ran trials on the new boats and fitted them out before they were loaded for shipment in New Orleans.

21. TENDERS

The first tenders were far from ideal, but they were the best available at the time. They were useful as communications centers—they could communicate with boats on patrol and at the same time receive orders from and pass information to higher echelons of command. They serviced torpedoes and performed a certain amount of engineering and electrical repair work. They could do some carpentry work, but unless they towed floating drydocks with them, could do little in the way of underwater repairs. They carried gasoline, supplies, and equipment in limited quantities. They messed the boat crews aboard, sparing the always overworked PT generators the added burden of supplying power to operate the electric stoves. Sometimes, when their

NR&L (MOD)—32486

The first PT tender, USS Niagara, *a converted yacht, with PT 17 alongside.*

evaporators were working well, they could offer the boat crews the luxury
of fresh water showers.

The first tender was the *Niagara,* the former Manville yacht *Hi-Esmaro.*
The *Niagara* was 253 feet long, 1,923 tons displacement.   Built at the Bath
Iron Works, Bath, Maine, in 1929, she was converted in New York in the
winter of 1940.   She was at Pearl Harbor for a time tending Squadron 1, then
went to Panama, and underwent further conversion in New York in the
summer of 1942.   In the winter of 1942 she was assigned to the South Pacific
area, where we shall meet her again.

The second tender was the *Jamestown,* the former yacht *Alder,* built by
Pusey & Jones, Wilmington, Del., in 1927.   She was 294 feet long, 2,386 tons.
After her conversion as a gunboat in May 1941, she was sent to the U.S. Naval
Academy at Annapolis for use in connection with midshipmen's cruises.
She underwent further conversion as a PT tender in the winter of 1941.   After
serving for a time as tender for Squadron 4 at Newport, the *Jamestown* sailed

80—G—248513

An LST-type PT tender, USS Silenus.

80—G—472496

PT tender Oyster Bay, first of a class originally laid down as seaplane tenders,
with a squadron of PT's in Leyte Gulf.

for the South Pacific, where she tended PT's until February 1944, when she
was transferred to the Southwest Pacific.

The third tender, and last of the yachts, was the *Hilo,* 278 feet long, 2,300
tons. She was built at the Bath Iron Works in 1931 as the Johnson yacht
Caroline. In 1938 she was purchased by William B. Leeds, who renamed her
Moana. Her conversion to a PT tender at Long Beach, Calif., early in 1942
was a horrible example of the frantic confusion of the early days of the war.
Capt. Frank A. Munroe, Jr., USNR, who as a lieutenant commander was her
first commanding officer, recalls that not an officer or man assigned to the
ship had ever seen a PT.

"Only vague specifications were received regarding what was required in
the ship to make it suitable as a tender," he said. "No one could be found in
the 11th Naval District who knew the first thing about PT's. BuPers was
asked to send a qualified officer and as a result Lt. (jg.) H. M. S. Swift, USNR,
was detached from Ron One at Pearl and ordered to temporary duty with
the ship. His knowledge and experience were invaluable and responsible

80–G–282678

USS Acontius, *a C–1–A-type PT tender. PT cradle may be seen under boom on foredeck.*

for what facilities the ship finally had. I had hoped to have him as my executive officer but he was ordered to Melville as an instructor about a month before commissioning."

The officers and men of the *Hilo* did not see a PT until early in July, when the ship arrived in Pearl Harbor. From Pearl Harbor the *Hilo* eventually made her way to New Guinea, where she became the first tender in the Southwest Pacific area.

An important step forward came with the commissioning of the USS *Portunus* in June 1943. This was a converted LST, 328 feet long, of 3,754 tons displacement. The large so-called "tank deck," used in LST's for cargo-carrying space, was converted to shop space. Here at last was a PT tender with adequate space and adequate machinery. One of her best features was an "A-frame," a heavy device on the port side that could lift a PT out of the water for repairs to the underwater structure.

The LST type was so satisfactory that eight more were built. Some of the later ones were equipped with two A-frames, one on each side, so that two boats could be raised from the water simultaneously.

Beginning with the *Oyster Bay,* commissioned in November 1943, four ships originally laid down as seaplane tenders were completed as PT tenders by their builder, the Lake Washington Shipyards, Houghton, Wash. These were 310 feet long, about 2,800 tons. They were fine, sleek ships, built along destroyer lines, and each carried, in addition to antiaircraft batteries, two 5-inch guns. Though they were faster than the ungainly LST type, they had limited shop space and had no means of raising a PT from the water unless they towed a drydock. In certain types of operations, however, where speed and firepower were required, they proved superior to the LST type.

Finally came two huge tenders, the *Acontius* and *Cyrene,* commissioned in June and September 1944. These were 413 feet long, with a full load displacement of 11,000 tons—converted Maritime Commission C–1 hulls. These were splendid ships, with extensive shops and a vast amount of storage space. There was a boom capable of lifting a PT out of the water and setting it down on the forecastle. The *Cyrene* obtained an extra cradle, so that it could set one boat down on the forecastle and lift another one alongside at the same time. The only disadvantage of these ships was that they were too big and valuable to risk in an area where concentrated enemy air attack was likely—but they were ideal in a rear area.

Thus each of the later three types had its uses; the seaplane-tender type for forward moves into areas where air attack was likely; the C–1 type as a rear area tender, and the LST type as a fairly successful compromise between the two—big enough to perform the tender function successfully, but not so valuable a ship that it could never be risked in a forward area.

22. BASES

The development of PT bases was a tiny part of the Navy's vast advance base program. Faced with the necessity of building hundreds of different types and sizes in all parts of the world, the Navy reduced each base to its simplest form: a combination of so-called functional components. A functional component is a collection of personnel and material designed to perform one of the specific tasks of an advance base. It may consist of one man with 100 pounds of equipment, or 1,000 officers and men with 10,000 tons of equipment.

Each functional component contains all of the personnel and equipment necessary for the performance of its particular task, including workshops, vehicles, boats, office equipment, and a 90-day initial supply of shop and office consumables. Housing and messing facilities for personnel, defensive ordnance, communication facilities, and in many cases powerplants and water supply usually are not provided with each functional component. These facilities are functional components in themselves and render services to all other functional components at the base.

All functional components were listed by designating letters and numbers in a large catalog, very similar to a mail-order catalog, so that area commanders or officers charged with the planning of operations could order the functional components which would fit together to give them exactly the type of bases they needed.

The Base Maintenance Section of the Office of the Chief of Naval Operations, working with representatives of the Bureau of Ships and assisted by the Training Center at Melville and officers with PT experience, developed seven functional components especially for PT's:

1. *A–4 Unit: Administration (PT Base):* This component directed and coordinated the activities of a PT base. It had a commanding officer (for the entire PT base), one other officer, and eight enlisted men. Its major material items included office equipment, a truck, motion picture projectors, a small boat, and housing for the office.

2. *E–11 Unit: PT Operating Base Repair Component:* This was a semimobile unit with facilities for major hull repair, minor engine repair, and replacement of engines for one squadron of PT's. It had no facilities for major engine overhaul. The component included 3 officers and 131 enlisted men, a machine shop, carpenter shop, spare parts for radio and radar, four 40- by 100-foot buildings, and utilities such as water, power, compressed air, and heat if necessary.

3. *E–12: PT Major Engine Overhaul Component:* This unit was designed to provide four squadrons with major engine overhaul facilities. It had 2 officers and 82 enlisted men. This component was designed to be used in conjunction with an E–11 unit. Its main material consisted of additional repair equipment for use in the machine and carpenter shops of the operating base repair unit.

4. *E–21 Unit: PT Squadron Portable Base Equipment:* This component was a portable base intended to provide a squadron of 8 to 12 boats with portable, lightweight repair and operating equipment. The unit could be carried aboard the PT's themselves and put ashore at a location as much as 350 miles in advance of the nearest PT boat operating base. The equipment of the organization allowed it to make frontline emergency repairs, such as replacing propellers and making hull repairs; and it could operate also as a temporary base where boats could obtain fuel, medical assistance, and communications support. Despite these extensive capabilities, the E–21 component had only one

officer and eight men.   However, it was expected that repair personnel of the PT squadron in the area would augment this unit as necessary.

5. *J–2B Unit: PT Base Ordnance Shop:* This unit had facilities to maintain and make minor repairs to all PT armament except torpedoes.   It had one officer and five men.

6. *J–5C Unit: Torpedo Depot Component, Small:* This unit provided facilities to service and ready 50 torpedoes a week.   It had 1 officer and 10 men.

7. *P–6D: Decontamination and Camouflage (PT Base):* This unit had decontamination apparatus for use in case of gas attack, and camouflage materials including paint, spray guns, and nets.   It had no regularly assigned personnel.

While other functional components were especially developed for PT's, a typical PT operating base would contain many standard functional components as well.   The following is a standard PT operating base, without main engine overhaul facilities, for one squadron of boats:

Designation	Components	Number required	Officers	Enlisted men	Long tons	Measurement tons
A–4	Administration (PT base)	1	2	8	12	20
C–3	Radio station—operating base (small)	1	1	13	20	40
C–8	Visual station—operating base (small)	1	0	8	9	23
D–9	Petroleum products	1	0	0	3,000	3,750
D–15	Cobbler and tailor shop (small)	1	0	5	15	25
D–22	Disbursing office (small)	1	1	5	6	9
E–11	PT operating base repair	1	3	131	1,000	2,500
G–10	Dispensary—10 bed—mobile	1	1	3	11	36
J–2B	PT base ordnance	1	1	5	25	30
J–4C	Base demolition	1	0	0	1	4
J–5C	Torpedo depot (small)	1	1	10	130	570
J–15A	Personal equipment for enlisted men	2	0	0	4	22
J–15B	Personal equipment for officers	10	0	0	1	2
N–1A	Camp (250 men)—tents	2	0	50	430	940
N–5B	Camp buildings (250 men)—tropical	2	0	0	300	446
N–20	Base recreation	1	1	3	2	4
P–6D	Decontamination and camouflage (PT)	1	0	0	40	100
P–12A	Fire protection (basic)	1	0	1	10	30
Q–2	Preembarkation (100 men)	2	0	0	1	3
	Total	11	242		5,017	8,554

It should be remembered that this is the standard operating base as planned, and that in practice components could be, and were, added or omitted. The E–11 unit in such a base was usually augmented by addition of one or more pontoon piers and drydocks. By no means all PT bases were as large as this one. Such a base as this would usually be augmented by one or more extra N–1A units and would be used as a main repair base for several squadrons which would operate from smaller bases in further advanced areas.

Like the tenders, the bases were not fully developed when the first squadrons were sent to the Pacific, and for many months PT's had to operate with inadequate base facilities. Once the functional component system was well underway, however, it provided as nearly perfect a solution to base problems as could be imagined, because it was possible merely by adding or subtracting components to form a base suited in size and capabilities for the performance of any required task.

23. HELLCAT AND ELCOPLANE

Although the Elco 80 and Higgins 78-foot boats remained standard throughout the war, the story of PT development would not be complete without mention of the Hellcat and Elcoplane, which exemplified the efforts of the two companies to improve their products.

Higgins Industries on their own initiative designed and built an entirely new boat, a 70-footer, which they called the Hellcat. Builder's trials, run on Lake Pontchartrain on June 30, 1943, were witnessed by officers of the Miami Shakedown Detail, who turned in an enthusiastic report to the Bureau of Ships. There was no doubt that the boat performed well: it made a top speed of 46 knots, and was able to reverse course in 9 seconds. A similar turn with a Higgins 78-footer (which could turn faster than the Elco 80) took 22 seconds. The boat had low silhouette and left little wake at idling speeds—good features for making a sneak attack. Visibility from the cockpit was superior to that of either of the standard boats.

On the basis of the report of the builder's trials, the Navy purchased the boat on August 26 and gave it a number, PT 564. A Board of Inspection and Survey ran trials for 5 days in September, during which the 564 averaged 47.825 knots on a full-throttle mile run, as compared with 40.12 knots averaged by a standard Higgins boat, PT 282. The smaller boat proved

PT 564, the 70-foot Higgins Hellcat.

itself considerably more maneuverable than the larger one, and was cheaper and easier to build.

The Board recommended that if it should pass rough water trials, the new boat be put into immediate production and that construction of the 78-foot Higgins boat be stopped. The Bureau of Ships made a more cautious approach, stating, "If the operating forces are assured that a smaller, faster boat is required and are satisfied to accept the lesser armament and accommodations which can be built into a smaller boat, the Bureau is assured that Higgins and other PT builders could build such a boat."

At a Navy Department conference in November it was decided not to put the new model in production. Various considerations favored continued production of the larger types. Most of the PT actions in the Pacific at that time were against barges—the boats were being used primarily as gunboats and had to carry considerable weight in guns and ammunition in addition to their torpedoes. A big boat was required to carry the load. In many forward areas the crews had to live and eat aboard the boats for weeks at a time. The Hellcat had no galley or refrigerator; its living accommodations were inadequate for that type of operation. A new boat would require retooling. And though it had passed its trials with flying colors, there was a possibility that performance in service would disclose defects not apparent in the trials.

Elco's contribution was the Elcoplane, a series of six steps fastened to the bottom and sides of a standard Elco boat, PT 487. In trials run on December 16, 1943, in Newark Bay for a Board of Inspection and Survey, the 487 made the amazing speeds of 55.95 knots (nearly 65 land-miles per hour) with light loading, and 53.62 knots at full warload. Even more impressive was the maneuverability at high speed. "Running at top speed," the Board reported, "threw helm hard over and reversed course. Turning both right and left, the boat turned 180 degrees in about 6 seconds, and completed the turn with sternway on. At all times during the turn, the boat banked inboard. The performance in this maneuver was spectacular."

The Board's report was so enthusiastic that the Bureau of Ships directed the Supervisor of Shipbuilding at Bayonne to expedite procurement of Elcoplane kits to send to squadrons in the operating areas for conversion of their boats. This project died aborning, however, on receipt of a report from the Commander Motor Torpedo Boat Squadron 29, four of whose boats. PT's 560 to 563, ran from New York to Miami with Elcoplanes.

These boats demonstrated that the Elcoplanes, ideal for high-speed operation, caused an increase of 25 percent in fuel consumption and 75 percent in lubricating oil consumption at cruising speeds. Also, at cruising speeds, the boats tended to root into heavy seas, steering was more difficult, and acceleration dropped off. The planes on the boats' sides warped and the supporting brackets cracked and loosened. The boats became sensitive to added weights and correct trim was an absolute necessity.

PART III

Guadalcanal and Beyond—*The Solomons Campaign*

Guadalcanal and Beyond—*The Solomons Campaign*

1. MIDWAY: BETWEEN TWO CAMPAIGNS

SIX MONTHS elapsed between the firing of PT 34's last torpedoes off Cebu and the first firing of torpedoes at Guadalcanal by boats of a new Squadron 3. During most of this time there were no bases from which the short-range PT's could go out to meet the enemy. They were not designed to patrol hundreds of miles to sea, but to deliver sudden punches close to shore and relatively near their bases. They met the enemy only once during these 6 months: on the fringe of the great Battle of Midway in June 1942.

Motor Torpedo Boat Squadron 1, then commanded by Lt. Clinton McKellar, Jr., was given 3 days' notice late in May to make its boats ready to proceed under their own power to Midway, 1,385 miles from Pearl Harbor. This was the longest run across open water that American PT's had ever made. Except for PT 23, which broke a crankshaft and had to turn back the first day, the boats made the run without strain, fueling from patrol vessels and a seaplane tender which met them at Necker Island, French Frigate Shoal, and Lisianski Island.

As at Pearl Harbor on December 7, breakfast was interrupted on the morning of June 4 by the arrival of Japanese planes. This time the air raid alarm gave the boat crews time to get their boats underway in the lagoon before the planes were overhead.

More than 60 Japanese Navy bombers came over, escorted by 50 Zero fighters. The first planes dropped bombs from high altitude along the north side of Eastern Island and in the hangar and barracks area on Sand Island. This attack was scarcely over when dive bombers swept down, scoring hits on the powerhouse on Eastern Island and on fuel tanks on Sand Island.

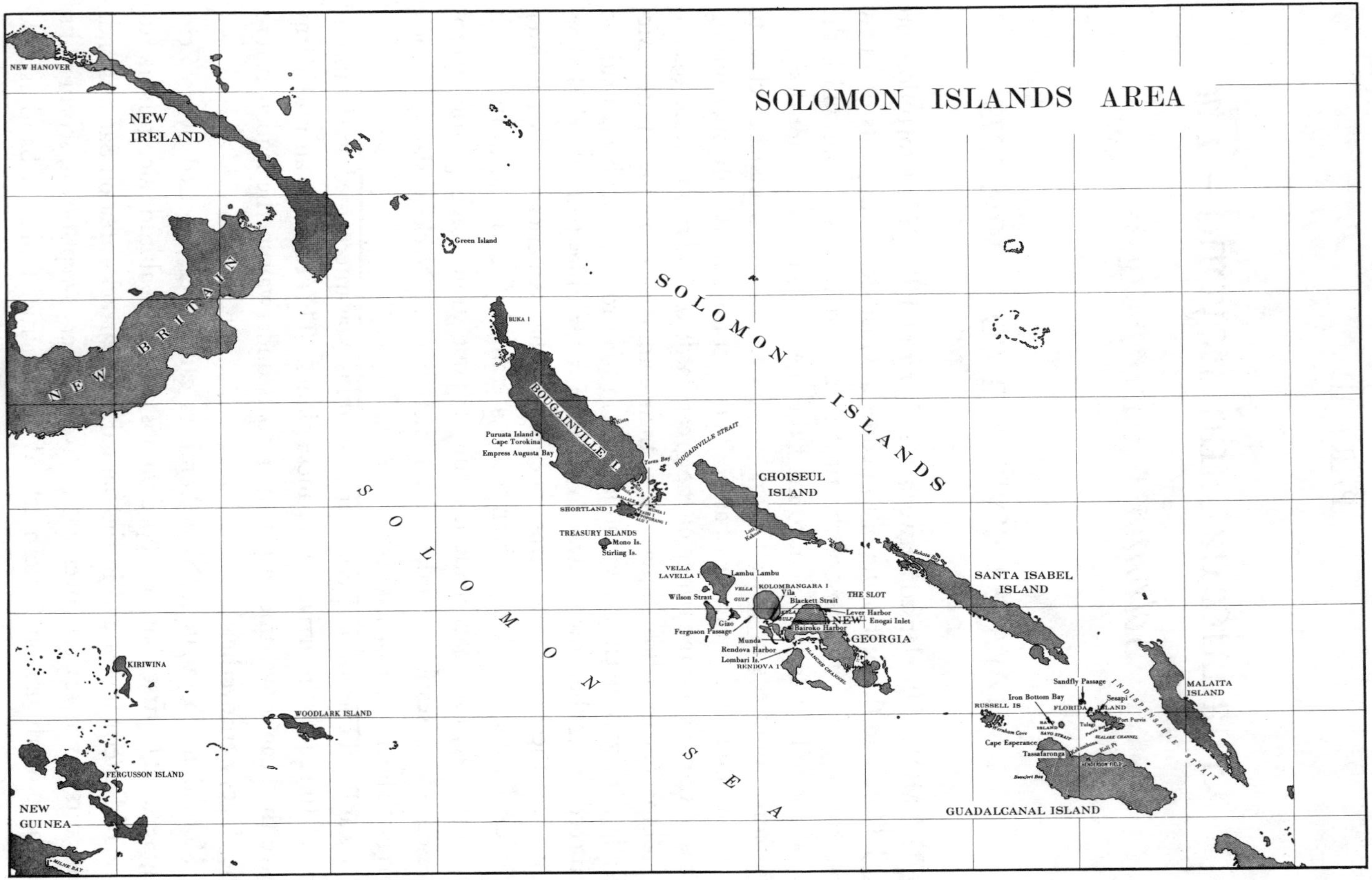

SOLOMON ISLANDS AREA
NEW HANOVER
NEW IRELAND
NEW BRITAIN
Green Island
BUKA I
BOUGAINVILLE I.
Puruata Island
Cape Torokina
Empress Augusta Bay
Torau Bay
BOUGAINVILLE STRAIT
SHORTLAND I
TREASURY ISLANDS
Mono Is.
Stirling Is.
SOLOMON ISLANDS
CHOISEUL ISLAND
SANTA ISABEL ISLAND
VELLA LAVELLA I
Lambu Lambu
VELLA GULF
KOLOMBANGARA I
Vila
Blackett Strait
THE SLOT
Lever Harbor
Enogai Inlet
Wilson Strait
Gizo
Ferguson Passage
Bairoko Harbor
NEW GEORGIA
Munda
Rendova Harbor
Lombari Is.
RENDOVA I
BLANCHE CHANNEL
Sandfly Passage
Iron Bottom Bay
RUSSELL IS
FLORIDA ISLAND
Sesapi
Port Purvis
Tulagi
SAVO ISLAND
SAVO STRAIT
SEALARK CHANNEL
Cape Esperance
Tassafaronga
Koli Pt
HENDERSON FIELD
INDISPENSABLE STRAIT
MALAITA ISLAND
GUADALCANAL ISLAND
KIRIWINA
WOODLARK ISLAND
FERGUSSON ISLAND
NEW GUINEA
MILNE BAY
SOLOMON SEA

The Solomons

As the dive bombers pulled out over the lagoon, the PT's opened with all their guns. PT's 21 and 22 concentrated their fire on a low-flying Zero, which crashed in the trees on Sand Island. Another Zero came out of a steep dive to strafe PT 25. The 25 took 30 small-caliber hits above the waterline; 1 officer and 2 men were slightly wounded by shrapnel. Planes several times started to dive on other boats, but swerved off as soon as the PT's opened fire.

Sixteen U.S. Marine planes had gone up to meet the attackers. Maj. Verne J. McCaul, USMC, Group Executive Officer, Aircraft Group 22, Second Marine Aircraft Wing, reported, "Each pilot made only one or two passes at the bombers and then spent the remainder of the time trying to shake from 1 to 5 Jap fighters off his tail. Most succeeded by using cloud cover, or, in two cases, by leading the Japs into fire from light anti-aircraft guns ashore and on PT boats."

When the raid was over, PT's 20, 22, and 28 returned to the Sand Island dock and sent fire and rescue parties ashore. Ens. D. J. Callaghan, USNR, and Ens. Clark W. Faulkner, USNR, salvaged rifles, ammunition, hand grenades, and Packard engine spares from a burning hangar. Lieutenant McKellar, with R. H. Lowell, MM2c; V. J. Miastowske, F3c; and J. B. Rodgers, S2c, cut a path through barbed wire to fight fires in a large fuel oil dump. PT's cruised around the bay, searching for downed Marine aviators. They picked up five pilots and two enlisted men.

During the rest of the day, far to the northwest, Army and Marine Corps planes from Midway and Navy planes from the *Enterprise, Yorktown,* and *Hornet* blasted the Japanese invasion force. At 1930 all 11 PT's got underway to search for damaged Japanese carriers reported 170 miles to the northwest. The weather was squally, with poor visibility. These conditions, excellent for PT attack, also made it difficult to find targets. Unable to find anything by dawn, the PT's turned back to Midway. On the way, PT's 20 and 21 sighted a column of smoke 50 miles to the west. They sped toward it at 40 knots, but when they arrived all they could see was a large expanse of fuel oil and floating wreckage, apparently Japanese. Probably no Japanese carriers were left afloat. The planes were credited with sinking two carriers, the *Kaga* and *Soryu,* on June 4, and another two, the *Hiryu,* and the *Akagi,* on the 5th.

On June 6 the PT's put to sea, each with a flag-draped coffin aboard, to bury at sea 11 Marines who had fallen in the air raid two days before.

2. TO THE SOUTH PACIFIC

The United States took its first offensive action of the Pacific war on August 7, 1942, with the landing of the First Marine Division on Guadalcanal and the neighboring islands of Tulagi and Florida. It was obvious that PT's could be used effectively in the Solomons. Squadron 2, in Panama, was alerted in July for a move to a combat area.

The squadron had been enlarged to 14 boats during the summer when Lt. Comdr. Henry Farrow brought PT's 59, 60, and 61 to Panama from Melville under their own power, to prove that boats could run to Panama on their own bottoms. The Chief of Naval Operations directed that eight boats be transferred from Squadron 2 to form a new Squadron 3, and that the new squadron prepare for immediate shipment. The remaining six boats were to remain in Panama. Lt. Comdr. Alan R. Montgomery, who had relieved Lieutenant Commander Caldwell as commander of Squadron 2 in June, was ordered to assume command of the new unit when it was commissioned on July 27. Lt. George A. Brackett, USNR, relieved him as commander of the parent squadron.

Designation of the new unit as Squadron 3 was unfortunate. Although all of the boats of the original Squadron 3 had been destroyed, the squadron was still carried on the books of the Bureau of Supplies and Accounts. Administrative confusion was inevitable. For example, when the new squadron requested its commissioning allotment, the Bureau of Supplies and Accounts tartly replied that this had already been granted to Squadron 3 in 1941, and that it was not the policy of the Navy Department to grant more than one commission allotment to any one command.

The first division of Squadron 3, PT's 38, 46, 48, and 60, departed Balboa on August 29 aboard the Navy oilers *Lackawanna* and *Tappahannock,* two PT's to a ship. They arrived September 19 at Noumea, New Caledonia, were unloaded, and were towed to Espiritu Santo by USS *Bellatrix,* a cargo ship, and the tender *Jamestown,* which had sailed from New York early in August to join the PT's in the Solomons. The boats were towed from Espiritu Santo by the fast minesweepers *Hovey* and *Southard,* converted four-stack destroyers, to a point 300 miles from Tulagi. There the boats were turned loose to proceed under their own power, arriving at Government Wharf, Tulagi, at daybreak on October 12.

The second division, PT's 37, 39, 45, and 61, was shipped to Noumea on a merchant ship and arrived at Tulagi on October 25.

80-G-26749

Squadron maneuvers were part of the Panama training for PTs en route to the Pacific.

Meanwhile Squadron 5, the first 12 Elco 80-foot boats, had arrived in Panama, scheduled for shipment to the Solomons.   On recommendation of the Commander Panama Sea Frontier, who considered Squadron 2 a more experienced unit than Squadron 5, the new squadron was directed late in September to remain in Panama, while Squadron 2 was designated for shipment to the combat area.   Six boats, PT's 109 to 114, were transferred to Squadron 2.   Lt. Rollin E. Westholm was detached as commander of the newly commissioned Squadron 7 in New York and flew to Panama to take command of Squadron 2.

The change in orders placed Squadron 2 in an unenviable position. Squadron 3 had left Panama with the lion's share of the available spare parts on the assumption that Squadron 2 would remain there.   Furthermore, Squadron 3 had taken the boats in best condition.   The remaining 77-footers needed complete overhaul, which could not be accomplished in the time available.   The squadron picked up the remnants, patched the boats as best it could, and departed for the combat area, arriving at Tulagi at the end of November.

3. THE STRUGGLE FOR GUADALCANAL

As Squadron 3's first division approached Tulagi from the southeast on the night of October 11/12, the cruisers *San Francisco, Boise, Salt Lake City,* and *Helena,* with accompanying destroyers, were blasting an enemy task force not 40 miles to the west, in what has come to be known as the Battle of Cape Esperance.

This action, which cost the enemy one heavy cruiser and three destroyers, was simply the latest manifestation of Japanese determination to regain control of the southern Solomons. The enemy had made his intentions clear the night following our original landings on Guadalcanal, when a cruiser task force struck swiftly and nearly disastrously, sinking our heavy cruisers *Astoria, Quincy,* and *Vincennes,* and the Australian heavy cruiser *Canberra.* Two weeks later a strong enemy force, including three or four carriers, was observed several hundred miles to the eastward, in the vicinity of the Santa Cruz Islands. Our carrier planes sank the carrier *Ryujo,* Army aircraft sank destroyer *Mutsuki,* and the rest of this force had to withdraw in the Battle of the Eastern Solomons.

During August the Japanese made many air attacks on Guadalcanal and attempted several landings. In September and early October they increased their efforts, sending cruisers and destroyers to make small night landings. This was the Bougainville Express—later renamed the Tokyo Express by Adm. William F. Halsey, Commander South Pacific Force. We had neither the seapower nor the airpower to counter all of these thrusts. Only when a major assault impended was it possible to send a heavy task force against the enemy.

It was such an assault that resulted in the Battle of Cape Esperance. The Japanese apparently had found reinforcement by cruisers and destroyers inadequate, and had resolved to make a major landing from large transports. A large-scale operation of this type demanded that our airpower on Guadalcanal be crippled, at least temporarily. So it came about that a carrier force was sent down to neutralize Henderson Field and was turned back by our cruisers.

Smashing as our victory was, it was not enough. We had lost the destroyer *Duncan,* and cruisers *Boise* and *Salt Lake City* had been heavily hit. The Japanese, with more ships immediately available, were able to send in another large task force 2 nights later to shell Henderson Field.

The noise of the shelling awoke the crews of the PT's at Tulagi at 0200 October 14. Lieutenant Commander Montgomery gave the order: "Prepare for action. All boats underway immediately."

Montgomery rode PT 60, with Lt. (jg.) John M. Searles, USNR. Following were Searles' brother, Lt. (jg.) Robert L. Searles, USNR, in PT 38; Lt. (jg.) Henry S. Taylor, USNR, in PT 46; and Lt. (jg.) Robert C. Wark, USNR, in PT 48. Midway between Tulagi and Guadalcanal, the tremendous orange flashes of Japanese guns became visible. Montgomery gave the signal to deploy for attack.

In the blackness of the night PT 38 became separated from the others. Bob Searles saw a Japanese searchlight flash on and sweep over his boat without picking it up. Seconds later he saw what appeared to be a light cruiser forward to his starboard beam. He eased his boat in at 10 knots, fired two torpedoes at 400 yards, two more at 200 yards, then shoved his throttles forward to full speed, turned right and passed 100 yards astern of the cruiser.

Searles saw a torpedo hit forward of the bridge, causing a violent double explosion. All hands on the PT felt the intense heat of the blast.

Montgomery attempted to close the only ship still shelling Guadalcanal, but a destroyer searchlight swept the water on PT 60's port hand, silhouetting the PT for another destroyer to starboard, which immediately opened fire. The 60 held her course until she could fire two torpedoes, then turned hard left and retired at high speed, under fire from the pursuing destroyer. H. M. Ramsdell, CMM, said he saw two explosions at the target. Taylor, in the 46, also saw explosions and was certain they were torpedo hits.

Montgomery, believing that he had shaken the destroyer, slowed the 60 and stopped laying smoke. Almost immediately another destroyer fixed the PT in its searchlight beam and opened fire. The first shell landed only 20 feet astern, almost lifting the PT out of the water. The 60 zigzagged at high speed, laid smoke, tried to shoot out the destroyer's searchlight, and finally discouraged pursuit by dropping two depth charges in the destroyer's path. Later still another destroyer was seen, patrolling Sandfly Passage, at the western end of Florida Island. The 60, idling close to the beach, washed aground on a coral reef.

Wark, in the 48, saw the first searchlight spot the 60. Just then the 46 cut across the 48's bow, forcing Wark to turn hard right to avoid collision. Wark lost contact with the destroyer and cruised slowly until another destroyer 200 yards away caught the 48 full in its searchlight and opened fire. C. E.

Todd, SC1c, poured .50 caliber into the destroyer's bridge and superstructure. The searchlight went out and the destroyer was not seen again.

Taylor, in the 46, had cut across the 48's bow to avoid collision with a destroyer which he saw only when it put its spotlight on PT 60. The 46 escaped detection and swung back to its original course to intercept the vessels shelling Guadalcanal. But the shelling had stopped, and with no gun flashes to silhouette the enemy ships, Taylor was unable to find them.

This was the first of many confused night actions, of which the results are uncertain. The squadron claimed three torpedo hits. A coastwatcher reported the next day that natives had seen a large vessel sink off New Georgia. Subsequent broadcasts by Radio Tokyo acknowledged the loss of one cruiser on the night of October 13/14, and stated that their ships had been attacked by 19 torpedo boats, of which they claimed to have destroyed 14. On the basis of these reports, the PT's claimed one cruiser damaged, one cruiser probably sunk. There is no conclusive evidence, however, that any major Japanese ship was sunk that night.

The PT's could not prevent the Japanese from sending in more cruisers and destroyers the following night to shell Henderson Field. PT 60 had been towed off the reef during the day, but it would be many weeks before she could patrol again; PT 38 had no torpedoes, and the other two boats were ordered to escort two small supply ships from Tulagi to Guadalcanal and return. On the return trip, the crews of the PT's watched the enemy shell the field. Their mission was to stand by their convoy, and they could not attack.

So effective was the bombardment that on the morning of the 15th it looked for a while as if no planes would be able to rise to oppose a Japanese landing from six transports west of Kokumbona. But soon Navy, Marine, and Army planes were in the air. They destroyed at least three transports, but the enemy had already landed thousands of troops.

4. MEETING THE TOKYO EXPRESS

Lt. Hugh M. Robinson, the squadron executive officer, relieved Lieutenant Commander Montgomery as squadron commander shortly after his arrival at Tulagi with the second group of four boats on October 25. Montgomery had contracted a fever in Panama, but got out of bed to sail with the first division. On the tanker the fever developed into pneumonia, which kept him flat on his back all the way across the Pacific. He insisted on making the long trip from Noumea to Tulagi with the boats, then forced himself to go out on patrol. He had lost 25 pounds and was living on nerves alone. Finally, at the end of October, he had to be shipped back to the United States for medical treatment.

The arrival of the second four boats permitted an increase in tempo of operations. While operations were varied, including courier and escort duties, and once even an attempt to tow a damaged destroyer, *McFarland,* the principal mission of the boats remained interception of the Tokyo Express.

Daily air reconnaissance of the Slot—the broad passage between New Georgia and Santa Isabel—and of the islands to the northwest, often gave warning of impending forays against Guadalcanal. Each evening the results of air reconnaissance were compared with late reports from coastwatchers on islands flanking the Slot, and the final report was forwarded to the PT's.

The sound between Florida Island and Guadalcanal, which came for obvious reasons to be known as Iron Bottom Bay, was geographically favorable for PT action. The two western entrances, between Cape Esperance and Savo Island to the south and between Savo Island and Sandfly Passage to the north, were relatively narrow. And the confinement of Japanese ground forces to the area between Kukum and Cape Esperance on northwestern Guadalcanal left little doubt as to the ultimate destination of enemy ships. Finally, Cape Esperance was less than 35 miles across smooth water from the PT base at Sesapi, on Tulagi.

It became a regular practice, on nights when the Tokyo Express was reported to be heading down the Slot, to place PT's as scouts in the entrance channels, or even outside the entrances, to the west of Savo Island, while other boats lay in wait inside the bay, ready to move toward either passage when the enemy was reported. On the night of October 29/30, when three enemy destroyers had been reported in the Slot, Lt. (jg.) James Brent Greene, USNR, in PT 39, went out to the west of Savo as an advance scout. Just after midnight he reported two ships 10 miles west of Cape Esperance heading for Savo at high speed.

Bob Searles, in the 38, was lying to between Esperance and Savo, watching for the enemy's approach from the west. Suddenly a friendly scoutplane swooped in and dropped a flare almost on the deck of a Japanese destroyer bearing down on the 38 at high speed from the east. No one had seen the destroyer enter the bay, and had it not been for the flare it undoubtedly would have run down the PT. The destroyer opened fire on the plane, giving the PT a chance to get underway. Then the destroyer shifted fire to the 38 and gave chase. The other boats heard the 38's radio: "One enemy can coming from east through Cape Esperance and Savo. Am being chased. Am being fired on. Course northeast. Hurry, Hurry!"

Five minutes later the destroyer swerved abruptly and shot out through the Savo-Esperance passage. Greene, having heard the 38's message, moved in to intercept. He picked up the destroyer's wake, bored in to 400 yards and fired three torpedoes. The destroyer replied with automatic weapons, holing the 39 in several places. As the 39 passed 200 yards astern, Greene thought that one of his torpedoes hit amidships and that he had damaged the ship. However, he was apparently mistaken.

Japanese cruisers and destroyers landed 1,500 men and some artillery east of Koli Point on the night of November 2. On the 4th, the cruisers *San Francisco* and *Helena,* with the destroyer *Sterett,* bombarded this new force, setting fire to supply and ammunition dumps. On the night of November 5/6, three PT's were ordered to patrol off Koli Point and one from Kokumbona to Cape Esperance, to guard against attempts to reinforce the newly landed troops.

Lack of radar, which seriously hampered PT operations throughout the Guadalcanal campaign, was sorely felt that night. Stilly Taylor, idling along in PT 39 on the Kokumbona to Cape Esperance patrol, learned that the enemy was in the vicinity only when his boat began to pitch and roll in what obviously was the wakes of two ships heading east at high speed. The wakes were visible, but not the ships. Later a searchlight at Henderson Field flashed on for an instant, silhouetting a destroyer, but Taylor could not find the destroyer again for another 40 minutes. Then, almost at the moment of sighting, the destroyer caught the 39 in its searchlight and blazed away with all guns. A shell exploded just off the PT's stern, knocking down the two torpedomen at the after tubes and hurling Teddy S. Kuharski, GM2c, right out of the starboard machinegun turret. Taylor tried to get his torpedoes away, but only one fired. As he swung the boat around, retiring in a wide turn, shells were dropping within 50 yards. Kuharski scrambled back into his turret and brought his guns to bear on the destroyer's bridge. After his first few bursts the searchlight went out and the destroyer ceased fire. A second destroyer also illuminated the 39 and fired at her, dropping heavy caliber shells in her wake and spraying the water all around with automatic fire. The 39 zigzagged to safety behind a smoke-screen.

The following night, off Koli Point, Lt. Lester H. Gamble, USNR, in PT 48, fired four torpedoes at a destroyer at less than 400 yards' range. He saw two hit amidships, causing a tremendous explosion and a geyser of water and foam. A single burst of shell-fire passed well overhead as the 48 retired at full speed. An oil slick and debris were sighted in the area at daybreak, but again there is no conclusive evidence that the ship was hit.

On the afternoon of November 8 the Commander Advance Naval Base Guadalcanal ordered all available PT's to intercept a reported enemy force of five destroyers heading for Guadalcanal. Only three boats were available. The condition of the squadron at the time was recorded by Lt. S. S. Savage, USNR, the squadron intelligence officer: "This was the third time in four nights that the PT boats had been out to clash with a strong enemy force. With the inadequacy of base facilities and the constant use of the boats, proper maintenance had become a problem. The boats' own officers and men, after spending a nerve-shattering night battling heavy Jap ships that repeatedly caught them in blinding lights, and on occasions, all but blew them out of the water with deadly salvos of explosive shells, would catch a few hours nap in the early morning, then spend the major portion of the day working to have the boats in shape for the night's patrol. Morale was high, but physical strain was beginning to show in men and boats."

Robinson led the night's patrol in PT 61, followed by Brent Greene in the 39 and Lt. (jg.) Leonard A. Nikoloric, USNR, in PT 37. Greene first reported an enemy destroyer south of Savo Island and, as the boats deployed in line abreast to attack, two more destroyers were sighted. The 39 fired two torpedoes, which missed the lead destroyer astern. The 61's line of sight was blocked by the 37, but the 37 let go two torpedoes at 500 yards and a third a few seconds later. The lead destroyer turned hard left, avoiding the torpedoes. Immediately the three destroyers turned on their searchlights and laid down a heavy barrage. A large caliber shell hit the 61, blowing off its bow. The boats escaped behind a smokescreen and, with the help of a calm sea, good boat handling, and sufficient speed to keep the bow out of water, Robinson brought the 61 safely to Tulagi. The 39, hit by shrapnel but not seriously damaged, remained on patrol until dawn. The action, which took only 8 minutes from first sighting to escape, was the quickest the squadron had had.

Two nights later Robinson led a three-boat division on patrol south of Savo Island where, for a moment, before they merged into the dark background of land, four destroyers could be seen in column close to the Guadal-

Only minor underwater repairs could be made without docking facilities. H. C. Zagary, CBM, puts on a diving helmet to inspect the bottom of a PT at a Solomons base.

canal shore. The PT's closed the range, but the destroyers saw them first. Robinson got two torpedoes away and Nikoloric one before the enemy fire forced the boats to retire. A shell exploded so close to Nikoloric's boat that everyone on deck was knocked down and stunned except John D. Legg, CQM, who had been hanging onto a guardrail in the cockpit. "I saw that we were going to get sunk," Legg said, "so I pushed the throttles down and gave her hard right."

Legg, whose quick action undoubtedly saved his boat from destruction, kept the PT zigzagging for 3 minutes before Nikoloric recovered sufficiently to take charge.

5. THE BATTLE OF GUADALCANAL

The enemy chose the middle of November for an all-out attempt to reinforce Guadalcanal. As early as November 9 it was obvious from air reconnaissance that a great amphibious offensive had been set in motion and might reach the Guadalcanal area on the 13th. We already had on the way to Guadalcanal transports carrying 6,000 men and thousands of tons of equipment, which had to be unloaded on November 11 and 12 if we were to continue to hold the island.

Rear Adm. Richmond K. Turner, in charge of the resupply operation, had 6 cruisers and 14 destroyers. Far to the south, at Noumea, Rear Adm. Thomas C. Kinkaid, had a supporting force of one aircraft carrier, two battleships, two cruisers, and eight destroyers. All available land-based planes were to attack Japanese airfields in range of Guadalcanal on November 11, 12, and 13. If Admiral Turner's force could turn back the enemy's thrust, expected on the 13th, then planes from Guadalcanal and Admiral Kinkaid's carrier, *Enterprise,* together with Admiral Kinkaid's battleships, might be able to handle the main Japanese force.

Despite Japanese air attacks, the transports were unloaded on schedule. On the evening of the 12th, Admiral Turner withdrew to the southwest with his transports. Five cruisers—*San Francisco, Portland, Helena, Juneau,* and *Atlanta*—with 8 destroyers—*Cushing, Laffey, Sterett, O'Bannon, Aaron Ward, Barton, Monssen,* and *Fletcher*—under Rear Adm. Daniel J. Callaghan, turned east to meet a far heavier enemy force of 17 ships, including 2 battleships, a light cruiser, and 14 destroyers. In the furious 34-minute action which followed, we lost *Atlanta, Barton, Cushing, Laffey,* and *Monssen,* and suffered damage to the *Portland, San Francisco, Helena, Juneau,*[4] and three destroyers. Admiral Callaghan was killed on his flagship, the *San Francisco.* The price was high, but the enemy also had been hurt, and his intended bombardment of Guadalcanal was completely frustrated.

One Japanese battleship, *Hiei,* had taken over 50 topside hits, but on the morning of the 13th was still afloat and heading toward Guadalcanal, possibly with the intention of bombarding Henderson Field. Throughout the day, planes from the *Enterprise,* Marine planes from Henderson Field, and Army B–17's made a total of seven torpedo, five dive-bombing, and two strafing attacks on the *Hiei.* By nightfall the apparently indestructible battleship had sunk.

That night the Japanese brought cruisers and destroyers into Iron Bottom Bay to shell Henderson Field. No big ships were available to stop them.

Stilly Taylor and Jack Searles were assigned to screen the heavy cruiser *Portland,* which had been damaged in the previous night's action and was being towed back to Tulagi. The boats separated, Taylor patrolling a north-south course and Searles an east-west course. "By about twelve-thirty," Taylor said, "we were secured from this job and immediately tried to locate each other again. However, before we were able to do so, the Nips began to shell Henderson Field, first putting a very bright flare in the vicinity of the field and naturally both of us started in on them independently.

"Apparently, I was much nearer to the Japs than Jack was because of where I had secured from patrol around the *Portland.* The best intelligence we had was that there was a Jap battleship on the way down from either Bougainville or Rabaul. It was supposed to have been accompanied by several escorts, probably destroyers. This intelligence report should not be confused with the battleship *Hiei,* which we knew was just the other side of Savo Island.

"As soon as the Japs opened fire, it was obvious to us that there was at least one fairly heavy ship. We thought, at the time, that it was probably the battleship referred to in the intelligence report. We could tell that it was definitely a heavy ship because of the long orange flash from its gunfire rather than the short white flash which we knew from experience was the smaller fire of the destroyers. As we started in to make our run on this formation, we thought that we saw a destroyer make a short scouting trip well ahead of the main formation. My quartermaster reported this and I could never be absolutely sure that it was not his imagination. However,

---

[4] The *Juneau* was sunk by an enemy torpedo the following morning during retirement toward Espiritu Santo.

due to the light put up by the Nips' flares, I was able to use my [torpedo] director for the first time. I set his speed at about 20 knots and I think that he was doing slightly more than this. I kept him in the director for approximately seven salvoes, and really had a beautiful line on him. After closing in to about a thousand yards, I decided that if we went in any further, we would get tangled up in the destroyer screen, which I knew would be surrounding him at about from five hundred to seven hundred yards. I, therefore, fired three torpedoes. The fourth misfired and never left the tube. The three fish landed beautifully and made no flash as we fired them. We immediately turned around and started back for the base, but we had the torpedoes running hot and straight towards the target. I am positive that at least one of them found its mark. Certainly the Nips ceased fire immediately and apparently turned right around and limped home. Jack who had been behind me, kept on going until he ran into one of the screening destroyers. He said that he had put two fish into him and left him sinking. As we were retiring, one of the Jap destroyers came up to a patch of smoke that we had laid to cover our retirement and fired a few rounds into the smoke, but we were, by this time, well on our way home.

"This was an easy attack for PT's because we were able to get within range unmolested with good visibility because of their flares and because of their gunfire. I do believe that the first they knew of our presence was when torpedoes hit them. It was the kind of attack that we had all been dreaming about. They usually came in under cover of bad weather, and we often found ourselves in the middle of them before we knew what was going on."

Here again, damage to the enemy cannot be stated with certainty. But the question of damage is secondary. The PT's had accomplished their primary purpose: to halt the bombardment of Henderson Field. Of that there is little doubt. As soon as Taylor and Searles attacked, the Japanese stopped shelling and retreated. If it seems incongruous that a major task force should retire precipitately as soon as attacked by two PT's, it must be remembered that the PT's achieved complete surprise. The Japanese did not know what was attacking them or what forces might be available to press the attack—they could have only an imperfect idea of how much damage they had inflicted on us the night before—and they were undoubtedly reluctant to risk action with an unknown force which seemed to have the drop on them.

The PT's interrupted the bombardment when 18 planes had been destroyed and 32 damaged. But Henderson Field was still usable. And during the day of the 14th, Henderson Field was used with great effectiveness, not only by the Marine planes based there, but by Navy planes from *Enterprise,* which landed at Henderson Field, refueled and took off again to make repeated attacks on Japanese task forces in the Slot.

Reports were conflicting as to the composition of these forces. One, apparently, was the cruiser task force heading back to base after its visit to Henderson Field; another was a large transport force convoyed by cruisers and destroyers and preceded by a separate force of cruisers, destroyers, and two battleships. Navy and Marine Corps planes made many torpedo and bomb hits on these ships, sinking the heavy cruiser *Kinugasa* and seven transports. The planes whittled down the Japanese forces, but could not stop them. At dusk they were still bearing down toward Iron Bottom Bay. Late in the afternoon of the 14th Lieutenant Robinson was ordered to send out all available PT's. He received reports of the transport task force coming down the Slot; of a battleship, cruiser, and destroyer force circling 150 miles to the north, and of a cruiser and destroyer task force approaching from the southwest. And there was a possibility that part of Admiral Kinkaid's force, the battleships *Washington* and *South Dakota* with four destroyers, under Rear Adm. Willis A. Lee, might be on its way.

Robinson, Greene, and Nikoloric took the only three boats still capable of operations to patrol north of Savo. Just as they arrived on station, Radio Tulagi informed Robinson that Admiral Lee's task force would be in the area and instructed him to withdraw to the east of Savo Island. As the boats withdrew, they saw *Washington* and *South Dakota* rounding the northern tip of Savo. Admiral Lee, in the *Washington,* apparently saw the boats at the same time. The Admiral himself called Guadalcanal headquarters saying, "Call off your boys."

Robinson, overhearing this, immediately assured Lee that they knew his identity.

The battleships decided the Battle of Guadalcanal, sinking the battleship *Kirishima* and battering the rest of the enemy task force so savagely that by the next day its remaining ships were in full retreat. During the day of the 15th, Army, Navy, and Marine planes blasted the remaining transports. The enemy's greatest attempt at reinforcement had ended in failure to land any substantial number of men or quantity of supplies.

6. AFTER TASSAFARONGA

The final major Japanese thrust at Guadalcanal was turned back by our cruisers in the Battle of Tassafaronga on November 30, but from that time until the final evacuation in early February, the Tokyo Express continued to run. During this period the PT's had some of their grimmest, as well as most successful, actions.

About the first of December the PT's received welcome assistance from half a dozen SOC's—Navy scout observation planes. The SOC's had been carried aboard cruisers damaged in the many actions around Guadalcanal, and were left behind with orders to work with the PT's when their cruisers left the area for repairs. Every night the PT's expected action, one or two SOC's flew up the Slot to spot enemy ships and report their position. It was a hazardous assignment for the SOC's, because the Japanese ships usually made their runs under cover of bad weather, and several were lost.

Further assistance was received about the first of January, with the arrival of a squadron of PBY's, Navy patrol bombers known as "Catalinas" or "Black Cats." The PBY's not only reported positions but heckled enemy ships by dropping flares and bombs, sometimes forcing the ships to reveal their positions by drawing fire from them. Once, toward the end of January, when a group of PT's was waiting near Savo to engage an approaching force of 12 enemy destroyers, the Black Cats bombed the destroyers so effectively that they turned and fled before they had come within 30 miles of Guadalcanal.

By December 7, when a reconnaissance plane reported at least nine destroyers heading down the Slot, the material condition of the Tulagi PT flotilla had been considerably improved by the arrival of Squadron 2, under Lt. R. E. Westholm. It was possible to send out eight PT's in three groups to meet the opposing force. Westholm, in PT 109, with Lt. Charles E. Tilden, USNR, in PT 43, patrolled between Kokumbona and Cape Esperance; Bob Searles, in PT 48, and Stilly Taylor, in PT 40, patrolled off the northwest tip of Guadalcanal, while four boats waited near Savo Island as a striking force: PT 59 (Jack Searles), PT 44 (Lt. Frank Freeland, USNR), PT 36 (Lt. (jg.) M. G. Pettit, USNR), and PT 37 (Lt. (jg.) Lester H. Gamble, USNR).

At 2320 the 48 and 40 sighted a group of enemy ships heading directly toward them from the northwest. As they started to move into firing position, one of PT 48's engines, then another, failed. The enemy ships, now seen to be destroyers, started firing at the 48. Taylor, realizing that the 48 was a sitting duck for the Japanese, swung the 40 back across the oncoming enemy's bows, laying a smokescreen, and then swerved to run south-south-east down the channel. Apparently unaware that the 48 was crippled, the destroyers pursued the 40, which easily outdistanced them. The 48 ran on one engine into the lee of Savo Island and anchored close to shore.

The striking group, advised of this contact by radio, deployed and at 2335 sighted the enemy force, which apparently consisted of five destroyers and a larger ship. As soon as the PT's came within effective range, the Japanese started firing at them. PT 37 fired two torpedoes at the leading ship with no observed results. PT 59 then let go two torpedoes at the nearest destroyer, which turned, avoiding the torpedoes, but exposing the large ship and another destroyer to the line of fire. As PT 59 swung to retire, it strafed the leading destroyer, a bare 100 yards away, and the destroyer returned the fire heavily. The PT was hit 10 times, but no one was injured. A machinegun bullet set fire to a belt of .50-caliber ammunition in one of the turrets. Cletus E. Osborne, GM2c, USNR, stayed in the turret, detached the blazing belt and threw it to the deck, where it was extinguished.

Barely 3 minutes after the 59 started her run, PT's 44 and 36 whipped in, fired four torpedoes each, and retired unscathed. Pettit claimed one probable and one possible hit; Freeland two certain hits. Westholm, approaching in the 109 from the southeast, heard a terrific explosion in the direction of the targets about the time that Freeland fired his torpedoes.

The enemy had had enough. The Japanese ships turned and withdrew precipitately to the north. Although damage to the enemy is uncertain, the PT's, with practically no damage to themselves, had frustrated the mission of a far superior force.

The Japanese also used submarines in their attempts to support Guadalcanal. A submarine would surface close to shore. Barges would come out to unload it. On the night of December 9, Jack Searles, in the 59, patrolling with PT 44 at Kamimbo Bay, sighted an enemy barge. As the PT's opened fire on the barge, Searles saw a surfaced submarine. He quickly fired two torpedoes, one of which hit amidships. A geyser of water spouted high in the air, followed by tremendous explosions and a huge oil slick that spread for an hour and a half. It has been confirmed that Searles sank the submarine I-3, a vessel 320 feet long, of 1,955 tons standard surface displacement.

Two nights later a sizable Japanese force again entered Iron Bottom Bay, and again the PT's were there to meet them. Les Gamble, Stilly Taylor, and Lt. (jg.) Williams E. Kreiner 3d, USNR, all claimed torpedo hits. It is known that the PT's sank the destroyer *Terutsuki*.

When this action began, Frank Freeland, in PT 44, and Charlie Tilden, in PT 110, were patrolling the Kamimbo Bay area, southwest of Cape Esperance. They turned back on receiving a radio report of the contact with the enemy, and headed into Iron Bottom Bay between Cape Esperance and Savo Island. As they came in, they passed astern of the burning cargo ship, still underway and heading slowly toward Cape Esperance. Lt. (jg.) Charles M. Melhorn, USNR, aboard the 44, became slightly perturbed when he saw tracer fire, apparently directed at Florida Island from a destroyer just off the port beam.

"We were throwing up quite a wake," he said, "and with the Jap cargo ship on our starboard quarter lighting up the whole area, I thought we would soon be easy pickings and I told the skipper so.

"Before he could reply, [Willard A.] Crowe, the quartermaster, who was at the wheel, pointed and yelled out, 'Destroyer on starboard bow. There's your target, Captain.'

"Through the glasses I could make out a DD [destroyer] two points on our starboard bow, distance about 8,000 yards, course SSW. We came right and started our run. We had no sooner steadied on our new course than I picked up two more destroyers through my glasses. They were in column, 30° on our port bow, target course 270°, coming up fast. The skipper and I both saw at once that continuing our present course would pin us against the beach and lay us wide open broadsides from at least three Jap cans. The skipper shifted targets to the two destroyers, still about 4,000 yards off, and we started in again. By this time we were directly between the blazing ship in toward Esperance and the two destroyers. As we started the run, I kept looking for the can that had fired toward Florida. I picked him up behind and to the left of our new targets. He was swinging apparently to form up in column astern of the other two. The trap was sprung and as I pointed out this fourth DD, the lead ship in column opened fire.

"The skipper ordered hard right rudder, increased speed, and smoke. We turned at right angles to the course of the column, and held until we were directly ahead of the lead ship who was firing steadily but over and astern. As we crossed his bow, we swung left again 90° to the west and retired behind our smoke. A few shots landed behind us as we turned, but they broke off firing at once, as soon as they saw we had gotten behind smoke. We retired at full throttle intending to get well under Savo before we made our next run. The AK [the cargo ship] under Esperance was burning fiercely and as we passed her again, she buckled amidships. We veered slightly to the right and when we were directly between Savo and Esperance, about 3 miles south of Savo, we turned right 180° and started back.

"Crowe was at the wheel, Ensign [John D.] Chester, [USNR] in the cockpit behind him, Lieutenant Freeland was at the throttles and I was standing on the transom between the machinegun stops. We had just come out of our turn when we were fired on by a ship to the east of, and behind, the burning AK. I saw the blast, yelled: 'That's for us!' and jumped down on the port side by the cockpit. We were hit aft in the engine room. I don't remember much. For a few seconds, nothing registered at all. I looked back and saw a gaping hole in what was once the engine room canopy. The perimeter of the hole in the canopy was ringed by little tongues of flame. I looked down into the water and saw we had practically lost way. Dowling, who was on the starboard side amidships when we were hit, said that the turrets were afire, but that both gunners had gotten out and went forward with him.

"Someone on the bow said, 'Shall we abandon ship?' Freeland gave the order to go ahead and abandon ship. Together with Crowe and Chester, Freeland jumped out of the cockpit and went aft on the port side. As he passed me he said something about 'getting the life raft.'

"I stayed by the cockpit, looking at the little group of men on the fore-castle and glancing over where the shell came from. He let go again. I glanced forward and dove. One man on the bow hit the water about a hand ahead of me as I dove, another man followed just behind me. I dove deep and was still under water when the salvo struck. The concussion jarred me badly, but I kept swimming under water. There was a tremendous explosion, paralyzing me from the waist down. The water around me went red. The life jacket took control and pulled me to the surface. I came up in a sea of fire, the flaming embers of the boat cascading all about me. I tried to get free of the life jacket, but couldn't. I started swimming feebly. I thought the game was up, but the water, which had shot sky high in the explosion, rained down and put out the fires around me. From the first hit to this point took less than 15 seconds.

"I took a few strokes away from the gasoline fire which was raging about 15 yards behind me and as I turned back, I saw two heads, one still helmeted, between me and the flames. I heard a cry which came from behind the flames. I called to the two men, told them that I expected the Japs to be over in short order to machinegun us, and to get their life jackets ready to slip. I told them to get clear of the reflection of the fire as quickly as possible and proceeded to do so myself.

"I struck out for Savo, whose skyline ridge I could see dimly, and gradually made headway towards shore. Every 2 or 3 minutes I stopped to look back for other survivors, or an approaching destroyer, but saw nothing save the boat which was burning steadily, and beyond it—slightly to the west—the Jap AK which burned and exploded all night long. Sometime shortly before dawn a PT boat cruised up and down Savo, came out and passed about 25 yards ahead of me. I was all set to hail him when I looked over my shoulder and saw a Jap can bearing down on his starboard quarter. I didn't know whether the PT was maneuvering to get a shot at him or not, so I kept my mouth shut, let him go by, slipped my life jacket and waited for the fireworks. The Jap can lay motionless for some minutes, and I finally made it out as nothing more than a destroyer-shaped shadow formed by the fires and smoke which etched the outline against Cape Esperance.

"I put my life jacket back on and started out again. I was being set down rapidly to the east and finally made Savo by swimming due west. The PT circled and came back behind me, I yelled, but he swung off toward the wrecked boat. Although I heard both him and the SOC droning around most of the night, they never came close.

"I saw no ships, nothing until after dawn when one of our DD's went west out through the groove. I judge that I finally got ashore on Savo about 0730 or 0800 in the morning. Lieutenant H. S. Taylor picked me up off the beach about an hour later."

Only one man besides Lieutenant Melhorn was picked up that morning. Two officers and seven enlisted men were lost with their boat.

On the night of January 2 the PT's met the Tokyo Express again; Gamble claimed damage to one destroyer. Then, on the evening of the 10th, Lieutenant Westholm received word that eight Japanese destroyers were expected to arrive in Iron Bottom Bay at midnight. Four boats were already out, patrolling in two groups to the west of the Savo Island-Cape Esperance line: Les Gamble, in PT 45, with Lt. (jg.) Ralph O. Amsden, Jr., USNR, in PT 39, to the west, and Bob Searles, in PT 48, with Ens. Bartholomew J. Connolly, III, in PT 115, to the east. Westholm, in PT 112, immediately got underway with Charlie Tilden in PT 43 and Lt. Clark W. Faulkner, USNR, in PT 40, to cover the Guadalcanal coast between Cape Esperance and Aruligo. He sent another group, Jack Searles, in PT 59; Taylor, in PT 46; and Pettit, in PT 36, to patrol just to the east, between Tassafaronga and Doma.[5]

Half an hour after midnight, Westholm's group, one-quarter mile offshore, sighted four destroyers heading slowly southeast, a mile offshore. The last ship turned back toward Savo Island; the other three presented perfect targets. Westholm gave the order, "Deploy to the right and make them good."

Tilden, easternmost of the group, closed to 400 yards and fired two torpedoes at the first ship in column. A tremendous crimson flash from his after port tube, caused perhaps by an imperfect impulse charge or too much oil in the tube, revealed his position to the enemy. The destroyer, which was not hit, opened with its main battery as Tilden turned hard right to retire. The second salvo hit the 43, slowing the boat so that it was just keeping headway. The destroyer closed fast. Tilden ordered abandon ship.

After Tilden jumped, he was fired on by Japanese machineguns. He dived as deep as he could, and saw and heard the bullets striking the surface above. Other members of the crew were so close to the destroyer that they could hear the Japanese talking.

Faulkner, whose boat was the center of the striking force, closed to 500 yards and fired four torpedoes at the second ship. He watched his after port torpedo hit solidly, shooting a column of water in the air. A moment later there was a second explosion at the same target. Faulkner turned hard right and retired at full speed along the coastline. Westholm bore in close to the third ship and fired four torpedoes, one of which hit, throwing a huge column of water in the air. He was so close that he had to turn hard left and pass astern of the destroyer. Ships to the west opened fire with large-caliber guns. He turned east and another ship toward Savo opened fire. Two shells hit the 112 almost simultaneously, one at the waterline amidships, the other near the forward bulkhead of the engineroom. C. A. Craig, MoMM1c, showed great courage and ability in subduing the fire in the engineroom, and when it appeared impossible to save the boat, he and Lieutenant Westholm were the last to abandon ship. The entire crew got off safely into a liferaft. At 0130 the boat was still afloat and Westholm decided to try to board her. As the raft drew within 100 feet, the 112 exploded and settled by the stern. She sank at daylight, 1 mile east of Cape Esperance.

[5] The PT flotilla by this time had been strengthened by the arrival of the first boats and personnel of Squadron 6. PT 115 was a Squadron 6 boat; Lieutenant Faulkner, though riding a Squadron 2 boat on this mission, was a Squadron 6 officer.

PT 46 was the only boat of the other striking group to make contact with the enemy. Taylor fired four torpedoes at 2,000 yards. One of his men saw two flashes at the target which might have been hits. Amsden and Gamble fired seven torpedoes from 2,000 yards at a ship between Esperance and Savo, with no observed results. Gamble fired his last torpedo at a ship 15 miles west of Savo, also at 2,000 yards' range, and without visible results. The other boats did not sight the enemy, but assisted in picking up survivors. The entire crew of the 112 was safe. One enlisted man was killed and 2 were missing from the crew of the 43. The 43 itself was seen in the morning on the beach in enemy territory near Cape Esperance, and was destroyed by gunfire from a New Zealand corvette to prevent capture.

The Japanese apparently had dumped overboard large quantities of supplies, trusting to the tide to float them ashore to their garrison on Guadalcanal. After daylight the PT's sank over 250 drums of supplies. The PT's claimed damage to three destroyers. All that can be definitely confirmed, however, is that the destroyer *Hatsukaze* was holed completely through both sides by a single torpedo hit, but was still able to retire at 18 knots.

Four nights later 13 PT's went out to meet a Japanese force consisting of 9 destroyers. The Searles brothers, with PT's 59 and 38, took the outer patrol off Kamimbo Bay. Clark Faulkner, in PT 39, with Bart Connolly in PT 115 formed the inner patrol 2 miles south of Savo Island. Strike group 1, led by Westholm in PT 109, with Gamble in PT 45 and Lt. John H. Clagett, USNR, in PT 37, took station 2 miles southwest of Savo; strike group 2, led by Lt. Allen H. Harris in PT 40, with Pettit in PT 36 and Ens. J. F. Kearny in PT 48, was 2 miles off Doma Reef on the Guadalcanal coast; and strike group 3, led by Hugh Robinson in PT 47, with Taylor in PT 46 and Ens. R. L. Richards, USNR, in PT 123, was midway between the inner patrol and strike group 2.

During the entire night visibility was practically zero, with occasional rain squalls so heavy that it was impossible to see the bow of the boat from the cockpit. But there were also occasional lightning flashes that silhouetted enemy ships.

Westholm, who left Clagett and Gamble to make a search northwest of Savo, had his only contact with the enemy when a plane dropped a bomb harmlessly 150 feet off his port quarter. Clagett and Gamble also were attacked by a plane which dropped two bombs at a safe distance and attempted to strafe the boats. Gamble returned the fire, ceasing abruptly when lightning flashes revealed five enemy ships standing in through the

Savo-Esperance Channel. Clagett fired three torpedoes without observed results; Gamble fired two, the first of which missed. The second was seen to hit the lead destroyer with a large explosion. As the PT's retired toward Savo, another destroyer fired on them from the east. The PT's swung left and up the west side of Savo. The destroyer kept them under heavy fire until they passed north of the island. Clagett retired successfully, but Gamble was taken under fire by a destroyer that came around the north tip of Savo from the east. He doubled back around the south of the island and retired toward Florida Island, where, in zero visibility, he ran aground. A Navy tug pulled the PT off the reef the following afternoon.

A few minutes after Clagett and Gamble made their attack, a flash of lightning silhouetted a ship between Savo and Esperance for Taylor and Richards. Taylor fired two torpedoes and Richards one—all misses. The ship opened fire, but in the extreme darkness was inaccurate. Richards made a wide circle, returning to the Savo-Esperance line. Several lightning flashes silhouetted another ship. Richards fired his remaining three torpedoes at 500 yards and as he withdrew at idling speed, saw one hit solidly aft of amidships. The target opened with all guns, but Richards believed that he was unobserved, as none of the fire came close.

Lieutenant Robinson, the third member of strike force 3, observed ships off the Guadalcanal coast, and repeatedly tried to close to firing range. Each time lightning flashes silhouetted him and enemy fire forced him to retire.

Lieutenant Harris was the only member of strike force 2 to sight the enemy. He fired two torpedoes at a ship standing in towards Tassafaronga, but was sure that neither hit.

Connolly, on the inner patrol 2 miles southeast of Savo, turned toward Esperance after observing gunfire from ships. He saw two enemy destroyers, closed to 1,000 yards and fired four torpedoes. While turning away to starboard he thought he saw a torpedo hit the first destroyer with a flash followed by a dull yellow glow. He retired under inaccurate fire.

Faulkner, who was patrolling with Connolly, picked up a destroyer in a flash of lightning. Just as he started to close, the destroyer poured heavy fire at him. The first salvo hit close aboard, throwing one of the gunner's mates to the deck. Several shells hit the beach on Savo, throwing up sand and rocks on their starboard hand. The PT went aground, but Faulkner succeeded in backing off with minor damage shortly before dawn.

The PT's had fired 17 torpedoes, claiming hits on 3 ships. Japanese records, however, show that no damage was inflicted.

7. EVACUATION

Toward the end of January, enemy activity gave the appearance of preparation for another major effort to regain Guadalcanal. Actually it was evacuation.

Reconnaissance aircraft and coastwatchers reported on the afternoon of February 1 that 20 destroyers were standing down the Slot at high speed. Forty-one fighters, scout bombers, and torpedo bombers from Henderson Field attacked the force at dusk, crippling one of the enemy. Thirty escorting Zeros shot down four of our planes and lost three of their own.

The destroyers *Fletcher, Radford,* and *Nicholas* stood out toward the Russell Islands to the west to intercept the Japanese. Every time they tried to close Cape Esperance, however, Japanese planes attacked them, forcing them to unmask their batteries. As soon as our destroyers opened fire, the planes would go away, only to return on the next attempt to work in toward Esperance. The planes also dropped flares to mark the track of our destroyers, and robbed them of surprise.

The light minelayers *Preble, Montgomery,* and *Tracy,* which had left Noumea on the 29th, arrived in Iron Bottom Bay early in the evening and dropped their mines from Doma Reef halfway to Cape Esperance, one of the earliest offensive minefields laid by our surface craft in the Pacific.

All available PT's were deployed in the Savo-Esperance area to meet the enemy. Bob Searles, in PT 47, and Taylor, in PT 39, were to take station 2 miles southeast of Savo; Clagett, in PT 111, and Gamble in PT 48, 2 miles southwest of Savo; Jack Searles in PT 59, Connolly in PT 115, and Ens. J. J. Kelly, USNR, in PT 37, 3 miles northwest of Esperance; Faulkner in PT 124 and Richards in PT 123, 3 miles south of Savo; Westholm in PT 109 and Tilden in PT 36, 2 miles north of Doma.

On the way to their patrol area, Clagett and Gamble were ineffectually strafed and bombed by a large monoplane. Forty minutes after arriving on station, Clagett sighted a destroyer 3 miles east of Cape Esperance and Gamble sighted 2 destroyers 2 miles west of Savo. The PT's separated, each to attack its own target. Gamble closed to 900 yards and fired his two after torpedoes at the first of the two destroyers. Both missed astern. He took more lead and fired his forward torpedoes. He was able to watch them only a few seconds before heavy fire from both ships forced him to retire behind a smokescreen. Then a steady rain of fire from another ship on his starboard bow forced him to turn left toward Savo to avoid being trapped. He nosed in to the beach and gave orders to abandon ship, expecting the enemy to pick up the boat in their searchlights and destroy it. But the Japanese failed to discover the boat, and it was pulled off the beach and returned to the base in the morning.

Clagett approached within 500 yards of his target and fired four torpedoes, but he too had no opportunity to observe the results because of the volume of fire directed at him. Thirteen minutes after firing its first torpedoes, PT 111 was hit by shellfire and burst into flames. Clagett, though thrown to the deck and severely burned about the face and arms, managed to crawl over the side and into the water. Unable to swim because of his burns, he was supported by Merle C. Elsass, TM2c, and Walter L. Long, S1c, until rescued by another PT. Russell J. Wackler, RM2c, suffered compound fractures of his legs. Ens. A. E. White, and Lamar H. Loggins, F2c, stayed with him, fighting off sharks for 2½ hours before he died. Except for Wackler and Lt. (jg.) Philip A. Shribman, who was missing, all of the crew of the 111 were rescued.

The 59, 115, and 37 were bombed and strafed, without damage, by enemy planes as they passed through the Savo-Esperance channel. An hour later they found themselves completely trapped by destroyers on three sides and the enemy-occupied Guadalcanal coast on the other. They counted as many as 12 destroyers circling them at a time.

Connolly closed within 500 yards of one destroyer, fired two torpedoes and reversed course. He thought that both hit. He saw the ship slow abruptly and start to list. Then another ship loomed up ahead. He fired two more torpedoes and reversed course again. Shellfire now seemed to be coming from all directions. He cut his speed and the destroyers lost his wake. The fire became increasingly inaccurate. A sudden, intense rain squall gave him a chance to slip through the ring of destroyers. He beached the 115 on the western shore of Savo. At dawn he backed her off and returned to base. During the same squall Jack Searles also escaped the trap, and hid north of Savo until dawn.

Ensign Kelly, in the 37, fired four torpedoes, but in retiring, the 37 received a direct hit in the gasoline tanks. The brilliant, blinding flash lighted the whole sky in the vicinity of Cape Esperance. Only one survivor of the 37 was picked up—Eldon O. Jenter, MM1c, who suffered serious shrapnel wounds and burns.

Faulkner and Richards were bombed and strafed ineffectually by enemy planes while proceeding to the patrol area. Soon after they arrived on station, Faulkner sighted a destroyer coming through the Savo-Esperance channel. He closed to 1,000 yards and fired three torpedoes. Two hit, sending up large columns of fire. The ship burst aflame and burned for more than 3 hours. Richards, following Faulkner in, was about to fire torpedoes at a second enemy ship when an enemy plane glided in silently and dropped a bomb squarely on the fantail of PT 123. Flames immediately swept the boat and the crew abandoned ship. Enemy planes bombed and strafed the men in the water. One enlisted man was killed, three were missing, and three others suffered serious injuries from shrapnel wounds, burns, or fractures.

The two remaining striking groups of PT's fired no torpedoes, but at dawn assisted in rescuing survivors. Taylor recovered three enemy landing barges with outboard motors, which appeared to have been hurriedly abandoned, as they contained Japanese rifles, knapsacks, and personal effects.

Of the 11 PT's that went out to meet the enemy, 5 had fired 19 torpedoes, and 3 PT's had been lost. Six men were killed, 3 officers and 6 men were missing, and 1 officer and 5 men were seriously injured. The PT's claimed to have sunk 2 destroyers and damaged 2 others. The only sinking that can be confirmed is that of the destroyer *Makigumo,* and the cause of her sinking was not entirely due to the PT's. A captured document indicates that the destroyer, while maneuvering to avoid PT torpedoes, struck one of the newly laid mines off the Guadalcanal coast, and that the enemy sank the damaged destroyer after futile efforts to tow it to safety.

This was the most violent action the PT's had at Guadalcanal, and it was their last. On the night of February 7/8, exactly 6 months after the Marines first landed, the Japanese completed their evacuation. Guadalcanal, stepping-stone for all of the Solomons, was ours.

8. A LULL IN OPERATIONS

The next 4 months were months of relative calm. Ousted from Guadalcanal, the Japanese devoted themselves to strengthening their positions in the upper Solomons and undertook no offensive action except for occasional air raids. This respite was sorely needed by the PT flotilla. The first squadrons had barely enough men to operate the boats, let alone maintain adequate base facilities. Crews became exhausted and were easy prey to malaria, dengue fever, and other tropical diseases. The boats, operating without adequate spares and repair facilities, were deteriorating.

Motor Torpedo Boat Flotilla 1, under command of Comdr. Allen P. Calvert, was activated on December 15, 1942, with headquarters at Sesapi, to bring all the squadrons under a single command. Operational control of the PT's remained, however, in the local naval base commanders (in the case of the Tulagi boats, Commander Naval Base Guadalcanal), a policy which, as will be seen, brought unfortunate results.

A month later, Capt. M. M. Dupre, Jr., was designated Commander Motor Torpedo Boat Squadrons, South Pacific (Administrative), in an attempt to improve the logistic support of PT's. Captain Dupre's organization was vitally needed. PT equipment was shipped from the United States to Noumea for off-loading and transshipment to the operating area. As the PT flotilla expanded, a centralized organization was needed to handle these transshipments.

Captain Dupre was also Chief of Staff to Commander Naval Bases, South Pacific, and this duality of command helped to insure consideration of PT requirements in the construction of new bases. Before Captain Dupre's appointment to the administrative command, there had been no one on South Pacific staff specifically charged with responsibility for PT bases, and the squadron commanders had been too much occupied with operations to have much time to spare for base problems. As a result, PT's were breaking down for lack of maintenance, although spares, material, and personnel to maintain them had already arrived in the South Pacific.

For example, when the first echelon of Motor Torpedo Boat Base 1, consisting of 4 officers, 21 men, and large quantities of spares and equipment arrived from the States and unloaded at Espiritu Santo, no one informed the PT squadrons of its arrival. Much of the base equipment was cannibalized by other commands at Espiritu Santo, PT spare parts deteriorated on the beach, and officers and men were assigned to other duties. Eventually, the remnants of material and personnel were collected and assimilated by the Motor Torpedo Boat Squadrons command, but during nearly all of the Guadalcanal campaign, the squadrons had to make out as best they could with entirely inadequate base facilities.

By March 1943, Base 2 and half of the salvaged personnel and material of Base 1 had been sent to Tulagi. Base 3, augmented by the other half of Base 1, was established as a main engine overhaul base at Espiritu Santo. By

*"Calvertville," the Tulagi PT base, named for Comdr. Allen P. Calvert,
Commander Motor Torpedo Boat Flotilla 1.*

May 1, the Espiritu Santo Base was overhauling 10 to 12 engines a month, and by November 1 was operating at full capacity of 54 engines a month.

The first four boats of Squadron 6 arrived at Tulagi on December 31, in time to go into action against the Tokyo Express. The squadron's second four boats, with PT's 113 and 114 of Squadron 2, were designated as Motor Torpedo Boat Division 17, and were sent to the Southwest Pacific. Under command of Lt. Daniel S. Baughman, executive officer of Squadron 6, Division 17 was the first PT unit to operate in the New Guinea area. The third division of Squadron 6 arrived at Tulagi in March. The squadron commander, Lt. Comdr. Clifton B. Maddox, was detached in February to become assistant to Captain Dupre, and Lt. Clark W. Faulkner, USNR, succeeded him as squadron commander.

Similarly, Lieutenant Westholm was detached from Squadron 2 for duty as operations officer on Captain Calvert's staff, and when that squadron took part in the occupation of the Russell Islands in February, Lt. Allen H. Harris, USNR, was squadron commander. Lieutenant Robinson became Captain Calvert's material officer, and was relieved as commander of Squadron 3 by Lt. John M. Searles, USNR.

The occupation of the Russells, roughly 35 miles west of Savo Island, was designed to deny the area to the enemy and to provide a staging point for future amphibious operations. Squadron 2 boats screened the transport group on its approach to the Russells on the night of February 20/21, and thereafter made regular nightly offshore patrols. The landings were entirely unopposed, and by the end of February the enemy still had not attacked, a fact which led to the belief that he was not even aware of our presence in the islands. The PT's had no action in the Russells. There were a few air raids, which caused no serious damage or losses.

Although the Guadalcanal PT's continued to run routine security patrols until July, they had no further action other than occasional air raids. On the night of March 5, a single plane dropped four bombs on Sesapi. The first three landed harmlessly in the water. The fourth hit the PT operations office, killing 1 officer and 3 enlisted men and seriously wounding 1 officer and 1 enlisted man. The hull of PT 118, moored in the slip alongside the operations office, was riddled with shrapnel.

On April 7 the Japanese raided the Guadalcanal-Tulagi area with 177 planes, of which about 25 were shot down. A group of dive bombers attacked shipping in Tulagi Harbor. Two bombs hit the New Zealand corvette *Moa*, sinking her in 4 minutes. Just to the north of the harbor the PT tender

Niagara was moored starboard side to the west bank of the Maliali River, heading downstream, with the minesweeper *Rail* tied up outboard, well aft. Nine planes came up the river, none of them over 150 feet off the water. The *Niagara* took them all under fire from her eight 20-mm. cannon, and the *Rail* fired at them with machineguns. The first plane, already in flames, crashed into the trees 1,000 yards astern of the ship. The second two were not damaged. The fourth, expelling a stream of white smoke, seemed unable to gain altitude and appeared to descend behind the hills to the north. The next two passed within 150 yards and attempted to strafe the ship, but their firing was erratic and they wobbled uncertainly as they passed through the *Niagara*'s heavy fire. Both crashed well back in the woods on the port quarter. The next two sheared up and to the right when taken under fire. One trailed light brown smoke as it disappeared close over the hilltops abaft the port beam; the other passed to starboard and crashed in the hills on the starboard quarter. This was the *Niagara*'s first action. It was also her next to last.

9. LOSS OF THE "NIAGARA"

Plans were being made in May 1943 for occupation of the New Georgia Group, 200 miles to the northwest of Guadalcanal. This was to be co-ordinated with operations in the Southwest Pacific area against Woodlark Island and the Trobriands, to the south of New Britain, and the Japanese bases of Lae and Salamaua on New Guinea. All of these moves were part of the overall strategy calling for eventual strangulation of the great Japanese stronghold of Rabaul, on the northwestern tip of New Britain.

Squadron 9, commanded by Lt. Comdr. Robert B. Kelly, arrived in the South Pacific in May and was assigned to the Russell Islands to stage there for forward movement in the New Georgia operation. In New Guinea, PT's already were patrolling off Lae and Salamaua. Other PT's were available for assignment to the Trobriand Islands. It would be spreading the Southwest Pacific PT's dangerously thin, however, to attempt to send any of them to Woodlark.

When Squadron 8, a Southwest Pacific squadron, passed through Noumea early in January, it transferred five boats, PT's 144–148, to Squadron 2 as compensation for the six boats of Division 17 that had been sent to the Southwest Pacific. By May Squadron 9 was in the Solomons, the first six boats of Squadron 10 were at Noumea, and the remainder of Squadron 10 and all of Squadron 5 were on their way. These increases in strength permitted reassignment of six PT's from South Pacific to Southwest Pacific for the Woodlark occupation. PT's 144–148, plus PT 110, were designated Motor Torpedo Boat Division 23, under command of Lt. Charles H. Jackson, USNR, and sailed from Tulagi for New Guinea, in company with the *Niagara,* on the afternoon of May 22.

The *Niagara* and the boats headed southeast toward Espiritu Santo, following a circuitous route intended to bring them south of the limit of enemy air activity before starting their open water passage westward to New Guinea. At 1135 on the morning of May 23, a high-flying Japanese twin-engine monoplane passed directly over the *Niagara,* headed north. Lt. Comdr. David B. Coleman, commanding officer of the *Niagara,* called his ship to general quarters and directed the PT's to take station in a wide circle around the tender. The plane turned, came back and dropped four bombs. Coleman held his ship in a hard right turn at maximum speed until the bombs were released, then swung his rudder amidships. Three were near-misses to starboard, the fourth a near-miss to port. They were close enough to disable the sound gear and the training mechanism of a 3-inch gun, and to knock out steering control temporarily. Half an hour later, when steering control had been regained, six more twin-engine planes approached from the northward at 12,000 feet altitude. The *Niagara* opened fire with her remaining 3-inch gun and all of her 20mms., but the planes were too high. The planes made a single pass, dropping 12 to 18 bombs. One hit directly on the forecastle. Several were damaging near-misses. From the PT's the ship appeared to be completely enveloped in a mass of water and smoke 250 feet high.

The *Niagara* listed rapidly to port. Water rushed through a 14-inch hole 6 feet below the waterline to flood two storerooms and a passageway. The engineroom also started flooding. All power and lighting failed and the main engines stopped. Fires below decks forward, caused by the direct hit, were out of control. Main engine and steering control were restored 7 minutes after the attack, but Lieutenant Commander Coleman ordered "abandon ship" because of the increasing list and the imminent danger of explosion if the flames should reach the tender's gasoline storage tanks.

Lieutenant Jackson brought PT 146 alongside the stern of the ship on the portside, and Lt. William E. Stedman, USNR, brought PT 147 alongside the

80-G-68537

The tender Niagara, *hit by Japanese bombs on May 23, 1943, burns as PT's come alongside to take off the crew.*

stern on the starboard side to take off some of the crew. Others went over the side into rafts and ship's boats, to be picked up by other PT's. The ship was then ablaze from bow to bridge, flames were spreading aft, and ammunition was exploding in the ready service boxes on the deck. Despite her heavy damage, the *Niagara* was lucky. Not one of her 136 officers and men was killed or even seriously injured.

Because of limited fuel and the distance from Tulagi—230 miles—the PT's had to head back without delay The *Niagara* was doomed, but might have stayed afloat for an hour or more. Lieutenant Commander Coleman decided to sink her. Lieutenant Stedman fired a torpedo which struck the *Niagara* in the gasoline tanks. The ship exploded with a sheet of flame 300 feet high, and went down in less than a minute.

The PT's arrived at Tulagi with the *Niagara*'s crew at 0200 on the 24th. A few days later they set out again with the seaplane tender *Ballard,* and arrived safely in Milne Bay, New Guinea, on May 31.

10. THE "STANVAC MANILA"

While the *Niagara* was being attacked, the SS *Stanvac Manila,* a merchant tanker, was approaching Noumea en route from Panama with the second division of Squadron 10 loaded in cradles on deck. PT's 167 and 172 were just forward of the bridge, headed forward. PT's 173 and 171 were just abaft the bridge, headed aft, and PT's 174 and 165 were just aft of them, headed forward.

At 0407 May 24 the *Stanvac Manila,* 100 miles south of Noumea, was hit by a torpedo in the port quarter. The events that followed were recounted by the squadron commander, Lt. Comdr. Thomas G. Warfield: [6]

About 2 minutes after the explosion, the stern was so low that the after portion of the well deck was awash. Apparently the engine room and fire room were flooded as all steam, light and power, and communications were lost. One of the *Manila*'s engineering officers had sounded abandon ship on a hand horn. The crews of the PT's 165 and 174 had freed their boats from the cradles and had then abandoned ship in compliance. The signal had not, however, been heard forward of the after section, so the remaining personnel busied themselves in casting their boats free and broadcasting on their radios. During this interval Ensign [Thomas E.] Falvey had noticed no crews aboard the after two boats and had made his way aft to check on their holding down gear in addition to freeing his own boat [PT 173]. Lt. (jg.) [Russel W.] Rome (Senior PT officer) had countermanded the abandon ship order. . . .

Until daylight the PT crews and the armed guards stood by their guns while the *Manila*'s officers and crew abandoned ship. . . . The forward 3-inch gun crew fired five rounds. About one hour after dawn the wind was freshening and the ship's bow had swung downwind. The stern had settled so that the stern of the PT 174 (lee side) had some buoyancy and was pounding lightly in her cradle. Ensign Falvey at considerable risk made his way to her, led her anchor cable from her sampson post to the stern of the PT 171 and then to the *Manila*'s bridge deck. Between 0800 and 0900 the PT 174 was pounding heavily in her cradle. Lt. (jg.) Rome, Ensign [Edward H.] Kruse (Boat Captain of the PT 171), and Ens. [Malcolm R.] McArdle were able to board her but being unable to cut the *Manila*'s shrouds the anchor cable was passed outboard of the shrouds. The bottom was sound under engine room and lazarette but gas fumes were extremely strong. The anchor cable was made fast to the 174's starboard quarter and all hands heaved from the *Manila*'s bridge deck until the boat was slewed around and lay athwartships. Her bow held fast to some of the *Manila*'s superstructure which prevented further outboard movement. It was apparent that her engines would have to be started, despite the loose gasoline, if she were to be saved. [Homer] Banks and [Harold E.] Hershey, both MoMM1c, and from other boat crews, volunteered to go below and to at-

[6] Lieutenant Commander Warfield had brought the first six boats of his squadron to the South Pacific and was already in Noumea at the time of the torpedoing of the *Stanvac Manila.*

tempt starting the engines. Without hesitation they started both wing engines and Ensign Kruse was able to back her clear. The effect upon morale was tremendous. A cheer from all hands went up.

The stern of the PT 165 was beginning to slap against the after deckhouse of the *Manila*. Her batteries had become wet as she had been damaged below the engine room but her engines were started with the auxiliary generator and by pushing her stern out she was backed clear. The water immediately rose to stop the engines. All attempts to stop the leaks and bail were unable to prevent her sinking. Even though watertight doors had been secured she had received too much bottom damage to remain afloat.

The first plane seen by boat crews reached the scene shortly after 1000. The possibility of launching additional boats seemed remote. Nevertheless, the boat crews busied themselves breaking loose shoring to prevent damage to the after hulls and fittings, and throwing off strongbacks.[7] Records, chronometers, binoculars, small arms, etc., were gathered from the remaining four boats and put in a lifeboat which had returned with the Chief Mate . . .

Waves breaking over the well deck lifted the PT 173 and set her down on two boat davits. Lt. (jg.) Rome and Ensign Falvey boarded her in spite of her precarious position, found her gas tanks and bottom ruptured beyond hope and flooded her with CO_2. The bow of the *Manila* now lifted to 45 or 50 degs. and she commenced to slip aft. The PT 173 broke loose and sank by the stern just as the two officers jumped clear. The PT 171 simultaneously broke loose and floated clear. Her engine room was taking water more rapidly and transverse bulkheads were probably rupturing. Abandon ship was ordered and carried out quickly and calmly.

As Lt. (jg.) Rome went down the falls into the last lifeboat a sea capsized it, pinning him underneath. He had a glimpse of the ship's master standing on the bridge and, when extricated from under the lifeboat and brought back to consciousness, he went back aboard the sinking *Manila* to save the Captain. He did not know that the Master had been taken off while he was beneath the lifeboat. The bridge of the ship was at this time awash and Rome was tossed about by the sea there but finally managed to swim clear as the tanker took her final plunge.

The *Manila* sank, slipping aft, at about 1205, corkscrewing to starboard as her bow heaved up. The motion threw the PT 172 clear but she broke her stem on the yardarm as she cleared. The PT 167 cleared from under the tanker's foremast in a remarkable manner, having been carried down with the ship. She shot clear of the water completely but stripped her topsides on the mast. Her hull was least damaged of any boat.

About 1300 a destroyer arrived taking the PT's 167, 171, and 174 in tow. The PT 172 made Noumea under her own power. During that day, all night, and the following day, exhaustive effort was displayed by the officers and men in keeping the damaged boats afloat.

Two boats (PT's 165 and 173) and one man were lost. The other four boats, with their crews, found haven in Noumea the following day.

---

[7] Large timbers laid athwartships and lashed down to keep PT's in transit from shifting in their cradles.

11. THE "McCAWLEY"

The occupation of New Georgia began quietly on June 21 with the unopposed landing of two companies of Marines at Segi, on the southern tip
of the island. The main landings were not made until June 30, when
troops were put ashore at Viru Harbor, to the northwest of Segi; at Wickham
Anchorage, on Vangunu Island to the southeast, and, most important of all,
at Rendova Harbor on the north side of Rendova Island, separated by only
a few miles of water from New Georgia. Rendova was to be the base for
the principal thrust against New Georgia. From there troops could be landed
a few miles east of the enemy airfield at Munda, which with the airfield at
Vila on the neighboring island of Kolombangara, was a primary objective
of the New Georgia campaign.

Leading the six large transports and cargo ships of the invasion force into
Rendova Harbor was USS *McCawley,* the former Grace liner *Santa Barbara,*
flagship of Rear Adm. Richmond K. Turner, Commander Amphibious
Force South Pacific. By midafternoon *McCawley,* first of the transports to
put men ashore, had landed about 1,200 troops and hundreds of tons of
cargo. The task force took up cruising formation and stood out through
Blanche Channel for Guadalcanal. Within an hour 25 torpedo bombers
swept in low and fast. One torpedo hit *McCawley* amidships in the engineroom, tearing a 20-foot hole in her side. The ship listed violently to port,
then righted herself, swinging to starboard with her rudder jammed hard
over and all engines stopped. Admiral Turner ordered the cargo ship
Libra to take the *McCawley* in tow and the destroyers *Ralph Talbot* and
McCalla to stand by to assist while he and his staff transferred to the destroyer
Farenholt, to proceed with the remainder of the task force. *Ralph Talbot*
took off all remaining personnel except the salvage crew, in charge of Rear
Adm. Theodore S. Wilkinson.

The *Libra* no sooner had the *McCawley* in tow than the group was attacked by eight dive bombers. The salvage crew manned the transport's
20mm. and .50 caliber guns, and, with the assistance of the two destroyers,
beat off the attack. The *McCawley* continued to settle. At 1850, with the
water still rising, Admiral Wilkinson had the *McCalla* come alongside and
ordered all hands to abandon ship. At 2002 he ordered the *McCalla* to prepare to torpedo the transport if she should settle to the point where she
could no longer be towed. Twenty minutes later, the *McCawley's* commanding officer reported, the transport "was struck by three torpedoes fired
by an enemy submarine and sank stern first in 340 fathoms of water."

The 12 boats of Motor Torpedo Boat Squadron 9 were part of the task force that entered Rendova Harbor on the morning of June 30. Lieutenant Commander Kelly was to establish a temporary base and operate as directed by the Commander Naval Base Rendova. Most of the first day was devoted to finding a suitable anchorage and fueling the boats from drums lightered out in LCM's. The Commander Naval Base at first told Kelly that there would be no PT patrols that night, but later Kelly received orders to establish a patrol from the northern tip of Rendova to Roviana Lagoon to screen landing craft that were to land troops on New Georgia, and another to the east and west of Mbalumbalu Island in Blanche Channel.

Kelly was shown a dispatch in which the Commander Amphibious Force directed that PT's intercept and destroy enemy forces which were expected to reinforce Viru Harbor from the north. He asked what friendly vessels might be encountered in the area, and was assured that there would be none operating north of Viru Harbor. He was specifically informed that all of our transports and their escorts would be well clear of the patrol areas.

Kelly sent six of his boats to patrol the Rendova-Roviana line, and himself took the other six, in two sections of three each, to patrol off Mbalumbalu Island. While passing through a light rain squall between Rendova and Mbalumbalu, Kelly's radar picked up surface targets 5 miles off the northeast tip of Rendova. On closing, the radar revealed what appeared to be a large ship lying to, surrounded by six to eight small craft* with two escorts patrolling about 1,500 yards to the eastward. Kelly had been told that none of our ships would be in the area—this must be an enemy transport landing troops on Rendova to the rear of our Army's positions.

Because of the overcast, Kelly had to close to 1,000 yards before he could identify the large ship as a transport. He ordered his first section to attack it and to retire at slow speed if undetected. The second section was to follow at 1,000 yard intervals and attack the escorts as opportunity permitted.

The first section closed to 600 yards, idling in with mufflers closed. Each boat fired four torpedoes. The attack was perfect. There were evenly spaced hits on the target, the transport sank, and the PT's idled away undetected. The second section gave chase to the larger of the two escorts which headed

---

*One must have been fleet tug *Pawnee* just arrived to take the tow from *Libra*. Maneuvering off *McCawley's* port bow to retrieve the line, which had parted, a *Pawnee* sailor sang out he heard engines idling and American voices; an instant later "tin fish" appeared from where he was pointing, phosphorescent trails spectacular in the darkness. The little ship rang full astern, almost ran into *McCalla* on her port quarter, but dodged the torpedoes, some of which her crew insist "porpoised" right under their tug. They say *Pawnee* was mistaken for an enemy vessel, silhouetted by a light bulb left hanging over the transport's side by the salvage party abandoning ship.

south at high speed. They were unable to close the range sufficiently to attack before it crossed a line between Rendova and Viru Harbor, the southern patrol area limit, so they returned to patrol east of Mbalumbalu.

During the rest of the night the six boats were harassed by enemy float-planes. One bomb dropped close aboard PT 162, mortally wounding the helmsman, wounding two men slightly, riddling mufflers, exhaust stacks and a gasoline tank with shrapnel. Near-misses ahead and astern lifted another boat practically out of water, causing only minor damage.

Returning to Rendova in the morning, Kelly saw a shattered landing craft adrift in Blanche Channel near the scene of the night's action, marked with the letters APA 4—the designation of the *McCawley*. And an officer aboard one of the PT's of Kelly's second section said he thought that the escort vessel he had pursued was a U.S. destroyer, but he could not be sure because of the distance and poor visibility. Kelly suspected something was amiss, and reported his doubts to the Commander Naval Base and the Commanding General Rendova. These officers assured him again that no friendly ships had been in the area, and congratulated him on a good night's work.

As soon as the action reports of the PT's and the *McCawley* were compared, of course, it was obvious that the transport had not been sunk by a submarine.

The incident demonstrated conclusively that Naval Base Commanders were not the proper authorities to exercise operational control over PT's. Essentially concerned with administration of a shore base, they did not always have the latest information regarding movements of forces afloat. After the sinking of the *McCawley,* operational control of PT's was vested in the Commander Amphibious Force, and a PT liaison officer was assigned to his staff. Specific operating areas were established for PT's, from which friendly surface and aircraft were warned to keep clear. PT's were kept advised of friendly shipping near their operating zones.

This system did not function perfectly in every instance, but was a vast improvement over the former method. The lesson cost one transport—a transport already so grievously wounded that the *McCalla* was standing by to torpedo it—without loss of life. The price might well have been higher.

12. TRANSITION

The first month after the New Georgia landings was a period of transition for the PT's. Their organization was strengthened on July 23, when Commodore Edward J. Moran, who had been commanding officer of the *Boise* in the Battle of Cape Esperance, reported for duty as Commander Motor Torpedo Boat Squadrons South Pacific Force. Operational control of the PT's remained in the Commander Amphibious Force, but Commodore Moran's appointment and subsequent organization of a capable staff brought about improvements in logistic support, standardized operating doctrine, and training programs.

During this period also, the PT's had their last actions with destroyers and their first with armored barges which were too small and of too shallow draft to be suitable torpedo targets and were more heavily gunned than the PT's. The boats started using PBY patrol planes, the "Black Cats," to locate and illuminate barges for them, and found that the Japanese floatplanes, which Kelly's boats met on their first patrol at Rendova, were to come over almost nightly to strafe and bomb them.

The situation had changed since the first days at Tulagi. Now we had the preponderance of seapower. Our cruisers and destroyers shelled enemy positions on New Georgia and Kolombangara at will, and in the Battle of Kula Gulf on July 5/6, the Battle of Kolombangara on 12/13 July, and the Battle of Vella Gulf, on August 6, in which they sank a total of three destroyers and a light cruiser, convinced the enemy that he would have to place his main reliance on coastal barges rather than the Tokyo Express to transport troops and supplies to his bases on New Georgia, Kolombangara, Arundel, Gizo, and the small neighboring islands. The barges were relatively expendable, and could operate close to shore in waters inaccessible to ships of deeper draft. Vulnerable to aircraft attack by day, they usually passed the daylight hours nestling against the shore, well camouflaged by freshly cut leaves and palm fronds, and made their runs at night, preferably in the dark of the moon. Barges became the Japanese lifeline. For the rest of the Solomons campaign, barge hunting was to be the principal mission of the PT's.

13. FIRST ACTION AT RENDOVA

Squadron 9 set up its base on Lumbari Island, on the north side of Rendova Harbor. Squadrons 5 and 10 arrived there in July 1943, and Squadron 11 in August. It soon became evident that while the boats could cover the western portion of the New Georgia Group from Rendova, they could not effectively cover the eastern coasts. Accordingly, a new operating point was established at Lever Harbor on the northeast coast of New Georgia.

Lt. Craig C. Smith, USNR, arrived there on July 24 with four boats of Squadron 6 and the APc 28, a small coastal transport which was to serve as tender, since it was not planned to establish a shore base. Lieutenant Commander Kelly, who had been relieved as area commander at Rendova by Lieutenant Commander Warfield, took command of the Lever Harbor boats on July 26.

The first action with enemy surface ships at Rendova was reminiscent of Tulagi. At dusk on July 3, Kelly took PT's 156, 157, and 161 to patrol off Baniata Point, the westernmost tip of Rendova. About midnight he received a radio message from the base: enemy destroyers were heading for Rendova. An hour later gun flashes were seen to the northwest. Kelly assumed that these were the enemy destroyers, but he could not be sure. He was not yet receiving complete information regarding movements of friendly forces. "The PT's," Kelly said, "were thus faced with the unpleasant task of advancing within visual distance of the unidentified ships and trying to make an identification."

The night was so black that the three PT's passed directly through the formation and were taken under fire before they could positively identify the ships as four Japanese destroyers. "The enemy destroyers apparently executed a turn movement bringing them into column," Kelly said, "and then proceeded to steam at high speed (20–25 knots) in a circle around the PT's. During the next 10-15 minutes a wild melee evolved. The PT's and their smoke puffs were kept almost constantly under fire. The enemy ships were for the most part so close and moving so rapidly that it was like trying to shoot ducks with a rifle to fire torpedoes at them. PT 156 fired two salvos of one torpedo each and missed on both occasions. PT 161 fired no torpedoes as it could never get a reasonable shot. PT 157 fired two two-torpedo salvos. The last of these was fired after that boat had had its center engine put out of commission when the supercharger was riddled by enemy machinegun fire. Its boat captain believed he obtained a hit with one torpedo on the second salvo as he saw a flash that seemed larger than the other main battery gun flashes. However, there is no assurance that such was the case except that the enemy immediately retired at high speed to the northwest."

The ability of the boats to survive more than 10 minutes of close-range fire from four destroyers, Kelly believed, was attributable to their tactic of maneuvering at slow speed, making frequent 90-degree turns after laying small smoke puffs. While speed may be a boat's only salvation once its position has been observed, slow maneuvers sometimes may be used to escape detection.

"It has never been determined," Kelly said, "whether or not the PT's obtained any torpedo hits on the enemy group. If one were obtained it must have been at the bow and have done relatively little damage due to the enemy's rapid retirement. However, despite this it is considered that it was an extremely successful engagement in that the enemy was forced to retire without ever having approached within range of our beach head. Had the PT's not intercepted them, the damage they might have inflicted would have been considerable. Our forces had not yet developed adequate defensive positions against bombardment and the beaches were still piled high with stores and munitions. The fact that the enemy was aware of this was indicated by the heavy air raids against these beaches that noon and the following day."

14. COSTLY ERRORS

On the night of July 17/18, three PT's (159, 157, and 160) patrolling the west side of Kolombangara erred to the north of their patrol area. A patrol plane sighted them and reported them as three enemy destroyers. Five of our destroyers which had been patrolling off the northern tip of New Georgia to screen a landing at Enogai Inlet proceeded at full speed toward the reported enemy, and opened fire at 20,000 yards. The PT's, thinking in turn that they had been taken under attack by the enemy, fired torpedoes and retired to the south. The destroyers, knowing that PT's were patrolling to the south, did not pursue them. Fortunately no hits were scored by either side.

A more serious error occurred on the morning of July 20, when three PT's just south of Ferguson Passage on their return from patrol were strafed by four Army B-25's. One PT held its fire; on the other two no order was given to fire, but some of the gunners, as yet with little experience in action, lost their heads and fired at the planes. "I got confused," one gunner said, "and thought it was a Jap plane with our insignia."

One plane crashed 5 miles from the boats. All of the boats were hit. PT 166 caught fire and exploded. All of its crew, some of them wounded, abandoned ship before the explosion. They were picked up by PT 164. Lt. Edward Macauley 3d, USNR, whose PT 168 had kept its guns silent, proceeded to the crashed bomber, despite the fact that his boat was afire. The crew extinguished the flames, and PT 168 picked up three survivors from the B–25. One PT and one B–25 were lost; 3 men of the B–25 were killed and 3 wounded, and 1 officer and 10 men of the PT's were wounded. The new operations setup was not yet working perfectly: the B–25 crews had been told that no friendly vessels would be operating in the area.

15. THEY DIDN'T PASS THE WORD

The PT's had their final all-out encounter with the Tokyo Express on the night of August 1/2, 1943, when four destroyers ran through Blackett Strait, on the west side of Kolombangara, to Vila, on the southern tip of the island. It was apparent that the Japanese knew that PT's would be their only opposition. Just before dusk on the afternoon of the 1st, 18 bombers made a strike on the PT base at Lumbari Island. One bomb blasted PT's 117 and 164 at their dock and killed two men. Two torpedoes blown off PT 164 by the bomb explosion ran erratically around the bay until they fetched up on the beach without detonating.

Even with the loss of two boats, it was possible to send 15 PT's out in 4 sections to meet the destroyers. Lt. Henry J. Brantingham, in PT 159, led PT 157 (Lt. (jg.) William F. Liebenow, Jr., USNR), PT 162 (Lt. (jg.) John R. Lowrey, USNR), and PT 109 (Lt. John F. Kennedy, USNR)* in the northernmost patrol in Blackett Strait, off Vanga Vanga on the Kolombangara coast. Lt. Arthur H. Berndtson, in PT 171, led a patrol a few miles to the south of Brantingham's division, with PT 169 (Lt. (jg.) Philip A. Potter, Jr., USNR), PT 172 (Lt. (jg.) Stuart Hamilton, USNR), and PT 163 (Ens. Edward H. Kruse, Jr., USNR). To the southeast of this patrol, still in Blackett Strait, Lt. Russel W. Rome, USNR, in PT 174, led PT 105 (Lt. (jg.) Richard E. Keresey, Jr., USNR) and PT 103 (Lt. (jg.) Joseph K.

---

*Who, 17 years later, was elected President of the United States. Several detailed accounts of President Kennedy's naval career have been published. These include John Hersey's moving and sensitive article "Survival" published in the *New Yorker* of 17 June 1944, and three books: Robert J. Donovan's *PT 109: John F. Kennedy in World War II* (New York: McGraw-Hill Book Co., 1961); Richard Tregaskis's *John F. Kennedy: War Hero* (New York: Dell Publishing Co., 1962); and Chandler Whipple's *Lt. John F. Kennedy—Expendable* (New York: Universal Publishing Corp., 1962).

*Results of enemy air attack on Rendova Harbor, August 1, 1943: Above,
PT 117, beached with a gaping hole in her bow; Below, PT 164, with bow
demolished.*

Roberts, USNR). South of Ferguson Passage, the southern entrance to Blackett Strait, were stationed Lt. George E. Cookman, USNR, in PT 107, with PT 104 (Lt. (jg.) Robert D. Shearer, USNR), PT 106 (Lt. (jg.) David M. Payne, USNR), and PT 108 (Lt. (jg.) Sidney D. Hix, USNR).

Brantingham made radar contact at midnight with ships approaching from the north, close to the Kolombangara coast. Soon afterward he saw four ships which he believed to be large landing craft. The 159 and 157 started to close the range to make a strafing run. The enemy ships opened fire with heavy guns, revealing themselves as destroyers. PT 159 fired four torpedoes and PT 157 fired two at 1,800 yards. As the boats retired to the northwest, a large explosion was seen at the target. PT 159, having fired all its torpedoes, returned to base. PT 157 attempted to rejoin PT's 162 and 109, but was unable to find them.

A few minutes later Berndtson's division sighted four destroyers, still heading down the Kolombangara coast. PT 171 closed to 1,500 yards. The destroyers fired starshells to illuminate the PT's and opened fire with their main batteries and automatic weapons. PT 171 fired four torpedoes at the second destroyer. Bright flashes from the tubes warned the destroyer, which turned toward the PT and avoided the torpedoes. The other three PT's in the division were not aware of the presence of the destroyers until they opened fire, and then could not fire torpedoes because PT 171 was crossing their bows. The 171 returned to base. The 159 proceeded north, joining PT's 162 and 109. PT's 170 and 172, straddled by gunfire from two destroyers, ran south through Ferguson Passage, where they were ineffectually attacked by four floatplanes, and eventually returned to their patrol station.

Lieutenant Cookman, whose PT 107 had the only radar in his section, had radar contact with two ships. He headed through Ferguson Passage at high speed to attack, leaving the other three boats of his section behind. Inside Ferguson Passage he fired four torpedoes by radar, and observed a dull red flash in the direction of the target. He reversed course and headed back for the base, passing his other three boats as they came north through the passage. These boats could find no targets, though they patrolled in Blackett Strait for more than an hour before returning to their original patrol station.

Lieutenant Rome's division saw the flashes of the destroyers firing on the boats to the north. At 0025 Rome saw a destroyer to the northeast, close to the Kolombangara shore, turn on its searchlight and start firing to the west. He fired four torpedoes at 1,000 yards and observed two explosions at the target. As he headed for Ferguson Passage, shells from the destroyer passed overhead and a plane strafed the boat. The 174 was not hit, but returned to base as it had no more torpedoes. PT 103 fired four torpedoes at 2 miles, and also returned to base. PT 105 was in an unfavorable position and could not attack.

An hour later the 105 was patrolling just inside Ferguson Passage. A flame flared up to the northwest in the middle of Blackett Strait, and gunfire flashed along the Kolombangara coast, silhouetting a destroyer moving slowly north, 2,000 yards away. PT 105 fired two torpedoes, but observed no hits.

To the north, PT 109 (Lieutenant Kennedy) was leading PT's 162 and 169 on a slow southward sweep. A destroyer suddenly knifed out of the darkness off PT 109's bow. Before Kennedy could turn his boat the destroyer rammed it at full speed. Gasoline burst into flames immediately. This was the flash which silhouetted a destroyer for the 105. Lowrey, in the 162, saw the destroyer as it bore down on Kennedy's boat. His torpedoes would not fire. He finally swerved off to the southwest to avoid collision with the destroyer, then only 100 yards away. Potter, in the 169, fired two torpedoes, but by then the destroyer was only 150 yards away, and the torpedoes probably would not have armed themselves in that distance even if they had hit. The destroyer opened fire on the 169, which zigzagged to the south behind smoke puffs. A few minutes later Potter saw the wake of another destroyer heading toward him from the south. He swung left and fired his last two torpedoes. The destroyer also turned left, just in time, Potter thought, for the torpedo to hit its bow and explode. The 169 continued to zigzag south, laying smoke.

PT 157, farther north than the other boats, fired two torpedoes at a ship close to the Kolombangara coast without observed results.

This was perhaps the most confused and least effectively executed action the PT's had been in. Eight PT's fired 30 torpedoes. The only confirmed results are the loss of PT 109 and damage to the Japanese destroyer *Amagiri*. The *Amagiri* was not hit by a torpedo, but vibrated so badly after ramming the 109 that she was unable to proceed at high speed. The chief fault of the PT's was that they didn't pass the word. Each boat attacked independently, leaving the others to discover the enemy for themselves.

16. THE 109 [8]

"The time was about 0230. Ensign Ross was on the bow as lookout; Ensign Thom was standing beside the cockpit; Lieutenant Kennedy was at the wheel, and with him in the cockpit was Maguire, his radioman; Marney was in the forward turret; Mauer, the quartermaster was standing beside Ensign Thom; Albert was in the after turret; and McMahon was in the engine room. The location of other members of the crew upon the boat is unknown. Suddenly a dark shape loomed up on PT 109's starboard bow 200–300 yards distance. At first this shape was believed to be other PT's. However, it was soon seen to be a destroyer identified as the *Ribiki* group of the *Fubuki* class [9] bearing down on PT 109 at high speed. The 109 had started to turn to starboard preparatory to firing torpedoes. However, when PT 109 had scarcely turned 30°, the destroyer rammed the PT, striking it forward of the forward starboard tube and shearing off the starboard side of the boat aft, including the starboard engine. The destroyer traveling at an estimated speed of 40 knots neither slowed nor fired as she split the PT, leaving part of the PT on one side and part on the other. Scarcely 10 seconds elapsed between time of sighting and the crash.

"A fire was immediately ignited, but, fortunately, it was gasoline burning on the water's surface at least 20 yards away from the remains of the PT which were still afloat. This fire burned brightly for 15–20 minutes and then died out. It is believed that the wake of the destroyer carried off the floating gasoline, thereby saving PT 109 from fire.

"Lt. Kennedy, Ensigns Thom and Ross, Mauer, Maguire and Albert still clung to the PT 109's hull. Lt. Kennedy ordered all hands to abandon ship when it appeared the fire would spread to it. All soon crawled back aboard when this danger passed. It was ascertained by shouting that Harris, McMahon and Starkey were in the water about 100 yards to the Southwest while Zinser and Johnson were an equal distance to the Southeast. Kennedy swam toward the group of three, and Thom and Ross struck out for the other two. Lt. Kennedy had to tow McMahon, who was helpless because of serious burns, back to the boat. A strong current impeded their progress, and it took

---

[8] This section is quoted from a report prepared on 22 August 1943, by Lt. (jg.) Byron R. White, USNR, and Lt. (jg.) J. C. McClure, USNR, intelligence officers of Motor Torpedo Boat Flotilla 1. In 1962, President Kennedy appointed Byron R. White an Associate Justice of the Supreme Court of the United States.

[9] Good identification. The *Amagiri* was of the *Amagiri* group of the *Fubuki* class, but practically identical in appearance with the destroyers of the *Ribiki* group.

about an hour to get McMahon aboard PT 109. Kennedy then returned for the other two men, one of whom was suffering from minor burns. He traded his life belt to Harris, who was uninjured, in return for Harris's water-logged kapok life jacket which was impeding the latter's swimming. Together they towed Starkey to the PT.

"Meanwhile, Ensigns Thom and Ross had reached Zinser and Johnson who were both helpless because of gas fumes. Thom towed Johnson, and Ross took Zinser. Both regained full consciousness by the time the boat was reached.

"Within 3 hours after the crash all survivors who could be located were brought aboard PT 109. Marney and Kirksey were never seen after the crash. During the 3 hours it took to gather the survivors together, nothing was seen or heard that indicated other boats or ships in the area. PT 109 did not fire its Very pistols for fear of giving away its position to the enemy.

"Meanwhile the IFF [10] and all codes aboard had been completely destroyed or sunk in the deep waters of Vella Gulf. Despite the fact that all water-tight doors were dogged down at the time of the crash, PT 109 was slowly taking on water. When daylight of August 2 arrived, the 11 survivors were still aboard PT 109. It was estimated that the boat lay about 4 miles north and slightly east of Gizo Anchorage and about 3 miles away from the reef along northeast Gizo.

"It was obvious that the PT 109 would sink on the 2d, and decision was made to abandon it in time to arrive before dark on one of the tiny islands east of Gizo. A small island 3½–4 miles to the southeast of Gizo was chosen on which to land, rather than one but 2½ miles away which was close to Gizo, and which, it was feared, might be occupied by the Japs.

"At 1400 Lt. Kennedy took the badly burned McMahon in tow and set out for land, intending to lead the way and scout the island in advance of the other survivors. Ensigns Ross and Thom followed with the other men. Johnson and Mauer, who could not swim, were tied to a float rigged from a 2 x 8 which was part of the 37mm. gun mount. Harris and Maguire were fair swimmers, but Zinser, Starkey and Albert were not so good. The strong swimmers pushed or towed the float to which the non-swimmers were tied.

"Lt. Kennedy was dressed only in skivvies, Ensign Thom, coveralls and shoes, Ensign Ross, trousers, and most of the men were dressed only in trou-

---

[10] IFF is an electronic recognition signaling device. The letters stand for "Identification, Friend or Foe."

sers and shirts. There were six 45's in the group (two of which were later lost before rescue), one 38, one flashlight, one large knife, one light knife and a pocket knife. The boat's first aid kit had been lost in the collision. All the group with the exception of McMahon, who suffered considerably from burns, were in fairly good condition, although weak and tired from their swim ashore.

"That evening Lt. Kennedy decided to swim into Ferguson Passage in an attempt to intercept PT boats proceeding to their patrol areas. He left about 1830, swam to a small island ½ mile to the southeast, proceeded along a reef which stretched out into Ferguson Passage, arriving there about 2000. No PT's were seen, but aircraft flares were observed which indicated that the PT's that night were operating in Gizo not Blackett Strait and were being harassed as usual by enemy float planes. Kennedy began his return over the same route he had previously used. While swimming the final lap to the island on which the other survivors were, he was caught in a current which swept him in a circle about 2 miles into Blackett Strait and back to the middle of Ferguson Passage, where he had to start his homeward trip all over again. On this trip he stopped on the small island just southeast of 'home' where he slept until dawn before covering the last ½ mile lap to join the rest of his group. He was completely exhausted, slightly feverish, and slept most of the day.

"Nothing was observed on August 2 or 3 which gave any hope of rescue. On the night of the 3d Ensign Ross decided to proceed into Ferguson Passage in another attempt to intercept PT patrols from Rendova. Using the same route as Kennedy had used and leaving about 1800, Ross 'patrolled' off the reefs on the west side of the Passage with negative results. In returning he wisely stopped on the islet southeast of 'home,' slept and thereby avoided the experience with the current which had swept Kennedy out to sea. He made the final lap next morning.

"The complete diet of the group on what came to be called Bird Island (because of the great abundance of droppings from the fine feathered friends) consisted of cocoanut milk and meat. As the cocoanut supply was running low and in order to get closer to Ferguson Passage, the group left Bird Island at noon, August 4th, and, using the same arrangements as before, headed for a small islet west of Cross Island. Kennedy, with McMahon in tow, arrived first. The rest of the group again experienced difficulty with a strong easterly current, but finally managed to make the eastern tip of the island.

"Their new home was slightly larger than their former, offered brush for protection and a few cocoanuts to eat, and had no Jap tenants. The night of August 4th was wet and cold, and no one ventured into Ferguson Passage that night. The next morning Kennedy and Ross decided to swim to Cross Island in search of food, boats or anything else which might be useful to their party. Prior to their leaving for Cross Island, one of three New Zealand P–40's made a strafing run on Cross Island. Although this indicated the possibility of Japs, because of the acute food shortage, the two set out, swam the channel and arrived on Cross Island about 1530. Immediately they ducked into the brush. Neither seeing nor hearing anything, the two officers sneaked through the brush to the east side of the island and peered from the brush onto the beach. A small rectangular box with Japanese writing on the side was seen which was quickly and furtively pulled into the bush. Its contents proved to be 30–40 small bags of crackers and candy. A little farther up the beach, alongside a native lean-to, a one-man canoe and a barrel of water were found. About this time a canoe containing two persons was sighted. Light showing between their legs revealed that they did not wear trousers and, therefore, must be natives. Despite all efforts of Kennedy and Ross to attract their attention, they paddled swiftly off to the northwest. Nevertheless, Kennedy and Ross, having obtained a canoe, food and water, considered their visit a success.

"That night Kennedy took the canoe and again proceeded into Ferguson Passage, waited there until 2100, but again no PT's appeared. He returned to his 'home' island via Cross Island where he picked up the food but left Ross who had decided to swim back the following morning. When Kennedy arrived at base at about 2330, he found that the two natives which he and Ross had sighted near Cross Island, had circled around and landed on the island where the rest of the group were. Ensign Thom, after telling the natives in as many ways as possible that he was an American and not a Jap, finally convinced them whereupon they landed and performed every service possible for the survivors.

"The next day, August 6, Kennedy and the natives paddled to Cross Island intercepting Ross, who was swimming back to the rest of the group. After Ross and Kennedy had thoroughly searched Cross Island for Japs and had found none, despite the natives' belief to the contrary, they showed the two PT survivors where a two-man native canoe was hidden.

"The natives were then sent with messages to the Coastwatcher. One was a pencilled note written the day before by Ensign Thom; the other was a message written on a green cocoanut husk by Kennedy, informing the coastwatcher that he and Ross were on Cross Island.

"After the natives left, Ross and Kennedy remained on the island until evening, when they set in the two-man canoe to again try their luck at intercepting PT's in Ferguson Passage. They paddled far out into Ferguson Passage, saw nothing, and were caught in a sudden rainsquall which eventually capsized the canoe. Swimming to land was difficult and treacherous as the sea swept the two officers against the reef on the south side of Cross Island. Ross received numerous cuts and bruises, but both managed to make land where they remained the rest of the night.

"On Saturday, August 7, eight natives arrived, bringing a message from the coastwatcher instructing the senior officer to go with the natives to Wana Wana. Kennedy and Ross had the natives paddle them to [the] island where the rest of the survivors were. The natives had brought food and other articles (including a cook stove) to make the survivors comfortable. They were extremely kind at all times.

"That afternoon, Kennedy, hidden under ferns in the native boat, was taken to the coastwatcher, arriving about 1600. There it was arranged that PT boats would rendezvous with him in Ferguson Passage that evening at 2230. Accordingly he was taken to the rendezvous point and finally managed to make contact with the PT's at 2315. He climbed aboard the PT and directed it to the rest of the survivors. The rescue was effected without mishap, and the Rendova base was reached at 0530, August 8, 7 days after the ramming of the PT 109 in Blackett Strait."

17. BARGE HUNTING

Barge hunting became the principal occupation of the PT's, both at Rendova and at Lever Harbor. From their first contact on July 21 until the end of August, the Rendova boats encountered 56 barges and 5 small auxiliary ships. They claimed 8 barges and 1 auxiliary sunk, 3 barges and 1 auxiliary probably sunk, and 6 barges and 1 auxiliary damaged. The Lever Harbor boats, which had their first barge action on August 3, engaged 43 or 44 barges from then until the end of the month, of which 2 were sunk, 1 was forced to be beached, and 8 to 16 were hit with possible damage.

These claims later proved to be conservative. On several occasions when our ground forces moved into previously enemy-held territory, they found beached or reefed barges which had been damaged beyond repair by PT gunfire, but which had not been claimed as destroyed. And frequently the boats disrupted Japanese plans by denying the enemy access to his island bases in actions which originally appeared to have caused little damage.

On the night of July 23/24, for example, PT's 117, 154, and 155, patrolling in Blackett Strait, west of Vila, encountered three barges, of which they sank one and chased the others back toward their base. Later they sighted three destroyers approaching from the north. The destroyers, apparently sighting the PT's at the same time, headed for Gizo and Wilson Straits at high speed and escaped to the west before the PT's could get into position to attack.

So far as anyone could tell at the time, this was not a particularly important engagement—only one barge sunk. But it gains significance in the light of a captured Japanese document, which says, "On 23 July 1943 Destroyer Division 16 was engaged in an urgent transport mission to Kolombangara, but was unable to fulfill it because a group of enemy PT boats, about 12, appeared just before we entered the base and interfered . . . The barges were thus late in assembling."

Thus, although only one barge was sunk, an "urgent transport mission" was utterly frustrated. Strangulation of the supply line was the paramount objective, and the boats accomplished this objective to a far greater degree than any mere "box score" of barge sinkings could possibly indicate.

The principal barge routes led from Choiseul Island across to the northern tip of Vella Lavella and down the west coast through Wilson, Gizo, and Blackett Straits to Vila on Kolombangara Island, and from Choiseul or northern Vella Lavella to the northern tip of Kolombangara and thence down the east coast to Vila. The Rendova boats attempted to intercept traffic on the first of these routes, the Lever Harbor boats on the other.

Although the Japanese airfield at Munda fell early in August, there remained a well-established enemy position at Bairoko Harbor on the north shore of New Georgia. With our ground forces advancing on Bairoko from Munda to the south and from Enogai Inlet to the east, the enemy attempted to evacuate his forces across Kula Gulf to Kolombangara. Many of the patrols from Lever Harbor were directed at interception of these operations.

Some of the barges were tough. On the night of July 26/27, PT's 106, 117, and 154 engaged six large barges so well armored that gunfire from the PT's ricocheted harmlessly off their sides. And these barges showed no hesitation, when the PT's stopped firing to reload, in closing the range and opening fire on the PT's. The PT's were hit many times by small-caliber fire, but suffered no casualties. Boat captains learned that the volume of return fire from barges could be reduced by keeping them constantly under fire. Every effort was made to prevent all guns from running out of ammunition at the same time, and to have supporting boats cover the retirement of an attacking PT.

Return fire from barges was not the only danger. Floatplanes harassed patrolling PT's almost every night, usually causing little damage, but frequently preventing the PT's from making an effective attack. On the night of August 2/3 six Rendova PT's were assigned to patrol south of Vella Lavella. PT 170 (Lt. (jg.) David M. Payne, USNR), PT 104 (Lt. (jg.) Robert D. Shearer, USNR), and PT 108 (Lt. (jg.) Sidney D. Hix, USNR) were to cover the northern portion of the area, and PT 172 (Lt. (jg.) Stuart Hamilton, USNR), PT 118 (Lt. (jg.) Douglas S. Kennedy, USNR), and PT 163 (Ens. Edward H. Kruse, Jr., USNR) the southern. For 4½ hours, each time the PT's attempted to approach the entrance to Wilson Strait or the north part of Gizo Strait they were attacked by planes, which made 27 separate strafing attacks and dropped 8 bombs and 25 flares and float lights.

The continued attacks separated the PT's; the flares disclosed their position. Ensign Kruse spotted two targets by radar off the southern end of Vella Lavella. A moment later his boat was attacked by a plane, and when the attack was over the radar contact was lost. An hour later all of the boats of the northern section picked up six barges by radar, but these boats too were strafed by aircraft and they lost their targets. Later the same boats sighted a column of eight barges heading from Vella Lavella toward Kolombangara. The PT's moved in for a strafing run. When they were 300 yards away all of the barges blazed into action with what appeared to be a solid sheet of fire from automatic weapons, which fortunately passed 10 feet over the PT's. A plane swept in, strafing the boats, and the barges escaped.

Boat captains learned to lie to when planes were overhead so that the white wakes of the PT's would not reveal them to the aircraft. Lt. (jg.) William F. Liebenow, Jr., USNR, in PT 157, and Lt. (jg.) Hamlin D. Smith, USNR, in PT 154, demonstrated the corollary of this doctrine on the night of August 15/16, when they escorted the APc 25 and LCT's 325 and 327 from Lever Harbor to Enogai Inlet. Twice planes came over to strafe and bomb. Each time the PT's created a diversion by zigzagging at high speed, laying puffs of smoke and leading the planes away from their convoy. Except for the wounding of two men of LCT 325 by shell fragments, the convoy suffered no damage.

Japanese countermeasures against PT's included the mounting of heavier guns—up to 40mm.—on their barges, and installation of shore batteries along the barge routes. Lieutenant Commander Kelly reported late in August, "A recent conference with the Commanding Officers of the First and Fourth Marine Raider Battalions at Enogai revealed that during the period 14–19 August, 28 barges have been observed by their Observation Post to enter and leave Bairoko. On three of these nights the PT's have attacked a total of 17 barges leaving Bairoko. On each occasion the return fire from the barges and shore batteries has been so heavy that the PT's have been unable to close to effective range. Only two barges were seen to be damaged and none are believed to have sunk or been seriously disabled. Without illumination it is impossible for the PT's to see the barges which closely hug the shore. However, the PT's themselves are clearly visible against the horizon in the moonlight. Heavily armored large barges with 40mm. and machineguns escort the medium barges which carry only machineguns and/or 20 mm. In order to sink a barge, the range must be closed well within 100 yards and more than 1,000 rounds of .50 caliber and 500 rounds of 20mm. are required . . . This requires laying to at point blank range of shore batteries and barges for approximately 10 minutes which is tantamount to sacrificing the PT boat. It is therefore believed that the only practical solution for combatting this barge traffic would be to employ similarly armored barges of our own or to install appropriate shore batteries capable of interdicting the barge route."

The Commander South Pacific Force, forwarding PT action reports for the month of August, agreed with Kelly only in part, saying, "The use of PT boats as barge destroyers leaves much to be desired. Such employment in daylight or bright moonlight is distinctly hazardous and frequently expensive to an unacceptable degree but Commander South Pacific does not agree that PT boats in anti-barge operations are ineffective and costly under all conditions. However, steps have been taken locally to improve their effectiveness, when so employed, by equipping them with a 37mm. or 40mm. single AA gun. Work is now underway on the conversion of three 77-foot MTB's into motor gunboats by removal of torpedo tubes and depth charges to provide space and weight compensation for an additional 40mm. single AA gun and armor."

After experimentation with the single-shot Army 37mm. cannon, which was not entirely satisfactory because of its slow rate of fire, the automatic Army Air Force 37mm. was made standard installation on PT's in the Solomons. Except for a few boats which had two 40mm. cannon, one forward and one aft, and no torpedoes, the 40mm. was not used by the South Pacific PT's until later squadrons came out from the States with them already installed. It will be seen later that in the Southwest Pacific the 40mm., a far more powerful weapon than the 37mm., became standard armament for PT's. This divergence in armament in the two areas resulted partly from differences in background, partly from differences in operating conditions.

In the Southwest Pacific PT's were used from the start and almost exclusively as barge destroyers. The 40mm. was the most potent and most accurate antibarge gun. Ergo, it was adopted. In the South Pacific, on the other hand, PT's had a background of action against destroyers and cruisers: the torpedo was regarded as the primary weapon. The 40mm. was a heavy gun, and it was feared that the extra weight would slow down the boats if they continued to carry four torpedoes. This fear was justified. Unless PT's are maintained in top condition, frequently a difficult thing to do under combat conditions in forward areas, extra weight does tend to slow them down. In many sections of the Southwest Pacific, PT's armed with the 40mm. were authorized to carry two, instead of the customary four, torpedoes. Although South Pacific PT's did not meet destroyers after August 1, 1943, the possibility that they would meet them still existed. The Japanese still had destroyers at Rabaul and could have run the Tokyo Express again had they been willing to risk their ships.

So much for differences in background. The difference in operating conditions was a matter of distance. South Pacific patrol areas were usually relatively close to the PT operating bases. So it was possible to act on Kelly's suggestion and convert some LCM's to gunboats to accompany the PT's on their missions. Each LCM gunboat carried a 3-inch gun, and their low speed was acceptable where distances were short. Later, larger landing craft, LCI's, were converted to gunboats to operate with the PT's. Similarly converted were some wooden-hulled 110-foot submarine chasers, which came to be known as PGM's. These were somewhat faster than the landing craft, and so could operate further from their base. Thus, in the South Pacific, the PT was preserved primarily as a torpedo boat, strengthened against barges by the 37mm. cannon, but largely dependent on slower gunboats for heavy firepower.   In the Southwest Pacific, where patrol areas usually were 100 to 150 miles from base, LCM and LCI gunboats and PGM's lacked the speed necessary to proceed to station and return during the hours of darkness. Consequently PT's had to carry their own heavy guns.

The 37mm., though inferior to the 40mm. in destructive power, was still a good antibarge gun.   Three Rendova boats used it on the night of August 29/30 to sink a heavily loaded barge off Vella Lavella.   Comdr. Henry Farrow, in submitting the action report, stated, "the barge probably would not have been sunk, except for the very effective fire of the aircraft type automatic 37mm. guns."

Another problem mentioned by Kelly—the inability of PT's to see barges against the dark background of land—was at least partially solved by increasing cooperation with Black Cats.   Each night one or more patrol planes were assigned to work with the PT's.   The Black Cats guided PT's to their targets and when directed by the senior PT officer dropped flares to illuminate barges and distract the attention of their crews.   Frequently the Black Cats would join in the attack, if requested to do so by the PT's, or they would bomb and strafe shore positions inaccessible to PT fire. Sometimes the planes would take over an action from PT's.   On the night of August 5/6, for example, a Black Cat had illuminated a 120-foot cargo ship for PT's 159 and 157.   The PT's exchanged fire with the ship and pursued it until it passed out of the limits of their prescribed patrol area.   The PT's informed the Black Cat that they could go no further, and the plane completed the attack.

With PT's patrolling every night except when destroyer operations were scheduled, it was to be expected that some men would be killed and others wounded, but considering the amount of lead and explosives thrown at the boats by floatplanes, shore batteries, and barges, the casualties were amazingly few.   The boats were hard to hit, and most of the hits they took were harmless.   Many times PT's returned to base riddled with bullets or sprayed with shrapnel, their crews unscathed.   The greatest hazard to the boats themselves was that of close inshore navigation at night in poorly charted reefy waters.   PT's 153 and 158 were reefed early in July and were destroyed to prevent capture, as were PT's 118 and 172 early in September, but their crews were brought safely to base by other PT's.

18. VELLA LAVELLA

The next major move of our forces up the Solomons chain was the occupation of Vella Lavella, northernmost of the New Georgia group, bypassing the island of Kolombangara where the Japanese still had upwards of 5,000 troops, strong fortifications, and an airfield at Vila. PT's landed six Army, Navy, and Marine officers on Vella Lavella on the night of July 21/22 to make a reconnaissance of the southern part of the island. Taken off by PT 6 days later, together with the rescued crew of a PBY plane, the party reported that the island was not occupied by the Japanese and that there were suitable landing beaches at Barakoma on the southeast coast.

D-day was set for August 15. On the night of August 12/13, PT 107 (Lt. (jg.) William F. Barrett, Jr., USNR), PT 169 (Lt. (jg.) Philip A. Potter, Jr., USNR), PT 168 (Ens. William F. Griffin, USNR), and PT 104 (Lt. (jg.) Robert D. Shearer, USNR), left Rendova with 45 Army and Navy personnel to be put ashore at Barakoma. This party was to mark the channels and beaches to be used by landing craft, select bivouac and dispersal areas and defense positions, and take into custody a large number of Japanese prisoners reported to be held by native sentries.

On their northern passage through Blackett Strait to Vella Gulf, the PT's were bombed and strafed for more than 2 hours in almost continuous aircraft attacks. One bomb exploded in the water 10 feet astern of PT 168, seriously wounding two crew members and two Army men. The blast holed the boat, punctured the gas tanks, riddled one engine with shrapnel and damaged the other two, putting all three out of commission. Ensign Griffin prepared to abandon ship, but eventually was able to start two engines. He did not know how long his engineers could keep them running, so he called for assistance by radio. The four boats had become separated during the attacks, and it was a boat from another patrol section, Lt. (jg.) David M. Payne's PT 106, that came to his aid. Payne located PT 169 and had it come alongside the 168 to take off the passengers for Barakoma. The 106 took the wounded aboard and, after escorting PT 168 through Ferguson Passage, put on speed to get the wounded back to the base.

PT 107 was the first to arrive at Barakoma, and put its passengers ashore without incident. While it was still unloading, PT's 169 and 104 arrived. They completed their mission at 0320 and departed for Rendova. At 0500 they found PT 103, which had been on another patrol, taking PT 168 in tow south of Ferguson Passage. The 168's engines had failed again. The

107 stood by until fighter cover arrived at 0630. The 103 towed the 168 in, arriving at Rendova at 0900.

Ashore on Vella Lavella, the advance party discovered that not only did the native police have no Japanese prisoners, but that several hundred Japanese, survivors of ships sunk in the Battle of Vella Gulf on August 6/7, were in the area selected for the landing. They were reported to be armed with hand grenades, clubs, and a few firearms. The advance party called by radio for help. At 0445 August 14, PT 103 (Lt. (jg.) Joseph K. Roberts, USNR), PT 169 (Lt. (jg.) Philip A. Potter, Jr., USNR), PT 175 (Ens. R. L. Balch, USNR), and PT 180 (Ens. S. Y. Carnes, USNR) left Rendova with reinforcements, landing them at Barakoma at 0940. This force was sufficient to insure that the Japanese in the area would not seriously interfere with the main landings, which were effected on the morning of August 15 with no opposition other than air attacks.

During September PT patrols from Rendova were gradually extended so that they included all of the Vella Lavella coast and portions of the Choiseul coast, 150 miles from the Rendova base. In order to reach these areas more easily, and to give the boats more hours to patrol them, Lt. Comdr. LeRoy Taylor, commander of Squadron 11, moved into Lambu Lambu Cove on the northeast coast of Vella Lavella on September 25, with seven PT's and one APc, to establish an advance operating base.

19. DAYLIGHT STRIKES

Rendova PT's made two daylight strikes in August and September. The first, made with air cover on the morning of August 22, was daring and very nearly disastrous. Comdr. Henry Farrow, in Lt. Robert D. Shearer's PT 104, led PT's 169 (Lt. (jg.) Douglas S. Kennedy, USNR) and PT 105 (Lt. (jg.) Richard E. Keresey, Jr., USNR), into Elliott Cove, just west of the Japanese stronghold of Vila on the south coast of Kolombangara. Lt. (jg.) David M. Payne, USNR, in Lt. (jg.) Sidney D. Hix's PT 108, led PT 125 (Lt. (jg.) C. Murray, USNR) and PT 124 (Lt. (jg.) Leighton C. Wood, USNR) into Webster Cove, just west of Elliott Cove. PT 107 (Lt. (jg.) William F. Barrett, Jr., USNR) and PT 118 (Lt. (jg.) B. P. Percy, USNR) were assigned to sweep the Kolombangara coast to the west and north of the two coves. Each boat carried Army demolition crews, which were to attempt destruction of enemy installations as opportunity presented.

PT's 104 and 169 started to enter Elliott Cove at 0725, leaving the 105 to patrol outside as cover. Shore guns opened on the 105 from the east but, since the alarm apparently had not been raised inside the cove itself, the other boats continued in. At the east side of the cove they saw four barges behind a large camouflage net suspended from trees at the water's edge. Many Japanese could be seen moving about on shore. As the boats swung toward the barges and opened fire with their 37's, they were taken under fire from machineguns and rifles on either side of the entrance. They continued shelling the barges, using their 20mm. and .50-caliber guns in an attempt to smother the fire from shore. Because of the heavy enemy fire the boats did not attempt to put Army demolition crews aboard the barges, but retired at high speed after completing their runs. As they emerged from the cove, PT 105 advanced, firing on the shore. When she had placed herself between the retiring boats and the shore batteries, she reversed course and laid a smokescreen behind which all three boats withdrew.

Of the second group, PT's 108 and 125 started to enter Webster Cove at 0730, leaving PT 124 to cover the entrance. As soon as the boats were well inside they were taken under murderous crossfire by machinegun positions all around the cove. The Japanese even had machinegun platforms in the trees. Lieutenant Payne was wounded immediately and fell into the charthouse. Lieutenant Hix, at the helm, was fatally wounded in the head. Before collapsing, he put the wheel hard over to withdraw. James G. Cannon, Jr., QM2c, although wounded in the arm, shoulder, and face, took the wheel and brought the boat out of the cove. Jack O. Bell, SC3c, one of the gunners, was killed, and all of the other gunners but one were wounded. Sgt. J. E. Rogers, of the Army demolition crew, was killed when he went forward to assist the wounded 37mm. gunner. Only one officer and two men were unhurt. As soon as the 108 cleared the area of heavy fire, all of the men still able to move went below and put out fires in the forepeak, crews quarters, officers quarters, and lazarette. The 125, which had been following the 108, started to turn as soon as she saw the lead boat turning and preceded her out. She took few hits and only one man aboard was wounded. The two boats patrolling further west had no action, but the 107 came alongside the 108 to carry her wounded back to the base.

The second daylight strike, a sweep of coves in the northern section of Vella Lavella, on the morning of September 15, met no opposition. Lt. Comdr. LeRoy Taylor, in Ens. W. Mills's PT 181, led PT 178 (Lt. (jg.) G. C. Miller, USNR) and PT 170 (Lt. (jg.) W. J. Maul, USNR), into six coves and inlets, strafing shore installations. In Susulantolo Bay the boats discovered a camouflaged barge filled with drums of rice. They tried to set it ablaze by gunfire, but it would not burn until the men threw a bucket of gasoline over it. In Warambari Bay they found another camouflaged barge, which blazed up immediately when they fired on it. A second section of boats, led by Lt. Leonard R. Hardy in PT 176 (Ens. W. E. Powell, USNR), with PT 175 (Ens. R. L. Balch, USNR), set three barges afire in Marisi Bay and destroyed two small boats in Karaka Bay.

20. END OF THE NEW GEORGIA CAMPAIGN

During the latter part of September the Japanese stopped trying to reinforce Kolombangara and began to evacuate their troops by barge, carrying them across to Choiseul, whence they could make their way to Bougainville. During the month the PT's had actions with 28 barges. They claimed 9 destroyed and 10 damaged. In October most of the work of intercepting the enemy evacuation from Kolombangara and Vella Lavella was assigned to destroyers. The only contact made by PT's with surface craft came when PT's 124 and 125 met two Japanese in a stolen native canoe, attempting to go from Kolombangara to Choiseul. Typically, these Japanese resisted all efforts to capture them, and were shot.

PT's made several reconnaissance missions, landing Marine scouting parties on Santa Isabel and Choiseul Islands; escorting supply echelons, and serving as rescue boats for downed fliers. Floatplanes continued to bomb and strafe them, but the PT's had the satisfaction of shooting down two of the hecklers.

In the Battle of Vella Lavella, on the night of October 6/7, three of our destroyers, *Selfridge, Chevalier,* and *O'Bannon,* intercepted and put to rout a Japanese force, estimated at nine destroyers, attempting to evacuate troops from Vella Lavella. One of the Japanese destroyers, *Yugumo,* was sunk. On the morning of the 7th, four PT's searched the waters northwest of Vella Lavella and picked up 78 survivors of the *Yugumo,* whom they brought back to Biloa on Vella Lavella, to turn them over to the Army. PT 163 had the most prisoners—36 of them lying face down on the deck forward, with 4 armed men standing guard over them. While the boats were lying to at Biloa, waiting for launches to disembark the prisoners, one of the Japanese on the 163 asked for a drink of water. Raymond Albert, S1c, one of the guards, handed him a canteen and permitted him to stand. As the prisoner returned the canteen, he whirled Albert around, snatched his submachine-gun and shot him in the head, fatally wounding him. Another guard instantly cut down the prisoner with a 45-caliber automatic.

With the end of resistance on Vella Lavella early in October and completion of the Japanese evacuation of Kolombangara, the PT bases at Lever Harbor and Rendova were no longer useful for patrols. The Lever Harbor base was rolled up, but not before another case of mistaken identity had cost four lives. Four PT's, returning from patrol on the morning of September 30, saw three Marine Corsair planes approaching. The boats recognized the planes as friendly, and the flight section leader recognized the boats, instructing the other two planes by radio, "Don't fire as they are our own PT boats."

The pilot of the second plane understood the message; the pilot of the third apparently did not. Although the PT's made a tight right turn, the standard recognition procedure, the third plane swept in and strafed PT 126, killing an officer and two men. The starboard gunner of the 126 opened fire without orders, putting one short burst into the plane. The plane exploded and the pilot was killed.

The Rendova base was kept for repair and supply. In January 1944, it was moved from Lumbari Island to Bau Island in Rendova Harbor, and with the installation of Motor Torpedo Boat Base 11 became the main repair and overhaul base in the area. Commodore Moran made it his headquarters, moving his staff up from Tulagi.

Operations from Lambu Lambu continued into December. Although the boats met few barges they harassed the enemy by strafing shore installations in Choiseul Bay. These missions were good training for the first Higgins squadrons to arrive in the Solomons: Squadron 19, under Lt. Comdr. Russell H. Smith, and Squadron 20, under Lt. Comdr. Glenn R. Van Ness, USNR. On December 14, the day the Commander Amphibious Force ordered abandonment of the Lambu Lambu base, fire broke out in the gasoline dump and swiftly enveloped the dock area and ammunition dump, which exploded for hours. Two boats were at the dock. PT 238, outboard, got underway, but the heat was so intense that the crew of the inboard boat, PT 239, could not cast off her lines. The 239 burned at the dock. The fire, burning at one side of the narrow entrance to Lambu Lambu Cove, prevented seven PT's and an APc from leaving the cove. Until the flames subsided, these craft stayed in the cove with engines running and fire hoses streaming water on their decks. The next day the bodies of two men were recovered from the scene of the fire.

21. TREASURY AND BOUGAINVILLE

The move to Bougainville, largest of the Solomons, had a double purpose. It was designed to cut Japanese communications with their forces on Choiseul, southern Bougainville, and the Shortland Islands, neutralizing thousands of troops in these areas, and to provide fields for land-based airstrikes on Rabaul. It was not necessary to conquer the entire island; a beachhead, airstrips, and a small defense perimeter would suffice. It was another step in the bypassing strategy, started at Vella Lavella, which was to leave tens of thousands of Japanese cut off not only from supply and reinforcement, but even from escape. Cape Torokina and the Empress Augusta Bay area, about halfway up the western side of Bougainville, were to be the beachhead.

Before landings could be made there, it was necessary to take the Treasury Islands, a small group directly between Vella Lavella and Empress Augusta Bay, for protection of our supply convoys to the Bougainville beachhead. PT's put a reconnaissance party ashore on Treasury on the night of October 21/22, and removed it the next night. The scouts reported that the

80—G—59340

Metalsmith and shipfitters shop at Torokina Base, Bougainville. Left to right, W. B. Bradley, SF2c; O. G. White, MoMM1c; R. C. Steen, CM3c.

enemy force amounted to only 235 men. They also brought back several natives of Mono Island, largest of the Treasury group, to serve as guides for the landing. On the night of October 25/26, PT's landed an advance party of New Zealand noncommissioned officers and native guides on Mono to cut enemy communication lines. On October 27, 1943, two PT's screened the fourth transport group for the landings on Stirling Island. The next day Lieutenant Commander Kelly arrived with Squadron 9, set up a temporary base on Stirling Island, and started patrols the same evening.

With the establishment of the Treasury base, the PT's were in position to blockade southern Bougainville, the Shortlands, and Choiseul Bay. Remnants of the enemy that had managed to escape from New Georgia to Choiseul were moving north on foot to the Choiseul Bay region where barges shuttled them by night across Bougainville Straits to Fauro Island, the Shortlands, and southern Bougainville.

80—G—59343

H. M. Garothorp, Bkr2c, bakes bread in ovens improvised from empty oil drums at Torokina PT base.

Our landings on Cape Torokina on November 1 met fierce resistance. Some of the bitterest fighting was on Puruata Island on the first day of the invasion. The island was cleared of the enemy by the night of November 2, and the following morning Comdr. Henry Farrow arrived there with eight PT's to set up a base. The enemy exerted constant pressure on our perimeter, and commenced concentrated bombing of the Cape Torokina area on the night of November 5/6. From then until the end of the month he dropped 600 bombs in 33 night attacks. PT's 124 and 187 were slightly damaged on the night of December 18/19 by a bomb at Puruata Island, but were able to go out on patrol the next night. Before the end of December we had gained superiority in the air and the night attacks dwindled to occasional nuisance raids.

Torokina PT's at first assisted in protecting the precarious Allied beachhead by patrolling 10 miles north and 10 miles south of the Cape. While barge contacts were few during November, the boats carried out a number of special missions, escorting convoys and covering minor landings. On six separate occasions they landed and picked up Marine reconnaissance parties on the Bougainville coast. On the afternoon of November 29, Lt. Comdr. LeRoy Taylor, who had relieved Commander Farrow at Bougainville, took PT 187 and two LCI gunboats to cover the evacuation of 700 Marines who had been trapped by superior enemy forces a few miles south of Cape Torokina.

In December both the Torokina and Treasury PT's extended their barge-hunting activities. The Torokina boats covered the western coast of Bougainville from Empress Augusta Bay to Buka Island to the north, and the Treasury boats stretched their patrol areas from the southwest coast of Bougainville through Bougainville Strait, and eventually to the eastern coast of Bougainville. During November and December the PT's claimed 6 barges sunk or destroyed, 11 barges damaged, 3 planes shot down, and 2 planes damaged.

22. A BRUSH WITH TORPEDO BOMBERS

One of the first escort jobs out of Torokina fell to Ens. Theodore Berlin, USNR, whose PT 167, with the LCI gunboat 70, was to accompany the LCT 68 to Treasury Island.* The little convoy left Torokina in the middle of

---

*The executive officer was Paul Burgess ("Red") Fay, Jr., later to be appointed Under Secretary of the Navy by President Kennedy.

the afternoon on November 5, and was 28 miles southwest of the Cape at twilight, when 12 Japanese torpedo bombers swept in from the west. They dived toward the 167, which opened fire on them. The first plane came in so low that its wing struck the PT's radio antenna. The plane wobbled and crashed into the sea. As it crashed the crew of the 167 felt a severe shock, as though their boat had been hit, but there was no explosion.

A few minutes later another group of planes attacked from the west but further astern. The 20mm. gunners on the fantail of the PT saw their shots go home in one of the planes, which crashed so close to the port quarter that the gunners were drenched by the splash. One of the gunners saw a torpedo wake pass under the stern of the boat. The 167 then lay to, firing at planes which seemed to be attacking the LCI 70 from every direction.

80–G–650957

Bow of Ens. Theodore Berlin's PT 167, holed clean through by an enemy torpedo which did not explode.

When the attack was over Ensign Berlin discovered what had jolted his boat. A torpedo had passed completely through the bow without exploding. It had ripped gaping holes through each side of the boat, leaving pieces of its fins and one of its rudders aboard as souvenirs. The holes were well above the waterline and forward of the forward watertight bulkhead, so the boat was in no danger of sinking. Ensign Berlin went alongside the LCI 70 and found that it also had taken a miraculously harmless hit, and had an unexploded torpedo lodged in its engineroom. He took aboard all of the LCI's crew, including two injured men, and proceeded to the LCT 68, which he found had not been attacked. One of the LCI's officers then took a volunteer crew back aboard the LCI so that the LCT could take it in tow.

The next day Radio Tokyo announced that their intrepid airmen had sunk one large carrier and one small carrier off Bougainville.

23. DESTROYERS AGAIN

The destroyers *Anthony* and *Hudson* were part of a screen of a supply echelon that left Guadalcanal at 0045 November 7, to arrive at Cape Torokina on the morning of November 8. During the night before their arrival the two destroyers were detached from the convoy to scout ahead and intercept any enemy barges that might be trying to land reinforcements in Empress Augusta Bay. The destroyers had been assured that the PT's would remain at their base.

A dispatch had, in fact, been sent from Guadalcanal, advising the PT's that destroyers would be in the area and instructing them not to patrol, but because of a breakdown in communications the message was not delivered until November 9. Ordinarily, if the PT's had received no instructions from the Commander Amphibious Force at Guadalcanal, they would have been bound to stay at their base anyway, and no harm would have been done. But a special situation existed at Torokina. For the first 2 days at the base, the boats received orders from the Commander Amphibious Force and patrolled 10 miles north and 10 miles south of Cape Torokina. Then communications collapsed and no operational orders were received for 3 days. The enemy lost no time in taking advantage of the inactivity, landing bargeloads of reinforcements near the savagely contested perimeter, first at night and then in broad daylight. The commanding general of the Marines became so incensed at this state of affairs that he ordered the boats to maintain continuous 24-hour patrols whether or not orders were received from Guadalcanal. Commander Farrow inquired whether friendly ships might be encountered in the area, but Marine headquarters had no information on ship movements.

So it happened that there were two patrols of two PT's each in Empress Augusta Bay when the destroyers arrived early on the morning of the 8th. The *Anthony*'s radar picked up a surface target lying to in the middle of the bay at 0315. The destroyers opened fire at 5,000 yards, and kept lobbing shells for 45 minutes. During this period the target divided into two distinct pips on the radar. When the pips indicated that the targets had increased speed to 20 knots and were still accelerating, the commanding officer of the *Anthony* realized they must be PT's. The destroyers ceased fire immediately.

PT's 170 and 169, of which Lt. Edward Macauley 3d was officer-in-tactical command, took evasive action, and when the firing ceased attempted to get in position to fire torpedoes at the "enemy" destroyers. Macauley called by radio to the two boats to the north, and PT 163 obligingly fired one torpedo, which missed. The *Anthony* could hear faintly the radio conversation between the PT's, so the destroyers turned to clear the area as quickly as possible. Eventually the *Anthony* made radio contact with the PT's, sending the message, "Humblest apologies, we are friendly vessels," just in time to forestall an attack by Macauley's boats.

This message came just after a new target, apparently a large ship, appeared on the 170's radar, 10,000 yards ahead, and projectiles which, Macauley said, looked like large ashcans passed over the boat. To this day no one knows what these projectiles were or who fired them.

The PT's and destroyers came unharmed to Cape Torokina. Shortly before noon on the 8th, 60 to 80 Japanese planes attacked. Many were shot down. Among the claims were 1 for PT's 103 and 163, 2 for the *Hudson,* and 11 for the *Anthony.*

On the night of November 24/25 two sections of PT's patrolling the Buka coast made radar contact with two large surface targets, but believed them to be friendly destroyers known to be in the area until two destroyers closed the southern section and attempted to ram Lt. (jg.) Charles A. Bernier, Jr.'s PT 318. The destroyers fired several 5-inch salvos at the three boats of the section. The boats still could not be sure that they were not our own destroyers, so except for one torpedo fired by PT 64 through a misunderstanding of orders by the torpedoman, the boats did not attempt to attack but laid smoke puffs and zigzagged to safety. The boats learned later that the destroyers were not our own.

The Commander Motor Torpedo Boat Squadrons South Pacific reported, "On the night of 7/8 November 1943, PT boats . . . were fired on for 45 minutes by some of our own destroyers. The fact that our own destroyers were known to be present on the night of 24/25 November and the previous experience of being fired upon by friendly forces, was undoubtedly the major contributing factor in failure to recognize the enemy ships . . . This occurrence and previous ones in which PT boats have had 'unhappy' incidents with our own surface and aircraft indicates the necessity for closer cooperation and coordination between our light surface forces and aircraft. This command is now endeavoring to obtain conduct of numerous training exercises in the back areas between PT boats and DD's [destroyers] and between the former and aircraft, particularly 'Black Cats' and 'Snoopers.' If cooperation is attained it is expected that much valuable information will be obtained and all personnel will have a more full and complete knowledge of capabilities and limitations of the other fellow as well as knowing what to do when they make contact with the enemy in the same area.

"For example, on the night of 24/25 November, it was later learned that one of our aircraft had been shadowing the enemy DD's and knew they were unfriendly. Had that particular aircraft imparted this knowledge to the PT boats and reported the approximate enemy position and course to the PT boat commander, the latter could have maneuvered the various sections in a favorable position to attack."

24. SHORE BATTERIES

As the boats had discovered at Rendova and Lever Harbor, wherever the enemy ran barges he ran them close to the beach and installed shore batteries for their protection. Shells from the shore guns seldom hit the boats, but frequently splashed close enough to force the boats further out to sea. The first boat—and one of the few—to receive a damaging direct hit from shore was PT 154 (Lt. (jg.) Hamlin D. Smith, USNR). The 154 and 155 (Lt. Michael R. Pessolano) were lying to 1 mile off the south coast of Shortland Island on the night of November 13/14. A 3-inch shore gun fired three rounds, the second of which hit the afterbody of the port forward torpedo, where it exploded, tearing a gaping hole in the deck and knocking out the steering control. Lieutenant Smith and six men were wounded. Lt. (jg.)

Joseph D. McLaughlin, USNR, the second officer, and Arthur J. Schwerdt, QM2c, were killed. John M. Nicholson, MM1c, senior man on the boat, less seriously injured than Lieutenant Smith, took charge and got the boat underway, heading out to sea.

As soon as Lieutenant Pessolano observed the firing he got the 155 underway, heading out, but when he saw the hit he reversed course to assist the 154. He did not realize that the 154 had no rudder control, and as the 154 increased speed, she collided with the 155, tearing off the 155's port after torpedo and tube. The boats separated and ran until they were well to seaward, when the 155 came alongside the 154. Lieutenant Pessolano went aboard the 154 and took command, transferring the wounded to the 155, which took them back to the Treasury base. Using emergency steering control, a hand tiller in the lazarette, the 154 slowly made its way to the base, arriving 2½ hours after the 155.

Frequently during the months that followed, PT's had the satisfaction of accompanying LCI gunboats and PGM's on missions to shell enemy shore batteries, and of working with Black Cats to bomb them. Yet the shore guns remained a constant menace. Commenting on an action on the night of January 7/8, 1944, in which heavy machinegun fire from shore twice prevented PT's from completing attacks on barges although the PT's were assisted by a Black Cat, Lieutenant Commander Kelly said, "It will be noted that the enemy has resorted to tactics similar to those employed during the enforced evacuation of Bairoko, New Georgia. Immediately preceding each barge movement machinegun positions are located along the entire evacuation route. Large caliber coastal batteries, placed at strategic positions, are also used to bombard the PT's, forcing them to keep outside their range. Float planes bomb the boats en route to their station and prior to barge movements. When passing fortified positions, the barges usually withhold their fire while the shore positions attempt to force the PT's to retire. When severely damaged the barges beach themselves in the vicinity of these protected areas until the attack has been driven off."

25. TO GREEN ISLAND

January was a month of rain and heavy winds with seas so high that sometimes PT's could not patrol. The Bougainville boats got the worst of it. During the first part of the month, northwest winds averaging 20 knots and gusting to 40 swept the exposed anchorage at Puruata Island, kicking up 3- to 5-foot seas. Nothing lighter than 500-pound anchors would hold the boats, and there were not enough of them. Lieutenant Commander Taylor sent in an urgent requisition for more anchors and moorings, saying, "boats cannot remain underway here indefinitely."

PT's 115 and 181 were blown on a reef at Torokina on January 7, and the LCI 67, attempting to pull them off, broached on the same reef. Six nights later heavy seas swept a depth charge off PT 189 and a 60mm. mortar off PT 178, broke the 178's 37mm. magazine and bent several 37mm. shells. It was small wonder that the number of barge contacts dropped. The PT's claimed only two barges destroyed and six damaged in January. The weather improved in February and for that month the claims were 13 destroyed, 3 possibly destroyed, and 15 damaged. During both months there were, of course, the usual brushes with float planes. The boats also rescued several downed fliers, and were more active in strafing enemy shore positions than they had been before.

Despite foul weather, the boats performed valuable service in the occupation of Green Island, to the north of Bougainville. Green is a circular atoll about 4 miles across, surrounding a deep lagoon, with two entrances on the west side. Since the enemy was present there in light strength, the Commander Amphibious Force resolved to make a reconnaissance in strength before the main landings, but he could not even plan a reconnaissance until he knew whether the lagoon entrances were deep enough for passage of landing craft. Accordingly, on the night of January 10/11, Lieutenant Commander Taylor and Lt. Leonard R. Hardy took PT 176 (Ens. W. E. Powell, USNR), PT 184 (Ens. E. C. Myers, USNR), and two of the 77-footers that had been converted to gunboats, PT 59 (Ens. J. Atkinson, USNR) and PT 61 (Lt. (jg.) R. L. Rhoads, USNR) to examine the channels.

The weather was too rough for the 77-footers, which had seen hard service and now were carrying the extra weight of two 40mm. guns, one fore and one aft. Seas tore their radar masts loose, fouled gears on the forward 40mm. guns, stripped beading from their chines, and opened seams. The 61's smoke screen generator broke loose and in going overboard carried away an exhaust stack. Water shorted out the 59's radio, starting a small fire in the charthouse. The gunboats could not keep up with the other PT's.

The 176 and 184 arrived at Green Island at 2230, entered the southern channel, took soundings, and departed at 0015 with the knowledge that there was 17 feet of water, ample for landing craft. There was no indication

that the enemy had been aware of their presence. Rear Adm. Theodore
S. Wilkinson, Commander Third Amphibious Force, said, "This passage
of the channel by two PT boats, within close rifle and machine gun range
of possible enemy positions on either side, was a bold exploit, consistent
with the reputation for courageous accomplishment of difficult and hazardous tasks which the MTB Squadrons have acquired and confirmed by their
operations throughout this area."

Because of the knowledge gained through this experience, Lieutenant
Commander Taylor and Lieutenant Hardy, in Ensign Powell's PT 176 and
PT 178 (Ens. J. S. Smith, USNR), led the way for our landing craft in the
reconnaissance in force on January 30/31. While destroyers screened our
transports outside the lagoon, the two PT's were the only covering force for
the landing craft inside the lagoon. Among those who went ashore with
the reconnaissance party were Comdr. William C. Specht, who had become
Commodore Moran's Chief Staff officer in November; Commander Farrow,
and Lt. (jg.) William F. Griffin, USNR. While reconnoitering for a PT
base site they helped destroy a Japanese machinegun nest.

For the landing itself, on the morning of February 15, Lieutenant Commander Taylor and Lieutenant Hardy, in PT 247 (Ens. R. B. Warnock,
USNR) and PT 249 (Lt. (jg.) M. S. Trimble, USNR) made a last-minute
investigation of the channel at 0200 to make sure there were no obstructions.
They reported to the approaching task force commander that the coast was
clear; the landing was made on schedule with little opposition. Motor
Torpedo Boat Base 7 was put ashore the first day, and, on February 16,
Squadron 10, under Lt. Comdr. Jack E. Gibson, arrived at Green Island
to start operations from the new base.

26. COLLISION

En route from Cape Torokina to patrol station off the Buka coast on the
night of February 11/12, 1944, with zero visibility because of a rain squall,
PT 282 rammed PT 279 in the engineroom. Jack D. Castleberry, TM3c, was
hurled overboard from PT 282, as, apparently, was Paul L. Spicher, RM3c,
from PT 279, though no one saw Spicher go. Lt. (jg.) John A. Doane,
USNR, boat captain of the 282, dived in after Castleberry and rescued him.
Spicher was never found, despite searches by PT's and aircraft.

Lt. Alan W. Ferron, USNR, and his PT 278, first to respond to PT 282's call for assistance, picked up the crew of the 279 from their liferaft. Before the 279 sank, 5½ hours after the collision, she was again boarded and a thorough search was made for the missing man. PT 282, heavily damaged in the bow, was towed to base stern first.

27. ACTION IN EMPRESS AUGUSTA BAY

The wide sweeping arc of the Bougainville coast between Cape Torokina on the north and Motupena Point on the south forms Empress Augusta Bay, which was a rewarding hunting ground for the Torokina PT's. Our defensive perimeter extended only a short distance south of Cape Torokina. Most of the coastline of the bay, from the Magine Islands, south of the Cape, past the mouths of the Jaba River, through Gazelle Harbor to Motupena Point, was firmly held by the Japanese. The PT's regularly strafed this coast, the LCI gunboats shelled it, and both PT's and LCI's met many barges running close inshore.

On the night of February 25/26, Lt. Jonathan S. Raymond, Jr., USNR, executive officer of Squadron 20, took PT's 251 (Lt. (jg.) Nixon Lee, Jr., USNR) and PT 252 (Ens. R. A. Hochberg, USNR) to Gazelle Harbor. Early in the evening the PT's sighted a barge running close to shore and sank it after two firing runs. Rifle fire from the barge and machinegun fire from the beach did no damage to the PT's.

Idling north, the boats arrived off the Jaba River mouth at 0150 and made radio contact with a Black Cat whose radio call was "Tarbaby," the call regularly assigned to the PBY detailed to work with the boats. Tarbaby dropped flares at the request of the PT's, illuminating three barges a mile south of the Jaba River, 300 yards offshore. Both boats started a port run, opening fire when abeam the barges. "Tarbaby" also strafed and dropped two bombs for near-misses. Enemy mortars and machineguns ashore attempted to make the boats withdraw. One barge beached itself and two headed for sea. The boats closed to 75 yards and saw one barge sink, but had to break off the engagement when guns on both boats jammed.

Half an hour later, a mile and a half farther south, the boats found two groups of three barges each, running within 100 yards of the beach. The boats strafed all of them, scoring many hits, and received machinegun fire from the beach and from one barge. Just after this run, the 251 sighted a large barge coming up astern, turned and strafed it with undetermined results. "Tarbaby" then dropped more flares for the boats, and directed them to a large barge between the flares and a signal light on the beach. The boats strafed this barge, again with undetermined results, and fired on the signal light on the beach for good measure. The 252 next attacked a barge that suddenly appeared 50 yards off its port beam. At the end of this run the barge's stern was under water and the 251 was on a reef. A few minutes later the 252, circling in an attempt to assist, went up on the same reef, but was able to back off. PT 251, hard aground, requested the base to send two relief boats.

Slowly working down the coast from the north was another patrol section, PT 246 (Lt. (jg.) R. S. Epperly, USNR), PT 254 (Ens. W. J. Harris, USNR), and LCI 24 (Lt. (jg.) O. O. Taylor, USNR). Also working with "Tarbaby," they made runs on four separate barges, as well as on a group of three or four other barges, destroying one and damaging others. Two of the barges beached themselves not far from the reef where the 251 had grounded. The LCI 24 tried to finish them off with its 3-inch guns, but gave up after five rounds because the 251 and 252 were too close to the line of fire.

Lt. Arthur H. Berndtson arrived at 0445 with two relief boats, PT 247 (Ens. R. B. Warnock, USNR) and PT 277 (Lt. J. M. Raine, USNR). Berndtson asked the base to send air cover at daylight. Then, for more than an hour, the boats attempted to sound their way to the 251 to put lines over to pull her off. PT 252 had come within 75 yards when a shore gun started firing. The first shot was over the 251, the second under, and the third a direct hit. The 251 exploded, blazing furiously.

The 252 backed off, firing all its guns at the shore position. PT 247 picked up three survivors from the water, and when air cover arrived at daylight the boats and planes searched for more survivors. They found none in the water, and there could be none on the flaming hulk of the 251. Two officers and eleven men were missing.

When the 252 arrived at the base, an unexploded 57mm. shell was found imbedded in the warhead of the port after torpedo.

28. RABAUL

February was the beginning of the end of Rabaul, the mighty bastion at the northeast tip of the Gazelle Peninsula on New Britain—ultimate objective of the Solomons campaign. Since mid-December, when fighter planes were able to take off from Torokina to escort bombers, airstrikes against Rabaul had mounted with increasing fury. In the Southwest Pacific, troops of the First Marine Division landed on Cape Gloucester, at the western end of New Britain, on December 26. They captured the Cape Gloucester airstrip 4 days later. Rabaul was doomed, and the enemy knew it. About the 19th of February he evacuated the major part of his air strength. On the night of February 29/March 1, Commander Specht led 12 PT's from Green Island in the first large-scale joint attack by destroyers and PT's in the South Pacific area. The weather was foul, with heavy rain, low visibility, strong winds, and heavy seas. After the destroyers shelled the coast from a distance, Commander Specht took six boats on a slow sweep down the coast and then took one boat, PT 319 (Ens. R. H. Lewin, USNR), into the vast and beautiful harbor of Rabaul. Visibility was only 100 yards; he found nothing in the harbor; but the search was significant in that the 319 was the first Allied warship to enter Rabaul since the Japanese occupation.

The other six boats on patrol, under Lt. Comdr. Jack E. Gibson, found three barges in the channel between Gazelle Peninsula and the Duke of York Islands to the east. The boats first became aware of the barges when one of them passed between Lt. (jg.) R. C. Simpson's PT 168 and Lt. (jg.) Edward H. Kruse, Jr.'s PT 163. All of the barges were damaged and probably sunk, but visibility was so bad that the boats could not be certain of their destruction.

With the landing of Southwest Pacific forces in the Admiralty Islands on February 29 and the occupation of Emirau Island by South Pacific forces on March 20, the noose around Rabaul was closed and 40,000 Japanese were left to wither on the vine.

Squadron 11 and the tender *Mobjack*, under tactical command of Commander Specht, moved into Homestead Lagoon, on the west end of Emirau, on March 25, and commenced patrols the following night. From that time on PT's in the South Pacific were to devote themselves to "containing" the Japanese in their sealed-off areas of occupation; disrupting any remaining barge traffic, and strafing coastal installations.

29. MARCH AND APRIL 1944

Operations in March continued along the familiar pattern, with the boats from Treasury, Torokina, and Green Island covering the coasts of Bougainville, southern New Ireland, and southeast New Britain. The PT's claimed 14 barges and 1 motor launch destroyed, 1 plane shot down, and 12 barges damaged. It was, on the whole, a good month for the boats, and, as usual, captured Japanese documents proved it was more successful than the PT personnel themselves realized. Witness the Japanese 17th Army Monthly Intendance Report for March, 1944:

> Lines of communications by sea maintained by large and small landing barges would appear to have great transportation capacity, but in view of constant hindrance by enemy planes and PT boats and occasional attacks by enemy destroyers with which airplanes cooperate by dropping flares, traffic was restricted to nights, particularly moonless nights. Transportation by sea also required such facilities as suitable debarkation points and barge hide-outs. Consequently, it is difficult to realize the transportation capacity theoretically possible . . . In defiance of the interference by enemy airplanes and PT boats, transportation was boldly carried out on moonless nights. Although we have sunk more than 10 enemy PT's since 1 February, we lost more than 20 large and small landing barges (about 90 percent of the total number of barges possessed by the Army) while engaged in this difficult transportation.

Actually, the only PT lost in the Solomons by enemy action during February and March was the 251. While the enemy multiplied his destruction of PT's tenfold, there is no reason to suppose he exaggerated his own losses.

An innovation in March was the beginning of destroyer cooperation with PT's. Two or three destroyers would patrol to seaward of several PT patrols. If the PT's should encounter barges or shore batteries too heavy for them to handle, they could call in the destroyers to assist them. This arrangement produced good results until the night of March 17/18, when Lt. Comdr. Ronald K. Irving, commander of Squadron 23, in PT 283 (Ens. William D. Schaffner, USNR), with PT 284 (Ens. L. R. Haspel, USNR), was patrolling with a Black Cat and the destroyer *Guest* in Empress Augusta Bay. The 283 was lying to 500 yards from a beached barge well loaded with supplies while Lieutenant Commander Irving directed the Black Cat to bombing position over the barge. *Guest,* with which the PT was having communication difficulties, fired a salvo which destroyed another barge several hundred yards down the beach. Irving told the destroyer about the barge which the Black Cat was about to attack. The *Guest* fired another salvo. At the

80—G—59347

Comdr. Thomas G. Warfield briefs boat captains about to go on night patrol of the Bougainville coast in March 1944.

same time Japanese machineguns opened fire from the shore. PT 283's gasoline tanks exploded and the boat burst into flames. One man was killed, three were missing, and three officers and two men, including Lieutenant Commander Irving and Ensign Schaffner, were seriously injured. Most of the crew was rescued by the skillful seamanship of Ensign Haspel in PT 284.

To this day Irving is not sure whether the boat was hit by a wild shot from *Guest* or by Japanese machinegun bullets.

In April the Japanese effort in the Solomons appeared to decline. Although an average of 18 PT's patrolled each night, searching the waters from Bougainville Strait to Emirau, they encountered only 8 barges, all of which they sank or destroyed. Lieutenant Hardy enlivened an otherwise dull month by maneuvering three of the Emirau boats close enough to a New Ireland coastal road to strafe and set fire to two trucks, one on the night of April 24/25, and one on the night of April 28/29.

The boats made several special reconnaissance missions. From Green Island, Lieutenant Commander Gibson took boats to the islands of the Carteret Group on March 29, and to the Nuguria Islands on April 9. At both of these island groups, well to the east of Green, they found friendly natives, who paddled out in canoes to greet the boats and exchange gifts. The natives said there never had been any Japanese in the Carterets, and the only ones who had ever been on Nuguria were three members of the crew of a crashed bomber, who had been taken off by barge.

At Emirau, one of the first missions for the PT's was to put a reconnaissance party ashore at Mussau, largest island of the St. Mathias Group, where the enemy had had a radio station and seaplane base. These installations had been shelled by our destroyers, *Franks* and *Haggard,* on March 23. Lieutenant Hardy, with PT 176 (Ens. M. D. Thompson, USNR) and PT 181 (Lt. (jg.) Edward Miller, USNR), put a party ashore on the night of March 27/28. The party learned from natives that *Franks* and *Haggard* had destroyed a ration dump and a fuel dump and damaged the radio station. There had been 40 to 50 Japanese, who escaped in 2 canoes. Three nights later Lieutenant Hardy brought a larger party to Mussau, again in Ens. Thompson's PT 176, with PT 175 (Lt. (jg.) T. B. Ashwell, USNR). The PT's took aboard 800 pounds of Japanese radio equipment, many documents, three machineguns, and several bombs. The reconnaissance party sketched and photographed the base and set fire to 8 buildings and 243 drums of gasoline. After the party was back aboard the boats, the PT's strafed the remaining installations, setting fire to a fuel dump.

30. THE RUGGED LIFE

PT sailors thought of themselves as having rugged duty. And so they had. When patrols were not dangerous, they were tedious. Officers and men alike had few comforts, and besides the obvious enemy they had to contend with such hazards and discomforts as heat, rains, uncharted reefs, dysentery, malaria, and a variety of tropical skin diseases known collectively as "the crud." They might have felt sorry for themselves except for their faith in the boats, their eagerness to inflict damage on the enemy, and the happy American habit of lightening one's burdens by exaggerating them. In this spirit Lt. Comdr. LeRoy Taylor, Commander of Squadron 11, wrote a brief history of his unit, which perhaps gives a truer picture of the rugged life than could be found in a more factual account.   He wrote:

Too Many Months in the Solomon Islands or *Sex Takes a Holiday*

This is about a squadron of MTB's.   There are no heroes in this group; no melo-dramatic book has been written about them.   They did their job as they saw it and at the same time tried to keep from going nuts by not letting it get them down.

Our squadron was formed at the Brooklyn Navy Yard where all good sailors go at least once in their lives.   Once is enough.   After struggling for 2 or 3 months, we were sent to Panama for 3 weeks' training and eventual transhipment to New Caledonia . . .

At Tulagi one finds what could have been a torpedo boat base.   There they open the conversation by "Now the trouble is—most people seem to take this place for granted." Then the lads who came out a while before, begin on the tall sea stories . . .   Fortu-nately we stayed only a week.

We arrived at Rendova just as the New Georgia Campaign was in full swing.   We got into the harbor at 9 o'clock at night without being shot up by our own guns there. At first the Japs used to dive bomb the boats in the harbor in daytime, coming in low just over the hills on Rendova Island where the radar couldn't pick them up.   One day two soldiers visited our camp on a little island in the harbor, a big soldier and a little soldier.   Someone yelled "Air Raid" and the little soldier jumped into the first hole he saw.   The big one jumped in on top of him.   The hole was our well, about 6 feet deep. The little one nearly drowned.   He got the Purple Heart.

There were plenty of flies which bred in the rotting cocoanuts.   Naturally there was also plenty of dysentery.   The privy was way out over the water.   To get to it, one had to walk a couple of cocoanut logs like a tightrope performer.   On a dark night one felt sorry for the lads who had to get there in a hurry and in such an unstable state, too.   It was a good place to sit and watch the people at Munda getting bombed at night, except that the duds from Munda's guns usually landed on Rendova.   In the daytime going out there was just like going to the aquarium.   All sorts of pretty fish swam around. When it rained it was bad.   Nothing gives you such a feeling of helplessness as a roll of wet toilet paper.

Hunting barges around Kolombangara and the Vella Gulf wasn't what one would call fun.   They traveled in convoys and carried plenty of machine guns.   One of the other squadrons operating in Kula Gulf had the worst time.   There, they had to contend not only with armed barges but with big guns and little guns on the beach.   And down near Diamond Narrows it wasn't so far from shore to shore.   There were Japs on both sides.   On our side there was a little more sea room . . .

The float planes used to chase our boats at night, bombing and strafing.   It was bad. Every time you opened fire on a barge you had a float plane on your neck in 2 minutes. It was a war of nerves.   Night fighters seemed to be a solution and a plan was arranged to get a float plane.   One of the section leaders volunteered to be the bait.   He would go out and raise a racket by steaming at high speeds and firing his guns.   Our night fighter would stay overhead waiting. The float plane would jump in to knock off a torpedo boat and the night fighter would shoot him down in the process. This first night everything went according to plan. The float plane came in and the night fighter was there. Then the first word from the night fighter came over the radio. "I'm being attacked by a float plane!" The word went back from the boat, "Bring him down to 2 feet and I'll get on his tail."

The charts of these islands are not what you'd call up to date. Probably because nobody was ever interested in them but a few traders. There are such reassuring notes as "Reefs reported 6 to 8 miles offshore," "Shoal sighted by H.M.S. *Dart*, 1792," "White water seen here by Capt. Bligh but position doubtful." These things don't help you much when you have to hunt three or four hundred yards off the coast at night. One goes slowly and somewhat nervously. Then some damn fool drops his tin hat or jumps down on deck and you go straight up in the air. You're sure you've hit a reef which is the surest way of finding it. This is the way we were so successful in locating most of the reefs around Vella and Choiseul. Once we made a daylight barge hunt around Vella and had such good luck that we asked to try the same thing at Choiseul. The answer was "No," because of the navigational hazards. The same night we were ordered to patrol the Choiseul coast arriving on station at midnight.

The local natives were good simple souls. We gave one a stick of gum. The next day he came back full of confidence and touched us for a pyramidal tent.

While at Vella we experimented with regular trench mortars mounted on our boats. Getting in to 500 yards of the beach and throwing mortar shells into enemy outposts was fun. The first night we heaved a few over onto the back side of Moli Island. After the first good explosion we heard a loud, exasperated voice scream, "Jesus Christ! What next?" We *knew* there were Japs in there.

After things quieted down at Vella the Bougainville show came off. We went there to relieve the squadron that had gone in on D-day. They had really caught it. Their base was on a little island which had been the Jap's "Target for Tonight" for 3 weeks. By the time we got there something new had been added. They liked the airstrip better than us but that didn't mean that a good many sticks didn't fall short. One night they got a gun on us. With shelling there's no Condition Red to give you warning. They just start landing. If there's just one gun you can stick your head up between salvos but it's harder when there are two.

Another danger was the cocoanut trees that had been weakened by shellfire and bombing. When the wind blew one always fell somewhere. During a very strong blow a large tree fell on a tent with two men in it. Each one thought the other was pinned under the wreckage and they both struggled frantically to move the tree. They quit when they looked up and saw each other.

By now we had learned that if you screen your privy and your galley right at first, you don't have so much dysentery. Consequently our binnacle list was rather small. But the food was dull so we planted a lettuce patch. In the morning after a particularly active night we noticed there were footprints in it pointing toward the nearest dugout. Then we rigged a string of baling wire around the crops. The next night was bright moonlight and Condition Red went. A white streak in skivvy pants headed through the lettuce patch and was brought up short on the wire. It was the intelligence officer, the vandal, going like a bat out of hell for his foxhole. Caught at last!

While we were there, one of the famous health and physical upkeep specialists sent out from Washington came to visit us. He made some profound observations. He said the men were in fine shape. (We had instructed the chief commissary steward, who hasn't seen his feet in 10 years, to walk by several times and be observed.) He also said that all the men needed was to have 10 days' leave in Sydney where they could have a beer and take a girl to the movie. To the movie? Some later did go to Sydney but they came home leaving their health behind them.

We had a movie there once. In one scene Greer Garson came tripping over the grass toward Ronald Colman, nudged him gently and opened a lunch basket. She took out the lunch and a bottle of milk. She was a very refreshing picture to war-tired minds. Mouths fell open. Then the audience gave voice. "Hey, look, fellas! Milk, fresh milk."

And so it goes with total warfare to maintain the American way of life and in which one gets to be like the Prisoner of Chillon whose hair was gray, but not with years.

Exaggerated, but not much.

31. TASK GROUP 30.3

After having had the title of Commander Motor Torpedo Boat Squadrons South Pacific Force for nearly a year, Commodore Moran at last was given full operational control of his boats on May 1, 1944, when he became commander of the newly formed Task Group 30.3. The task group's mission was to blockade the enemy held coasts of Bougainville, New Hanover, New Ireland, and adjacent island groups to the northeastward, and to destroy all enemy shipping encountered.

During May an average of 24 PT's patrolled nightly. The boats claimed 46 barges destroyed, 14 probably destroyed, and 8 damaged. "The increased number of barges destroyed during May," Commodore Moran reported, "might indicate greater enemy barge activity during the month, but is more likely due to the larger number of boats dispatched on nightly patrols and a more thorough covering of all areas in which barges were likely to be encountered."

Besides barge actions, the boats had their usual share of strafing shore installations and tangling with floatplanes, and the Emirau boats accounted for another truck on the road to Kavieng on New Ireland. PT men from Emirau also boarded several wrecked Japanese ships off New Hanover and stripped them of equipment, publications, and code books. Treasury boats, with PGM's, on three successive nights entered the mouths of the Puriata, Hongorai,

Mobiai, and Mibo Rivers on the southwest coast of Bougainville, in preparation for minelaying operations designed to disrupt enemy barge traffic and to force the barges away from shore into the open where PT's could find them more easily. The PGM's took fathometer readings near the river mouths and the PT's put dinghies over the side to take leadline soundings close inshore. On the fourth night three LCI gunboats, covered by two PT's and a PGM, laid mines in the four river mouths.

It would be well at this time to review the state of Commodore Moran's command. Besides PT's, Task Group 30.3 comprised 2 tenders, *Mobjack* and *Varuna;* 6 PGM's; 12 LCI gunboats; 1 LCM gunboat; and 1 APc, a small coastal transport used to carry priority cargo from base to base. The *Mobjack*, a seaplane-tender type, had reported to Rendova on January 14, 1944, and was now at Green Island. Her arrival had permitted the original South Pacific PT tender, *Jamestown,* to sail for the United States for a well-earned overhaul, after which she was to be reassigned to the Southwest Pacific. *Varuna,* an LST type, had arrived on February 13 and was now at Emirau.

Despite the increased number of barge actions during May, it was clear that with the Solomons and the Bismarck Archipelago entirely sealed off, the South Pacific would be an area of declining activity. The Southwest Pacific, on the other hand, was an expanding area. In April, General MacArthur's forces occupied Aitape and Hollandia on the New Guinea coast, isolating some 45,000 Japanese troops between Aitape and Madang, and in May swept forward 115 miles along the New Guinea coast to take Wakde Island, and thence another 180 miles to land on Biak Island. These developments dictated the transfer of PT squadrons from South to Southwest Pacific. Squadron 10 left Green Island for Dreger Harbor, New Guinea, on April 19, and Squadrons 6 and 9 followed a month later.

As for the other squadrons, Squadron 2 had been decommissioned on November 11, 1943. Its 80-foot boats already had been lost in action or transferred to other squadrons; of the eight 77-footers remaining, four, in poor condition, were reclassified as small boats and the others were transferred to Squadron 3. Squadron 3 thus comprised all of the 77-footers in the area. All of these boats had seen hard service and were no longer considered adequate for combat. Squadron 3 therefore was kept at Rendova for training purposes.

Squadrons 5 and 11 were at Emirau. When Squadron 11 first arrived in the area, four of its boats had been sent to Funafuti, one of the Ellice Islands, as Squadron 11–2, to relieve four 77-footers which had been moved there in December 1942 from Pearl Harbor. These 77-footers had been transferred from Squadron 1 to Squadron 3 when they moved to Funafuti. None of the boats at Funafuti had any contact with the enemy; they were there primarily for crashboat duty under operational control of the Commanding General Samoan Defense Area. By May of 1944 there was no longer any necessity for keeping PT's tied up in such a quiet backwater, so the four boats of 11–2 joined the parent squadron at Emirau.

The three Higgins Squadrons, 19, 20, and 23, were divided between Treasury and Bougainville until the end of April, when the Bougainville base was closed. Squadrons 19 and 20 had been commissioned with only 10 boats each, and by the middle of May the 3 squadrons had lost a total of 5 boats. In order to consolidate the Higgins boats, the lowest numbered squadron, 19, was decommissioned on May 15 and its remaining boats were divided between the other two units.

Two new Elco Squadrons, 27 and 28, arrived, respectively, at Treasury Island early in May, and at Green Island in April.

32. A TRAP

At the beginning of May the Treasury boats found considerable activity in the waters around Rantan Island, 3 miles off the southeast coast of Bougainville. In the first 4 nights of the month they encountered eight large, fast, heavily armed barges near the island, of which they probably sank one and damaged the others. On each of these nights they also encountered floatplanes in the channel between Rantan and Bougainville, and usually were taken under fire by guns on the shores of one or both of the islands.

On the night of May 5/6, Lt. Jonathan S. Raymond, Jr., USNR, who had miraculously survived the destruction of PT 251 just 10 weeks earlier, led a section of three boats to the Rantan area. He rode PT 247 (Lt. (jg.) A. W. MacLean, USNR). With the 247 were PT 245 (Lt. (jg.) C. A. Hastings, USNR) and PT 250 (Ens. F. H. Kaul, USNR). As the boats passed between Rantan Island and Bougainville, they sighted three barges, close together, 600 yards east of Rantan. The boats turned southeast to make a run on them, passing within three-quarters of a mile north of Rantan Island. Then a fourth barge was seen advancing around the northwest tip of the island, and a fifth around the northeast tip. At the same time two or three other barges appeared to the north of them. By the time the boats were ready to attack, they were in an obvious trap. With barges on all sides of them, machineguns on Rantan and heavy shore batteries on Bougainville, the PT's could be caught in enemy crossfire no matter which group of barges they attacked.

Lieutenant Raymond continued to lead the way in for a run on the first three barges. Even before the PT's started firing, all of the barges opened on them with a tremendous volume of machinegun, 20mm., and 37mm. fire; machineguns poured lead at them from Rantan and the coastal guns on Bougainville started shelling them. At the end of the run the 247 was hit in the engineroom by a large-caliber tracer projectile from Bougainville. The hit caused a large explosion in the engine room, set an engine on fire, reduced the boat's speed to 3 knots, blew the port turret loose, and threw the radar mast forward across the wheel, separating Lieutenant MacLean from Lieutenant Raymond and Ens. R. J. Griebel, USNR, second officer of the 247. Ensign Griebel was mortally wounded.

With the engineroom in flames, the boat practically dead in the water and still under heavy fire, all hands abandoned ship. Lieutenant Raymond, who had been crouching in the chartroom hatch attempting to communicate with another section of PT's to the northward, was last seen heading aft on the starboard side of the boat.

The 245 and 250 had lost contact with the 247 and did not know she had been hit. They turned and made a second, then a third run on the barges, with PT 250 falling rapidly behind, because one of her engines had been hit on the first run. PT 245 made a fourth run on the easternmost of the three barges and was preparing for a fifth when she saw the 247 burning and dead in the water, just north of Rantan, with one barge half a mile southeast of her and another three-quarters of a mile to the northwest. The 245 made runs on each of these barges, and at the end of them the 250 approached from the northeast. The two boats picked up 13 survivors, accounting for all hands except Lieutenant Raymond.

Shortly afterwards, in response to Lieutenant Raymond's call for assistance, Lt. John S. Bonte, USNR, arrived with PT's 374 (Ens. D. A. Boyd, USNR) and PT 357 (Lt. (jg.) W. J. Mullen, USNR). These boats searched for Lieutenant Raymond until the 247, which had been burning brightly with ammunition bursting in all directions, exploded. Survivors then were transferred to the 357, except for Ensign Griebel, who was too seriously wounded to be moved from the damaged 250. The 357 and 250 left for the base.

Curiously, during these operations the barges withdrew without firing on the boats and no fire was received from shore except for one large-caliber shell from Bougainville.

On the return trip a floatplane dropped a bomb near the 250 and attempted to strafe the boat, but caused no damage. A shore gun fired six rounds in the general direction of the 357. PT's 374 and 245 remained to search for Lieutenant Raymond for 4½ hours, but could find no sign of him. A Black Cat assisted them by dropping flares and then dropped six bombs in the vicinity of the Bougainville gun positions, starting a large fire which burned with loud explosions.

On succeeding nights PT's returned with PGM's and LCI gunboats to shell the gun positions, but were unable to assess the results of their firing with any degree of certainty.

33. TASK GROUP 70.8

Task Group 30.3 existed for only 6 weeks. In June 1944, the major part of Admiral Halsey's Third Fleet moved to greener pastures. From the beginning of the New Georgia campaign a year earlier, South Pacific Forces had continually operated to the west of 159° east longitude, which was technically part of the Southwest Pacific area. Thus ships and aircraft when in this area had been under the strategic direction of General Mac-Arthur as Supreme Commander Allied Forces Southwest Pacific Area, but had been under the tactical command of Admiral Halsey as Commander South Pacific Area and South Pacific Force. By June, with our activities in the Solomons and Bismarck Archipelago almost entirely confined to blockading, the high command decided to unify these activities under the Southwest Pacific Forces. Accordingly, all military responsibility for the area west of 159° east longitude and south of the Equator passed on June 15 to General MacArthur. All naval ships, aircraft, and bases were transferred at the same time to Vice Adm. Thomas C. Kinkaid's Seventh Fleet, which was part of General MacArthur's command.

Commodore Moran had had conferences in Brisbane, Australia, with Admiral Kinkaid, and when the transfer was made he was designated Commander Allied Naval Forces Northern Solomons Area and Commander Task Group 70.8. His task group comprised all of the naval vessels in the northern Solomons, from New Georgia to Emirau. Besides the PT's, LCI's, and PGM's, he had command of a division of five destroyers and a division of six destroyer escorts. He was assigned further duties as Subordinate Commander Service Force Seventh Fleet, and so also had command of the naval bases at Rendova, Treasury, Torokina, Green, and Emirau. On June 15 he moved his headquarters from Bau Island in Rendova Harbor to Torokina, in order to maintain closer liaison with the headquarters of the XIV U.S. Army Corps and the Commander Aircraft Northern Solomons already established there.

Although Commodore Moran's PT's were now part of the Seventh Fleet, they were not immediately put under the operational or administrative control of the Commander Motor Torpedo Boat Squadrons Seventh Fleet. This seeming anomaly had a very simple explanation. The Commander Seventh Fleet planned to have PT's continue to operate in the Northern Solomons for a time, and to withdraw the squadrons gradually as they could be more profitably employed in the waters to the westward. As long as they remained in the Northern Solomons he wished them to be under command of Commodore Moran, who was thoroughly familiar with PT operations in that area. And he could not make Commodore Moran subordinate to the Commander Motor Torpedo Boat Squadrons Seventh Fleet, who held the junior rank of commander. Thus the PT's of Task Group 70.8, though part of the Seventh Fleet, did not become part of the Motor Torpedo Boat Squadrons Seventh Fleet until they were withdrawn from Commodore Moran's area of command, the Northern Solomons.

The increased barge activity of May was like the final flareup of a candle before it gutters out. In June the boats destroyed only three barges and damaged only one. "The marked decline in enemy barge sightings and contacts in the area," Commodore Moran reported, "significantly indicates a practical cessation of enemy barge traffic in this area . . .

"The barges destroyed were sunk in St. George Channel between the Duke of York Islands and Southwest New Ireland, where the only known barge traffic in the area was encountered during the period. Because the excessive distances from the PT base at Green Island or Emirau Island to this barge route considerably reduced the period of effective patrol, and since the enemy barges were frequently accompanied by heavily armed . . . escort barges which demonstrated a superiority in fire power over PT's as well as the ability to withstand gunfire, task units of LCI and PGM gunboats are being employed to intercept and destroy this barge traffic. From dusk to dawn these units patrol close inshore along New Ireland between Huru Point and Labur Bay and retire northwestward out of sight of land during daylight for a period of 3 to 4 days and nights. On the final night of the patrol the gunboats bombard piers, loading areas and barge hideouts along the New Ireland coast before returning to their bases via St. George Channel.

"Although enemy float planes continued to harass the boats, particularly in St. George Channel, the presence of covering friendly night fighters appeared effective in preventing bombing attacks by the enemy."

But the PGM's had no better luck than the PT's. From June until they ceased patrolling in February 1945, the PGM's claimed only 14 barges destroyed.

The Commander Seventh Fleet ordered *Mobjack* to New Guinea in July, and in August directed Squadrons 27 and 28, with *Varuna*, to report to the Commander Third Fleet at Manus, in the Admiralties, for temporary duty. After an uneventful sojourn in Manus, Squadron 27 and *Varuna* went to Palau, in the Marianas, and operated there until the end of December, when they joined the Seventh Fleet PT's in the Philippines. Squadron 28 reported to the Commander Motor Torpedo Boat Squadrons Seventh Fleet in October.

Also in August came the decommissioning of Squadron 3, now down to four superannuated 77-footers, PT's 39, 47, 48, and 59, battered veterans that had tangled with the Tokyo Express at Guadalcanal. The four old boats were shipped back to the Training Center at Melville, R.I., where they were used as guinea pigs for training repair personnel.

From July to October the boats claimed only 15 barges destroyed. And not only were there no barges, but at last the floatplane menace subsided. After the first of August there were no plane attacks at all. A new hazard came from drifting mines when Japanese minefields in the Shortland Islands area began to break up. Fortunately no boats struck mines, but the PT's sank about 50 of them during July, August, and September.

For the most part, the boats strafed the Japanese-held beaches. Reconnaissance parties, captured documents, and the native grapevine sometimes brought word that they had caused damage, but usually it was impossible to assess damage with any accuracy at the time of the strafing.

Squadrons 5 and 11, at Emirau, had the most varied missions. They caught 5 more trucks on the New Ireland coastal road, claiming 3 destroyed and 2 damaged and possibly destroyed. They undertook a continuous evacuation of natives from New Hanover, to reduce the Japanese labor supply on the island—and, incidentally, food supply, for the remaining Japanese were reduced to obtaining their food from the natives. In July and August the

NR&L (MOD) –32491

A Japanese storehouse on New Ireland, set ablaze by a landing party of PT personnel.

Emirau boats stole 283 natives and 16 Chinese from under the enemy's nose on New Hanover and took them to Mussau Island. Emirau boats also landed raiding groups, which the PT officers and men frequently accompanied, to destroy Japanese supplies on the small islands off the New Hanover coast.

It was at Emirau that the only losses occurred. PT's 63 and 107 returned on the morning of June 18 from a patrol off the New Ireland coast, and fueled at the dock at Hamburg Bay. A defective valve in the fuel line permitted gasoline to leak into the water. When PT 107 started its engines, the exhaust blast lighted the gasoline on the surface. Both boats burned and sank within an hour, and the fuel dock was destroyed, but there was no loss of life nor serious injuries.

The landing of American forces in the Philippines in October made the war seem remote indeed from the Solomons. It also created a new and expanding area for PT's. Commodore Moran discontinued all PT patrols in the Northern Solomons on November 24. In December Squadrons 5, 11, 20, and 23 departed for duty under the Commander Motor Torpedo Boat Squadrons Seventh Fleet.

Meanwhile, Squadron 31, 15 Higgins boats, arrived at Tulagi in October with the tender *Acontius;* Squadron 37, 12 Elcos, in November with the tender *Silenus;* and Squadron 32, 12 Higgins, in December. These three squadrons were commanded by officers who had been in the heavy fighting when Tulagi was the forward base, Lts. John M. Searles, Clark W. Faulkner, and Robert C. Wark, all USNR.

This time their duty was to be less strenuous. Commodore Moran assigned the three squadrons to "combat training" at the Treasury base. The boats made nightly patrols of the Bougainville and Choiseul coasts, but the barges had vanished.

Squadron 31 left Treasury with the *Acontius* on December 1 for Palau in the Marianas, to relieve Squadron 27 and the *Varuna.* The squadron stayed there until the end of February, when it proceeded to Leyte Gulf in the Philippines, and from there was shipped in June to Okinawa. Squadrons 32 and 37 left Treasury with the *Silenus* on February 15 for Espiritu Santo to await forward movement to Okinawa. The PT campaign in the Solomons was over.

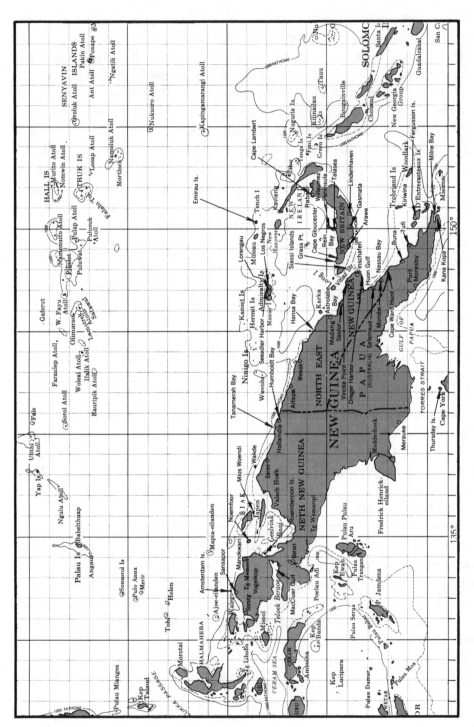

The Southwest Pacific Area.

PART IV

Southwest Pacific—*Conquest of New Guinea*

1. TO THE BUNA CAMPAIGN

THE JAPANESE did not wait for the end of the Philippine campaign to launch their engulfing sweep to the south. Three weeks after the fall of Manila they made their first landings on Rabaul in New Britain and Kavieng in New Ireland. From Rabaul they spearheaded twin advances, one southeast through the Solomons, the other southwest into New Guinea. The objective of both was the isolation or conquest of Australia.

New Guinea, which bars the approach at Australia from the north, is one of the world's largest, least-developed, and least-known islands, extending for nearly 1,500 miles on a northwest-southeast line and containing more than 300,000 square miles. Dense jungles and rugged mountains make its interior all but impassable and, for the most part, limited the Japanese advance to the coastline.

Early in March of 1942 the enemy landed on New Guinea at Lae and Salamaua in Huon Gulf and began to develop these bases as staging points for further moves down the Papuan coast. So compelling was his advance that in Australia serious consideration was given to plans to abandon most of Australia's northern province of Queensland and to fall back on a defense line just north of Brisbane.

At the time of the fall of Corregidor on May 6, there was in progress a naval battle, the first in history to be decided entirely by carrier planes, which for the time being checked the march toward Australia. This action, now known as the Battle of the Coral Sea, was fought from the 4th to the 8th of May in waters to the southeast of New Guinea. We lost the carrier *Lexington* and suffered damage to the carrier *Yorktown,* but the enemy was turned back with loss of the carrier *Shoho* and damage to other ships.

For the first time in the Pacific war, we had inflicted an important setback on the enemy. Still, he was only checked; not stopped. On July 21 and 22 he landed troops at Gona, Buna, and Sanananda on the northern Papuan coast and began his drive across the Kokoda trail through the Owen Stanley Mountains toward Port Moresby on the south coast, the last Allied base north of Australia. He almost succeeded. The drive was stopped only 32 miles from Port Moresby.

In connection with the overland advance, the enemy landed troops in Milne Bay at the southeastern end of New Guinea, apparently in preparation for an amphibious assault on Port Moresby. Two Australian brigades engaged these forces so effectively that, after 3 days of fighting, Japanese destroyers evacuated them. The destroyers came into Milne Bay again on 3 nights early in September to shell the Australians. Destroyer Squadron 4, under Capt. Cornelius W. Flynn, moved north on September 11 to intercept the enemy surface forces, but could not find them. The Japanese never again attempted to send ships into Milne Bay.

This unusual lack of persistence on the part of the Japanese was un-doubtedly a result of the fierceness of the struggle for Guadalcanal, to which the enemy was devoting all available sea, air, and land strength. With the major part of the enemy's forces committed to the Guadalcanal campaign, and with the arrival of U.S. ground forces in the Southwest Pacific, Ameri-can and Australian troops were able to concentrate on clearing the enemy from eastern New Guinea. They pushed him back across the Kokoda trail and at the same time moved up the northern Papuan coast in a flanking movement aimed at Buna. After a long and bitter struggle, in which the rains and swamps and jungles proved to be enemies as formidable as the Japanese, Allied troops took Buna Mission on January 2 and completed mopping up the remaining enemy forces at Sanananda on January 23.

PT's were the first naval vessels to have action in New Guinea waters, and their first actions were in support of the coastal advance toward Buna.

2. THE CRUISE OF THE *"HILO"*

To bring the first PT's to New Guinea, it is necessary to go back to Pearl Harbor, where, it will be remembered, the captain and crew of the tender *Hilo* saw their first PT on July 5, 1942. Ten days later the *Hilo* left Pearl Harbor with PT's 21, 23, 25, and 26, which comprised MTB Division 2 of Squadron 1, under command of Lt. Jonathan F. Rice, USNR, for duty in

Palmyra Island, 1,100 miles to the southwest. *Hilo* towed two boats; the other two ran free, fueling from *Hilo* each morning while under way. At midpoint in the passage, the boats exchanged places to share equally the discomforts of towing.

Palmyra was quiet. There was nothing for the boats to do there but take part in the island's weekly battle problem and run as practice targets for the shore radar station. Lt. Comdr. Frank A. Munroe, Jr., USNR, commanding officer of *Hilo,* recalled later that "About the middle of September, Admiral Nimitz stopped overnight en route to Guadalcanal. He gave a talk to all the officers and afterwards [Lt. (jg.) Alvin P.] Cluster button-holed him and persuaded him that the boats would be more useful farther south. So the Admiral wrote out a dispatch to the Staff in Pearl telling them to send the boats southward. I got in my two-bits worth for drydocking and a radar."

Hilo made a quick run to Pearl Harbor for docking and radar, then returned to Palmyra to pick up the boats. They left Palmyra on October 25 and arrived at their new base, Funafuti, in the Ellice Islands, on November 2. On the way out they kept a sharp lookout for the plane in which Capt. Eddie Rickenbacker had been flying across the Pacific on a special mission for the War Department. It had not been heard from since October 21, when the pilot reported he was lost and running low on gasoline.

No trace of the plane was seen and nothing more was heard of it until November 11, when Lt. (jg.) Frederick E. Woodward, USNR, pilot of a Navy Kingfisher scout plane based at Funafuti, reported after an afternoon patrol that he had seen a yellow raft a few miles south of the atoll. Lieutenant Cluster got PT 21 underway, found the raft, and returned to *Hilo* with a very sick man. After treatment by *Hilo's* medical officer, Lt. Richard W. Garrity (MC), he revived sufficiently to say that he was Capt. William T. Cherry, Jr., pilot of the Rickenbacker plane; the other survivors were in two rafts; they had separated two days before; the rafts should be southwest of the point where the PT 21 had found him.

At first light on the 12th, Lieutenant Commander Munroe got underway with the *Hilo* and the four PT's. At 1630 he received a dispatch from the island saying a Kingfisher plane had found another raft northwest of the island and was landing near it. The four PT's took off at top speed. Just before dark Ens. J. M. Weeks, USNR, in PT 26, found the plane.

The pilot of the Kingfisher, Lt. William F. Eadie, knew when he saw the raft that he could not fly with extra passengers in his two-seater plane, but he was afraid that if he did not pick up the survivors, the PT's might miss them

in the approaching darkness.   So he set his plane down on the water and took
three men aboard.   They were "Captain" Rickenbacker; his aide, Col. Hans
C. Adamson; and Pvt. John F. Bartek, the flight engineer.   Colonel Adamson, in great pain from a back injury, was put in the back seat of the Kingfisher with Eadie's radioman, L. H. Boutte, ARM1c, USNR.   Then Eadie
lashed Rickenbacker to the starboard wing and Bartek to the port wing, and
began to taxi back to Funafuti, 40 miles away.   Within minutes, PT 26 arrived.   Rickenbacker and Bartek were transferred to the PT, but it was decided that the plane should continue taxiing to the base rather than risk
moving the injured Adamson again.

Lt. Edward M. Gordon, USNR, executive officer of the *Hilo,* recalled that
"One interesting sidelight on Captain Rickenbacker's condition was that
when he was taken aboard he said that he had never seen a PT boat before,
and, therefore, he would like to inspect it, in spite of the fact that he had been
on this raft 21 days, and the captain of the PT boat took him all over his ship,
showing him the various features."

As soon as *Hilo* anchored at Funafuti the next morning, Lt. Col. J. Franklin Good, USMC, came aboard to tell Lieutenant Commander Munroe that
a coastwatcher on Nuku Fetau, 60 miles to the northwest, had reported that
the third raft, with three survivors, had washed ashore there.

"I got underway immediately," Munroe said, "and arrived off the island
in the middle of the afternoon.   The lagoon looked too dirty so I sent in the
whale boat with Mack Gordon and Dr. Garrity.   They returned in about an
hour with three survivors, Lt. J. C. Whittaker, the copilot, Lt. J. I. DeAngelis,
and Staff Sgt. J. W. Reynolds.   Whittaker was in quite good shape, but the
other two were in a very bad state—very thin and badly ulcerated.   I had not
realized that living bodies could smell so putrid and still be alive.   It was
remarkable that the two oldest men in the party, Rickenbacker and Whittaker, were in the best shape.

"Gordon and Garrity returned with very smug expressions and a tall tale
of an extraordinarily beautiful native girl who had spoken to them in excellent English, asked them to have a drink, and perhaps spend the night.   No
further details could be drawn from either officer.

"I remained underway overnight and returned to Funafuti in the morning.
Whittaker and DeAngelis were taken to the hospital but Reynolds was in
such bad shape that it was necessary to keep him aboard for several days
while Garrity gave him plasma and glucose.

"On 24 November I received a dispatch from ComSoPac directing me to proceed to Noumea, leaving the four boats at Funafuti. That left the boats in a grim fix. There was no pier or jetty, no bulk gasoline, no torpedo compressor, no drydock, no shop, no living or messing facilities and water had to be delivered in gas drums. The Marines and SeaBees were helpful and cooperative and gave the boats whatever they could of their limited facilities. I off-loaded all spare engines, torpedoes and all Packard and Elco parts.

"*Hilo* left Funafuti the next day and arrived in Noumea on 2 December."

Lieutenant Commander Munroe was ordered to take the *Hilo* and four boats of Division 17 to Cairns, Australia, and report to the Commander Southwest Pacific Forces for duty. Division 17, it will be remembered, was made up of PT's 113 and 114 of Squadron 2 and PT's 119–122, of Squadron 6, and was commanded by Lt. Daniel S. Baughman,[11] who had been executive officer of Squadron 6.

"I found that PT's 121 and 122 had departed for Cairns a few days previously in tow of a Liberty ship, with a substantial part of the division's spares in the Liberty," Munroe said. "*Hilo* fueled and then went alongside another Liberty to load the balance of the spares. Many of the vital Packard spares were missing as the result of a barge capsizing the previous day. Loading was accomplished with the usual confusion, and a small base force came aboard.

"*Hilo* and the four boats departed Noumea late in the afternoon of 3 December. Tow lines were passed to two of the boats and we proceeded at the usual 5 knots. We had an escort this time—USS *Aaron Ward*. Weather was unfavorable, generally poor visibility with frequent squalls. None of the personnel in the boats had ever been to sea in them before, and considerable difficulty was had in keeping stations. One particularly dirty night, one of the boats was continually dropping out of sight. The boat quartermaster was green and unable to read blinker. It took 3 hours to get a visual message through to him that I desired the boat to come within hailing distance, and another hour for the boat to get there. When he was finally alongside I told the boat captain in an emphatic manner that he was to stay within 200 yards of *Hilo,* period. After we arrived in Cairns and we were holding a conference about the next leg, this particular boat captain, who shall be nameless, told me that he took exception to the tone of voice which I had used in

---

[11] Lieutenant Baughman later entered the submarine service, and died in action when the USS *Swordfish* was lost in January 1945.

talking to him by megaphone! It was quite a trip. In the 7 days underway I had 21 hours sleep. When tow lines were not parting boat engines were failing. I had several consoling messages from the skipper of the escorting destroyer."

Hilo and the PT's arrived at Cairns on the morning of December 11, and the next day received orders to proceed as soon as possible to Milne Bay and to report there to the Commander Task Group 50.1, which was to be the PT task group in New Guinea. PT's 121 and 122 had left for Milne Bay 3 days earlier in tow of the gunboat *Tulsa*.

Also at Cairns was the advance echelon of PT Base 4. "Confusion reigned supreme," Munroe said. "The base site was in a mangrove swamp; there was no construction equipment; the squadron equipment which had accompanied the first two boats had been off-loaded into a municipal warehouse and thoroughly rifled. We took aboard as much gear as we could and an Advance Communications Unit with Ensign Simons in charge, plus one bottle of Australian beer and a Red Cross Christmas package per man. It was in Cairns that we first encountered HMAS *Arunta* [destroyer], and her doughty skipper, Comdr. J. D. Morrow, RAN, and his formidable wine mess. An evening aboard *Arunta* was a hair-raising experience.

"We left Cairns late on the 15th and picked up our escort outside, USS *Patterson,* commanded by a classmate, Lt. Comdr. W. C. Schultz, USN. On account of the comparatively short distance involved, and the possibility of enemy air attack, all boats ran under their own power, all being refueled during the 16th. The weather was quite dirty and many insulting remarks came from Schultz to the effect that it was a poor hen that couldn't keep its chickens under its wings.

"The New Guinea coast was picked up in the morning of the 17th, and position fixed. Whereupon Schultz turned around and said, 'Goodbye now, this is as far as I'm allowed to go.' That made us feel just wonderful. And that was the last U.S. naval vessel, other than the *Tulsa* and an occasional SC or YP, we saw until *Rigel* arrived late in May."

3. TUFI

Milne Bay offered any number of good anchorages for *Hilo,* but was already too far behind the lines to be used as an operating base for PT's. Ground forces had driven 200 miles up the coast and were in possession of Oro Bay, only 15 miles from Buna. The boats needed an operating base farther up the coast.

On December 13, PT's 121 and 122, which had arrived in Milne Bay 2 days earlier, were sent to Porlock Harbor, on the west side of the Cape Nelson Peninsula, to establish an advance base. The 121 and 122 made the first patrol in New Guinea waters on the night of December 18/19. They sighted a surfaced submarine and fired two torpedoes. The boat captains thought the torpedoes hit, but were certain they did not explode.

It soon was apparent that Porlock Harbor would not do. The land was swampy, there were no dispersal areas for the boats, and the water was so shallow that even a small Army supply ship could not enter the harbor to unload drum gasoline. The only way to get gasoline ashore was to dump drums over the side and have boat crews swim them to the beach. On December 18, Comdr. Edgar T. Neale, Commander Task Group 50.1, left Milne Bay with two PT's to explore the Cape Nelson area to find a more suitable base. He found it the next day at Tufi, on the east side of the cape.

Tufi Inlet resembled a fjord: narrow and winding, deep water, with hills rising abruptly on either side. Near the entrance was a little jetty and a small flat plot of land at the base of a steep hill, that could be used for a gasoline dump. Farther up the inlet there were places where the boats could tie up against the bank, reasonably secure from detection by enemy planes. A little fall of pure cold water cascaded into the inlet. Tufi was the government station for that section of New Guinea, with a resident representative of ANGAU (Australia-New Guinea Administrative Unit), who could arrange for native labor to roll gasoline drums and do other heavy work. The boats abandoned Porlock Harbor and moved to Tufi immediately. Within a few days *Tulsa* brought a load of base equipment and the Mobile Communications Unit to the new base.

The patrol on the night of December 23/24 reported sighting what might have been an enemy submarine. The following night, Christmas Eve, Lieutenant Baughman patrolled up the coast in PT 122 (Ens. Robert F. Lynch, USNR). Off the mouth of the Kumusi River, 15 miles beyond Buna, he saw a large submarine, fully surfaced, with a dark object beyond which he thought might be another submarine. While Ens. Theodore F. Bruno, USNR, guided the boat in, Lynch set up the torpedo director and fired his two after torpedoes at 1,000 yards. There was a geyser of water at the target and a small flash, but the submarine did not sink. Bruno continued in to 500 yards and

NR&L (MOD)−32493

The jetty at Tufi, first PT advance base in New Guinea.

Lynch fired his forward torpedoes. The starboard torpedo hit with a solid explosion, which was immediately followed by a second explosion. Large sheets of flame shot upwards and the submarine broke in half and sank. Immediately after the war, PT 122 was given official credit for sinking in this attack I–22, a submarine of 2,180 standard tons. More recent investigations, however, have thrown doubt on this assessment. The object of the 122's attack and the degree of damage inflicted must still be considered uncertain.

Ten minutes after the submarine exploded, the 122 had to maneuver to avoid four torpedoes. Apparently the other submarine had submerged and was trying to pay back the PT in kind.

On the same night PT's 114 and 121 had the first barge action in New Guinea, sinking two troop-laden landing craft at Douglas Harbor. The Japanese fired at the boats with small arms, but caused no damage or casualties. "The tactics used by both sides," Commander Neale reported, "may best be described as a melee."

Early in January it became apparent that the fall of Buna would not be long delayed. It was reported on January 6 that a Japanese force of two cruisers, four destroyers, and four merchant ships were approaching from Gasmata, on the south coast of New Britain, possibly to attempt evacuation of Buna. PT's prepared to attack, but the threat did not materialize. It was learned later that the enemy convoy had put into Lae after suffering minor damage from our aircraft.

On the night of January 17/18, PT 120 intercepted three barges loaded with Japanese Army officers near Douglas Harbor. The 120 sank two of them and set the third afire, under heavy machinegun and 20mm. fire which fatally wounded John J. Masters, Jr., CMoMM. Masters was awarded the Silver Star posthumously, with the citation: "Although mortally wounded at the outset of the action, he held valiantly to his battle station until he was too weak from loss of blood to carry on effectively. Even then, in the face of acute pain and imminent danger of falling overboard, he withheld an appeal for aid until the engagement was broken off, bravely devoting his last hours to the instruction of an inexperienced assistant to replace him. By his unyielding devotion to duty and cool courage under fire, he was in a large measure responsible for the sinking of two landing craft and the immobilization of the third."

As in the Philippines, lack of boats and insufficiency of repair facilities forced the PT's to make many patrols alone, instead of in the customary pairs. By the first of February, PT's 113 and 122 had been so badly reefed that they had to be towed back to Cairns for rebuilding. That left only four boats in operation. But this was not the Philippines, 1942; it was New Guinea, 1943—more PT's were on the way.

4. TASK GROUP 70.1

Commander Neale was relieved as Commander Task Group 50.1 on February 5, 1943, by Comdr. Morton C. Mumma, Jr., who had been commanding officer of the submarine *Sailfish* in the Philippines, and then had been on the Southwest Pacific submarine staff in western Australia and naval liaison officer at the Fifth Air Force Advance Headquarters at Port Moresby. On March 15, when the U.S. naval forces in the Southwest Pacific became the

Seventh Fleet, under command of Rear Adm. Arthur S. Carpender, Task Group 50.1 was changed to Task Group 70.1. Motor Torpedo Boat Squadrons Seventh Fleet were to be so designated until the end of the war.

Task Force 70 existed only on paper and never operated as a tactical unit. It was composed of several independent task groups under direct operational control of the task force commander, who was the Commander Seventh Fleet. In this respect the New Guinea PT's were more fortunate than the Solomons PT's; the Commander Motor Torpedo Boat Squadrons Seventh Fleet was responsible directly to, and only to, the Commander Seventh Fleet. Furthermore, from the start he had full operational control of his boats, and specific areas were assigned for PT operations. As a task group commander he received complete information as to the movements of other naval vessels. While it is impossible in wartime to insure against every contingency, this operational plan reduced to a minimum the possibility of clashes between PT's and friendly surface forces. During the entire New Guinea campaign there was not a single instance of PT's firing on, or being fired on, by our own ships. Three years later, in the Philippines, two PT's were destroyed by our own ships, but that was caused by local confusion and not by any defect in the operational plan.

The closing days of February saw the arrival in Milne Bay of Squadron 8, under Lt. Comdr. Barry K. Atkins; the first three boats of Squadron 7, under Lt. Comdr. John D. Bulkeley; and *Tulsa,* carrying the advance echelon of PT Base 6, under Lt. (jg.) Ralph S. Cooley, USNR. Because of an acute shortage of cargo carriers, Bulkeley returned to Cairns with *Tulsa* to try to expedite the shipment of supplies, spares, and base material to Milne Bay. Early in March the *Tulsa* again entered Milne Bay, with three more boats of Squadron 7. It was planned for the time being to send to New Guinea six of Squadron 7's boats, under Lt. Robert J. Bulkley, Jr., USNR, the squadron executive officer. John Bulkeley was to keep the other six boats at Cairns until such time as Base 6 should be sufficiently developed to support more boats.

Kana Kopa, a tiny circular bay, 250 yards across, at the southeastern end of Milne Bay, was selected as the site for Base 6. On the whole, it was a good site, as sites in New Guinea go, but for the first few months everyone ashore wallowed in apparently bottomless mud. One truck was actually lost in the mud of Kana Kopa. Eventually this became the main repair base; while it was building, *Hilo* did the best it could with its limited facilities.

Mud was a problem at Kana Kopa, New Guinea's first PT base.

Some of the repair and overhaul procedures were quaintly primitive. If a boat needed an engine changed, for example, it borrowed a chief motor machinist's mate from *Hilo* to supervise the installation, and ran down to Gili Gili, at the western end of Milne Bay. There the boat captain would borrow a small crane from the Army, select a new engine from a small store of crates piled under a tree, pick it up with the crane and carry it to the jetty. The boat crew would unbutton the old engine, install the new one, and put the old one back in the crate. Then the boat would return to *Hilo* for tuning and adjustments.

Hilo's lack of a drydock was compensated for by an ancient marine railway on the island of Sariba in the China Strait off the entrance to Milne Bay. A hand winch, manned by frizzle-topped Papuans, was the sole motive power. On each end of the drum of the winch was a long crank handle. Two natives faced each other across each crank handle and started winding slowly. A fifth native blew a conch shell at intervals. After each blast the men on the crank handles increased their tempo, until at last they were spinning the drum in frenzy. After 10 or 15 minutes they sank to the ground exhausted. After a 15-minute rest they started all over again: slow turning, tooting on the conch shell, gradual acceleration to unbearable speed, and finally exhaustion. It took 2 hours to haul a boat; even then the railway was so short that the stern was barely clear of the water and men working on propellers and struts had to stand in water up to their waists. Eventually a kerosene engine was installed to supplant the native crank turners. It was less picturesque, but cut the hauling time in half. By the time Base 6 got its first drydock operating about the first of June, every PT in New Guinea had been hauled at least once on the marine railway at Sariba.

Quaintly primitive, yes—but only in retrospect. At the time it was a pain in the neck. There weren't enough tools, there weren't enough spares. There wasn't enough of anything, except, by some vagary of supply, hose clamps. There were enough hose clamps to hitch up a pipeline to the moon, but PT's couldn't run on hose clamps alone. Commander Mumma's letters to members of the Seventh Fleet Staff in Brisbane tell of the constant shortages. On March 5 he reported that gasoline delivered to the Advance Base at Tufi was 320 drums short of requirements. On April 23, he wrote, "I do not have a single shaft left to put in an 80-foot boat. At the moment I am converting two 77-foot shafts, which were damaged, to use as center shafts on two 80-foot boats."

A week later he wrote that the Seabees, scheduled to complete the construction of the Kana Kopa base, had again been delayed in arriving, "for the same old reason: no transportation."

As time went on progress was made on the base and it took over an increasing amount of the repair and overhaul of the boats. At the insistence of Commander Mumma, who as early as February had said that the Cairns base "at this stage is so far in the rear as to be practically useless," Base 4 was moved from Cairns to Kana Kopa on October 18 and eventually absorbed Base 6. In the meantime enough boats were kept in operation to maintain nightly patrols, through the ingenuity and determination of the squadron base forces, *Hilo* repair personnel, and the boat crews themselves.

For example, there was long a critical shortage of auxiliary generators, without which the boats could not operate. There just were not enough to go around. For a time it was standard practice for a boat, on its return from a night's patrol, to transfer its generator to another boat so that boat could make a patrol. The next day the generator would be switched back again, or even to a third boat. This practice was not confined to generators. Radar and radio sets, and many other items of equipment were freely shifted from boat to boat so that patrols could be maintained. Any boat that was going

80–G–472468

PT crewmen lower hot food and coffee over side of a tender. Whenever possible, boat crews ate in the general mess at bases or aboard tenders to save wear on the auxiliary generators of the PT's.

to be laid up for any length of time for hull repairs would quickly be stripped of parts to keep other boats in operation. By the time the hull repairs were completed, there probably would be other boats laid up from which it could replenish itself.

5. BATTLE OF THE BISMARCK SEA

On the afternoon of March 1 a large convoy was sighted by reconnaissance planes north of Cape Gloucester, New Britain, apparently bound for Lae. The convoy consisted of 8 destroyers and 8 merchant vessels carrying a force of 6,912 troops to reinforce the enemy garrisons at Lae and Salamaua. Beginning at dawn of the 2d, every American and Australian plane that could take to the air, more than 100 in all, made repeated attacks on the convoy and fought off counterattacks by the enemy air cover, which slightly outnumbered our own planes.

Bad weather in the afternoon made the air attacks more difficult and less effective. During the night the convoy was shadowed by Catalina flying boats, which dropped bombs from time to time without results. At dawn of the 3d, the large-scale attack began again. All day long fighters and bombers shuttled over the Owen Stanley Mountains between Port Moresby and Huon Gulf. By nightfall it was reported that only three destroyers and two cargo vessels were still afloat. Both of the cargo vessels were on fire; one destroyer had a large hole in its side and another was surrounded by an oil slick.

Dispatches received at Milne Bay and Tufi indicated that the remaining Japanese force would be within striking distance of the PT's on the night of the 3d. Lieutenant Commander Atkins, who had relieved Lieutenant Baughman as commander of the advance base, readied the seven boats at Tufi. Commander Mumma arrived from Milne Bay with 3 additional boats and all 10 set out late in the afternoon in 3 sections, to take positions on a line in Huon Gulf. Atkins, with Lt. (jg.) John S. Baylis, USNR, in PT 143, led PT 119 (Ens. R. L. Jackson, USNR), PT 150 (Lt. (jg.) Russell E. Hamachek, USNR, and PT 132 (Ens. F. Gardner Cox, Jr., USNR). PT's 119 and 132 struck submerged objects, probably logs, and had to turn back.

At 2310 the 143 and 150 saw a fire ahead, to the north. On close approach they saw it was a cargo ship, *Oigawa Maru* of 6,493 tons, dead in the water, with a large fire in the forward hold and a smaller fire aft. It seemed to be abandoned. At 800 yards the 143 fired a torpedo which exploded near the stern and the ship began to heel to port and settle in the water. Five minutes later the 150 fired a torpedo at 700 yards. This one exploded amidships and the ship sank, stern first, with a brilliant blaze of fire just before she went under.

The second group of boats, PT 149 (Lt. William J. Flittie, USNR), PT 66 (Lt. (jg.) William C. Quinby, USNR), PT 121 (Ens. Edward R. Bergin, Jr.,

USNR), and PT 68 (Lt. (jg.) Robert L. Childs, USNR), also saw the fire and began to approach it at slow speed. To Lieutenant Flittie, on the 149, the fire appeared as several lights on a stationary ship, and when it blazed up before taking its final plunge he thought the ship had put a searchlight on him. He fired one torpedo, the light went out immediately, and he could not find the target again.

The third group, PT 67 (Ens. James W. Emmons, USNR) and PT 128 (Ens. James W. Herring), also saw the fire. PT 128 fired two torpedoes at long range, 1,500 yards, the second at about the same time the 143 fired. Both of the 128's torpedoes missed, but, seeing the explosion from the 143's torpedo, the crew of the 128 thought for a time that their torpedo had hit.

After the sinking Lieutenant Commander Atkins ordered the three groups to search an area further to the west. All boats encountered heavy seas and frequent rain squalls, but found no more ships.

It was learned later that there were only two ships still afloat when the PT's arrived in the area: the damaged cargo ship which they sank, and a destroyer which was finished off by planes the following morning.

On the 4th of March our planes returned and strafed everything afloat in Huon Gulf. Thousands of Japanese troops from the sunken transports were adrift in collapsible boats. For several days, the PT's, too, met many of these troop-filled boats and sank them. It was an unpleasant task, but there was no alternative. If the boats were permitted to reach shore, the troops, who were armed with rifles, would constitute a serious menace to our lightly held positions along the coast.

At daylight on March 5, Jack Baylis in PT 143 and Russ Hamachek in PT 150 sighted a large submarine on the surface well out to sea, 25 miles northeast of Cape Ward Hunt. Near it were three boats: a large one with more than 100 Japanese soldiers and two smaller ones with about 20 soldiers in each. The men were survivors of the Bismarck Sea battle; the submarine was taking them aboard. Each PT fired a torpedo. The 143's ran erratically. The 150's ran true, but missed as the submarine crash dived. The PT's strafed the conning tower as it submerged, then sank the three boats with machinegun fire and depth charges.

Five days later Comdr. Geoffrey C. F. Branson, RN, Naval Officer in Charge, Milne Bay, received intelligence that a lifeboat containing 18 survivors of the battle had drifted ashore on Kiriwina, in the Trobriand Islands, 120 miles to the north of Milne Bay. The Trobriands were then a sort of no-man's land; the Japanese held New Britain to the north, we held the New

Guinea coast to the south. The only military installation in the Trobriands was an Allied radar station on Kiriwina, which might be endangered by the new arrivals. Ens. Frank H. Dean, Jr.,[12] took Commander Branson to Kiriwina in PT 114, captured the 18 Japanese, who were in a docile mood, and returned to Milne Bay the next day. One of the prisoners, who had been badly wounded a week earlier in the Bismarck Sea and almost certainly would have died had he not been captured, later sent his American-made money belt to "Skipper" Dean as a token of gratitude.

The Battle of the Bismarck Sea, a striking victory for airpower, convinced the enemy that he could no longer run surface ships from Rabaul to Lae. He never tried to again. The Fifth Air Force began operating from Dobodura, near Buna, in April, and thereafter the enemy was unable to send cargo ships or destroyers anywhere on the north coast of New Guinea east of Wewak. He could still move some supplies overland through the Ramu and Markham River Valleys, a slow and arduous undertaking, and he could operate a submarine shuttle service between Rabaul and Lae, but the great bulk of supplies had to be moved by coastal barges. The Air Force was to prevent the barges from operating by day, and the PT's were to cut down the night traffic to such a thin trickle as literally to starve the enemy out.

6. SOME BARGES AND A FIRE

On the night of March 15/16, "Skipper" Dean in PT 114 and Lt. (jg.) Francis H. McAdoo, Jr., USNR, in PT 129, tried a new tactic, that of lying in wait to ambush barges in Mai-ama Bay, a suspected unloading point on the southern shore of Huon Gulf. The current kept setting the boats into the bay, so the 114 dropped anchor and the 129 idled out on one engine to see if any barges might be unloading on the beach outside the southern side of the entrance.

It was raining and visibility was so poor that neither boat realized six barges had entered the bay until two of them bumped into the side of the 114. Dean said later that the barges must have taken the PT for a Japanese vessel, because their crews were chattering unconcernedly and made no attempt to attack. The barges were so close, right up under the flare of the PT's side, that the

---

[12] Dean, one of the outstanding boat captains in early PT actions in New Guinea, later became a naval aviator. He came through the war unscathed, and was killed in a plane crash on Sept. 7, 1945.

forward .50-caliber guns could not immediately be depressed to bear on them. The PT crew hosed down the barges with submachineguns and got their boat underway, cutting their anchor line when the anchor refused to budge from the bottom. One of the two barges alongside was sunk by fire from the after .50-caliber turret and from submachineguns; the other one caught under the bow of the 114, and as the boat got underway was pushed under the surface and sank. Fire from the forward .50's sank two other barges as the 114 cleared the bay to rendezvous with the 129. Both boats returned, and each sank one of the two remaining barges.

Late in the afternoon of March 17, PT's 67 and 119 had completed fueling at the Tufi jetty, when a sheet of flames leaped up between the two boats. The flames spread so rapidly that the boats could not even be cast off. Their crews had barely enough time to go over the side. Ammunition and gasoline tanks exploded and the boats sank at the jetty. A small Australian cargo ship, the AS16, which had been unloading supplies just astern of the PT's, also caught fire and was destroyed. The flames spread quickly to the dock and to the gasoline dump ashore. Six depth charges stored ashore exploded in one mighty blast, spreading the fire still further. Soon the entire stock of gasoline, except for 700 or 800 drums on the far side of the cove, was ablaze. Gasoline from exploded drums seeped into the ground and the whole area continued to burn until late the next afternoon. Losses were the 2 PT's, the Australian AS16, 4,000 drums of gasoline, 6 depth charges, the jetty and a shack containing tools, spares, fueling pumps, and ammunition. In view of the rapid spread of the flames and complete destruction of everything at the base of the hill, it is almost miraculous that no one was killed or even injured. It was believed that the fire started when a native lighted a cigarette and threw his match into the water, touching off gasoline on the surface.

7. DOUGLAS HARBOR AND MOROBE

After the end of the Buna campaign our ground forces continued their slow advance up the coast, making possible the establishment of a further advanced operating base. From Tufi the boats patrolled into Huon Gulf, but the distance was so great that most of their time was used up in getting to their stations and returning, with only a few hours left for useful patrol. A base in the vicinity of Cape Ward Hunt would bring the boats 90 miles closer to Huon Gulf, and save 180 miles on each patrol.

On March 24, Commander Mumma took PT 142 into Douglas Harbor, on the east side of Cape Ward Hunt, and remained there overnight. The harbor was suitable for a PT base and apparently was free of Japanese. Within a few days MS *Masaya* steamed into Tufi and took aboard supplies, equipment, and a small base force under Ens. Donald F. Galloway, USNR. *Masaya* was an interesting old ship, World War I four-stack destroyer *Dale* (290) converted to diesel power in 1933 and used in South and Central American banana trade for some years before she wound up in Australasia. She left Tufi on March 28 for Oro Bay to take aboard 50 Army troops who were to be the local defense force for the Douglas Harbor PT base.

When the *Masaya* was still 6 or 7 miles off Oro Bay, a flight of enemy dive bombers swept in to raid Army installations ashore. As soon as the pilots saw the old banana boat, whose destroyer lines had not changed with the years, they pounced on her with obvious glee, thinking that they had caught a warship out alone. The *Masaya* took several direct hits and sank. There were some casualties to her own crew, but only one of the PT men was injured. All were rescued and brought to Oro Bay.

Lost with the *Masaya* were 400 drums of gasoline, a radio transmitter and receiver, and all of the tools, spare parts, fuel pumps, and other equipment for the advance base. Equipment was so scarce that it was almost another month before enough could be assembled to try again to establish a new base. The Japanese fliers had not, as they thought, sunk a destroyer, but they had put a nasty crimp in PT activity in Huon Gulf.

On April 8, Lieutenant Commander Atkins, with Maj. Gen. Horace H. Fuller, Commanding General of the 41st Infantry Division, made a reconnaissance of Morobe Harbor, 40 miles beyond Cape Ward Hunt, in Ensign Dean's PT 114. It appeared to be clear of the enemy and was a better site than Douglas Harbor. It was closer to Huon Gulf, and would cut more than 200 miles off each patrol. The Morobe River, flowing into the harbor, had deep water right up to the banks and lofty trees on either side. PT's moored to the riverbank and a base built under the trees would be practically invisible from the air.

Commander Mumma inspected Morobe in Jim Herring's PT 128 on

80–G–53846

PT's lie hidden under trees in the Morobe River.

April 14, and arranged with General Fuller to have troops of the 41st Division occupy and defend the harbor. On April 20 Atkins, with PT's 142, 66, and 149, started to set up the advance base. From that time Tufi was used only as an emergency fueling station between Milne Bay and Morobe.

8. THURSDAY ISLAND

On the southwest coast of New Guinea the enemy pressed forward to Kaukenau, and sent reconnaissance parties up the rivers and eastward toward Tanahmerah, a Dutch settlement in the interior, situated on the broad and swift Merauke River. If troops could make their way in any numbers to Tanahmerah, they could easily float downstream in barges, or on rafts and

NR&L (MOD)−32481

A PT is hauled on the marine railway at Thursday Island. Lt. Thomas A. Arnold, USNR, Squadron 7 engineering officer, looks on.

capture Merauke, the capital of Dutch New Guinea, on the southern coast. Such a move would put them within 250 miles of the York Peninsula, Australia's northeastern extremity. Whether by land or by sea, it was feared that the enemy might attempt to force the Torres Straits, the reef-studded expanse of water separating the York Peninsula from New Guinea. It was also possible that he might land on Australia in the broad Gulf of Carpentaria, or make an all-out assault on Darwin, to the west.

Australian ground troops were moved into Merauke, and U.S. Army Engineers began construction of fighter strips there. On April 16, 1943, Lieutenant Commander Bulkeley's second six boats, PT's 133–138, were towed from Cairns to Thursday Island, in the Torres Straits off the tip of the York Peninsula, with orders to prepare to base at Merauke. On May 1 the other six boats of Squadron 7, PT's 127–132, left Milne Bay for Thursday Island, towed by *Tulsa* and two minesweepers. PT Base 10 was sent to Darwin so that the boats would have an operating base and repair facilities ready should it become necessary to move them suddenly westward.

By the end of May the enemy was still 1,000 miles away, and more boats were needed in eastern New Guinea for use in connection with the occupation of Kiriwina and Woodlark Islands. John Bulkeley took PT's 133–138 to Milne Bay on June 6, leaving PT's 127–132 and a base force in command of Lt. Robert J. Bulkley, Jr., USNR. These boats, later designated Motor Torpedo Boat Division 19, remained at Thursday Island in view of the possibility that the enemy might make a diversionary attack on the Torres Straits while the major part of the Southwest Pacific Forces was committed to the Kiriwina-Woodlark operation.

There never was any action at Thursday Island; the enemy never came within range. Perhaps it was just as well. It would have been impossible to fire a torpedo anywhere within 15 miles of the southern coast of New Guinea. The water is so shallow that a torpedo would have buried itself in mud on its initial dive. Off Frederik Hendrik Island shoal water extends so far to sea, and the shoreline is so low, that a ship can go aground out of sight of land. Merauke itself is a miasmic little settlement built on a narrow bar of land a few feet above the level of the swamp which covers thousands of square miles of southern New Guinea.

The Merauke River is strange and wonderful. A few miles above the town the river crosses itself at right angles. Floating islands, logs and all manner of debris (very hazardous to PT's) sweep majestically downstream, east to west, eddy about at the crossing, continue westward and float for several miles around a large island, then return to the crossing, this time from north to south, and after eddying about again, proceed southward to the sea.

By the end of July, Australian troops were well established at Merauke, the RAAF was flying planes from the new airstrips, and the enemy appeared to be too heavily committed elsewhere to be capable of mounting a serious assault on the Torres Straits. The PT's, towed by three minesweepers, returned to Milne Bay. The threat to Darwin, though diminished, had not entirely disappeared. Although no PT's were ever sent to Darwin, PT Base 10 remained there, servicing patrol planes, throughout the New Guinea campaign.

9. KIRIWINA, WOODLARK, AND NASSAU BAY

The occupation of Kiriwina and Woodlark Islands, and of Nassau Bay, 15 miles southeast of Salamaua on the New Guinea coast, were coordinated with the South Pacific landings in the New Georgia group.

Kiriwina and Woodlark were desired as bases for air operations against New Britain. Since neither island was occupied by the enemy, it was not expected that he would react in force to our invasion. There was, however, the possibility that, once alerted, the enemy might send submarines and even destroyers from New Britain to strike at our supply ships. To guard against such a move, PT's accompanied the landing forces on June 30 and established nightly patrols off the islands. Lieutenant Pat Munroe, USNR, set up a base at Woodlark with the six boats of Division 23. Because of lack of suitable anchorage and difficulty of gasoline supply, no base was established at Kiriwina at the time of the landing. Instead, John Bulkeley took his boats to Kola Kola, on Fergusson Island, 70 miles south of Kiriwina, and started shuttle patrols which kept two boats each night on station off the north coast of Kiriwina. These security patrols continued until the end of September, without any contacts with the enemy.

Nassau Bay was desired as a supply point for the 7th Australian Division, which was working its way over the mountains and into the area back of Salamaua. All supplies for the division were being flown from Port Moresby to Wau, an airstrip 25 miles inland from Salamaua, and transported from the airstrip to the 7th Division positions by native carriers. It was impossible to handle sufficient quantities of 75mm. and 105mm. artillery ammunition by this method. The Nassau Bay landing was the result of Commander Mumma's suggestion that a beachhead there would greatly shorten the supply line to the 7th Australian Division.

In this operation PT's were used for the first time as troop carriers. Army landing craft of the 2d Engineer Special Brigade were to move troops of the 41st Division to Nassau Bay from Mort Bay,[13] 15 miles north of Morobe. PT's were to screen the landing craft and carry troops who would be taken ashore by the landing craft as soon as they had landed the first wave. Four PT's, the 142, 143, 120, and 68, were to take part in the initial landings on

---

[13] Mort Bay, which previously was not shown on navigational charts, was discovered and reconnoitered by Comdr. Morton C. Mumma, Jr., in a PT. Australian hydrographers then put it on the charts and named it Mort Bay, in Commander Mumma's honor.

Lt. E. B. Proctor, USNR, gives orders of the day to native working party at Fergusson Island PT advance base.

the night of June 29/30. Each of the 80-foot boats was to carry 70 men. PT 68, a 77-footer, was to patrol ahead and to seaward to intercept any enemy craft that might attempt to move down from Salamaua.

The seas were rough, it was raining hard, and visibility was extremely limited. The 68 lost visual contact with the other PT's after leaving Mort Bay, but continued to patrol through the night without sighting anything. The 142, with Lieutenant Commander Atkins aboard, led the first wave of landing craft out of Mort Bay, and because of poor visibility overshot Nassau Bay by about 3 miles. Some time was lost in getting all of the landing craft headed back for Nassau Bay. By the time they got there, PT 143 was arriving with the second wave of 12 landing craft. The landing craft of the first wave became alarmed and scattered. The 142 rounded them up again and

80—G—52526

A PT disembarks troops into a landing craft at Nassau Bay, July 6, 1943.

led them into the bay.   They landed their troops at 0130, came out to the 142, disembarked its troops and landed them.   Then the landing craft of the second wave went in to the beach.   In the meantime PT 120 arrived with the third wave.   At 0250, PT's 143 and 120, still standing by to disembark their troops, received a radio communication from the beach, telling them that all of the landing craft had broached in the heavy surf and could not get off the beach.   The 143 and 120 returned to Morobe, while the 142 set up a security patrol offshore for the rest of the night.   Fortunately the landing was unopposed.

Subsequent reinforcement operations were more successful.   In the early morning hours of July 2, PT 149, with Atkins aboard, and PT 142 covered the landing of 11 landing craft at Nassau Bay, strafed 2 enemy-held villages on the southern side of the bay, and then covered the arrival of 2 trawlers with more landing craft in tow. On the afternoon of July 4, PT's 120 and 152 each carried 70 troops to Nassau Bay. The troops were successfully disembarked by Higgins landing boats. On the morning of the 6th, PT's 149 and 120 carried a total of 135 men to Nassau Bay and covered the landing of 11 landing craft which, after putting their own troops ashore, disembarked the men from the PT's.

Arrival of the reinforcements assured the success of the operation. Within a few days our forces at Nassau Bay were joined by Australian troops moving east from the Mubo area in a drive to strike at Salamaua from the south.

10. ACTIONS IN HUON GULF

During the period they operated from Tufi, the PT's sank 1 submarine and claimed 18 barges sunk and 2 more possibly sunk. Oddly enough, during the first 2 months of operations from Morobe, they sank no barges at all. Perhaps the barge traffic had not yet grown to the proportions it was later to assume; also, it is a good guess than the PT's, in their anxiety to intercept surfaced submarines on the Rabaul-Lae shuttle, spent too much time on the offshore submarine lanes and not enough on the close-inshore barge routes. There was no doubt the submarines were running. PT's often saw them lying on the surface, but it was like chasing a will-of-the-wisp. Usually the target vanished in a crash dive before the boats could come close enough to launch a torpedo.

On the night of May 13/14, Commander Mumma in Russ Hamachek's PT 150 and Lieutenant Commander Atkins in PT 152 (Ens. Herbert P. Knight, USNR) went sub hunting 5 miles off Lae, and met a smart submarine skipper. They saw a large submarine 6,000 yards away, proceeding on the surface at an estimated speed of 12 knots. Each boat lined up its sights and fired two torpedoes in a long-range shot. The submarine stopped. All torpedoes passed ahead. Closing the range to 4,000 yards, the 150 fired one torpedo at the stationary target. The submarine immediately increased speed to maximum, with sparks trailing from her exhaust. The torpedo missed astern. The boats ran parallel to the submarine's course to gain a favorable firing position and then turned to decrease the range. The submarine crash dived. As the PT's lay to, wondering what the next move

80–G–53876

PT's leave the Morobe base at dusk to patrol in Huon Gulf.

would be, a torpedo from the submarine passed under the bow of PT 150. The PT was saved by her shallow draft at the bow.

"By God!" exclaimed Commander Mumma, himself an old submarine skipper, "I wish I had that fellow working for me!"

Later a division of Australian ML's, small wooden-hulled antisubmarine vessels equipped with sound gear, somewhat similar to our SC's, joined the task group at Morobe. Many joint PT–ML patrols were made in Huon Gulf, and on several occasions the ML's depth charged submarines, but never with any confirmable results. ML operations were greatly hampered by an almost complete lack of spare parts.

Barge actions began to pick up in July. During July, August, and September, the boats claimed 44 barges sunk or destroyed, 7 possibly sunk or destroyed, and 1 damaged, as well as one 120-foot cargo ship sunk. Even earlier than in the Solomons, the New Guinea boats had started mounting 37mm.

80—G—55627

A shower in the jungle at Morobe. Note PT moored to riverbank in background.

cannon on the bow for antibarge work.   Late in August, Squadron 12, under Lt. Comdr. John Harllee, arrived in the combat area.   Four of the squadron's boats had been equipped with a 40mm. gun as an experimental mounting before leaving the United States.   Comdr. Selman S. Bowling, whose Squadron 21 followed shortly after Squadron 12, admired Harllee's 40mms. so much that he got 12 Australian-built guns in Brisbane and had them mounted on his boats.   Thereafter, as rapidly as guns could be obtained, every PT in the Southwest Pacific was equipped with a 40mm. on the stern and a 37mm. on the bow.   In time these installations were accepted as standard and all PT's were fitted with them before leaving the United States.

An unusual action was fought on the night of July 28/29, when Barry Atkins, in the PT 149 of Lt. (jg.) James W. ("Tex") Emmons, USNR, with PT 142 (Lt. (jg.) John L. Carey, USNR), ran into a flotilla of 30 or more heavily laden barges bound from the direction of Cape Busching, New Britain, toward Finschhafen, New Guinea. The night was so dark and rainy that the PT's were not aware of the barges until they were in the midst of the formation and saw lights blinking on their port beam and port and starboard quarters. The PT's sank six of them under extremely heavy return fire. Several barges tried to ram the PT's. One tried to ram the 149, firing 20mm. as it came. The PT sank it when it was only 10 feet away. One man was wounded on the 142. An enemy 20mm. shell exploded in the engineroom of the 149, severing a throttle rod, carrying away water lines and electrical connections and piercing exhaust stacks. For a time the boat had only one engine running. Charles E. Neff, MoMM1c, USNR, and Edward L. Bernie, MoMM2c, worked like beavers, repairing the wiring and taping up the throttle rod, water lines, and exhaust stacks. When they ran out of friction tape they robbed the first-aid kit of adhesive tape. Soon they had all engines back in commission and the 149 was able to make 24 knots on its return trip to Morobe.

On the following night, Lt. George E. Cox, Jr., USNR, in his first action since he left the Philippines, took his PT 135 with PT 143 to patrol the coast east of Lae. The boats sank three barges, two loaded with troops and one loaded with supplies. All of the barges returned heavy fire and one of them came close to ramming the 135, sinking just as the 135's stern cleared it. During the action, shore guns were firing at the PT's.

It was apparent that the Japanese were employing tactics similar to those adopted in the Solomons. Lieutenant Commander Atkins, in forwarding Cox's action report, commented, "The gunfire received from the beach in this action and from other points on the coast in previous encounters would indicate an effort on the part of the enemy to protect his line of communications by fortifying strategic points along the coast."

Another PT was lost early in August when the 113, which had been thoroughly rebuilt in Cairns, ran high and dry on Veale Reef, near Tufi, before she had a chance to make even a single patrol. All efforts to salvage the boat failed, so she was stripped of all equipment and parts that might be useful to other PT's, and the bare hull was left to decay on the reef.

Although the boats extended their patrols northward along the Huon Peninsula into Vitiaz Strait, they found fewer barges in August than they had in July. They began strafing shore installations with greater frequency, and often started sizable fires in Japanese camps and supply dumps. On the night of August 23/24, George Cox in PT 135, with Lt. (jg.) Ray F.

Boat captains report to intelligence officers at Morobe after a night's patrol.

Smith, destroyed a large beached barge and sank a small one at Walingai. Flames from the beached barge illuminated the shore and the boats strafed the beach area heavily, starting a large fire that burned with dense white smoke and red flames hundreds of feet in the air. The fire was still visible when the boats were 30 miles away.

On the night of August 28/29, John Bulkeley, who had been transferred to Morobe from Fergusson Island, patrolled Vitiaz Strait in PT 142 (Lt. (jg.) John L. Carey), with Ens. Herbert P. Knight, USNR, in PT 152. As they were passing Finschhafen on their return from patrol, they saw three barges, one of which they sank on their first run. Gunfire seemed ineffective against the other two barges, so at the end of the third run PT 152 dropped a depth charge near each barge without noticeable effect. The 142 then made two runs, dropping depth charges and sinking one barge. The third barge still floated, so the 142 pulled alongside and Bulkeley, followed by

Lt. (jg.) Joseph L. Broderick, USNR, and Lt. (jg.) Oliver B. Crager, USNR, boarded it. A man in the barge made a suspicious move and Bulkeley shot him with a 45. It turned out that the other occupants, 12 fully equipped soldiers, were already dead. The PT officers reboarded the 142 and pulled away while the 152 fired 37mm. at close range until the barge sank.

A wistful commentary on this action appears in the captured diary of a Japanese officer named Kobayashi, under date of August 29. "Last night," Kobayashi wrote, "with the utmost precautions, we were without incident fortunately transported safely by barge between Sio and Finschhafen. So far, there has not been a time during such trips when barges had not been attacked by enemy torpedo boats. However, it was reported that the barge unit which transported us was attacked and sunk on the return trip last night, and the barge commanding officer and his men were all lost."

11. LAE, SALAMAUA, AND FINSCHHAFEN

As a preliminary to the amphibious operations against Lae, four destroyers of Destroyer Squadron 5, *Perkins, Smith, Conyngham,* and *Mahan,* were directed to make a sweep of Huon Gulf and to bombard the Finschhafen area, paying particular attention to barge hideouts. The destroyers arrived at Buna on the morning of August 22. The squadron commander, Capt. Jesse H. Carter, conferred with Commander Mumma and went with him to the Fifth Air Force Headquarters at Dobodura to select targets for the night's bombardment. When the destroyers stood out from Buna late in the afternoon, Commander Mumma acompanied Captain Carter in the *Perkins* to assist in locating targets. The sweep of Huon Gulf was negative, but the shelling of Finschhafen achieved complete surprise and the shore area was well covered.

Ships of the Seventh Amphibious Force put troops of the 9th Australian Division ashore on beaches 14 and 18 miles east of Lae on the morning of September 4. Within 3 days 14,000 men had been landed. The main thrust of these forces was westward toward Lae; a subsidiary movement was started eastward toward Finschhafen. Meanwhile troops of the 7th Australian Division made parachute landings at Nadzab, behind Lae, and moved down the Markham Valley from the west. Other troops mounted a drive against Salamaua from the south.

Members of a PT crew inspect a Japanese 5-inch gun after the fall of Lae.
Guns of this type frequently fired on PT's patrolling in Huon Gulf.

Salamaua fell on September 11.   Advance units of the 7th Australian Division entered Lae on the 16th.   The occupation was completed 3 days later. PT's supported the operations by nightly patrols in Huon Gulf and northward into Vitiaz Strait.   Between the 3d and 20th of September they claimed six barges destroyed, three probables and one damaged.   During this period also, PT 136 (Lt. (jg.) Roger H. Hallowell, USNR) was lost.   She went hard aground on an uncharted reef while on patrol in Vitiaz Strait on the night of September 16/17 and, since these were enemy waters, had to be destroyed. Her crew was taken aboard other PT's without casualties, and PT 142 set the 136 ablaze by gunfire.

The early fall of Lae and Salamaua cleared the way for the next major move, the occupation of Finschhafen.   PT's already had helped prepare for this operation by landing six American and Australian scouts and four natives on the proposed beach north of Finschhafen on the night of September 11/12 and taking them off again on the 14th.   On the night of September 21/22, while the ships of the Seventh Amphibious Force were approaching the landing beach, three sections of two PT's each set up a defensive screen to the northward in Vitiaz Strait.

Lieutenant Commander Harllee, in PT 191 (Ens. Rumsey Ewing, USNR), with Lt. (jg.) Robert R. Read, USNR, in PT 133, encountered a 120-foot cargo ship 10 miles off Vincke Point. "Upon sighting ship," Ewing reported, "PT 191 followed by PT 133 closed it at high speed and then slowed to make a firing run to starboard. Light machinegun fire was encountered on this run, but none thereafter. After the first run, two more runs were made at closer ranges and fire was directed inside the boat as much of previous fire had glanced off side. After the third run, the ship caught fire and lost headway, and the PT's lay off in case of an explosion. Attempts to extinguish the blaze were observed on the ship. Another run and a depth charge set at 30 ft. was dropped, but was a little too far off to be destructive. About seven men attempted to embark in a dinghy and this was sunk, the men either regaining the ship or jumping into the water. Although the ship was well ablaze and had settled, it did not appear to be going to sink and another depth charge was dropped close to the bow, blowing it out of the water and apparently breaking the keel. When last seen, she was low in the water and still burning. It is considered that she was destroyed beyond further use."

An hour after this action ended, troops of the 9th Australian Division began to pour ashore at Finschhafen. The Japanese, after 18 months of occupation, had been cleared from Huon Gulf.

12. MOROBE: OCTOBER AND NOVEMBER

The liberation of Huon Gulf forced the PT's to extend their patrols further up the coast of the Huon Peninsula; to the islands to the north, Long Island, Umboi, Tolokiwa, and Sakar; and to the southern and western shores of New Britain. The patrols were long and rugged; the boats had to go at least 100 miles to get on station. But the crews were eager and there were plenty of barges—the Japanese were making a determined stand in the Huon Peninsula and attempting to reinforce their garrison with bargeloads of troops and supplies from New Britain and from Madang and Wewak on the New Guinea coast.

New boats came to Morobe and the old ones were gradually withdrawn. By the end of October, Squadron 8, which had absorbed Division 17, went to Kana Kopa for overhaul. The boats of Squadron 7, which had been divided between Morobe and Fergusson Island, were moved to a new base at Kiriwina.

80–G–53793

A boat crew relaxes on deck of a PT under camouflage net in the Morobe River.

Soon after these moves, Lt. Robert L. Childs, USNR, relieved Lieutenant Commander Atkins as commander of Squadron 8, and Lt. Edward W. Roberts, USNR, relieved Lieutenant Commander Bulkeley as commander of Squadron 7. Squadron 12, which had started patrols from Morobe with four boats at the end of August, had all of its boats operating in October. Squadron 21, the first to have a 40mm. on every boat, arrived at Morobe early in November.

Squadron 21's arrival was greeted with astonishment, not because of the size of its guns, but because of the size of its officers. Commander Bowling first became acquainted with PT's when, as a staff communications officer with the South Pacific Amphibious Force, he voluntarily went out on patrols with the Tulagi boats. He decided that PT officers should be tough, and when he returned to the United States to fit out his own squadron, he chose as officers the biggest, toughest athletes he could find.

Among them were Ens. Ernest W. Pannell, USNR, all-American tackle from Texas A.&M., who had played professional football with the Green Bay Packers; Ens. Alex Schibanoff, USNR, of Franklin & Marshall College and the Detroit Lions; and Ens. Steven J. Levanitis, USNR, of Boston College and the Philadelphia Eagles. Other football players included Ens. Bernard A. Crimmins, USNR, all-American, of Notre Dame; Lt. (jg.) Paul B. Lillis, USNR, Notre Dame captain; Ens. Louis E. Smith, USNR, University of California halfback; Ens. Kermit W. Montz, USNR, Franklin & Marshall; Ens. John M. Eastham, Jr., USNR, Texas A.&M.; Ens. Stuart A. Lewis, USNR, University of California; Ens. Cedric J. Janien, USNR, Harvard; and Ens. William P. Hall, USNR, Wabash.

Other sports were represented by Ens. Joseph W. Burk, USNR, holder of the world's record for single sculls; Ens. Kenneth D. Molloy, USNR, all-American lacrosse player from Syracuse University; Lt. John B. Williams, USNR, Olympic swimmer from Oregon State; and Ens. James F. Foran, USNR, Princeton swimmer.

Whether athletes, as a class, could operate PT's any better than nonathletes is still open to debate. There is no doubt that Squadron 21 was a smart and efficient outfit.

New and old, the PT's had good hunting in the last months at Morobe. In October they claimed nine barges sunk or destroyed, one plane shot down, and one plane possibly damaged. In November the claims jumped to 45 barges sunk or destroyed, 6 damaged, and 1 plane possibly damaged.

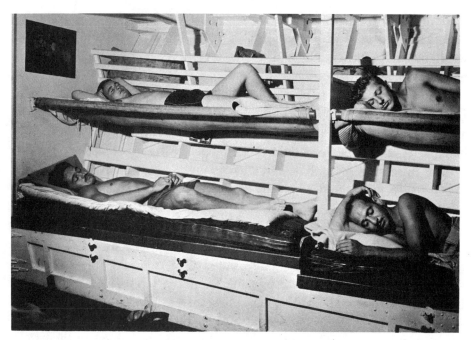

"Sack drill" aboard a New Guinea PT.

The sudden increase was caused by a variety of factors. As our ground forces increased their pressure, the Japanese undoubtedly made more vigorous efforts to supply their troops, and sent more barges into the area. At the same time, the PT's became more efficient barge-destroyers by installation of 40mm. guns and a new and improved type of radar which greatly increased their ability to locate the enemy and aided in navigation as well. And, finally, the PT's improved their tactics by patrolling closer inshore, close enough to make sure that no barges could pass undetected between them and the beach, and to be able to see any barges that might be unloading on the beach. This doctrine, as will be seen, resulted in the loss of several PT's by grounding on uncharted reefs. In fact, more PT's were lost through grounding in enemy waters than from any other single cause, but the risk was acceptable in view of the vastly greater amount of damage inflicted on the enemy. Danger to crews was reduced by having boats patrol in echelon formation, with the following boat or boats farther offshore than the lead boat. In this formation, even if the lead boat should go aground, a following boat probably would not, and would be able to tow the lead boat off the reef or, failing in that, to rescue its crew.

Running close to shore was not, of course, a new invention in November. The tactic had been used with success many times before, and was used with greater frequency and with increasing success until by November it had become standard doctrine.

On the night of September 30/October 1, Lt. (jg.) Robert F. Lynch, USNR, in PT 68, with Ens. Rumsey Ewing, USNR, in PT 191, attacked and sank two barges near Vincke Point. During their run on the second barge, they sighted a third unloading troops on the beach. They opened fire on it, scoring many hits, and then swung to port to head out to sea. When the 68 had almost completed its turn, it ran hard aground, 40 yards offshore.

"PT 68 called PT 191 and the latter stood in to attempt to pull PT 68 free," Lynch reported. "At 0125 lines were passed from PT 68 to PT 191 and for 25 minutes PT 191 attempted to pull PT 68 free, but the latter could not be moved. It did not seem probable from the first that PT 68 could be freed, but all efforts were made, regardless of this. During this time, about 100 men, deduced to be Japanese troops by their shouts and chatter, collected on the beach. PT 68 kept its guns manned and trained on the beach, but did not open fire as it was feared that by doing so return fire from the beach would have ended all chance at salvage and would have unnecessarily endangered PT 191.

"At 0155, I ordered the crew of PT 68 to abandon ship, transferring to PT 191. The two anchor lines were still across, and PT 191 again tried to work PT 68 loose, but within a minute a gun judged to be 37mm. opened fire on the boats from the beach on the southwest shore and a light machine-gun was heard on the northeast side, and the lines were cut. I ordered PT 191 to destroy PT 68, which she did by opening fire on it and setting fires on it which very quickly spread completely over the boat. At 0220, PT 68 was a complete mass of flames and ammunition on board was exploding . . . At 0225, PT 191 left the scene of action and returned to base.

"During the second run on the barges, five large fires were started on the beach. These continued to grow in intensity and could still be seen from 35 to 40 miles away. One fire appeared to be oil stores, the others general stores but no ammunition."

On the night of October 8/9, Lt. (jg.) Lawrence M. Stutsman, USNR, in PT 128, and Ens. Robert M. Hursh, Jr., USNR, in PT 194, had the only contact with destroyers during the entire New Guinea campaign. The boats were guided to the western end of New Britain through the narrow passages of the Siassi Islands by Lt. George O. Walbridge 2d, USNR, radar officer of Squadron 7, who was aboard Hursh's boat. Walbridge had made so many patrols to test radar equipment that he knew the coast better than most of the boat captains, and Lieutenant Commander Harllee, then in charge of operations at Morobe, used to send him out as a pilot.

The boats were lying to off Grass Point, New Britain, when to the north, off Lagoon Point, they observed a column of black smoke, similar to that made by a ship blowing its tubes. As the boats proceeded slowly northward, pips appeared on their radar screens, indicating the presence of six large ships near Lagoon Point. The boats lay to, trying to track the targets, when one of the "targets" opened fire at a range of 3½ miles. The first shell, apparently 5-inch, landed within 25 yards of the 194 and threw everyone to the deck. At least three more shells fell close before the boats could even get their engines in gear to get underway.

By the time the PT's brought their speed up to 40 knots, two destroyers, making not less than 35 knots, had closed within less than a mile, and were bracketing the boats with rapid salvos. One destroyer held the 194 in its searchlight beam. At first the PT's had not opened fire because it was thought that gun flashes might give the enemy a point of aim, but now the 194 poured 60 rounds of 40mm. at the searchlight, and it went out.

A second searchlight caught the 194, followed immediately by a shell which landed not more than 15 yards astern, lifting the stern out of the water and piercing the transom with many shrapnel holes. Soon afterwards another shell landed close astern, spraying shrapnel which killed two men and wounded two other men and an officer.

Both boats had been laying smoke, the 128 heading northwest and the 194 southwest. The 194's smoke generator jammed and could not be turned off. The continued emission of smoke was giving the destroyers a point of aim. Lieutenant Walbridge, though wounded, grabbed a fire ax, hacked the smoke bottle loose from the deck and kicked it over the stern. He then advised Hursh that his best escape route lay to the northwest. Hursh swung his boat northwards, passing through his smokescreen. Stutsman had just turned to the south to get behind his smoke. As they came through the screens the boats all but crashed head on. Each boat captain put his helm hard over. The boats responded instantly, and though they collided, it was a glancing blow. The bow of the 194 was damaged and there was a gaping hole in the portside of the 128 above the waterline, but the boats could still make top speed. Once the boats were behind the smoke, the destroyer fire became increasingly inaccurate and the boats ran to safety behind Sakar Island.

At no time did the boats have a chance to fire torpedoes. The destroyers had the drop on them and fired with great accuracy from the first salvo. "We thought about firing torpedoes," Stutsman said, "but any attempt to turn simply brought a slight turn from the destroyer, and she remained head-on."

Several submarines were sighted during the period, but always dived before the boats could get a good shot at them. Lt. Charles H. Jackson, Jr., USNR, in PT 147 and Lt. (jg.) Raymond C. Turnbull, USNR, in PT 195, came closest to a kill on the night of November 5/6 when they sighted two surfaced submarines in column off Nunzen Plantation, north of Blucher Point. The boats closed to 800 yards and fired torpedoes, the 147 at the first submarine, the 195 at the second. One of Jackson's torpedoes missed. The other, he said "ran true, and hit. The explosion was accompanied by a flash of flame and the column of water was black . . . The target sank immediately."

Turnbull fired only one torpedo. "The torpedo run," he said, "was hot, straight and normal, followed to its target by boat captain and seen to explode on target with accompanying geyser of white water. No flash was observed. Thirty seconds later, a geyser of black water was observed broad on the port bow, which was the result of PT 147's torpedo hit. The submarines did not open fire during the attack, neither were targets sighted after the torpedo explosions. A search of the vicinity disclosed a large patch of white, boiling, phosphorescent water at the spot of the contact."

The following night PT's observed a large oil slick in the area.

The evidence is good as far as it goes but, lacking confirmation, is insufficient to support any definite claim.

Just 2 weeks later, on the night of November 19/20, while patrolling with Ensign Hursh's PT 194, Jackson drove the 147 aground off Teliata Point. PT's 144, 322, and 331 joined PT 194 in trying to pull her off the reef. The boats worked for 3 hours attempting to free the boat under intermittent sniper fire from shore. Then, as the tide was still running out, Jackson transferred his crew to the 194 and set a landmine next to a gasoline tank. The boat exploded and burned for 45 minutes.

Lieutenant Commander Harllee, in forwarding Jackson's report, said, "It is not felt that the officer-in-tactical-command is deserving of censure for this grounding, as PT's have had to take such risks in order to effectively attack Japanese coastal barge traffic. In the past, these risks have proven worthwhile. On the other hand, it is felt that both boat captains deserve commendation for their prolonged efforts under fire to refloat the boat."

Less than a week later, on the night of November 23/24, Ens. John M. Eastham, USNR, in PT 322 went aground near Hardenberg Point, just after the 322, with Ens. Ernest W. Pannell's PT 324, had sunk two barges. The 322 also had to be destroyed after all efforts to refloat her failed.

13. A LETTER FROM GENERAL BERRYMAN

Costly as it sometimes proved, barge hunting was paying off. The barges that the PT's were sinking were vital to the entire Japanese effort in the area. Unless they got through, that effort must fail. The importance of the PT's role is emphasized by a letter from Maj. Gen. F. H. Berryman, Commanding General of the 2d Australian Corps, who was in charge of the ground forces in the Huon Peninsula campaign:

H.Q. 2 AUST CORPS, 1 Dec. 43.

Commander M. C. MUMMA USN,
Comd MTB Squadrons, Seventh Fleet, US NAVY

1. On behalf of 2 Aust Corps I wish to express appreciation of the excellent work being done by units of your command in the VITIAZ STRAITS area.

2. The immediate success of their operations will have been evident to the personnel as witness the continual and steady destruction of the enemy's barges over the last few months.

3. But there is another and more far reaching aspect of these operations which I feel should be made known to all taking part, and that is the telling effect which has been wrought upon the enemy's land forces in the FINSCHHAFEN area.

4. The following evidence emerging from the recent operations will illustrate the cumulative effect of the activities of your command.

(a) The small degree to which the enemy has used artillery indicates a shortage of ammunition.

(b) The enemy, in an endeavour to protect his barges, has been forced to dispose his normal field artillery over 50 miles of coast when those guns might well have been used in the coastal sector against our land troops.

(c) Many Japanese diary entries describe the shortage of rations and the regular fatigues of foraging parties to collect native food, which are becoming increasingly difficult to obtain.

(d) A Japanese PW* stated that three days rice augmented by native food now has to last 9 days, this is supported by the absence of food and the presence of native roots on enemy dead.

---

*PW: Prisoner of War.

(e) There is definite evidence that the enemy has in one area slaughtered and eaten his pack-carrying animals.

(f) There is evidence that reinforcements have arrived in the WEWAK area, but, it is believed, the enemy has been unable to send large numbers forward because of his inability to maintain larger forces in the forward area.

(g) A PW states that the enemy has been forced to send carrying parties back to KANOMI to carry supplies, thus reducing the fighting troops capable of being placed against our land troops.

From the above you will see how effective has been the work of your squadrons, and how it has contributed to the recent defeat of the enemy.

5. Without your willing cooperation it would not have been possible for our officers to visit FINSCHHAFEN quickly or to have ensured the timely arrival of urgently needed medical supplies such as blood plasma. The number of officers you have carried from BUNA to FINSCHHAFEN has been considerable and must at times have been a strain on the food supplies in your PT Boats, but at all times the courtesy and open hearted hospitality has been most marked and has been deeply appreciated.

6. All ranks of 2 Aust Corps appreciate your help, and, I know, will join me in wishing you every continued success. I would be grateful if you would convey to your officers and crews our appreciation of their cooperation, courtesy and hospitality.

F. H. BERRYMAN,
Maj-Gen, Comd 2 Aust Corps.

14. TENDERS, STAFF, AND LOGISTICS

By the middle of August the Fifth Air Force had its strips at Dobodura in full operation, and it was considered safe to move *Hilo* and a drydock forward from Milne Bay to Buna. This was a great economy. Morobe boats in need of repair had only to run 75 miles to Buna instead of 300 to Kana Kopa.

"Safe" is, of course, a relative term. The enemy still made raids on the Buna area from time to time. On the morning of October 14 *Hilo* was just leaving Oro Bay, where she had gone to take on fresh water, when 45 enemy planes came over. Our fighters were already in the air, about to set out on a strike against Rabaul. They shot down every enemy plane. *Hilo* scored several hits on one, but could not claim it because one of our P–38's finished it off; conversely, SS *John Ross,* riding low at anchor with a load of bombs and mustard gas, claimed an already crippled plane that narrowly missed her stack as the pilot was riddled by the Liberty ship's 20mm. guns at point-blank range. "At one time," Commander Munroe said, "we could see 10 planes burning on the water."

Three days later, when the *Hilo* was back at Buna, there was another raid, mostly over Dobodura. A P–38 crashed into the sea about 8 miles from the *Hilo.* Herb Knight took PT 152 to the scene of the crash and rescued the

Hilo *in Buna Roads.*

pilot, 1st Lt. Tommy McGuire, USAAF, who had shot down his 10th and 11th Japanese planes that morning.

USS *Portunus,* first of the LST-type tenders assigned to the Southwest Pacific, arrived in Milne Bay on October 18 and put ashore officers and men of PT Base 4. Commander Mumma, who had begun to assemble a staff to assist him in the administration of his growing task group, wished to use *Portunus* as his command ship. Although far superior to *Hilo* in the matter of shop space, *Portunus* had almost no room for office space or living quarters for staff personnel. Commander Mumma resolved the difficulty by having a 20- by 40-foot quonset hut erected on the forward deck, enhancing the already arklike appearance of the ungainly tender.

Portunus arrived at Buna on October 20. Commander Mumma shifted his pennant to her November 3, permitting *Hilo* to leave for Sydney for well-earned overhaul and liberty for her crew. She arrived in Sydney on November 13, exactly 333 days after she had stood out from Cairns with the boats of Division 17. En route to Brisbane, *Hilo* stopped briefly at Milne Bay. "I found Base 6 still without torpedo tools, parts and equipment," Commander Munroe wrote to Commander Mumma, "so I completely stripped the torpedo shop. All engine parts and tools also were transferred, some to LST 201, mostly to Base 6."

The LST 201, mentioned by Commander Munroe, was in many ways the most unusual of all PT tenders. Commander Mumma was to receive increasing numbers of boats, which in all probability would be moving

NR&L (MOD)—32483

An LST-type tender lifts a PT with its A*-frame for repairs.*

fairly quickly from base to base. He foresaw that he would need more
tenders than he was scheduled to receive from the United States. When
PT Base 14, under Lt. William B. Cameron, USNR, arrived in Australia,
Commander Mumma obtained from the Commander Service Force Seventh
Fleet the assignment of the Coast Guard-manned LST 201, commanded by
Lt. S. D. LaRoue, USCGR. Under the general supervision of Lt. William
J. Flittie, USNR, who had been taken from Squadron 8 to become the Task
Group material officer, the LST 201 was fitted out in Australia and at Milne
Bay as a PT tender, using as much of Base 14's equipment as possible.
The personnel of Base 14 went aboard as the repair crew. It was not feasible
to manufacture and mount an A-frame for lifting PT's, so the 201 towed
a drydock with her wherever she went. She did acquire one superior piece
of equipment, an 11-ton crane with a 50-foot boom, mounted on deck forward, which could be operated by one man. The other LST-type tenders
had only an inconveniently short boom, which could not be operated by
less than seven men. Despite her hybrid character—a Coast Guard crew
operated the ship and a Navy crew handled the PT repair work—the LST
201 performed her function well, and in August 1944 was officially designated
as a PT tender and dignified with a name, USS *Pontus.*

A PT is raised in a pontoon drydock. Lacking an A-frame, LST 201, later USS Pontus, *towed a drydock wherever she went. Note 40mm. gun on stern of PT.*

The LST 201 completed her fitting out in Milne Bay and arrived at Buna on November 18. Five days later both *Portunus* and LST 201 moved to Morobe.

Soon after taking command of the Task Group, Commander Mumma realized it would be many months before adequate amounts of spare parts could be shipped to New Guinea from the United States. He worked out a plan for manufacture of essential spares in Australia, and sent Lieutenant Flittie to Australia to assist the Commander Service Force in getting the spares into production. Many Australian-built spares eventually were used on the boats. Mufflers and struts compared favorably with those of U.S. manufacture, and the propellers, though usually not perfectly balanced, were far better than none at all. Only the shafts, made of bronze instead of monel, which was not available in Australia, were entirely unsatisfactory. They were more apt than not to shear off after the first hour or so of operation.

Besides spare parts and tenders, advance base equipment was needed for future moves. Late in 1943 Commander Mumma arranged with the Commander Service Force for the assembly at Milne Bay of a number of advance base units, each of which could be loaded for transportation on one LST, and would be capable of supporting two operating squadrons. These units contained only the barest essentials to keep squadrons in operation—tents, galley gear, a mobile communications unit, a field torpedo unit, and a small medical unit—for any major repairs the boats would have to return to the repair base.

In addition to the equipment that would be put ashore at the base, Commander Mumma had various types of pontoon floating equipment constructed. These included drydocks; barges with two 1,000-barrel gasoline tanks on them, which, from their strange appearance, came to be known as "double bubbles"; self-propelled barges with a motor-driven crane and a quonset hut machine shop aboard, useful for changing engines and minor repairs; and small barges fitted out as radar shops.

An advance base unit of this type, with its floating equipment, could be set up as soon as a beachhead was established, and because it could be well dispersed was far less vulnerable to air attack than a tender.

Supervision of the assembly of the advance base units at Milne Bay originally was under Lt. Philip Q. Sawin, USNR, who succeeded Lieutenant Flittie as Task Group material officer, and later under Lt. Comdr. Herman F. Straw, USNR, who not only assembled the materials but went ashore with one base after another as officer in charge.

Commander Mumma built up his staff gradually over a period of months. Commander Munroe was his Chief Staff Officer; most of the other members of the staff were drawn from the squadrons. Two staff officers who should be mentioned were Maj. James T. Throsby, AIF, who joined the task group late in December 1942, to provide liaison between the PT's and the Australian ground forces, and Lt. Eric M. Howitt, RANVR, who joined the boats at Morobe as a pilot. Major Throsby had longer continuous service

80-G-257011

A tug (left) arrives at Amsterdam Island, Dutch New Guinea, towing a floating drydock, a "double-bubble" gasoline barge, a crane barge, and a radar repair barge.

in Task Group 70.1 than any other person, American or Australian. He accompanied the boats all the way up the New Guinea coast, into Morotai in the Halmaheras, and finally to Balikpapan in Borneo. Lieutenant Howitt, who in peacetime had been, among other things, a master of vessels engaged in interisland trade, knew the New Guinea and New Britain coasts like the back of his hand. He guided the boats through reefs and into harbors at night with uncanny accuracy, and usually was the coolest person on the boat when the shooting began. For their invaluable assistance both of these officers were awarded the Legion of Merit; Throsby in the degree of Legionnaire, Howitt in the degree of Officer.

On May 18 the task group acquired the first of an odd collection of cargo craft, HMAS *Potrero,* a 70-foot, wooden-hull, diesel-driven coaster that could carry 30 to 40 tons. Theoretically it was the job of the Service Force to see that the squadrons got what they needed where and when they needed it, but PT's needed so many special spares that were not common to the rest of the Navy, and so frequently were operating in advance of the places ordinarily reached by Navy supply, that it turned out to be simpler and more satisfactory for all concerned to have the Task Group run its own cargo carriers between bases. Eventually the Task Group was operating the equivalent of a small shipping line to keep its forward bases supplied.

15. KIRIWINA

Since the first of July, two PT's from Fergusson Island had patrolled off the north shore of Kiriwina each night. By the end of September the Royal Australian Air Force was getting ample supplies of gasoline at Kiriwina, and was willing to allocate some of it to the PT's in order to have them at hand for air-sea rescue work.

Kiriwina was far from ideal for a PT base. The only anchorage was in the open roadstead on the north side of the island. But it had one advantage: the Japanese base of Gasmata on New Britain lay across 130 miles of open water to the north. It might be possible to intercept barges running from Rabaul to Gasmata. Accordingly, with the six boats of Squadron 7 from Fergusson Island and the six boats of Division 23 from Woodlark, a base was set up at Kiriwina on October 2, under Lt. Comdr. Robert J. Bulkley, Jr., USNR. Lt. Edward W. Roberts, USNR, took over the base on October 17 and Bulkley became Task Group operations officer. Roberts was relieved in January by Lt. Robert L. Childs, USNR.

At the time the base was established, plans were being made for the invasion of New Britain, and the first task of the boats was to land a party of American, Australian, and native scouts at Ablingi Harbor, west of Gasmata. The scouts were taken out by PT's 2 weeks later, after collecting considerable information on enemy dispositions in the Gasmata area.

Results from Kiriwina were, on the whole, disappointing. During nearly 5 months of operation, the PT's claimed only 1 lugger and 2 barges sunk or destroyed, 1 barge probably destroyed, and 3 barges damaged. On three occasions they attacked submarines with undetermined results. To a greater extent than anywhere else in the New Guinea campaign, the PT's were harassed by enemy planes, which twice dropped bombs close enough to wound men on the boats. Lt. (jg.) Joseph R. Ellicott, USNR, in PT 131 and Lt. (jg.) Robert R. Read, USNR, in PT 133 evened the score on the night of December 15/16 when they shot down an enemy four-engine seaplane off Gasmata.

One of the worst accidents of the New Guinea campaign occurred during a patrol in Ablingi Harbor on the night of January 25/26, when PT's 110 and 114 collided. A depth charge, which had been set in ready condition because of the likelihood of submarine contacts, was broken loose and exploded under the 110, blowing the boat out of the water and breaking it in two pieces. The 114 was heavily jolted, but not damaged. Two officers and one enlisted man of the 110 were missing, one man killed, and one officer and six men wounded.

Because of the infrequency of barge contacts, as well as the fact that by then the south coast of New Britain could be covered as well from Dreger Harbor as from Kiriwina, the Kiriwina base was closed on February 27, 1944.

16. DREGER HARBOR

Dreger Harbor, which eventually was to supplant Kana Kopa as the main PT supply and repair base in New Guinea, was established as an advance base on November 25 when Commander Bowling moved there with boats of Squadron 21 and two LCT loads of base equipment. Boats of Squadrons 12 and 21 began patrols from Dreger Harbor 5 days later. The new base added 65 miles to the distance the boats could patrol along the New Guinea and New Britain coasts. It is not surprising, therefore, that after December 5 Morobe was abandoned as an operating base.

The length of patrols was further extended after the U.S. Army landings at Arawe, on the southwestern coast of New Britain, on December 15, and at Saidor, on the New Guinea coast, on January 2, 1944. Fuel barges were placed at both of these points so that PT's could leave Dreger Harbor in the morning or early afternoon, top off their tanks at Arawe or Saidor, and then start their patrol. Arawe was about 75 miles from Dreger Harbor; Saidor 110. The Task Group acquired operational control of an APc (small transport), which was kept busy most of the time towing fuel barges back and forth between Dreger Harbor and the advance fueling points. She was always escorted by PT's on these missions, and as she could barely make 5 knots while towing, this was one of the least coveted assignments for PT skippers. When not engaged in towing, the APc, like *Potrero,* was used for carrying supplies between bases.

Portunus moved to Dreger on January 6, followed within a week by the LST 201. Our air strength had developed to such an extent that the Japa-

PT crewmen came young. Forrest Hall, S1c, USNR (left), 17 years old, helps Charles Ferguson, GM2c, USNR (right), and Carl Ochsner, CMM, USNR, bring .50-caliber ammunition aboard his boat at Dreger Harbor.

nese made no large raids on the Dreger-Finschhafen area, but many times during the first few months they sent one or two planes in for a nuisance raid. On the evening of January 23, enemy planes which sneaked past the warning system dropped several bombs in Dreger Harbor. Two fell within 25 yards of LST 201 without causing damage. Another, a small fragmentation bomb, hit squarely on the deck of LST 201, causing minor damage to the ship and wounding five men. A fourth bomb fell harmlessly between the LST 201 and *Portunus,* and a fifth killed several men on a dock at the north end of the harbor, where the Liberty ship *John Muir* was being unloaded.

Operations at Dreger were started by Squadrons 12 and 21. During the latter part of December and most of January, they were joined by PT's 127, 134, and 138 of Squadron 7, and PT's 110 and 144 of Squadron 8. In addition, three new squadrons began their operations from Dreger Harbor: Squadron 18, under Lt. Henry M. S. Swift, USNR, on December 14; Squadron 24, under Lt. Comdr. N. Burt Davis, Jr., on January 10; and Squadron 25, under Lt. James R. Thompson, USNR, on February 28.

The PT's continued to extend their patrols until they were covering most of the south coast of New Britain and the north coast as far east as the Willaumez Peninsula, and were traveling 200 miles and more up the New Guinea coast. And the patrols continued to pay off. In December the boats claimed 55 barges sunk or destroyed, 14 damaged, and 4 aircraft shot down; in January 47 barges sunk or destroyed, 7 damaged, and 3 aircraft possibly damaged; and in February, 17 barges sunk or destroyed, 1 damaged and 1 aircraft possibly damaged. The slump in February was attributed primarily to the withdrawal of the enemy.

On February 8, Commander Mumma, who had had 3 years of duty in the Pacific, was relieved as Commander Motor Torpedo Boat Squadrons Seventh Fleet and Commander Task Group 70.1 by Commander Bowling. Commander Bowling, in turn, was relieved of command of Squadron 21 by Lt. Paul T. Rennell, USNR, who had been his executive officer.

17. ACTION ON A REEF

On the night of December 18/19, Lieutenant Swift, in PT 369 (Lt. (jg.) John F. Ganong, USNR), with PT 323 (Ens. James F. Foran, USNR), patrolled up the Huon Peninsula from Wandokai. The 369 opened fire on a small barge near the beach at Walingai, and while maneuvering to get in position for a second run, went aground on a reef. Foran brought the 323 in close and put lines over, but after breaking two anchor lines without budging the 369, stood off a few hundred yards to call other PT's to the scene by radio.

About an hour and a half after the grounding, a small loaded barge came past, running down the coast 200 yards offshore. The 323 made one run on it and sank it. An hour later eight more barges passed the 369, 250 yards to seaward. As he did not then know the location of the other PT, Swift held the 369's fire until the barges opened fire on the 323 and the 323 returned the fire. The 369 then opened fire with all the guns it could bring to bear from its stationary position. The 323 was having engine trouble, and so made a very slow run past the barges, firing with all guns. Because of the darkness and great volume of tracer fire from both sides, it was not possible to determine the results of the action accurately, but from the 369 one barge was seen to sink and it was believed that the others were at least heavily damaged. The 323 stood by for another 2 hours, until Ray Turnbull's PT 195 arrived and assisted the 323 in freeing the 369 from the reef. The 195 towed the 369 back to base.

18. A SUBMERSIBLE

Ens. Rumsey Ewing, USNR, in PT 191, and Ens. Herbert P. Knight, USNR, in PT 152, were returning from an uneventful patrol on the morning of December 24, when, shortly after daylight, one of the lookouts on the 191 saw a barge making for the beach at Gneisenau Point.

"Both boats closed the beach from about 2½ miles out," Ewing reported, "and saw another object which at first looked like a large barge. In the meanwhile, the barge had arrived at the beach and three men appeared to leave it and run to the bush.

"On approaching more closely, the object which at first had appeared to be a large barge was identified as a submarine about 100 feet long. At the same time a picket boat was seen on the beach with a large pile of stores next to it. The stores were contained in what seemed to be gunny sacks.

"Both boats opened fire on the submarine, and a loud hissing noise comparable to the sound of escaping compressed air was heard during a lull in the firing. The submarine had its stern to the beach, and began to settle by the bow. It only went down about 4 feet when it hit the bottom. The hull was shot up badly, and fire was now turned on the barge and picket boat, riddling both with 37mm., 20mm., and .50-caliber fire. Both of these latter craft were made definitely unserviceable for further use.

"The PT's 191 and 152 were about 50 to 75 yards from their targets at all times, laying to while firing. No shore fire was encountered."

Three weeks later, after Allied ground forces had taken Gneisenau Point, Major Throsby, with Lt. George Vanderbilt, USNR, intelligence officer of Squadron 12, examined the vessel sunk by the 191 and 152. They found it lying heeled over on its side in 8 feet of water, and learned that it was not a submarine, but a curious type of submersible, capable of carrying either fuel or cargo, but having no propulsion machinery of its own. The vessel, 104 feet long, was equipped with fixed horizontal stabilizers so that if it were towed by a surface vessel its superstructure would be awash, and if towed by a submarine it would travel beneath the surface. It was equipped with a heavy bollard aft, which suggested the possibility that two or more submersible carriers might be towed in line.

19. PLANES AT ARAWE

Immediately following the landing of our troops at Arawe, New Britain, on December 15, PT's instituted regular nightly patrols of the Arawe area to forestall any attempts by the enemy to move troops in by barge. Lt. William C. Quinby, USNR, in PT 110 and Lt. (jg.) Elliott H. Goodwin, USNR, in PT 138 made one of these patrols on the night of December 25/26, and in the morning stopped at Arawe to embark 16 passengers for Dreger, including several wounded soldiers.

As the PT's stood out of Arawe Harbor, 15 to 20 enemy dive bombers flew directly out of the sun, attacking the PT's, the APc 15, the SC 747, and an LCT. The attack was so sudden that the first bombs dropped before the PT's could open fire. The first bomb hit only 30 feet from the 110, severely jolting the boat and crew, and knocking the 20mm. gunner, Stephen P. LeFebvre, TM3c, down the engineroom hatch. As other bombs were dropping 50 and 75 feet away, LeFebvre scrambled back to his gun and opened fire on a plane off the port quarter, following it around to the starboard bow. The plane caught fire and crashed ashore.

Several bombs fell near the 138, exploding under water and spraying fragments, opening up seams, and piercing the hull. One small bomb landed on the deck forward, falling at an angle, and passed through the deck and out the starboard side of the boat above the waterline without exploding. The 138 was taking on water so rapidly that Goodwin ran her bow up on a reef on the south side of Arawe Island.

The planes made only one pass and then went away. Aboard the 110, Quinby and William F. Lohman, GM2c, USNR had suffered superficial wounds. LeFebvre had a bruised shoulder from a bullet which hit the shoulder rest of his gun, missing him by less than an inch. No one was injured on the 138.

In a few minutes it was apparent that the leaks in the 138 could be controlled. The SC 747 pulled her off the reef and she returned to Dreger Harbor under her own power.

Twenty-four hours later Lieutenant Swift, in PT 190 (Lt. Edward I. Farley, USNR) with Ens. Ewing's PT 191, were 25 miles northwest of Arawe, on the way back to Dreger Harbor after an uneventful patrol. A large flight of enemy dive bombers and fighters—estimates ran from 30 to 38—came in from the north and began to bomb and strafe the boats in groups of three and four. The PT's separated, increased speed, and started zigzagging toward a bank of low-hanging clouds 12 miles away.

Unlike the planes of the day before, these made repeated dives, strafing and dropping a total of forty 100-pound bombs. As soon as the attack began, the boats asked for fighter cover, but they had difficulty getting the message through, and it was 40 minutes before a flight of P-47's arrived from Finschhafen.

The 191 took the heaviest part of the attack. Ensign Ewing was wounded in the lung early in the action, and his second officer, Ens. Fred Calhoun, USNR, took charge of the boat. Himself hit in the thigh by a machinegun bullet, Calhoun stuck to the wheel, watching each bomb drop and twisting the PT out of its path. Bomb fragments ricocheted from the 20mm. magazine, putting the gun out of action and severely wounding Thomas H. Dean, CMoMM, USNR, the gunner, and August Sciutto, MoMM2c, the loader. Other near-misses blew an 18-inch hole in the portside and peppered the entire boat with fragments.

On the third and fourth run, the port and starboard engine water jackets were hit, and jets of hot water spurted through the engineroom. The starboard intake manifold also was hit, and the supercharger forced gasoline fumes into the engineroom. Victor A. Bloom, MoMM1c, USNR, despite bomb splinters and bullets, fumes and spraying hot water, swiftly taped and stuffed the leaks, keeping the engines running. Then, fearing that the fumes might explode, he closed off the fuel tank compartment and pulled the release valve to smother it with carbon dioxide. Finally, when he had brought order to his engineroom, he went to work to give first aid to the wounded.

The action was far from one sided, however. The gunners on both boats met every attacking plane with a withering blast of fire. Four Japanese planes crashed into the sea near the boats. "Toward the end of the attack," Lieutenant Farley reported, "the enemy became more and more inaccurate and less willing to close us. It is possible that we may have knocked down the squadron leader as the planes milled about in considerable confusion, as if lacking leadership."

The remaining planes were routed by our P–47's, which shot down at least one more of the enemy. One P–47, hit by an enemy plane, made a belly landing half a mile from the 190. The pilot, though badly cut in the head and wounded in the arm, freed himself just before his plane sank. The 190 sped to him, and Lieutenant Swift and Joe H. Cope, S1c, USNR, dived into the water and towed him to the PT.

The 190 was undamaged. The 191, thanks to the accuracy of her gunners, the skillful boat handling of Ensign Calhoun, and the remarkable performance of Bloom, was able to return to base under her own power.

"This action," Commander Mumma reported, "is believed to be one of the outstanding fights between PT boats and aircraft. It has shown that the automatic weapon armament is most effective. It has demonstrated that ably handled PT's can in daylight withstand heavy air attack, however not without disabling damage."

20. ACTIONS ALONG THE NEW GUINEA COAST

The New Guinea coast gave the boats the best hunting until the barge traffic declined in February 1944. Although our forces had landed at Saidor on January 2, there were still long stretches of enemy-held coastline to the east, as well as to the west, of Saidor. Scarcely a night went by in January without the PT's meeting barges.

On the night of January 3/4, Ens. Oliver J. Schnieders, USNR, in PT 145, and Lt. Laurence B. Green, in PT 370, patrolled to the west of Saidor. The boats, with 145 leading, made a run on a barge close to shore off Mindiri

Village and sank it. Just as his boat opened fire, Schneiders saw foul water ahead. He ordered the helmsman to come to port and attempted to back down, but the boat was already on a reef. Heavy swells caused the PT to broach and drove her further aground. Green tried to come in to put lines over, and also went on the reef, but was able to back off. By the time he was clear, the 145 had pounded holes in her bottom and was taking on water rapidly. The crew swam to the 370, which fired 20mm. into the 145 until she burned and exploded.

Four nights later, Ens. Ernest W. Pannell, USNR, in PT 324, and Ens. Frederick C. Feeser, USNR, in PT 363, sank five 80-foot barges loaded with personnel and supplies 3 miles north of Pommern Bay. There was some return fire from the barges, and during the first few seconds of the action, Frank C. Walker, GM1c, USNR, manning the 37mm. gun on the 363, was fatally wounded. He kept firing accurately at the barges until the first run was over. Then he collapsed on the deck. Later he recovered consciousness for a time and asked, "Did we get them? How did my guns fire?" He spoke his last words to the man who was to succeed him as gunner's mate. "Get those guns cleaned up, son," he said.

On the same night, Lt. John K. Williams, USNR, in PT 134, and Ens. James R. McCafferty, USNR, in PT 146, stopped to investigate two rafts near Nambariwa. The rafts were piled with rubber bags of rice, and near them were floating tins of dried fish and waterproof boxes of medical supplies. While they were examining these supplies, the 146 picked up a radar pip, 2½ miles away. The boats started toward it and soon sighted a submarine, the I–177, which dived immediately. As the boats returned they had another radar contact, this time only a mile away. They proceeded toward it, and saw a periscope only 200 yards away. Each boat dropped two depth charges, with no apparent results. At daylight they sank the food rafts. Apparently the submarines, instead of waiting to be unloaded, had adopted a new technique of dumping supplies overboard in waterproof containers and trusting to the tide to float them ashore.

Ens. Joseph W. Burk, USNR, one of the coolest boat captains in the business, added to his already impressive score on the night of January 8/9, when he led his own PT 320 and Ens. James F. Foran, USNR, in PT 323 to destroy 10 barges and to silence a shore battery that was trying to break up the attack.

"At 2225, four barges were sighted 1 mile north of Mindiri, about one-quarter mile offshore and headed south," Burk reported. "All barges were about 70–80 feet in length and one was definitely seen to be carrying troops. As the PT's closed for a port run, the troop-carrying barge opened fire with light machinegun fire and a huge amount of rifle fire. On the first run three of the barges were sunk, one exploding when hit by the 323's 40mm. gun. The fourth barge made the beach but was destroyed by the PT 320 on its second run. There was an explosion of what appeared to be ammunition on this barge. All barges had been loaded. The barges took no evasive tactics other than to head for the beach and to fire upon the PT 320, which was the lead boat.

"At 0030, three barges were sighted about ¾ mile off the beach at Maragum, 4 miles north of Enke Point. By the time the 320 and 323 closed to attacking distance, the barges were ¼ mile from the beach, proceeding very rapidly. They were close aboard when both PT's opened fire, and there was no doubt about all three barges having taken plenty of hits. One was definitely hit by a 40mm. When the PT's returned immediately after the first run, none of the three was observed floating. However, three other barges were seen lined up on the beach, ramps down and stern seaward. These barges were empty while the others were loaded. While destroying the three barges on the beach, a shore gun that seemed to be about 3-inch in size opened fire from a position 2½ miles north of Enke Point. Both boats proceeded to close in on the shore gun at high speed, firing .50-caliber, 20 and 40mm. shells. This caused the shore battery to cease firing at both PT's, and they proceeded to finish the task of destroying the beached barges. All barges involved in this action were of 70 to 80 foot length.

"At 0400, in Pommern Bay, about 50 boxes of Japanese foodstuffs were sighted and after collecting 8 samples, the remainder was destroyed by light machinegun and small arms fire.

"The personnel of both boats acquitted themselves very well, especially in view of the fact that so much of the action took place while under return fire."

The boxes of foodstuffs were the same type waterproof containers that Williams and McCafferty had met the previous night. After sinking 10 barges, silencing the shore batteries, and destroying 50 food containers, the boats were completely out of ammunition. "If a plane had jumped us on the way home," Foran said later, "we'd have had to throw rocks at it."

21. EXPANSION

By March 1944, Dreger Harbor was becoming a rear area. Most of the Japanese had been forced from the Huon Peninsula to Madang, in Astrolabe Bay. The next job for the boats—already they had started to work on it from Dreger—was to cut the barge supply line to Madang.

On March 4, Squadron 24, under Lt. Comdr. N. Burt Davis, Jr., started operations from a new base at Saidor, the first of the advance base units planned by Commander Mumma and assembled in Milne Bay. On March 17 LST 201 arrived at the new base. The site was Nom Plantation. Squadron humorists called it Nom de Nom Plantation, a name that later found its way into many official reports.

Army units landed February 29 on Los Negros Island in the Admiralties, nearly 300 miles to the north of Dreger Harbor. What was planned as a reconnaissance in force became a full-fledged occupation when enemy resistance proved less formidable than had been anticipated. Fifteen PT's of Squadrons 18 and 21, under Lt. Henry M. S. Swift, USNR, and Lt. Paul T. Rennell, USNR, left Dreger on March 9 for Seeadler Harbor in the Admiralties. With the PT's went the tender *Oyster Bay* (Lt. Comdr. Walter W. Holroyd, USNR), a new seaplane-type tender which had arrived at Dreger Harbor on February 21.

On New Britain, PT's from Dreger had landed and picked up reconnaissance parties in preparation for the Cape Gloucester landings on December 26. As our troops moved eastward in northwestern New Britain, Dreger PT's swept the coast past Rein Bay, 50 miles to the east of Cape Gloucester. Finally the distance between Dreger Harbor and enemy territory became too great, and it was necessary to move the operating point forward. *Hilo* arrived at Dreger on March 7 fresh from overhaul. A week later, after Lt. Comdr. Herrmann G. Page relieved Commander Munroe, *Hilo* left for Rein Bay with Squadron 8, under Lt. Edward I. Farley, USNR, and Squadron 25, under Lt. James R. Thompson, USNR.

On March 26 *Hilo* and the two squadrons again moved forward to Talasea, on the eastern side of the Willaumez Peninsula. From there the boats could patrol the entire northern New Britain coast as far east as the dividing line between Southwest Pacific and South Pacific waters at Cape Lambert, only 40 miles from Rabaul.

Dreger then became primarily a supply and repair base. It was used as an operating base for patrols against the southern coast of New Britain until

80—G—58532

A crane barge lowers a new Packard engine into PT 242 at a Pacific base.

April 14, when patrols were secured for lack of targets. Some of the southern New Britain patrols were among the longest ever undertaken by PT's, extending all the way to the Southwest Pacific-South Pacific dividing line at Cape Archway, more than 350 miles from Dreger Harbor.

Operating in four distinct areas—New Guinea, the Admiralties, northern New Britain, and southern New Britain—the PTs' claims in March were 17 barges, 3 luggers, 1 175-foot cargo ship, 1 plane, and 31 canoes destroyed; 1 barge damaged; and 1 barge captured. In April the boats claimed destruction of 44 barges and a picket boat, and damage to 8 barges.

22. DESTRUCTION IN HANSA BAY

On the night of March 5/6, Lt. R. H. Miller, USNR, in PT 335 (Lt. Bernard C. Denvir, USNR), with PT 343 (Ens. Fred L. Jacobson, USNR), destroyed two enemy luggers and set fire to a storehouse, a fuel dump, and an ammunition dump at Bogia Harbor, 125 miles northwest of Saidor. On the following night, Lieutenant Commander Davis, in PT 338 (Lt. (jg.) Carl T. Gleason), with PT 337 (Ens. Henry W. Cutter, USNR), went 10 miles farther up the coast to Hansa Bay, a known enemy strongpoint.

The boats idled into the bay at 0200, the 338 leading. They picked up a radar target a mile and a quarter ahead, close to shore. Closing to 400 yards, they saw two heavily camouflaged luggers moored together. Heavy machinegun fire opened from the beach. As the PT's turned and started to strafe the beach, more machineguns started firing along the shore, and a heavy-caliber battery opened from Awar Point, at the northwestern entrance of the bay.

The first shell hit so close to the port bow of the 337 that some of the crew were splashed with water and heard fragments whizzing overhead. Three or four more shells dropped near the 337; then one hit the tank compartment just below the port turret, going through the engineroom. All engines were knocked out and the tanks burst into flame. Ensign Cutter pulled the carbon dioxide release, but the blaze already was too furious to be checked.

Francis C. Watson, MoMM3c, USNR, who had been thrown from the port turret, got to his feet and saw William Daley, Jr., MoMM1c, USNR, staggering out of the flaming engineroom, badly wounded in the neck and jaw. Watson guided Daley forward, slipped to the deck and shouted to Morgan J.

Canterbury, TM2c, USNR, to help the wounded man. In the meantime Cutter gave the order to abandon ship and the men put the liferaft over the starboard, or offshore, side, and began taking to the water. Daley was dazed but obedient. He got in the water by himself, and Ensign Cutter and Ens. Robert W. Hyde, USNR, towed him to the raft.

The crew paddled and swam, trying to guide the raft away from the exploding boat and out to sea. They must have been working against the current, because after 2 hours they were only 700 yards away from the boat, and were considerably shaken by a tremendous explosion. After the explosion the flames subsided somewhat, but the hulk was still burning at dawn.

Several times the survivors saw searchlights sweep the bay from shore and heard the shore guns firing. They did not know the guns were firing at the 338, outside the bay. When the heavy battery had first opened on the boats, Davis ordered a high-speed retirement and the 338 laid a smokescreen. When the 337 did not come through the screen, Davis tried repeatedly to reenter the bay, but every time the 338 approached the entrance, the shore battery bracketed the PT so closely that it had to retire. Finally, knowing that the 338 would be a sitting duck not only for shore guns but enemy planes in daylight, Davis set course back to Saidor.

Daley died before dawn and was committed to the sea. That left three officers and eight men in the raft. Besides Cutter, Hyde, Watson, and Canterbury, there were Ens. Bruce S. Bales, USNR; Allen B. Gregory, QM2c, USNR; Harry E. Barnett, RM2c, USNR; Henry S. Timmons, Y2c; Edgar L. Schmidt, TM3c, USNR; Evo A. Fucili, MoMM3c, USNR; and James P. Mitchell, SC3c.

To say that the men were *in* the raft perhaps gives an exaggerated impression of comfort. It was an oval of balsa, 7 feet by 3, with a slatted bottom open to the waves. With 11 men, it was awash. Usually they did not even try to stay in it at the same time. Some stayed in it and paddled, others tried to guide it by swimming.

At dawn on the 7th the raft still was less than a mile off the entrance of Hansa Bay. During the morning the current carried it toward Manam Island, 6 miles offshore. Cutter wanted to go ashore on Manam, thinking it would be easier to escape detection in the woods than on the surface so close to Hansa Bay. Besides, the men could find food, water, and shelter ashore, and might be able to steal a canoe or a sailboat. All afternoon they paddled and swam, but whenever they came close to shore another current pushed them out again.

That night Cutter and Bales tried to paddle ashore on logs. If they could get ashore they would try to find a boat and come back for the others. After 3 hours the unaccountable currents swept the two exhausted officers and the raft together again. While they were away, Hyde and Gregory set out to swim to the island. They were not seen again.

During the night the men saw gunfire toward Hansa Bay, as though PT's and shore batteries were firing at each other, but they saw no PT's. By dawn of the 8th the raft had drifted around to the north side of Manam, no more than a mile from the beach. Mitchell already had set out to swim to the island. Cutter, Schmidt, and Canterbury were delirious that night. During the storm Canterbury suddenly swam away. Barnett, a strong swimmer, tried to save him, but could not find him. Soon after dawn, Bales, Fucili, and Schmidt also set out for shore. The others were too weak to move. Most of the men thought that Bales, Fucili, and Schmidt reached the island, but Watson, who said he saw Bales walking on the beach, is the only one who claimed to have seen any of them ashore. Soon afterward Japanese were seen on the beach.

Mitchell returned to the raft in the middle of the morning. He was only 75 yards from shore when he saw several Japanese working on the beach, apparently building boats. Plans to go to Manam were abandoned.

Soon after dark that night a small boat put out from shore, circled the raft and stood off at about 200 yards. There were two men in it who, some of the men said, were armed with machineguns. They made no attempt to molest the men in the raft, but kept close to them until about 0400, when a sudden squall blew up, with 6- to 8-foot waves. When calm came again the boat was nowhere to be seen.

On the morning of the 9th the remaining men, Cutter, Barnett, Timmons, Watson, and Mitchell, saw an overturned Japanese collapsible boat floating a few yards away. It was only 15 feet long, but it looked luxurious in comparison with the raft. They righted it, bailed it and boarded it. Mitchell saw a crab clinging to the boat, and in catching it let the raft slip away. No one thought it was worth retrieving.

The crab was not the only food during the day. Later the men picked up a drifting cocoanut. The food helped some, but the men were tortured by thirst. They had lost their waterbreaker in the storm, and the cocoanut was dry. They were suffering, too, from exposure. Scorched by day and chilled at night, they were covered with salt water sores.

The night of the 9th and the morning of the 10th were monotonous agony. At noon, three Army B–25's flew over, wheeled about and circled the boat. Cutter waved his arms, trying to identify himself by semaphore. One of the bombers came in low and dropped a box. It collapsed and sank on hitting the water. Then came two more boxes and a small package attached to a life preserver, all within 10 feet of the boat. The boxes contained food, water, cigarettes, and medicines. In the package was a chart showing their position and a message saying that a Catalina would come to pick them up.

The next morning a Catalina, covered by two P–47's, circled the boat. The Catalina picked up the five men. Within 2½ hours they were back in Dreger Harbor.

A liferaft is a hard thing to spot. During the 5 days since the loss of the 337, planes by day and PT's by night had searched for the survivors. Of those who tried to go ashore at Manam, little is known. A captured document indicates that 1 officer and 2 enlisted men were taken prisoner by the Japanese, but none of the crew of the 337 was reported as a prisoner of war.

23. THE ADMIRALTIES

Oyster Bay and 15 PT's of Squadrons 18 and 21 arrived March 10 in Seeadler Harbor, the elbow of Los Negros Island in the Admiralties. Although the 1st Cavalry Division, under Maj. Gen. Innis P. Swift, had landed on Los Negros 10 days before, the island was not yet under control. The perimeter defenses of the harbor were still in dispute. Snipers still fired occasionally at the tender and PT's at anchor. Fortunately, there were no casualties.

It was unlikely that the Japanese could bring reinforcements to the Admiralties, separated by more than 150 miles of open water from New Guinea to the south, and by almost the same distance from New Hanover to the east. The boats were there to prevent interisland reinforcement or evacuation, to land scouting parties, and to provide fire support for a series of minor amphibious landings on small islands around Manus. Enemy airstrips at Momote on Los Negros and at Lorengau on the adjoining island of Manus, largest of the group, had been thoroughly bombed out before the initial landings. With no air opposition, the boats could operate as well by day as by night. Apparently the Japanese had resigned themselves to the loss of the Admiralties and were unwilling to risk any of their dwindling hoard of planes on New Guinea in a futile defense of the islands to the north.

When the PT's arrived, the Army was planning an amphibious assault on Lorengau, just west of Seeadler Harbor.   On the morning of March 11, PT's were assigned to escort Army reconnaissance parties in LCV's to Butjo Luo Island, Bear Point, and Hauwei Island.   PT 366 strafed Butjo Luo, scouts went ashore and found the island suitable for an artillery emplacement.   At Bear Point the 323 strafed the shore, scouts completed their mission without opposition, but found that there was no beach for bringing artillery ashore. After the scouts had withdrawn, the 323 destroyed two barges on the beach a quarter mile southeast of Bear Point.   The party escorted to Hauwei Island by PT 329 ran into trouble.   As soon as it had advanced 100 yards inland, it was taken under heavy machinegun and rifle fire from a large enemy force in well-fortified positions.   The PT crew heard the fire, but could not bring the boat closer than a quarter of a mile because of wide fringing reefs.   The island was very small and covered with dense underbrush.   It was impossible to see anyone ashore, so the boat had to hold its fire.   A sniper bullet from shore bored through the left ankle of the boat captain, who then committed an unfortunate error in judgment.   Unable to give fire support because he could not distinguish friend from foe, he thought his boat could be of no further use.   He ordered it to return to the tender.

The reconnaissance party already was trying to withdraw, but was cut off by the enemy.   After a bitter fight the men reached the beach to find that their LCV had been sunk by a mortar shell.   They waded out into the water and stayed there several hours under mortar and machinegun fire until PT's 366 and 328 arrived from the tender to pick them up.   Of 35 men in the party, 11 had been killed and 15 wounded.   The 366 returned the wounded to the tender while the 328 strafed the island, destroying a pillbox.

The next day, after the island had been worked over by an artillery barrage and by RAAF P-40's from Momote, Army troops went ashore.   Despite strong opposition they cleaned out the enemy by the afternoon of the 13th. Artillery was set up on Hauwei and Butjo Luo in time to join B-25's and five destroyers in bombarding Lorengau in preparation for landings on the morning of March 15.

During the landings at Lorengau, PT 323 (Lt. (jg.) Emery M. Newton, USNR), was used as an observation boat by Capt. Karl J. Christoph, senior naval officer in the Admiralties.   PT 363 (Lt. Laurence B. Green, USNR) with Lt. Eric M. Howitt, RANVR, and Lt. H. M. S. Swift, USNR, aboard, laid marker buoys to show the landing craft the way to the beaches, and PT

325 (Lt. (jg.) Stuart A. Lewis, USNR), with Lt. Rennell aboard, anchored 2 miles off the beach and directed movements of landing craft to the beaches. After laying its buoys, the 363 strafed and mortared the coastline as the landing craft approached. Some of the first troops ashore informed the 363 that there was a sniper's nest at Lugos Mission. Green brought his boat within 75 yards of the beach, strafed the area, and had the satisfaction of seeing a sniper fall out of a tree.

The boats met few barges in the Admiralties. Lieutenant Green's PT 363 and Lt. (jg.) Lawrence J. Kelley's PT 330 got credit for the only one sunk underway, on the night of March 11/12. The boats also strafed a jetty, house, and lookout tower on Pak Island, to the east of Los Negros.

On the night of March 16/17, Lieutenant Swift, in PT 367 (Lt. (jg.) Eugene E. Klecan, USNR), with Lewis's PT 325, intercepted nine Japanese in a native canoe south of Pak Island. As the PT's approached, one of the Japanese committed suicide with a hand grenade, killing three of his fellows as well. Of those who survived the grenade, one was shot when he refused to be taken prisoner, and the others were captured. One of the prisoners asked for pencil and paper and wrote an odd little note. It was later translated:

My name is Kaminaga. After finishing Ota High School I worked in a Yokohama Army factory as an American spy. I set fire to Yokohama's arsenal. Later, I was conscripted into Japanese Army, unfortunately. I was very unhappy, but now I am very happy because I was saved by American Army. To repay your kindness I will work as a spy for your American Army.

Kaminaga was turned over to Army authorities, who did not accept his offer.

On the morning of March 20, Lt. (jg.) Cedric J. Janien, USNR, in PT 321, and Lt. (jg.) John F. Ganong, USNR, in PT 369, strafed enemy installations at Loniu Village, on Los Negros Island. Finding that he could not set fire to the buildings by gunfire, Janien decided to take more direct action. He and Ganong went ashore in a dinghy with a volunteer crew, taking two buckets of gasoline with them. They found 25 buildings, under which were stored 30 new canoes, each capable of carrying 35 men. They set fire to the canoes and some of the buildings, among them one which housed an ammunition dump, and returned to the PT's to get more gasoline. They had heard sniper fire ashore, and when they returned to the boats learned that an officer on the 321 had been grazed by a sniper bullet.

After the ammunition dump stopped exploding, they went ashore again, and examined the remaining buildings. They found several tons of food and supplies, and in one building picked up a Japanese naval code book, which they took with them. From time to time they heard the whine of a sniper bullet, but did not leave the beach until they had made certain of the destruction of all the buildings and stores.

Organized resistance to the Army's advance on Manus collapsed on March 25 with the enemy's flight to the southwest. The Army then turned its attention to cleaning up the outlying islands, of which the most important were Koruniat, Ndrilo, and Pityili Islands in Seeadler Harbor, and Tong, Pak, and Rambutyo Islands to the southeast.

On the morning of March 23, Lt. (jg.) Ernest W. Pannell, USNR, in PT 324, and Lt. (jg.) Stuart A. Lewis, USNR, in PT 325, landed Army, ANGAU, and native scouts on Tong Island, and native scouts on Rambutyo, picking them up the same day except for the natives on Tong, who said they had seen four Japanese armed with two rifles. Three days later Joe Burk's PT 320 and Ens. Francis L. Cappaert, USNR, in PT 370 picked up the natives, who had captured the four Japanese, thus clearing the island of the enemy. Some of the natives had given food to the Japanese. As soon as the Japanese laid down their rifles to eat, they were surrounded by armed natives.

Pityilu Island had been bombed and strafed by aircraft and shelled by destroyers at intervals for more than 2 weeks before the landings on March 30. The *Oyster Bay* had been pressed into service on March 14 to knock out enemy positions on the island with 60 rounds from her 5-inch guns. On the morning of March 30, 10 PT's got underway to support the landings. Joe Burk's PT 320 dropped a marker buoy to guide the amphibious craft through a channel between two reefs. PT's 324 and 326, patrolling the southeast tip of the island to prevent evacuation, quickly silenced light sniper fire with their guns. After the island had been shelled by destroyers and strafed by P-40's and Spitfires, PT's 320, 325, 328, 362, 363, 365, and 367 moved in ahead of the landing craft and mortared and strafed the beach. Machine-guns fired inaccurately at the boats from shore. PT 331 (Lt. (jg.) Bernard A. Crimmins, USNR), with General Swift aboard, was used as an observation post for the high command in the immediate vicinity of the landing area. The troops met stiff resistance, but by nightfall had gained complete control of the island.

The following morning PT's 362, 363, 365, 366, and 367 bombarded Koruniat Island with mortars, and *Oyster Bay,* with PT's 320, 321, 325, and 326, shelled and strafed Ndrilo Island. On April 1 an Army combat team went ashore on Koruniat and later moved to Ndrilo. Both islands were deserted.

On April 2 PT's 366 and 326 put ANGAU and native scouts ashore on Rambutyo and Tong Islands. They reported that the Japanese were concentrated at Malambok Village. The boats strafed the village without visible results. The next morning PT's 365, 323, 331, and 364 covered the landing of troops by LCV's and LCM's. There were only about 40 Japanese on the island, but it took 3 weeks to ferret them out because of difficult terrain and dense vegetation. One of the natives landed by the PT's was to make his way to the adjoining island of Bundro, where eight Japanese had been reported. He planned to feed the Japanese drugged cocoanuts, tie them up, and bring them out to the PT's in a canoe. That was the last the PT's saw of the scout. It was later learned that the native succeeded in part of his mission. The eight Japs were easily duped and trussed up. But when the native went for help, renegade natives came along and cut their bonds, allowing them to escape.

On the morning of April 9, PT's 324 and 328 strafed the beach of Pak Island for 15 minutes before troops went ashore. The landing was unopposed, and the island was secured by April 12.

Squadron 21 was withdrawn to Dreger Harbor on April 11, and Squadron 16 and *Oyster Bay* on the 17th.

24. REIN BAY AND TALASEA

Early in March, PT's from Dreger Harbor were active in the waters off northwest New Britain, patrolling as far as Cape Hollman, on the northern tip of the Willaumez Peninsula. They landed scouts on Garowe Island, 50 miles to the north of New Britain, and helped prepare for landings on the Willaumez Peninsula by putting scouts ashore at Cape Schellong on the night of March 2/3 and picking them up the following night. On the night of March 5/6, PT's 323, 326, 329, 331, 347, and 370 took part in the landing operations, escorting 5 LCT's, 48 LCM's, 2 picket boats, and 18 LCV's to Volupai and covering them while a landing force of the Fifth Marine Regiment went ashore.

On March 17 the *Hilo,* with Squadrons 8 and 25, arrived at Rein Bay, and on the 26th moved to Talasea, on the eastern side of the Willaumez

Peninsula. There was little barge traffic in the area, however. PT's patrolled the coast until the end of May, but destroyed only two barges in March, seven in April, and none in May.

On the night of April 2/3, Lieutenant Thompson, in PT 355 (Ens. J. T. Cressey), with PT 120 (Ens. W. T. Shine, Jr., USNR) and PT 352 (Ens. T. A. Tucker, USNR), sighted a surfaced submarine standing out to sea from Hixon Bay and fired a spread of seven torpedoes at a range of 2 miles. The submarine appeared to lose headway, then slowly submerged. Five minutes after the torpedoes were released, the proper interval for a run to the target, all hands felt a heavy concussion. There were no reefs or land within 9 miles that could have detonated the torpedoes.

A few minutes later the boats sighted a barge half a mile to seaward. They sank it with gunfire and took one prisoner. Although PT's could find no signs of damage to the submarine, the next day aircraft sighted an oil slick half a mile square, which persisted and spread for several days. This, again, was not sufficient evidence to support a claim of damage or destruction.

Late in May two PT's landed Army commando troops at Ea Ea, 75 miles east of Talasea, and on the neighboring island of Lolobau.

For more than a year PT's had operated in the Southwest Pacific without casualties from mistaken identification. At Talasea, in little more than a month, two cruel errors cost 24 lives, 25 wounded, 4 PT's, and 2 aircraft.

On the morning of March 27, Lt. Crowell C. Hall, USNR, executive officer of Squadron 25, in PT 353 (Ens. George H. Guckert, USNR), with PT 121 (Ens. Richard B. Secrest, USNR), was trying to thread a way through reefs to Ewasse, in Bangula Bay, to investigate a reported enemy schooner. At 0745 four P-40's of the 78th Squadron, Royal Australian Air Force, operating out of Kiriwina, flew over and Lieutenant Hall asked them by radio to investigate the schooner. The planes complied, and reported it had been strafed previously and was no longer a worthwhile target. No sooner had the boats turned to leave than they were attacked by four other P-40's of the 78th Squadron and a Beaufighter of the 30th Squadron, RAAF. A second Beaufighter recognized the PT's and throughout the attack attempted to call off the other Beaufighter by radio and to maneuver to head off the P-40's.

No order to open fire was given on either boat. After the planes made several runs, gunners on the 353 fired seven or eight rounds of 40 mm. and five rounds of 37mm., and those on the 121 fired seven rounds of 20mm. and three short bursts of .50 caliber. Lieutenant Hall on the 353 and Ensign Secrest on the 121 stopped the firing immediately. Both boats burned, exploded, and sank, except for a portion of the bow of the 121. Shortly after the attack two P-40's of the group that had investigated the schooner returned. They dropped a liferaft to the survivors and sent in a radio report of the tragedy. Five hours later a P-40 guided PT's 346 and 354 to the survivors.

Four officers and four enlisted men were dead; four officers and eight enlisted men were wounded; two PT's were completely destroyed. In part the losses were caused by a failure in communications. The message reporting the intended movements of PT's had been placed in the wrong file at 78th Squadron headquarters, so the pilots had not been told that PT's would be operating in the area. In part the losses were caused by failure of the pilots to recognize the PT's. The first P-40's recognized them and gave them a helping hand. One Beaufighter in the second group recognized them and tried to stop the attack. The other pilots simply mistook them for enemy craft.

On the night of April 28/29, PT 347 (Lt. (jg.) Robert J. Williams), while patrolling with PT 350 (Lt. (jg.) Stanley L. Manning, USNR), went on a reef at Cape Pomas, 5 miles from the Southwest Pacific-South Pacific dividing line at Cape Lambert. The 350 was still trying to tow off the 347 when, at 0700, two Marine Corps Corsairs attacked the boats. The PT's did not recognize the planes as our own until the attack was over, and shot one of them down. Three men were killed aboard the 350, and the boat was damaged, so it set out at once for Talasea.

Lieutenant Thompson, aboard *Hilo* at Talasea, received word of the attack by radio. He requested air cover from Cape Gloucester and immediately got underway for Cape Pomas in PT 346 (Lt. (jg.) James R. Burk, USNR).

In the meantime, the pilot of the remaining Corsair reported to his base at Green Island in the Solomons that he had attacked two enemy gunboats, 125 feet long, in Lassul Bay. He was guilty not only of mistaken identification; he had placed the attack 15 miles inside of South Pacific territory, and 20 miles from Cape Pomas. As a result, four Corsairs, six Avengers, four Hellcats, and eight Dauntless dive bombers were ordered to strike immediately to finish off the gunboats. They did not find the targets in Lassul Bay, but eventually located them in Southwest Pacific waters, at Cape Pomas.

By then Lieutenant Thompson had arrived and was attempting to free the 347. Lieutenant Williams told him that planes were approaching from the north. Thompson recognized them as friendly, told Williams that they were the air cover he had requested, and gave instructions for the salvage work to continue. Then the planes attacked, so quickly that the boats had no time even to try to identify themselves until bombs were dropping all around them. When all attempts at identification failed, the 346, in desperation, opened fire and shot down one Hellcat. This only aggravated the attack. The planes strafed and bombed until both boats were completely destroyed.

The flight commander notified the Green Island base of the loss of the Hellcat, and a Catalina was sent to try to find the pilot. The Catalina failed in this, but brought back 13 survivors from the PT's. Their arrival at Green Island was the first intimation to the air operations office there that the plane targets had not been enemy vessels.

Three PT officers, 11 PT enlisted men, and 2 plane pilots were dead; 4 PT officers and 9 PT enlisted men were wounded; 2 PT's and 2 planes were completely destroyed. The primary causes of the losses were failure to identify the boats, faulty navigation, and failure of the pilots to observe the dividing line between the two operating areas.

25. NEW BRITAIN: SOUTH COAST

During March and April, PT's from Dreger made 28 patrols along the south coast of New Britain, and claimed destruction of one 175-foot cargo ship, a lugger, 9 barges, and a floatplane. While there was not enough enemy activity to justify nightly patrols, occasional patrols paid off. Also, there was ample evidence that the mere presence of PT's served to hold down the barge traffic.

The patrols were intended to cut the supply line from Rabaul to Gasmata, which still was believed to be the principal Japanese stronghold on the south coast. On the night of March 16/17, Lt. (jg.) Raymond C. Turnbull, USNR, in PT 146 (Ens. George W. Burgers, USNR), with PT 353, set out to patrol from Gasmata eastward to Rainbow Bay. The boats became separated about 0230, and at daylight the 353 returned to Dreger Harbor, but Turnbull kept the 146 at Fulleborn Harbor, 25 miles east of Gasmata, until 0830, when he started a slow daylight sweep westward. Five miles east of Lindenhaven the 146 sank a 35-foot landing craft, and half a mile east of Lindenhaven sank two more barges of the same type.

Crew members dine aboard a New Guinea PT in informal attire. The tropical sun beating down on the decks made shirts an unbearable discomfort.

The 146 continued slowly west until it was just east of Gasmata. Turnbull saw a large, freshly camouflaged barge on the beach at the Anwek River mouth, and another, 60 yards up the river. He took the 146 in to close range and destroyed both barges. Since there had been no resistance, or indeed any signs of enemy activity whatsoever, he continued into the harbor of Gasmata, passing 75mm. gun emplacements at the entrance. The waterfront was studded with machinegun nests and pillboxes. None of them was manned. Finally the 146 tied up at the jetty on Gasmata Island. Turnbull led a party of men ashore to make a close inspection. When he returned to Dreger Harbor he brought surprising and wonderful news: Gasmata had been completely evacuated.

Turnbull's exploit led the next day to a close reconnaissance of Lindenhaven, an enemy base 10 miles east of Gasmata, by Lt. (jg.) Roland B. Steele, USNR, in PT 150 (Lt. (jg.) Robert S. Milford, USNR), with PT 192 (Lt. (jg.) T. J. Lovvorn, USNR). The boats tested out the harbor defenses with close-range gunfire, scoring hits on nine pillboxes, a large storage tank, a heavy gun emplacement, a supply dump, and a bivouac area. They found that Lindenhaven, like Gasmata, had been recently but thoroughly evacuated.

Thereafter the southern New Britain patrols had to extend further eastward to find targets. On one of these patrols, on the night of April 12/13, Lt. Robert Leeson, USNR, who had relieved Lt. Edward W. Roberts, USNR, as commander of Squadron 7, ran PT 135 aground near Crater Point, during a rain squall. Heavy surf drove the 135 up on the beach and the accompanying boat, PT 137, could not pull it off. The 137 took the 135's crew aboard and set the grounded boat ablaze with gunfire.

As had been the case in the past, when the boats were operating from Kiriwina, the south coast of New Britain continued to be the only area where enemy planes attempted to harass the PT's with any regularity. The planes caused no damage, and on the night of March 12/13, Lt. (jg.) Alfred G. Vanderbilt, USNR, in PT 196, and Lt. (jg.) Cyrus R. Taylor, USNR, in PT 193, had the satisfaction of shooting down a floatplane in flames after it had dropped a bomb 150 yards astern of the 193.

On the night of April 13/14, Lt. (jg.) Julius O. Aschenbach, USNR, in PT 132, and Ens. Fendall M. Clagett, USNR, in PT 133, attacked eight barges in Henry Reid Bay, sinking four, destroying two on the beach, and damaging the other two. During repeated runs on the barges, the PT's were attacked by an enemy plane which dropped four bombs and made two strafing runs. The PT's refused to be diverted from their own attack and kept blasting away at the barges until they were out of ammunition.

26. SAIDOR

Saidor continued as an operating base longer than any other location in eastern New Guinea. From the establishment of the base in March until the end of June, Saidor PT's made 185 patrols, extending up the coast as far as Cape Girgir, 30 miles beyond Hansa Bay. Squadron 24 remained at Saidor until June 17, when it was withdrawn to Dreger for overhaul. Squadron 10, under Lt. Comdr. Jack E. Gibson, first of the Solomons squadrons to be transferred to New Guinea, joined Squadron 24 at Saidor on April 28. Heavy barge traffic made Saidor a productive operating point; the strongly defended coastline—PT's drew shore fire at least 64 times in March, April, and May—made it a dangerous one.

On the night of April 2/3, Lt. (jg.) Henry M. Curry 3d, USNR, in PT 339, with PT 341 (Ens. Oscar C. Blanchard, USNR), found four barges in Sarang

Harbor. As the PT's closed to 50 yards to make their first run, the barges opened fire. Before the run was completed, the boats met heavy fire from 37mm. batteries and machineguns on shore. The 339 made a high-speed firing run on the batteries, while the 341 concentrated on the barges. The boats then made five more runs, dividing their fire between shore and barges. Return fire from the barges ceased after the first run, and the shore batteries were silenced on the third run. The 341 was hit three times by 37 mm. shells on the second run and two men were slightly wounded by fragments, but the boat kept fighting until three barges had been sunk. The fourth barge, damaged, escaped behind reefs in the harbor. Besides silencing the shore batteries, the PT's started a large fire on the beach, apparently a fuel dump, which burned brilliantly for three-quarters of an hour.

On the night of April 4/5, Lt. (jg.) Roman G. Mislicky, in PT 334, and Ens. Edward F. Lyons, USNR, in PT 340, sank two of three 110-foot barges near Puttkamer Point, 15 miles beyond Sarang Harbor, despite heavy fire from the barges and from shore. The boats broke off the action when a hit on the 334 started a fire in the crew's quarters. Heading out to sea, Mislicky found that he had very little rudder control. It turned out that the fire was confined to three mattresses, which were heaved over the side, but a rudder bar had been shot away, so the boats could not return to pursue the third barge. During this action the 334 fired 25 rounds from its new 75mm. gun at the shore batteries. Although the 75 operated well and carried a terrific punch, it eventually was discarded in favor of the 40mm., which was faster firing and had tracer control.

On the night of April 8/9, Lt. (jg.) Elmer L. Douglas, USNR, in PT 336, and Ens. Oscar C. Blanchard, USNR, in PT 341, were searching for barges close to shore near Cape Gourdon, 20 miles beyond Puttkamer Point, when three shore batteries started firing 3-inch shells at them. The 341 pumped over 50 rounds of 40mm. into the first one and silenced it. On the 336, Richard E. Betty, MoMM1c, the 20mm. gunner, was hit by shell fragments in the right arm and ankle and was thrown to the deck. He picked himself up and returned to his gun, firing until he was out of ammunition.

Several of the Saidor boats were hit by shore fire, but none sustained serious damage except the 337, lost in Hansa Bay on the night of March 6/7, 1944. The only other PT lost during the operations from Saidor was PT 339 (Lt. Henry M. Curry, USNR), which grounded on a sandbar on the night of May 26/27 while preparing to strafe the beach at Purpur, at the mouth of the Ramu River. The crew was taken aboard PT 335 and the boat was destroyed to prevent possible capture.

Besides the usual barge patrols, the Saidor boats performed a variety of missions, including the rescue of several downed aviators; landing scouting parties, frequently composed of PT personnel, in the Bogadjim-Erima area in Astrolabe Bay; and a close-range dawn bombardment of the beach in support of an Army landing at Yalau Plantation, 20 miles above Saidor. These boats were particularly well equipped for work against shore installations. Starting with Lt. (jg.) Elmer L. Douglass's PT 336, five boats of Squadron 24 were armed with racks for 4.5-inch barrage rockets. Although not sufficiently accurate for regular employment against surface targets, the rockets were excellent for shore bombardment. A barrage of 24 rockets, each weighing 27 pounds, could be released in 4 seconds to blanket a wide area with high explosives.

At dawn on April 7, 10 PT's and 11 B–25 bombers made a coordinated strike against Japanese shore positions on Karkar Island, and on June 2 6 PT's participated in amphibious landings by units of the Fifth Australian Division at Biu and Kavilo Bays on Karkar. On April 10, Lieutenant Commander Davis boarded the destroyer *Hutchins* to pinpoint coastal targets for the *Hutchins, Bache,* and *Daly* at Hansa Bay, Ulingan Harbor, Alexishafen, and Madang. Capt. Kenmore M. McManes, Commander Destroyer Squadron 24, reported, "His assistance, backed by his familiarity with the targets all along this long coast, was invaluable in making the small ammunition allowance count. Lieutenant Commander Davis was particularly pleased at the opportunity to range shots into the confines of Ulingen Harbor where MTB's have been unable to penetrate because of the narrow entrance."

Allied troops drove overland to Madang on April 24 and Alexishafen on April 26, clearing Astrolabe Bay of the Japanese. For another month the Saidor boats had good hunting along the coast beyond Astrolabe Bay, claiming 19 barges destroyed and 5 damaged in the 75-mile stretch between Dove Point and the mouth of the Sepik River. In June the enemy, trapped in the Wewak area by new Allied landings, was forced to withdraw his remaining barges to the west. The Saidor PT's found barges only once during the month, on the night of June 4/5, when Lt. (jg.) Otis J. Hiebeler, USNR, in PT 338, and Ens. E. L. Mills, USNR, in PT 332, destroyed two of them near the mouth of the Sepik River. The enemy also withdrew his artillery; the boats encountered no shore fire except at Hansa Bay. Patrols from Saidor were discontinued on June 25 for lack of targets.

27. AITAPE

By the middle of April, Allied forces controlled the New Guinea coast past Saidor and were pushing toward Madang and Alexishafen. The occupation of western New Britain, the Admiralties, and Emirau Island had effectively neutralized Rabaul. The growing Southwest Pacific Forces were ready to strike again, in a bypassing operation of far greater magnitude than any they had been able to undertake in the past.

Supported by warships, including carriers, of the Fifth and Seventh Fleets, the Seventh Amphibious Force landed units of the Sixth Army on the morning of April 22 at Humboldt and Tanahmerah Bays, more than 500 miles to the northwest of Dreger Harbor, and at Aitape, about 400 miles northwest of Dreger. The landings isolated the 18th Imperial Japanese Army, some 50,000 strong, in the area between Wewak and Hansa Bay. This force had no aircraft and no naval vessels except barges, but it had vast supplies of stores and equipment at Wewak. During May and June the enemy moved westward and launched a powerful and determined drive toward Aitape, defended by the 32d Infantry Division.

As usual, the enemy depended heavily on barges to maintain his supply line, and in this region, to a greater extent than anywhere else in the Southwest Pacific, attempted to protect his barges with shore batteries. In 8 out of 10 attacks the PT's were under fire from enemy guns. The boats of Squadron 7 alone were fired on by shore batteries on 64 out of 100 nights.

Squadron 7, under Lt. Comdr. Robert Leeson, USNR, and Squadron 18, under Lt. Comdr. Henry M. S. Swift, USNR, arrived at Aitape with *Oyster Bay* on April 26, 4 days after the first landings. Squadron 8, under Lt. Edward I. Farley, USNR, arrived on May 1 with the LST 201, and the next day Squadron 18 and *Oyster Bay* moved up the line to Hollandia, in Humboldt Bay.

The boats had their first action on the night of April 28/29, when Ens. Francis L. Cappaert, USNR, in PT 370, and Ens. Louis A. Fanget, USNR, in PT 368, sank three barges in Nightingale Bay, east of Wewak. One of the barges had been loaded with two 75mm. fieldpieces and 45 soldiers. The boats tried to take prisoners, but could only get two. The others resisted capture and some deliberately drowned themselves rather than be taken aboard the boats.

One of the prisoners announced, "Me officer," and after questioning told Cappaert that more barges were headed toward Nightingale Bay. The boats waited, and sure enough, three more barges arrived. The PT's sank them and took a third prisoner, who was clutching a box of documents which he was reluctant to give up. His reluctance was understandable. It was learned later that he was one of three men assigned to guard a box of secret Army documents being sent from Hansa Bay to Wewak.

When the PT's returned to Aitape the officer who had so obligingly told Cappaert that more barges were on the way was questioned further in Japanese by Army authorities. In his own language he was even more voluble. He dictated a barge movement schedule which greatly aided the PT's in intercepting and destroying 15 barges and a picket boat, and damaging 8 barges during the next 5 nights.

That was an odd trait of Japanese prisoners. Most of them preferred death to capture but, once captured, they usually were docile and willing, almost eager, to give information. And while their information might be limited, it was generally reliable. They seldom attempted deception. The big job was to capture them, and PT crews became fairly adept at it. One method was to crack a man over the head with a boathook and haul him up on deck. Another technique, more certain, was to drop a cargo net over the bow. Two men climbed down on the net. Other members of the crew held them by lines around their waists, so that their hands were free. They would blackjack a floating Japanese and put a line on him so that he could be hauled aboard. These were rough methods, but gentle ones didn't work. The Japanese almost never took a line willingly, and as long as they were conscious would fight to free themselves from a boathook.

On the night of May 2, PT's 114 and 144 sank two barges and damaged four more on the beach west of Bogia Harbor. Three hours later, at 0130, the 114 went aground on a fringing reef 400 yards offshore from Yarin, on Kairiru Island. The 114 jettisoned its torpedoes and depth charges, and at 0630 was pulled off the reef by the 144. Preparations had been made to abandon ship, and by the time the boat was freed, the crew of the 114 had carelessly permitted a raft containing the boat's codes and other confidential publications to drift away.

As soon as the boats returned to the tender and reported their loss, Lieutenant Commander Leeson set out to recover the publications in PT 129, of which his brother, Ens. A. Dix Leeson, USNR, was boat captain. With the 129 was Ens. Edmund F. Wakelin, USNR, in PT 134. Late in the afternoon the boats sighted the raft on the beach at Yarin. With knowledge that the Japanese had big guns nearby, and in full view of a native village and a Japanese military lean-to within 600 yards of the raft, Bob Leeson swam 400 yards across the reef in daylight to tow the raft back to the waiting PT's. The publications were intact.   Ten minutes after Leeson's return, a 3-inch gun opened fire on the boats from a position half a mile from Yarin.   The boats returned fire and withdrew to seaward.   After dark they again closed the coast of Kairiru Island when they sighted three heavily laden barges, which ran toward the beach to get under cover of shore batteries.   The PT's sank two of them and damaged the third before damage to the 129 forced them to retire.   A 20mm. shell had blown a 14-inch hole in an exhaust stack and started a small fire under the starboard engine.   Clarence L. Nelson, MoMM2c, USNR, put out the fire with a hand extinguisher before he was overcome by exhaust fumes and carbon dioxide from the extinguisher. A. F. Hall, MoMM3c, USNR, also was overcome.   Ens. Richard Holt, USNR, third officer of the 129, quickly revived both men by artificial respiration.   The squadron medical officer said that Holt's prompt action saved Hall's life.

After the engineroom had been aired out, the 129 led the way back to the beach on two engines to launch a salvo of 24 rockets against several beached barges and shore guns that were still firing at the boats.   The rocket barrage silenced the enemy fire.   During the entire action the boats also had been under inaccurate fire from large naval guns situated on the beach several miles away.

There were many actions of this type at Aitape.   Nowhere else were the Japanese so determined to maintain their coastal supply line and to protect their barges with shore batteries; nowhere else were the PT's more determined to strangle the supply.   PT's were in action almost every night, and the action was usually violent.   During 5 months at Aitape (most of the actions took place in the first 3), the PT's claimed 115 barges sunk or destroyed, more than a dozen trucks destroyed or damaged on the coastal roads, and damage to many coastal installations.   In view of the intensity of enemy resistance, the PT's suffered remarkably few losses.   Three men were killed and seven were wounded.   Eleven PT's were hit by enemy fire, but only one, the 133, was destroyed.

Lt. (jg.) Fendall M. Clagett, USNR, in PT 133, with Ens. T. E. Moran, USNR, in PT 128, attacked three barges near Cape Pus, in Muschu Strait, on the night of 15/16 July, sinking one and damaging the other two on their first run.   As the PT's were circling for a second run, a 40mm. gun opened fire from shore.   The first round hit the 133 amidships, setting the gasoline tanks ablaze. For 5 minutes the crew tried to bring the flames under control. Then Clagett gave the order to abandon ship. The entire crew, except for one man lost overboard immediately after the hit, got away in two rubber liferafts. Ten minutes later the boat started exploding. In another 10 minutes a huge explosion split it in two sections, which sank at once. The 128 was holed in four places and had two men wounded. PT 143, called in by radio from an adjoining patrol area, picked up the crew of the 133.

Throughout the Aitape campaign the PT's worked in close cooperation with the 32d Infantry Division, which was meeting the drive of the 18th Japanese Army. Our Army found that air reconnaissance was not particularly satisfactory because of dense jungle growth right down to the shoreline. "PT boat reconnaissance," the 32d Division's report on the Aitape operation said, "provided considerable information of the enemy movements during the periods of darkness. These boats, observing from 100 to 800 yards offshore between our front lines and the enemy troop concentrations in the vicinity of Wewak, were more able to report accurately on the location of enemy troops and supply movements and enemy bivouac areas."

As usual, the PT's landed and picked up many Army scouting parties, and on several occasions provided fire support for minor amphibious operations. In the early hours of May 15, Leeson received an urgent request from the Army for PT's to cover the withdrawal of 300 men surrounded near Ulau Mission, 25 miles east of Aitape and at Marubian Mission, another mile and a half east. Leeson, in PT 131; Farley, in PT 149, with PT's 120, 127, 132, and 142, escorted two LCT's and two LCM's to Marubian and Ulau. The PT's strafed enemy positions heavily and laid a smokescreen which enabled the landing craft to beach and evacuate the troops without casualty despite heavy enemy mortar and small arms fire.

PT's also worked closely with Beaufighters and P-39's of the 78th Wing, Royal Australian Air Force, based at Aitape. Covered by these planes the boats could make daylight strikes without undue risk. The enemy was reluctant to unmask his coastal guns while the planes were overhead. The most successful of these strikes was made late in the afternoon of June 26, when Beaufighters on patrol with PT 130 (Lt. (jg.) Ian D. Malcolm, USNR) and PT 132 (Ens. Paul H. Jones, USNR) asked the boats to investigate a possible target on the coast of Muschu Island. The boats had to close within 75 yards of the beach before they could see two barges behind nets of fresh green foliage strung down to the water from overhanging trees. Further investigation located several more camouflaged nests. The boats made four deliberate firing runs. Camouflage nets came tumbling down, revealing at least 14 barges shot up, of which 6 were ablaze. Ricochets from the 20mm. guns started a grass fire ashore which in turn touched off a concealed ammunition dump. After the first explosion flames billowed 100 feet in the air, with great clouds of smoke rising above them. Four more tremendous explosions followed. By this time it was dark and the boats were low on ammunition, so they returned to the tender, took on a fresh supply, and came back to Muschu after daylight under cover of four P–39's. The boats made four more slow firing runs, completing the destruction of 15 barges. Then they rocketed a supply dump and withdrew while the P–39's bombed and strafed the area. The boats received considerable sniper fire from shore, which did no damage, and a few inaccurate rounds of 40mm. fire from Cape Pus, across Muschu Strait.

Night-flying Beaufort bombers of the 71st Wing, RAAF, also cooperated with the boats. On the night of July 2/3, a Beaufort told PT 134 (Ens. Edmund F. Wakelin, USNR) and PT 189 (Lt. (jg.) Joseph J. Fitzpatrick, USNR) that six barges were moving close to the beach at Sowam, 7 miles east of the PT's. As the boats approached Sowam, the Beaufort dropped a flare and reported that there were now eight barges. The PT's still were not close enough to see them, so the Beaufort dropped a bomb on the barges. The boats headed for the spot where the bomb exploded. The Beaufort told them that the barges then were half a mile further east. The PT's found five barges and sank three of them in two gunnery runs. The 134 then fired 12 rockets which exploded all around the remaining barges. The Beaufort reported that both had sunk. Soon afterwards the Beaufort reported that the last three of the original eight barges were escaping to the east, and dropped a flare 500 feet over them. The PT's forced them to the beach, made 2 strafing runs on them, and fired a salvo of 10 rockets around them. The Beaufort dropped a bomb near them. The PT's returned to the tender, 40 miles away, for more ammunition, and first thing in the morning came back with two P–39's to finish off the barges. They had been removed from the beach, so the PT's strafed and rocketed and the planes strafed and bombed two possible barge hideouts nearby. From time to time during the night action, 75mm. and machineguns started to fire on the boats from shore. The Beaufort promptly strafed and silenced every gun that opened fire, permitting the PT's to continue their runs on the barges.

Sometimes the PT's were able to give the Air Force a hand. PT's 128 and 131 had started out to patrol on the afternoon of May 28 when they received word from the base that an RAAF pilot, Flight Officer R. A. Graetz, had been forced down at the mouth of the Danmap River, in enemy territory 35 miles east of Aitape. The boats found the flier on the beach. He was injured and could not swim out to them or haul in a line which the boats shot to him with a line-throwing gun. Lt. William W. Stewart, USNR, and Ens. Gregory J. Azarigian, USNR, disregarding sniper fire from the beach, paddled ashore in a rubber raft and rescued the pilot.

Lieutenant Farley made an interesting experiment, having a 60-inch Army searchlight mounted on one of the boats of his squadron, PT 143, to aid the boats in spotting barges close to the beach. "We used it for about 2 weeks on about six patrols with no tangible results," Farley said. "This was not so much the fault of the light but the fact that there seemed to be little barge movement during that period. By the time the barge traffic started up, the boys on the 143 had tired a little of being the guinea pigs and we were also afraid of causing some permanent strain on the hull so we dismounted the light and generator and considered the test a success insofar as being able to prove that the boats could handle the light and that control of the beam by radio instructions was practical. The searchlight boat would stay two to five thousand yards offshore—the two accompanying boats close inshore. The control boat would call for illumination of suspicious areas and direct the beam by a fairly simple system of training and elevating orders. The searchlight was fired at several times but the boys doused the light quick and being pretty far out it wasn't very dangerous. The beam was amply effective at a mile and a half range. Of course the water had to be calm to use it effectively."

The Aitape boats made several joint patrols with the Australian destroyers, HMAS *Arunta* and HMAS *Warramunga*. On the night of 19/20 July, PT 144 (Lt. (jg.) J. K. Cunningham, USNR) and PT 149 (Ens. Mason H. Blandford, USNR), patrolling with the *Warramunga*, attacked a group of barges at the mouth of the Ninahau River. On their first run the boats made many hits on two barges, but the fire from shore batteries was so intense that *Warramunga* ordered the PT's to pull out while the destroyer shelled the batteries and silenced them. *Warramunga* then fired starshell to illuminate the barges, but the boats were unable to find them. Later, when the patrol had proceeded 15 miles to the east, *Warramunga* picked up a radar target close to the beach and vectored the boats toward it. The boats found the target, a group of three barges, and sank two of them. The third escaped to the beach. At the request of the PT's *Warramunga* fired star-shell. Under this illumination the PT's sighted the barge on the beach and destroyed it. The boats received light fire from shore batteries, so when they had completed their run they withdrew and *Warramunga* bombarded the area.

On May 11, Destroyer Division 48, comprising the *Abner Read, Bache,* and *Beale,* under Comdr. John B. McLean, was ordered to shell the coast in the Wewak area to destroy gun positions which were endangering PT operations. Four PT officers went aboard each destroyer to point out targets. The destroyers shelled 29 target areas in which 39 shore batteries were known to be situated. Similar missions were carried out, again with PT officers aboard to pinpoint targets, on the night of June 18/19 by *Abner Read, Ammen, Bache,* and HMS *Ariadne* and on the night of August 31/September 1 by *Lang, Stack,* and *Murray* and again HMS *Ariadne.*

In operations ashore, the enemy made his most ambitious strike on the night of July 10/11, when two regiments, supported by a heavy artillery barrage, broke through the center of our lines on the Driniumor River, 10 miles from Aitape. Many enemy troops crossed the river and penetrated several miles toward Aitape. By July 19 the enemy had been pushed back again across the Driniumor River. His attack, originally successful, had been turned to disaster. The two regiments that broke through our lines were nearly annihilated. By the middle of August the enemy was being driven south and east toward the Torricelli Mountains and the 18th Japanese Army was no longer an effective threat. Wewak, like Rabaul, was neutralized.

Barge contacts in the Aitape area were few after the end of July. The PT's continued to harass the enemy during August and September by strafing and rocketing shore installations, frequently in daylight strikes with Beaufighters and P–39's. Squadrons 7 and 8 were joined on July 18 by Squadron 33, a new squadron freshly arrived from the United States, commanded by Lt. A. Murray Preston, USNR. The tender *Mobjack* arrived from the South Pacific on August 1, and later in the month *Orestes,* a new LST-type tender, arrived to relieve the LST 201, which by then had been renamed USS *Pontus.* The *Pontus* departed Aitape on August 22 for overhaul in Brisbane. Squadron 33 and the *Mobjack* moved 380 miles up the line at the end of August to a new base at Mios Woendi, where they were joined a month later by Squadrons 7 and 8 and *Orestes.*

28. MIOS WOENDI

Squadron 18 and *Oyster Bay* had moved to Hollandia on May 2. On the 11th they were joined by Squadron 12, under Lt. Comdr. Robert J. Bulkley, Jr., USNR. The area was not a rewarding one. There were no great concentrations of the enemy along the coast, and almost no barge traffic. The boats landed several Army scouting parties and made nightly patrols, but by June 5 had sighted only eight barges, of which they claimed to have destroyed seven.

Army forces occupied Wakde Island, 115 miles beyond Hollandia, on May 18th, and 9 days later moved another 180 miles up the line to land at Bosnek, on Biak Island in Geelvink Bay.

The great distance of Hollandia, Wakde, and Biak from Dreger Harbor made it imperative to establish a new major repair and supply base. PT Base 21, under Lt. David M. Alexander, USNR, was sent into Hollandia on a Liberty ship, *James Buchanan,* but because of the difficult terrain and the greater need of other units for the few suitable base sites, was not unloaded from the ship. When plans were made for the Biak operation, it seemed likely that Mios Woendi, a small island in a coral atoll 10 miles south of Biak, would be a suitable location for the new base. Army forces occupied Mios Woendi without opposition on June 2. The flat, sandy island, situated on a deep water lagoon, was the finest base site the boats had had in New Guinea.

The original plan was to reserve Mios Woendi for the repair and supply base, and to establish a small operating base at Sorido Lagoon, on Biak. The Army met unexpectedly stiff resistance on Biak, however, and did not take Sorido on schedule, so when it came time for the PT's to move into Geelvink Bay, they went to Mios Woendi.

Patrols from Hollandia were secured June 5 and *Oyster Bay* and Squadrons 12 and 18 moved to Wakde. Squadron 12 moved on to Mios Woendi the following day and started patrols on the 8th. Squadron 21, under Lt. Paul T. Rennell, USNR, arrived on June 11, and Squadron 9, under Lt. Michael R. Pessolano, on June 19.

The threat of enemy air attack made it unwise to send in a tender at the beginning. PT Advance Base 2, under Lt. Comdr. Herman F. Straw, USNR, was put ashore on June 6. With the base came a newly formed unit, the PT Advance Base Construction Detachment of the 113th Naval Construction Battalion, under Lt. Harold F. Liberty, USNR. This Seabee detachment, comprising 2 officers and 55 men with construction equipment, set up the base facilities and built piers in record time. Later in the month, when we had gained sufficient control of the air to permit bringing the Liberty ship with Base 21 into the lagoon, the Seabees greatly expedited the construction of the repair and overhaul base. The unit was retained as part of Task Group 70.1 until the end of the war, and contributed greatly to the success of PT operations by rapid construction of operating bases throughout the Philippines.

The same considerations that led to the establishment of a major base at Mios Woendi led to the disestablishment of PT Base 4 at Kana Kopa. Base 4 was so far behind the scene of action as to be practically useless as a repair base. Port facilities at Finschhafen and Langemak Bay had been developed to the point where supply ships arrived there directly from the United States, so Dreger Harbor became a more favorable site for a rear supply base than Kana Kopa. On June 15 Base 4 was decommissioned and all personnel and equipment were moved to Dreger Harbor except for the main engine overhaul shop, which was consolidated with other Navy repair facilities at Ladava

NR&L (MOD)−32496

Torpedo dump at Mios Woendi.

Mission, Milne Bay. On the same day, the base at Dreger Harbor, which until then technically was an advance base under Task Group 70.1, was commissioned as a regular PT base under the administrative jurisdiction of the Commander Service Force Seventh Fleet.

Squadrons and tenders arriving from the Solomons and the United States staged through Dreger Harbor. Squadron 6, which arrived at Dreger on May 20, was decommissioned on May 29, and its eight boats were distributed among Squadrons 8, 9, 10, and 25, which had suffered operational losses.

As the supply line lengthened and the number of boats increased, it became imperative to acquire more cargo ships to carry spare parts and other special PT equipment between bases. At the time of the Aitape and Hollandia landings, Commander Bowling obtained from the Sixth Army the assignment of four F-ships, little freighters built on the lines of a Dutch wooden shoe, each of which had a capacity of about 100 tons. For the rest of the war these little ships plied back and forth between PT bases, making a maximum speed of 8 knots.

With the expansion of the task group, the staff grew, and *Portunus,* with its quonset hut on deck, became more and more congested. The arrival of new tenders made it possible to convert *Hilo,* which had never been entirely adequate as a tender, to a command ship. Shops and repair equipment were removed and the space was used for staff offices. Commander Bowling shifted his pennant to *Hilo* on June 20, and early in July moved the base of his command from Dreger Harbor to Mios Woendi, arriving there in *Hilo* on the 9th.

29. OPERATIONS IN GEELVINK BAY

The first action at Mios Woendi came unexpectedly on the morning of June 12, when Lieutenant Rennell, in Lt. (jg.) Kenneth D. Molloy's PT 326, set out for Biak for a meeting with Army officers. On the way four enemy planes dived out of the sun and dropped four bombs which landed within 75 feet of the boat. The 326 scored a 40mm. hit on one plane, which fell into the sea in flames. The remaining planes attacked the destroyer *Kalk,* patrolling 2 miles to the west. The *Kalk* shot down another plane, but herself took a direct bomb hit amidships which heavily damaged her superstructure and started fires below decks. Four officers and 26 men were killed; 4 officers and 36 men were wounded.

The entire action was visible from Mios Woendi. As soon as *Kalk* was hit, every PT in the lagoon got underway at top speed for the stricken ship. One after another the PT's drew alongside *Kalk*, which was still underway, and removed wounded. The PT's carried them to Bosnek and transferred them to the LST 469, which had a surgical team on board. En route boat officers gave first aid, administering plasma to the more seriously wounded.

That night Lt. (jg.) William N. Bannard, USNR, in PT 190, and Lt. (jg.) James C. Higgins, USNR, in PT 146, had the first barge action in the area, sinking three large barges on the north coast of Biak. A prisoner of war later reported that these barges had been carrying 200 men of the 202d Pioneer Unit. He said that the commanding officer, a Lieutenant Commander Nagata, and most of his men had been killed.

Geelvink Bay was not as productive an area as Aitape, but for several months the boats did a steady business in destroying barges. During June the enemy made sporadic attempts to reinforce his garrison on Biak, sending barges from Manokwari, at the northwestern end of Geelvink Bay, via the island of Noemfoor to the west of Biak. The boats' claims for the month were seven barges destroyed around Biak, three near Noemfoor and three in the vicinity of Manokwari. Attempts at reinforcement ended about the first of July. By then most of the remaining Japanese forces on Biak were bottled up in the northern part of the island, and on July 2 our Army occupied Noemfoor. Thereafter the PT's had practically all of their barge contacts on the western shores of Geelvink Bay. The enemy was trying to evacuate the entire area, running bargeloads of personnel and supplies to the western side of the bay, south of Manokwari, whence they could travel overland across the narrow neck of the Vogelkop (head of the New Guinea bird) to MacCluer Gulf, out of reach of our surface forces.

In July the PT's claimed 16 barges destroyed. There was also ample evidence from scouts, prisoners of war, and liberated Javanese that the threat of PT's was forcing the enemy to conduct most of his evacuation overland. This meant, of course, abandonment of most of his equipment, and a slow and dangerous trek for personnel—besides the natural hazards of overland travel in New Guinea, there was constant daylight coverage of evacuation routes by our aircraft.

Squadron 18 boats made shuttle patrols between Wakde and Mios Woendi in June. Leaving Wakde, the boats followed the New Guinea coast to the eastern entrance of Geelvink Bay, and then patrolled either the eastern

80—G—258692

Evaporator and water tower at Mios Woendi. Here, as at many bases, there was not enough natural fresh water and it was necessary to distill sea water.

shore of the bay or the coast of Japen Island, south of Mios Woendi. The boats arrived at Mios Woendi in the morning, laid over for the day and patrolled back to Wakde the following night. Although Catalinas joined the boats in these searches, the patrols were unproductive.

On July 9, Squadron 18, *Oyster Bay, Portunus,* and *Hilo* moved into Mios Woendi. Squadron 25, under Lt. Comdr. Richard E. Johnson, had arrived 2 days earlier. Squadron 24, under Lt. Comdr. N. Burt Davis, Jr., arrived on the 22d to stage for a new move up the coast to Sansapor.

While barge actions around Biak were few, the PT's carried out a variety of other missions. It was believed that the Japanese would try to evacuate key personnel by submarine from Korim Bay, on the north coast, so PT's kept a round-the-clock patrol off Korim Bay for a week, pairs of boats relieving one another on station. The boats saw no sign of enemy craft, but it was learned later that a submarine had approached and turned back without attempting to enter the bay, because of the presence of the PT's.

From NICA (Netherlands Indies Civil Administration) the PT's received interpreters. Natives, extremely loyal to the Dutch, would paddle out from shore in canoes and tell the interpreters where there were concentrations of Japanese along the shore. Sometimes they would come aboard the boats and help pilot them within range of the enemy camps. The boats would strafe the area and come back in a day or two, when the natives would give them a detailed account of the damage they had done. As time went on the Japanese on Biak ran low on rations. It was easy for natives to lure small groups of them away from their camps with promises of food. The natives overpowered the weakened Japanese and kept them in stockades until the next PT came by. Several times the natives turned over groups of prisoners to the PT's, as many as 30 at a time, with the promise that they would have more next time the PT's came to see them.

Of the barge actions at Biak, the most unusual was fought on the night of June 20/21 by Lt. (jg.) Joseph W. Burk, USNR, in PT 320, with PT 161 (Lt. (jg.) Rogers V. Waugh, USNR). Burk led the way into the Sorendidori River mouth on southern Biak, looking for suspected barge hideouts, and set the 320 on a reef. Soon afterwards three barges loaded with personnel and supplies approached from seaward. Although the 320 was stuck fast and could not maneuver, both PT's opened fire and the 320 illuminated the barges with mortar flares. Within 20 minutes the PT's sank all three barges. Then the 161 pulled the 320 off the reef.

As part of the preparations for Army landings on Noemfoor, PT's landed and picked up several scouting parties. Lt. Cyrus R. Taylor, USNR, in PT 193, with Lt. (jg.) Kermit W. Montz, USNR, in PT 331, put one of these parties ashore at Bani Point on the night of June 24/25. After picking up the scouts again the boats patrolled the north coast of Noemfoor, and attacked two barges. One sank quickly, the other ran up on a reef. As Taylor started his third run on this barge, the 193 also went hard aground. For over 3 hours the barge, which had been loaded with ammunition, burned and exploded, illuminating the 193. The 331 and the crew of the 193 kept working to refloat the PT until they saw enemy trucks move up and come to a stop on the beach half a mile away. It seemed probable that the enemy was moving up guns to shell the boat. All of the crew was put aboard the 331, except Taylor and three others who remained behind to destroy confidential material.

80-G-258662

The waterfront at Camp Taylor, Mios Woendi, largest PT base in New Guinea. The base was named for Lt. Cyrus R. Taylor, USNR, who was fatally wounded in action.

When this had been done Taylor released gasoline into the bilges to make sure that the boat would be thoroughly destroyed. Taylor was still below decks when there was a premature explosion. He made his way topside and into the water, and was taken, with the others, to the 331, but he was fatally burned.

Taylor was a brave and capable officer, who had been through many engagements with barges, aircraft, and shore batteries. The PT base at Mios Woendi was named Camp Taylor in his memory.

After the occupation of Noemfoor, when the boats had to go to the western shores of Geelvink Bay to find barges, encounters with shore batteries were not infrequent. On the night of July 6/7, Lieutenant (jg.) Burk, in PT 320, and Ens. Emil O. Sommer, Jr., USNR, in PT 160, fired mortar flares to illuminate a large barge on the beach at Waren Plantation. Immediately six to eight 90mm. guns back of the beach and several 3-inch guns on the beach itself opened fire on the boats. Burk kept his 40mm. firing at the shore batteries while the rest of his guns and all of the guns of the 160 concentrated on the barge. The boats kept firing until they thought they had rendered the barge unserviceable and then withdrew. Three hours later, after a sweep down the coast, they returned and saw another barge, 2 miles south of the first one. This time they used no flares, and destroyed the barge before the shore guns opened fire, but shells fell close during their retirement.

On the night of July 7/8, Lt. (jg.) William P. Hall, USNR, in PT 329, with Lt. (jg.) Rogers V. Waugh, USNR, in PT 161, sank a 130-foot lugger south of Cape Oransbari by gunfire and a well-placed depth charge from the 329. The boats took four prisoners, one of whom was a lieutenant colonel, one of the highest ranking Japanese prisoners taken in the entire New Guinea campaign. Hall won his Purple Heart in a peculiar way that night, being quite literally "wounded in the face of the enemy." One of the prisoners tried to attack him. Hall knocked him cold with a well-placed right to the mouth, but in doing so sprained his thumb and gashed his hand badly on the prisoner's teeth.

That was not the only case of hand-to-hand combat. PT personnel sometimes accompanied the NICA scouts on their reconnaissance missions to the islands of southwestern Geelvink Bay. Lt. Charles A. Black, USNR, was with a scouting party that surprised three Japanese sentries on the beach on Roemberpon Island. One of the sentries ran. Black chased him down the beach and clubbed him over the head with the butt of his rifle. In the meantime the scouts took the other two sentries, and within an hour Black, scouts, and captured sentries were aboard a PT on their way back to Mios Woendi.

30. AMSTERDAM ISLAND

The final amphibious operation of the New Guinea campaign was the landing on July 30, 1944, in the vicinity of Cape Sansapor, 250 miles west of Mios Woendi. The primary purpose of the landings, which completed Allied domination of the north coast of New Guinea, was to take a site for construction of an airfield from which fighter planes could take off to cover the projected invasion of the island of Morotai, in the Halmaheras.

PT's from Mios Woendi put a reconnaissance party ashore east of Cape Opmarai, near Cape Sansapor, on the night of July 14/15, and picked it up 2 nights later. The party found that there were suitable landing beaches, a good site for an airstrip, and no enemy troops in the immediate vicinity. Troops of the 6th Infantry Division went ashore on the morning of July 30 near Cape Opmari without opposition, and on the same day took three nearby islands, Mios Soe, Amsterdam, and Middleburg. The next day, in a shore-to-shore landing, troops occupied Cape Sansapor.

The Army had agreed to take a cove near Cape Sansapor for a PT base, but discovered that the cove was full of reefs which had not been apparent in aerial photographs. PT Advance Base 3, under Lt. Comdr. Herman F. Straw, USNR, arrived in LST 546 on the morning of August 2 with Squadron 24, under Lieutenant Commander Davis, and Squadron 25, under Lieutenant Commander Johnson. On the Army's recommendation, Davis accepted Amsterdam Island as a site for the base. The site was, indeed, the best in the area, but it offered little protection from shifting winds and seas. During the 2 months the base was in operation, there was a constant struggle to keep boats and floating equipment from blowing aground on reefs.

Although Amsterdam Island was favorably situated for interception of barge traffic between Manokwari and Sorong, the principal enemy base on the western end of the Vogelkop, the boats found only a few surface targets. They claimed eight barges and two 100-foot luggers in August, and three barges in September. They also claimed one of the largest vessels of the New Guinea campaign, a 200-foot ship, believed to be a minelayer, torpedoed on the night of September 21/22 by PT 342 (Lt. (jg.) Herbert W. Punches, USNR). Aerial reconnaissance on September 22 showed that this ship was sunk, resting on the bottom in shallow water.

The boats frequently met fire from heavy shore guns in the Sorong area, but the only damage to any boats came on the afternoon of August 30,

80–G–257024

PT's nose up on beach for unloading of camp gear to set up advance base at Amsterdam Island.

when three enemy planes attacked PT 344 (Lt. (jg.) John R. Tennant, USNR) and PT 115 (Ens. Robert G. Kittrell, USNR). The boats were only slightly damaged; one officer and six men were wounded, none critically.

PT's made 20 special missions to land and retrieve Army and NICA scouts, and on 11 occasions put ashore reconnaissance and raiding forces composed of PT personnel and led by Lieutenant Commander Davis. This force took 11 prisoners, killed perhaps twice that many Japanese, destroyed enemy stores and equipment, and captured many military documents, all without loss or injury to its own personnel.

A typical report is that of the action of September 20, when Davis, in Lt. (jg.) Herbert W. Punches's PT 342, with PT 341 (Lt. (jg.) Oscar C. Blanchard, USNR), led a daylight reconnaissance of the coast eastward from Cape of Good Hope to Cape Boropen.

"At 1310," the report said, "the patrol reached Cape Boropen, its eastern limit, and was about to return when the hull of a partially camouflaged lugger was sighted near the reef. While approaching the lugger for closer inspection, a small tent was sighted on the beach. It was immediately taken under fire by the 40mm.'s from both boats at a range of about 400 yards. A landing party of 10 men and 2 officers was then landed through the surf in rubber life rafts. A thorough search revealed the recent and hurried evacuation of the area by the enemy. In addition to the tent first sighted, which contained a portable radio station, a bivouac and stores area composed of eight shacks were located about a hundred yards inland. Some sniper fire was experienced and three Japs were sighted by the landing party. One was killed and the others, believed wounded, escaped inland. It is believed about 50 of the enemy were encamped at this outpost. The main camp, to a distance of about 100 yards outside its perimeter, was protected by slit trenches and pill boxes. Two large bomb shelters were located near the central and largest shack. At 1350, the landing party withdrew after capturing one Japanese Army 7.7 model 29 machine gun intact, destroying the drinking well and the majority of the stores sighted and setting fire to the largest shacks. Boats then proceeded in company to the base, arriving at 1730. All captured documents were turned over to the Army . . . The main radio set was destroyed by the opening barrage fire from the boats and hence no attempt was made to salvage."

Combat patrols were secured at Amsterdam on September 28, and in October the two squadrons returned to Mios Woendi for overhaul.

31. END OF THE NEW GUINEA CAMPAIGN

August was the best month at Mios Woendi, with claims of 26 barges destroyed. By September the Japanese evacuation was nearly completed, and the boats claimed only eight barges. Squadrons 9, 10, 12, 18, and 21 conducted 133 patrols during the 2 months. They were joined in September by part of Squadron 36, under Lt. Comdr. Francis D. Tappaan, USNR, and by the first two Higgins squadrons to arrive in the Southwest Pacific, squadrons that previously had served in the Aleutians. These were Squadron 13, under Lt. Comdr. Alvin W. Fargo, Jr., USNR, and Squadron 16, under Lt. Comdr. Almer P. Colvin.

Since June the Mios Woendi PT's had been assisted by night-flying Catalinas. Late in July, RAAF Beaufort bombers and Beaufighters began to work with them so they could do some of their hunting in daylight. Lt. (jg.) Kenneth D. Molloy, USNR, in PT 326, and Lt. (jg.) James N. Elliott, Jr., USNR, in PT 325, had had an unproductive night patrol when, on the morning of August 10, they met natives in canoes off the southern end of Roemberpon Island. The natives told them where a camouflaged barge was hidden and piloted the boats as far as they could through the reefs. The boats still could not reach the hideout, so Lieutenant Molloy, William Boldt, GM2c, and Richard Lawrence, MoMM1c, went with some natives in a dugout to inspect the barge. The natives showed them where the barge was, but refused to approach closer than 35 yards for fear of snipers. Molloy returned to the PT and directed two Beauforts to the barge. They strafed it several times but soon had to leave because they were low on gasoline. Boldt, Peter Kolar, TM2c, and Wilbur Burkett, TM3c, then went ashore in a native canoe with a .30-caliber machinegun. They set it up 50 yards from the barge and pumped 500 rounds into it, leaving it smoking. Before the boats left for the base, natives turned over to them a Javanese laborer who had escaped from the Japanese.

The most concentrated destruction of barges came on August 17 and 18. Lt. Malcolm Toon, USNR, in PT 155, and Lt. (jg.) Rex L. Anderson, USNR, in PT 156, entered Dore Bay, near Manokwari, on the morning of the 17th covered by one Beaufighter. The boats found 18 serviceable barges on the beach of Mansinam Island, and made 3 runs, concentrating their fire on 12 of them. Increasingly accurate fire from 90mm. shore batteries forced the boats to retire before they could make an accurate assessment of the results

80—G—256496

PT's from Mios Woendi fire at beached barges in daylight strike on August 17, 1944.

of their fire, but it was a fair estimate that they had destroyed six barges and damaged three more.

The following morning Lieutenant (jg.) Molloy, in PT 326, with Ens. Nelson Davis, USNR, in PT 191, swept the coast of Mansinam Island, strafing nine barges, two marine railways, a fuel dump, a floating platform, and several buildings. Three of the barges were sunk and the others damaged. The boats received desultory fire from 90mm. guns on the mainland, and heavy machinegun fire from several points on Mansinam. As they withdrew, they met two Beaufighters and directed them to a barge the PT's had been unable to reach because of reefs. Lt. (jg.) Emery M. Newton, Jr., USNR, in PT 323, with Lt. (jg.) Robert L. Lanning, Jr., USNR, in PT 329, followed the Beaufighters into the bay. These boats, under machinegun fire from Mansinam and 90mm. fire from the mainland, made a firing run along the whole western side of the island, scoring many hits on four barges which showed signs of previous damage, and definitely destroying a fifth with 40mm. hits. At one point on the shore, three men, attempting to set up a machinegun on the beach, were seen to fall. The 323 was hit in several places by fragments and one man was slightly wounded.

Barge contacts dwindled into insignificance after September, but the boats continued making special missions to evacuate Javanese, Formosans, and Indian Army personnel who had been impressed as laborers by the Japanese and who had escaped with the assistance of natives, coastwatchers, or NICA or U.S. Army scouts. Accurate figures are not available before October, but in October and November alone, the boats evacuated 782 former prisoners of the Japanese.

PT 301 was lost at Mios Woendi as a result of an accidental engineroom explosion on November 4, which killed two men and damaged the boat so badly that it had to be scrapped.

On September 12 Commander Bowling temporarily shifted his pennant to *Oyster Bay* and sailed with the *Mobjack* and Squadrons 9, 10, 18, and 33 for Morotai in the Halmaheras, arriving there September 16, the day after the initial amphibious landings. *Oyster Bay* with 10 boats of Squadron 33 returned to Mios Woendi on October 6, and a week later, with Commander Bowling again aboard, departed with two new seaplane-type tenders, *Wachapreague* and *Willoughby,* and 45 PT's of Squadrons 7, 12, 21, 33, and 36, for Leyte Gulf in the Philippines. They arrived there at dawn on October 21, a day after the major assault landings on the island of Leyte.

Combat patrols from Mios Woendi, last operating base in New Guinea, were secured on November 16. It was not quite 23 months since PT's 121 and 122 had made their first patrol from Porlock Harbor. During that time the Task Group had expanded from 1 small tender and 6 PT's to 8 tenders and 14 squadrons of PT's. Its boats had had almost nightly action along 1,500 miles of the coastline of New Guinea, and along the coasts of New Britain and the Admiralties as well. From first to last they met and overcame the bitterest opposition the enemy could mount against them; with relatively little damage to themselves they took terrible toll of the Japanese. Along the coastline was the wreckage of hundreds of blasted barges; in former enemy encampments were bodies of thousands of soldiers who died for lack of supplies.

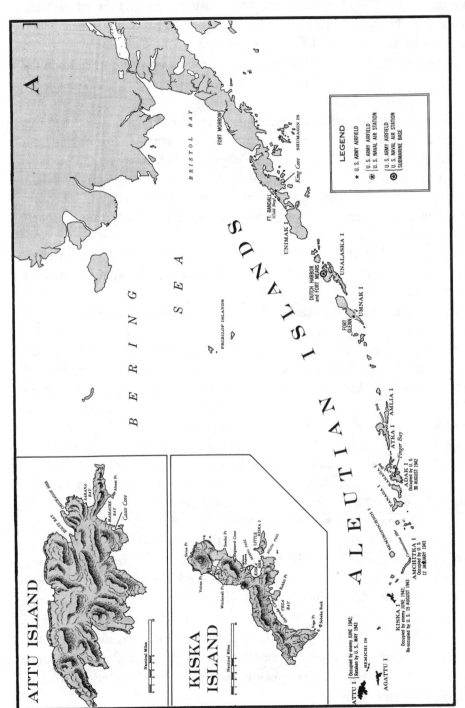

The Aleutians.

PART V

The Aleutians—*A Battle Against Weather*

1. A RACE FOR ISLANDS

IT IS FARTHER from the southeastern tip of the Alaskan Panhandle to Attu, westernmost of the Aleutians, than from Savannah to Los Angeles. Nearly half the distance is covered by the arc of the Aleutians, more than 100 small, rocky, desolate islands which form the shortest land route between the American mainland and the Japanese Empire. Attu, nearly 1,000 miles from the Alaskan mainland, is only 650 miles from the northernmost of the Kurile Islands, where the Japanese had a large naval base at Paramushiru.

Aleutian weather, particularly toward the western part of the chain, is the worst in the world. Nowhere else are storms so numerous and so intense. Squalls known as "williwaws" sweep down from the mountains with terrifying speed, building up to gale proportions in half an hour. Winds of 100 knots are not uncommon. The accompanying heavy seas, with strong currents running through the passes and channels, the jagged shorelines and submerged rock formations, make navigation extremely hazardous. In the western islands, when it is not raining, there is usually fog, and it is a peculiarity of the Aleutians that fog and wind may persist together for many days at a time.

Coordinated with their massive and futile assault on Midway, the Japanese made two damaging but inconclusive attacks on our naval base at Dutch Harbor on the island of Unalaska on June 3 and 4, 1942. Weather caused many enemy planes to miss their carriers and fall into the sea. It also prevented our planes, flying from Cold Bay and Umnak, from making effective attacks on the enemy carrier force.

The raids on Dutch Harbor were the enemy's only strikes at the central and eastern Aleutians. Possibly his defeat at Midway and his discovery that we had an airbase at Umnak, 100 miles west of Dutch Harbor, caused the cancellation of more ambitious plans. To the westward, however, a race for islands quickly developed. On June 6, under cover of fog, the enemy began the occupation of Attu and Kiska, where our only installations were small meteorological outposts. Reports from these stations ceased on the 7th, but it was not until the 10th that the weather cleared sufficiently for our patrol planes to confirm the fact that the enemy had landed substantial forces on both islands.

With the greater part of our available forces committed to the impending campaign in the Solomons, no immediate major countermove was possible. Navy Catalinas and Army bombers of the 11th Air Force bombed and strafed Attu and Kiska when weather permitted; submarines attacked enemy shipping, and on August 7 our heavy cruisers *Indianapolis* and *Louisville,* with the light cruisers *Honolulu, St. Louis,* and *Nashville,* and nine destroyer types, shelled Kiska Harbor.

Army Forces occupied Adak, 200 miles east of Kiska, on August 30 without opposition. Once ashore, the Army performed a miraculous feat of engineering, building an airstrip in 12 days. Thereafter, whenever it was possible to fly, our planes bombed Kiska and Attu. The planes could not drive the Japanese from the islands, but, with our submarines, they kept the enemy from building up his bases to the point where he would be able to undertake further offensive action.

On December 17, American reconnaissance parties surveyed Amchitka Island, only 70 miles east of Kiska, and found that the Japanese had already been there, digging test holes for possible airfield sites. On January 12 Army forces made unopposed landings at Constantine Harbor, on the eastern end of Amchitka. Twelve days later the enemy began a series of minor air attacks on Amchitka, but by February 16 a new fighter strip was placed in operation on the island, and the enemy bombings ceased. The occupation of Amchitka further accelerated the bombing schedule of the 11th Air Force and proportionately increased the enemy's supply problems.

2. MTB DIVISION 1

On July 28, 1942, 13 days after *Hilo* left Pearl Harbor for Palmyra with PT's 21, 23, 25, and 26, four other boats of Squadron 1 were loaded on SS *Irvin MacDowell* at Pearl Harbor. These boats, PT's 22, 24, 27, and 28, were designated Motor Torpedo Boat Division 1, under command of the squadron commander, Lt. Clinton McKellar, Jr. *Irvin MacDowell* sailed from Pearl Harbor on July 30 and arrived at Seattle on August 11.

After overhaul and installation of 20mm. guns at the Olson-Winge Marine Works in Seattle, the boats got underway on August 20, following the British Columbia and Alaskan Panhandle coast northward into the Gulf of Alaska, and then heading southwestward down the Alaska Peninsula to Dutch Harbor. They stopped at Vancouver, Prince Rupert, Ketchikan, Juneau, Yakutat, Seward, and Kodiak, covering more than 2,500 miles and arriving at Dutch Harbor on September 1.

There an aircraft radar was mounted on PT 28, as an aid to navigation in the Aleutian fogs, but the 28 went aground and could not leave for Adak with the other boats on September 5. PT's 22, 24, and 27 arrived at Adak on September 9. The 28 joined them 3 weeks later. They were held at Adak as a striking force to be used if the Japanese should attempt to occupy Amchitka. During September they carried out reconnaissance and supply missions for the Army.

On September 21, PT 22 (Lt. John W. Ewell, USNR) and PT 27 (Lt. George A. Matteson, USNR) carried an Army supply party to outposts in Shagak Bay, on the west side of Adak. In the course of this mission an Army skiff capsized, throwing nine men into the icy water. The 22 rescued all of them, but damaged her propellers and bottom and had to be sent back to King Cove, on the Alaska Peninsula, for repairs.

On October 25, PT's 24, 27, and 28 laid mines in Umak Pass and in Kagalaska Strait, to the east of Adak.

As fall turned to winter, life on the boats became less and less comfortable. The only heat came from the two-burner gasoline stove in the galley—a little alcove off the crew's quarters. Most of the time there was a heavy layer of frost on the inside of the bulkheads. The boats, which were among the first of the Elco 77-footers, had had fairly hard service for over a year, and with the combination of extremely heavy seas and no repair facilities at Adak, soon required extensive overhaul. They arrived at King Cove on December 18.

Repairs to all four boats were completed on January 5, and at 0200 the next day they got underway for Dutch Harbor. During the early morning hours the boats were lashed by hail and snow, they were pounded by a heavy sea from the north, and they became coated with ice 2 to 4 inches thick. In a squall at 0645, PT 24 (Lt. (jg.) Lawrence F. Jones, USNR) rammed Lieutenant Ewell's PT 22 on the port bow, damaging her own bow, tearing a hole in the side of the 22, ripping off a 4- by 6-foot section of the 22's deck, and carrying away the 22's steering control. One man on the 22, J. C. Rothery, F1c, USNR, suffered a fractured rib.

The 22 rigged emergency collision mats of mattresses, and with the 24 and 28 headed for shelter at Dora Harbor, a little cove on the southeastern end of Unimak Island. During the afternoon the gale increased, and water poured through the gaping side of the 22. The crew formed a bucket brigade, bailing until they reached Dora Harbor at 1745 with water 2 inches over the floorplates in the crew's quarters.

Lieutenant Matteson's PT 27 took Rothery to Seal Cape, 50 miles away at the western end of Unimak, and put him aboard the gunboat *Charleston* for treatment. Matteson arranged to have the YP 149 bring materials for emergency repairs and then rejoined the other boats at Dora Harbor, anchoring alongside the 22 to shelter the injured boat.

During the next 4 days all of the boats had trouble with dragging anchors as the wind steadily increased. On the 10th the wind was gusting to 80 knots. The 22 and 27, still moored together, had a particularly difficult time that day. Their anchor lines parted several times. Once, in a snow squall, they drifted into a snowbank on an overhanging cliff. Later, after they had anchored in the lee of the cliff, their anchors dragged again and both boats went aground. The 27's struts and propellers were damaged, and her bottom was holed in three places by jagged rocks. The crew patched the holes from the inside, and both boats kedged off on a rising tide. On the same day PT 28 (Lt. Robert A. Williamson, USNR), with Lieutenant McKellar aboard, was swept aground near the southern entrance of the harbor. Williamson managed to back off under his own power, but the boat was leaking badly in the lazarette.

By the 12th, the weather had moderated sufficiently for Jones' PT 24, which had completed temporary repairs, to run to Seal Cape for assistance. The 24 returned early on the morning of the 14th with a YP and YMS. In the meantime the boats at Dora Harbor had more trouble.

Just before midnight on the night of January 12/13, the 22 was set on a reef. The 28, attempting to pull her off, also went hard aground. The 27 tried to move the boats off. First the towlines parted; then, when the lines had been doubled up, the cleats pulled right out of the decks. The receding tide made further attempts useless. The 27 took off the crews of the 22 and 28 and headed for King Cove.

On the 14th, the YMS 125 freed the 22 from the reef and pumped her dry. The 22 was then towed to King Cove by the cannery tender *Virginia E.* When the 22 was safely in tow, the YMS 125 pulled the 28 off. The towline broke and the 28 started to drift back toward the reef. The 24 got her in tow and took her alongside the YMS. The 28 again broke away, and again the 24 took her alongside the YMS, but in clearing the side the towline fouled the 24's screws. The 28 drifted away, and this time the 24, herself disabled, could do nothing for the 28. The 24 managed to put over a mooring line to the YP 575, but the 28 washed up on the rocks on the northwest shore of the harbor. All further attempts at salvage failed. The 24 was towed back to King Cove, but the 28 was abandoned and later broke up on the rocks.

The damage to PT's 24 and 27 could be repaired in Alaska; that to the 22 could not. The ill-fated 22 was written off as a complete loss when it was dropped from a crane while being loaded on a Liberty ship for return to the United States.

3. SQUADRON 13

Motor Torpedo Boat Squadron 13, the first squadron of Higgins PT's, was commissioned on September 18, 1942, in New Orleans, with Lt. James B. Denny as squadron commander. The first boats were far from satisfactory, particularly in the matter of speed. Lieutenant Denny, working closely with Lt. Richard J. Dressling, officer in charge of the PT Commissioning Detail at New Orleans, made many recommendations for removal of excess weight, and redesign and relocation of items of equipment. The recommendations were approved by the Bureau of Ships, and thereafter were incorporated into the standard design of the Higgins boats. The necessity for alterations meant that the first six boats did not leave New Orleans until November 30, and the second six did not leave until December 17.

Squadron 13 was the first squadron to run on its own bottoms to Taboga. The boats proceeded by way of Pensacola, Tampa, and Key West, Fla.; La Fe, Cuba; Grand Cayman Island; Portland Bight, Jamaica; Barranquilla, Colombia; and Coco Solo, C.Z., a distance of nearly 2,500 miles. The trip demonstrated both the strength and a fault of the Higgins PT's. The boats were sturdy—they stood up well in heavy seas—but they had a tendency to nose under at low speeds, drenching the crews. Lieutenant Denny, after completing the Pensacola-to-Tampa leg, wrote to his executive officer, Lt. James A. Danver, USNR, who was still in New Orleans, "I am surprised and pleased. These little ships ride like destroyers. However, most of this run we made at periscope depth."

The first division reached Taboga on December 20 and the second on January 16. The voyage had been so successful that thereafter all Higgins' squadrons assigned to the Pacific and, later, Elco squadrons as well, ran under their own power to Taboga.

The squadron had several weeks of training at Taboga and then was

NR&L (MOD)—32497

Unloading a Squadron 13 boat from a merchant ship at Seattle. The boats were shipped to Seattle and ran from there to the Aleutians on their own bottoms.

NR&L (MOD)—32498

PT's of Squadron 13 proceed northward through the inland passage.

shipped to Seattle. The first boats left Panama on January 26, and the last arrived in Seattle early in April. Denny, promoted to lieutenant commander, left Seattle on February 28 with PT's 73, 74, 75, and 76, and took the boats under their own power to Adak, via Hardy Bay, Bella Bella, Ketchikan, Juneau, Yakutat, Cordova, Kodiak, Sand Point, King Cove, Dutch Harbor, and Atka, arriving at Adak on March 31. Lieutenant Danver followed with PT's 77, 78, 79, and 80, leaving Seattle on March 21 and arriving at Adak on May 1. Lt. Charles A. Mills, Jr., USNR, left Seattle on May 10 with PT's 81, 82, 83, and 84, and arrived at Adak on the 27th.

PT's 75 and 79 acquired aircraft radar sets at Dutch Harbor, as the 28 had done the preceding September. While Danver's division was at Dutch Harbor, Lieutenant McKellar, who had been ordered back to the United States, turned over to him PT's 24 and 27, repaired again after their damage at Dora Harbor.

Messhall at Adak PT base.

Before the division left Dutch Harbor, however, the 24 damaged a propeller on a submerged rock. "We thought the shaft would be all right after we changed the propeller," Danver said, "but on trial she vibrated so badly we could not keep the bolts in that held the strut. The bolts would break, the water would fountain in, and of course it was necessary to secure the engine. Anyway, both PT's 24 and 27 were so old and had seen so much service that they actually weaved as they went through the water, opening seams in their decks and allowing water to pour through. I reported . . . that they could not keep up with the newer PT's and I did not consider it safe to take them along. We frankly advised that both boats have their nice new engines removed and the boats be put out of service as PT's. The hull officer of the Commander Alaskan Sector was called in to the conference and said he could fix the 24. We took the 27 with us."

PT 24 eventually was sent to Adak. Lieutenant Commander Denny joined in recommending that the two old 77-footers were no longer useful for service in the Aleutians, but it was not until June that the boats were ordered out of the area. Lt. (jg.) Charles R. White, Jr., USNR, took them under their own power to Seattle, where they were rebuilt. Later they were shipped back to Pearl Harbor to rejoin the remaining four boats of Squadron 1.

Although no PT's were well suited for Aleutian operations, the boats of Squadron 13 were far better than those of Division 1. They were new boats, of sturdier construction, and they were fitted with motor-driven hot air heaters. A defect in the heater design, which permitted exhaust fumes from the motor to mingle with the hot air being circulated through the boat, gave trouble at first, knocking the entire crew of PT 80 (Lt. (jg.) William G. Jens, USNR) into a stupor. Once discovered, this defect was quickly corrected, and the heaters greatly improved the habitability of the boats.

80–G–220314

PT base at Adak. In background is USS Tatoosh, *which served as tender during building of base.*

PT Base 5 was moved into Finger Bay soon after the arrival of the first Squadron 13 boats at Adak. While the base was being constructed the boats had the district craft, USS *Tatoosh,* as a tender. Although its facilities were limited, it did have good food, hot showers, and motion pictures every night.

The boats made a few uneventful patrols out of Adak soon after their arrival there but, for most of the time, Adak was regarded as a rear base, used primarily for repair and training.

For the invasion of Attu, scheduled for May 11, the PT's were assigned the task of protecting Amchitka against possible counterthrusts by the enemy, and of patrolling to keep the enemy from sending reinforcements to Kiska. Lieutenant Commander Denny took PT's 79, 74, 75, and 76 to Constantine Harbor, Amchitka, on May 3 to start an operating base with personnel and equipment from PT Base 5. Lieutenant Danver joined him there on May 14 with PT's 73 and 80. The boats patrolled Oglala Pass and Rat Island Pass, logical approaches to Kiska Harbor, but had no contacts with the enemy.

The Army landings on Attu were made on schedule. Despite fierce resistance the island was secured by the end of May. Lieutenant Commander Denny left Constantine Harbor on June 3 with PT's 79, 75, 77, and 82 for Casco Cove in Massacre Bay, Attu, where PT Base 13 was already being installed. Patrols from Attu were entirely negative, as the Japanese never again attempted to send ships there. The boats were used principally for escorting ships through the thick fog from Massacre Bay to Shemya Island, where an airstrip was being constructed, and for transportation of high-ranking officers between Massacre Bay and Shemya, and to Holtz Bay, on the northern side of Attu. With only two boats, the 75 and 79, fitted with radar, it was remarkable how accurately the boats were able to find their way through the fog. The boats returned to Adak in September, when they were relieved by PT's 219 to 224, of Squadron 16, under Lt. Almer P. Colvin.

The boats of Squadron 16 saw no more action than their predecessors, but took a worse beating from the weather. On the morning of September 14, PT 219 (Ens. Harold F. Grove, USNR) was moored to a buoy in Casco Cove, 350 yards from shore. The wind velocity was 40 knots, with gusts to 55 knots. One gust parted the cable between anchor and buoy, and though the 219 lighted off her engines within a minute, the boat was already aground on a rocky spit. Five hours later the seaplane tender *Casco* pulled

80—G—53215

A PT breaks through leading boat's wake off coast of Attu.

the 219 off the rocks and started to bring her alongside. The bottom had been badly holed, and as *Casco* hauled the PT toward her, water rushed into the hull and built up air pressure until the engineroom vent covers blew off. The engineroom immediately filled with water and the boat sank by the stern, leaving the forecastle deck awash. The *Casco* got her alongside and tried to pump her out. After 2 hours with no improvement, the *Casco* cast off the 219, and the boat sank in 25 feet. Four days later the weather moderated sufficiently to send down a diver. The seaplane wrecking derrick YSD 26 raised the 219 on the 20th, and pumped out enough water to put the boat in drydock. Later a heavy wind swept the drydock ashore. The boat was eventually scrapped.

As the 11th Air Force stepped up its bombing of Kiska, the PT's organized a crashboat service at Amchitka. Two boats were kept on station at Bird Cape, on the western end of the island. When the weather plane returned from its early morning run to Kiska, it would run northward over the PT's if the weather was satisfactory for flying, and to the southward if it was not. If the flight was northward, the PT's moved out to the west, where they could see the enemy's guns firing at our planes over Kiska. As it turned out, boats were required only once for rescue work, but officers of the 11th

Air Force believed their presence contributed to the efficiency of the bombing of Kiska. The bomber crews knew they stood a good chance of rescue if they should be forced down by antiaircraft fire.

Lt. (jg.) Louis R. Fockele, USNR, in PT 76 was on one of these missions on the afternoon of July 11, when an Army Liberator flew over, circled and came back to strafe the boat. The bomber made three more runs, but did not fire during any of them. The 76 answered with a short burst of fire to try to chase the plane away. There was no damage either to boat or bomber. After this exchange all aircraft pilots on the Kiska run were ordered to visit the PT base and inspect the PT's so that they would recognize them when they saw them from the air.

On the evening of the same day the Army asked for a PT to go to the assistance of the crew of a Liberator forced down by lack of fuel near Little Sitkin Island. Guided by a Catalina, which had been unable to make the rescue because the water was too rough for a landing, Lt. (jg.) William R. McQuilkin, in PT 73, ran from Bird Cape to the north coast of Little Sitkin, where he found the bomber crew safe ashore. The pilot had set his plane down in a little cove. It sank quickly, but the crew got ashore in a rubber raft.

In July, PT's from Amchitka covered small Army landings on Rat and Semisopochnoi Islands, to the northwest and northeast of Amchitka. They saw no sign of the enemy.

The Aleutians campaign entered its final phase on August 15, 1943, with the American occupation of Kiska. For a time it appeared that the PT's at last would have some action, since it was estimated that the Japanese had 4,000 to 7,000 troops on the island. While the main landings were being made to the north, five PT's were to join a group of transports in a feint at Vega Point, the southeastern extremity of the island, to draw enemy reserves from the north and prevent concentration of defenses against the main landings. Strips of plywood cut out to resemble the sides of barges surmounted by rows of soldiers' heads were tacked to the gunwales of the PT's, outboard of the torpedo tubes. The camouflage was crude close-to, but at a little distance gave the PT's the appearance of loaded landing craft.

Lieutenant Commander Denny, in PT 81 (Lt. (jg.) Elbert S. Churchill, USNR), with PT 73 (Lt. (jg.) William R. McQuilkin); PT 76 (Lt. (jg.) Louis R. Fockele, USNR); PT 80 (Lt. (jg.) William G. Jens, USNR); and PT 84 (Lt. (jg.) Joseph A. Sheehan, USNR), left Bird Cape at 0330 on August 15 and entered Vega Bay ahead of the transports at 0715 to begin their demonstration. In a heavy haze the boats closed within 100 yards of shore and intermittently strafed the beach until 1100. In the afternoon they made several strafing runs in Gertrude Cove, to the north. No matter how close to shore they went, they drew no return fire. That night the boats returned to Constantine Harbor. The landings at Kiska, to the surprise of everyone who took part in them, were entirely unopposed. The enemy had evacuated the island, secretly and completely.

After Kiska the boats devoted themselves entirely to operational training. Even these exercises frequently had to be canceled because of high winds and heavy seas. The base at Amchitka was abandoned after a heavy storm in mid-September wrecked the breakwater. In April 1944, the boats at Adak maintained an antisubmarine patrol between Adak Strait and Atka Pass when weather permitted, but had no sightings.

In May 1944, Squadron 13 was withdrawn from Adak and Squadron 16 was withdrawn from Attu. The boats ran under their own power to Seattle

NR&L (MOD)—32499

PT's with sides built up to resemble landing barges filled with troops, ready for diversionary operations in the reoccupation of Kiska.

At Adak base, a tractor hauls a PT up a ramp in a rubber-tired cradle
for repairs.

for overhaul and shipment to the Southwest Pacific. Squadron 16B, a group of six boats under Lt. James H. Van Sicklen, USNR, which was to be placed out of separate commission on joining Squadron 16, came up the Alaskan coast in April as far as Sitka, en route to Attu, when orders were received to return to Seattle to await the arrival of the parent squadron there. The last boats of Squadron 16 arrived at Seattle at the end of May, and those of Squadron 13 in June.

PART VI

The Mediterranean—*Torpedo War*

646674 O—63———20

The Mediterranean.

PART VI

The Mediterranean—*Torpedo War*

1. SQUADRON 15

WHILE THE boats of Squadron 13 were still fitting out at New Orleans, Higgins Industries began to deliver boats for Squadron 14, of which Lt. Comdr. Stanley M. Barnes was to be squadron commander.

The squadron was to be assigned to the Hawaiian Sea Frontier for duty at Midway. But before it could be commissioned, Barnes received orders to fit out the boats and deliver them to New York for transfer under lend-lease. Then he and his officers and men were to return to New Orleans to fit out Squadron 15.

The orders were a shock and a disappointment. Later everyone realized that the experience of fitting out 12 boats and taking them on a 2,000-mile trip was the best possible training for fitting out a new squadron. "The boats of Squadron 15 were better in every way than the ones we fitted out for the Russians," Barnes said, "simply because we knew what to look for and insisted that the job be done right."

Squadron 15 was commissioned on January 20, 1943, at the Municipal Yacht Basin in Lake Pontchartrain. The new squadron also was scheduled for assignment to the Hawaiian Sea Frontier, and when Lieutenant Commander Barnes said at the commissioning ceremony that somehow, somewhere, the squadron was going to find somebody to fight, no one—not even himself—quite believed it.

On February 12 Barnes left New Orleans for Panama with his first six boats, PT's 201 to 206. That night, between Pensacola and Tampa, the boats ran into such heavy seas that four boats cracked frames. The division returned to New Orleans for repairs. Lt. John B. Mutty, the squadron executive officer, left New Orleans on February 26 with PT's 207 to 212. The first division was ready to go again on the 28th, and the following day the two divisions passed each other in Tampa Channel, Barnes's boats entering and Mutty's standing out for Key West. Mutty's division had reached Guantanamo, Cuba, and Barnes's division was at Key West when both received dispatches canceling previous orders and instructing them to stand

277

80–G–21109

Launching PT's at Higgins Industries, New Orleans.

by until further notice. After several days all boats were ordered to report to the Commander in Chief Atlantic Fleet at Norfolk. Barnes's boats arrived there on March 16 and Mutty's 3 days later. At Norfolk, Barnes learned what he had hardly dared hope for—his squadron was, after all, going to find somebody to fight. Squadron 15 was going to the Mediterranean. As the first American squadron in the European theater, it was to be enlarged by the addition of six more boats, PT's 213 to 218.

2. NORTH AFRICA

PT's 201 to 204, in charge of Lt. (jg.) Robert B. Reade, USNR (later relieved by Lt. Edwin A. DuBose, USNR), were loaded on the oiler *Enoree,* and PT's 205 to 208, under Lieutenant Commander Barnes, were put aboard *Housatonic,* while Lieutenant Mutty was left in Norfolk to take care of shipment of the remaining 10 boats. The two oilers went to New York to join separate convoys for the Mediterranean, *Enoree* sailing from New York on April 1 and *Housatonic* on April 2.

The *Housatonic* arrived at Gibraltar on April 13 and the boats were put in the water the next day. After readying their torpedoes at the British Coastal Forces base at Gibraltar, the boats proceeded to Oran, where Barnes reported to the Commander Amphibious Force Northwest African Waters on April 17. *Enoree* arrived at Casablanca on April 20 only to find that the floating crane there was too short to lift the boats from her deck. The ship was rerouted to Gibraltar, where the boats were unloaded on the 22d and 23rd.

Barnes learned that the Commander Amphibious Force planned to establish a PT base at Cherchel, 150 miles east of Oran and 50 miles west of Algiers, and to keep the boats there for an indefinite period for training. Protesting that Cherchel was already 300 miles behind the lines of the North African fighting, he persuaded the Commander Amphibious Force to recommend to the Commander U.S. Naval Forces Northwest African Waters, Vice Adm. Henry K. Hewitt, that the PT's be sent to Bone, the most advanced port in Allied hands, 265 miles east of Cherchel. But his orders remained unchanged, and he took his four boats to Cherchel on April 23.

"I decided to take the bull by the horns and bum a ride down to Algiers in an Army truck the following morning to see Admiral Hewitt and try to get released for duty at Bone," Barnes said. "That trip took me several hours and by the time I got there I was chagrined to find that orders had already been issued and Lt. Richard H. O'Brien, who was my next senior, had gotten the boats underway and was in Algiers before me. The Admiral himself brought me up to date with the information that my boats were already there, most embarrassing. We tied up that night alongside the British Coastal Forces tender HMS *Vienna*. The next day we went on to Bone, arriving late in the afternoon and reported to the Advanced Coastal Forces Base for duty."

DuBose's boats arrived at Bone on April 27, and the next night made their first patrol. For several weeks Bone had been a base for MTB's and MGB's of the British Coastal Forces. Most of the early PT patrols were made in company with these boats, with British officers aboard to give them advantage of their experience.[14]

---

[14] The British MTB, or motor torpedo boat, carried two torpedoes and light machineguns. The MGB, or motor gunboat, carried heavier guns but no torpedoes. The U.S. Navy attempted and, by and large, succeeded in combining in its PT's the functions of both MTB and MGB. It is interesting to note that among the MTB's operating at Bone when the PT's arrived were 70-foot Elco boats transferred to Britain in April and June 1941, from Squadron 2, and 77-foot boats built by Elco and transferred to Britain in February and March 1942.

The North African campaign was drawing to a close, and it was expected that the Germans would try a final evacuation by sea. The Coastal Forces, which at that time included the PT's, were assigned small patrol areas within 5 miles of the coast, which were to be occupied every night regardless of weather. PT's patrolled nearly every night, but had no action until the night of May 8/9, when Lieutenant Commander Barnes, in PT 206 (Lt. (jg.) John W. Oswald, USNR), patrolled the eastern side of Cape Bon, east of Tunis, with MTB's 265, 316, and 317, and Lt. (jg.) Robert B. Reade, USNR, in PT 203, patrolled an adjacent area to the south with MTB's 61 and 77.

Barnes's group made a sweep up the coast, and then Lt. Dennis Germaine, RN, took MTB's 316 and 317 into Ras Idda Bay to investigate a possible target, leaving PT 206 and MTB 265 outside. "Pretty soon," Barnes said, "Germaine came up on the radio with the startling statement that 'There are lots of ships in here.' So I took the remaining British boat with me and started on in. It was as black as the inside of your pocket, but sure enough right there in front of me was a ship. By the time we saw it against the dark background of land, we were inside the torpedo aiming range and had to go all the way around the other side of it before getting a good shot. Thinking there were other targets around, I lined up and fired only one torpedo, our first. It ran hot and straight and after what seemed like an interminable time made a beautiful hit forward and the whole ship blew up in our faces, scattering pieces of debris all around us and on deck. Just like the movies." German records list two war tankers as missing in the Cape Bon area at this time. Barnes must have been responsible for the disappearance of one of them.

"We immediately started to look for other ships," wrote Barnes, "but could find none. Neither could we find our British friend who, it turned out, was temporarily aground. So we just eased around trying to rendezvous. Pretty soon he found us and promptly fired two fish, one of which passed right under our bow and the other under the stern, much to our alarm and his subsequent embarrassment. About half an hour later bombers started working over the airfield a couple of miles away and with the light of the flares we managed to join up with Germaine. I personally think that ship was aground although it certainly made a fine spectacle going up and one of our officers who was along that night subsequently flew over the area in a plane and reported it sitting nicely on the bottom. Actually Germaine had not seen any ship and had mistaken some peculiar rock formations for a group of enemy vessels. Nothing much else happened that night except that there was a mysterious fire to the south of us which blazed away for over an hour."

The mysterious fire came from Reade's division. While Reade's 203 and MTB 77 waited outside, MTB 61 went into Kelibia Roads to investigate the anchorage. The boat went aground only 250 yards from a German-occupied fortress and called by radio for help. Reade worked the 203 within 15 yards of the MTB and began to pick up her crew from the water. The boat captain of the MTB set fire to his boat prematurely, and it exploded and burned, illuminating the PT while most of the crew were still in the water. "The PT 203," the action report said, "remained to recover all personnel despite the fact that the enemy was alerted and engaging the boat with rifle fire from the beach. Apparently the big guns commanding the harbor could not be depressed sufficiently to take the boat under fire. A Heinkel 111, attracted by the fire, circled continuously."

While the MTB was burning, Ens. Ernest W. Olson, USNR, second officer of the 203, went over the side to help the men of the MTB. When all were safely aboard, the 203 pulled out of the bay at top speed.

Two nights later Lieutenant DuBose, in PT 202, with PT 204 (Lt. (jg.) Eugene S. A. Clifford, USNR) and PT 205 (Lt. Richard H. O'Brien), completed a patrol off Cape Bon and headed back toward Bone, cutting deep into the Gulf of Tunis to keep clear of an area in which British destroyers were operating. Suddenly two British destroyers loomed up out of the night, passing on opposite course, 900 yards away. The destroyers opened fire with machineguns as they passed. DuBose fired a two-star emergency recognition cartridge and ordered all boats to increase speed and lay smoke. No sooner had the PT's pushed up their throttles than two German E-boats [15] started firing at them.

The British destroyers kept blazing away at PT's and E-boats alike. The PT's tried at the same time to dodge the destroyers and engage the E-boats. Clifford turned back through his smokescreen to strafe an E-boat at close quarters and then withdrew at high speed. The E-boat was seen to burn by the destroyers, which pursued the PT's for nearly an hour, firing starshell and salvos from their main batteries. The PT's received a few machinegun hits which did no significant damage.

---

[15] The E-boat was the German counterpart of the PT. It was a larger boat, 106 feet long, displacing 95 tons, and its speed was about the same as that of the PT's. It was driven by three diesel engines, and was heavily armed, usually carrying four torpedoes, a 40mm. and one or more 20mm. guns. The designation "E-boat" was adopted by the British early in the war as an abbreviation for "Enemy war motorboat." The German name was "Schnellboot" (fast boat).

Several days later one of the destroyer captains offered his apologies, explaining that the destroyers had found no enemy activity in their assigned area and had gone south "to have a bit of a look." They had been attacked by three E-boats at the precise moment DuBose's boats appeared, and had just heard the enemy discussing attack plans by radio. The destroyers saw DuBose's recognition flare but, as so often happened with this type of recognition signal, mistook it for tracer fire.

The boats became separated in the melee. O'Brien, whose PT 205 was running low on gasoline, decided to put into Bizerte, which had been taken only a few hours before by Allied ground forces. "Friendly" shore batteries fired a few rounds as he entered the harbor, but the shots were wide, so he continued in and tied up at the dock. Two hours later he was asked to move his boat out of the way so newsreel photographers could take pictures of the first Allied vessels to enter Bizerte—some British landing craft which were just arriving.

3. BIZERTE

Plans called for establishment of a PT base at Bizerte, 100 miles east of Bone. On May 18, Barnes went there in Reade's PT 203 with Lt. Comdr. Robert A. Allan, RNVR, commander of the Coastal Forces Base at Bone, to investigate base facilities. The Commander Advanced Amphibious Training Base assigned the entire Karouba seaplane base to the PT's and told Barnes that all the material for PT Base 12 was already in the harbor, on board the LST 381.

Barnes decided to stay at Bizerte to get the base started, while Lieutenant Commander Allan returned to Bone in the 203. On the way back, the 203 investigated the island of Galite, 20 miles offshore, and discovered that all of the enemy occupation troops had been evacuated by E-boat several days earlier.

"Karouba," Barnes said, "was an enormous place formerly used by the French Navy and later the Italians and Germans for a seaplane base and aircraft repair depot. It was almost totally wrecked by our bombing and most of what little remained had been dynamited by the Italians before they evacuated, but it suited us right down to the ground and I began making plans for the future. Pretty soon I found a Lieutenant (jg.) USNR, by the name of Harry Gorsuch and 75 men wandering about the place looking very lost. It turned out they were our PT Base 12 personnel recently released from a month in the tent city at Oran. They knew nothing at all about our base equipment which they had never seen but were only too happy to find someone to belong to. So we started right then and there to clean out of one of the few intact buildings.

"Bizerte was subsequently to be the principal jumping-off place for the Sicilian invasion, at least for landing craft, and the Army and Navy began moving in in force. The harbor entrance and the channel to the excellent deep water lake behind it were completely jammed with sunken wrecks. For weeks it was impossible to move anything larger than PT's and small landing craft into the lake, and it was only by intensive demolition that a channel was finally cleared for deep draft vessels.

"We set up shop immediately, salvaging a galley and galley gear from bombed-out buildings. We made our own arrangements with the British port director to get our LST into the beach and finagled direct with the Army for trucks with which we unloaded our gear on a 24-hour basis. No sooner had we got it all off the ship and into one of the few hangars with a roof on it than the squeeze began and we had to move everything half a mile down the other end of the base into another hangar. We cleaned out half the buildings in the area, but ended up with only a fraction of our original space, fighting tooth and nail all the way along the line, but we did have good dock space."

PT Base 12 was the principal PT base during the first year in the Mediterranean. Until the end of the Mediterranean campaign all PT engines were overhauled there. Every item of equipment used by the PT's came through Bizerte and was forwarded to the advanced bases.

Soon the PT's, MTB's, and MGB's were patrolling nightly from Bizerte to the west coast of Sicily. The rest of the squadron's boats arrived late in May, already equipped with radar, which was to be of vital importance to PT operations in the Mediterranean. Gradually radar was installed on the first eight boats at Base 12.

On June 30 the squadron performed one of its many missions for the Office of Strategic Services, when Lieutenant Mutty took three boats (PT's 210, 214, 218) to land five agents halfway up the west coast of Sardinia, a 505-mile round trip. The boats made several similar missions to the northwest coast of Sicily. On the night of June 9/10, Barnes took PT's 206 and 203 right into Palermo Harbor, but found no ships there. For these long-range missions the boats carried extra fuel in rubber tanks and in drums on deck, sometimes as many as 12 drums on each boat.

Allied forces landed on Pantelleria, about halfway between Cape Bon and Sicily, on June 11, 1943, and took the island without resistance from the dispirited Italian garrison. That night four divisions of coastal forces, two of PT's and two of British MTB's and MGB's, were ordered to patrol between Pantelleria and the Sicilian coast, 60 miles away, to prevent any attempts at evacuation or enemy interference. As senior officer, Barnes was in charge of the leading division, in PT 216 (Lt. (jg.) Cecil C. Sanders, USNR), with Reade's PT 203 and Oswald's PT 206.

"About half an hour after sunset we passed Pantelleria and were steaming along strung out in a column with the divisions about 500 yards apart," Barnes said. "The radioman on my boat reported a possible air target about 4 miles ahead and shortly thereafter, I saw a couple of bombs land a few hundred yards off our port bow. Seconds later a plane was heard diving on us. The first thing I knew a bomb dropped close astern completely enveloping the other two boats of my division in a cloud of smoke and water. I thought sure they were goners. It was just at last light; too dark for us to see the planes until they pulled out overhead and just light enough for them to see us. That was the beginning of continuous dive bombing which lasted about 15 minutes, all of it directed against my lead group. The other boats just lay off and watched, wondering when it was going to be their turn. It was hell on wheels for a while. I couldn't make up my mind whether to lie to and hope they couldn't see us without a wake or just push up the throttles and try to dodge. We ended up by doing both and by some extraordinary fate got no direct hits, although there were many near-misses. They must have dropped between 30 and 40 bombs altogether from what appeared to be about 8 planes. Most of the bombs were the contact type, but at least two were either depth charges or delayed action bombs which looked for all the world like mines going up. My boats stuck generally together for mutual antiaircraft support, but we just couldn't see enough to do any good. PT 203 was pretty well riddled by shrapnel. Lewis J. Bendl, seaman second class, who had volunteered for the mission to take the place of a sick friend, was badly wounded in the throat. I sent the boat right back but Bendl died before they could reach a doctor. The 206 had a few shrapnel holes in it, one prop knocked off, and the rudder bent by those delayed action bombs, but I kept it to make a group of two for the patrol."

The patrol itself was without further incident until the next morning when MGB 643 intercepted a small boat and captured seven Italians, including the harbormaster of Pantelleria, trying to escape to Sicily.

4. SICILIAN INVASION

The occupation of Pantelleria was a mere preliminary to the invasion of Sicily, scheduled for July 10, 1943. Toward the end of June the PT's were withdrawn from operations under the British Coastal Forces to give them time to prepare for Sicily. "Our principal difficulty," Barnes said, "was docking the boats since we had no drydock. But we pulled one of those unbelievable jobs and made a marine railway out of two large French seaplane dollies bolted together and run up and down a seaplane ramp by trucks. I also sent DuBose and four boats back to Bone where they docked themselves on a marine railway previously condemned by the British as being beyond repair. The boys had to get the French collaborationist owner out of a concentration camp for that period but they managed somehow."

More than 3,200 ships, boats, and landing craft made up the Allied Naval Forces for the invasion of Sicily, of which 1,700 were in the Western Naval Task Force, the U.S. force which was to effect landings in the Gela area of south central Sicily. This force in turn was divided into three separate task forces, of which the westernmost, under Rear Adm. Richard L. Conolly, was to carry out landings in the vicinity of Licata. The PT's of Squadron 15, with the destroyer *Ordronaux,* were designated as the western screen for Admiral Conolly's task force, with the special mission of guarding against attacks by E-boats believed to be based at Porto Empedocle.

Leaving Bizerte on the morning of July 9, the PT's had a wet and miserable trip to the Sicilian coast, wallowing through seas 12 to 16 feet high, with a 30-knot following wind. That night 17 PT's patrolled the western flank of their task force while the *Ordronaux* shelled Porto Empedocle. The PT's saw no enemy ships. It was learned later that the E-boat flotilla had withdrawn, leaving dummy boats to confuse air reconnaissance that night from Porto Empedocle. One group of PT's saw two American destroyers approaching at high speed. Before they came close, the destroyers collided and withdrew. Several weeks later the PT's learned that the destroyers had not received word of a late change in PT patrol areas and until the collision had every intention of blasting the unsuspecting boats out of the water.

On the day of the 10th, the PT's withdrew to Pantelleria, where they fueled from a little British tanker, *Empire Bairn,* and that night returned to the patrol line with *Ordronaux.*

On the night of July 12/13, eight PT's carried out diversionary operations with a group of specially equipped ASRC's (air-sea rescue craft) off two enemy-held beaches near Cape Granitola. The equipment of the ASRC's included rockets, smoke pots, equipment to simulate the noises of a large assault force, and radio circuits to direct (for the benefit of enemy interception) the movements of a fleet of imaginary landing craft. Their purpose was to force the enemy to keep troops at beaches where no landing was to be made—troops that might otherwise be thrown into combat at the real beachhead.

Two divisions, each containing five PT's and four ASRC's, were to make simultaneous demonstrations, one to the east and one to the west of Cape Granitola. The PT's were to run parallel to the beach, 2,000 yards offshore, laying smoke and firing all guns toward the beach. Then they were to close to 1,000 yards and reverse course for a second run. The ASRC's were to follow behind the smokescreen to complete the demonstration with their sound and pyrotechnic equipment.

The first division, under Comdr. H. R. Robinson, USNR, commander of the diversion group, carried out its demonstration according to plan but a few minutes ahead of schedule. Searchlights blazed from the shore and heavy batteries opened fire. The first few salvos were wild but toward the end of the second run the shells dropped so close—one of them only 15 yards ahead of the 208—that the boats had to open the range.

Barnes, leading the second group, arrived a few minutes late. "The shore batteries by this time were completely alerted," he said in his action report. "Apparently the enemy was convinced that a landing was about to take place when it detected the large number of boats constituting the second group approaching the beach, for they opened a heavy and accurate fire with radar control before the second demonstration could begin. Course was immediately reversed and the range opened. Salvos of 6-inch and smaller guns were observed. One shell damaged the rudders of an ASRC and another fell 10 yards astern of a PT. It was considered that the purpose of the demonstration had been accomplished and both groups withdrew, the ASRC's returning to Pantelleria and the PT's to Bizerte."

There was some gratification in enemy press reports that an attempted landing on the southwest coast of Sicily had been repulsed.

5. PALERMO

On July 14 Admiral Hewitt ordered the PT's to operate against enemy surface units attempting to reinforce Sicily through its western ports, including Palermo. Distance made this a difficult assignment. The PT's, still based at Bizerte, each had to carry at least 500 gallons of gasoline on deck for each patrol. A week later Barnes went to Algiers and obtained Admiral Hewitt's permission to set up an operating base at Palermo as soon as the port was taken.

Palermo fell on July 23. On the evening of the 23d, Barnes set out from Bizerte with eight boats. "At dawn the next day we were off Ustica," he said. "First thing off we saw a fishing boat putt-putting toward Italy. Going over we found a handful of very scared individuals crawling out from under the floor plates hopefully waving white handkerchiefs. This was the staff of the Italian Admiral at Trapani. The only reason we didn't get the Admiral was that he was late getting down to the dock and his staff said to hell with him. In addition to a few souvenir pistols and binoculars we captured a whole fruit crate of thousand-lira notes which we reluctantly turned over to the Army authorities later. While this was going on, one of the other boats spotted a raft with seven Germans on it feebly paddling out to sea. We picked those up too."

The boats put into Palermo at 0800, and that night Lt. Ernest C. Arbuckle, USNR, in PT 209 (Lt. (jg.) W. Knox Eldredge, USNR), led PT's 216 (Lt. (jg.) Cecil C. Sanders, USNR) and PT 204 (Lt. (jg.) Eugene S. A. Clifford, USNR) eastward to the Italian coast just north of the Strait of Messina, the narrow strip of water separating Sicily from the toe of the Italian boot. On arrival at Palermo the boats had undertaken a new mission—to prevent enemy supply and evacuation of Sicily by patrolling the northern approaches to the Strait of Messina.

Half a mile off the coast near Palmi the boats found a tug towing the 8,800-ton Italian merchant ship *Viminale*. Sanders scored a torpedo hit on the ship, and then under ineffective fire from shore batteries, the boats strafed the tug until it was smoking and dead in the water. As the boats retired they saw the *Viminale* sink stern first. Later, the tug also sank.

Two nights later Lieutenant Mutty, in PT 202 (Lt. (jg.) Robert D. McLeod, USNR), with PT 210 (Lt. (jg.) John L. Davis, Jr., USNR) and PT 214 (Lt. (jg.) Ernest W. Olson, USNR), had the squadron's first encounter with F-lighters. The F-lighters, which from this time on became the principal prey of the Mediterranean PT's, were somewhat similar to, but considerably larger than, our LCT's. They were 170 feet long, with a cargo-carrying capacity of about 120 tons, and their hulls were so well compartmented that it was impossible for PT's to sink them with anything less than a torpedo hit. The PT's learned after their first few engagements with F-lighters that it was foolish to try to fight them with guns; the F-lighters were far more heavily armed than the PT's and far less vulnerable to gunfire.

Mutty's division found seven F-lighters in column northeast of Stromboli and sneaked in to 500 yards. Each boat fired two torpedoes, and at 300 yards started to turn away. During the turn, the second lighter in column sent up a flare, apparently a signal to open fire. All of the lighters immediately opened with a great volume of 76mm., 20mm., and machinegun fire, which the PT's returned. Although it was felt that two torpedoes hit home, German records show that they all missed. A few seconds later it became apparent that the fire from the PT's, while hitting the F-lighters, was also giving them a point of aim. The PT's ceased fire and laid smoke, and the enemy fire became inaccurate. The 202 had a punctured gasoline tank, several holes in the hull, and one man wounded. The other boats were not hit.

On the following night, July 28/29, Lieutenant Arbuckle, in PT 218 (Lt. (jg.) Donald W. Henry, USNR), with Olson's 214 and Reade's 203 made a torpedo attack on three Italian MAS boats.[16] The torpedoes were well aimed but passed under the enemy without exploding. The PT's idled away and Arbuckle decided to attack again, making a gunnery run with the 218, while the other two boats maneuvered for a torpedo attack. He closed to 100 yards and began to strafe the lighters. "This," said the action report, "was immediately returned with a heavy volume of fire from all enemy vessels . . . directed principally at PT 218. The boat was hit repeatedly with 20mm. and suffered considerable damage which included the holing of the vessel below the waterline forward, puncturing of both forward gas tanks, and disabling of one engine. The engagement was broken off in confusion."

Arbuckle, Henry, and Ens. Edmund F. Jacobs, USNR, second officer of the 218, were wounded. Henry and Jacobs were flat on the deck, but Ar-

[16] The Italian MAS boats which the PT's met in the Mediterranean were the direct descendants of the boats the Italians used with some success in World War I. The World War II MAS boats were about 60 feet long and carried two torpedo tubes and light machineguns. They had a top speed of about 42 knots, and usually could outrun the Mediterranean PT's.

NR&L (MOD)—32501

PT torpedo storehouse at Palermo, Sicily.

buckle, painfully wounded in the heel, propped himself up and organized the crew to save the boat. The crew's quarters were flooding, one engine was knocked out, and several hundreds of gallons of gasoline had drained into the bilges. Under Arbuckle's direction the crew partially bailed out the flooded compartment and plugged the biggest holes. Three hours later Arbuckle brought his boat alongside the destroyer *Wainwright* at Palermo. Then he collapsed.

On the night of July 29/30, PT's again met F-lighters. This time Lt. (jg.) Richard H. O'Brien, in Clifford's PT 204, with Lt. Norman DeVol's PT 217, engaged two F-lighters escorted by four MAS boats, firing six torpedoes and strafing the MAS boats before heavy fire from one of the lighters forced them to retire. The Italian officer commanding the MAS boats in this action was later interviewed in Capri. He said one F-lighter had been sunk and one MAS boat had been so badly damaged that it was abandoned and sunk by the other MAS boats.

"It seemed after that last engagement," Barnes said, "that the enemy finally got the idea that we weren't going to let them make that northern run any more. They confined their future efforts almost exclusively to running back and forth inside the strait below Messina where nobody could get at them except aircraft."

During this period the squadron continued to undertake special missions for the Office of Strategic Services. "A team under Lieutenant John Shaheen, USNR, arrived quietly and mysteriously for a venture called 'Operation MacGregor,'" Barnes said. "Essentially the idea was to get a letter from our Government through to a certain Rear Admiral in the Italian Navy suggesting that the Italian Navy call it quits and offering certain inducements to that end. Our part of the operation was to land and recover an agent with the letter and to bring someone out for a parley. I gave O'Brien the job of putting the thing over. He trained with members of the team while waiting for a suitable dark moon period, teaching them to handle and navigate a rubber boat. The first attempt [August 10, 1943] at landing in the Gulf of Gaeta failed when the boats ran into numerous fishing or patrol craft which made an unobserved landing impossible but the second attempt [August 12] was successful. The agent never did meet the rendezvous although the boats were there waiting for him. As it turned out the letter reached the proper hands and, although somewhat late, apparently had considerable influence on the subsequent surrender of the Italian Navy."

At the end of July, Rear Adm. Lyal A. Davidson arrived at Palermo with Task Force 88—two cruisers, several destroyers, and an assortment of landing craft—to support the eastward advance of Lt. Gen. George S. Patton's Seventh Army by fire support and a series of leapfrog landings along the northern coast of Sicily. On the night of 15/16 August, six PT's were assigned to screen one of these landings at Spadafora from possible enemy E-boat attacks. Lieutenant DuBose, commanding the northern PT group, PT 205 (Ens. Robert T. Boebel, USNR), PT 215 (Lt. George A. Steele, Jr., USNR), and PT 216 (Lt. (jg.) Cecil C. Sanders, USNR), sighted and gave chase to two German E-boats off the Italian coast.

"The Germans opened a heavy and accurate fire with 40mm., 20mm., and smaller guns and headed south at high speed," Barnes reported. "Fire was returned with all guns that could bear in the overtaking chase and the range closed to 400 yards. The enemy turned away, laid smoke and dropped depth charges, employing every possible evasive maneuver. The PT's were handicapped by their inability to make more than 25 knots, the 216 lagging the other PT's to such an extent that it was unable to take part in the engagement for any length of time. . . . All PT's were hit repeatedly but miraculously no serious damage was incurred. Four men were wounded on the PT 216. Subsequent interview with an Italian E-boat flotilla commander after the capitulation of Italy revealed that in the engagement the German E-boats suffered heavy casualties totalling 14. These included the German flotilla commander who was killed."

Lack of speed prevented the PT's from conclusive action against the E-boats but, in forcing them to retire, the PT's accomplished their primary mission of protecting our assault forces from E-boat attack. None of the squadron's boats could make more than 27 or 28 knots during the summer of 1943. The boats were overloaded, maintenance facilities were limited, and the engines would not give top performance in the heat of the Mediterranean summer.

Two and a half hours after the engagement with the E-boats, PT 205 intercepted a small sailboat and captured a German officer and six Italian merchant sailors who had been en route to Italy from the island of Lipari, one of the Eolie group to the north of Sicily. Questioning of the sailors indicated that no Germans remained in the islands and that the Italian inhabitants would welcome a chance to surrender to Americans.

Accordingly, under orders from Admiral Davidson to effect surrender of the Eolie Islands, DuBose set out from Palermo on the morning of August 17 in Lieutenant Steele's PT 215, with Lieutenant (jg.) Sanders' PT 216 and Lieutenant DeVol's PT 217. The boats carried an American military government representative, 1 other Army officer, 7 Army enlisted men, and 17 extra enlisted men from the squadron. The destroyer *Trippe* was assigned as a supporting force for the PT's.

The boats entered Lipari Harbor without opposition and found the Italian Naval Commandant of the islands waiting for them on the dock. Within 10 minutes he had surrendered unconditionally the islands of Alicudi, Filicudi, Salina, Stromboli, Lipari, and Vulcano. While the military government officer negotiated with the mayor for establishment of a new civil government for the islands, the PT men rounded up 19 prisoners, and after the commandant had sent radio messages demanding concurrence of the other islands in the surrender, put the radio station out of commission. Only the island of Stromboli refused to agree to the surrender.

The PT's occupied Stromboli late in the afternoon. They found that an Italian chief petty officer and his 30 men had destroyed barracks and confidential papers. The PT men took 19 more prisoners, destroyed a radio station, and the military government officer advised the mayor of the agreement reached at Lipari for civil administration. Then the PT's returned to Palermo to find that Messina had fallen that day. The Sicilian campaign was over.

6. INVASION OF ITALY

Seventeen PT's got underway from Palermo on the morning of September 8, 1943, to take part in the amphibious invasion of Italy at Salerno, scheduled to begin on the morning of the 9th. One PT, Lieutenant (jg.) Olson's PT 214, joined the Diversion Group and participated in a demonstration near the Volturno River and in the capture of the island of Ventotene; the other 16 boats, under Lieutenant Commander Barnes, patrolled in 5 groups off the Bay of Naples to screen the landings in Salerno Bay against interference from the north.

"It seemed as if every plane the Germans had flew low over us that night," Barnes said. "A couple of them dropped a casual bomb or two in our midst but did no damage. Their objectives were the hundreds of ships to the southwest of us from which we could see clouds of brilliant flak going up as they were attacked.

"Nothing much really happened. First of all I picked up an Italian officer trying to get from Capri to Naples in a small picket boat. Later I saw something by radar come out of the harbor entrance but as soon as I approached, it went right back in. However, an F-lighter did come out and head west, very close to the beach. I went up and fired one torpedo from 500 yards without effect and then had another boat do the same thing, after which the F-lighter ran into the shore and beached itself. O'Brien spent a quiet night until he found a trawler trying to work its way out. Rather than waste a torpedo on it, he decided to gun it up. He had his three boats lie off that thing while it was dead in the water and pour shells into it for half an hour at point blank range. It was a very illuminating example of how ineffective our gunfire really was. Not only did it not sink but it didn't even catch on fire.[17] Later we found out that there was a crew of

---

[17] At this time Squadron 15 had no guns heavier than 20mm. Early in 1944 a 40mm. cannon was mounted on each boat.

80—G—87333

Two PT's slide past an LST in Salerno harbor during the invasion of Italy.

three on board who abandoned the ship in a rowboat on the opposite side and just lay off until O'Brien quit; then they went back on board and got it underway again for Capri where we found it a few days later riddled with holes but still serviceable. Except for the time when I found O'Brien tracking and about to attack my own group, there was little other excitement that evening. At dawn we pulled out and headed around for Salerno."

During the next week PT operations were considerably limited by failure of gasoline tankers to arrive on schedule. The PT's did maintain anti-E-boat screens each night north of the Bay of Salerno, but sighted no enemy ships. When they were not patrolling, the boats anchored off the towns of Minori, Maori, and Amalfi on the south side of the Sorrento Peninsula in the Gulf of Salerno. Large flights of enemy planes came over regularly on the way to the assault beaches, but seldom tried to bomb the boats, which were somewhat protected by high hills close to shore. One Messerschmidt 109 dropped a bomb close enough to Lt. (jg.) Page H. Tulloch's 211 to bend the boat's rudders. The 211 retaliated by shooting the plane down.

80-G-87326

A PT lays smoke at Salerno to shield ships of invasion force from air attack.
Mast of USS Ancon, *flagship of the Commander Eighth Fleet, is just visible*
over top of screen.

PT's, along with other types, were used daily to lay smokescreens around assault shipping at dawn, dusk, and moonrise, and at other times when air raids were expected. Admiral Hewitt reported that the smoke was especially valuable in protecting against night air attacks.

On September 20, Lt. (jg.) W. Knox Eldredge, USNR, in PT 209, and Lt. (jg.) Eugene S. A. Clifford, USNR, in PT 204, felt out the Bay of Naples to determine whether minesweeping operations could be conducted there in daylight. The Germans let them come in until they had four shore guns bearing on them, and then opened fire, dropping shells so close that the boats were drenched by the splashes. The boats maneuvered out independently, refusing to lay smoke until they had the four gun positions pinpointed on their charts.

On September 15 the PT's moved to Capri, and started patrolling further to the north, but had no more surface contacts during the month.

7. MADDALENA AND BASTIA

About the first of October, Barnes was ordered to proceed to Maddalena, on northwest Sardinia, to report to the Advanced Coastal Forces Base for operations. He arrived there with four PT's on October 4 and reported to Comdr. Robert A. Allan, RNVR, commander of the base, who had recently arrived from Sicily with an advanced base party and a few MTB's and MGB's.[18]

By the middle of the month the PT's and British Coastal Forces had set up a still further advanced base 100 miles to the north at Bastia, Corsica, which brought the entire Gulf of Genoa within easy patrolling distance. The German-held island of Elba, only 20 miles from Bastia, was used as an operational dividing line between the bases, boats from Maddalena covering the territory to the south and boats from Bastia that to the north. Enemy surface activity gradually became concentrated more and more to the north, and by the middle of December all PT patrols went out from Bastia.

The boats had hard sledding during their first few months at the new bases. The difficulty of finding suitable shelter ashore led Barnes to remark, "Our bases were hewn out of proprietary resistance as much as they were out of rubble."

The squadron had received no replacements of officers or men, and was operating far below complement. And it was not until the middle of November that Barnes succeeded in having the squadron's advanced base equipment moved up from Palermo. For any but minor repairs the boats had to go all the way to Bizerte. Worst of all, torpedoes could not be maintained properly until the base equipment arrived from Palermo. The British Coastal Forces Base did what it could, but lacked tools, parts, and experience to do a proper job on American torpedoes.

A torpedo is a complex and delicate machine. The old Mark VIII's, most of them built in the early 1920's, required constant maintenance and adjustment to give satisfactory performance. Furthermore, the Mark VIII was designed to run several feet below the surface, where the surrounding water,

---

[18] At this time Commander Allan, as Commander Advanced Coastal Forces Base, was operating directly under the Commander in Chief, Mediterranean (Admiral Sir Andrew Cunningham, RN). Later the command, Senior Officer Inshore Squadron, was established at Bastia, with operational control of Coastal Forces, including PT's. Except during special operations, such as the invasion of Sicily, Italy, and southern France, American PT's operated as part of the British Coastal Forces during the entire Mediterranean campaign. The only operations of MTB's and MGB's that will be mentioned here are those undertaken jointly with PT's. The brilliant accomplishments of the British Coastal Forces, not only in western Italy, but in Tunisia, Sicily, the Adriatic, and eastern Mediterranean, are another story, outside the scope of this volume.

itself noncompressible, would direct the full force of the explosion against the hull of the target ship. F-lighters, which had become the principal targets of the PT's, were of such shallow draft that the PT's had to adjust their torpedoes to run almost on the surface—otherwise they would pass harmlessly under the F-lighters. But the Mark VIII torpedo simply would not run at fixed depth with a shallow setting. If a boat captain was lucky, his torpedo would porpoise when it reached the F-lighter; if unlucky, it would pass below the target. Besides, without proper maintenance, it was to be expected that many torpedoes would run erratically. Many did.

"I remember one of the first times we went out," Barnes said. "I took three boats up off Leghorn and distinguished myself by throwing four torpedoes at a wreck on the Meloria Banks off the harbor entrance. If I do say so myself, it was a very realistic target and looked for all the world like something headed into port. We frequently torpedoed wrecks in new

NR&L (MOD)—32500

PT's at Maddalena, Sardinia, with surrendered Italian corvette in background. The blasted building at left was repaired and used for a PT engineering repair shop.

80—G—23442

PT 211 in Bastia harbor, Corsica. Note rocket launchers on forward deck.

areas until we had them properly marked down and got the word around. Only one of these four fish hit and two of them ran erratic."

Lieutenant O'Brien had even worse luck on the night of October 19/20, when he led a three-boat division (PT's 217, 211, and 208) that fired eight torpedoes at merchant ship *Giorgio* escorted by three E- or R-boats and a flak lighter north of Leghorn.[19] Six of the eight torpedoes were erratic, one of them circling the PT formation and forcing the boats to maneuver to avoid their own torpedo. The other two missed the enemy.

Lieutenant DuBose made the first definite kill in the Maddalena-Bastia area on the night of October 22/23, when, in Oswald's PT 206, he led Sanders's PT 216 and PT 212 (Lt. (jg.) T. Lowry Sinclair, USNR) in an attack on a cargo ship escorted by four E- or R-boats south of Giglio Island.

---

[19] The R-boat, frequently used as an escort vessel, was 120 to 150 feet in length, and was armed with 37mm. or 40mm. and heavier guns, up to 76mm. or 88mm. Its designation is an abbreviation of the German "Raumboot," or "sweeping boat." The flak lighters were identical in appearance with ordinary F-lighters, but were far more heavily armed, their decks bristling with guns up to 88mm.

The 206 and 216 each fired two torpedoes, and as the 212, third boat in formation, was getting its sights lined up for a shot, one of the 206's torpedoes, running wild, porpoised alongside it. Sinclair swung his boat hard right as the torpedo passed, and then came back to firing course. DuBose, impatient, asked Sinclair by radio, "How many have you fired?"

"None yet," Sinclair replied. "I'm too damned busy dodging yours."

Sinclair finally managed to get off two torpedoes and joined the other boats in a slow retirement. "Two torpedoes are believed to have hit," the action report said. "One hit was observed forward followed by a violent explosion and the ship disintegrated. The retirement was made at slow speed on the beam. The enemy did not open fire and it is believed that the attack was completely unobserved."

Prisoner-of-war interrogation later indicated that this ship was a corvette converted for use as a cargo carrier.

On the night of November 2/3, Lieutenant O'Brien, patrolling in Lt. (jg.) Page Tulloch's PT 211, with Lt. (jg.) Frederick W. Rosen's PT 207, attacked a ship initially identified as a tanker, which he estimated at 4,000 tons, escorted by three E- or R-boats, off the north shore of Giglio Island. The 211 fired four torpedoes and the 207 two, all within 450 yards. "As the last torpedoes were fired," the action report said, "fire was opened by the tanker with one major caliber gun and several machine guns. Shortly after, the escort opened fire with 40mm. and 20mm. and the division increased speed to maximum and laid smoke. . .

"As speed was increased, one torpedo hit was observed at the tanker's bow. A few seconds later another hit amidships which caused an explosion. This was quickly followed by another which precipitated a violent explosion sending flames 150 feet into the air. The entire superstructure of the tanker was thrown bodily into the air and it sank within a few seconds. The explosion was of such force that the PT's were severely shaken at 800 yards. The escort ceased firing at this time." German records reveal that the "tanker" was actually Submarine Chaser 2206.

An incendiary bullet, unnoticed at the time, had passed through a gasoline tank of the 207, through an ammunition locker, and into the officers' quarters, where it set some clothing smoldering. Gasoline poured through the bullet hole into the bilges, and soon there was an explosion that blew open the deck hatch to the officers' quarters and projected the ladder straight up through the hatch and over the side. Flames leaped up through the hatch as high as the top of the radar mast. Edward B. Farley, RM2c, grabbed a fire extinguisher from the charthouse, opened its nozzle, dropped it into the compartment, and slammed down the hatch. At the same time the torpedoman pulled the release lever to blanket the tank compartment with carbon dioxide. The flames were smothered. As soon as he saw the flareup on the 207, O'Brien cut across Rosen's bow, laying smoke. A moment later the 207 passed through the screen, perfectly concealed from the enemy and miraculously intact. The inside of the officers' quarters was completely burned out. Why the whole boat didn't explode no one ever knew.

8. WINTER OPERATIONS

On the Italian mainland Allied forces drove the Germans from the beaches of the Gulf of Salerno, past Naples, and across the Volturno River. Then the American Fifth Army on the west and the British Eighth Army on the east began their slow and painful advance toward Rome, fighting the Germans on the roads and in the mountains, in the villages and across the rivers, cracking through the Winter Line barrier of mountains only to have the enemy withdraw into the even more formidable Gustav Line behind the Garigliano and Rapido Rivers.

Constant Allied air attacks disrupted enemy supply by rail and road from Genoa to Rome and the forward lines. More and more the Germans had to rely on waterborne transport, F-lighters and cargo ships running down the coast by night behind a barrier of minefields and under the protection of heavy shore batteries. The minefields made it too risky to send destroyers in to stop the traffic; the job had to be done by PT's, MTB's, and MGB's, shallow-draft vessels that could pass over the deep-set mines without detonating them.

Strategically, the German supply problem bore some resemblance to that of the Japanese in New Guinea. But the tactics for cutting the supply, even though the job was to be done by PT's and their British counterparts, had to be different. The Japanese barges were too small to be considered as torpedo targets, and could not stand up to the PT's in a gunnery engagement, even though some of them were more heavily gunned than the PT's. F-lighters, on the other hand, were almost invulnerable to PT gunfire. It took torpedoes to sink them and the PT's had to get their torpedoes away before they themselves were taken under the intense, accurate, heavy-caliber fire of the F-lighters. In New Guinea the PT's sometimes stood up against the

3-inch shore guns of the Japanese and silenced them with their 40mms. Along the Italian coast south of Genoa the Germans protected their F-lighters with 6-inch and 8-inch guns. The boats were forced to develop a sneak technique—tracking the target by radar to learn its course and speed and the most favorable angle of approach, then idling in and firing torpedoes before the enemy became aware of their presence.

Early in November Lieutenant Commander Barnes realized that the PT's, because they were equipped with radar and the British boats were not, were superior to the British boats in the matter of finding enemy vessels and in executing the necessary maneuvers for a sneak attack. He also realized that the MTB's were superior to the PT's in the matter of torpedoes—the British torpedoes were more reliable than the Mark VIII's, were faster, and carried a heavier explosive charge—and that the MGB's were superior to the PT's in the matter of firepower—their guns included 6-pounders, ancient but powerful. Barnes proposed to Commander Allan that a PT accompany each group of British boats to serve as a scout and a tracker.

From November until the end of April, joint PT-British patrols resulted in 14 actions with the enemy, in which the boats claimed 15 F-lighters, 2 E-boats, a tug, and an oil barge sunk; 3 F-lighters, a destroyer, a trawler, and an E-boat damaged; and 2 destroyers possibly damaged. During the same period PT's patrolling alone were in action with the enemy 10 times, claiming 1 F-lighter sunk, 1 E-boat damaged, and a possible torpedo hit on a small coaster. The PT's also conducted many special missions, landing or picking up agents, coastwatchers, and commandos on at least 18 occasions.

Throughout the winter, operations were severely limited by foul weather. The Gulf of Genoa is the stormiest part of the Mediterranean, and on many nights the seas raged so high that the boats could not go out at all. Often they started out in calm seas, only to have the wind blow up to gale force before they reached patrol stations. The heavy winds and seas created a further hazard by setting adrift many mines from the German fields. The danger was particularly acute at Bastia, where a German minefield gradually broke up during the winter storms. Several drifting mines exploded right on the Bastia breakwater. During the first few months the British lost six minesweepers in the Maddalena-Bastia area.

On the morning of December 31, a small tanker bringing gasoline for the PT's and a British LST, escorted by two British minesweepers, approached Bastia. Shortly before the convoy arrived at the entrance to the swept channel, the weather, which had been calm and clear, began to blow up for a gale. The ships missed the channel entrance and drifted into the minefield. One of the minesweepers hit a mine and went down. Then the LST hit a mine and almost broke in two. "When the news of this disaster reached Bastia," Barnes said, "all boats were ordered to stand by, but the PT's were the only available that could weather that kind of a sea. I remember standing on the sea wall watching two RAF crashboats trying to get out. One of them almost broke itself up before it had gone more than a few hundred yards and the other one cut up some members of its crew so badly that it had to turn back."

PT's 206, 214, 215, and 216 battled 20-foot seas and 40-knot winds for more than 3 hours, picking up 12 survivors from the water and towing two liferafts each containing 20 men to the remaining minesweeper. "I've never seen a bunch of people so exhausted in my life as they were when they got back," Barnes said. "I remember Oswald with the blind staggers and mumbling incoherently about his rocket racks which had been swept off the boat. He really must have been in a bad way because that certainly was the last thing any boat captain would worry about losing."

Ill as this wind was, it blew its pittance of good. Men from the PT base stripped the abandoned LST of its galley, pots and pans, plates and cutlery, to the incalculable improvement of their own primitive mess.

9. COLLISION WITH A MINESWEEPER

On the evening of November 29, Lieutenant DuBose, in Lt. (jg.) Page H. Tulloch's PT 211, set out with Lt. (jg.) Eugene S. A. Clifford's PT 204 to patrol near Genoa. When they left Bastia the sea was moderate and the wind light. Within 2 hours a 35-knot wind was blowing and both boats were making heavy weather. Water came over the bows in sheets and short circuited the radars. With visibility less than 100 yards, the boats were ordered to return to port.

They became separated on their return trip, the 211 running ahead of the 204. When the 204 was 3½ miles from the harbor entrance, a group of enemy motor minesweepers and E-boats loomed out of the darkness, running on an opposite course 75 yards away. Then another motor minesweeper appeared just off the starboard bow crossing to port. The PT turned hard left and struck the other a glancing blow by the bows. As they sheared off they exchanged heavy machinegun fire at a range of 10 yards. The other minesweepers joined in the action almost immediately, but their fire was inaccurate and, in the low visibility, contact with all of the boats was lost in about 15 seconds.

Torpedo tubes, ventilators, gun mounts, and the deck of the 204 were riddled with bullet holes, and 100 bullets passed through the side of the boat into the engineroom. There were no hits in the gasoline tanks; the engines, though hit, kept running, and not an officer or man was scratched.

10. ANZIO

In the closing days of 1943 it became apparent that the American Fifth and British Eighth Armies' drive on Rome had hit a brick wall. If there was to be a decision in the Italian campaign, there would have to be another major amphibious landing behind the right flank of the enemy's Gustav Line. Early on the morning of January 22, 1944, ships of the Eighth Amphibious Force (Rear Adm. Frank J. Lowry) began to land elements of the Fifth Army's VI Corps at Anzio, 37 miles south of Rome. Later that morning Lt. Gen. Mark Clark, Commanding General of the Fifth Army, and members of his staff, arrived at the beachhead aboard a PT and were taken ashore in a small landing craft.

General Clark had asked for, and received, the assignment of two PT's to his operational control. Until March he always had two PT's, though not always the same two, at his disposal. They were used primarily as fast passenger craft to carry the General and other ranking officers between Naples and Anzio, and occasionally were sent on intelligence and rescue missions. Their work usually was uneventful, but not always—one morning they almost lost General Clark.

The General left from the mouth of the Volturno River at 0825 on January 28 in PT 201 (Lt. (jg.) George E. Patterson, Jr., USNR), accompanied by Sanders's PT 216, heading north toward Anzio. As the boats approached Cape Circeo, 25 miles below Anzio, they were sighted by the minesweeper *Sway,* patrolling the southern approaches to Anzio. Now *Sway* had just been warned that enemy aircraft were attacking Anzio and might carry the attack to shipping; it was known that the enemy sometimes coordinated air and E-boat strikes, and the captain of *Sway* saw two small boats approaching at high speed out of the sun. He challenged the PT's by signal light. Without reducing his speed, Patterson replied to the challenge with a 6-inch signal light. He did not realize that, with the sun at his back, the small light could not be seen aboard the *Sway*. *Sway,* receiving no reply to the challenge and seeing the boats continuing their approach, opened fire. Patterson fired an emergency identification flare, but again the glare of the sun prevented the crew of the *Sway* from seeing the signal. The 201 reduced speed and almost immediately a shell hit the boat in the chart-house, wounding Patterson, his second officer, and one man, and fatally wounding another man and an officer passenger.

"Let's get the hell out of here," General Clark said.*

Ens. Paul R. Benson, USNR, the wounded executive officer, maneuvered away at full speed until the boats were out of range of *Sway's* guns. After the wounded were put aboard a British minesweeper a few miles down the coast, Sanders took over the 201 and returned, proceeding cautiously until the boats had established their identity with a 12-inch searchlight. The sun by this time was higher in the sky and *Sway* was able to read the larger light without difficulty. The boats proceeded to Anzio without further mishap.

11. TB DESTROYERS

The German Tenth Torpedo Boat Flotilla started operations in the Gulf of Genoa in the fall of 1943. Though manned by German personnel, its ships were almost all former Italian warships, most of them of a type peculiar to the Italian Navy, called torpedo boats by the Italians but in reality small destroyers. The Americans referred to them variously as destroyers, TB's (for torpedo boats), or TB destroyers.

The first encounter with them came on the night of December 11/12, when Lt. (jg.) John M. Torrance, USNR, in PT 208, and Lt. (jg.) Frederick W. Rosen, USNR, in PT 207, were patrolling between Elba and Leghorn. The PT radars were not working properly and the boats were taken by surprise when two destroyers opened fire on them at a range of 2½ miles. The PT's headed out to sea. The destroyers gave chase for a few minutes and then turned away.

On the night of December 16/17, two destroyers came down to Bastia and lobbed shells into the town for 15 minutes, with no harm to the PT's

---

*General Clark, in his book, *Calculated Risk,* Harper & Bros., New York, 1950, records (p. 293) that he said, "Well, let's run for it." I prefer the saltier language of the contemporaneous PT report.

and little to the town. Because the shelling was brief and ineffective, and because of heavy seas, which had kept all the boats in port since the 13th, no attempt was made to intercept the destroyers. Two nights later the weather moderated somewhat, and though one patrol was turned back by heavy seas, another group, MGB's 659 and 663, and MTB 655, with Eldredge's PT 209 as scout and tracker, was able to remain on station in the channel between Elba and the Italian mainland. Just after midnight, Barnes, in PT 210 (Lt. John L. Davis, Jr., USNR), went out with Olson's 214, Torrance's 208, and Oswald's 206 as a reception committee in case the destroyers should decide to pay another visit to Bastia.

Less than 10 minutes after arriving on station, the boats sighted two destroyers steaming toward Bastia at better than 20 knots. Barnes tried to move in from the west with the 210 and 214 to attack on the bow, ordering the other two boats to get in position for an attack if the enemy should reverse course. The destroyers headed toward Barnes's section and opened fire on the PT's. The turn gave the other boats a chance to fire seven torpedoes, which the destroyers avoided by swinging south again. This turn left Barnes's boats in a poor position for firing torpedoes. With destroyer shells dropping uncomfortably close, Barnes retired to the west behind smoke.

Barnes sent the 208 and 206, which had fired all but one of their torpedoes, back to Bastia, and when the enemy fire ceased, turned eastward with the 210 and 214 to pursue the destroyers. The destroyer speed was such that he could not hope to hit them with an overtaking shot, but thought he might be able to work up ahead of them into good firing position, or to head them off toward Elba, where the 209 was patrolling with the British boats. The destroyers ran east, with the PT's gradually overtaking them on a parallel course to the north. Off the northwest corner of Elba the destroyers began to turn north. Barnes closed the range to force them to turn right toward the other group of boats to the east. The destroyers again opened fire on the PT's, but the stratagem worked. The destroyers turned to the east.

The second group of boats met the destroyers a mile off the north coast of Elba. Eldredge's 209 and MTB 655 each launched two torpedoes, while the MGB's took the destroyers under fire with their guns. Barnes's boats, closing in from the west, each fired four torpedoes. For a few minutes there was wild confusion, with the torpedo boats laying smoke, the gunboats and destroyers blazing away at each other, the brilliant beam of a searchlight sweeping the water from the Elba shore, and shore batteries firing in the general direction of the boats.

The action was a disappointing one, resulting in no damage to the enemy. However, the boats had influenced the Germans to abandon their plans to bombard Bastia.

PT's did not meet destroyers again until the night of February 17/18, when the Senior Officer Inshore Squadron again told Barnes to intercept two destroyers approaching Bastia from the north. Three PT's (the 211, 203 and 202) chased two destroyers for more than 2 hours, firing five torpedoes and finally abandoning pursuit because the boats were taking terrific punishment from mounting seas. Some months later, when Barnes prepared a summary of his squadron's actions, he characterized this one succinctly: "No hits, everybody running; all errors."

These actions proved that PT's could harass TB destroyers. They also demonstrated the extreme difficulty of attacking a fast target with a slow torpedo.

12. FUN WITH ROCKETS

Squadron 15 experimented with rockets as a desperate measure to find a weapon that would be effective against F-lighters. They were used only twice, however, since their accuracy left something to be desired, and they took off with such a blaze of flame that the position of the PT's was revealed to the enemy. The squadron first used rockets on the night of February 18/19, in one of the strangest actions of the Mediterranean campaign.

Lieutenant Commander Barnes was patrolling between Giglio Island and the Argentario Peninsula on the Italian coast in PT 211 (Lt. (jg.) Page H. Tulloch, USNR), with PT 203 (Lt. Robert B. Reade, USNR) and PT 202 (Lt. (jg.) Robert D. McLeod, USNR). "I saw a small radar target come out from behind the peninsula and head over toward one of the small islands south of Giglio," Barnes said. "Thinking it might be an F-lighter I ordered the rocket racks loaded and started over. I think he must have seen us because whatever it was—probably an E-boat—speeded up and ducked into the island before we could make contact. That presented the first difficulty of our rocket installation. There we were with the racks all loaded and the safety pins out. The weather had picked up a little and getting those pins back and the racks unloaded was going to be a touchy job in the pitch darkness on wet tossing decks. I decided to leave them there for a while to see what would happen.

"Around about midnight it started to kick up a good deal more. I had just about made up my mind that whatever it was we were looking for wasn't going to show and was getting pretty worried about the rockets heaving out of the racks and rolling around in a semi-armed condition on deck. I decided to make one turn around our patrol area and head for the barn. On our last southerly leg we picked up a target coming north at about 8 knots and I closed right away thinking to spend all our rockets on whatever it was. As we got in closer it appeared to be two small targets in column—a conclusion which I later used as an outstanding example of 'don't trust your interpretation of radar too blindly.'

"Just about the time we got to the 1,000-yard firing range the lookouts started reporting vessels everywhere, all the way from our port back around to our starboard bow. I had arranged the other two boats one on either side in line abreast and ordered them to stand by to fire on my order over the radio. I gave the order and we all let go together. During the 11 seconds the rockets were in flight nobody fired a shot, but a couple of seconds after the rockets landed what seemed like a dozen enemy craft opened up. The formation was probably three or four F-lighters escorted by two groups of E-boats. We had passed through the two groups of escorts on the way to our firing position.

"Now it came time to turn away and as my boat turned to the right, we found that the 202 was steaming right into the convoy. To avoid collision we had to turn back and parallel the 202. Just at that time the engines on my boat started to labor and unbelievably coughed and died—all three of them. All during this time we were smack dab in the center of the whole outfit with the enemy shooting from all sides. Never in my life will I see anything like it. The volume was terrific. Meanwhile the 203 on my port hand had lost all electrical power including the radar and compass lights. As she started to turn away she saw the two of us going off on our original course and came back to join us, making a wide circle at high speed and laying smoke.

"It is impossible to say just what happened. The melee was too terrific. The 202 had a jammed rudder which they were able to clear in a minute or so. She eventually got out by ducking around several vessels, passing a number as close as 100 yards. The 203 likewise got clear dodging in and out of the enemy but we on the 211 just sat there helpless watching the whole show. This business lasted for at least 4 or 5 minutes and even the shore batteries came in to illuminate the whole area with starshells. Fortunately by that time there was enough smoke in the air to keep the issue confused. That confusion was the only thing that saved us. None of our boats were using their guns at all and it was obvious that the enemy was frightfully confused with us weaving through the formation and were hard at work shooting up each other. I am sure they sank at least one of their E-boats because several minutes later they started firing again off to the north and there was a large gasoline fire in the channel which burned for a long time. We got clear by the simple process of just sitting still and letting the enemy pass around us and continue north.

"I finally got one engine going and went out to our previously designated rendezvous which was only a couple of miles away. By the time I got there I could just see the other two boats on the radar screen off to the left. I tried to reach them by radio. I tried to call them back but I couldn't get a soul and waited around for some time thinking they would come back. They didn't, however, and went on back individually for which they got a little private hell from me later. I had no alternative now but to go on back myself so I went. I expected to find the other two boats pretty well shot up as it was a miracle that we weren't lost ourselves. Strangely enough I found that they were not damaged and except for the fantastic coincidence of all three of us being more or less disabled simultaneously in the instant of contact we were O.K."

13. OPERATION GUN

Capt. J. F. Stevens, RN, Captain Coastal Forces, Mediterranean,[20] reporting on operations during January and February 1944, said, "There can be no question but that the interruption of the enemy's sea communications off the West Coast of Italy presents a difficult problem. He has made extensive use of minefields to cover his shipping route and while Coastal Forces are the most suitable forces to operate in mined areas, the enemy has so strengthened his escorts and armed his 'shipping' that our coastal craft find themselves up against considerably heavier metal. Furthermore, the enemy's use of 'F-lighters' of shallow draft does not provide good torpedo targets.

---

[20] The Captain Coastal Forces, Mediterranean, was the administrative commander of the MTB's and MGB's. Although the PT's were under the operational control of the British Coastal Forces, they remained under the Commander U.S. Eighth Fleet for administration.

Everything that can be done to improve our chances of successful attack is being done. Plans for diversionary attacks in the hope of breaking up an enemy convoy and cutting off stragglers have been made. Torpedoes will, if possible, be fired at even shallower settings. Meanwhile, if they cannot achieve destruction, Coastal Forces will harry the enemy and endeavour to cause him the utmost possible alarm, damage and casualties."

Within a month of this report, the Coastal Forces developed a new technique with which they did "achieve destruction." "Operation Gun" was built around three British LCG's, landing craft each of which had been fitted out with two 4.7-inch guns and two 40mm. guns, manned by Royal Marine gun crews. The Battle Group, LCG's 14, 19, and 20, was to be screened from possible E-boat attack during the operation by an Escort Group, MTB 634 and MGB's 662, 660, and 659. A Scouting Group, PT 212 (Lt. (jg.) T. Lowry Sinclair, USNR) and PT 214 (Lt. (jg.) Robert T. Boebel, USNR), under command of Lt. Edwin A. DuBose, USNR, in PT 212, was to search ahead of the main group and report targets, and, in the event of contact with the enemy, to act as a screen against destroyers. Finally, there was a Control Group, PT 218 (Lt. (jg.) Thaddeus Grundy, USNR) and PT 208 (Lt. (jg.) John M. Torrance, USNR), with Comdr. Robert A. Allan, RNVR, commanding the entire operation, in PT 218. Besides directing the operation as a whole, this group was to control the fire of the LCG's, passing to the LCG's by radio all target ranges and bearings received on the PT radar.

The force arrived off San Vincenzo on the Italian coast early on the evening of March 27, and the Scouting Group was detached to patrol to the north. At 2200 DuBose reported that six F-lighters were proceeding southward along the coast. The main force moved into position to intercept them, and at 2300 DuBose reported that the F-lighters had a seaward escort of two destroyers, which he was preparing to attack. Within 10 minutes the Control Group picked up both destroyers and F-lighters by radar. Commander Allan led the main force into position between the convoy and the escort and waited for DuBose to attack the destroyers. "Until he carried out this attack," Commander Allan reported, "it was not possible for us to engage the convoy as our Starshells, being fired inshore over the target, would serve to illuminate us for the escorting destroyers which were to seaward. Fire was therefore held during many anxious minutes."

Actually, he waited only 10 "anxious minutes." The Scouting Group fired three torpedoes at the destroyers at less than 400 yards range, retiring behind a smokescreen under heavy fire. A 37mm. shell hit the 214 in the engineroom, wounding the engineer, Joseph F. Grossman, MoMM2c, USNR, and damaging the center engine. Grossman kept the engine running and did not even report his wounds until the boat was out of danger. As the PT's retired they saw a large explosion on the second destroyer, but because of the smoke could not estimate the extent of the damage. Damage or not, the destroyers reversed course and ran up the coast.

As soon as DuBose delivered his attack, Commander Allan ordered the LCG's to open fire. Their first starshells, fired on bearings and ranges given to them by the Control Group, illuminated the targets perfectly. The F-lighters, taken completely by surprise, apparently mistook the starshells for aircraft flares and fired their guns furiously straight up in the air. That gave the Royal Marine gunners on the LCG's all the opportunity they needed. Within 30 seconds one of the F-lighters blew up with a tremendous explosion. Within 10 minutes three others had been set afire. The LCG's then reversed course and caught the last two as they attempted to retire from the action. "Of the six destroyed," Commander Allan reported, "two, judging by the impressive explosions, were carrying petrol, two ammunition, and one a mixed cargo of both. The sixth sank without exploding."

The final score was an entire convoy of four F-lighters wiped out, accomplished at a cost of two men wounded and trifling damage to PT 214.

"The outstanding feature of the operation," Commander Allan said, "was the remarkable accuracy of the LCG's gunfire, but to enable this to function two most important factors cannot be overlooked. One was the excellent manner in which the LCG's carried out rather hurried manoeuvers. The other was the attack on the escorts by the Scouting PT's. This episode allowed the LCG's to fire undisturbed at the convoy and but for it the action might have developed very differently. It was, in fact, the crucial point of the whole engagement and Lt. E. A. DuBose, USNR, and Lt. (jg.) R. T. Boebel, USNR, are to be commended on their skill and courage in carrying out this attack. Also to be commended is Lt. (jg.) T. Grundy, USNR, who commanded the controlling PT with coolness and skill."

A repeat performance on the night of April 24/25 was equally successful. Commander Allan again led the force in PT 218, this time accompanied by PT 209. DuBose, in PT 212, led the 202 and 213 as the Scouting Group. The Battle Group, LCG's 14, 19, and 20, were escorted by PT's 211 and 216, MTB's 640, 633, and 655, and MGB's 657, 660, and 662.

The Scouting Group reported at 2205 that a convoy was proceeding south from Vada Rocks along the Italian coast. A few minutes later the Control

Group, in close company with the Battle and Escort Groups, made radar contact not only with this convoy but with a northbound target near Piombino on the Italian coast opposite Elba, 25 miles south of Vada Rocks. Commander Allan thought that this was a screening group for the southbound convoy, so with considerable maneuvering he managed to pass astern of it, permitting it to continue on to the north before he attempted to attack the southbound targets. When it was safely past, he moved in on the convoy and gave the order for the LCG's to open fire at 3,000 yards range.

The first starshells illuminated two F-lighters. In less than 3 minutes they were hit by the LCG's and exploded. Starshells landed on high wooded ground near the beach and started large brush fires which, with the burning and exploding F-lighters, made a vast and brilliant glow visible in Bastia, 50 miles away. A large oceangoing tug and more F-lighters were illuminated to the north. The tug was hit repeatedly by the LCG's and sank, one F-lighter blew up, and another burned furiously and then exploded. Smoke from the brush fires and exploding F-lighters spread over the water near the beach, so the MGB's of the Escort Group went in for a close inshore search while the rest of the force moved offshore to intercept still another radar target moving up from the south. The MGB's found an undamaged F-lighter, abandoned except for a few hands. They set it ablaze with gunfire, and after burning for some time it blew up with a tremendous blast. The MGB's picked up 12 survivors, 6 of the German sailors from the F-lighters, and 6 impressed Dutch seamen from the tug.

Meanwhile the Battle Group closed the target approaching from the north. Starshells revealed three flak lighters. The LCG's hit two of them on the first salvo and they burned from stem to stern in a wild fury of exploding ammunition. They never had a chance to fire a shot. The third lighter was not hit for 2 minutes. During that time it poured out shells with surprising intensity. Commander Allan, in PT 218, increased speed ahead of the LCG's and drew most of the fire; 20mm., 40mm., and 88mm. shells came screaming over, some landing within 10 yards. Finally the flak lighter was hit and it withdrew behind a smokescreen. The LCG's ceased fire and PT 209 led the MTB's through the smokescreen. The 209 fired a torpedo which caught the lighter squarely and sank it.

To the north, DuBose's Scouting Group intercepted the northbound flak lighter screening group which Commander Allan had avoided earlier. The PT's fired three torpedoes. While the boats were retiring at idling speed, one battle lighter disintegrated in an impressive explosion.

Two and one-half hours after this attack Radio Bastia reported that shore radar had picked up an enemy contact near the island of Capraia, to the west of the boats. DuBose's group investigated and found two destroyers and an E-boat proceeding in column. When the PT's were still 2,500 yards away, the destroyers illuminated them with starshells. The 202 fired a captured five-star recognition flare, which apparently satisfied the enemy. The boats moved in to 1,700 yards and launched four torpedoes. As they retired they felt a heavy underwater explosion, which was followed immediately by intense fire from the destroyers.

The force claimed to have sunk five F-lighters, four flak lighters, and a tug. Considering the difficulties of assessing damage in a night action, the claims were close to the actual fact. German records available since the war show that three F-lighters, two flak lighters, and one tug were lost with heavy personnel casualties.

14. EXPANSION

PT operations were stepped up in May with addition of two new squadrons to the available forces. The first boats of Squadron 22, a Higgins squadron under Lt. Comdr. Richard J. Dressling, arrived at Oran from the United States on April 21, and the first boats of Squadron 29, an Elco squadron under Lt. Comdr. S. Stephen Daunis, arrived at Bizerte on April 30.

Squadron 22 was brought to Bastia, and a new base was started for Squadron 29 at Calvi, on the western side of Corsica, where the boats would be closer to the French coast and the Italian coast west of Genoa. The boats of Squadron 15 were split between Bastia and Calvi according to operational requirements. Lieutenant Commander Barnes was designated Commander Boat Squadrons Eighth Fleet, in operational command of all three squadrons.

The new boats had modern Mark XIII torpedoes, faster, lighter, harder hitting, and infinitely more reliable than the old Mark VIII's. By early May, most of the boats of Squadron 15, too, had been to Bizerte to have their heavy torpedo tubes replaced by light racks for the new torpedoes and to have a 40mm. gun mounted on the stern. The Mark XIII's were not, of course, infallible. On the night of May 18/19, Lt. Eugene S. A. Clifford, USNR, in PT 204, led PT's 213 and 304 in an attack on two flak lighters near Vada Rocks. The boats were under heavy fire from the flak lighters and shore batteries when they fired their torpedoes at a range of 1,500 yards. A

Mark XIII from the 304 ran wild and hit the 204 in the stern. Happily, it had not run far enough to arm itself, so instead of blowing the boat out of the water, it merely lodged with its warhead in the lazarette and the after-body hanging in the water. Lewis H. Riggsby, TM2c, USNR, went down into the rapidly flooding compartment and stuffed a towel into the vanes of the impeller to avoid any possibility of the torpedo arming itself. The flak lighters pursued the boats briefly, scoring one 20mm. hit on the 204 but, despite the reduced speed of the 204, the boats retired safely behind smoke, with no personnel casualties.

By and large, however, the new torpedoes were a vast improvement over the old ones. And not only were there more boats and better armed, but the boats were faster. The new PT's arrived with 1,500-horsepower engines; Squadron 15's boats had their engines converted from 1,350 to 1,500 horse-power at Bizerte, raising their top speed by about 5 knots. Finally, with the approach of summer, the storms abated and the seas quieted.

All these factors helped the three squadrons run up an impressive score during May, June, and July. In May, PT's claimed one corvette and four F-lighters sunk; one corvette, two F-lighters, and two cargo ships damaged; and one R-boat possibly damaged. In June the PT's operating alone claimed one corvette and two F-lighters sunk; one MAS boat captured; two corvettes, four F-lighters, and two cargo ships damaged; and one F-lighter probably damaged. In operations with the British they claimed one F-lighter sunk, one probably sunk, and a corvette damaged.

In July the PT's alone claimed five F-lighters, a cargo ship, a large self-propelled barge, and two small patrol craft sunk; one F-lighter probably sunk and another possibly sunk; one corvette, three F-lighters, two cargo ships, and an R-boat damaged; an F-lighter probably damaged; and two corvettes and an F-lighter possibly damaged. In joint operations with the British they claimed one corvette, two F-lighters, and an E-boat damaged.

15. CORVETTES AND DESTROYERS

In May and June the boats had more encounters with TB destroyers and with corvettes as well. The corvettes were not as fast as the destroyers and were not quite as heavily armed, but it was simply a matter of degree—they were still difficult and dangerous targets. One of the most successful engagements came on the night of May 23/24, in an action patterned after Operation Gun, in which, however, the PT Scouting Force fought the entire action.

As usual, Commander Allan, this time in PT 217, was the senior officer, with a Battle Force of three LCG's escorted by five MGB's and three MTB's. There was a Southern Scouting Force of two PT's and a Northern Scouting Force of six PT's, divided in two groups. The first group was PT's 202, 213, and 218, led by Lieutenant DuBose in PT 202; the second, PT's 302, 303, and 304, led by Lieutenant Commander Dressling, in PT 302. The Northern Scouting Force made radar contact with two southbound corvettes near Vada Rocks, and DuBose's group was directed to attack. The 202 and 213 each fired four torpedoes and the 218 fired three. As the boats retired, they saw two torpedoes hit the leading corvette. Immediately after the first hit the second corvette laid down a heavy barrage, firing very accurately at the puffs of smoke released by the PT's.

The boats rendezvoused with Dressling's group and a few minutes later saw the damaged corvette disappear from the radar screen. Dressling, whose boats were carrying only two torpedoes each, obtained permission from Commander Allan to attack the remaining corvette. Since the target was alerted, Dressling decided to make a long-range attack, not attempting to close to visual range but directing the torpedoes entirely by radar bearings. Each boat fired two torpedoes at $1\frac{1}{2}$ miles. Even at that range shells from the corvette were bursting furiously off the starboard bow of the PT formation. As the boats retired they saw a yellow flash in the direction of the target, and on their radar screens saw the corvette come to a dead stop. Ten minutes later the 218 was sent back to fire her one remaining torpedo. The PT closed unobserved within 1,000 yards of the motionless target and had a perfect chance—but the torpedo ran erratically to the right and missed far astern.

By the time Lt. (jg.) John W. Oswald reached the scene with PT's 201 and 216, the Southern Scouting Force, the boats had lost contact with the second corvette. Oswald's boats picked up 19 Germans from the water. Ten of them were from the corvette UJ–2223 which had sunk after two torpedo hits, and nine had been blown over the side of the corvette UJ–2222, when it was hit by a torpedo. Many weeks later it was learned from other prisoners of war that the UJ–2222 had limped home to Leghorn, so badly damaged that she was stripped and abandoned there.*

---

*UJ (Unterseeboot-Jäger) is translated "U-boat Chaser" but the category was of mixed origin, ranging from corvettes to trawlers and drifters. The "Torpedoboot"(T) and "Torpedoboot-Ausland"(TA) are better understood in English as "Coastal Destroyers"—"Ausland" indicating a foreign destroyer-type (Italian) pressed into German service and covering both DD's and coastal DD's.

That these attacks were hitting home can be gathered from the fact that on May 24 the German Naval Command in Italy made an urgent request for air strikes on Bastia, saying that unless something was done to stop the PT's the entire supply system along the coast would be wrecked.

A week after this action, Lt. Edwin W. Snodgress, USNR, patrolling between Leghorn and La Spezia in PT 304, with PT's 306 and 307, found a destroyer and a corvette moving southward and began to close the range for an attack. The newly risen moon revealed the PT's to the enemy. The destroyer and corvette opened fire. The 306 and 307 slowed down while the 304 increased speed. The 304 fired two torpedoes at long range, and then, when it was again taken under fire, tried to lead the enemy ships back past the other two PT's. Again the high visibility favored the enemy. The 306 launched two torpedoes at 1,600 yards range, but the torpedoman on the 307, William I. Fuller, TM2c, was wounded by a 20mm. shell from the corvette before he could get his torpedoes away. The destroyer and corvette turned toward the 307 and raked it with 20mm. and 40mm., closing to 300 yards before the PT began to pull away. The 307 fired all its guns as it retired. The 306, which was not hit, dropped two smoke pots over the side and these drew most of the enemy fire, permitting the 307 to escape. Three men were killed and five wounded on the 307. The boat captain, Lt. (jg.) Paul F. Fidler, USNR, wounded in the leg, head, and shoulder, refused first aid until all the others had been treated and remained at the conn until he had brought his boat back to Bastia, 90 miles away. It was learned later from prisoners of war that the German TB destroyer T–29 had been considerably damaged by 40mm. hits from the 307, and that two men were killed and a dozen or more wounded. The Germans, no doubt misled by the smoke pots, thought that one PT had been sunk.

On the night of June 14/15, Lt. Bruce P. Van Buskirk, USNR, leading a patrol out of Bastia in PT 558, with PT's 552 and 559, made a nearly perfect attack on two corvettes between La Spezia and Genoa. The PT's tracked the corvettes by radar for 25 minutes, finally idling in to firing range and releasing two torpedoes each. As the boats sneaked away they saw the leading corvette disintegrate with a violent explosion, and immediately afterwards saw an explosion on the other corvette. Ten minutes later the boats saw gunfire, apparently from the second corvette, but it was not even in the direction of the PT's. Then there was another explosion in the direction of the corvette, and the ship disappeared from the radar screen. The PT's were certain of destruction of one corvette, and thought they might have sunk the other, but could not stop to investigate because the first light of dawn was breaking. It is now known that both enemy ships (TA 26 and TA 30) were sunk.

16. ELBA

Fifth Army units entered Rome on June 4, 1944, just under 9 months after the first landings at Salerno. Less than 2 weeks later, on the morning of the 17th of June, Senegalese troops of the French 9th Colonial Infantry Division landed on the south coast of Elba and quickly overran the island, bringing all organized resistance to an end in 2 days. Subsequent establishment of Allied heavy guns on Elba denied the Germans the use of the coastal waters to the south, and greatly facilitated the Allied advance up the Italian coast.

Because of the great number of mines the Germans had laid about Elba, the risk of using deep-draft vessels in the invasion of the island was considered unacceptable, so nearly all of the surface support for the operation was provided by Coastal Forces. Thirty-seven PT's took part in the operation, on the night of June 16/17, with the following missions:

GROUP 1: PT's 556, 557, 558, 559, 563. To launch rubber rafts carrying French raiders ashore at Cape Enfola, on the northern coast of Elba, then to join Group 1A.

GROUP 1A: PT's 552, 553, 554, 555, 562. Senior Officer in charge of Groups 1 and 1A, Lt. Comdr. S. Stephen Daunis, in PT 553. With Group 1 to threaten a landing and create a diversion along the north coast of Elba while the actual landing was accomplished on the south coast.

GROUP 2: PT's 201, 211, 217. Senior Officer, Lt. Donald M. Craig, USNR, in PT 201. To establish a light on Africa Rock, 25 miles south of Elba, as a navigational aid to landing craft approaching the invasion beaches from Porto Vecchio, Corsica; PT 201 to stand by to take off the light party in the morning; PT's 211 and 217 to guide small landing craft to designated points on the beach.

GROUP 2A: PT's 308, 309, 310, 311, 312, 313. Senior Officer, Lt. Comdr. Richard J. Dressling, in PT 309. To patrol south of Vada Rocks and destroy any enemy vessels encountered.

GROUP 3: PT 203, Lt. (jg.) Norman G. Hickman, USNR. To escort LCG's 8 and 14 and to assist them in bombardment of coastal batteries on Pta. dei Riparti, the southeastern extremity of Elba.

GROUP 5: PT's 204, 207, 213, 215, 218. Senior Officer, Lt. Gilbert L. Reed, USNR, in PT 218. To escort landing craft from Porto Vecchio to Elba and then patrol off the south central coast of Elba.

GROUP 7: PT's 202, 208, 214, 216. Senior Officer, Lt. Comdr. Stanley M. Barnes, in PT 216. To patrol off the southeast coast of Elba and destroy any enemy ships attempting to enter the area.

FOLBOT GROUP: PT's 209 and 210. Senior Officer, Lt. (jg.) Harold J. Nugent, USNR, in PT 210. To disembark six commandos in two small boats near Capo di Poro, on the southern coast of Elba.

ESCORT GROUP: PT's 302, 303, 304, 305, 306, 307. Senior Officer, Lt. Thomas B. Creede, USNR, in PT 303. To escort the second wave of landing craft from Porto Vecchio to Elba, and to escort four British rocket barges from Elba to Porto Vecchio.

Group 1 approached Cape Enfola on the north coast at midnight and half a mile from shore disembarked 87 French raiders in rubber rafts. The boats then moved slowly to the east, joining Group 1A off Cape Vita, the north-eastern extremity of Elba, at 0200. The group began its demonstration at 0320, with three PT's running southwest at 40 knots, laying a dense smoke screen along the coast from Cape Vita across the harbor of Portoferraia. Each boat carried two smoke generators which were kept wide open during the run, and 54 floating smoke pots, which the crews dropped over the side. The boats met no opposition until the leading PT was almost across the harbor of Portoferraia. Then a searchlight ashore caught the leading boat and a 40mm. shore battery began dropping shells so close that the PT had to double back behind the screen.

The screen was perfect, 14,000 yards long and gradually rising to a height of 200 feet. A light breeze from the east swept it slowly westward across the harbor. Four other PT's followed down behind the screen, with special sound apparatus blaring forth a multitude of noises that would sound to the defenders of the island like a great fleet of landing craft approaching the beaches. These boats were also equipped with rockets, which they fired toward shore at intervals to simulate a preinvasion barrage rolling up the coast. To confuse the enemy further, three other PT's carried on continuous radio conversations from 0320 to 0440, directing the movements of the imaginary invasion fleet.

The deception apparently was a complete success. Searchlights swept across the water trying to stab through the blanket of smoke. Guns in Portoferraia and in the mountains to the west fired steadily though blindly into the screen until 0400, when Allied planes arrived to bomb the port from the air.

PT 201, of Group 2, put the light party and its equipment ashore on Africa Rock without opposition. Soon afterwards, while Group 7 was passing Africa Rock en route to its patrol station, one of its boats, PT 208, had a propeller shaft shear off, so Barnes ordered the 208 to stand by to remove the light party at dawn, and took the 201 with him on patrol.

PT's 211 and 217 went on from Africa Rock and took separate positions off the south coast of Elba to guide landing craft to the beaches. Just as the first craft were beginning their approach, the 211's radar picked up a target coming out of Marina di Campo Harbor. Lt. (jg.) Eads Poitevent, Jr., USNR, boat captain of the 211, knew that he must avoid engagement lest the beach be alerted, and at the same time must keep the enemy vessel away from the landing craft. He used his boat as a decoy, flashing a signal light at the enemy vessel. It took the bait. When it came within 500 yards, Poitevent saw that it was an MAS boat. He steered the 211 west and south, away from the landing craft and the invasion beach, with the MAS following. After 15 minutes he shook off the MAS and returned to the landing area.

Just to the west of Marina di Campo Harbor, Lt. (jg.) Harold J. Nugent's PT 210 and Lt. (jg.) James K. McArthur's PT 209 were moving in to land, at points 3 miles apart, British commandos who were to act as beach markers for the invasion forces. After putting the commandos ashore, the boats were to rendezvous and patrol between Elba and the island of Pianosa, 15 miles to the southwest.

"When the 210 arrived at the spot to debark the Commandos," Nugent said, "I found a German E boat patrolling the area, so after a hasty conference with the senior Commando, decided to put them down about three-quarters of a mile further out from the original pin-point. This was accomplished without being detected by the E-boat, which made me breathe much easier as the task force commander had impressed me with the importance of not alerting the enemy shore garrison at this stage of the operation.

"Then I went to the rendezvous point and watched the E boat on the radar as he patrolled in an east and west direction off the mouth of Campo Bay. When Lieutenant McArthur on the 209 boat completed the landing of his Commandos, he proceeded to the rendezvous point, narrowly missing an engagement with the E-boat in doing so, as he thought it was my boat still in the process of landing Commandoes, and was attempting to join in column with them. It was necessary at this time for me to break radio silence and warn him of his mistake.

"At 2359 we completed the rendezvous and started our patrol. At this time I still had the E boat on the radar screen and another large target approaching directly up our patrol line from Pianosa. I signaled the 209 to form a left echelon and prepare for a torpedo attack and started a run on

the starboard bow of the target. Since the course of the target indicated that
it could be ships from our invasion convoy also approaching from the direction of Pianosa, I challenged the ships by blinker at a distance of 400 yards.
The closest ship immediately flashed back the correct recognition for that
period and a few seconds later repeated it.

"Thus being convinced that the ships were part of the invasion convoy
who had probably become lost in rounding Pianosa, I called to my executive
officer, Lt. (jg.) Joel W. Bloom, to be ready to look up the ships' correct
position in our copy of the invasion plan. I brought the 210 up to the
starboard side of the nearest ship, took off my helmet, put the megaphone
to my mouth and called over, 'What ship are you?'

"The answer I received was one I shall never forget. First there was
a string of guttural words followed immediately by a broadside from the
ship's two 88mm. guns and five or six 20mm. guns. The first blast carried
the megaphone away and tore off the right side of a pair of binoculars that
I was wearing around my neck. It also tore through the bridge of the boat,
jamming the helm, knocking out the bridge engine controls, and scored
a direct hit on the three engine emergency cut-out switches (Higgins boat)
which stopped the engines.

"I immediately gave the order to open fire, and although we were dead in
the water and had no way of controlling the boat, she was in such a position
as to deliver a full broadside. After a few minutes of heavy fire we had reduced the fire power of the closest ship to one wildly wavering 20mm. and
one 88mm. which continued to fire over our heads throughout the engagement. At this time it was easy to identify the ships as the scene was well
lighted with tracers. There were three traveling in a close, flat V, an E-boat
in the center with an F-ship on either flank. We were engaging the
F-lighter on the starboard flank of the formation.

"As the ships continued to move toward our stern, the injured F-ship
screened us from the fire of the other two ships, so I gave the order to cease
fire and in the ensuing silence clearly heard screams and cries from the
F-ship.

"Two members of the engine room crew who were loaders at general quarters were sent to the engine room to relieve the chief engineer who I thought
had been killed or wounded. However, he had been working on the engines
throughout the engagement and had already located the trouble when his
relief arrived. We immediately got under way but found that the wheel
was jammed in a dead ahead position, so I dropped a couple of smoke pots

over the side and we moved off in a dead ahead direction which fortunately was in the opposite direction from the German ships. They then switched their fire to the smoke pots and we lay to and started repairs.

"Much to our surprise, we found that none of us had even been wounded, but the boat had absorbed a great deal of punishment. A burst of 20mm. had ripped through the chart house, torn the chart table to bits, knocked out the lighting system, and detuned and scarred the radio and radar. Another burst had gone through the engine room but had only damaged the panel board and torn the hull up a bit along the waterline. The rest of the hull had been hit on the starboard side, but the holes were high enough to be ignored for the time being. The turret, turret lockers, and vents on deck had also been holed.

"I then called the 209 boat alongside, sent off a radio report to the flagship concerning the action and the direction in which the ships had retired, and received Lieutenant McArthur's report on the damage he had sustained. The 209 had been hit only twice, but, unfortunately, one of them had been a direct hit on the 40mm. loader and had killed him instantly."

As the 210 was completing its emergency repairs preparatory to resuming patrol with the 209, Nugent and McArthur saw heavy gunfire in the direction of Marina di Campo Harbor.

Poitevent's 211, returning to guide landing craft to the beaches after shaking off the MAS, had picked up another target approaching from the west and hugging the shore. As he moved in to investigate, an F-lighter suddenly turned toward the landing craft's escort and opened fire. The escort returned fire, joined immediately by the 211. The PT scored eight or ten 40mm. hits on the F-lighter and it broke off the engagement abruptly, retiring into Marina di Campo Harbor. The landing craft proceeded without further interference.

Although the 211 sighted only one F-lighter, it is likely that it was one of the two that had engaged the 210 and 209. Damage suffered in that engagement would explain its reluctance to slug it out with the 211.

Lt. (jg.) Norman G. Hickman's PT 203 accompanied LCG's 8 and 14 to a point 1,800 yards off Pta. dei Riparti and passed radar ranges and bearings to the LCG's while they bombarded shore gun positions. During the bombardment the PT and LCG's were under continuous starshell illumination and heavy caliber fire, which the 203 diverted to some extent by laying puffs of smoke astern of the LCG's.

At first light the 203 returned to the point to see whether the bombardment had knocked out the coastal batteries. One and one-half miles offshore Hickman learned that it had not. He withdrew under heavy fire. The LCG's came in and laid down another barrage. The 203 again went in to see whether the bombardment had been successful. When the boat was a mile offshore the shore guns again opened fire, but this time in the direction of landing craft lying several miles off, waiting to be called in to the beaches. Hickman fired several bursts of 40mm. at the emplacements trying to divert the fire from the landing craft, and to his surprise drew fire from other positions which up to then had been unobserved. He withdrew, firing at and observing hits in the immediate area of the new positions. After another bombardment the 203 again tested out the shore batteries, and again drew fire from them, though considerably lighter in volume than before.

The PT's of Groups 2A, 5, 7, and the Escort Group carried out their missions according to plan and without opposition by the enemy.

During the next few nights, before the conquest of Elba was complete, the boats patrolled east of the island to prevent evacuation of troops to the Italian mainland. On the night of June 17/18, Lt. (jg.) Judson S. Lyon's PT 207 acted as scout and tracker for MTB's 633, 640, 655, and MGB 658, which damaged a corvette and sank an F-lighter. On the night of June 19/20, Lt. Gilbert L. Reed, USNR, led a patrol of PT's 203, 204, and 214, which took three prisoners and inflicted minor damage on F-lighters evacuating German troops from Elba.

17. CAPTURE OF AN MAS

Elba was entirely under Allied control by the night of June 29/30, when Lt. John Newell, USNR, led PT 308 (Lt. (jg.) Charles H. Murphy, USNR) and PT 309 (Lt. (jg.) Wayne E. Barber, USNR) on a patrol between Cape Falcone on the Italian mainland and the northeast corner of Elba. Investigating a radar contact, the PT's found two MAS boats trying to sneak into the harbor of Portoferraia on Elba.

The PT's opened fire on the MAS boats at 800 yards, and the enemy craft ran north at high speed, shooting back with 20mm. The PT's chased them north for 10 miles in a running gun battle, until one of the MAS boats began to lose speed and the PT's slowed to concentrate their attack on it. As they closed the range, the PT's found that the entire crew of MAS

NR&L (MOD)—32503

MAS 562, Italian motor torpedo boat captured by PT's on June 30, 1944.

562 had gone over the side into a liferaft. The PT's took them prisoner—14 in all, including the commander of the Italian MAS flotilla based at La Spezia. The PT's by then were nearly out of ammunition, and there appeared to be a fire on the MAS, so they abandoned it and returned to port.

The next morning a reconnaissance plane reported that the MAS was still afloat. Lt. Thomas B. Creede took PT 306 out and found the MAS, with a fire still smoldering in the engineroom. Men from the 306 went aboard and put out the fire, which had been a small one causing remarkably little damage. The 306 towed the prize into Bastia. Just what the MAS boats were doing in Portoferraia was not determined with certainty, though there was reason to believe that they had gone there to evacuate high-ranking German officers who had evaded capture by the occupying forces.

18. THE THUNDERBOLT

Four boats of Squadron 29, PT's 556–559, were equipped with the Elco Thunderbolt, a power-driven mount holding four 20mm. cannon. In the torpedo war of the Mediterranean, where even the 40mm. gun was ineffective against the heavily armed and well-compartmented F-lighters, it was obvious that this would be a weapon of limited usefulness. Twice in July, however, Squadron 29 boats used the Thunderbolt against smaller targets with great success. In both of these actions, one Thunderbolt PT accompanied two 40mm. PT's. The combination of the Thunderbolt's withering volume of

20mm. fire and the slower but more potent 40mm. fire from the other boats proved particularly effective.

On the night of July 15/16, Lt. Stanley Livingston, Jr., USNR, in Ens. Aalton D. Monaghan's PT 558, a Thunderbolt boat, led PT 552 (Lt. Carl A. Whitman, USNR) and PT 555 (Ens. Howard H. Boyle, Jr., USNR), 40mm. boats, on patrol off the French coast with the British destroyers *Terpsichore* and *Kimberley*. Near Nice the group picked up two small radar targets, one of which the destroyers sank by 4.7-inch gunfire. Comdr. A. C. Banague, RN, tactical commander of the group, in the *Terpsichore,* ordered the PT's to attack the second target.

The PT's closed the target, a 70-foot patrol craft, and made three firing runs on it at a range of about 500 yards. At the end of the runs the target was still underway but appeared to be out of control. Livingston brought the 558 alongside and found one badly wounded man on deck and two dead below. The all-metal hull of the patrol craft had taken some twenty-five 40mm. hits, seventy 20mm. hits, and over two hundred .50-caliber hits, and was listing badly. The 558 took off the wounded man and all documents aboard, including a photograph of the boat with a crew of seven men. Apparently some of the crew had gone over the side, but none could be found. The 558 pulled away and PT 552 sank the vessel with 40mm. fire.

Two nights later Lieutenant Livingston, again in Ensign Monaghan's PT 558, with two 40mm. boats, Ens. J. L. McCullough, Jr.'s PT 561, and Ens. Robert F. Morton's PT 562, found a similar patrol craft 3 miles east of Antibes. The boats fired at it for 5 minutes at a range of 250 yards. Then Morton took the 562 alongside and found one badly wounded man and three dead on deck, all grouped around the patrol craft's forward 20mm. gun. The 562 took off the wounded man and pulled away. Three minutes later the vessel capsized and sank.

"The Elco Thunderbolt mount," Lieutenant Commander Daunis reported, "has been used in two gunnery attacks and has proven to be an exceptional weapon."

19. SOUTHERN FRANCE

All PT's were withdrawn from operations on August 1 to prepare for the invasion of southern France, scheduled for the morning of August 15, 1944. Plans called for the simultaneous landing by three great naval task forces, designated the Alpha, Delta, and Camel Attack Forces, of the 3d, 45th, and

36th U.S. Infantry Divisions, on a 25-mile stretch of coast between Cape Cavalaire and Cape Roux—roughly midway between Toulon on the west and Cannes on the east.

On the night before the landings, most of the PT's were assigned to special duties either with the Diversion Group, which was to try to throw the enemy off balance with demonstrations to the east and west of the landing beaches, or with Task Force 86, the Support Force, which was to make advance landings of small numbers of troops on the Île de Port Cros, Île de Levant, and on Cap Negre to capture heavy enemy coastal batteries and thereby remove a serious threat to the left flank of the main assault forces.

On the morning of D-day, August 15, all of the boats except eight which were to remain temporarily with the Diversion Group were to report back to Lieutenant Commander Barnes, who had been designated Commander Screening Group. His duties included the screening of assault forces against enemy surface attack; the establishment of a boat pool in the Baie de Briande, from which PT's would be made available for duty as courier boats, and maintenance of a daily blood bank shuttle between Calvi and the Delta beaches.

20. THE ADVANCE LANDINGS

Sixteen PT's assisted in the operations of the Support Force, which made advance landings of 700 men on Île de Port Cros, 1,400 men on Île de Levant, and 800 men near Cap Negre on the mainland. These landings were to be made by stealth, without preliminary bombardment, 6½ hours before the main assault landings. The troops were to paddle ashore silently in rubber boats, towed from transports to points half a mile from the beaches by small landing craft, and guided by PT's.

While some of the PT's patrolled to the south and west to guard against interference by enemy ships, others waited in the transport area for the troops to be embarked in their rubber boats. At 2317 the first waves headed for the two islands, the PT's leading the way followed by the landing craft towing the rubber boats. The PT's stopped 3,000 yards from shore, took final bearings by radar and, as the towing craft came alongside, told them what courses to follow. The towing craft went shoreward another 2,000 yards and then released the rafts to travel the last half mile in complete silence. The PT's remained on their stations to guide succeeding waves to the proper beaches.

Cap Negre was considerably further than the islands from the transport area, so to expedite the landing of an advance party of 75 men, PT's carried the men and towed the landing craft which were, in turn, to tow the rubber boats from a point 3,000 yards offshore. When the PT's were on station, they unloaded the men into rubber boats, the landing craft towed them within 1,000 yards of shore, and the men paddled the rest of the way.

The landings were entirely successful. None of the PT's had any action with the enemy, but some of the PT's of the screen to the south and west assisted in picking up 99 survivors from the German Auxiliary *Escaburt** and UJ 6081 (ex-Italian corvette *Camoscio*), sunk in the early morning hours 5 miles southeast of the Île de Port Cros by the U.S. destroyer *Somers*.

21. DIVERSIONARY OPERATIONS

Diversionary operations to the east and west of the landing beaches were undertaken to present multiple threats to the enemy so that he would be confused as to the location and extent of the actual assault and not know where to concentrate his forces to meet it. The Eastern Diversion Unit, consisting of two gunboats, one fighter director ship, and three British ML's [21] left Ajaccio, Corsica, on the morning of August 14 and sailed northward until 2130, when it was joined by the PT's of Squadron 22 from Bastia. Three PT's were detached to patrol as an anti-E-boat screen off Nice, and 4 others headed for the Gulf of Napoule to put 70 French commandos ashore in rubber boats at Pointe des Deux Freres. The rest of the force continued northward as though bound for Genoa, trailing balloons as artificial radar targets to give the enemy the impression that a large invasion force was approaching.

When the group had advanced far enough northward so that its presence presumably had become known to the enemy, it shifted its threat by turning westward from Genoa toward the Nice-Cannes area. The four PT's that had landed the French commandos crossed to the eastern flank of the group and took stations as an anti-E-boat patrol. The ML's and remaining PT's deployed off Antibes, trailing balloons so that the enemy would be confused by a multiplicity of radar targets, while the two gunboats, HMS *Aphis* and HMS *Scarab,* bombarded targets between Antibes and the Var River.

---

*Probably a former or local name; otherwise described in action reports as *SG–21* (*Schnellgeleit* vessel or fast escort).

[21] Although there were several types of British ML's (motor launches), most of them were larger and slower vessels than the MTB's or MGB's, and carried heavier guns.

Capt. Henry C. Johnson, commander of the Diversion Group, reported that the "decoy screen" of ML's and PT's "proved effective as, in addition to several enemy salvos falling short of or bursting in the air over the gunboats, the PT's and ML's were subjected to a considerable degree of large-caliber fire which passed well over them."

After an hour's bombardment, the Eastern Diversion Unit departed for the Baie de Briande, in the assault area, to rendezvous with the Western Diversion Unit.

The mission of the Western Diversion Unit was very similar to that of the Eastern Unit. Four ML's and one destroyer sailed from Ajaccio on the morning of August 14, and were joined at 1255 by 8 PT's of Squadron 29 and 11 ASRC's, 63-foot air-sea rescue craft, from Calvi. It is worth noting that the commanding officer of the destroyer, USS *Endicott,* was Comdr. John D. Bulkeley, who, it will be remembered, had had some previous experience with PT's.

The Western Unit proceeded westward, streaming balloons to give the appearance, on enemy radar screens, of a convoy 10 miles long and 8 miles wide. As the Eastern Unit at first had made for Genoa, the Western Unit headed for the Sete-Agde area deep in the Gulf of Lions, then shifted its threat towards the Baie de la Ciotat, between Marseille and Toulon.

On arrival off the Baie de la Ciotat at 0300, the *Endicott* and the ML's were to deploy as a gunfire support force would, while the PT's screened them to east and west and the ASRC's entered the bay in waves, laying smoke-screens, firing barrage rockets, placing special delayed-action demolition charges close inshore, and using sonic apparatus to reproduce the noises of many landing craft. Meanwhile, *Endicott* and the ML's were to bombard coastal defenses. At 0400 a squadron of troop-carrier aircraft was to fly over the town of Ciotat and drop 300 dummy paratroops rigged with demolition charges northwest of Toulon. The operation was carried out according to plan, except that because of dense fog and radar failures, only one ASRC actually entered the Baie de la Ciotat.

The Western Diversion Unit was scheduled to make a repeat performance on the night of August 15/16, but the gasoline tanker that was to fuel the PT's and ASRC's did not arrive on schedule. The operation was postponed for 24 hours. Even with the postponement, fueling was so slow that after 13 ASRC's had fueled, only 2 PT's, Lt. (jg.) Comer A. Trimm's PT 553 and Lt. (jg.) Byron K. Burke's PT 554, were able to fuel in time to take part in the operation.

This time the demonstration went smoothly, the ASRC's entering the bay in waves, while the *Endicott* shelled the town of Ciotat and the gunboats *Aphis* and *Scarab* bombarded the east coast of the bay. The shelling provoked heavy return fire from enemy shore guns as big as 240mm., most of it directed toward *Endicott*.

The unit began its withdrawal about 0430. The ASRC 21 started to steer toward a radar pip believed to be *Endicott*. As the range closed, the pip divided to represent two ships. The skipper of the ASRC continued to head toward them, thinking that they must be ML's. He had closed the range to 1,500 yards when both ships opened fire on the ASRC. Realizing at last that the ships were enemy corvettes, the captain of the ASRC called for help. *Aphis* and *Scarab* arrived within 10 minutes and engaged the corvettes. Gunboats and corvettes fought a running battle for nearly 20 minutes until *Endicott*, steaming up from the south at 36 knots, took the corvettes under fire at 15,000 yards.

At first *Endicott*'s fire was slow, because in her attempt to simulate a group of fire support ships in the night's demonstration, she had fired so rapidly that her guns became badly overheated. Now only one of her 5-inch guns was operative; the other three had jammed breechblocks. She shifted fire with her one gun from one corvette to the other, gradually closing the range to 3,000 yards. The two PT's, which had been acting as a screen for *Endicott*, started to move in on the corvettes, but were taken under such heavy and accurate fire after advancing 300 yards that they quickly fired two torpedoes and retired. *Endicott*, straddled by shells from the corvettes, also fired two torpedoes, one at each ship.

The corvettes had to turn bow on to *Endicott* to avoid the torpedoes; in doing so they masked their main batteries. This gave *Endicott* a chance to close the range to 1,500 yards, where she was able to use her 40mm. and 20mm. guns to rake the decks of the corvettes. Prisoners of war later told Bulkeley that this automatic gunfire was decisive, making it impossible to keep the corvettes' exposed gun stations manned.

As the corvettes turned to flee, *Aphis* and *Scarab* rejoined the action. The three ships pounded the corvettes until they sank. *Endicott, Aphis, Scarab,* and PT's 553 and 554 picked up 211 prisoners, who identified the ships as the *Nimet Allah,* a former Egyptian Khedivial yacht, and the *Capriolo,* a former Italian ship, pressed into service by the Germans.

Reporting on the results of the three demonstrations, Captain Johnson said, "On the early morning of D-Day, Berlin Radio broadcast . . . that the

Allies were landing forces from 'west of Toulon to east of Cannes.' The bitter shore reaction of enemy defenses substantiated their fears of such a wide front. The presence of French commandos near Antibes also apparently created a wide and general alarm.

"This same broadcast also announced that 'thousands of enemy paratroops are being dropped in areas northwest of Toulon.' Five hours later this broadcast was corrected with the words, 'these paratroops were found later to be only dummies which had booby-traps attached and which subsequently killed scores of innocent civilians. This deception could only have been conceived in the sinister Anglo-Saxon mind.'

"At 2000 of the same day Radio Berlin broadcast stated that a 'large assault force had attempted to breach defenses west of Toulon' but 'as the first waves had been wiped out by minefields, the rest lost heart and withdrew and returned to areas in the east.'

"For the first 2 days the Germans stated that our main intentions were a direct assault on Toulon and Marseilles, and that we had 'captured Cannes' after bombarding Antibes and Nice with 'four or five large battleships.'

"A great deal of mobile artillery and infantry units remained or were sent to reinforce this area. Four or five enemy combatant ships in the area were ordered to stand by and assault the flanks of the Allied attacking forces when they returned, according to statements by enemy prisoners. . . .

"On the 1100 broadcast of 19 August, Radio Berlin claimed that 'an additional and futile attempt of the American forces to land large bodies of troops west of Toulon has failed miserably.'

" 'Lord Haw-Haw' commented on this 'attempt' later, stating that the assault convoy, which had the Toulon-Marseilles area as its target, was '12 miles long' but that for a second time in 3 nights the 'Allies have learned of the determined resistance of the Wehrmacht, to their cost.'

"Prisoners rescued from the sunken German ships expressed amazement at the types of ships we employed and stated that the other ships ordered out to the attack failed to obey because, as a result of their reports, they 'lost heart.' "

22. MINES

The gasoline tanker intended for the PT's failed to sail because of engineering difficulties. That meant that when Barnes set up his boat pool in the Baie de Briande, the PT's had to hunt out tankers assigned to other assault areas.

On the evening of August 16, Lt. (jg.) Wesley J. H. Gallagher, USNR, in PT 202, and Lt. Robert A. Dearth, USNR, in PT 218, set out from the Baie de Briande to find a tanker reported to be in the Gulf of Frejus, 15 miles to the northeast. At 2050, when the boats were 2½ miles off Pte. St. Aygulf, at the western side of the Gulf of Frejus, the bow lookout on PT 202 reported a floating boxlike object 150 yards dead ahead. Gallagher immediately altered course to the right to avoid it. During its turn the boat ran over a mine which blew the stern right off, knocked several men overboard, and catapulted a column of water, smoke, and debris hundreds of feet in the air.

Francis A. Kowalski, TM2c, USNR; Francis J. Cavanaugh, RM3c, USNR; Dante Alfieri, QM2c, USNR, and Nicholas J. Massiello, TM2c, USNR, unhesitatingly went over the side to the aid of the men in the water. Dearth brought the 218 in and picked up all of the men from the water. He was proceeding toward the 202 to take off the rest of the crew when his boat also ran over a mine which blew off her stern. Gallagher had started to try to signal to other ships in the bay to get help. As soon as the 218 was mined he stopped, considering it unsafe for any other ships to come into the area.

The boat captains inspected their boats to make sure that no personnel remained below, and then got their crews into liferafts. They tied the liferafts together and held a muster. Only one man was missing. One officer and five enlisted men were injured. By amazing luck the engineer on watch in the engineroom of each boat survived, although on one boat the force of the blast tossed a bank of storage batteries right out of the engineroom and onto the forecastle.

Both boats were obviously sinking, so the boat captains turned their rafts shorewards. An air raid was then in progress, and fragments from anti-aircraft projectiles were falling all about the rafts. The crews made shore three-quarters of an hour after midnight, choosing as a landing place a barren, rocky point that they thought was the least likely terrain for landmines. Gallagher picked his way through barbed wire entanglements and found an abandoned, partially destroyed cottage not far from the beach. The crews stayed in the cottage for the night, since they had no way of knowing whether they were in friendly or enemy territory. Soon after daylight the boat captains found an advanced U.S. Army unit half a mile away. The wounded were transferred by ambulance to a first-aid station and a nearby Navy beach-master found transportation for the rest of the crews back to the Baie de Briande.

23. PORQUEROLLES

On August 18, Rear Adm. L. A. Davidson, Commander Task Force 86, the Support Force, attempted the reduction of Porquerolles, an island just to the west of the Île de Port Cros on the left flank of the invasion forces as a preliminary to the occupation of the Toulon-Marseille area. After preliminary bombardment of Porquerolles by the U.S. cruiser *Augusta* and the French cruiser *Emile Bertin,* a demand for surrender was carried to the island by a party aboard PT 215. As the PT approached the shore it was taken under heavy fire from big guns on the mainland peninsula of Giens to the northwest and was forced to retire. "Giens," Admiral Davidson reported, "appeared to be as important a thorn as Porquerolles and more difficult to remove."

During the next few days ships of Task Force 86 tried to soften up both Giens and Porquerolles, but were unable to silence permanently the guns on Giens. On the afternoon of the 21st the destroyer *Eberle* saw a small group of men on the southwest point of Porquerolles waving a white flag. An officer sent ashore to investigate reported that a group of Armenians in the German service wished to surrender. *Eberle* took 57 Armenian prisoners, who said that 150 Germans remained in a fort on the island and were planning to move to the mainland that night in 3 small boats. *Eberle* went around to the north side of the island and destroyed the boats. That night PT's 553 and 556 patrolled between Porquerolles and the mainland to prevent evacuation, but saw nothing of the enemy.

On the 22d, after the French battleship *Lorraine* and U.S. cruiser *Philadelphia* had shelled the fort on Porquerolles, Ens. William A. Klopman's PT 556 landed a flag-of-truce party which demanded and received the surrender of the 158 Germans remaining on the island. Later in the afternoon the big guns on Giens opened up on the ships carrying troops to garrison Porquerolles. They were silenced, at least temporarily, by well-placed salvos from the cruiser *Omaha.*

24. THE GULF OF FOS

On August 23, Admiral Davidson received information that Port de Bouc in the Gulf of Fos, to the west of Marseille, was in the hands of French patriots. On the same day he was ordered to start minesweeping operations to open the Port de Bouc and Gulf of Fos. Accordingly, on August 24, he sent Capitaine de Fregate M.J.B. Bataille, French naval liaison officer on his staff, and Lt. Bayard Walker, USNR, to make a reconnaissance of Port de Bouc aboard PT 555. Lieutenant Walker's report to Admiral Davidson follows:

"Pursuant to your verbal orders of 24 August 1944, I accompanied Cap. aine de Fregate Bataille, French Navy, on a mission to Port de Bouc on the PT 555 to determine whether the port was actually in the hands of the FFI [22] as reported, and if so, to what extent it could be used. We departed from alongside the USS *Augusta* at approximately 1300.

"We proceeded westward past Marseilles and then northwards towards the Gulf de Fos through a north-south channel in the process of being cleared of enemy mines by a large sweeping force. Near the end of this channel we came close aboard a U.S. destroyer who notified us that coastal batteries to the eastward had straddled ships coming near the entrance of the Gulf de Fos. It is believed that the batteries were those in the Niolan or Cape Mejean area.

"The other officers aboard the PT 555 were Lt. Stanley Livingston, [Jr.], Division Commander; Ens. Howard [H.] Boyle, [Jr.]; and Ens. [Charles H.] Stearns, [Jr.], Executive Officer.

"It was decided that we could enter the Gulf de Fos despite fire from enemy coastal batteries since we presented such a small target at long range. We entered the bay cautiously and proceeded close to the port without drawing enemy fire. Despite a two-man mine watch, we passed over a shallow mine which just cleared the bottom of the boat.

"The French flag could be seen flying in more than a dozen places as we neared the port, demolished by the enemy when they left. A pilot and a fisherman opened the boom and allowed us to enter the harbor. We were welcomed by cheering crowds waving French flags.

"At Port de Bouc Capitaine Bataille and myself got the necessary information regarding the condition and usefulness of the port from the local authorities which included Lieutenant Granry, French Navy, in civilian clothes, who had parachuted in this area some weeks before. Through his efforts, much of the enemy attempts to make the ports useless were countered. We learned that the last of the Germans had left the town on 21 August.

"After about a half hour ashore, gathering the above information, we got underway to return to the *Augusta*. Shortly after clearing the harbor entrance the Commanding Officer called all hands to general quarters, set

---

[22] FFI: French Forces of the Interior.

a two-man mine watch at the bow, and began steaming at 1500 RPM, about 29 knots. A minutes later (about 1715) a terrific blast exploded beneath our stern, carrying away the 40mm. gun and gun crew and almost everything up to the forward bulkhead of the engine room. Enough framework remained to hold the engines, now submerged. The four torpedoes were immediately jettisoned and we anchored with two anchors from separate lines.

"A rubber life boat was then lowered as was a life raft to search for the missing men. Four men were missing. One man with a broken leg, an uninjured man and a body were brought back aboard after a thorough search by those in the life raft. Due to the strong current the life rafts were not only unable to make headway towards the ship but were drifting away. Lieutenant Livingston, an expert swimmer, swam over to the rubber raft, a distance of over 300 yards, with the bitter end of a line to which we added all the spare line, electric cable, halyards, etc., available to make it reach. The line was kept buoyed by floatable material such as 'Mae Wests' and regular life jackets at varying intervals. This made possible the return of the above mentioned men.

"A French pilot boat and an open fishing boat stood out from Port de Bouc, rescuing the other searcher in the regular life raft, thence coming alongside.

"During this time we were constantly covered by a large number of fighter planes who had been attracted to us by the explosion. A Navy spotting plane flew very close to us but was unable to read our light. A Navy plane from the USS *Philadelphia* landed and came close aboard to get our message concerning Port de Bouc for relay to Commander Task Force 86.

"It was decided that I should attempt to make Port de Bouc, aiding an interpreter for the injured man who needed medical attention. We left with the Pharmacist's Mate and the body in the open boat. When we had gone scarcely 100 yards from the PT, a violent explosion lifted the boat in the air and threw us all headlong into the water. The time was about 1805. An instant before the explosion I saw a greenish line with green floats spaced about every foot get tangled in our screw astern. I came up under the boat which seemed to be coming down on me and quickly freed my foot which got caught somewhere for an instant. The water was black in spots from the residue of the charge as I shot up nearer the surface.

"As I gathered my senses I realized that everyone seemed to be all right and accounted for. The body disappeared never to be seen again and the injured man was placed on the bottom of the overturned boat where he appeared to be comfortable. The Pharmacist's Mate who was about 60 feet away from me called for help as he couldn't swim. I swam to him and reassured him he was doing fine, but got ducked under a few times in attempting to help him. Fortunately, an inflated 'Mae West' floated by and then an empty 10 gallon can, all of which helped calm him and keep him afloat. As a matter of fact, the situation seemed so good at this point that I decided not to take off my pistol and belt. We began drifting rapidly from the others, clinging to the boat, but the pilot boat came to our rescue, picking us up first and then those in the overturned fisherman. The injured man was put aboard without further harm and the boat up-ended and sank as the last man let go.

"Right after the explosion the *Philadelphia* plane took off before receiving our message, I learned later with regret, as we were most anxious to complete the mission by getting the word through.

"We had two narrow escapes getting back to the PT—coming very close to similar lines and floats as I had seen before. I requested the pilot, Ensign Moneglia, French Navy, also in civilian clothes, to go between two sets of lines rather than back down and turn around as the majority seemed to wish. It proved to be the safe way between two mines whose floats we could actually see.

"Another fishing boat with Lieutenant Granry aboard came out and tied alongside. Lieutenant Livingston and Ensign Boyle attempted for a long time to get word to a U.S. cruiser which was with the sweeping group out in the swept channel, but our portable light was not strong enough and attempts with a mirror received only spasmodic dashes, but no Roger.

"We continued to jettison topside weights as the stern of the remainder of the boat sank lower. Eventually, two twin .50 caliber machine guns and the 20mm. gun and ammunition together with other topside weights were jettisoned. One twin .50 caliber machine gun and some ammunition was not jettisoned at the request of the Commanding Officer in order to have something to open up with in case of attack. K-rations and fruit juices were brought topside to feed the crew and Frenchmen.

"Commander Bataille and Lieutenant Livingston set off for Carro [23] in the rubber boat in an attempt to get the message through if they could find transportation or communication facilities of the Army. I remained aboard

---

[23] Carro is at the eastern entrance of the Gulf of Fos, about 5 miles south of Port de Bouc.

with a duplicate message in case of visual contact with Allied craft and also to serve as interpreter with the French patriots alongside.

"We had two teams of bucket brigades that night. One was composed of the Commanding Officer and the crew and the other of the Frenchmen and myself. About midnight the trim looked as though we might have to abandon ship prior to dawn despite the calm sea, so all preparations were made for such an event. The radar set and aerial were dismantled, destroyed and jettisoned and secret and classified publications and charts were made ready to be deep-sixed.

"We were able to keep ahead of the water coming in, however, and the weather continued fair until daylight. The bilge pump aft had been shot away and the one forward couldn't make suction due to our being so far down by the stern.

"The night was quiet except for the flashes and vibrations of the aerial bombardment which appeared to be going on in Marseille. It was chilly and damp, but we made out fairly well by sharing blankets.

"About an hour after sunrise, Commander Bataille and Lieutenant Livingston returned in a fishing boat followed by another boat. They reported that they hadn't been able to get the message through, but told of their experience of paddling by a mined gate and finding an almost deserted village.

"It was decided to tow the PT to Port de Bouc with two of the boats, using the other two boats ahead to search for mine lines. Commander Bataille and Lieutenant Livingston stood in the bows of the two searching craft. After going only a short distance so many of these lines were encountered that we abandoned the plan of going to Port de Bouc and headed instead for Carro, near Cap Couronne.

"On arrival at Carro the PT boat was moored alongside the dock with the stern settled on the bottom. An abandoned house next to the dock was turned over to us to quarter the officers and men. Personal and living gear was taken to the house which we cleared out with the help of five Italian prisoners put at our disposal by the FFI. There were sufficient provisions aboard to take ashore to feed the men for several days.

"The Commanding Officer of the *Philadelphia* sent Ensign Pitcher and a radioman with a . . . radio ashore at the time of our arrival at Carro, to attempt to get information regarding troop dispositions and targets along the coast. It was by means of this radio that we were able to communicate with Commander Task Force 86 via the *Philadelphia*. My . . . [dispatch] reported the pocket of 3,000 enemy troops in the area bounded by Ensues, La Redenne, and Rouet, only a few kilometers away, whose escape was anticipated on the northern road via Martiques. The FFI strongly desired air support to prevent this maneuver as there were no Allied troops in the vicinity.

"Saturday morning 26 August I proceeded to Port de Bouc to gather information . . . I returned . . . to Carro for the night and to pick up my gear and returned to Port de Bouc the next day as U.S. Naval Liaison Officer.

"I had asked the pastor of the Catholic Church at La Couronne to say a mass on Sunday morning for the five men we had lost. A high mass was celebrated in the church, crowded to the doors at ten-thirty. The pastor and local people had gone [to] considerable effort to decorate the church with French and American flags and flowers. The choir sang despite the broken organ and the Curé gave a moving sermon in French. Four FFI men, gotten up in a uniform of French helmets, blue shirts and white trousers, stood as a guard of honor before the draped coffin on which was an American flag.

"After mass, our men fell in ranks behind a platoon of FFI followed by what seemed to be the whole town and marched to the World War monument. There, a little ceremony was held and a wreath was placed in honor of the five American sailors. We were told that a collection was in the process of being taken up amongst the local people in order to have a plaque made for the monument with the names of the five Americans who had given their lives for the liberation of France."

25. EXPLOSIVE BOATS AND HUMAN TORPEDOES

The trip of PT 555 to Port de Bouc and those of PT's 215 and 556 to Porquerolles were among the missions performed by the PT's in the boat pool in the Baie de Briande. Other boats were assigned as required to flagships of the various task forces and groups for use as courier boats and close night screens. PT 208 had a close call on the evening of August 18, when it carried Vice Admiral Hewitt, Lt. Gen. Ira Baker and Lt. Gen. Jacob L. Devers to the USS *Catoctin*, Admiral Hewitt's flagship anchored in the Gulf of St. Tropez. An air raid had just started when the PT put the admiral and the two generals aboard the flagship. Within a minute after they went aboard, a bomb hit the flagship, killing 2 men and wounding 3 officers and 32 men aboard *Catoctin,* and wounding 4 men on PT 208.

Most of the courier duty was uneventful, however, as were the nightly patrols in the Rade d'Hyeres, to the west of the assault area. The PT blood bank shuttle made daily deliveries to the Delta beaches from Calvi. Three PT's of Squadron 29 were released from the assault area on August 19, at the request of the Senior Officer Inshore Squadron at Bastia, to serve as radar scouts and trackers for the British boats operating against enemy shipping in the Gulf of Genoa, and later other boats of Squadron 29 were placed under operational control of the Senior Officer Inshore Squadron at Bastia.

On August 23 all of the remaining boats were moved from the Baie de Briande to St. Maxime, in the Gulf of St. Tropez; the patrols in the Rade d'Hyeres were discontinued, and the blood bank shuttle was taken over by aircraft, so that the PT's could start close inshore patrols on the eastern flank of the assault area to guard against attacks by two new and alarming types of enemy vessels: explosive boats and human torpedoes.

NR&L (MOD)—32502

PT's at St. Maxime in the Gulf of St. Tropez, Southern France.

The explosive boat, it was learned later, had a plywood hull about 18 feet long, with 600 to 700 pounds of explosives in the bow section which would detonate when the boat was driven head on into its target. There were two types, one controlled by a single operator who jumped overboard after setting his boat on collision course with a target; the other a drone type, of which several could be directed and detonated by radio from a slightly larger control boat. The explosive boats, driven by gasoline engines, had a top speed of 25 to 30 knots.

The human torpedoes were in effect one torpedo suspended from another. The upper torpedo, which had no warhead and was for propulsion only, floated with its topside awash. From it was suspended the missile torpedo, which could be released by the operator, who sat astride the upper torpedo, enclosed in a watertight casing with his head above the surface in a transparent plastic dome 18 inches in diameter. Top speed was about 4 knots and the operator had only limited visibility.

PT's first encountered explosive boats on the night of August 24/25, when the 552, 553, 554 and 564 broke up a group of them without actually engaging them. One explosive boat narrowly missed a PT and then disappeared in the darkness. Shortly afterwards there were three large explosions in the area, possibly caused by a control boat detonating its drones. Two nights later PT's 210 and 213 intercepted five explosive boats traveling slowly in column. The PT's crossed ahead of the column, dropping a float flare with a 5-minute delay fuse. As soon as the flare ignited, the PT's opened fire. Four of the boats blew up almost immediately, apparently by remote control from the remaining boat, which escaped to the beach. On the night of September 7/8, PT's 215 and 216 made contact with two separate groups of boats. Three boats in the first group blew up, and the control boat again escaped to the beach. Of the second group, one blew up and another was left in flames. The second engagement was confused by a smokescreen laid by the enemy.

On the night of September 9/10, PT's 206 and 214, under Lieutenant Reed, chased and fired on three explosive boats which headed for the beach at 30 knots. The PT's gradually closed the range to 100 yards, when one of the boats stopped dead in the water and blew up with a terrific explosion. A few minutes later another boat turned and headed for the PT's. As it passed close aboard, the crew of the leading PT could see clearly that it was unmanned.

At daylight the PT's reported to the destroyers *Madison* and *Hilary P. Jones,* which were closing the beach for a bombardment. *Madison* sighted a human torpedo 500 yards off her port beam and maneuvered at high speed to avoid it. Both *Madison* and PT 206 opened fire, and the operator of the torpedo jumped out of his transparent dome as his craft sank. PT 206 took him prisoner. A few minutes later a Navy scouting plane spotted another human torpedo. PT 206 went alongside it and DuBose motioned to the operator to abandon ship. He refused and the 206 sank the torpedo by close-range gunfire. During the rest of the morning, planes kept spotting more torpedoes, of which eight were destroyed by PT gunfire or destroyer depth charges.

The PT's thereafter had two more inconclusive engagements with explosive boats. While these actions were usually inconclusive, and the control boats usually managed to escape, the PT's accomplished their purpose of thwarting the enemy attacks. Neither explosive boats nor human torpedoes inflicted any damage on our forces in the invasion of southern France.

26. LAST DAYS AT BASTIA

While PT's continued to operate from St. Maxime until September 28, when the base was moved to Gulf Juan, the PT's operating from Bastia were the only ones to encounter surface targets other than explosive boats and human torpedoes. During the last week in August the Bastia boats met TB destroyers on 3 nights, and on the night of August 27/28 had their first engagement with a new type of craft, Rhône River barges 250 feet long, which the Germans were pressing into service as a substitute for their dwindling fleet of F-lighters. Then contacts dropped off for a few days until, starting on the night of September 10/11, the boats engaged F-lighters or Rhône River barges on nine consecutive nights. The rest of the month was quiet except for the night of September 26/27, when an oil barge (GPS 256) carrying 140 tons of badly needed oil exploded after being hit by two torpedoes. All of these engagements took place within a 50-mile radius of Genoa, between Cape Mele on the west and La Spezia on the east.

Damage to the enemy was estimated at one destroyer and two barges sunk, and one destroyer and one barge damaged, during the last week in August; eight barges and four F-lighters sunk, one F-lighter probably sunk, one corvette, three F-lighters and two barges damaged during the 9-night run in

September; and one tanker sunk at the end of the month. While we now know that these claims were high, the remarkable thing about these actions is that of the considerable damage inflicted almost all was by joint patrols of one of the three Squadron 29 PT's assigned to Bastia and two or three MTB's. While many factors contributed to this result, one of the obvious and most important is that the British division commanders had been patrolling these waters for nearly a year and had acquired greater skill than the relatively inexperienced officers of Squadrons 22 and 29.

The importance of the division leader is illustrated by the repeated successes during this period of Lt. A. C. Blomfield, RN, riding as division leader with Lt. Robert E. Nagle, USNR, in PT 559. The 559 led MTB 423 to Genoa Harbor on the night of August 24/25 (MTB 420 had started with them and returned to Bastia because of an engine casualty). There they sighted a harbor defense ship escorted by a small craft 1,500 yards east of the harbor breakwater. Each boat fired two torpedoes at 1,300 yards and retired undetected, observing three apparent hits on the target. Intelligence sources later confirmed the sinking of this craft.

Three nights later Blomfield and Nagle in PT 559, with MTB's 423 and 375, made another undetected torpedo attack, this time on three Rhône River barges and claimed to have sunk two of them. On the night of September 10/11, the 559, with MTB's 422 and 376, fired five torpedoes at a convoy of one F-lighter and one Rhône River barge with several small escorts. Nagle and Blomfield claimed to have sunk both the barge and the lighter, but German sources do not confirm the claim.

On the night of September 13/14, the same three boats each fired two torpedoes at a convoy of three F-lighters and heard four explosions as they retired. Half an hour later the boats closed the same formation, the MTB's following the 559 although the only torpedoes remaining in the group were two aboard the PT. This time there were only two F-lighters in the convoy. Just as Nagle was about to take another shot at them, a lookout reported an enemy corvette (later established as UJ 2216) closing fast on the starboard bow. Nagle swung his boat toward the corvette and fired one torpedo at 400 yards range. It hit the corvette's port side and a mass of flames shot up through the stern of the ship, blasting the stern gun clear of the deck and hurling a man high into the air. The corvette soon sank. Nagle turned the 559 back toward the F-lighters, fired his last torpedo at them and retired under fire from the corvettes and F-lighters.

Another example of Anglo-American cooperation occurred on the night of September 11/12 when PT 558 (Ensign C. C. McPherson) together with MTB's 419 and 423 attacked and sank two Rhône River barges off Spezia. Lieutenant T. Finch, RNVR, in the 558 was the tactical commander.

Back in the early days of the Mediterranean campaign, when the PT's first started to work with the British boats at Bone, Barnes had been of the opinion that joint patrols would not work. "The radical differences," he wrote, "which exist between British and U.S. boats with regard to communication equipment and procedure, military characteristics of boats, and tactical doctrine made it undesirable to include units of both nations in the same task group and this was avoided whenever possible."

That was before the PT's had radar. At Bastia joint patrols were resumed to combine the advantages of American radar and British torpedoes. In time the PT's and British boats worked out their own joint tactical doctrines, and proved beyond a doubt that boats of different types could operate together with utmost efficiency, provided there was teamwork between the types. Commenting on the action in which PT 559 and MTB 423 sank a harbor defense ship, Barnes wrote, "Lieutenant Blomfield, RN, is an exceedingly capable and aggressive Coastal Force officer with 3 years of experience in this type of craft. The PT's working with this and other British groups have been more or less permanently assigned. Since the normal operating group is a U.S. Elco, a British Higgins and a British Vosper, with the British Senior Officer embarked in the U.S. Elco, it is obvious that successful operations require only tactical unity and not homogeneous types."

27. LEGHORN

Commander Allan relieved Capt. N. Vincent Dickinson, RN, as Senior Officer Inshore Squadron on September 8 and at the same time received orders to prepare plans to move the Inshore Squadron to Leghorn, on the Italian mainland, where the boats would be closer to the Gulf of Genoa patrol areas than they had been at Bastia. Barnes closed out the PT base at Calvi on September 22—now that there was a base in southern France, Calvi was no longer needed—and on September 28 recommended to the Commander Eighth Fleet that the PT's move to Leghorn with the British Coastal Forces. On September 29 the Commander Eighth Fleet granted authority to close the PT base at Bastia and to establish a temporary operating base at Leghorn.

Squadron 15 did not go to Leghorn. Now that southern France was taken, German coastal traffic in the western Mediterranean was limited almost entirely to the Gulf of Genoa, and less PT's were required. On October 1 Barnes learned from the Commander Eighth Fleet that the 16 remaining boats of the squadron were to be transferred under lend-lease to the Captain Coastal Forces Mediterranean. He sailed his PT's for Malta, decommissioned the squadron on October 17, and completed the transfer on October 25, 1944, 18 months to the day after his first boats arrived at Bone, the scene of their first actions.

Leghorn was in operation by October 10. During the rest of the month the boats of Squadrons 22 and 29 patrolled from there and from St. Maxime, and later from Gulf Juan, in southern France. The forces claimed heavy damage on two F-lighters and probable damage to one barge.

Squadron 29 was withdrawn from operations on October 28, with orders to turn over eight boats to the Commander Twelfth Fleet for further transfer under lend-lease to Russia, and to ship its remaining four boats back to the United States for duty with Squadron 4 at the Training Center at Melville. The squadron was decommissioned on November 23. Lieutenant Commander Daunis had relieved Barnes as Commander Boat Squadrons Eighth Fleet on October 22. He in turn was relieved by Lieutenant Commander Dressling on November 23.

Dressling, whose boats had been at St. Maxime and then at Gulf Juan during October, was ordered to move six of them to Leghorn early in November. Throughout the winter Leghorn remained the principal offensive base, with PT's rotating between the bases to permit training at Gulf Juan. The Gulf Juan boats occasionally were permitted to make offensive sweeps into the Gulf of Genoa, but saw little action.

The winter patrols were hampered by bad weather—worse, if anything, than that of the year before. Commander Allan estimated that in the 150 days between October and March, it was possible to maintain full patrols on only 57 nights. A week of severe storms from November 10 to 16 increased the normal hazards by setting many mines adrift.

On the night of November 17/18, Lt. (jg.) Brenton W. Creelman's PT 311 set out with MTB's 378 and 420 for a patrol of the Portofino-Spezia area, but at 0230 was ordered back to Leghorn by the division commander in MTB 420 because of a steering casualty which had been affecting the boat's operations all night. At 0330 the PT sent a radio dispatch to Leghorn, giving its estimated time of arrival as 0515. At noon the 311 still had not arrived, so Commander Allan sent PT's 312 and 307, under Lt. Daniel L. Fleming, USNR, to search for it. At 1305 the boats sighted the bow section of the 311 adrift 35 miles northwest of Leghorn. The PT had hit a mine at 0400. The entire boat aft of the crew's quarters was completely destroyed. Clinging to the bow were the survivors—five men who had been in their bunks in the crew's quarters at the time of the explosion. Both officers and eight men were missing.

The PT's had only one successful action in November, 2 nights after the loss of the 311, when Lt. (jg.) Charles H. Murphy's PT 308, with MTB's 420 and 422, claimed five torpedo hits on two enemy convoys joining each other off Portofino resulting, it was believed at the time, in the sinking of an F-lighter and a coaster, and the possible sinking of a second F-lighter. German records show that the submarine chaser UJ 2207 was the actual and only victim of this attack.

By the middle of November the Germans had installed more and heavier shore guns along the coastal routes and had rearmed their F-lighters so that most of them were the equivalent of the old flak lighters, carrying two 88mm. guns and several 40mm. and 20mm. guns. To counter the increased armament, Commander Allan requested heavier ships. He was assigned five British trawlers, three mounting 4-inch guns and two mounting 12-pounders. In November, Commander Allan reported, "exercises, much hampered by bad weather, were carried out with some of the trawlers which had been allocated. These ships were unaccustomed to night maneuvering, and so every chance was taken to exercise them. This entailed the controlling PT going out in more weather than she could stand, or more properly than the stomach of the Senior Officer could stand. I regret to say that the sight of a 'limey' succumbing to the weather, gave an accountable pleasure to our allies (though at the time they hardly appeared as such) and the fact has been duly recorded in their annals."

The trawlers, fairly deep-draft vessels, could not pass over the minefields as did the PT's and British coastal craft, so before they could be used it was necessary to sweep a channel for them. On the night of December 15/16, four minesweeping ML's swept a channel into Mesco Point, guided by Lt. (jg.) Robert Spangenberg's PT 302. The ML's were screened on the north by Lt. (jg.) Edward Groweg's PT 306 and MTB 419, under Lt. Edwin

W. Snodgress, USNR, and on the south by Lt. (jg.) Robert Wallace's PT 310 and MTB 422, under Lt. N. Ilett, RNVR.

The ML's completed their sweep by 0200 without encountering any mines, and set course for Leghorn, accompanied by the northern covering force. The southern covering force remained on patrol, and found four F-lighters off Moneglia Point. As the boats closed the range, the F-lighters and shore batteries took them under heavy fire. Each boat got two torpedoes away. There were two huge explosions in the direction of the target but apparently these resulted from the torpedoes exploding on the beach.

On the following night a striking force of the trawlers *Minuet, Hornpipe, Twostep, Gulland,* and *Ailsa Craig,* rendezvoused with the control group, Commander Allan in PT 302, with MTB 419; the northern escort group, Lt. E. Good, RNVR, in PT 306, with MTB's 377 and 421, and the southern escort group, Lt. N. Ilett, RNVR, in MTB 420, with MTB 376 and PT 309. Ahead of the main body ranged the northern scouting group, Lt. Eugene G. Wilson, USNR, in PT 304, with PT 313 and MTB 422, and the southern scouting group, Lieutenant Commander Dressling in PT 310, with MTB's 378 and 375. The 17th Squadron, South African Air Force, was to have sent a flight of bombers to illuminate the enemy by starting brush fires ashore with incendiary bombs, but because of low visibility was unable to take part in the operation.

Dressling's scouting group picked up a southbound F-lighter convoy, only to lose it when it moved in close to the beach. Later it picked up a north-bound convoy of F-lighters and a coaster escorted by an R-boat, and shadowed it for three-quarters of an hour, giving constant reports of its position to Commander Allan's control group. When the convoy came within range of the trawlers, Commander Allan ordered Dressling's group to retire to sea-ward. Two of the trawlers illuminated the convoy with starshell and the other three immediately opened fire with their 4-inch guns. The F-lighters fought back savagely with their 88mm. guns, but the trawlers had the advantage of surprise and scored many hits, whereas the best the F-lighters could do was to spray one of the trawlers with shell fragments, slightly damaging its bridge and wounding one officer. By the time the F-lighters began to get the range, Commander Allan ordered MTB 420 to lay a smoke-screen to cover the retirement of the trawlers. Commander Allan assessed the damage to the enemy as two F-lighters and one R-boat sunk, but again German records do not confirm this claim.

During 3 weeks of December, three U.S. destroyers were held available to move into the Italian coast to attack convoys if minesweeping ML's could find a gap in the minefields. The ML's carried out two difficult night sweeps. "Unfortunately," Commander Allan reported, "on both occasions, they encountered mines. The proposed employment of the destroyers was, much to their disgust, thereafter abandoned."

In January 1945, two patrols met the enemy: one on the night of January 10/11, in which PT 304 and MTB 422, under Lt. (jg.) Lawrence F. Knorr, USNR, fired four torpedoes at a convoy of five F-lighters off Mesco Point, and one on the night of January 15/16, when PT 313 and MTB 378, under Lt. William B. Borsdorff, USNR, fired six torpedoes at five F-lighters off Corneglia. Again torpedo explosions on the shore were confused by our forces with hits on the enemy. German sources indicate that no damage was suffered.

"During the latter half of January and the first weeks of February," Commander Allan reported, "a flotilla of Royal Yugo-Slav MGB's was allocated. Despite their great keenness these boats never made contact with the enemy although they were out on many patrols. They did, however, in their behaviour both afloat and ashore, create an exceptionally fine impression by their alertness, cleanness, and general enthusiasm."

During January, to counter the bad weather nearly always experienced on passage from Leghorn across the Gulf of Genoa, Commander Allan sent some British boats to Gulf Juan, whence they could more easily attack enemy traffic between Genoa and Savona. On the night of January 7/8, PT 303 (Lt. (jg.) David R. Campbell, USNR), PT 304 (Lt. (jg.) Lawrence F. Knorr, USNR), and MTB 422, under Lt. Stanmore B. Marshall, USNR, fired five torpedoes at three coasters half a mile off Savona Harbor. It was felt that two of the ships were sunk but this cannot be confirmed. A searchlight flashed on from the harbor and the patrol retired under heavy shore battery fire without damage.

Squadron 22 boats from Leghorn were in action on February 5/6, when PT 308 (Lt. (jg.) Charles H. Murphy, USNR) and PT 310 (Lt. (jg.) Robert Wallace, USNR), under Lt. Eugene G. Wilson, USNR, made an attack on a fast coaster but inflicted no damage. On February 8/9, Lieutenant (jg.) Murphy's PT 308, with MTB's 376 and 423, under Lt. N. Good, RNVR, attacked three F-lighters under heavy enemy fire but the enemy was able to escape damage.

During February, six British destroyers were assigned to the Inshore Squadron. Though their operations were severely limited by minefields, they were able, at extreme range, and with illumination by scouting aircraft, to engage convoys passing the Portofino Promontory, 12 miles east of Genoa. "During these patrols," Commander Allan reported, "two convoys were engaged, and Genoa and Sestri Levante were bombarded, all with uncertain results, although an apparent fire in a ship in convoy indicated a probable hit . . . Even if they achieved no great direct result, these patrols, which were almost continuous, very definitely curtailed the enemy's coastal traffic . . . ."

Early in March the destroyers were transferred to operate under Rear Adm. Robert Jaujard, FN, commander of the Flank Force, which was engaged in harassing the enemy coast and attacking such enemy shipping as it could find. On March 19 the PT's were also transferred to Admiral Jaujard's command, to operate from Gulf Juan. They had one last good action from Leghorn before they departed, on the night of March 9/10, when Lieutenant (jg.) Knorr's PT 304, Lieutenant (jg.) Murphy's PT 308, and Lt. (jg.) Richard L. Noble's PT 313, under Lt. William T. Davies, USNR, made two attacks on a convoy of eight ships off Mesco Point and sank one Rhône River barge.

Two of the Flank Force destroyers, HMS *Lookout* and HMS *Meteor,* sank two German TB destroyers, the TA–24 and TA–29, southeast of Genoa on the night of March 17/18. One hundred and eight prisoners were taken, including the commander of the German 10th Torpedo Boat Flotilla. The statements of the prisoners regarding the effectiveness of Coastal Forces operations during the winter were of particular interest. Almost every convoy sailing between Genoa and La Spezia, they said, had been subjected to motor torpedo boat or air attack, and the greatest threats to their coastwise traffic were groups of motor torpedo boats and medium bombers.

That gave the boats a good sendoff as they finally parted company with the British Coastal Forces. Commander Allan gave them another: "It is impossible," he said in reporting on Coastal Forces operations, "to refrain from once more emphasizing the very real cooperation which we have had throughout our associations with them, from all officers and men of PT squadrons serving on the station. From the maker of ice-cream and the barber, to the radar technicians and the storemen, we have had nothing but help and goodwill. The officers have always been considered as good friends rather than brave Allies, which they undoubtedly have proved themselves to be. There are innumerable memories of great occasions both afloat and ashore, which I am confident will never fade. Although all those who served under him, and who followed him, fully maintained the high standard which he set, it is to Commander S. M. Barnes, USN, that we owe the greatest gratitude for laying the sure foundations of what has been perfect inter-Allied harmony of design and action."

28. TORPEDOING THE HARBORS

Admiral Jaujard gave Lieutenant Commander Dressling a novel assignment—to harass the enemy by firing the PT's remaining store of Mark VIII torpedoes into the German-held harbors between Genoa and the French-Italian border. On the night of March 21/22, Lt. Stanmore B. Marshall, USNR, in PT 310 (Lt. (jg.) Robert Wallace, USNR), with PT 312 (Lt. (jg.) William J. Shea, USNR), fired four torpedoes at a range of 2 miles into the harbor of Savona, and observed three explosions. On the night of April 4/5, the same boats, under Lt. John Newell, USNR, fired four torpedoes into the harbor of San Remo and saw two explosions, of which the second was so powerful that it jarred the boats.

On the night of April 11/12, Lieutenant Marshall led PT 313 (Lt. (jg.) Erling Gamborg, USNR) and PT 309 (Lt. Roscoe T. Avery, USNR) to fire four torpedoes into Vado harbor. There was one large explosion, followed immediately by three or four smaller ones. Thirty seconds later there was a single explosion of great intensity. Lieutenant Commander Dressling led PT 302 (Lt. (jg.) Robert Spangenberg, USNR) and PT 305 (Lt. (jg.) Richard A. Hamilton, USNR) on the night of April 19/20 to fire the last three Mark VIII's in the stockpile into the harbor of Porto Maurizio, where a single loud explosion was heard.

"During these actions," Dressling reported, "Italian partisans were rising against the Germans, and there is little doubt that the explosions of our torpedoes were taken by the enemy as sabotage attempts by partisans. At no time were we fired on, despite the fact that we were well inside the range of many enemy shore batteries. Our boats were apparently never detected.

"It is the opinion of this command that to a small extent the . . . actions assisted the partisans in taking over the Italian ports on 27 April 1945."

29. THE LAST PATROLS

Several times during April the PT's had fleeting contacts with fast small craft thought to be MAS boats, and on the night of April 16/17, PT's 302 and 308 went to the assistance of the French destroyer *Trombe,* which had been torpedoed by an MAS or an E-boat. On the night of April 23/24, PT 307 (Lt. (jg.) Walter E. Powell, USNR) and PT 305 (Lt. (jg.) Richard A. Hamilton, USNR), under Lt. Robert E. Nagle, USNR, patrolling the Italian coast, gave chase to an MAS which tried to discourage pursuit by dropping a depth charge in their path. The MAS was gradually pulling away from the PT's when it was hit and stopped dead in the water. The PT's closed the range, intending to board it, but the MAS was already afire, so they stood off and pumped 40mm. into it until it exploded and sank.

The boats moved westward to Nice, where they communicated with French SC's which apparently were engaging enemy small craft in the Cannes area. The PT's were ordered to maintain a patrol to the east of the area of the action. Their own patrol was without incident, but the French SC's sank six E-boats, and seven others were run aground on the French coast or scuttled as a result of the engagement.

"It is interesting to note," Dressling reported, "that a life ring picked up a few days later had the number 'MAS 561.' We had previously captured the MAS 562 in an engagement off Elba."

On April 28/29, Lieutenant Commander Dressling led 10 of his boats in a special sweep of the French-Italian coast in company with 2 French cruisers, 3 French destroyers, and 10 French PC's. All of the coastline, formerly held by the enemy, apparently was in the hands of the Partisans.

That was the last patrol of PT's in the Mediterranean. They were released from operations on May 4 and in June were assembled at Oran for shipment to the United States. Back in New York, the boats were being readied for duty in the Pacific when hostilities ended in August. Squadron 22 was decommissioned in New York on November 15, 1945.

The three squadrons had operated in the Mediterranean for 2 years. Their losses were 4 boats destroyed by mines; 5 officers and 19 men killed in action; 7 officers and 28 men wounded in action. They fired 354 torpedoes and claimed on their own to have sunk 38 vessels totaling 23,700 tons and to have damaged 49, totaling 22,600 tons; and in joint patrols with British boats to have sunk 15 vessels totaling 13,000 tons and to have damaged 17, totaling 5,650 tons.

The English Channel—*D-Day and After*

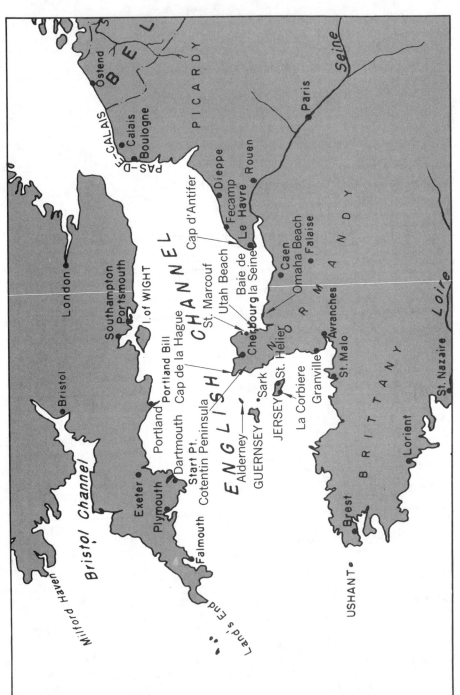

The English Channel.

PART VII

The English Channel—*D-Day and After*

I. D-DAY AND THE MASON LINE

THE ENGLISH Channel was the British Coastal Forces' own backyard. From the summer of 1940, when the German blitzkrieg flashed across the Low Countries and northern France, until the end of the war in Europe, the MTB's, MGB's, and ML's fought 464 actions in British home waters, claiming 269 enemy vessels sunk or probably sunk, as against the loss of 76 Coastal Force craft.[24] With the British boats carrying out the double mission of preying on enemy coastal convoys and protecting Allied shipping from E-boat attack, there was no need for American PT's in the Channel until the spring of 1944, when the invasion of Normandy was imminent.

An urgent request by the Office of Strategic Services for PT's to land and pick up agents on the French coast resulted in the hasty commissioning of a new Squadron 2 (the original squadron had been decommissioned in the Solomons in November 1943) on March 23, 1944, at Fyfe's Shipyard, Glenwood Landing, Long Island. The squadron, commanded by Lt. Comdr. John D. Bulkeley, was made up of three early Higgins boats, PT's 71, 72, and 199, which had had almost 2 years of service as training boats in Squadron 4 at Melville. After a rapid overhaul at Fyfe's Shipyard, the boats were shipped to England, arriving at Dartmouth on April 24. There they were fitted with special navigational equipment to give them pinpoint accuracy in locating their objectives on the French coast. Officers and men practiced launching, rowing, loading, and unloading four-oared pulling boats, constructed with padded sides and muffled oarlocks, until they could land men and equipment on a beach swiftly and silently on the darkest night.

---

[24] These figures are taken from *The Battle of the Narrow Seas,* by Lt. Comdr. Peter Scott, RNVR, published by Country Life Limited, London, 1945: a thorough and vivid account of operations of British Coastal Forces in the English Channel and North Sea.

PT 71 made the first trip across the Channel on the night of May 19/20, carrying agents and several hundreds of pounds of equipment. The 71 crossed German convoy lanes and minefields, anchored within 500 yards of a beach commanded by German shore guns and a radar station, landed the men and their gear under the noses of German sentries, and returned to Dartmouth without discovery. That was typical of the 19 missions Squadron 2 performed for the Office of Strategic Services between May and November. Sometimes they put men ashore, sometimes they took them out of France. The boat officers and men never knew the identity of their passengers or the exact nature of their missions. The job of the boats was to land their passengers or to pick them up at precisely the right position on the coast, and to do it without being detected. The squadron completed its 19 missions without once making contact with the enemy, which is entirely as it should have been.

Three more squadrons of PT's were sent to the Channel to join the screening forces in the invasion of Normandy, though only one of them, Squadron 34, 12 Elco boats, commanded by Lt. Allen H. Harris, USNR, was in time to take part in the operations on D-day, June 6, 1944. Squadron 34 arrived in England in May; Squadron 35, 12 Elco boats, under Lt. Comdr. Richard Davis, Jr., on June 4; and Squadron 30, 6 Higgins boats, under Lt. Robert L. Searles, USNR, on June 7. Also in June, Lieutenant Commander Bulkeley was designated a task group commander in charge of all PT operations during the invasion of Normandy.

Invasion plans called for landings by five great task forces in the Baie de la Seine, which was divided into the British assault area on the east and the American assault area on the west. Admiral Sir Philip Vian, RN, Commander Eastern Task Force, was in command of the three task forces in the British area; Rear Adm. Alan G. Kirk, in command of the two task forces in the American area. Admiral Kirk's forces were Task Force U, commanded by Rear Adm. Don P. Moon, to land troops at Utah Beach, westernmost of the invasion beaches, and Task Force O, under Rear Adm. John L. Hall, Jr., to effect landings at Omaha Beach, between Utah Beach and the British area.

The PT's of Squadron 34, in divisions of three, were to escort four groups of minesweepers in advance of the invasion fleet to clear a broad sealane to the beaches and the fire support areas offshore. The first group, PT's 500, 498, and 509, under Lt. Herbert J. Sherertz, USNR, nearly invaded France a day too soon. D-day had been scheduled for June 5, so early on the morning

NR&L (MOD)—32504

PT's cross English Channel on D-day as Army bombers pass overhead.

of the 4th the boats rendezvoused with their minesweepers and set out from the Isle of Wight for the Baie de la Seine. Later in the morning the PT base at Portland received belated notice that D-day had been postponed until June 6. Fortunately a patrolling destroyer was able to intercept the boats, already halfway to France, and send them back to Portland.

They made a fresh start on the morning of June 5, and stayed with their minesweepers through the night of the 5th and morning of the 6th, at times approaching within half a mile of the French coast, protected from shore batteries by a tremendous naval and aerial bombardment. The only casualty was the minesweeper *Osprey,* which struck a mine and sank just as she took station on the evening of the 5th. PT's 505 and 508 picked up six of her survivors.

The boats of Squadron 2 crossed the Channel on the night of June 5/6 with flagships to which they had been assigned as dispatch boats. PT 71 accompanied the USS *Augusta,* Admiral Kirk's flagship; PT 72, the USS *Ancon,* Admiral Hall's flagship; and PT 199, the USS *Bayfield,* flagship

of Admiral Moon.   After taking an Army officer from the *Bayfield* to Utah
Beach on the morning of June 6, PT 199 rescued 61 survivors of the destroyer
Corry, which had been mined.

Except for these rescue operations, D-day turned out to be a routine affair
for the PT's.   "We might have had trouble with mines, with shore batteries
or with E-boats," Bulkeley said.   "As it was, we didn't have any trouble
at all."

At 1600 on D-day the PT's of Squadron 34 joined the Western Task Force
Area screen, which included destroyers, destroyer escorts, PC's, and British
steam gunboats.   The PT's were stationed on the "Mason Line," extending
6½ miles to seaward from the beach near St. Marcouf, as an inner defense
against infiltration by E-boats into the convoy unloading area.   They were
joined on June 7 and 8 by boats of Squadron 35, and on the 10th by those of
Squadron 30.   Until the end of the month, an average of 19 PT's remained on
the line at all times.   Boats rotated between the Mason Line and the Portland Base, usually patrolling for a week at a time, although some boats stayed
on the line for as long as 3 weeks without relief.   E-boats made so few attempts to penetrate the screen that PT's had no contact with enemy surface
craft.   In the midst of the greatest invasion in history, however, their duty
was seldom dull.

On the evening of June 7, Lt. William C. Godfrey's PT 505 gave chase to
what appeared to be a submarine periscope cutting through the water near
St. Marcouf Island.   The periscope disappeared when the 505 came within
75 yards, and Godfrey was about to give the order to release depth charges
when the 505 ran over a mine.   A violent explosion lifted the stern of the
PT out of the water, injured two men, tore loose one depth charge, snapped
the warheads off the torpedoes, threw the engine beds awry, and caused some
damage to practically every part of the boat.   The PT went down quickly
by the stern until the base of the 40mm. gun was awash.   Godfrey jettisoned
his torpedoes and his other depth charge, and transferred his forward guns,
radar, and radio equipment to PT 507, which towed the 505 to anchorage
in the lee of St. Marcouf Island.   Although there was some danger that the
boat would sink, Godfrey, two other officers, and one enlisted man remained
aboard that night.   The next morning two LCM's towed the 505 onto the
invasion beach at high tide.   Low tide left the boat high and dry for 6 hours,
time enough for the crew to put emergency patches on the hull and to paint
the side with the legend, "PORTLAND OR BUST!"   PT 500 towed the

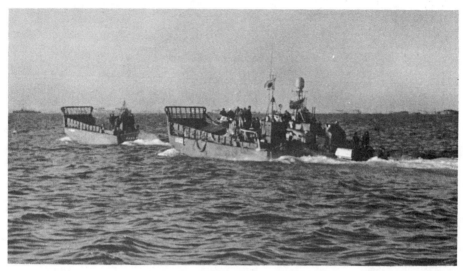

NR&L (MOD)−32506

PT 505, damaged by a mine off Normandy, is towed to the beach by two LCM's, her stern awash.

505 back to Portland on June 11, in a crossing made miserable by four partings of the towline in heavy seas.

Mines were perhaps the greatest single menace in the Baie de la Seine. During the month of June, PT's rescued 203 survivors of mined ships. On the morning of June 8, the destroyer *Glennon* hit a mine and began to settle by the stern. The destroyer escort *Rich,* preceded by two minesweepers, approached *Glennon* and was passing a towline to the destroyer when a mine exploded 50 yards to starboard. *Rich* was shaken, but not damaged. PT 504 (Lt. (jg.) Harold B. Sherwood, Jr., USNR) at this time was drawing near to *Rich* to offer assistance. Two minutes later another mine blew the stern off *Rich.* PT 504 circled *Rich,* and within 3 minutes still another mine caught *Rich* amidships. PT 504, joined by PT 502 (Lt. Charles E. Twadell, Jr., USNR) and PT 506 (Lt. Jaquelin J. Daniel, USNR), made fast to the sinking ship and sent rescue parties aboard. The boats took off 69 wounded men, casting off their lines only when the decks of the *Rich* were awash. R. W. Gretter, QM2c, of the 504, and Paul E. Cayer, S1c, of the 506, did not hear the order to abandon the *Rich,* and were still aboard when the ship sank. They were picked up by a Coast Guard vessel. Cayer was cited for removing "nine crew members who would have died without his aid." PT 508 (Lt.

NR&L (MOD)—32507

The destroyer Glennon (right) *has just struck a mine and is down by the stern.* Destroyer escort Rich, *a British ML, and PT's are going to her assistance.* Rich *soon hit a mine, which blew off her stern.*

NR&L (MOD)—32508

Minutes later, Rich *hit another mine, shown here exploding amidships.*

(jg.) Calvin R. Whorton, USNR) rescued the last two survivors aboard the detached stern section of the ship.

On the night of June 14/15, German planes tried something new in the way of illumination for night bombing attacks on shipping, dropping brilliant and long-burning float flares in two rows in the assault area. Capt. Harry Sanders, commander of the Western Task Force Area Screen, ordered PT's to sink the flares if the enemy should attempt a repeat performance. The next night the Germans again dropped two long rows of flares on the water and the PT's went alongside them and sank them with submachineguns before the bombers came over. On the night of June 16/17, PT's again extinguished flares, with the result that the German planes dropped their bombs in empty water well clear of shipping. "Thereafter," Captain Sanders reported, "the Germans dropped no more floating flares. I believe that the frustration of bombing attacks by extinguishing marker flares is a new achievement for PT boats."

NR&L (MOD)–32509

PT 504 and British ML 116 pick up survivors of the Rich.

80–G–253227

PT 199 carries Adm. Harold R. Stark to Allied invasion beachhead, June 14, 1944.

Boats of Squadron 34 relieved PT's 71, 72, and 199 of their routine but exacting duties as dispatch boats on June 17, and the Squadron 2 boats returned to Portland for repairs and resumption of their special work for the Office of Strategic Services. Lt. William M. Snelling, USNR, boat captain of PT 71, claimed the all-time PT record for carrying gold braid. On June 12, he had as passengers for an inspection tour of the invasion beaches, Admirals King, Stark, Kirk, Moon, and Wilkes, and Generals Marshall, Eisenhower, Arnold, Bradley, and Hodges.

The boats on the Mason Line took a beating from June 19 to 22, during what Prime Minister Churchill described as the "worst Channel storm in 40 years." Many boats suffered hull damage from gale-lashed debris and narrowly missed being crushed by drifting ships and barges, but 11 boats of Squadron 34, eight of Squadron 35, and two of Squadron 30 rode out the 4-day storm maintaining their positions on the line.

In addition to the Mason Line assignment, PT's patrolled in divisions of two or three to the northwest during most of June. Toward the end of the month they began to cover the approaches to Cherbourg in the hope of catching Germans attempting to evacuate by sea, but none of these patrols was productive. On June 25 a force of American battleships, cruisers, and destroyers, bombarded Cherbourg for more than 3 hours, knocking out most of the big coastal guns. By nightfall American troops had entered the city and were fighting in the streets. That night PT's patrolling with destroyers drew fire from shore batteries on Cap de la Hague, to the west of Cherbourg, and on the evening of the 27th went right up to the Cherbourg breakwater to learn whether any enemy guns were still active.

While four other PT's patrolled offshore with the destroyer *Shubrick,* Lieutenant Commander Bulkeley, in PT 510 (Lt. (jg.) Elliott B. MacSwan, USNR), with PT 521 (Lt. (jg.) Peter S. Zaley, USNR), maneuvered for 25 minutes within a quarter mile of the breakwater, at times approaching within 150 yards. Then a large-caliber battery in the harbor fort opened on the boats, dropping one explosive shell 30 feet ahead and another 20 feet behind the 521, which was following 200 yards behind the 510. The explosions stopped all three of the 521's engines, bent the throttle rods, loosened the deck planking, and jarred the port torpedo halfway out of its rack. PT 510 laid a smokescreen around the 521, whose engineers got her underway again in 5 minutes. Bulkeley ordered the 521 to launch her dangling port torpedo toward the breakwater and the boats retired, zigzagging away behind

NR&L (MOD)—32505

A PT maneuvers off the German fort at Cherbourg to see if its guns are still active. They were.

smoke. Because of the smoke and noise it was impossible to observe the effect of the torpedo on the breakwater.

"We decided then and there that that fort had not fallen," Bulkeley said, "and waited until the next day to pay our next call. This time we saw a white flag in the fort so we went right into the harbor."

While the 510 and 521 were drawing fire from the fort, *Shubrick* and the other four PT's continued westward toward Cap de la Hague. When they were 2½ miles off the cape, a heavy shore battery opened fire, dropping shells within 30 yards of Lt. (jg.) Stewart J. Moulin's PT 459 and 300 yards from *Shubrick*. The group took evasive action, with the *Shubrick* retiring behind a smokescreen. A few minutes later PT 457 (Lt. (jg.) Waldemar A. Tomski, USNR) observed the position of the shore guns and reported it to *Shubrick*. The destroyer came about through the smoke, fired a salvo, and then was forced to retire by renewed fire from shore.

Patrolling on the Mason Line continued through July without incident. Bulkeley, promoted to commander, was detached in the middle of July to take command of the destroyer *Endicott*. He was succeeded as overall commander of PT's in the Channel by Lt. Allen H. Harris, USNR. He previously had been relieved as commander of Squadron 2 by Lt. Robert R. Read, USNR. Lt. Herbert J. Sherertz, USNR, relieved Harris as commander of Squadron 34. Squadron 35 had had a change of command on June 11, when Lt. Arthur N. Barnes, USNR, relieved Lieutenant Commander Davis as squadron commander and Davis assumed command of the PT base at Portland. Lt. Ralph S. Duley, USNR, succeeded Davis as base commander in mid-July.

Admiral Kirk, his duties as Commander Western Task Force completed, wrote on July 5:

DEAR BULKELEY:

As you know, I have turned over command off the beaches and at Cherbourg to Admiral Wilkes, and have withdrawn from the assault area. I cannot leave without congratulating you, and, through you, all your men, on the very fine job done by PT boats during the first month of the campaign. Your boys have fully justified our very high expectations, and if they have not had as much direct action as we had all hoped, that in itself is a tribute to the high respect the German has for them.

Whether in the Area Screen or on Advanced Patrol, or in the dull but demanding business of ferrying old men around the bay, your boys have done themselves proud. I wish you and them all the luck in the world.

Sincerely,

ALAN KIRK

2. THE CHANNEL ISLANDS

At the beginning of August the PT's were withdrawn from the Normandy invasion area. Nine were transferred to Portsmouth, England, to work with British MTB's and MGB's patrolling off LeHavre, and 18 were assigned to Cherbourg, to replace British Coastal Forces in disrupting enemy shipping between the Channel Islands—Jersey, Guernsey, and Alderney—and between the islands and the German hold-out garrisons at St. Malo and the Île de Cezembre.

At both of these bases, the PT's learned a patrolling technique new to them, which had been developed by the British Coastal Forces: the use of a destroyer or frigate to control the PT attack. A destroyer or frigate patrolled a line several miles long, with a division of PT's stationed at each end of the line. The destroyer, with radar superior to that of the PT's, spotted enemy targets and vectored the PT's in to the attack, passing ranges and bearings to them by radio. At Cherbourg, Lieutenant Sherertz rode the destroyer during these operations as officer in tactical command of the PT's, with Lt. Comdr. Peter Scott, RNVR, a veteran Coastal Forces officer, loaned to the task group as vector controller.

On the night of August 8/9, destroyer *Maloy* patrolled a north-south line 6 miles long, west of the Island of Jersey. PT's 503 (Lt. James A. Doherty, USNR), 500 (Lt. Douglas S. Kennedy, USNR), and 507 (Ens. Buell T. Heminway, USNR) were stationed at the north end of the line, and PT's 509 (Lt. Harry M. Crist, USNR) and 508 (Lt. (jg.) Calvin R. Whorton, USNR) at the south. At 0530 the *Maloy* vectored the northern group to attack a group of six minesweepers moving south toward La Corbiere, the southwestern point of Jersey. The boats, running through a pea-soup fog, were unable to see the enemy and fired their torpedoes by radar, with no apparent results. Half an hour later *Maloy* vectored the southern pair of boats in to attack.

Lieutenant Crist led them in through fog that limited visibility to 150 yards. PT 509 released one torpedo one-quarter mile off the enemy's port bow. PT 508's radar was not working and the minesweepers were not visible in the fog, so the 508 fired no torpedoes. The boats circled and went in for another attack. PT 508 still did not sight the enemy, but launched one torpedo on radio orders from Lieutenant Crist, who said the enemy ships were dead ahead. As the 508 turned away there was heavy firing between the 509 and a minesweeper on her port bow. The 508 could not engage the enemy im-

mediately, since the 509 was directly in her line of fire. PT 508 heard the
509 report by radio, "I am directly in the middle," but when she had circled
to port, could find no trace of the 509. The 508 rejoined *Maloy* at 0710.

Fifteen minutes later Lieutenant Sherertz got underway in PT 503, with
PT 507, to search the southern coast of Jersey for the missing boat. At 0800
the boats picked up a radar target in St. Helier roadstead. Just as they closed
to 200 yards, the thick fog bank ledged off and an enemy minesweeper appeared dead ahead and bow on. The 503 fired one torpedo. Both boats
opened fire with all guns, scoring many hits on the minesweeper's bridge
structure, and retired under heavy return fire. Both PT's were hit. Two
men were killed and four were wounded on the 503, and one was wounded
on the 507.

On August 10 a searchplane found the body of one of the men of the 509,
and on the 20th a bullet-riddled portion of the hull of the 509 was found
floating in the Channel.

The full story of the 509 will never be known, but part of it was learned
after V–E Day, when prisoners of war on the Island of Jersey were liberated,
among them John L. Page, RdM2c, USNR, the sole survivor of PT 509.

After firing one torpedo by radar, Page said, the 509 circled and came in
for a gunnery run. Page was in the charthouse, manning the radar; Lt. (jg.)
John K. Pavlis, USNR, was at the wheel. Page remembered that the PT
was moving along at a good clip and that it got up pretty close to the enemy
and opened fire before there was any return fire from the minesweeper. But
when the return fire came it was heavy and it was accurate. One shell exploded in the charthouse, knocking Page out. When he came to he was
trying to beat out flames with his hands. He was wounded and the boat was
on fire, but he still remembered to pull the detonator switch to destroy his
radar set before he tried to crawl out on deck.

When he reached the deck he found that the bow of the boat was hung up
on the side of a 180-foot minesweeper. Everything aft of the cockpit was in
flames. From the deck of the minesweeper, Germans were blazing away
with small arms and tossing hand grenades down on the PT. Page chose
the lesser hell and struggled painfully forward through the rain of bullets
and exploding grenades. When he reached the bow—he has no idea whether
it took him 15 seconds or 15 minutes—the Germans tossed him a line. He
still had strength to take it, and they hauled him aboard the minesweeper.
By the time they stretched him out on the deck his right arm and leg were

broken and he had been wounded in 37 places. One heavy slug had ripped a hole through his back and lodged in his right lung.

German sailors were working frantically with crowbars to free the flaming PT from the side. Eventually they worked it loose and almost immediately it exploded with a mighty roar. "I couldn't see it," Page said, "but I felt the heat of the blast."

Page was taken to the crew's quarters, along with the German wounded and dead. "I managed to count the dead," he said. "There were 15 of them, and a good number of wounded—it's difficult to estimate how many, because they kept milling around. I guess I conked out for a while. The first thing I remember is the first-aid man putting a pack on my back and arm. Then I could hear the noise of the ship docking. After they removed their dead and wounded, they took me ashore at St. Helier.

"They laid me out on the dock for quite a while and a couple of civilians— I found out later that they were Gestapo agents—tried to question me, but they saw I was badly shot up, so they didn't try to question me any further."

Page was taken to the former English hospital at St. Helier, where a skillful German surgeon performed many operations on him, removing dozens of bullets and fragments from every part of his body. He did not have his final operation until December 27, and though he was released to prison camp on January 2, he had to report back to the hospital for dressings every other day until the middle of March. While he was in the hospital the bodies of three of his shipmates washed ashore on Jersey. The British Red Cross took charge and saw that they were buried with full military honors.

Page was annoyed from time to time by the Gestapo agents, but, he said, "I found that being very correct and stressing the fact that my Government didn't permit me to answer questions was very effective. They tried a few times and finally left me alone."

He was liberated from prison camp upon the surrender of Germany on May 8, 1945.

During the week that followed the destruction of the 509, PT's from Cherbourg had two more actions with minesweepers. On the night of August 11/12, PT 500 (Lt. Douglas S. Kennedy, USNR) and PT 502 (Lt. Charles E. Twadell, Jr., USNR) were vectored by the destroyer escort *Borum* to attack two vessels off La Corbiere. Each boat fired two torpedoes, scoring no damage, and retired under fire which wounded three men on PT 502 and one on PT 500. Two nights later, Lt. William C. Godfrey's PT 505, which had had its mine damage repaired at the British Power Boat Co. at Poole, England, patrolling with PT 498 (Lt. (jg.) William S. Squire, USNR), was vectored by the *Borum* to attack five ships off the Jersey coast. The enemy illuminated the boats with starshell when they were 2½ miles away, but the PT's continued in to three-quarters of a mile and fired a spread of four torpedoes without results. The boats retired unscathed as the enemy fired furiously into puffs of smoke laid by the 505.

St. Malo fell on August 18, and by the end of the month traffic between the Channel Islands virtually dried up. PT patrols with destroyers and destroyer escorts were discontinued. Thereafter, Lieutenant Harris reported, the boats "were used for convoys going north and for a defense line against the escape of army personnel from Île de Cezembre, farther south. No further actions ensued except for dodging shore batteries which were frequently pretty accurate."

3. THE EASTERN FLANK

While the PT's on the Mason Line waited for the E-boats that did not attack, British boats were having a hot time on the eastern flank of the invasion. A tight blockade of LeHavre was being maintained. Night after night, during all of June and July, they engaged the enemy off LeHavre and along the coast to the northeast, principally between Cap d'Antifer and Fécamp, fighting pitched battles with E-boats, R-boats, trawlers, minelayers, explosive boats, and occasional destroyers. It was to assist the British boats in operations off LeHavre that most of the Squadron 35 boats were moved to Portsmouth on August 4. Later, boats from Squadron 30 also were thrown into the battle.

At 1700 of the day of their arrival, the PT officers assembled with Coastal Forces officers in the briefing room of HMS *Dolphin,* the Coastal Forces base at Portsmouth, to receive orders for their first mission. An hour and 20 minutes later, four PT's stood out for LeHavre with a division of MTB's and HMS *Stayner,* their vectoring frigate. The PT's were not to see LeHavre that night, however. Enroute, *Stayner* made sound contact with a submarine and, with HMS *Wensley Dale,* repeatedly attacked it for nearly 5 hours, dropping 140 explosive charges. The PT's and MTB's, lying to 3 miles away, were severely shaken, though not damaged, by the explosions. The attack resulted in the positive sinking of the German submarine U–671, from which *Stayner* captured four survivors.

The PT's had their first action 2 nights later when HMS *Thornborough* vectored PT's 510, 512, and 514, led by Lt. James C. Mountcastle, USNR, to attack three E-boats coming out of LeHavre. The PT's made two runs on the E-boats, apparently scoring several 40mm. hits. The E-boats retired into the harbor.

On the night of August 8/9, Lt. Sidney I. Saltsman, USNR, led PT's 520, 521, and 511 to attack a convoy of one auxiliary vessel and five R-boats off Cap d'Antifer. The boats were illuminated and taken under fire by shore guns when they were more than a mile from the targets. Saltsman decided that he had lost his chance for a successful torpedo attack and led the boats in two gunnery runs on the targets. During the second run, Saltsman's PT 520 and Lt. (jg.) Peter S. Zaley's PT 521 were hit. One man was wounded on the 521 and two engines stopped. The boats retired slowly behind a smokescreen laid by Lt. (jg.) Robert S. Taft's PT 511.

On the night of August 10/11, Lieutenant Jones led PT's 515, 513, and 518 in a torpedo and gunnery attack on an armed trawler, four R-boats, and one E-boat, with no damage although the convoy was apparently forced into LeHavre. PT's 515 and 513 were hit by enemy fire and three men were wounded.

The PT's had no more action until the last week in August, when the Germans attempted first to reinforce, then to evacuate, LeHavre. From August 23 to September 1, Coastal Forces, together with British destroyers and frigates and one French destroyer, *La Combattante,* claimed to have sunk 4 coasters, 9 tank landing craft, 2 trawlers, 2 R-boats, and an E-boat, and to have driven aground a coaster, a tank landing craft, and an R-boat.[25] While the major share of the victory unquestionably belongs to the MTB's and destroyers, the PT's were in action for 4 nights running and contributed to the successful bottling up of the Germans in LeHavre.

On the night of August 24/25 Lieutenant Sidney I. Saltsman, USNR, in PT 520, led PT 511 (Lieutenant (jg.) Robert S. Taft, USNR) and PT 514 (Lieutenant (jg.) George E. Fowler, USNR) in three separate gunnery attacks on a group of four E-boats. One of the enemy boats, S–91, was so seriously damaged that it was abandoned and blown up by her crew. The PT's were forced to break off each attack by heavy fire from shore. PT 520

[25] These figures are taken from Lt. Comdr. Peter Scott's *The Battle of the Narrow Seas.*

took one direct hit, which tore a large hole in her starboard side, without injury to any of her crew. The next night Lieutenant William J. Ryan, Jr., USNR, in PT 519, led PT's 513 and 516 in an unsuccessful torpedo attack on two R-boats and two E-boats, and followed it up with a gunnery run, during which several hits were made on an R-boat. The 513 had a large hole shot in its hull and the 516 had two men wounded by shrapnel.

The enemy's last attempt to reinforce LeHavre was made on the night of August 26/27, when a group of tank landing craft escorted by R-boats were attacked first by 2 MTB's, then by the destroyer HMS *Middleton,* and finally by 2 more MTB's. The upshot of this complicated action, according to German records, was the loss of two tank landing craft, AF–98 and AF–108. Lieutenant Saltsman led the PT attack in Lieutenant (jg.) Fowler's PT 514, with Lieutenant (jg.) Taft's PT 511 and Lt. (jg.) William F. Ryder's PT 520. Vectored onto their targets by the *Retalick,* the PT's fired six torpedoes and started their retirement without discovery. "PT's were rewarded with a tremendous explosion in target area," Saltsman reported, "followed by sparks and debris; a second explosion was observed soon after, not as large as the first. PT's by this time had turned stern to target and were idling away. After the explosion occurred, the enemy convoy opened up with gunfire attack on PT's, distance 2,500 yards. PT's continued to idle away, not returning fire because of inaccuracy of enemy gunfire. PT's were then illuminated and began retirement at 43 knots. PT's were subjected to intense, accurate and heavy-caliber gunfire until range became 4 miles. Several shells fell within 20 yards of PT 514. No damage was sustained."

The following night PT's 519 and 512 fired torpedoes at a group of R-boats off Fécamp—without hits. They were the last torpedoes fired by PT's in the Channel. The Canadian First Army sealed off the Germans in LeHavre with the capture of Dieppe on September 1, and carried LeHavre itself by assault a week later.

4. END OF THE CAMPAIGN

Squadron 2 remained at Dartmouth, continuing its missions for the Office of Strategic Services until so much of the French coast was in our hands that there was no more work for the boats to do. The squadron eventually was shipped back to New York, where it was decommissioned in September 1945. Its most spectacular projected mission, which might have come off except for an engine casualty, was that of running the German North Sea blockade with arms and ammunition for the resistance movement in Denmark. It was expected that even if the PT succeeded in running the gauntlet of German ships, planes, mines, and shore batteries, the crew would be interned in Sweden for the duration, since the boat could not possibly carry enough fuel for a round trip. Nevertheless, there was no difficulty in assembling a volunteer crew under Lt. William M. Snelling, USNR; Lt. Joseph R. Ellicott, USNR; and Lt. (jg.) Redmond J. Reilly, USNR. PT 72 was fitted out with extra gasoline tanks and was actually loaded with her cargo of arms and ammunition. On her final check run, however, she had a serious engine casualty. Before it could be repaired the Office of Strategic Services canceled the mission.

In November 1944, Squadrons 34 and 35, less PT 505, sailed for Roseneath, Scotland, where, after many delays, the boats were transferred under lend-lease to the Russian Government. PT 505's bottom had opened up again during patrols in heavy weather during August and September, and she was not considered in good enough condition for transfer. She was shipped back to the United States where she was repaired and turned over to Squadron 4 at Melville.

Squadron 30 remained at Cherbourg during the winter and spring of 1945, patrolling for the protection of shipping in and out of Cherbourg, Le-Havre, and Granville. Several times during the winter, Squadron 30 boats went to the aid of torpedoed ships, rescuing many survivors. Their only actions with the enemy resulted from patrols to prevent possible enemy landings on the Cotentin Peninsula by small craft from the Channel Islands. On the night of February 27/28, 1945, PT's 457 and 459, under Lt. (jg.) J. M. Boone, USNR, attacked and claimed to have sunk two small landing craft off Cap de la Hague, and on the night of April 10/11, Lt. (jg.) Sydney E. Garner's PT 458 exchanged fire with a 100-foot trawler northeast of the Island of Sark.

On May 12, after the German surrender, the PT's had the pleasant duty of escorting the first Allied ships into St. Peter Port on the Island of Guernsey, and into St. Helier on the Island of Jersey. In June the boats were shipped back to the United States to be overhauled for assignment to the Pacific. The war ended while they were still in New York, and Squadron 30 was decommissioned there on November 15, 1945.

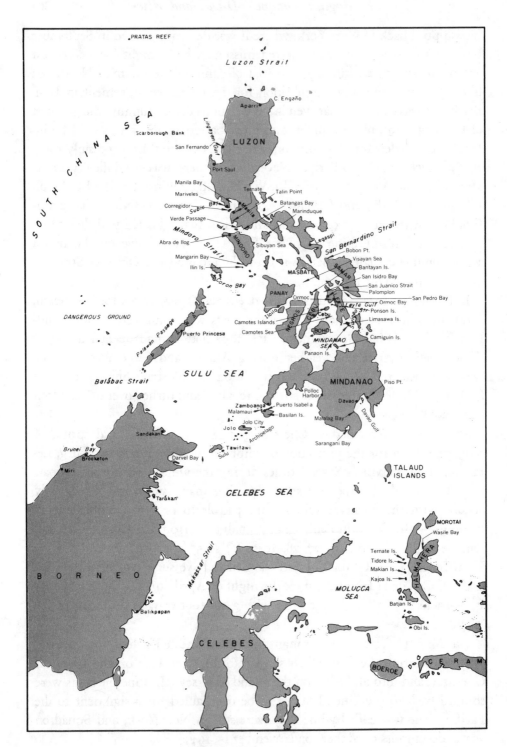

Southwest Pacific Area.

PART VIII

Southwest Pacific—*Return to the Philippines*

1. MOROTAI

NORTHWEST OF New Guinea's Vogelkop lies Halmahera, an island shaped like a rude K, extending 170 miles from north to south. Morotai, an egg-shaped island some 40 miles long, is separated by 12 miles of water from the northernmost tip of Halmahera, and lies roughly halfway between Cape Sansapor in New Guinea and Davao Gulf in Mindanao, southernmost of the Philippines. Seizure of a base on Halmahera or Morotai was considered necessary to provide land-based air support and flank protection for invasion of the Philippines, which was to begin with landings on Mindanao.

Lt. Gen. Walter Krueger, Commanding General Sixth Army, reported that "The successful fulfillment of this requirement would necessitate an amphibious operation in force to seize and hold an area as close to the Philippines as possible, but within fighter aircraft range of Cape Sansapor, where elements of the Allied Air Forces would be established to provide land-based air support. Furthermore, the area selected should be suitable for the development or construction of necessary airfields, for the employment of light naval forces required to prevent enemy reinforcement by small craft, and for maintenance of the forces committed.

"With these factors in view, GHQ, SWPA, thus restricted the choice of an objective to either northern Halmahera or to Morotai Island. Although northern Halmahera possessed a sufficient number of developed airfields, the capture of any one of these would require a large force. Even after an area had been captured, its defense would present a major problem: the enemy, by utilizing overland routes or by employing shore-to-shore overwater operations, could easily concentrate superior numbers to oppose our forces.

"Plans were therefore made in July 1944, to bypass the main island of Halmahera and to secure objectives on the weakly garrisoned Morotai Island . . ."

The Morotai Task Force, under the command of Rear Adm. Daniel E. Barbey, landed on the southwestern shore of the island on September 15, 1944. The next day Comdr. Selman S. Bowling, who commanded the Motor Torpedo Boat Squadrons of the Seventh Fleet, arrived in the PT-boat tender *Oyster Bay* with *Mobjack,* another tender, and 41 PT's of Squadrons 9, 10, 18, and 33. From the night of September 16/17, when 16 PT's went out on patrol, until the cessation of hostilities 11 months later, the PT's operated regularly as the "light naval forces" mentioned by General Krueger, preventing the numerically superior Japanese on Halmahera from attacking our forces on Morotai. Estimates of Japanese strength on Halmahera ran as high as 31,000 troops, but it was not until August 1945 that the PT's learned that they had "contained" 37,000 Japanese on Halmahera for nearly a year, rendering this huge force impotent by denying it passage across the 12-mile strait between the two islands.

2. RESCUE IN WASILE BAY

The landings of the Morotai Task Force were supported not only by land-based planes from Cape Sansapor but by Navy planes from six escort carriers.

Carrierborne fighters made an early morning sweep over Halmahera on September 16, and one of them was shot down by antiaircraft fire over Wasile Bay, 60 miles south of Morotai. The pilot, Ens. Harold A. Thompson, USNR, of Fighter Squadron 26 was wounded, but parachuted into the water several hundred yards from the shore. Soon a Catalina rescue plane arrived on the scene and dropped a rubber raft to Thompson. Thompson drifted shorewards until his raft fetched up against the side of a small unmanned cargo ship 200 yards from the enemy-occupied beach. He tied the raft to the ship's anchor chain to keep from drifting ashore.

As long as their fuel held out, his squadron mates circled the area, strafing Japanese gun positions and keeping Thompson in sight. When the squadron's fuel ran low, planes from other units arrived on the scene to continue harassing the Japanese. About noon a Navy Catalina tried to land to rescue him, but was driven off by heavy antiaircraft fire.

In the meantime Thompson's plight was reported to *Oyster Bay*. Early in the afternoon Lt. A. Murray Preston, USNR, commander of Squadron 33, got underway for Wasile Bay in PT 489 (Lt. Wilfred B. Tatro, USNR) accompanied by PT 363 (Lt. (jg.) Hershel F. Boyd, USNR). Every officer and man aboard the two PT's had volunteered for the dangerous daylight mission.

Arriving at the 4-mile-wide entrance to the bay ahead of their air cover, the boats started to run in close to the western side to avoid minefields and shore batteries to the east. When the PT's were still 4 miles from the narrows, a heavy gun opened fire from the western shore. Preston turned eastward, leading his boats at high speed across a suspected minefield to try the other side. Not one, but three heavy guns opened fire from the eastern shore. The boats were forced to retire. They had hardly pulled out of range of the guns before fighter planes arrived to cover them. They turned and started in again.

It took the PT's 20 minutes to pass through the straits and enter Wasile Bay. The planes strafed both sides of the entrance but the big guns kept blazing away from both sides, dropping their shells much closer to the PT's than they had on the first approach. Once inside the bay, which is nowhere more than 7 miles across, the boats were brought under heavy fire by many guns from both the northern and southern coasts. A fighter plane laid smoke along the shore and guided the PT's to Thompson's raft. Shore batteries, planes, and PT's were all firing furiously as PT 489 came close aboard the cargo ship. Lt. Donald F. Seaman, USNR, the Task Group Intelligence Officer, and Charles D. Day, MoMM1c, USNR, dived overboard from the 489, swam to the raft and towed it back to the 489. During the 5 minutes that the PT's had to lie to while Thompson was being brought aboard, the boats raked the beach with their 40mm. guns, starting several fires. As a parting gesture they gunned up the cargo ship and left it ablaze.

Getting out of the bay was worse than getting in. The fighter planes were running low on fuel and had to streak back to their carriers. Now the shore batteries were free to fire in full volume. For 20 minutes the PT's zigzagged at high speed across the minefield, big shells dropping within 10 yards of them. At last they were out of range. They had been under almost constant shellfire in broad daylight for 2½ hours.

There were no casualties on either PT. The boat's themselves were unharmed save for superficial damage from shell fragments. Rear Adm. C. A. F. Sprague, commander of the carrier task force, said in a letter to

Lt. Comdr. A. Murray Preston, USNR, receives the Medal of Honor from President Harry S. Truman.

Commander Bowling, "The consummation of this rescue in the face of the tremendous odds is characteristic of the highest traditions of our Navy. The PT Squadron may well be proud of this act which is considered one of the most daring and skillfully executed rescues of the war."

For this action, Lieutenant Preston was awarded the "Congressional" Medal of Honor.   Tatro, Boyd, Seaman, and Day were awarded Navy Crosses.

3. LOSSES

Three PT's were lost at Morotai, all of them during the first 3 months of the campaign. PT 371, on 18/19 September, and PT 368, on 10/11 October, went aground on uncharted reefs close to the Halmahera coast and had to be destroyed. Lt. (jg.) Robert J. Lyon, USNR, boat captain of the 368, believed that his boat could have been towed off had it not been for rifle, machinegun, mortar, and 75mm. fire from the beach, which hit the 368 many times, mortally wounded one man on PT 365, which was standing by to assist, and forced Lyon to transfer the rest of his crew to the accompanying PT and to destroy his boat.

The third loss was that of PT 363, commanded by Lt. Frank Kendall Mitchell, USNR. Lieutenant Mitchell had come to Mios Woendi in June as executive officer of PT Base 21. His enthusiasm for the boats and his determination to get into the fighting gained him a transfer to Squadron 18, where his ability soon led to appointment as a boat captain and section leader. On the morning of November 25 his boat was returning from patrol, leading Lt. (jg.) William K. Paynter's PT 362, when a lookout sighted a barge beached on the Halmahera shore. Although it was after daylight, Mitchell did not hesitate in leading the boats in to strafe the barge.

Halfway through the first run, machineguns opened fire from shore and the 363 stopped dead in the water. Mitchell called Paynter by radio: "Our engines are conked out. We are working on them."

Paynter pushed up his throttles and made two daring runs between the disabled PT and the beach, blazing away at the shore guns to distract their attention from the 363. It would have been useless to lay smoke; there was a strong offshore breeze that would have blown the screen away. The shore guns spoke back, hitting the 362 and setting fire to the pyrotechnic signals in the charthouse. David W. Knowles, S1c, USNR, serving as quartermaster of the 362, coolly helped put out the fire with a hand extinguisher, although his left arm was badly burned.

At the end of the second run, word came from the 363: "Come alongside and throw us a tow. After we get out of here we can fix it in 10 minutes."

Paynter rigged towlines and approached the disabled boat, but it was not ready for him. He was circling again, firing at the shore, when a desperate message came from the 363: "For God's sake come alongside and take us off of here."

As Paynter brought his boat alongside, two 3-inch guns added their fire to the storm of machinegun bullets that were ripping into the boats. Lieutenant Mitchell had been mortally wounded and one man, David L. Friedman, QM3c, USNR, was missing. The 363's second officer, Ens. Edwin W. Polk, USNR, wounded in the right wrist and leg, remained standing in the cockpit, supporting the stricken boat captain and directing the evacuation of his crew.

Knowles, despite his burns and constant enemy fire, boarded the 363 and inspected the boat topside to make sure that none of the crew was left aboard. Francis O. Cooper, TM3c, USNR, pointer of the 40mm. gun on the 362, found that his gun was masked and useless while the boats were together. Although wounded in both feet, he made his way to the 363 and helped carry Mitchell to the 362. Then he returned to his gun. Alfred R. McClure, MoMM3c, USNR, whose bow .50-caliber gun had been the only one on the 362 that was not masked or out of action while his boat was alongside the 363, kept up a steady fire, the only cover during the transfer of the crew. As his boat headed out to sea he could no longer bring his own gun to bear on the shore. He ran aft and took the place of the fallen trainer of the 40mm. gun. Cooper and McClure kept the gun blazing away at the shore until the 362 pulled out of range.

Besides Mitchell, Friedman, Polk, Knowles, and Cooper, the shore fire had wounded one officer and 10 men.

"The batteries which were responsible for the destruction of subject boat were known to exist," Lieutenant Commander Swift, commander of Squadron 18, said in forwarding the action report, "for in the early stages of operations in the Halmahera Island area, shore fire was frequently observed to come from the Galela-Miti Island vicinity. In the 2 weeks previous to subject incident, boats had been in this vicinity without receiving fire of any kind and it was considered that the positions had been wiped out by known aerial strikes. The crafty enemy was evidently waiting just such an opportunity as presented itself on the morning of 25 November, before again revealing his guns. It is considered even possible that the barge on which the run was being made had been previously placed there as a decoy, for no reports had previously been made of enemy craft in that area on the beach."

Both Paynter and Swift felt that this action pointed up the dangers of PT operations during daylight against enemy coastal defenses. But Paynter, possibly thinking of the highly successful rescue in Wasile Bay, also pointed out that effective daytime PT action against fortified beach areas was entirely possible with good air support.

4. CONTAINING AND HARASSING

Establishment of air and PT bases at Morotai did not require clearing the entire island. Thus, until the end of the war, there was a Japanese garrison on Morotai. Because of the great numbers of Japanese on Halmahera and their persistent efforts to reinforce the Morotai garrison, this remained a productive operating point for PT's far longer than any other base in the Southwest Pacific. In their 11 months at Morotai, the PT's made nearly 1,300 patrols and special missions, destroying over 50 barges and 150 other miscellaneous small craft, harassing the Japanese on Halmahera by raids and beach strafing, preventing efforts to supply or evacuate troops, and, most important of all, effectively preventing reinforcement of the Morotai garrison.

The PT detachment of the 116th Seabees built PT Advance Base 4 on the little island of Soemoe Soemoe, inside the fringing reef off the southwest end of Morotai. Development of the base permitted withdrawal of the *Oyster Bay* on October 3, 1944. Squadron 33 departed with the *Oyster Bay.* By February, barge traffic declined to the point where two squadrons could handle it. Squadrons 9 and 10 departed in that month, leaving Squadrons 11 (which had arrived on 17 February) and 18 to handle the Japanese. Since the base was capable of handling two squadrons, *Mobjack* was also withdrawn in February. Squadron 18 was relieved for overhaul in June 1945 by Squadron 25.[26]

Operations from September to May in general followed the familiar pattern of barge hunting established in New Guinea. In addition to their nightly patrols, the PT's made many sweeps of the Halmahera coast. Some of these were with fighters, which protected the PT's from shore batteries; others, where the shore guns were not so much to be feared, were with the little "liaison" planes, L-4's and L-5's, which spotted targets for the PT's and directed their fire. These planes sometimes discovered barges hidden away near the mouths of winding rivers and dropped smoke bombs on them to give the PT's aiming points for targets which they could not see.

---

[26] Senior squadron commanders in operational command of the Morotai PT's were:
  Lt. Comdr. Henry M. S. Swift, USNR, Commander Squadron 18, Sept. 16 to Dec. 6, 1944.
  Lt. Hamilton H. Wood, USNR, Commander Squadron 9, Dec. 6, 1944 to Feb. 10, 1945.
  Lt. Edward Macauley III, USNR, Commander Squadron 18, Feb. 10 to 17, 1945.
  Lt. John W. Ewell, USNR, Commander Squadron 11, Feb. 17 to June 10, 1945.
  Lt. Comdr. Theodore R. Stansbury, USNR, Commander Squadron 25, June 10 to Sept. 11, 1945.

The PT's worked closely with Australian, Dutch, and native scouts, putting them ashore and retrieving them from the Talaud Islands to the north and several of the small islands around Halmahera. Early in April scouts brought word that the Sultan of Ternate, who before the war had governed the entire area under the controlling influence of the Dutch, was being badly treated by the Japanese. On 8/9 April, PT's 364 and 178 carried a rescue team of Australian, Dutch, and native scouts to the island of Hiri just north of Ternate. The team removed the Sultan and his wives and on April 11 the same PT's picked up the entire party and returned to base. This is the only case in history in which PT's were used to transport a harem.

Early in July 1945, the PT's learned of the Nanyo Kaihatsu Kaisha, and set out to wreck it. The "South Seas Development Co." was a civilian trading firm with stores and warehouses scattered through Halmahera and the small islands off the west coast, and was an important link in the Japanese food supply system for all of Halmahera. The company impressed food from the natives of the islands and stored it in warehouses under supervision of native collaborators or a few Japanese. When military outposts needed food the company hired natives to haul it from the warehouses in large out-rigger canoes or in so-called "Sopi" class prahaus, 30 to 40 feet long and capable of carrying a load of over a ton.

On July 5, Lt. Joseph W. Burk, USNR, took a Dutch lieutenant and 37 native scouts aboard Lt. (jg.) J. L. Grubbs's PT 351 and Lt. (jg.) E. F. Shaw's PT 348 for a raid on Makian Island. Near the island they overhauled two supply-laden prahaus. The badly scared native crews told them the supplies were Japanese, so they took the natives aboard and sank the prahaus. The boats tied up at the Makian Island dock and their scouts went to work on two warehouses and the Japanese headquarters building, loading the PT's with bundles of documents and samples of stores before setting the buildings afire. When the headquarters and storehouses were blazing nicely, the boats shot up three empty prahaus on the beach and towed five loaded ones into deep water, where they sank them.

Two days later Joe Burk struck again, taking landing parties of Australian and Dutch scouts on five PT's covered by three RAAF fighter planes, for a barnstorming tour of the western islands.[27] All of the boats carried extra fuel in deck tanks to permit them to carry their strike as far south as Obit

[27] PT 350, Lt. (jg.) R. H. Moeller, USNR; PT 349, Ens. C. W. Bullard, USNR; PT 179, Ens. William A. Klopman, USNR; PT 180, Lt. (jg.) C. C. Hamberger, USNR; PT 182, Lt. (jg.) Steve L. Hudacek, USNR.

Island off the southwestern end of Halmahera, 200 miles from the Morotai base.

At Badjoe, Obit Island, the landing party destroyed a warehouse and a sago mill, and PT 182 ripped six beached prahaus to pieces with its 40mm. A machinegun opened fire from the beach. The 182 and the three planes strafed and silenced it. The group then moved south to the town of Amasing, on Batjan Island, where the planes directed fire of the boats' guns and rockets against a radio station and several warehouses. It was impossible to observe the full results of the attack, but it could be seen that two warehouses were riddled by shells and rockets and that two 20-foot canoes were destroyed. While the other boats were occupied with this action, PT 182 moved a few miles up the coast of Batjan and destroyed 13 more canoes at Belang Belang.

Turning northward, the group divided, with PT's 350, 349, and 182 proceeding to the village of Kotta, on Moti Island, and PT's 179 and 180 going to Toloemaoe, on Tidore Island. At Kotta the scouts seized enemy documents and supplies and burned a warehouse without opposition. At Toloemaoe a party of 10 men went ashore and captured a quantity of documents from Japanese headquarters. As they were returning to the PT's, six Japanese armed with rifles charged them, and two machineguns started firing from the underbrush. The men of the landing party ran for it. As they swarmed aboard PT 180 at the dock, E. D. McKeever, MM2c, USNR, opened fire with the 180's bow 37mm. gun, killing all six Japanese. Other guns of the 180 silenced the machinegun emplacements.

Lt. Redmond J. Reilly, USNR, hit the jackpot on July 10 when he took Lt. (jg.) Kermit W. Montz's PT 355 and Lt. (jg.) William D. Finan's PT 178 on a daylight patrol of the western Halmahera coast and Tidore Island. The boats destroyed nine prahaus on the Halmahera beach and 42 more drawn up on the Tidore shore. There was no enemy return fire and the PT's had plenty of time to blast the prahaus to pieces. Two followup raids in the same area also produced results. On July 14, Lt. Wendell E. Carroll, commander of Squadron 11, led two PT's [28] in destroying 15 prahaus, 2 sailboats, and a whaleboat, and damaging 6 more prahaus, opposed only by light and inaccurate machinegun fire. On the 25th, Lieutenant Montz, in PT 355, led Lt. (jg.) Wayne H. Meagher's PT 134 to destroy 12 prahaus and 3 canoes and to damage a warehouse and 2 pillboxes. Both boats were hit by machinegun bullets, suffering only superficial damage.

---

[28] PT 186, Lt. (jg.) E. R. Freeman, USNR; PT 175, Lt. (jg.) P. R. Washburn, USNR.

The final raid was made on July 30, when Lt. (jg.) T. J. Lovvorn, USNR, in PT 177, with Lt. (jg.) R. C. Fisher's PT 176, shelled and heavily damaged 3 barracks buildings at Taroaoe, on Ternate Island, and then put 14 scouts and 6 PT men ashore at Goeroeapin, on Kajoa Island, to set fire to 5 warehouses bulging with foodstuffs, copra, oil, and clothing.

Scouts and friendly natives brought reports to the PT base that the raids had caused the entire supply system of the Nanyo Kaihatsu Kaisha to be abandoned. As of August 1, 1945, it was reported that only one supply center was still operating and it had been moved so far inland that it was impossible to reach by PT attack.

5. BATTLE OF SURIGAO STRAIT

During the early part of September, Admiral Halsey's Third Fleet swept into the Japanese defense zone like an avenging whirlwind. His carrier planes battered shore installations in the Palaus, Mindanao, and the Visayas, sank many ships, and shot down or destroyed on the ground about 200 enemy planes. Admiral Halsey, impressed by the damage inflicted and by the light opposition encountered, then made an extremely significant recommendation for the future course of the war. On September 13 he stated to Admiral Nimitz, Commander in Chief, Pacific, that the original plan to secure a position in Mindanao prior to seizing Leyte was no longer necessary. Mindanao could be bypassed and the Leyte operation proceed 2 months earlier than planned originally. Immediately, Nimitz, who approved this bold plan, obtained the concurrence of General MacArthur. On September 15 the Joint Chiefs of Staff authorized the cancellation of the Mindanao landings and set October 20 as the target date for the attack on Leyte.

Under the overall command of General MacArthur, the Seventh Fleet, commanded by Adm. Thomas C. Kinkaid, was to land troops of Lt. Gen. Walter Krueger's Sixth Army. For the operation the Seventh Fleet was augumented by many ships normally assigned in the Central Pacific. By agreement with Admiral Nimitz, Admiral Halsey's powerful Third Fleet was to provide naval cover and support for the landings.

The first troops were landed on October 17 on Dinaget and Suluan Islands, commanding the approaches to Leyte Gulf. On the 18th troops were landed on Homonhon Island, at the entrance of the Gulf; minesweepers entered the gulf and underwater demolition teams went to work to investigate landing beaches; bombardment ships entered and began to lay down a withering barrage on the shore. At the same time, planes from the escort carriers of the Seventh Fleet ranged over the central Philippines, blasting enemy airfields and bombing enemy shipping. Ships of the Northern Attack Force, under Rear Adm. Daniel E. Barbey, and the Southern Attack Force, under Vice Adm. Theodore S. Wilkinson, entered Leyte Gulf on the night of October 19/20. By 1000, October 20, troops were pouring ashore on beaches on the west side of Leyte Gulf.

Movement of PT's from Mios Woendi, New Guinea, to Leyte, some 1,200 miles away, presented a difficult problem. "It was considered too far for the boats to make in one hop, even if escorted by tenders," Commander Bowling reported, "because, although possible of accomplishment if continuously good weather were had, by fueling at sea, the boat personnel would be too tired to commence combat operations efficiently after the trip, and so much gasoline would be used from the tenders that too little would remain in the tenders for combat operations of the boats for more than a day or so. The margin of safety was too thin to make this acceptable."

Consideration was also given to transporting PT's by LSD, the war-born combination of ship and floating drydock which could swallow half a dozen PT's in its maw, but the few available LSD's were urgently needed for other purposes. It was finally decided to send the boats with tenders by way of Palau, in the Marianas, which had been taken by Central Pacific Forces at the same time that Southwest Pacific Forces were invading Morotai.

On Friday the 13th of October 1944, Commander Bowling sailed from Mios Woendi in the *Oyster Bay,* with two other PT tenders, *Willoughby* and *Wachapreague,* a seaplane tender (*Half Moon*), two Army craft, and 45 PT's under tactical command of Lt. Comdr. Robert Leeson, USNR.[29] The PT's fueled from the tenders in Kossol Roads, Palau, and the tenders in turn fueled from tankers. En route from Palau to Leyte Gulf, the PT's fueled at sea from the tenders in order to arrive with enough gasoline to start operations immediately. The boats arrived in Leyte Gulf on the morning of October 21 and started patrols that night. This was the largest and longest mass movement of PT's under their own power during the war, and every one of the 45 boats covered the full distance under its own power.

---

[29] The 45 PT's included: Squadron 7 (9 PT's), Lt. Comdr. Robert Leeson, USNR; Squadron 12 (10 PT's), Lt. Weston C. Pullen, Jr., USNR; Squadron 21 (11 PT's), Lt. Carl T. Gleason; Squadron 33 (10 PT's), Lt. A. Murray Preston, USNR; Squadron 36 (5 PT's), Lt. Comdr. Francis D. Tappaan, USNR.

NR&L (MOD)—32510

PT 194 refuels from tender en route from Palau to Leyte Gulf.

During their first 3 nights at Leyte, the PT's claimed to have sunk seven barges and a small freighter, and claimed damage to several other small craft. On the 23d, Squadron 12, with five boats of Squadron 7 and the *Wachapreague,* moved to Liloan, on Panaon Island, off southern Leyte, which the Army had taken so that the PT's could guard Surigao Strait, between Leyte and Mindanao.

This passage, and the waters of the Mindanao Sea to the south, was the scene of one of three great naval engagements, fought almost simultaneously, which collectively have been designated as the Battle for Leyte Gulf. The battle opened in the early morning hours of October 23, when the submarines *Darter* and *Dace* discovered an enemy task force of battleships, cruisers, and destroyers far to the southwest of Leyte. The submarines sank two cruisers.

On the 24th carrier planes found the enemy's southern force heading through the Sulu Sea in the direction of Surigao Strait, and his central force steaming through the Sibuyan Sea toward San Bernardino Strait, to the north of Leyte and Samar. During the day planes from Vice Adm. Marc A. Mitscher's fast carrier task force attacked and inflicted substantial damage on both enemy forces. It was decided that Admiral Halsey would meet the central force, the more powerful of the two, with ships of the Third Fleet, while Admiral Kinkaid would send Rear Adm. Jesse B. Oldendorf, with the Seventh Fleet's 6 old battleships, 8 cruisers, 25 destroyers, and PT's, to meet the force approaching Surigao Strait.

It was apparent that the enemy was undertaking major attack. Admiral Halsey, certain that the enemy must use carriers in such an effort, sent searchplanes far to the north. There, late in the afternoon of the 24th, the planes found a mighty force of carriers, battleships, cruisers, and destroyers. Three great task forces were converging on Leyte Gulf, one from the south, one from the west, and one from the north. Now that his inner defenses had been breached, the enemy, for the first time since Guadalcanal, was ready to risk an all-out naval engagement in an attempt to recapture a beachhead.

*   *   *   *   *

Rear Admiral Oldendorf disposed his battleships, cruisers, and destroyers across the northern end of Surigao Strait. These ships normally had greater firepower than the reported Japanese force, but they had used up most of their ammunition during the invasion bombardment. On the night of October 24/25, every shell had to count.

South of the main force were 39 PT's deployed in sections of three through the strait and along the coasts of Mindanao, Leyte, and Bohol far into the Mindanao Sea. They were a scouting force, to detect the approach of the enemy and to keep our heavy ships at the head of the strait informed of the enemy's advance. Scouting and reporting was their primary mission; their secondary mission was to attack.

In broad outline, the Battle of Surigao Strait is clear enough. Two Japanese task forces steamed through the Mindanao Sea with the objective of forcing Surigao Strait and destroying our transport shipping in Leyte Gulf. In the van was Vice Adm. Shoji Nishimura's task force, comprising the battleships *Yamashiro* and *Fuso,* heavy cruiser *Mogami,* and four destroyers, *Michishio, Asagumo, Yamagumo,* and *Shigure.* Following 20 or 30 miles behind was Vice Adm. Kiyohide Shima's task force, consisting of the heavy cruisers *Nachi* and *Ashigara,* the light cruiser *Abukuma,* and the destroyers *Shiranuhi, Kasumi, Ushio,* and *Akebono.* The almost complete lack of coordination between these two groups greatly facilitated the complete rout of the enemy.

The battle was succinctly outlined by Fleet Adm. Ernest J. King in a report to the Secretary of the Navy: "The enemy was first met by our PT boats, then in succession by three coordinated destroyer torpedo attacks, and finally by devastating gunfire from our cruisers and battleships which had been disposed across the northern end of the strait by the officer in tactical command, Rear Adm. (now Vice Admiral) J. B. Oldendorf. The enemy was utterly defeated. This action is an exemplification of the classical naval tactics of 'crossing the T.' Rear Admiral Oldendorf had deployed his light forces on each flank of the approaching column and had sealed off the enemy's advance through the strait with his cruisers and battleships. By means of this deployment he was able to concentrate his fire, both guns and torpedoes, on the enemy units before they were able to extricate themselves from the trap. The Japanese lost two battleships and three destroyers almost before they could open fire. The heavy cruiser and one destroyer escaped, but the cruiser was sunk on the 26th by our planes."

The destroyer *Shigure* was the only ship of Admiral Nishimura's force that survived the battle.

Admiral Shima's force never really got into action. It was thrown off balance during its approach when a PT torpedo ripped into *Abukuma,* slowing the cruiser down so that it had to drop out of formation. Admiral Shima did reach the head of the strait, but no sooner had his cruisers launched a single ineffectual salvo of torpedoes than his flagship, *Nachi,* collided with the burning *Mogami,* of Admiral Nishimura's force. With his flagship damaged and slowed to 18 knots, and surmising the destruction of Nishimura's fleet, Shima fled, saving all of his ships except for *Abukuma* and destroyer *Shiranuhi,* which were sunk by planes during their retreat.

So much for the broad picture; many details of the individual PT actions, however, were obscure. For instance, it was known beyond a doubt that it was a PT torpedo that hit the *Abukuma.* First, we had no craft except PT's within range of the *Abukuma* at the time she was hit. Second, Comdr. Kokichi Mori, Admiral Shima's staff torpedo officer, said he saw the PT's attack, and gave this account of the damage: "The wireless room which was under the bridge structure was hit and water came in and the crew in this room were all killed, and those above that room were suffocated by gas. She was down at the bow, reduced to about 10 knots, about 30 were killed . . . The remainder of the fleet went on leaving *Abukuma* with no escort. On a course of 010 after the attack, we increased speed to 26 knots and very frequently received torpedo attacks from the vicinity of Panaon Island, but no damage was done."

So many PT's were attacking enemy ships that at the time it was impossible to determine which one made the hit. It now has been established, however, that Lt. (jg.) Isadore M. Kovar, USNR, in PT 137 was responsible.

The boat captains were working under difficulties, and it is small wonder that some confusion crept into their action reports. In forwarding the reports, Commander Bowling said: "The weather was fairly clear until about midnight when it became dark, with frequent rain. Because of the darkness, rain squalls, short radar range, low height of eye, small crews with no facilities for accurate observations and records, and the confusion caused by enemy gun fire, the estimate of numbers and types of enemy ships is not considered too accurate. It is also believed that some of the stated times of sighting may be in error by as much as 15 to 30 minutes."

Here are some accounts of what the boat crews saw and did:

*   *   *   *   *

The two southernmost sections, nearest the enemy's line of approach, were stationed where Camiguin Island narrows the Mindanao Sea between Mindanao and Bohol. Lt. Weston C. Pullen, Jr., USNR, led the boats on the Bohol side: Lt. (jg.) Joseph A. Eddins's PT 152, Lt. (jg.) Ian D. Malcolm's PT 130, and Ens. Peter R. Gadd's PT 131. At 2215, when the boats were about 18 miles off the Bohol coast, PT 131's radar picked up two targets between them and Bohol. As the PT's approached, the two pips divided into five. A light haze lifted, revealing what appeared to be a destroyer, two cruisers, and two battleships. The PT's were still 3 miles away, too far for an effective torpedo shot, when the enemy's big guns opened fire.

The first salvo straddled the boats. The PT's retired behind smoke, pursued by the destroyer and cruisers, while the battleships sat back firing at them and illuminating them with starshell. An 8-inch shell struck a glancing blow on the forward port torpedo of the 130, shattering the warhead, ripping up deck planking, and passing through the bow above the water-line. Neither the shell nor the torpedo exploded; no one was injured. The 152 was not so fortunate. A 4.7-inch shell tore away the 37mm. gun from the bow, fatally wounded the gunner, stunned the loader, and set fire to the boat. The destroyer bore down on the 152, spotting it in a searchlight beam. "Enemy destroyer sheared off when PT 152 dropped two depth charges set

80–G–345822

Forward deck of PT 152, showing effect of enemy 4.7-inch shell in the Battle of Surigao Strait.

at 100 feet," Eddins reported, "and return 40mm. PT fire made enemy reluctant to continue use of searchlight."

The chase lasted for 23 minutes.   Just before it broke off, the last two ships of Admiral Nishimura's fleet appeared on the radar.   The PT's had been unable to reach friendly forces by radio before the action; after it their radios were out of commission, damaged by the concussion of bursting shells.   Lieutenant Malcolm, finding that the 152 had become separated from the group, took the 130 and 131 southward until he found Lt. (jg.) John A. Cady's section of PT's near Camiguin Island.   He boarded Ens. Dudley J. Johnson's PT 127, and at 0010 the 127 made the first radio report of the position, course, and speed of the enemy ships.

Aboard the 152, the crew put out the fire and surveyed the damage.   The bow was stove in, but the boat could still make 24 knots.   Pullen tried for an hour to close the enemy for a torpedo attack, but the ships were making at least 22 knots and he could not overtake them.

* * * * *

Lt. (jg.) Dwight H. Owen, USNR, aboard PT 151, was in charge of a section stationed to the northeast, south of Limasawa Island: Ens. John M. Ladd's PT 151, Ens. Buford M. Grosscup's PT 146, and Ens. Edward S. Haugen's PT 190. "At approximately 2330," Owen said, "the prologue began. Off to the southwest over the horizon we saw distant flashes of gunfire, starshells bursting and far-off sweep of searchlights . . . The display continued about 15 minutes, then blacked out. Squalls came and went. One moment the moon shone bright as day and the next you couldn't make out the bow of your boat. Then the radar developed the sort of pips you read about."

At range of 2 miles, Owen identified the targets as a battleship, a cruiser, and three destroyers. Because of interference and enemy jamming of circuits, it was 3 hours before PT 190 succeeded in reporting the sighting. In the meantime the boats deployed for attack. When they came within 1,800 yards a searchlight swept the water on their right hand. PT 146 got off one torpedo, which ran erratically. PT 151 launched one which ran straight, but there was no time to watch it run its course. It was no sooner away than a destroyer caught the 151 and 190 square in its searchlight. The 146 and 190 scored many 40mm. hits on the destroyer superstructure and the light went out. Immediately the battleship turned a light on the 151 and took it under heavy fire. The 151 ran behind smoke on a zigzag course, unharmed except for minor damage from shell fragments. During the encounter another group of ships, about 6 miles to the southwest, fired 15 or 20 rounds at the PT's without effect.

* * * * *

The southern entrance to Surigao Strait was guarded on the west by Lt. Comdr. Robert Leeson's section: Lt. (jg.) Edmund F. Wakelin's PT 134, Ens. Paul H. Jones's PT 132, and Lt. (jg.) Isadore M. Kovar's PT 137. Leeson saw the gun flashes of the Japanese ships firing on Owen's boats, and reported this by radio. Thereafter both the 134 and 132 were able to report promptly all of their sightings. The 137's auxiliary generator had failed, leaving it without radio transmitter or radar.

Half an hour after seeing the flashes, Leeson picked up radar targets 10 miles away. While tracking the targets the three PT's became separated, and thereafter operated independently. Leeson, in PT 134, had approached within 3,000 yards of what he believed to be two battleships and three destroyers, when the PT was caught in a searchlight beam. Shells fell all about the boat, bursting in the water on both sides and in the air overhead. The 134, firing its 40mm., 37mm., and 20mm., bored in for another 500 yards and launched three torpedoes. Between 3 and 4 minutes later the 134 was jolted by three underwater explosions. No explosion was visible, however, and the enemy ships appeared to continue on course. The 134 shook off the enemy fire and lay to close to the coast of Panaon Island. Soon four destroyers filed past, 1,000 yards away. Leeson launched his last remaining torpedo at the lead destroyer and watched it miss astern. During the next hour the men on the 134 saw other large ships, possibly Admiral Shima's force, pass through the strait, but they had no more torpedoes and could not attack.

PT 132 found a destroyer lying to a mile off the southern tip of Panaon Island and closed to 1,200 yards. As Ensign Jones maneuvered his boat into firing position, the destroyer turned toward him, but did not open fire. Jones launched four torpedoes. One was erratic and the other three narrowly missed. He withdrew, then circled to return for a rocket attack, but could not find the destroyer again.

Two destroyers almost slipped past the radarless 137 before Lieutenant Kovar spotted them. As it was, he was able to get away only one overtaking shot which missed astern. Two hours and 20 minutes later, at 0335, he saw an enemy destroyer coming back down the strait. He closed within 900 yards and fired one torpedo which, he said, "was observed to pass under the beam of the destroyer." A heavy underwater concussion jarred the PT, but there was no visible explosion. The destroyer illuminated the PT with starshell and fired several salvos at it before entering a cloud of heavy smoke which hung over the strait. Mike Kovar's torpedo, while missing the destroyer, was no dud. It plowed on through the sea and ripped into light cruiser *Abukuma*. The explosion killed about 30 men and slowed the cruiser to 10 knots. *Abukuma* fell out of formation and put into port. She was sunk off Mindanao on October 26 by Air Force bombers.

*   *   *   *   *

Guarding the eastern entrance to Surigao Strait, about 10 miles from Leeson's section, were Lt. Robert W. Orrell's PT 523, Lt. (jg.) James P. Wolf's PT 524, and Lt. Donald Hamilton, Jr.'s PT 526, led by Lt. Comdr. Francis D. Tappaan, USNR. About the time Leeson was moving in with the 134 for his torpedo attack, Tappaan's boats picked up radar targets 8 miles away. When the PT's had closed to a mile and an eighth, the enemy fired starshell to the west, no doubt to illuminate the 134 and, in so doing, silhouetted his ships to Tappaan's group on the east.

With this illumination, there was surprising lack of agreement among the PT officers as to the composition of the enemy force. Tappaan identified the ships as "two battleships and three small war vessels of the size of destroyers or larger." Orrell identified them as two cruisers and two destroyers; Wolf as one battleship, two cruisers, and two destroyers; Hamilton as one battleship, one cruiser, and one destroyer.

With the enemy already occupied on his portside, each of Tappaan's PT's was able to get two torpedoes away before being taken under fire. As the boats retired, enemy shells began to walk up the wake of PT 526. The 526 laid two short puffs of smoke, which absorbed most of the enemy fire but prevented the boats from observing the effect of their torpedoes. During their retirement all three boats saw five more pips on their radar screens, following 3 miles astern of the first group of enemy ships.

*   *   *   *   *

Lt. (jg.) John M. McElfresh, USNR, in PT 490, was stationed in the middle of Surigao Strait with Lt. (jg.) Harley A. Thronson's PT 491 and Lt. (jg.) Richard W. Brown's PT 493, about 10 miles north of the sections led by Leeson and Tappaan. Picking up four radar targets rounding the end of Panaon Island, 8 miles to the south, the boats deployed to intercept them. A rain squall so reduced visibility that the boats closed within 700 yards of the enemy before they could see the ships, which they identified as a cruiser and three destroyers.

The 490 launched two torpedoes at the leading destroyer. Immediately a ship in another group a mile and a half to 2 miles to the south turned on a searchlight. A moment later the leading destroyer caught the PT in its searchlight and enemy guns fired heavily on the PT's. The 490 launched two more torpedoes at the leading ship, then only 400 yards away, and opened fire on the searchlight with all guns.

The 491, a little further off, launched two torpedoes at the second ship after the enemy opened fire. The 493, still further away, tried to launch a torpedo, but it hung in the rack, and then the enemy fire was so intense that the boat was forced to retire. The 490 shot out the destroyer searchlight, only to be spotted by another. Just before the 490 ran behind a smokescreen laid by the 493, Lieutenant Brown saw a large flash on the destroyer's side, heard a loud explosion, and the second searchlight went out. He believed that one of his torpedoes had hit.

The enemy's fire was accurate. The 490's searchlight was shot off and the boat was holed above the waterline. On the first broadside, Arthur G. Peterson, TM3c, was knocked down and wounded by shell fragments. He picked himself up and turned on the smokescreen generator before reporting his injuries.

A 4.7-inch shell passed through the 493 from side to side, above the waterline. Almost immediately another shell tore clean through the engineroom, carrying away the auxiliary generator, ripping a hole below the waterline, and causing some damage to the engines. Albert W. Brunelle, MoMM2c, USNR, whipped off his own lifejacket, stuffed it into the hole in the side, and went to work to keep his damaged engines running. A third shell carried away the charthouse canopy, killing two men and wounding the boat captain, second officer, and three men. Everyone in the cockpit was blown aft by the blast. Ens. Robert E. Carter, USNR, the second officer, although wounded, quickly returned to the cockpit and regained control of the boat, heading for the Panaon shore. Brunelle kept the engines running until Carter beached the boat. By that time water had seeped in past Brunelle's lifejacket until the engines were almost submerged. The dead and wounded were taken ashore.

The 491, undamaged, continued on patrol until 0530, when it sighted an enemy cruiser, probably the damaged *Mogami,* steaming slowly southwards. There appeared to be a small fire on the cruiser, aft of the stacks. The cruiser opened up on the 491, bracketing it with 8-inch shells. The PT fired two torpedoes and withdrew behind smoke, following the Panaon coast to the north. Soon the 491 came upon the beached 493 and picked up the survivors. The tide lifted the 493 off the beach, and it sank in deep water soon after daylight.

McElfresh, in the 490, lay to off the Panaon coast, and some 2 hours after his own action had a radar sighting of four ships passing northward through the strait. He saw nothing more until morning, when four enemy dive bombers attacked his boat. The first two dropped bombs, missing the PT by 200 yards. The 490's gunfire made the other two planes turn away.

* * * * *

Commander Bowling reported that there was "a fair agreement between Lieutenant McElfresh aboard the PT 490, Lieutenant Commander Leeson aboard the PT 134, and Lieutenant Commander Tappaan aboard the PT 523, that at the time Lieutenant McElfresh was attacking what he believed to be one cruiser and three destroyers, he saw Lieutenant Commander Leeson, under enemy illumination and well to the south, attacking from the west, and being fired upon by what Lieutenant Commander Leeson believed to be two battleships and three destroyers. At the same time, Lieutenant Commander Tappaan attacked the same two battleships and three destroyers from the east—these ships having silhouetted themselves to Lieutenant Commander Tappaan's group by illuminating Lieutenant Commander Leeson to the west."

*   *   *   *   *

Eight miles north of McElfresh's section were three boats led by Lt. Carl T. Gleason: Lt. (jg.) Kenneth B. Sharpe's PT 327, Ens. Louis E. Thomas's PT 321, and Lt. (jg.) H. L. Terry's PT 326. This section sighted the advancing enemy about 0300 by radar, and made a prompt report to the Commander Destroyer Squadron 54, who advised the boats that he would attack and ordered them to stand clear. The PT's lay to and watched three destroyers, a battleship, and another large warship file past. By 0400, four burning enemy ships were visible. Half an hour later the PT's found a burning destroyer accompanied by an apparently undamaged destroyer. They moved in to attack the undamaged ship, but were taken under such heavy and accurate fire, which wounded a torpedoman on the 321, that they were forced to launch their torpedoes at ranges of 3,000 to 4,000 yards and to retire without waiting to watch the results.

*   *   *   *   *

The northernmost sections of PT's were the 320, 330, and 331, led by Lt. G. W. Hogan, USNR, and the 328, 323, and 329, led by Lt. H. G. Young, USNR, stationed south and east of Amagusan Point on Leyte. During the night, our destroyers were ranging down into the strait and told these sections to stand clear. At 0630, Lt. (jg.) Herbert Stadler's PT 323, which had become separated from the other boats, sighted destroyer *Asagumo* standing by a large burning ship, the Japanese battlewagon *Fuso,* a few miles to the south. *Asagumo* was already badly damaged and dead in the water.

The destroyer took the 323 under fire at 3,000 yards, but Stadler moved in another 1,500 yards and made three torpedo runs, firing one torpedo on each run. The third torpedo hit *Asagumo* in the stern. As Stadler retired, a group of our cruisers and destroyers moved down the strait to finish off the enemy ship. At 0722 *Asagumo* sank.

Hogan's section, joined by PT's 328 and 489, was returning to Leyte Gulf after daylight when five enemy dive bombers made a strafing and bombing run on the boats. Two bombs dropped 10 yards astern of PT 330, but both were duds, and the planes did no damage.

* * * * *

A few miles to the west of Leeson's section off the southern tip of Panaon Island were three boats led by Lt. Roman G. Mislicky: Lt. Thomas C. Hall's PT 194, Ens. James R. Beck's PT 196, and Lt. William J. West, Jr.'s PT 150. During most of the night these boats were hemmed in by clouds and squalls, so it was not until 0500 that they made their first sighting, a large fire in Surigao Strait.

The boats moved out into the strait and soon saw two vessels which they thought might be PT's. As they closed the range to 1,200 yards, they recognized them as enemy destroyers, and at the same time the destroyers laid down a terrific barrage of fire. The 194's 40mm. gun was carried away by the first salvo, and the boat retired behind smoke. Only the 150 was able to get a torpedo away. A 4.7-inch shell ripped through the stern of the 194 below the waterline and the boat began to settle and lose speed. A 40mm. shell exploded in the cockpit and charthouse, setting off a box of 20mm. ammunition. Two men were seriously injured, Lieutenant Mislicky was knocked unconscious, and Lieutenant Hall, his second officer, and four men were wounded by fragments. The exploding 20mm. ammunition cut the emergency CO_2 release and carbon dioxide blanketed the engineroom, smothering the engines. Earl R. Welker, MoMM1c, USNR, and John O. Bozman, MoMM1c, USNR, quickly aired out the engineroom, got their engines running, and then went to work like beavers to keep the engineroom from flooding. The 194 was under fire for half an hour.

Lieutenant West, in the 150, cruised along the Panaon shore trying to find the damaged 194. During his search he was taken under fire by a burning cruiser and four destroyers proceeding southward through the strait.

PT 190, from Lieutenant Owen's section on the west, and PT 137, from Lieutenant Commander Leeson's section on the east, heard the 194's report of damage and also tried to find her. The 190 apparently encountered the same force that had fired on the 150, with an added cruiser. Two of the destroyers chased the 190 for a few minutes, bracketing the boat with

8 or 10 salvos. The 137 sighted only a destroyer and a burning cruiser, both of which fired a few inaccurate rounds at the PT.

*   *   *   *   *

Of the 39 PT's that participated in the battle, 30 were under enemy fire and 10 were hit. One boat, the 493, was lost after three hits by 4.7-inch shells. Three men were killed, 3 officers and 17 men were wounded. Fifteen boats fired 35 torpedoes. Fourteen are known to have missed, 1 ran erratically, 1 had a hot run on deck, 11 were unobserved, and 7 were claimed as possible hits.

This much is certain: Admiral Nishimura's ships were flushed by PT's as soon as they passed between the islands of Bohol and Camiguin in the northern Mindanao Sea. For the rest of their passage to and through Surigao Strait their positions were reported by PT's with such accuracy that our heavy forces were able to estimate within 3 minutes the time of their initial salvos. In addition, the enemy ships time and again were forced to reveal

80–G–285970

PT 321 picks up a Japanese survivor of the Battle of Surigao Strait. Note second man still in water.

themselves by firing at PT's. And it is certain that PT torpedoes ripped into *Abukuma* and *Asagumo,* putting them out of action.

Admiral Nimitz, reporting on the battle, said, "The skill, determination and courage displayed by the personnel of these small boats is worthy of the highest praise. Their contact reports, as well as the firing and illumination which they drew from the enemy, gave ample warning to our own main body; and while the issue of the later main engagement was never in doubt, the PT's action very probably threw the Japanese command off balance and contributed to the completeness of their subsequent defeat."

*   *   *   *   *

In the Battle of Surigao Strait and subsequent air attacks, the enemy lost two battleships, two cruisers, and four destroyers. To the north, Rear Adm. C. A. F. Sprague's escort carriers, destroyers, and destroyer escorts gallantly and almost unbelievably held off a far more powerful Japanese battleship and cruiser task force off Samar, while Admiral Halsey cut down an enemy carrier and battleship task force off Cape Engaño. In these actions and ensuing air attacks, the Japanese lost four carriers, a battleship, six cruisers, and four destroyers, and suffered damage to three carriers, five cruisers, and seven destroyers.

"Our invasion of the Philippines was not even slowed down," Admiral Nimitz reported, "and the losses sustained by the Japanese reduced their fleet from what had been at least a potential menace to the mere nuisance level."

6. AIR ATTACKS

In the days following the first landings in the Philippines, the Japanese launched air attacks of unprecedented fury against our shipping in Leyte Gulf. Because of losses in the air and damage to their fields, they could no longer mount large-scale raids. Nevertheless, they attacked persistently with small numbers of planes, not only bombing but employing the suicide dive for the first time as part of a definite program of attack.

While they attacked all types of ships, PT's and PT tenders seemed to be particularly desirable targets. Lt. Comdr. H. A. Stewart, USNR, commanding officer of the *Wachapreague,* which was under air attack for 2 hours on the morning of October 26, stated with classic simplicity, "Apparently the enemy were somewhat hostile to anything connected with PT operations."

80-G-47007

Two PT's stand by during a bombing attack on shipping in Leyte Gulf. The Liberty ship in left background was hit in this attack.

80-G-258299

An LCI, hit by an enemy suicide plane in Leyte Gulf, burns as PT's move in to pick up survivors.

80-G-325823

An enemy suicide plane, shot down by PT tender Oyster Bay, crashes in the water close aboard an LST. The tenders Oyster Bay and Hilo are at left, Orestes center. This was the third plane shot down by Oyster Bay on the morning of November 24, 1944.

Willoughby, in Leyte Gulf, shot down one plane on October 24 and another on the 25th. The attacks on *Wachapreague* started the morning after the Battle of Surigao Strait, while the tender was anchored at Liloan, and continued during the morning as the tender proceeded to Leyte Gulf with a group of PT's. *Wachapreague* was credited with one plane shot down, two probables, and one damaged. The tender was undamaged, but a fragmentation bomb killed one man and wounded four aboard one of the accompanying PT's, the 134.

On the night of October 26/27, Ens. Paul H. Jones, USNR, led PT's 132 and 326 in a patrol that resulted in destruction of two barges loaded with fuel and ammunition. As the boats were returning in the morning, a Japanese Zero dropped a fragmentation bomb 10 yards off the 132. Two men were killed; Ensign Jones, his second officer, and eight men were wounded. On the following evening Lieutenant Commander Tappaan was taking PT's 525 and 523 to patrol station on the north of Leyte in a heavy rain. The

NR&L (MOD)—32517

Wreckage of PT 320, victim of a direct bomb hit in Leyte Gulf, November 5, 1944.

rain cleared for 5 minutes, just long enough for four planes to sneak in to bomb and strafe the boats. Eight men aboard the 523 were killed; three officers, six men and an Australian war correspondent were wounded.

Whenever possible, PT's going to and returning from patrol stations by daylight had aircraft cover. They could not be covered constantly, however, and the attacks continued. The attacks were not entirely one-sided. PT's 195, 522, and 324 each shot down a plane. *Oyster Bay* shot one down on November 24 and, assisted by the fire of several PT's and other tenders, shot down three more on November 26. Each of these three tried to crashdive *Oyster Bay,* the last one falling so close aboard that flying fragments caused minor damage to the ship and wounded 11 men.

Early on the morning of November 5 a high-flying plane dropped a bomb squarely on the deck of PT 320, anchored in Leyte Gulf. The boat was completely destroyed, with loss of 2 officers and 12 men. Only one man of the crew was saved.

On the night of November 19/20, Lt. Frank H. Olton, USNR, led PT's 495, 491, and 489 on a successful sweep of Ormoc Bay and the Camotes Islands. The boats sank one barge, blew up another, left two ablaze and sinking, and damaged a fifth. Later the boats found two luggers and a barge. They sank the barge and one lugger, and were scoring many hits on the second lugger when a plane dropped a fragmentation bomb alongside PT 495. One man was killed and 17 were wounded.

Late in the afternoon of December 5, a "Zeke"-type fighter plane tried to make a suicide dive on Lt. Joseph H. Moran II's PT 494, after the 494 and Lt. William H. Von Bergen, Jr.'s PT 531 opened fire on it. "At the start of this dive," Moran reported, "the plane was still under control and followed every move of PT 494. Both boats then resumed fire, very accurately. A piece was torn out of the Zeke's wing and it was seen that the Zeke was plunging straight down. PT 494 turned to the left and the Zeke crashed about 25 yards off the PT 494's starboard beam. A few parts from the plane were thrown over the bow of PT 494."

On the afternoon of December 10, PT's 323 and 327 were underway for patrol station, with PT's 528 and 532 following 200 yards astern, when four planes attacked them. One crashed the 323 amidships, damaging the boat beyond repair. Lt. (jg.) Herbert Stadler, USNR, the boat captain, was killed; Ens. William I. Adelman, USNR, the second officer, was missing; 11 men were wounded, including two Army officers who were passengers on the 323. Another plane dived at Lt. (jg.) Benjamin M. Stephens's PT 532.

PT 323, cut almost in half by a Kamikaze plane on December 10, 1944.

"As the plane closed to approximately 500 yards," Stephens reported, "we turned hard left and the plane hit the water directly in our wake, distance 25 yards. The plane exploded on contact with the sea."

U.S. forces landed on the island of Mindoro on December 15. Practically all of the available Japanese air strength was shifted to counter the new landings; enemy air attacks around Leyte dwindled into relative insignificance.

7. LEYTE AND CEBU

During October, U.S. Army troops pushed inland on Leyte against increasing resistance. The enemy's stronghold was at Ormoc Bay, on the west side of the island, and there he brought in reinforcements and supplies from Cebu and the other islands to the west by a variety of craft, ranging from barges and luggers to transports and destroyers. Until the end of December, PT's from Leyte Gulf hunted this shipping every night and for the first time in the Southwest Pacific had frequent contact with destroyers.

On the night of November 9/10, Lt. Alexander W. Wells, USNR, patrolled with PT's 524 and 525 on the east side of Ponson Island near the southern entrance to Ormoc Bay, while Lt. A. Murray Preston, USNR, covered the

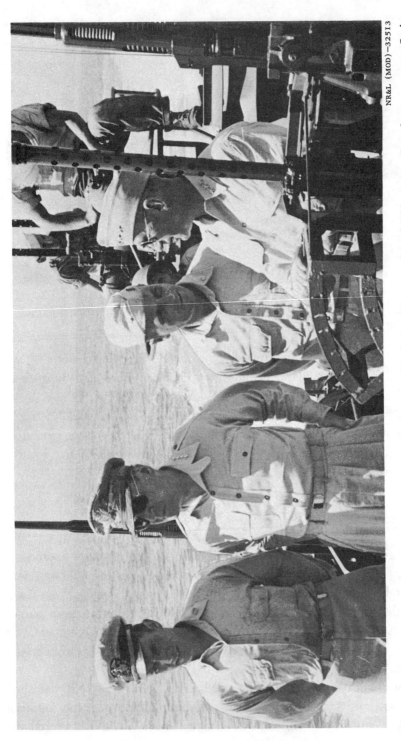

NR&L (MOD)–32513

General Douglas MacArthur returns to the Philippines at Tacloban, Leyte, aboard PT 525 on October 24, 1944. Left to right, Lt. Alexander W. Wells, USNR, boat captain of PT 525; General MacArthur; Comdr. Selman S. Bowling, Commander MTB Squadrons Seventh Fleet; Lt. Gen. Walter Krueger, Commanding General Sixth Army.

west side of the island with PT's 497 and 492. Just after midnight the 525 fired two torpedoes at a transport entering the bay, but apparently these missed. At the same time the 524 fired two torpedoes at a destroyer, missing astern. The 525 retired under fire from a destroyer and a ship that the boat captain, Ens. Gervis S. Brady, USNR, believed to be a light cruiser. The 524 was pursued by a destroyer for 45 minutes.

An hour after this attack, Preston's boats saw three destroyers round the northern end of Ponson Island. Each boat launched four torpedoes. Great silver blasts leaped up from the last destroyer in column, followed by an orange blaze and clouds of black smoke. As the other two destroyers opened fire and started to chase the boats, the third disappeared from the PT radar screens. Looking back through binoculars, Preston could see only two destroyers where three had been before. The destroyers pursued the boats down the coast of Ponson Island, giving up the chase when the PT's slipped through narrow Kawit Strait between Ponson and Poro Islands.

Preston's attack illustrates the extreme difficulty of accurate assessment of damage. There is no confirmation from Japanese sources of loss or damage in this action. Yet, Preston says, the explosion "was like the Fourth of July— it looked just like an Elco advertisement." Before the explosion he saw three destroyers on his radar screen and through his binoculars; afterwards, only two.

On the following night several boats sighted destroyers near Ormoc Bay. Some of the boats fired torpedoes, but all were certain misses. PT 321 (Ens. Louis E. Thomas, USNR) and PT 324 (Ens. Harrell F. Dumas, USNR) were maneuvering to get a shot at two destroyers near Gigantangan Island, off northwest Leyte, when the destroyers bracketed the boats with a well-placed salvo. The PT's ran southward, with the destroyers in pursuit. Off the entrance to San Isidro Bay on the Leyte coast, they saw two more destroyers. The boats ducked into the bay and the 321 ran aground near the entrance. Two of the destroyers approached the mouth of the bay. Then the tide washed the 324 aground 100 yards from the 321. A destroyer swept the beach with its searchlight without picking up the boats. The crews set demolition charges on their boats and went ashore. The 321 exploded, but the demolition charges on the 324 failed to detonate.

At daylight friendly Filipinos found the boat crews. About 100 of them helped free the 324, and pilots guided the PT to a little cove at the south of the bay. Its propellers damaged, the boat could still move slowly on two engines. During this passage destroyers again fired on the boat. Assisted by the Filipinos, the crew camouflaged the boat with branches, and a runner set out to inform the nearest Army outpost of their plight. On the evening of the following day an Army officer, Lt. Robert Schermerhorn, arrived at San Isidro and told the boat captains he would send a report to Sixth Army headquarters. The next morning a runner brought word that their squadron commander, Lt. Carl T. Gleason, was in Arevalo Bay, a few miles to the south. Lieutenant Schermerhorn took Thomas and Dumas to Arevalo Bay in a captured Japanese launch. They found Gleason, who told them to be ready to leave San Isidro Bay at 1900.

The 324, with both crews aboard, was nosing out of San Isidro Bay at 1900 when a Filipino came alongside in a canoe. He brought a message from Lieutenant Gleason: "Nip destroyers around, get back in bay."

Two and a half hours later Gleason arrived at the entrance of the bay with PT's 325, 326, 327, 330, and 190. He blinked word to the 324 to get underway, and the boats returned to Leyte Gulf without interference at 0930, November 14.

On the night of November 28/29, Lt. Roger H. Hallowell, who 2 days earlier had relieved Lieutenant Commander Leeson as commander of Squadron 7, took Ens. Dudley J. Johnson's PT 127 and Lt. (jg.) William P. West's PT 331 to Ormoc Bay. The 127 fired four torpedoes and the 331 fired two at a warship, and the 331 fired two torpedoes at what appeared to be a transport. As the boats retired under heavy fire, explosions were observed on both targets. Hallowell intercepted Lt. (jg.) Gregory J. Azarigian's PT 128 and Lt. (jg.) Nelson Davis's PT 191, patrolling the Camotes Islands. He boarded the 128 and returned to Ormoc Bay, where the PT's, under heavy fire, launched seven torpedoes at three ships at anchor. As the boats retired they saw a large explosion on one of the targets.

After the fall of Ormoc, Hallowell dived for the warship hit by the 127 and found a ship some 200 feet long, similar to a minesweeper, with a large torpedo hole amidships. Captain Bowling assessed the damage as one escort vessel similar to a minesweeper probably sunk by a PT torpedo, one medium transport probably hit and damaged. Information from Japanese sources indicates that Submarine Chaser No. 53 and Patrol Boat No. 105 were sunk by PT's at Ormoc Bay on November 28/29.

The final destroyer action in the Leyte area came on the night of December 11/12, when Lt. Melvin W. Haines, USNR, in PT 492, led Lt. John M. McElfresh's PT 490 in a perfect attack on a single destroyer lying to near Palomplon, on the west coast of Leyte. Sighting his target by radar at a

80-G-472485

A Japanese lugger in flames off the coast of Cebu. This was one of five luggers destroyed by PT's 491 and 494 on December 31, 1944.

range of 4 miles, Haines skillfully worked the PT's between the destroyer and the beach, so as to silhouette the destroyer against the horizon and make the PT's difficult to detect against the shore. He let the boats idle in until they were 1,000 yards from the target; then the 490 launched four torpedoes and the 492 launched two.

One exploded with a great flash directly beneath the bridge. Immediately afterwards a second torpedo exploded amidships, sending oil, water, and debris hundreds of feet in the air. The destroyer sank immediately, and 3 minutes later the boats were jarred by three underwater explosions. At no time had the destroyer given any indication that it was aware of the presence of the PT's. This sinking has been confirmed as that of the destroyer *Uzuki,* a ship 330 feet long, of 1,315 tons standard displacement.

All this time the PT's had been running up an impressive score against small freighters, barges, luggers, and other small craft in the Camotes Sea. On New Year's Eve, for example, Lt. Joseph H. Moran II, USNR, in PT 494, with PT 491, found five luggers anchored at Daanbantayan, on the west coast of Cebu. The boats claimed destruction of all the luggers, as well as a small motor launch. The light of explosions from the luggers and flares from the PT's illuminated a number of small craft on the beach, which the PT's strafed heavily without observed results.

By the end of December the Eighth Army had taken Ormoc and practically overrun Leyte, compressing the remaining enemy troops into a few isolated pockets in the central mountain range. The enemy's attempt to reinforce Leyte had failed. Squadrons 7 and 12 started operating from a small advance base at Ormoc on December 28. On February 21 they were relieved by Squadron 25.[30] The Ormoc boats had good hunting, destroying barges and luggers and harassing the enemy ashore, until the end of March, when units of the Eighth Army entered Cebu City.

The boats ranged through the Camotes Sea, preventing evacuation from Leyte and disrupting enemy supply along the coasts of Cebu, Negros, Bohol, Mindanao, and the lesser islands contiguous to them. Close liaison with guerrilla leaders on Cebu and with Marine Air Group 12, whose Corsairs flew over the area daily, helped the PT's to find and destroy many camouflaged and hidden Japanese small craft. The most productive area was

[30] Officers in operation command of Ormoc PT's were:
 Lt. Weston C. Pullen, Jr., USNR, Commander Squadron 12, Dec. 28, 1944 to Mar. 7, 1945.
 Lt. Comdr. Theodore R. Stansbury, USNR, Commander Squadron 25, Mar. 7 to May 4, 1945.
 Lt. John J. McGlynn, USNR, Commander Squadron 12, May 4 to July 25, 1945.

around the well-defended harbor of Cebu City, principal enemy supply base for the neighboring islands.

Many of these actions were carried out with great daring. For example: On the evening of March 24, 1945, Lt. Joseph W. Burk, USNR, entered the harbor of Cebu City with Lt. (jg.) Leo A. Anderson's PT 348 and Lt. Edward J. Pope, Jr.'s PT 134. The boats drew within half a mile of the southern wharf. There were two freight cars on the wharf and two barges tied up alongside. As the boats tried to approach closer, several machineguns opened fire on them from shore, joined almost immediately by a 37mm. and a 75mm. gun. The PT's turned, firing deliberately at the freight cars and barges with their 40mm. guns, while their other guns returned the enemy fire. They destroyed the barges and set the freight cars ablaze before they speeded up to clear the harbor. After Cebu City had been taken, the gutted freight cars were found on the wharf, with the shattered barges lying on the bottom alongside.

80–G–424230

PT's returning to base after supporting landings of Army troops at Palomplon, Leyte, Christmas Day, 1944.

In addition to attacks on shipping and shore installations, the PT's supported several minor landings by Army and guerrilla forces. The most unusual of these missions was on the night of May 13/14, when PT's 190 and 192 spearheaded the guerrilla invasion of Guintacan Island, in the Visayan Sea, by towing eight 60-foot fishing boats, loaded with a total of 200 guerrillas, from Bantayan Island to Langob on Guintacan Island.

Lt. Gen. Robert L. Eichelberger, Commanding General Eighth Army, reported at the end of the campaign: "The cooperation of Motor Torpedo Boats throughout all operations on the western half of Leyte provided invaluable support to elements of the XXIV Corps. PT squadrons located at Ormoc conducted continuous nightly sorties, sinking over 200 Japanese barges and over 200 other miscellaneous craft loaded with reinforcements, equipment and supplies. The eagerness of the crews to close with the enemy and furnish aid to our ground forces was outstanding throughout." [31]

8. FIRST DAYS AT MINDORO

Wachapreague and *Willoughby* sailed from Leyte Gulf for Mios Woendi on November 13, returning 2 weeks later with *Pontus;* Squadrons 13, 16, and 28; six boats of Squadron 36, and PT's 227 and 230 of Squadron 17. The PT's of Squadrons 13, 16, and 36 had had some action in the New Guinea campaign; Squadron 28 was newly arrived from the Solomons, and PT's 227 and 230 were the first boats to be transferred to the Southwest Pacific from the Hawaiian Sea Frontier. Squadron 17 had been based at Majuro Atoll in the Marshall Islands from February to April 1944, and since then had been at Pearl Harbor, but had not yet been in action.

Squadrons 13 and 16, with PT's 227 and 230, under operational command of Lt. Comdr. N. Burt Davis, Jr., got underway from Leyte Gulf on the afternoon of December 12 in the convoy carrying the Eighth Army's Western Visayan Task Force to the invasion of Mindoro, 300 miles to the northwest. Because of the likelihood of heavy enemy air attacks, the PT's had no tender; instead, an advance base unit was loaded in LST 605 with the PT Detachment of the 113th Naval Construction Battalion.

---

[31] General Eichelberger gave the PT's more credit than they claimed. Task Group 70.1's estimate of damage inflicted by PT's operating from Leyte Gulf and Ormoc was: 140 barges, 63 other surface craft, and 6 planes destroyed; 18 barges, 16 other surface craft, and 4 planes damaged or probably destroyed.

The invasion convoy had a portent of enemy intentions on the afternoon of the 13th, when a suicide plane crashed into the flagship, *Nashville,* before it could be taken under fire. Later in the afternoon a flight of 12 enemy planes was driven off by the convoy's air cover, assisted by antiaircraft fire of escort vessels and the PT's. Three of the enemy were shot down.

Troops began to pour ashore on the southwest corner of Mindoro at 0700, December 15, meeting little opposition at the beachhead. Half an hour later Lieutenant Commander Davis went ahead with five PT's, accompanying several of the escort vessels into Mangarin Bay, the prospective site of the PT base, while the other 18 PT's remained with a group of LST's approaching Mangarin Bay. Eleven Japanese planes came over, 4 attacking ships in the bay and the other 7 concentrating on the LST's outside.

Three of the planes over the bay tried to dive on a destroyer, and were shot down by combined fire of all ships. The fourth swooped in over the stern of Ens. J. P. Rafferty's PT 221. The 221 shot it down in flames.

Outside the bay, Lt. Comdr. Alvin W. Fargo, Jr., USNR, commander of Squadron 13, ordered the PT's to speed up to get between the LST's and the approaching planes. The seven planes peeled off and strafed the PT's ineffectively. The PT's shot down three of them. Of the four that got through, two were brought down by combined fire of the PT's and LST 605, crashing in the water close aboard the LST. The other two dived into LST's 472 and 738, ahead and astern of LST 605, setting them ablaze and sinking them. The PT's picked up more than 200 survivors from the 2 ships.

The next morning all of the PT's were in Mangarin Bay and LST 605 was unloading base equipment on the beach. PT's 230 and 300 had just entered the bay, returning from patrol, when a single plane strafed the 230 without causing any damage, made a complete circle and started to dive on LST 605. The LST and all of the PT's opened fire, shooting off part of the plane's tail. It crashed on the beach 50 yards from the LST, killing 5 men and wounding 11.

Half an hour later eight planes attacked the PT's. Lt. (jg.) Byron F. Kent, USNR, boat captain of PT 230, reported: "Three of the planes chose PT 230 as their target. All fire was concentrated on the first as it dove for the boat in a gradual sweep increasing to an angle of about 70 degrees. The boat was maneuvered at high speed to present a starboard broadside to the oncoming plane. When it became apparent that the plane would not pull out of the dive, the boat feinted in several directions and then turned hard right rudder

PT 297 picks up survivors of an LST hit by a suicide plane during invasion of Mindoro, December 15, 1944.

80—G—294583

under the plane. The boat's speed carried it partly around the plane as it struck the water 30 feet off the starboard bow.

"About 1 minute later the second plane began its dive following somewhat the same tactics as the first. When the pilot finally committed himself as to his final direction, the boat was swung to the opposite direction of the plane's slight bank. The plane struck 50 feet off the port beam.

"The third plane came in 30 seconds later at a 70 degree angle. After zigzagging rapidly as the plane came down, the boat swung suddenly at right angles to the plane, which by then had finally committed itself. The plane landed in the water just off the boat's stern, raising the stern out of the water and showering the 40mm. crew with flame, smoke, debris and water. All personnel on the boat were slightly dazed, but there were no injuries, and the boat was undamaged."

Lt. (jg.) Frank A. Tredinnick, USNR, whose PT 77 was under attack by a single plane, waited until the last second and pulled down his throttles, causing the plane to crash in the water 10 yards ahead of the boat. Lt. (jg.) Harry E. Griffin, Jr., USNR, similarly avoided a plane by swinging the rudder of his PT 223 hard right. The plane missed by about 10 feet. Lt. (jg.) J. R. Erickson, USNR, with two planes heading for his PT 298, maneuvered at top speed to avoid them. "The gunners fired a steady stream of shells into one plane," he reported, "as it came down in a steep dive and crashed 15 feet off the port bow. Just then the second plane circled once and dived down on our stern, strafing as he dove. The gunners fired on him until he crashed about 3 feet off the starboard bow, spraying the deck with debris and water. One man was blown over the side by the concussion but was rescued uninjured."

The eighth plane was shot down by the combined fire of several PT's.

That afternoon, as PT's 224 and 297 were departing for the night's patrol, two planes dropped three bombs near them. The two PT's, assisted by other PT's in the bay, shot down one plane in the water, which narrowly missed the 224, and saw the other glide over the treetops on Mindoro, on fire and losing altitude.

On the afternoon of December 17, three planes attacked the boats in Mangarin Bay. The boats shot one down and the other two crashed in the water trying to dive on PT's 75 and 84. One man on PT 224 was wounded by strafing, and four men on PT 75 suffered minor wounds from flying debris.

On December 18 three planes came over. Only one went into a suicide dive. Lt. Comdr. Almer P. Colvin, commander of Squadron 16, gave PT 300 a last-second swing to the right. The plane apparently had anticipated the maneuver. It swung right with the PT and crashed into the engine-room, splitting the boat in half. The stern sank immediately; the bow burned for 8 hours. Colvin was seriously wounded, four men were killed, four men were missing, and two officers and four men were wounded. Only one man of the crew of PT 300 escaped without injury.

That night planes dropped bombs on Mangarin Bay, wounding three men. The PT's withheld their fire to avoid revealing their positions. The Mindoro airstrip began operations on December 20, but even the presence of locally based fighters could not immediately stop the enemy attacks. Between the 19th and 26th of December, the PT's shot down five more planes at no cost to themselves.

9. A JAPANESE TASK FORCE

Late in the afternoon of December 26 an Army pilot returning from a reconnaissance flight reported that an enemy task force of one battleship, one cruiser, and six destroyers was only 80 miles to the northwest of Mindoro, bearing down at a speed of 20 knots. It was the second enemy force sighted that day in Philippine waters. The other, a group of cargo ships and transports off Subic Bay, Luzon, already was under air attack by Mindoro-based planes. It seemed likely that the enemy planned an amphibious landing to regain control of Mindoro.

All available planes were sent out to bomb and strafe the task force. When planes returned from Subic Bay, they were refueled, reloaded, and sent out to join the attack. Through most of the night the planes shuttled between the Japanese ships and the Mindoro strip, dropping their bombs and returning for more.

While the Army ground forces deployed to meet the landing ashore, the PT's, the only Allied naval forces present, prepared to disrupt any invasion forces before they hit the beach. Lieutenant Commander Davis sent Lieutenant Commander Fargo with four PT's (80, 77, 84 and 192) to patrol to the north, and Lt. John H. Stillman, USNR, who succeeded Lieutenant Commander Colvin as commander of Squadron 16, with PT's 78, 76 and 81 to patrol near Ilin Island, off the entrance to Mangarin Bay. PT's 230 and 227 were stationed in outer Mangarin Bay, ready to support either Fargo or

Stillman. Eleven other boats, all in poor condition because of hull or engine casualties suffered during the past 12 days' operations, were dispersed about the inner bay to protect the inner anchorage and to counter any landings on the southwestern coast of Mindoro below the main Allied defense perimeter. The two remaining boats of the task unit, PT's 223 and 221, already had departed from the base to carry an Army radar team and several guerrillas to Abra de Ilog, on northern Mindoro, and could not be reached immediately by radio when word of the aproaching enemy was received.

Davis reasoned correctly that if a landing were attempted, the PT's would be of greatest value when the transports closed the beach to put troops ashore. Then the PT's could attack the transports with torpedoes and use their machineguns and depth charges against any ships' boats or landing barges that the transports might put in the water. For this reason and because the battleship, cruiser, and destroyer force already was under air attack, he instructed Fargo and Stillman to scout and report on this force, but not to attack until the enemy should approach the beach in the probable landing area.

At 2030 Fargo's boats saw antiaircraft fire on the horizon, 40 miles to the northwest of Mangarin Bay. The firing continued intermittently for an hour, as the enemy fought off repeated air attacks. At 2115 there was a large flash followed by a steady glow in the sky, indicating that one of the ships had been hit and was burning. Then Fargo's boats picked up the enemy ships on their radars, and at 2150 clearly saw six ships 4 miles away. Five minutes later the enemy took Fargo's boats under intense and accurate fire, straddling the PT's on the first salvo. The boats were under fire for 80 minutes as they zigzagged to the south, and for nearly an hour they were under bombing attack by aircraft as well. Fearing that the aircraft might be our own, the PT's did not fire on them. While the shellfire was close, the only casualties were caused by aerial bombs. One exploded just off the stern of PT 77, damaging the boat and wounding the boat captain and 11 men. Another dropped close aboard PT 84, blowing a man overboard. Lieutenant Commander Davis, advised of the casualties by radio, instructed PT 84 to escort PT 77 back to the base. Fargo requested permission to attack, but was ordered to proceed with PT's 80 and 82 southward through the strait between Ilin Island and Mindoro in case the enemy should attempt an assault on the southern beaches. On their passage through the strait the boats were bombed by an enemy floatplane. They zigzagged at high speed and escaped damage.

Stillman's boats, north of Ilin Island, observed the approach of the enemy and were taken under sporadic shellfire. None of the shells came closer than 100 yards. During the 2 hours that Stillman had the enemy in sight, the enemy ships were under almost constant air attack, a circumstance which undoubtedly affected the accuracy of shellfire. Stillman requested permission to attack. Davis, preferring to hold his boats in reserve for a last-ditch stand, ordered Stillman not to attack as long as our planes were still in action. Soon after midnight the enemy succumbed to the air attack and fled northward at high speed, shelling the beach on the way. The Army requested Stillman to search the southwest coast of Mindoro for evidences of a landing. He found nothing.

The boats that had set out for Abra de Ilog with the Army radar team, Lt. (jg.) Harry E. Griffin, Jr.'s PT 223 and Lt. (jg.) E. H. Lockwood's PT 221, with Lt. Philip A. Swart, USNR, as section leader, had reached the northwestern tip of Mindoro before they received orders by radio to return to the base. They met the enemy task force as it steamed northward. Since the force was retiring, Davis gave permission to attack. As the PT's closed, the 221 was taken under heavy shellfire and retired, laying smoke. The 223, apparently unobserved, got two torpedoes away. There was a bright orange-red flash on the third ship in line, followed by the sound of a heavy explosion.

PT's searched the scene of action on the 27th. They picked up the man who had been blown over the side of PT 84. He was slightly waterlogged, but uninjured. They also picked up five Japanese sailors, survivors of the 2,100-ton destroyer *Kiyoshimo,* one of the newest and most powerful in the Japanese Navy. It had been damaged during the air attack and sank after being hit by one of PT 223's torpedoes.

After the action, it was apparent that no invasion had been contemplated, and that the sole intention of the enemy had been to shell the airstrip. The enemy ships were so occupied with fighting off air attacks, however, that their bombardment was ineffective.

10. MINDORO CONVOY

Squadrons 8, 24, and 25 arrived in Leyte Gulf from Mios Woendi on December 23 and were transferred the same day with the tender *Orestes* to the operational control of Capt. George F. Mentz's Task Group 77.11. Captain Mentz's group was to make diversionary strikes against southern Luzon as a preliminary to the main assault on the island, scheduled for January 9 in Lingayen Gulf. On December 27, the squadrons and *Orestes* sailed in convoy for Mindoro.[32]

Air attacks on the convoy began on the morning of December 28, when suicide planes crashed on LST 750 and the Liberty ships *John Burke* and *William Ahearn*. *John Burke*, loaded with ammunition, literally disintegrated with a mighty roar, sinking a small Army freighter immediately astern. The concussion opened seams in PT 332 although 500 yards away. *William Ahearn*, no longer able to keep up with the convoy, returned independently to Leyte. The LST, less severely damaged, continued in convoy.

Five times during the afternoon and evening, small groups of planes attacked or threatened the convoy. An aerial torpedo hit LST 750 in the engineroom. Other ships removed the crew and our destroyers sank the damaged ship. Another torpedo grazed the bottom of LCI 624 from stem to stern without exploding. Four PT's were damaged slightly by strafing attacks. Six planes were shot down during the night.

On the morning of the 29th the convoy was under attack for an hour and a half. Three planes were shot down by ships in convoy, one of them by PT 352 when the plane tried to dive on an LST. The convoy's air cover shot down a fourth plane. That afternoon air cover turned back five flights of planes before they could reach the convoy, but for 8 hours during the night, crews of all ships were at battle stations fighting off bombers, torpedo planes, and suicide planes. Six more aircraft were shot down, one by PT 355 when it attempted to crash a destroyer.

There were more attacks during the early morning of the 30th, as the convoy stood into Mangarin Bay, and three planes were shot down. The rest of the day was quiet until midafternoon, when three planes dived at ships in the bay. One crashed on tanker *Porcupine*, one on destroyer *Gansevoort*, and the third, set ablaze by fire from *Orestes* and nearby PT's, hit the water alongside the tender. It skipped on the water and crashed into the starboard side of *Orestes*. Its bombs, deflected upward, exploded inside the tender, blowing many of the crew overboard and engulfing the ship in flames. The blaze spread almost instantly to the ready ammunition boxes on the deck, and for a time the ship was an inferno of exploding 40mm. and 20mm. shells.

---

[32] The squadron commanders and tender commanding officer were: Squadron 8, Lt. Robert A. Williamson, USNR; Squadron 24, Lt. Stanley C. Thomas, USNR; Squadron 25, Lt. Comdr. Theodore R. Stansbury, USNR; *Orestes*, Lt. Kenneth N. Mueller, USNR.

Captain Mentz, standing on the bridge, was seriously injured; his chief staff officer, Comdr. John Kremer, Jr., USNR, was fatally wounded. In all, 6 officers and 14 men were killed; 37 were missing, and 7 officers and 86 men were wounded.

Despite imminent danger of explosion from 37,000 gallons of high-octane gasoline and stores of PT ammunition and torpedo warheads aboard the tender, PT's came alongside to take off the survivors. Led by Lieutenant Commander Davis, many PT officers and men went aboard to search for wounded. Comdr. A. Vernon Jannotta, USNR, on whom command of the task group devolved when Captain Mentz and Commander Kremer were put out of action, brought LCI's 624 and 636 alongside and carried hoses aboard *Orestes* to fight the flames. After an hour and a half the blaze was under control and the LCI's beached the tender.

Gansevoort, which had been hit amidships, was beached and abandoned. *Porcupine* was totally destroyed by fire.

Since there were no salvage facilities at Mindoro, the men of the PT Advance Base Construction Detachment, 113th Naval Construction Battalion, squared their shoulders and went to work on *Orestes* and *Gansevoort.* They got *Orestes* in shape to be towed back to Leyte Gulf by LST 708 at the end of January, and *Gansevoort* at the beginning of February. Since there was no other ship available to tow *Gansevoort,* PT tender *Willoughby* made a special trip from Leyte to do the job.

The air attacks on Mangarin Bay were not quite over. On December 30, PT's 75, 78, 220, and 224 shot down a plane as they left the bay to go on patrol. In the early morning hours of January 1, bombers were over the base. A single fragmentation bomb killed 11 men and seriously wounded 10 others, most of them survivors of the *Orestes.* There was more bombing during the next couple of days, but no more damage until the afternoon of January 4, when PT's 78 and 81 set fire to one of four enemy fighters which flew over the bay. Trailing a plume of smoke and flame, the plane glided into the side of an ammunition ship anchored a quarter of a mile from the two PT's. The ship exploded with a thunderous roar. The PT's were lifted out of the water and were badly damaged by the concussion and falling debris. On the PT's, two men were killed and three officers and seven men were wounded.

Although there were many red alerts in the days to follow, and further air attacks on the Mindoro airstrips, this was the last time that Japanese planes visited Mangarin Bay.

11. TASK GROUP 77.11

The PT's and LCI's of Task Group 77.11 performed all the shore-to-shore movements of troops and supplies required by the Western Visayan Task Force, including reinforcement of Mindoro forces from Leyte, securing the central portion of Mindoro's eastern coast, and seizure of the island of Marinduque, between Mindoro and the Bondoc Peninsula of southern Luzon. In all, there were 27 of these shore-to-shore operations. For the larger ones, when from 100 to 800 troops and large quantities of supplies were to be carried to the objectives, PT's escorted LCI's to the landing beaches. On a few smaller operations, involving the movement of 60 men or less and only 1 or 2 tons of supplies, PT's performed the missions unassisted.

The PT's landed scouts and raiders behind enemy lines on Mindoro and the surrounding islands, established and maintained contacts with guerrilla forces on northern Mindanao and southern Luzon, and reconnoitered all of the principal anchorages of Mindoro, Marinduque, and southern Luzon, bringing back valuable information concerning beach approaches, minefields, and shore defenses. Some of their most valuable reconnaissance work was in preparation for two major diversionary operations undertaken by the task group in the eastern Tayabas Bay area of southern Luzon at the time of the Army landings in force at San Antonio and Nasugbu on the western coast of Luzon late in January. Commander Jannotta expressed the belief that these operations made the enemy uncertain as to our strategic intent, diverted his attention from the actual target areas, and immobilized elements of his forces in the Tayabas-Batangas area.

As part of the preparation for the first of these missions, PT's 188 and 149, led by Ens. William H. Suttenfield, Jr., USNR, made the first daylight transit by Allied vessels of Verde Passage, between Mindoro and Luzon, since the enemy occupied the central Philippines. On the way back to the base the boats destroyed 16 sailing vessels on the beach of Verde Island and pinpointed the position of a heavy gun that fired at them so that fighter bombers of the 310th Bomb Wing were able to destroy it.

The task group suffered the loss of PT 338 on January 25 when the boat ran aground near Semirara Island, off southern Mindoro, and was so badly damaged that it could not be salvaged.

The PT's were released from Task Group 77.11 on February 10 and returned to Leyte Gulf to prepare for further operations.

12. MINDORO PATROLS

Squadrons 13 and 16, with the boats of Squadron 17 increased to six in February, continued patrols in Verde Passage and the Sibuyan Sea until April with good results. For the most part their work consisted of close scanning of enemy-held bays and inlets, since Japanese small craft no longer dared venture into the open sea. The boats found some of their best hunting in Coron Bay, southeast of Mindoro, which as recently as the time of the Battle for Leyte Gulf had been a major Japanese Fleet anchorage.

On the night of January 8/9, Lt. (jg.) R. H. Beasley, Jr.'s PT 220, with Lt. Philip A. Swart, USNR, aboard as officer in tactical command, accompanied by PT 223, made an unusual attack on a 2,000-ton freighter in Coron Bay. Earlier in the patrol the 220 had torn a hole in her bottom on an uncharted reef, and was in imminent danger of sinking as she approached the freighter and fired four torpedoes. While it was claimed that three torpedoes hit the target and destroyed it, this is not confirmed. As the 220 limped homewards, the crew bailed with buckets for 5 hours until PT's 75 and 83 arrived, bringing pumps from the base.

Of the many daylight air-sea strikes, two of the most successful were led by Lt. Robert J. Wehrli, USNR, aboard PT 222. On January 29 he led four PT's, covered by two P–38's and two B–25's, into Batangas Bay on southern Luzon.[33] The boats were in the bay for 67 minutes, making repeated strafing attacks on small craft and dock areas. For 37 minutes they were under intense fire from shore. The PT's destroyed 2 luggers, 3 barges, 24 sailing vessels, and an undetermined number of suicide boats hidden in huts along the shore. In cooperation with their covering aircraft, they knocked out several gun positions, damaged buildings and a dock, and started eight fires, one of them in a large oil dump. The cost to the PT's was one officer wounded.

On February 23, Wehrli visited Coron town, in Coron Bay, with six PT's and two P–47's.[34] With no damage to themselves, the PT's destroyed three motor launches, a whaleboat, a gig, two barges, and two 70-foot lighters, and set fire to a fuel dump ashore.

---

[33] The PT's were: PT 77, Ens. Allen Slickers, USNR; PT 81, Lt. (jg.) Richard H. Dunlap, USNR; PT 222, Lt. (jg.) Robert Roth, USNR; PT 230, Lt. (jg.) William J. Bursaw, Jr., USNR.

[34] The PT's were: PT 76, Lt. (jg.) William S. Wilkinson, USNR; PT 78, Lt. (jg.) Charles W. Sparaco, USNR; PT 83, Lt. (jg.) James W. Stitt, USNR; PT 224, Lt. R. H. Lewis, USNR; PT 229, Lt. (jg.) J. H. Brodahl, USNR; PT 298, Lt. (jg) J. R. Erickson, USNR.

The Japanese suicide boat, which appeared in the Mindoro area for the first time in the Southwest Pacific, apparently was intended as the marine counterpart of the Kamikaze plane. Fortunately it was far less effective. It was a small motorboat with a large explosive charge in the bow, designed to detonate when the boat was driven into a ship's side. The PT's made a series of strikes on suicide boats hideouts, claiming destruction of more than 40 explosive boats.

Three more PT's were lost at Mindoro. On the night of January 14/15, PT's 73 and 75 delivered supplies to the Mindoro guerrillas at Abra de Ilog, and took the guerrilla leader, Lt. Comdr. George Rowe, aboard for their patrol. Near Lubang Island, to the northwest of Mindoro, the 73 ran hard aground. Lieutenant Commander Rowe said there were 300 Japanese on Lubang, who undoubtedly would attack as soon as daylight revealed the boat's position. PT 75 took the 73's crew aboard and set the grounded boat on fire.

The other two boats, the last PT's lost in the war, were destroyed by our own warships as a result of mistaken identification. Troops landed at Nasugbu, on western Luzon, on January 31, and that night ships of the screen were attacked by 20 or more suicide boats. One rammed and sank PC 1129; the rest were destroyed or driven off. The following night, Lt. John H. Stillman, USNR, was ordered to patrol with PT's 77 and 79 against suicide boats south of the landing beaches. He was not to go north of Talin Point, because our destroyers and destroyer escorts were patrolling north of the point.

Three miles south of Talin Point the PT's were illuminated by starshell, and were taken under fire by ships that they recognized as our own. The PT's fled southward at top speed, trying to identify themselves by radio and by signal light. It turned out later that the ships that fired on them, a destroyer and a destroyer escort, had tried repeatedly to reach the boats by radio, and failing to get an answer, had concluded that they were enemy PT's or suicide boats. The destroyer and destroyer escort did not see the visual recognition signals from the PT's.

Even then the PT's might have outrun pursuit, if the 77 had not run up on a reef. The crew abandoned ship. Ten minutes later a shell hit the boat amidships. The boat burned all night. The 79, following 100 yards astern of the 77, swung hard right and reduced speed to avoid the reef. Running slowly, she was an easy mark. A shell hit her squarely on the port side. The 79 exploded and burned.

Lieutenant Stillman, who had been aboard the 77, was never seen again. The boat captain of the 79, Lt. (jg.) Michael A. Haughian, USNR, and two men of his crew, Joseph E. Klesh, MoMM1c, USNR, and Vincent A. Berra, QM3c, USNR, were killed when the boat exploded. All of the other officers and men of the 2 boats, 30 in all, swam to the enemy-held shore 2 miles away. With the aid of guerrillas they evaded capture until February 3, when they were picked up by PT's 227 and 230.

Both in lives and materiel, the Mindoro campaign was the most costly that the PT's had had in the Southwest Pacific. Yet the damage they did far overbalanced their losses. They met and overcame the most savage air attacks the enemy could mount, causing destruction of more than 20 enemy aircraft. Together with Army bombers, they sank one of the newest and finest destroyers in the Japanese Navy. They stopped Japanese interisland traffic, cut off evacuation from Mindoro to Luzon, and ferreted out and destroyed small craft in the harbors. They cleaned out whole nests of suicide boats. They supported the guerrillas on Mindoro and Luzon, and carried out many valuable reconnaissance missions.

Task Unit 70.1.4, comprising Squadrons 13 and 16 and PT's 227 and 230, received a Navy Unit Commendation, which read in part: "As the only Naval force present following the retirement of the invasion convoys, this Task Unit served as the major obstruction to enemy counter-landings from nearby Luzon, Panay and Palawan and bore the brunt of concentrated hostile air attacks throughout a 5-day period. Providing the only anti-aircraft protection available for personnel ashore engaged in the establishment of a motor torpedo boat operating and repair base, the gallant officers and men who commanded and staffed the Task Unit and who manned the boats maintained the vigilant watch by night and stood out in the open waters close to base by day to fight off repeated Japanese bombing, strafing and suicide attacks, expending in 3 days the ammunition which had been expected to last approximately 3 weeks in the destruction or damaging of a large percentage of the attacking planes. Their invaluable service in support of the expeditious completion of operations ashore vital to the furtherance of the Mindoro Campaign reflects the highest credit upon the United States Naval Service."

13. BASES AND LOGISTICS

With the ending of the New Guinea campaign and the beginning of operations in the Philippines, plans were made to establish both an advance base and a large operating, repair, and supply base for PT's in the Leyte Gulf area and to move all available squadrons and floating equipment to Leyte as rapidly as possible. Binatac Point in San Juanico Strait, the narrow strip of water separating Leyte from Samar, was selected as the site. PT Advance Base 5 was to be constructed immediately, and the large base was to be put on the same site when it arrived.

"PT base construction in the Leyte area was one disappointment after another during the first several months," Captain Bowling wrote. "The day before the LST's carrying the advance base arrived, the Naval Base Commander notified the Task Group Commander that the place desired at Binatac Point was required for Naval Base construction and was not available for a PT base. A quick survey was made that afternoon to locate another site agreeable to him. Tinaogan Point further up the strait was finally agreed upon.

"This base site proved almost impossible. The base equipment was unloaded during one typhoon and another typhoon occurred shortly afterwards during base construction. It was the height of the rainy season and there was no coral or rock fill available in the area for roads or walks. The terrain was very hilly. The base was constructed, after a fashion, but never satisfactorily completed. It was necessary to base some squadrons and floating equipment here, however, and the conditions were very detrimental to morale with the sides of the hills mere mud slides and the flat places morasses of mud. The large operating and repair base, PT Base 17, arrived in stages— personnel first, by about a month, so that they had to be housed and fed at the advance base, and were a hindrance instead of a help. A battalion of Seabees worked several weeks with a great deal of equipment building themselves a camp just below the PT Base site on a knoll which had some coral in the water just off the beach. They dredged up coral to make usable roads. When the Seabees vacated this spot very soon after they had it set up, the PT advance base moved there, with an exchange of tentage, lumber, etc.

"When it was finally decided by the higher commands, because of the difficulties of construction on Samar near Tacloban, to shift the Naval Base, the Naval Supply Depot and air strip construction to the Guiuan area of

USS Cyrene *lifts a PT aboard for major hull repair.*

Samar, a fast survey was made and a PT base site was selected near Bobon Point . . . The advance base was left in San Juanico Strait. The first equipment for PT Base 17 did not arrive at Bobon Point until January 26, 1945.

"The period from 21 October through January 1945 presented the most acute problems ever encountered by the task group during the writer's experience in it. Rains, typhoons and frequent air raids interfered greatly with the servicing of boats by tenders. The advance base was a sea of mud, making it an effort just to exist there. The two typhoons, heavy enemy air oppositions, the Battle of Surigao Strait, and operations against enemy surface ships in the Camotes Sea quickly built up an unusually heavy load and backlog of repair work. All repair work and servicing was done by the tenders anchored in San Juanico Strait or San Pedro Bay, and by the floating work shop barges, crane barges, radar barges, fuel barges and drydocks anchored near the advance base. The handling of spare parts and material was a heartbreaking job, getting them ashore, sorting and distributing them in one inadequate warehouse which had been borrowed from the Army and

19–N–78876

Cyrene could dock two PT's at a time. PT 325 rests in cradle alongside, suspended from boom; another PT, with corner of stern just visible, rests in cradle on deck.

put up at the advance base. During this period almost all PT spares came from Woendi, a few straight from Manus.

"To accentuate all problems, it was necessary during this period, in addition to supporting current operations, to stage the PT's and supporting equipment through Leyte for the Mindoro, Ormoc, Lingayen Gulf, and Subic Bay operations, and on top of that one tender and three squadrons of PT's were transferred temporarily to operational control of Commander Task Group 77.11 for a special operation from Mindoro. The early arrival of PT Base 17 would have helped immeasurably. This base was of little value to the task group until some time in March 1945. The floating equipment—drydocks, radar barges, ramp barges, crane barges, gas barges, work shop barges and the four F ships and two FS ships assigned to the task group were the saving features during this period. It would not have been possible to meet our requirements without this equipment. The arrival of the USS *Cyrene* in San Pedro Bay about 1 January was a tremendous help, with its major repair facilities, large provision storage capacity and berthing capacity."

Cyrene, commanded by Comdr. Frank A. Munroe, Jr., USNR, former skipper of *Hilo*, looked like a floating navy yard to the PT's.[35] She carried a heavy part of the repair load during her first weeks in Leyte Gulf, and had more adequate quarters for Captain Bowling and his staff than they had ever had before. Captain Bowling shifted his pennant from *Hilo* to *Cyrene* on January 17.

The "acute problems" of the first weeks in Leyte Gulf were gradually overcome during the early part of 1945. Once it began to function, Base 17, at Bobon Point, Samar, became the biggest and most complete PT base in the world. Its warehouses bulged with supplies, spares, and ammunition. To supply its advance bases, the task group operated what amounted to a private shipping line, using the four F ships acquired from the Army at the time of the Aitape and Hollandia landings and two larger freighters, FS ships, assigned to operational control of the task group by the Commander Service Force. The converted yachts *Hilo* and *Jamestown*, though still carried on the books as tenders, had been rendered obsolete as tenders by the arrival of larger and more efficient vessels, and were used as utility ships to shuttle personnel and cargo between bases.

The task group had grown to mammoth size. At its peak in mid-1945, it had 212 PT's, 11 tenders, 46 functional components, and, not counting

---

[35] For a description of the *Cyrene*, see p. 73.

NR&L (MOD)–3254

PT Base 17, Bobon Point, Samar.

the major bases which were administered by the Commander Service Force, had more than 1,000 officers and 10,000 men. At the beginning of the year, there were 20 squadrons of PT's. In February, the 2 lowest numbered squadrons, 5 and 7, were decommissioned and their 16 boats were apportioned among 8 other squadrons which had suffered losses. In May the number of squadrons was raised to 19 with the arrival of the first boats of Squadron 38 from the United States.

With so many PT's, more major bases were required. The Dreger Harbor base was rolled up and shipped to Mindoro in January. This became the principal repair and staging base for the task group's five squadrons of Higgins PT's. It was planned to divide the Elco squadrons between Base 17 and PT Base 16, which was established in March as a major repair base at Puerto Isabela on Basilan Island, off the southern end of the Zamboanga Peninsula. Although some squadrons did base there for a time, construction of PT Base 16 had not been completed at the end of hostilities in August, and the base did not play as important a role in the support of PT operations as did the bases at Bobon Point and Mindoro.

14. LINGAYEN GULF

American reoccupation of the island of Luzon began on January 9, 1945, with the landing of the XIV and I Corps of Lt. Gen. Walter Krueger's Sixth Army in Lingayen Gulf. Motor Torpedo Boat Squadrons 28 and 36 and the tender *Wachapreague,* under tactical command of Lt. Comdr. Francis D. Tappaan, USNR, arrived 4 days later.[36]

The PT's sank four barges on their first patrol on the night of January 14/15. Thereafter they found few targets on their nightly patrols. With his navy reduced to impotence, the enemy made no attempt to reinforce Luzon, and with good internal communications on the island did not risk his small craft at sea. A shining exception to the general unproductiveness of patrols came on the night of January 23/24, when Lt. G. S. Wright's PT 528 and Lt. (jg.) B. M. Stevens's PT 532 fired eight torpedoes at a 6,000-ton freighter, scoring two hits on the bow. Several weeks later Lt. John W. Morrison, Jr., USNR, commander of Squadron 36, had an opportunity to

[36] The squadron commanders and tender commanding officer were: Squadron 28, Lt. Comdr. George A. Matteson, Jr., USNR; Squadron 36, Lt. John W. Morrison, Jr., USNR; *Wachapreague,* Lt. Comdr. H. A. Stewart, USNR.

NR&L (MOD)—32512

A Japanese suicide boat on the beach of Lingayen Gulf. PT's destroyed many of these explosive craft throughout the Philippines.

examine this freighter by daylight. It was aground and abandoned, with the entire bow blown off.

Aside from the freighter and a few barges, all enemy surface craft destroyed by the Lingayen PT's were encountered in a series of four daylight air-sea strikes during a 2-week period in January and February. On the afternoon of January 29, Lt. R. C. Castle, USNR, led Lt. N. J. Russell, Jr.'s PT 523 and Lt. (jg.) James P. Wolf's PT 524 on a sweep of the beach near San Fernando. Covered by aircraft of the 85th Fighter Command, the PT's sank 6 barges, destroyed 4 more on the beach, sank 1 lugger and damaged another beyond repair, destroyed 10 beached suicide boats, and set fire to 3 fuel dumps and 1 ammunition dump.

Two days later Lt. Comdr. Frank B. Gass, USNR, led Lt. (jg.) E. H. Olson's PT 551 and Lt. Walter F. Brown's PT 547 on another strike at the San Fernando area. The boats sank or destroyed 21 barges and 5 suicide boats, holed a water tower with several 40mm. hits, and started a huge fire near the tower. P–38's of the 308th Bomb Wing sank a lugger that was screened by a dock from the fire of the PT's. Two more strikes in the same area, on February 8 and 11, resulted in destruction of 16 barges, 9 suicide boats, a 100-foot lugger, and a 40-foot motor launch, and damage to a warehouse, a garage, and a truck. The patrol of February 11 was the last in which the Lingayen boats sighted enemy surface craft.

Construction of PT Advance Base 6 at Port Sual, in Lingayen Gulf, permitted *Wachapreague* to return to Leyte Gulf in March. The boats continued their patrols of the west coast of Luzon and, with the establishment of a fueling station in Santiago Cove in guerrilla territory 100 miles north of the base, extended their patrol area to include the entire northern coast of the island. Most of their activity was confined to strafing enemy shore installations, supplying guerrilla forces and obtaining guerrilla intelligence of Japanese troop dispositions. For several months the PT's were a vital part of the day-and-night air-surface blockade to forestall any enemy attempts at evacuation from northern Luzon to Formosa.

The PT's made several rescues of personnel of aircraft forced down at sea. Lieutenant Commander Gass led PT's 379 and 551 on a mission on March 17, picking up 12 crew members and passengers of a Navy PBM in seas so heavy that the PT's were considerably damaged and every officer and man of the PT crews suffered minor injuries. In a series of three operations off northern Luzon from the 5th to 13th of June, PT's rescued a total of 20 aircrewmen.

PT's supported the Army's eastward drive along the northern Luzon coastline in June by carrying Army officers who spotted targets and directed fire of Army fieldpieces ashore while the boats illuminated enemy concentration areas with flares and strafed them. During the latter part of July, elements of the Philippine Army and the U.S. 11th Airborne Division completed the occupation of the north coast, and PT patrols from Lingayen were discontinued on July 31.

15. RETURN TO MANILA BAY

Landings by the XI Corps of the Sixth Army in the San Antonio-San Narciso area of Luzon on January 29 reopened Subic Bay as an American naval base and, in conjunction with the landings of the 11th Airborne Division 2 days later at Nasugbu to the south, marked the opening of the drive to liberate Manila. Squadrons 21 and 27, under Lt. Henry S. Taylor, USNR, arrived in Subic Bay with the tender *Varuna* on February 3. Patrolling to the south,

80–G–273306

Lt. John A. Mapp's PT 376 approaches Corregidor on February 16, 1945, to rescue paratroopers who overshot the top of the island and were taken under enemy sniper fire.

these PT's became the first Allied war vessels to enter Manila Bay since the surrender of Corregidor in May 1942.[37]

While the battle for Manila was raging, the Sixth Army started operations to open Manila Bay to Allied shipping. In a combined overland and amphibious assault, which the PT's had helped prepare with a thorough reconnaissance of Mariveles Harbor early in February, Sixth Army forces established control over the southern Bataan Peninsula on February 15, and followed up this success a day later with a combined airborne and amphibious assault on Corregidor.

Japanese experience 3 years earlier had indicated how costly an amphibious assault on Corregidor could be. It was decided, therefore, to drop 2,000 paratroopers to seize key positions by surprise before the enemy had time

---

[37] The squadron commanders and tender commanding officer were: Squadron 21, Lt. Carl T. Gleason, USNR; Squadron 27, Lt. Henry S. Taylor, USNR; *Varuna*, Lt. Carl J. Kalb.

80—G—273308

Lt. Raymond P. Shafer, USNR, and Lt. (jg.) Charles Adams, USNR, approach Corregidor beach to pick up paratroopers under Japanese sniper fire.

to react. The only good drop site was at Kindley Field, but if the paratroopers landed there, the enemy could direct fire at them from above and they would have to attack against the heavily defended higher ground. It was necessary, therefore, to make the drop on the very top of the rock, even though the only suitable spots there were the Parade Ground, measuring 150 by 250 yards, and the golf course, 150 by 325 yards. These fields were surrounded by splintered trees, tangled undergrowth, and wrecked buildings, and had the added disadvantage of sloping off suddenly in almost perpendicular cliffs. It was to be expected that some paratroopers would miss the fields and find themselves on the cliffside.

As the paratroopers began their descent, PT's waited close to shore. Lt. John A. Mapp's PT 376 spotted a group of paratroopers picking their way down the face of the cliff as enemy snipers took pot shots at them. The 376 moved in and 50 yards from shore put a rubber raft over the side. Lt. Raymond P. Shafer, USNR, executive officer of Squadron 27, and Lt. (jg.) Charles Adams, USNR, paddled ashore and picked up the men. Shortly afterwards they paddled in again for a second group. On the 2 trips, they rescued 17 paratroopers under enemy sniper fire.

Corregidor was taken after a ferocious 12-day battle. General MacArthur, who had left the Rock in PT 41 on March 11, 1942, returned to it in PT 373 on March 2, 1945.

After the fall of Corregidor the Army began a series of shore-to-shore movements to liberate the rest of the islands of Manila Bay. The PT's supported these operations, making close reconnaissance of the entire shoreline of the bay and the islands, and reporting enemy positions and installations to the Army. They sank several barges, suicide boats, and other small craft; prevented reinforcement or escape of the Japanese on the islands, and took many prisoners who were trying to escape from the islands by rafts and canoes, or even by swimming. Interrogation of these prisoners gave much valuable information as to the enemy situation in the bay. The PT's also gave direct support to some of the shore-to-shore movements by strafing and rocketing the beaches in preparation for landings.

The boats helped to acquire further information by putting intelligence teams aboard Japanese hulks in the harbor. Occasionally the boats had to clean out snipers on the hulks before they could put the intelligence teams aboard.

Manila fell on March 3, and the Army completed the liberation of the bay islands on April 16. PT combat patrols ended on April 27.

16. PALAWAN

Squadrons 20 and 23, under tactical command of Lt. James H. Van Sicklen, USNR, and supported by the tender *Willoughby,* began operations from Puerto Princesa on Palawan, westernmost of the major islands of the Philippines, on March 1, 1945, 1 day after the initial landings by units of the Eighth Army.[38] The Army found few Japanese ashore; the PT's, though they patrolled from one end of the island to the other, found none afloat.

Eventually the PT's located a Japanese garrison on Pandanan Island, off the southern tip of Paláwan, and strafed it repeatedly. During their first strikes, the PT's drew heavy fire from Pandanan. As time went on the volume of enemy fire slackened, and finally ceased altogether. Late in April, PT's put a landing party ashore and found that the island had been evacuated. With no enemy left to fight, patrols were secured on April 28.

---

[38] The squadron commanders and tender commanding officer were: Squadron 20, Lt. Robert C. Harris, USNR; Squadron 23, Lt. James H. Van Sicklen, USNR; *Willoughby,* Lt. Joseph P. E. Brouillette.

17. ZAMBOANGA

Rear Adm. Forrest B. Royal, commander of the amphibious group that was to put troops of the Eighth Army's 41st Infantry Division ashore at Zamboanga, on Mindanao, requested that PT's start operations as early as possible, to work with aircraft in destroying any enemy suicide boats or PT's that might imperil the invasion forces. Since little enemy air reaction was anticipated, Squadrons 8 and 24, under Lt. Robert A. Williamson, USNR, arrived in the assault area with *Oyster Bay* on March 9, the day before the first landings.[39]   For the first few days *Oyster Bay* remained in the assault area during the day and retired at night to guerrilla-held Sibuco Bay on the west side of Zamboanga Peninsula. Later the tender shifted to a sheltered anchorage in the Pilas Islands to the southwest of Zamboanga.

Operating independently at night and in cooperation with Morotai-based Army bombers during the daytime, the PT's destroyed many small craft around Zamboanga, at Basilan Island to the south, and in the Sulu Archipelago to the southwest. Several fruitful air-sea strikes were made in narrow Isabela Channel, between Basilan and the smaller island of Malamaui. The bag for these forays included two enemy PT boats and a number of smaller craft believed to be suicide boats.

On March 15, Lt. (jg.) William H. Suttenfield, Jr., USNR, with Lt. (jg.) R. B. Mack's PT 114 and Ens. George J. Larson's PT 189, covered by two Mitchell bombers, struck at Jolo City, 80 miles southwest of Zamboanga in the Sulu Archipelago. While the PT's destroyed two luggers, a barge, and six other small craft at the docks, the Mitchells dropped bombs on supply dumps, starting several large fires and setting off one ammunition dump with a blast that threw flame and smoke thousands of feet in the air. Guerrilla reports later indicated that this patrol had wiped out all of the craft owned by the Japanese on Jolo, and that the Japanese thereafter had to resort to native canoes and small sailboats for movement of their troops.

"The immense success of Motor Torpedo Boat-Plane Patrol Teams was clearly illustrated during this operation," Admiral Royal said in his report of the invasion of Zamboanga. "The fine cooperation that was accomplished resulted in the destruction of many prime targets, inland and along the beaches, especially the destruction of small surface craft, and contributed to making this operation free from suicide boat attacks."

---

[39] The squadron commanders and tender commanding officer were: Squadron 8, Lt. Robert A. Williamson, USNR, Squadron 24, Lt. Edgar D. Hogland, USNR; *Oyster Bay*, Lt. Comdr. Walter W. Holroyd, USNR.

It was planned to install an advance base for PT's at Caldera Point, 7 miles east of the town of Zamboanga, and the advance base unit was unloaded on the beach. Japanese infiltrated through the thinly held defense perimeter of the 41st Division and brought the camp area under heavy mortar and 75mm. fire. Seabees of the PT Advance Base Construction Detachment and base personnel worked swiftly under enemy fire to move the base equipment to safety. They saved more than two-thirds of the equipment and suffered only two minor casualties to personnel.

The Army made unopposed landings on Basilan Island on March 16, and on Malamaui on the 18th. Since plans called for establishment of a major repair and overhaul PT base at Puerto Isabela on Basilan Island, the advance base was installed on Malamaui Island, across Isabela Channel from Puerto Isabela.

By the end of March, enemy water traffic along the Zamboanga Peninsula and through the Sulu Archipelago had dried up. Seaplane tender *Pocomoke* anchored on April 25 at Tawi Tawi at the southern end of the archipelago to service Navy patrol planes for operations over Borneo. Afterwards PT's began to run down the archipelago from Malamaui, refuel from *Pocomoke,* and strike at targets in northeastern Borneo, usually by daylight, under cover of Army fighters from Zamboanga or Navy patrol bombers from *Pocomoke.*

On the morning of April 26, Lt. (jg.) Earle P. Brown's PT 122 and Ens. George J. Larson's PT 189, patrolling in Darvel Bay, Borneo, pounded a small freighter to pieces with repeated 40mm. and 37mm. hits, and on the following morning destroyed a 100-foot junk in the same area. One of the most successful of the early Borneo strikes was that led by Lt. F. Gardner Cox, USNR, against the town of Lahad Datu in Darvel Bay during daylight on April 30 and May 1. On this patrol Ens. George I. Cook's PT 129 and Ens. B. E. Burtch's PT 144 destroyed 12 small craft and damaged 3 more while the covering Mariner patrol bomber of VPB 20 strafed 6 barges anchored up a river and set fire to a fuel dump. As the boats were returning from patrol, they intercepted a raft and an outrigger canoe, from which they captured 12 Japanese sailors attempting to escape from Bongao Island, near Tawi Tawi, to Borneo.

18. PANAY

The situation in the Philippines after the Zamboanga landings was summarized in a report by Lt. Gen. Robert L. Eichelberger, Commanding General Eighth Army. "By the middle of March 1945," he said, "the campaign

for the liberation of the Philippines had successfully passed the climactic
stage. The original American toeholds on the periphery of the archipelago
had, by a combination of multiple amphibious assaults on the beaches and
protracted engagements in the mountains, been expanded until they formed
an almost continuous ring around the islands.

"On Leyte and Samar to the east, the last of the Japanese remnants were
being destroyed. On Luzon to the north, the enemy defenses were disin-
tegrating as Manila fell to the forces of liberation. Mindoro, Marinduque,
and the miscellaneous island groups astride the overwater routes through the
Visayas were in the final mop-up stage. The enemy's grip on Palawan on
the western edge of the archipelago had been broken and our operations
in Zamboanga (western Mindanao) and the Sulu Archipelago had disrupted
his communication and evacuation routes to the south. With the only remaining escape route to eastern Mindanao dominated by our motor torpedo boats
and our air superiority established everywhere, the central Philippines had
been turned into a vast trap. Embattled conquerors but a few months before,
the Japanese garrisons in the islands were now condemned prisoners facing
ultimate capture or annihilation."

The PT's at Ormoc already were lending support to the Army's mopping-
up operations in the eastern part of the central Philippines. On March 18,
when elements of the Eighth Army landed in the Tigbauan area of the island
of Panay, Squadron 33, under Lt. A. Murray Preston, USNR, arrived off
the southwestern coast of Panay with tender *Portunus* (Lt. Comdr. Ralph E.
McKinnie, USNR) to support the consolidation of the western portion of
the central Philippines. After the Army took Iloilo City on March 20, a
small advance base was installed there for the PT's, permitting withdrawal
of the *Portunus* on April 2.

Since the Japanese in the islands were, as Lieutenant General Eichelberger
said, "condemned prisoners" and had no hope of reinforcement, there was
little for the PT's to do. Although they patrolled the coasts of Panay
and Negros religiously from the middle of March to the middle of July,
they found less than a dozen surface craft, all of which they sank or
destroyed.

19. EAST TO DAVAO

Our holdings in Mindanao were advanced 140 miles eastward on April 17,
when the 24th Division landed at Malabang and Parang, across Moro Gulf
from eastern Zamboanga. Accompanying the invaders were Squadron 24,

under Lt. Edgar D. Hogland, USNR, and *Portunus* (Lt. Comdr. Ralph E. McKinnie, USNR). A small advance base was shipped in, for installation at Polloc Harbor, but in view of the Army's rapid overland advance to the east and the complete absence of enemy waterborne traffic, the base equipment was not even unloaded.

Since there was little likelihood of encountering Japanese aircraft or submarines off the southern Mindanao coast, Captain Bowling tried a new experiment: using a tender as a mobile base to support a long-range strike into Davao Gulf and at the islands off the southern tip of Mindanao. On the morning of April 26, *Oyster Bay* (Lt. Comdr. Walter W. Holroyd, USNR) rendezvoused with PT's 343, 332, 334, 336, 340 and 342 of Squadron 24 twenty miles south of Matil Point, Mindanao, and began fueling them. That night *Oyster Bay* retired to sea and two sections of PT's patrolled in Davao Gulf, the first Allied surface units to enter the gulf since the Japanese occupation. Each patrol was bombed ineffectively by a Japanese plane, in the first and last attacks on PT's by enemy aircraft in the Davao area. After the first night, *Oyster Bay* moved into Canalasan Cove in Sarangani Bay, which was found to be held by guerrillas, but continued to retire seaward at night after she had finished fueling and servicing the boats. The experiment was entirely successful, though something of a disappointment, since the PT's found no enemy shipping.

Oyster Bay and the six boats returned to Polloc Harbor on April 30. Two days later the entire squadron moved with *Portunus* to Sarangani Bay. In the meantime the Army's overland drive had reached Davao Gulf, and by May 6 *Portunus* was able to move into the gulf and drop anchor in Malalag Bay.

Lacking enemy surface contacts, the PT's performed many special missions, landing Army scouts and Navy intelligence personnel around Davao Gulf to gather information of Japanese troop movements. They also launched a series of air-sea strikes with Navy bombers, damaging shore installations in Davao Gulf and the Sarangani Islands.

The most spectacular of these strikes, which developed into a series of actions continuing over a period of 7 days, began on May 14, when Lieutenant Hogland, with Lt. (jg.) Luther C. Evans's PT 343, Lt. (jg.) Byrne C. Fernelius's PT 335, and the LCI gunboat 21, rendezvoused with a Navy Mitchell bomber in northeastern Davao Gulf. At Piso Point the PT's destroyed a cargo barge and launch on the beach and all units of the group strafed buildings and three pillboxes. The PT's approached a little cove behind Piso Point but did not enter because of shoal water at the entrance. Hogland surveyed the shoreline of the cove with binoculars at a distance of 400 yards. Seeing nothing but a dense growth of mangroves, he pulled out and continued his patrol to the north. The LCI, remaining behind, destroyed a 50-foot launch and set fire to an oil dump at nearby Pangasinan Point. Just before noon the Mitchell bomber reported that it had discovered two enemy PT's hidden in the mangroves at Piso Point.

PT's 343 and 335 returned, and searched out a deep narrow channel leading through the shoals into the cove. There they found six Japanese PT's tucked away under the mangroves, so cleverly camouflaged with green netting, freshly cut brush, and palm leaves that they could not be seen at a distance greater than 100 yards, and then only with the aid of binoculars. Soon after the boats opened fire they shot away the camouflage from an enemy PT, which was then seen to be resting in a graving dock. A moment later they exploded its gasoline tanks with 40mm. hits. The boats discovered some gasoline drums on the beach, hit them and set them ablaze. This fire spread to an ammunition dump. There was a tremendous blast of flame, smoke, and debris, rising 300 feet in the air, followed by a series of lesser explosions for the next 3 hours. A second enemy PT blew up with the ammunition dump, and two torpedoes with freshly painted warheads were engulfed in the flames. The boats poured 40mm. shells into four more enemy PT's and a 30-foot launch, and set fire to a chemical dump which threw out billowing clouds of pure white smoke. After our boats had been in the cove for nearly 3 hours, three more Mitchell bombers arrived. Hogland withdrew and directed the planes to the targets. They bombed, rocketed, and strafed the area, exploding an inland gasoline and ammunition dump and setting fire to an oil dump.

Early the next morning, Ens. John Adams, USNR, returning with PT's 332 and 334 from a night patrol in northern Davao Gulf, approached Piso Point. He observed seven small explosions in the inner cove and a huge explosion of an ammunition dump near a dock in the outer cove. The enemy apparently was destroying his own material. PT's 332 and 334 strafed the shoreline of the outer cove and returned to Malalag Bay.

Two hours later Lieutenant Hogland, in Lt. (jg.) Donald Maley's PT 106, with Ens. D. A. Zoeller's PT 341, rendezvoused off Piso Point with the destroyer escort *Key*, the LCI gunboats 21 and 22, and four Navy Mitchell bombers. Hogland took PT 106 within 400 yards of the cove and began strafing to feel out the enemy. Whereas he had met no return fire the day before, this time he was greeted by steady streams of machinegun and rifle fire. With bullets splashing 10 feet from the 106, he withdrew and boarded the *Key* to spot targets. The *Key* shelled the cove at 1,800 yards range, starting three large fires and blowing up a gasoline dump. Hogland then transferred to LCI gunboat 21 and took her within 400 yards of the beach for closer bombardment. Her guns exploded a chemical dump and set fire to an oil dump. After the bombardment Hogland took PT's 106 and 341 into the inner cove under close air support, and at 75 yards range shelled the four enemy PT's damaged the previous day. Three of them caught fire and burned with heavy explosions. The fourth was seen to be one-third consumed by fire from the previous day's shelling. The boats riddled the remaining portion with 40mm. hits and it was considered destroyed. The boats discovered still another heavily camouflaged PT, and it, too, was set afire and burned with many explosions. By the time the PT's withdrew, the destroyer *Flusser* had arrived. With Hogland aboard to spot targets, the *Flusser* shelled the cove from 4,000 yards, exploding a chemical dump. The Mitchell bombers touched off an ammunition dump.

On the morning of May 16, Hogland was back at Piso Point with PT's 334 and 340. Since it was raining hard and visibility was poor, he did not enter the inner cove, but stood off and strafed the point. At noon four Corsair fighters bombed and strafed the cove, starting an oil fire. Then, as the weather continued to close in, the boats and planes departed.

The next morning Hogland returned with Lieutenant Evans's PT 343 and Lt. (jg.) R. J. Lewis's PT 336, under cover of four Navy Mitchell bombers. Hogland and his squadron intelligence officer, Lt. Hugh Kenworthy, Jr., USNR, paddled toward shore in a canoe to inspect the enemy PT hulks. Twenty yards from shore, five sniper bullets splashed near the canoe. Startled, the officers capsized their craft. They righted it and took shelter on the offshore side of one of the hulks. They were about to board it when they discovered that it was boobytrapped, with wires leading to two mines in the water. Before further sniper fire persuaded them to return to PT 343, they saw a camouflaged barge hidden away 10 yards inland. The boats fired 100 rounds of 40mm. in the direction of the barge, though they were unable to see it. The planes, trying to hit the barge with bombs, touched off another ammunition dump.

On the morning of May 18, Hogland, with Ens. John Adams's PT 332 and Ens. R. M. Brittingham's PT 334, covered by three Dauntless scout bombers.

discovered and sank two more camouflaged barges, and, with the help of the planes, located the barge they had been firing at blindly the previous day. The boats had damaged it severely when a Navy Mitchell bomber arrived and made a direct hit with a 250-pound bomb. On the same day other PT's on an intelligence mission at the nearby village of Magdug interrogated a local resident of Russian extraction, who told them that the Japanese had been evacuating Piso Point since the first strike on May 14.

Hogland again brought two PT's, the 343 and 106, to Piso Point on the 19th and strafed the entire area at range of 100 yards, receiving no return fire. The boats destroyed a 30-foot sailboat on the beach 1 mile north of the point. The climactic end of the strikes against Piso Point came on the following morning, May 20, when Hogland, with the same two PT's, vectored 24 Liberator bombers onto the target. The planes saturated the entire area with 36 tons of bombs. Subsequent inspection by the PT's revealed that the enemy's PT base had ceased to exist.

Thereafter the Davao boats continued their scouting missions and strafing of shore installations, and supported several minor landings by Army units in mopping-up operations, but they had almost no contacts with enemy surface craft.

20. TARAKAN

With the Philippine campaign drawing to a close, the Allied invasion of Borneo was ready to get underway. An American Naval Task Force under Rear Adm. Forrest B. Royal was to transport Australian troops from Morotai and land them on the island of Tarakan, northeast Borneo, on May 1, 1945. Admiral Royal requested that PT's start operations in the Tarakan area in advance of the landings as a precaution against suicide boats and enemy PT's, and to prevent the Japanese from repairing the gaps which Allied Engineer Assault Teams were to make in the beach obstacles in preparation for the invasion.

Squadron 36 and *Wachapreague,* under tactical command of Lt. Comdr. Francis D. Tappaan, USNR, arrived at Tawi Tawi in the Sulu Archipelago on April 27. PT's began moving down to Tarakan on the 28th to illuminate and strafe the beaches at night to prevent the Japanese from repairing their obstacles. Until the arrival of the *Wachapreague* on May 1, these boats refueled from cruisers of the covering force.

80–G–345827

A 5-inch rocket blazes ahead of a PT in test firing in the Philippines. Tubes of the port rocket launcher may be seen at extreme left. Just to their right is a 20mm. gun. In center is a mortar, used for firing illuminating flares and lobbing explosive shells. On bow is a 37mm. gun and aft of it another 20mm. The boat also carries a rocket launcher and 20mm. gun on the starboard side, two pairs of .50-caliber machineguns, a 40mm. gun, and two depth charges.

On the night of April 29/30, Lt. John W. Morrison, USNR, the squadron commander, patrolled Tarakan Roads with Lt. N. J. Russell, Jr.'s PT 523 and Lt. (jg.) B. M. Stephens's PT 532. Early in the evening they set fire to a small anchored freighter with a 37mm. hit. It burned for more than 9 hours, emitting great clouds of dense black smoke. Ten minutes after setting the freighter ablaze, the boats found five luggers and a motor launch near a pier at Lingkas Town on Tarakan. Because of reported minefields near the shore, Morrison stood off at 800 yards and opened fire on the luggers, but scored only a few scattered hits. He decided to try the new 5-inch spin stabilized rockets carried by the 532. The 532 fired a full load of 16 rockets, sinking 1 lugger and damaging 2 others beyond repair. The 523 then sank the motor launch and damaged the other two luggers with 40mm. hits. On the following night Lt. (jg.) A. J. Hanes's PT 525 together with 529, 522 and 531, found one of the two damaged luggers and finished it off with gunfire.

The landings went off on schedule and with little opposition. The PT's found no suicide boats or enemy PT's, but during their first 10 days at Tarakan sank or destroyed a dozen or more small craft—luggers, barges, and lighters—in addition to those destroyed during the preinvasion patrols. In May the PT's found that they had to search out their targets by patrolling up the Sesajap and Sekata Rivers and in the narrow channels of the deltas of these rivers. On May 8, Lt. G. S. Wright's PT 528 and Lt. (jg.) B. M. Stephens's PT 532 found a small freighter 4 miles up the Morutai River and sank it with gunfire.

On most of their patrols the PT's carried NICA interpreters who interrogated natives and asked them to capture and hold Japanese prisoners for the PT's. The natives, friendly to the Dutch, were only too happy to comply. A prize catch came on June 12, when natives handed over a prisoner who had in his possession an excellent map of the remaining Japanese defenses on Tarakan Island.

As Japanese resistance on Tarakan came to an end, the Australian Army requested the PT's to patrol the northeastern side of the island to prevent the escape of enemy personnel to the Borneo mainland. The boats captured many Japanese trying to paddle away in dugouts and canoes, and killed others who resisted capture. One morning shortly after dawn, a PT patrol spotted a floating clump of nipa palms, a sight not unusual in those waters. The boats investigated it and found that it was actually a camouflaged raft, with nine Japanese in the water clinging to one side. The Japanese fired at the PT's with rifles. The PT's killed four of them and took the other five prisoner.

21. TAWI TAWI

While the Tarakan PT's patrolled the Borneo coast as far north as Cowie Bay, the boats from Zamboanga, fueling from *Pocomoke* at Tawi Tawi, were striking at targets along the coast above Cowie Bay, principally in the Darvel Bay region. In order to facilitate these operations and to extend the range of the patrols along the northeastern Borneo coast, Squadron 8, under Lt. William C. Godfrey, moved on May 21 with the *Oyster Bay* to an anchorage in Chongos Bay, Tawi Tawi. Boats of Squadron 9, under Lt. Richard M. Monahon, USNR, arrived in Chongos Bay 2 days later.

The most successful of their early operations began at dawn on May 27, when Lieutenant Monahon led nine PT's, covered by eight RAAF Kittyhawk fighters and four Navy Mariner bombers, into the harbor of Sandakan.[40] The PT's ran at 35 knots through the narrow harbor entrance, laying smoke as a protection against the enemy fortifications. Several 75mm. shells dropped near the boats without causing damage. PT's 126, 154, and 155 each fired two torpedoes at harbor installations. Two hit the government dock, shattering pilings, leaving the dock sagging, and sinking three small launches alongside. Another overturned a 300-foot finger pier, sank three launches alongside, ripped up the tracks of a marine railway, and blew the stern off a small freighter on the railway. For 2½ hours, under spasmodic machinegun fire from shore, the PT's strafed and rocketed harbor installations. They destroyed three more launches, heavily damaged a 100-foot lugger, and set fire to warehouses, buildings, and a sawmill which was reported to house enemy suicide craft. The planes strafed and bombed the town heavily, damaging other buildings and knocking out a shore battery that was giving the boats trouble. The cost to the PT's was minor wounds to one officer and three men.

Two days later Lt. (jg.) F. W. Weidmann's PT 130 and Ens. B. E. Burtch's PT 144 entered Sandakan Harbor and observed nine large fires burning in the town. The boats destroyed a canoe and damaged a 60-foot sea truck, two barges, three sloops, two canoes, a motor launch, and a gig. These and subsequent raids caused the enemy to evacuate the town.

During their first 2 weeks at Tawi Tawi, the PT's destroyed or damaged upwards of 70 surface craft. Thereafter most of their activity was restricted, for lack of other targets, to strafing and rocketing shore installations, usually in cooperation with aircraft. These strikes eventually resulted in Japanese evacuation of Lahad Datu and several other coastal towns.

The PT's performed many special missions for guerrilla forces and for the Australian Intelligence Bureau. A few examples:

On June 3, Lieutenant Weidmann's PT 130 and Ens. George J. Larson's PT 189, escorted by PT's 142 and 143, towed four native craft loaded with guerrilla troops to Banguey Island, where the guerrillas landed and captured a Japanese fish cannery.

On the mornings of June 26 and 27, Lt. Mack L. Kennedy, USNR, led Lt. (jg.) Richard M. Dicke's PT 187 and Lt. (jg.) Charles J. Moran, Jr.'s PT 160 in close-range strafing of the town of Beluran in Labuk Bay to

---

[40] PT 126, Lt. (jg.) J. L. McKay, USNR; PT 154, Lt. (jg.) J. Harvey DuBose, USNR; PT 155, Lt. (jg.)P. A. Rodgers, USNR; PT 114, Lt. (jg.) M. H. Berry, USNR; PT 12, Lt. (jg.) M. R. Allen, USNR; PT 130, Lt. (jg.) F. W. Weidmann, USNR; PT 142, Lt. (jg.) R. W. Clifford, USNR; PT 149, Lt. (jg.) A. D. Brice, USNR; PT 189, Ens. George J. Larson, Jr., USNR.

distract attention from the landing of an Australian scouting party at nearby Samarang Point. The diversionary operation was entirely successful and the boats did considerable damage to buildings in Beluran. During the runs on the second morning, made only 50 yards offshore in daylight, one man was killed by a rifle bullet and two were wounded by shell fragments.

Lt. (jg.) J. Harvey DuBose's PT 154, searching for a downed Navy Mariner patrol bomber on July 2, found it north of Labuk Bay, afloat but unable to take off. PT 154 towed the plane back to its tender, the *Pocomoke*, at Tawi Tawi, covering the distance of more than 200 miles in a little less than 23 hours.

22. BRUNEI BAY

Troops of the 9th Australian Division landed at Brunei Bay, on the western coast of Borneo, on June 10. PT's 78, 81, 82 and 84 which had staged from Mindoro and refueled at Puerto Princesa on Palawan patrolled the assault area on the night before the invasion, and were joined at Brunei Bay on the 10th by other boats of Squadrons 13 and 16 and the tender *Willoughby*.[41]

---

[41] The squadron commanders and tender commanding officer were: Squadron 13, Lt. Comdr. Alvin W. Fargo, Jr., USNR; Squadron 16, Lt. Roger H. Hallowell, USNR; *Willoughby*, Lt. Joseph P. E. Brouillette.

NR&L (MOD)—32515

PT advance base at Brunei Bay, Borneo. The terrain was low and swampy, so most of the men lived in tents on the dock.

During the first few days the boats destroyed a 60-foot sailing vessel and damaged half a dozen barges. On the night of June 18, in a heavy rain with low visibility, PT's 241 and 223 on patrol twice sighted the periscope of a midget submarine and attacked with depth charges, but the water was so shallow that the charges, set to detonate at 30 feet, did not explode.

After that the PT's ran out of targets. The disheartened Japanese were making their retreat to the southward by land, and little remained for the PT's to do except strafe and mortar enemy positions along the coast and make strikes with RAAF planes against shore installations at enemy-held oil centers such as Jesselton, Miri, and Kudat.

23. BALIKPAPAN

The final invasion in the Southwest Pacific Area was made on July 1, 1945, when troops of the 7th Australian Division were landed at the great oil port of Balikpapan in southeastern Borneo. As at Tarakan, the amphibious attack group commander wished PT's to start patrolling before the landings to prevent the enemy from rebuilding beach obstacles destroyed by our underwater demolition teams, and to forestall any attempt by the enemy to molest navigational buoys laid by our minesweepers. Accordingly, four PT's of Squadron 10, four of Squadron 27, and the tender *Mobjack,* under tactical command of Lt. Comdr. Francis D. Tappaan, USNR, arrived in the assault area on June 27. The boats had no contact with enemy surface craft in the immediate vicinity of Balikpapan. By strafing and rocketing the shore, however, they accomplished their primary mission of keeping the enemy away from the beaches.

On the day of the landings, *Varuna* arrived with eight more PT's, and the task unit was brought up to full strength on July 6 with the arrival of the last seven boats of the two squadrons.[42]

Early in July, patrols were extended to the Little Paternoster Islands in Macassar Strait and to the western coast of Celebes, across the strait from Borneo. On the night of July 9/10, Lt. Alexander W. Allison's PT 373 and Lt. (jg.) Charles S. Welsh's PT 359, with Lt. Frank I. Manter, USNR, as section leader, were sent to destroy a reported enemy radar station on Bala-

---

[42] The squadron commanders and tender commanding officers were: Squadron 10, Lt. Francis H. McAdoo Jr., USNR; Squadron 27, Lt. Henry S. Taylor, USNR; *Mobjack,* Lt. Comdr. John H. McClain, USNR; *Varuna,* Lt. Carl J. Kalb.

balagan Island in the Little Paternoster group. The boats did a thorough job of strafing huts and buildings and a 130-foot tower on the island, in the face of machinegun and rifle fire that killed one man and wounded another. On the morning of July 14, Lt. Rogers V. Waugh, in PT 163, with Lt. (jg.) Harold A. Sparks's PT 167 and Lt. E. L. Harrison's PT 170, returned to the island and gave the buildings and tower a working over with rockets and mortar shells as well as with guns. A subsequent landing on the island revealed that electronic equipment in the buildings and tower had been destroyed. There were six fresh graves and one dead Japanese soldier on the island.

The patrols to the western coast of Celebes were so long that the boats had to run to and from station on two engines to save fuel. Yet it was only along the Celebes coast that the PT's found any enemy shipping, and even there the traffic quickly dried up after the boats sank a few large prahaus. The boats had their most rewarding action on July 22 when Lieutenant Waugh's PT 163, Lieutenant Harrison's PT 170, and Lt. (jg.) Robert L. Baker's PT 174 made a daylight strike on Paloe Bay, Celebes, with RAAF Kittyhawk fighters. The combined boat-and-plane attack resulted in the destruction of four prahaus and heavy damage to a hotel, a dock, and many houses in Dongala town. As the boats made their way back to Balikpapan, they could see smoke from four large fires 30 miles at sea.

24. MTBRONSPAC

The period of June and July 1945 was characterized by the disappearance of PT targets in all operating areas of the Southwest Pacific except for Morotai, where the boats continued to encounter enemy small craft because of the static land situation and the imminence of large enemy concentrations on Halmahera. As the Philippine campaign drew to a close, plans were made to transfer squadrons and tenders from the Seventh Fleet to the Pacific Fleet for operations to the North in which the Seventh Fleet would not take part. The command, Motor Torpedo Boat Squadrons Pacific Fleet, had been revived after a period of desuetude, and was preparing to assume the major burden of PT warfare in the Pacific.

This command had its beginning on May 1, 1944, when Commodore Edward J. Moran reported for additional duty as Commander Motor Torpedo Boat Squadrons Pacific Fleet (ComMTBRonsPac). In effect, Commodore Moran acquired a title only, since he was already Commander Motor Torpedo Boat Squadrons South Pacific, and he did not gain jurisdiction over any more squadrons in his new command than he had in his old one. By the first of December 1944, he had transferred all of his old squadrons and tenders to the Seventh Fleet, and his command was reduced to Squadrons 31, 32, and 37, and the tenders *Acontius* and *Silenus,* newly arrived in the Solomons from the United States.

By March 1, 1945, Squadron 31 had been sent to Palau, under operational command of the local naval commander, and the other two squadrons were at Espiritu Santo, New Hebrides, under operational control of the Commander South Pacific Force, awaiting transportation to an operating area. Commodore Moran had been given administrative control of a fourth squadron, Squadron 26 at Pearl Harbor, but this unit was under operational control of the Commander Destroyers Pacific Fleet.

Commodore Moran left the Solomons in March under orders to report to the Navy Department for temporary duty. Since only four squadrons remained under the administrative control and none under the operational control of ComMTBRonsPac, and no decision had been reached as to the future of the command, he detached all his staff personnel except one supply officer, Lt. J. I. Everest, USNR, and one chief yeoman. He ordered Lieutenant Everest to assume temporary additional duty as ComMTBRonsPac (Administrative), and to hold down the fort until such time as the status of the command might be clarified.

Lieutenant Everest held down the fort until May 20, 1945, when Commodore Richard W. Bates assumed duties as ComMTBRonsPac. After inspecting the units of his command, Commodore Bates prepared for the Commander in Chief Pacific Fleet an estimate for motor torpedo boat operations in the invasion of the Japanese home island of Kyushu. He then went to work to form his staff organization aboard his flagship, *Acontius,* which he had had moved to Leyte Gulf.

In June, Commodore Bates began moving his squadrons to Okinawa. Squadron 31, commanded by Lt. Robert L. Searles, USNR, had moved from Palau to Leyte Gulf in March. Its first boats, shipped from Leyte by LSD *Whitemarsh,* arrived in Okinawa on June 18. During July, PT's of Squadron 31 carried out several successful air-sea rescue missions and maintained nightly "fly-catcher patrols" to stop evacuation from Okinawa. In the course of these patrols they sank a lugger and six canoes, all loaded with troops seeking to escape.

80-G-326551

PT's of Squadron 37 being eased into their cradles in Oak Hill (LSD 7) *at Espiritu Santo on July 24, 1945, for shipment to Okinawa. The LSD submerges to let the PT's enter her well deck. When six PT's are safely aboard in their cradles, the LSD refloats herself and is ready to get underway.*

The first boats of Squadron 37, shipped by LSD *Oak Hill* from Espiritu Santo, arrived at Okinawa on August 8. They had no action with the enemy. Squadron 32, the rest of Squadron 37, and the tenders *Silenus* and *Antigone,* did not reach Okinawa until after the end of hostilities.

Besides these three squadrons, Commodore Bates had two new squadrons, 39 and 40, en route to Leyte from the United States, and the Huckins Squadron 26, a permanent fixture at Pearl Harbor.

Captain Bowling was ordered in June to transfer a tender to Commodore Bates to take care of Squadron 31. The *Portunus* was transferred on July 15, and arrived at Okinawa on July 21. On the same day Captain Bowling received orders to prepare to transfer eight squadrons of Elco PT's three squadrons of Higgins PT's, and five tenders to ComMTBRonsPac. Commodore Bates requested, however, that these squadrons and tenders remain in the Seventh Fleet organization until such time as he might need them for combat operations.

The original plans for Operation Olympic, the projected invasion of the Japanese home islands, made no provision for PT operations. Subsequent to the drafting of the operation plan, however, the Commander Amphibious Force Pacific Fleet asked Commodore Bates to submit a plan for use of PT's off Japan, and subordinate commanders of the Amphibious Force made requests on him to provide more than 200 PT's for use in connection with the invasion. Hostilities ended before the plan could be submitted.

25. SURRENDER

After the cessation of hostilities, the Seventh Fleet prepared to move westward from the Philippines to patrol Chinese and Korean waters. Admiral Kinkaid, foreseeing no need for PT's in this assignment, ordered Captain Bowling to report with his squadrons and tenders to the Commander Philippine Sea Frontier for duty. On the morning of August 28, 1945, Motor Torpedo Boat Squadrons Seventh Fleet became Motor Torpedo Boat Squadrons Philippine Sea Frontier.

The shooting was over, but there were still a few jobs for the boats to do in connection with the surrender of Japanese forces in the islands.

At Morotai, on the morning of August 25, 16 PT's under Lt. Comdr. Theodore R. Stansbury, USNR, got underway for a rendezvous with the

commanders of the Japanese forces on Halmahera. With Stansbury on PT
115 were Maj. Gen. Harry H. Johnson, Commanding General of the Morotai-
based 93d Division, and members of his staff. Near Miti Island off northeast
Halmahera, the PT's met a party of Japanese officers in two small barges.
The meeting was a disappointment, as the Japanese commanding general
had not come himself, but had sent his chief of staff and operations officer.
General Johnson gave the Japanese firm instructions to have the Army and
Navy commanders present on the following morning.

The next day General Johnson sent Brig. Gen. Warren H. McNaught with
six PT's to fetch the Japanese. This time Lieutenant General Ishii, Commanding General, Japanese Forces, Halmahera, and Captain Fujita, Naval
Commander, Japanese Forces, Halmahera, were waiting for the PT's. The
boats carried them to 93d Division headquarters on Morotai, where they surrendered 37,000 troops, 4,000 Japanese civilians, and a vast quantity of
equipment, including 19,000 rifles, 900 cannon, and 600 machineguns. Such
was the size of the force that the Morotai PT's had held at bay for almost
a year.

While the PT's took no part in the surrender of the Morotai garrison, this
surrender brought them an interesting bit of news. The garrison commander, Colonel Ouchi, reported that since May 12, when three barges
brought sorely needed supplies from Halmahera, not a single barge had
crossed the 12-mile strait between the two islands. And of those three barges,
two were destroyed by PT's while attempting to return to Halmahera.

In the central Philippines, PT's 489 and 492 of Squadron 33 under Lt.
Comdr. Edwin A. DuBose, USNR, carried U.S. Army personnel and members of a Japanese surrender commission to isolated enemy outposts on the
islands of Samar, Masbate, and Romblon, to accept surrender of more than
500 Japanese troops.

At Balikpapan on the morning of September 8, Lt. Comdr. Henry S.
Taylor, USNR, led seven PT's to a rendezvous in the delta of the Koetai
River with Vice Admiral Kamada and his party. The boats carried the Japa-
nese to HMAS *Burdekin* at Balikpapan and slowly circled the ship as
Admiral Kamada signed documents surrendering all Japanese forces in the
area.

The most extensive operations in connection with the surrender were carried out by *Willoughby* and the Brunei Bay PT's, under Lt. Comdr. Alvin W.
Fargo, Jr., USNR, in the vicinity of Kuching, capital of Sarawak.

"On 10 September 1945," Captain Bowling reported, "the USS *Wil-*

loughby, after loading 50 tons of supplies and embarking 38 officers and 318 men of the 9th Australian Division at Labuan Island [Brunei Bay], got underway for Tanjong Po, off the mouth of the Sarawak River. Six PT's rendezvoused en route. Upon arrival at Tanjong Po, on the 11th of September, five of the PT's took aboard 180 troops from the USS *Willoughby.* The sixth boat embarked Capt. W. C. Jennings, USN; Comdr. J. P. Engle, USNR, and Lt. Comdr. A. W. Fargo, USNR, who were the naval officers invited to attend the surrender ceremonies set for 1400 the same day aboard HMAS *Kapunda,* an Australian corvette. This latter PT also carried officers and men charged with press coverage of the surrender. The six PT's and HMAS *Kapunda* then proceeded up the Sarawak River to Pending (the junction of the Kuap and Sarawak Rivers) where the Japanese surrender party was scheduled to board the *Kapunda.* After arrival at Pending, three of the PT's continued up river to Kuching, for reconnaissance purposes, then returned to Pending. Although both river banks and the docks at Kuching were found crowded with cheering natives and scattered Jap troops, no incident occurred.

"At 1430 the Japanese surrender party had not yet arrived and an Australian crash boat was despatched to bring Major General Yamamura, the Jap com-

In September 1945, PT's from Brunei Bay evacuated hundreds of internees, including women and children, from Kuching, Borneo.

mander, and his party to HMAS *Kapunda*. When the boat returned and reported General Yamamura was indisposed, Brigadier T. C. Eastrick, commander of the Kuching force, ordered Yamamura aboard. At 1500 the Jap commander, his chief of staff and two other officers arrived. After a short discussion the surrender was signed. The Jap party left the ship at 1600. Shortly thereafter the six PT's proceeded to Kuching and disembarked the first Australian reoccupation troops in the Sarawak capital.

"On the following morning the majority of the remaining Australian troops on the USS *Willoughby* were taken aboard the PT's and transported to Kuching. Two LCT's unloaded the *Willoughby*'s 50 tons of stores and few remaining troops.

"On the 12th and 13th of September the PT's evacuated 210 Allied prisoners-of-war and internees from Kuching and loaded them aboard the USS *Willoughby*. Included in the group were Harry H. Stone, SC2c, of Peoria, Ill., and Harold E. McManus, S1c, of Cherokee, Iowa, two enlisted survivors of the USS *Houston,* who had been captured 2 March 1942. Several additional stretcher cases were discharged by the boats aboard the Australian hospital ship *Manunda* off Tanjong Po. The USS *Willoughby* and her PT's got underway on the afternoon of 13 September for Labuan Island. On the evening of the 14th, the *Willoughby* stood into Victoria Harbor, Labuan Island, and discharged all evacuees.

"On the 18th the USS *Willoughby*, with 15 officers and 325 men of the 9th Australian Division and 50 tons of supplies, departed Labuan Island for Tanjong Po. The tender was joined en route by four PT's. All arrived on the morning of the 19th. Each of the 4 PT's took aboard 50 troops from the *Willoughby* and proceeded to Kuching when they backloaded with 97 evacuees, including 2 women, all of whom were transferred to the *Willoughby*. The *Willoughby*'s 50 tons of supplies were loaded on the Australian corvette. That afternoon the four PT's returned to Kuching and the USS *Willoughby* got underway for Brunei Bay.

"On the afternoon of 20 September the *Willoughby* arrived at Victoria Harbor, Labuan Island, and discharged her 201 evacuees.

"Again on 22 September, the *Willoughby* stood out of Victoria Harbor with 8 officers and 194 men of the 9th Australian Division and another 50 tons of supplies aboard, for Tanjong Po. She arrived on the morning of the 23d and rendezvoused with the four PT's previously left behind. The 4 boats immediately loaded 182 of the *Willoughby*'s troops and transported them to Kuching. An Australian lugger removed the *Willoughby*'s 50 tons of supplies and remaining 20 troops. On that afternoon the four PT's returned from Kuching with 133 Allied prisoners-of-war and internees plus 34 Australian Army personnel, all of whom were transferred to the *Willoughby*. At 1330, the *Willoughby* and the four PT's departed Tanjong Po for Brunei Bay. They arrived on the 24th, and the evacuees and Australian personnel were disembarked at Victoria Harbor, Labuan Island."

26. THE END AND THE BEGINNING

In mid-August 1945, 30 squadrons of PT's were in commission. Nineteen were in the Seventh Fleet, six in the Pacific Fleet, three were being reconditioned in the United States for Pacific duty after combat in the European theater, one was shaking down in Miami, and one was the training squadron at Melville. By the end of the year all had been decommissioned except Squadron 4, the training squadron, and the brand new Squadron 41. In addition there was Squadron 42, which had been fitting out in New York in August, and which was the only PT unit placed in commission after the end of hostilities.

The Navy Department properly got rid of most of its PT's. Their job was done, and because of their light wooden construction, they could not be stored away against future need as the steel-hulled ships of the fleet. Indeed, many of the older boats, which had been kept running because of combat necessity, were no longer worth saving for any purpose. All the boats in the western Pacific were carefully surveyed. It was found that 118 hulls were defective because of broken frames, worms and dry rot, broken keels, cracked longitudinals, or battle damage. These boats were stripped of all salvageable material and the bare hulls were burned on the beach at Samar.

The serviceable boats in the Pacific, after being stripped of armament and other military equipment, were turned over to the Foreign Liquidation Commission, and those in the United States to the War Shipping Administration, for disposal.

Squadrons 4, 41, and 42 were being saved for training purposes but, early in 1946, the Navy Department decided to retain only a few PT's for experimental work. Squadrons 41 and 42 were decommissioned in February and Squadron 4 in April. PT's 613, 616, 619, and 620, new Elco boats originally in Squadron 42 and later in Squadron 4, were transferred to the Operational Development Force—the last PT's remaining in service.

Behind the decision to cut the PT force so drastically there was, besides the obvious reason of economy, a realization that in the end of the old boats was the beginning of a new PT. Because of wartime need for standardization, there had been no major changes in PT design since adoption of the 80-foot Elco and 78-foot Higgins designs in 1941. With the war ended, the Navy could afford to take time to redesign its PT's in the light of 4 years of combat experience.

With increased speed in other combat types, particularly destroyers, PT's too should have more speed. It would be highly desirable to increase their range and improve their sea-keeping qualities as well. At the same time, they should retain their high maneuverability and small size for their own protection, and their shallow draft to permit them to work close to shore. These requirements suggest the possibility that gas turbines may someday replace the present gasoline engines as a method of propulsion.

There undoubtedly will be many developments in armament. Torpedoes should be faster, more powerful, and more reliable. And it may be that rockets someday will supplant torpedoes as the heavy armament of the PT's. This possibility was foreseen by Captain Bowling in October 1944, when he wrote: "Rockets are generally regarded in the Task Group as the greatest potential PT weapon of the war. Their high fire power and low recoil make them ideal for MTB armament. Because of the continuing development of larger caliber and greater range rockets, it is impossible to standardize on a particular type for use by MTB's at this time. However, rockets of sufficient size, power, and range are now available or under development to make replacement of the torpedoes and heavy automatic weapons seem entirely feasible.

"Commander Motor Torpedo Boat Squadrons Seventh Fleet has requested that every rocket development be thoroughly investigated with a view to possible employment by PT's and that the development of a 'motor rocket boat' be considered. If the present ratio of launcher to projector weight is maintained, and all PT armament except the turret twin fifties is removed, it would be possible to carry 5 tons of rocket equipment and deliver 4 tons of projectiles at the target at ranges in excess of 5,000 yards. This would give PT's tremendous fire power—greatly in excess of what they now have.

"The speed of rockets as compared with that of torpedoes should make them easier to hit targets with. With the development of radar on enemy ships, it may be difficult to close them to a few hundred yards for a torpedo hit. Also the reliability of rockets would seem to be much greater than that of torpedoes and they will not require the same painstaking care. It is believed that all these advantages plus the greater weight of explosive which can be delivered to the target, more than compensates for the torpedoes' single advantage of underwater destructive power."

Whatever the details of their construction and armament, the PT's should always be small, fast, shallow draft, highly maneuverable craft, elusive targets themselves, able to hit the enemy hard, and possessing a high degree of versatility. For such craft, until either "pushbutton war" becomes a reality, or until we have achieved everlasting peace, there always will be a use.

Finally, it must be remembered that the best PT is no better than its crew. The success of the PT's depended and always will depend on the ability and valor of their officers and men, on their eagerness to seek out the enemy and to engage him at close quarters. The spirit of their courage and determination, a spirit old in the Navy, was expressed on a sign at the PT base at Bougainville in the Solomons:

80-G-59332

Postscript

Shortly after August 1945, when the construction of four experimental PT boats was authorized, work was begun on several completely new designs that incorporated lessons learned in World War II. In 1951 the Navy accepted these boats—the first post-World War II PT's. All of the boats had aluminum hulls, were powered by four Packard engines of considerably higher horsepower ratings than those used in the older boats, and had speeds in excess of 40 knots. Beyond these characteristics, however, the boats showed considerable variation.

PT 809, the first of the new boats to be tested, was built by the Electric Boat Co. It had a riveted hull which through the use of airframe construction principles was notably lightweight. The overall length of the boat was 98 feet and the maximum beam was 26 feet.

PT 810 was a Bath Iron Works (Bath, Maine) boat whose hull was partly riveted and partly welded. It was a shorter and broader boat than the rest, with dimensions of 89 feet in overall length and 24 feet at the extreme beam.

PT 811 was built by John Trumpy & Sons, Annapolis, Md. An all-welded boat, it was 94 feet in length and 25 feet in its maximum beam.

The last of the experimental boats, and also the largest, was PT 812. This boat was built by the Philadelphia Naval Shipyard and had an overall length of 105 feet and a maximum beam of only 21 feet. It had an all-welded hull with a shape designed to assure high speed in rough seas. However, its speed in calm water did not equal that of the other boats. The 812 was later equipped with gas turbines in lieu of its four Packard engines.

From 1954 to 1959, these boats operated as Motor Torpedo Squadron 1 under the Navy's Operational Development Force. They were thoroughly evaluated both from a tactical and material point of view.

As of 1962, the lessons learned from these boats, as well as their predecessors, continue to be of great value in the never-ending efforts of the Navy to maintain versatile and highly effective seagoing forces.

Composition of the Squadrons

MOTOR TORPEDO BOAT SQUADRON 1

Commissioned July 24, 1940; decommissioned February 9, 1945.
Squadron Commanders:
Lt. EARL S. CALDWELL
July 24, 1940–February 1941
Lt. WILLIAM C. SPECHT
February 1941–February 19, 1942
Lt. CLINTON McKELLAR, Jr.
February 19–24, 1942
Lt. JOHN HARLLEE
February 24–March 12, 1942
Lt. Comdr. CLINTON McKELLAR, Jr.
March 12, 1942–May 1943
Lt. HERBERT J. SHERERTZ, USNR
May–October 1943
Lt. EDWARD M. ERIKSON, USNR
October 1943–February 9, 1945

PT 58' Fisher Boat Works

3, 4 Placed in service July 24, 1940. Transferred under lend-lease to Britain, April 19, 1941.

81' Higgins (Sparkman & Stephens design)

5 Placed in service March 17, 1941. Transferred under lend-lease to Britain, April 19, 1941.

81' Higgins (Higgins design)

6 Placed in service March 6, 1941. This was the second PT 6. The first one, also built by Higgins, but of Sparkman & Stephens design, was sold to Finland in 1940. Transferred under lend-lease to Britain, July 29, 1941.

PT 81' Philadelphia Navy Yard

7 Placed in service November 20, 1940. Transferred under lend-lease to Britain, July 19, 1941.
8 Placed in service October 29, 1940. The only aluminum-hull PT. Transferred to Squadron 2, August 13, 1941.

70' Scott-Paine

9 Placed in service July 24, 1940. Built by British Power Boat Co. Transferred to Squadron 2, November 8, 1940.

77' Elco

20 Transferred from Squadron 2, August 13, 1941. Stricken from Navy Register because of obsolescence, December 22, 1944.
21 Placed in service June 21, 1941. Transferred to Squadron 3(2),* December 22, 1942.
22 Transferred from Squadron 2, August 13, 1941. Badly damaged in storm January 12, 1943; scrapped.
23 Placed in service June 25, 1941. Transferred to Squadron 3(2), December 22, 1942.
24 Transferred from Squadron 2, August 13, 1941. Reclassified as small boat December 12, 1944.

---

*Two squadrons had the number 3 and two had the number 2. The designations "2(2)" and "3(2)" will be used to distinguish the second squadrons from the first.

PT 77' Elco

25 Placed in service June 11, 1941. Transferred to Squadron 3(2), December 22, 1942.

26 Transferred from Squadron 2, August 13, 1941. Transferred to Squadron 3(2), December 22, 1942.

27 Placed in service June 27, 1941. Reclassified as small boat December 12, 1944.

28 Transferred from Squadron 2, August 13, 1941. Wrecked in storm, January 12, 1943.

29 Placed in service July 2, 1941. Stricken from Navy Register because of obsolescence, December 22, 1944.

30 Transferred from Squadron 2, August 13, 1941. Stricken from Navy Register because of obsolesence, March 6, 1944.

31 Placed in service July 8, 1941. Transferred to Squadron 3, August 12, 1941.

33 Placed in service July 11, 1941. Transferred to Squadron 3, August 12, 1941.

35 Placed in service July 16, 1941. Transferred to Squadron 3, August 12, 1941.

37 Placed in service July 18, 1941. Transferred to Squadron 2, August 13, 1941.

39 Placed in service July 21, 1941. Transferred to Squadron 2, August 13, 1941.

PT 77' Elco

41 Placed in service July 23, 1941. Transferred to Squadron 3, August 12, 1941.

42 Transferred from Squadron 2, August 13, 1941. Stricken from Navy Register because of obsolesence, December 12, 1944.

43 Placed in service July 26, 1941. Transferred to Squadron 2, August 13, 1941.

PT's 1 and 2 originally were assigned to Squadron 1. Their completion was so delayed, waiting for their Vimalert engines, that they were outmoded by the time they were delivered. They were not placed in squadron service, but were reclassified as small boats.

Squadron 1 was the first squadron commissioned, and originally was made up of experimental boats. Later, when it was composed of 77' Elco boats, the squadron was sent to Pearl Harbor, where it was in action on December 7, 1941. Its boats again saw action at the Battle of Midway, and participated in the Aleutian campaign. PT's 21, 23, 25, and 26 were on detached duty under command of Lt. Jonathan F. Rice, USNR, at Palmyra Island from July to October 1942. They moved to Funafuti, in the Ellice Group, in November 1942, and were transferred to Squadron 3(2) on December 22, 1942.

MOTOR TORPEDO BOAT SQUADRON 2

Commissioned November 8, 1940; decommissioned November 11, 1943.
Squadron Commanders:
  Lt. Comdr. EARL S. CALDWELL
    November 8, 1940–May 1942.
  Lt. HUGH M. ROBINSON
    May–June 1942.
  Lt. Comdr. ALAN R. MONTGOMERY
    June–July 1942.
  Lt. GEORGE A. BRACKETT, USNR
    July–September 1942.

  Lt. ROLLIN E. WESTHOLM
    September–December 1942.
  Lt. ALLEN H. HARRIS, USNR
    December 1942–April 1943.
  Lt. ALVIN P. CLUSTER
    April–November 11, 1943.

PT 81' Philadelphia Navy Yard

8 Transferred from Squadron 1, August 13, 1941. Reclassified as district patrol vessel, YP 110, October 14, 1941.

PT *70′ Scott-Paine*

9 Transferred from Squadron 1, November 8, 1940. Transferred under lend-lease to Britain, April 11, 1941.

70′ Elco

10 Placed in service November 7, 1940. Transferred under lend-lease to Britain, April 11, 1941.
11 Placed in service November 12, 1940. Transferred under lend-lease to Britain, April 11, 1941.
12 Placed in service November 14, 1940. Transferred under lend-lease to Britain, April 11, 1941.
13 Placed in service November 26, 1940. Transferred under lend-lease to Britain, April 11, 1941.
14 Placed in service November 29, 1940. Transferred under lend-lease to Britain, April 11, 1941.
15 Placed in service December 5, 1940. Transferred under lend-lease to Britain, April 11, 1941.
16 Placed in service December 31, 1940. Transferred under lend-lease to Britain, July 11, 1941.
17 Placed in service December 16, 1940. Transferred under lend-lease to Britain, July 11, 1941.
18 Placed in service December 30, 1940. Transferred under lend-lease to Britain, July 11, 1941.
19 Placed in service December 31, 1940. Placed out of service July 2, 1941; later transferred under lend-lease to Britain.

77′ Elco

20 Placed in service June 20, 1941. Transferred to Squadron 1, August 13, 1941.
21 Transferred from Squadron 3(2) September 27, 1943. Stricken from Navy Register because of obsolescence, October 11, 1943.
22 Placed in service June 21, 1941. Transferred to Squadron 1, August 13, 1941.

PT *77′ Elco*

23 Transferred from Squadron 3(2), September 27, 1943. Reclassified as small boat, October 6, 1943.
24 Placed in service June 26, 1941. Transferred to Squadron 1, August 13, 1941.
25 Transferred from Squadron 3(2), September 27, 1943. Reclassified as small boat, October 6, 1943.
26 Placed in service June 18, 1941. Transferred to Squadron 1, August 13, 1941. Transferred from Squadron 3(2), September 27, 1943. Reclassified as small boat October 6, 1943.
28 Placed in service June 30, 1941. Transferred to Squadron 1, August 13, 1941.
30 Placed in service July 3, 1941. Transferred to Squadron 1, August 13, 1941.
32 Placed in service July 10, 1941. Transferred to Squadron 3, August 12, 1941.
34 Placed in service July 12, 1941. Transferred to Squadron 3, August 12, 1941.
36 Placed in service August 27, 1941. Transferred to Squadron 3(2), November 11, 1943.
37 Transferred from Squadron 1, August 13, 1941. Transferred to Squadron 3(2), July 27, 1942.
38 Placed in service July 18, 1941. Transferred to Squadron 3(2), July 27, 1942.
39 Transferred from Squadron 1, August 13, 1941. Transferred to Squadron 3(2), July 27, 1942.
40 Placed in service July 22, 1941. Transferred to Squadron 3(2), November 11, 1943.
42 Placed in service July 25, 1941. Transferred to Squadron 1, August 13, 1941.
43 Transferred from Squadron 1, August 13, 1941. Damaged by enemy warships, beached and destroyed to prevent capture January 11, 1943.

PT 77' Elco

44 Placed in service July 31, 1941. Destroyed by enemy warships, December 12, 1942.

45 Placed in service September 3, 1941. Transferred to Squadron 3(2), July 27, 1942.

46 Placed in service September 6, 1941. Transferred to Squadron 3(2), July 27, 1942.

47 Placed in service September 9, 1941. Transferred to Squadron 3(2), November 11, 1943.

48 Placed in service September 15, 1941. Transferred to Squadron 3(2), July 27, 1942.

59 Transferred from Squadron 4, May 7, 1942. Transferred to Squadron 3(2), November 11, 1943.

60, 61 Transferred from Squadron 4, May 7, 1942. Transferred to Squadron 3(2), July 27, 1942.

PT 80' Elco

109 Transferred from Squadron 5, September 22, 1942. Destroyed by enemy warship, August 2, 1943.

110 Transferred from Squadron 5, September 22, 1942. Transferred to Squadron 8, June 1, 1943.

111 Transferred from Squadron 5, September 22, 1942. Destroyed by enemy warships, February 1, 1943.

PT 80' Elco

112 Transferred from Squadron 5, September 22, 1942. Destroyed by enemy warships, January 11, 1943.

113, 114 Transferred from Squadron 5, September 22, 1942. Transferred to Squadron 8, April 1, 1943.

144 Transferred from Squadron 8, January, 1943. Transferred to Squadron 8, June 1, 1943.

145, 146 Transferred from Squadron 8, January, 1943. Transferred to Squadron 12, June 1, 1943.

147, 148 Transferred from Squadron 8, January, 1943. Transferred to Squadron 18, June 1, 1943.

Squadron 2 tested the first 70' Elco boats in Florida and Caribbean waters in the winter of 1940/41. In December 1941, with 11 new 77' Elco boats, the squadron was assigned to the Panama Sea Frontier. Then, late in 1942, with six 77' Elco boats and six 80' Elco boats, it was shipped to the South Pacific, where it was active in the Solomons campaign, engaging in many strenuous night actions with the Tokyo Express in the defense of Guadalcanal. PT's 113 and 114 operated from December 1942 to April 1943 as part of Motor Torpedo Boat Division 17, in turn part of Squadron 6, on detached duty in New Guinea waters. Earl S. Caldwell, then a lieutenant, was for a time commander of both Squadrons 1 and 2.

MOTOR TORPEDO BOAT SQUADRON 2(2)

Commissioned March 23, 1944: decommissioned September 21, 1945.

Squadron Commanders:

Comdr. JOHN D. BULKELEY
March 23–July 15, 1944

Lt. ROBERT R. READ, USNR
July 15, 1944–February 2, 1945

Lt. JOSEPH R. ELLICOTT, USNR
February 2–September 21, 1945.

PT 78' Higgins

71, 72 Transferred from Squadron 4, March 18, 1944. Stricken from Navy Register October 11, 1945.

199 Transferred from Squadron 4, March 18, 1944. Placed out of service September 21, 1945.

The second Squadron 2, the smallest in number of boats ever commissioned, was organized for special duty with the Office of Strategic Services in the English Channel area. From May to October 1944, the squadron engaged in 20 special missions, landing personnel and supplies in enemy-occupied territory.

MOTOR TORPEDO BOAT SQUADRON 3

Commissioned August 12, 1941. All boats expended by April 15, 1942.
Squadron Commander:
Lt. JOHN D. BULKELEY
August 12, 1941–April 15, 1942

PT 77' Elco

31 Transferred from Squadron 1, August 12, 1941. Destroyed to prevent capture, January 20, 1942.

32 Transferred from Squadron 2, August 12, 1941. Destroyed to prevent capture, March 13, 1942.

33 Transferred from Squadron 1, August 12, 1941. Destroyed to prevent capture, December 26, 1941.

PT 77' Elco

34 Transferred from Squadron 2, August 12, 1941. Destroyed by enemy aircraft, April 9, 1942.

35 Transferred from Squadron 1, August 12, 1941. Destroyed to prevent capture, April 12, 1942.

41 Transfererd from Squadron 1, August 12, 1941. Transferred to U.S. Army April 13, 1942; later destroyed to prevent capture.

Squadron 3 was the only PT squadron engaged in the defense of the Philippines. Among its important missions was the evacuation of Gen. Douglas MacArthur from Corregidor in March 1942.

MOTOR TORPEDO BOAT SQUADRON 3(2)

Commissioned July 27, 1942; decommissioned August 7, 1944.
Squadron Commanders:
Lt. Comdr. ALAN R. MONTGOMERY
July 27–October 1942
Lt. HUGH M. ROBINSON
October 1942–January 1943
Lt. JOHN M. SEARLES, USNR
January–August 1943.
Lt. RICHARD E. JOHNSON
August–November 1943.
Lt. ALVIN P. CLUSTER
November 1943–February 1, 1944
Lt. Comdr. GEORGE A. BRACKETT, USNR
February 1–July 22, 1944
Lt. (jg.) JAY J. REYNOLDS, Jr., USNR
July 22–August 7, 1944

PT 77' Elco

21, 23, 25, 26 Transferred from Squadron 1, December 22, 1942. Transferred to Squadron 2, September 27, 1943.

PT 77' Elco

36 Transferred from Squadron 2, November 11, 1943. Reclassified as small boat, April 15, 1944.

37 Transferred from Squadron 2, July 27, 1942. Destroyed by enemy warships, February 1, 1943.

38 Transferred from Squadron 2, July 27, 1942. Reclassified as small boat, February 16, 1944.

39 Transferred from Squadron 2, July 27, 1942. Transferred to MTB Squadrons Training Center, August 7, 1944, for training repair personnel; reclassified as small boat, October 14, 1944.

40 Transferred from Squadron 2, November 11, 1943. Reclassified as small boat, April 15, 1944.

45 Transferred from Squadron 2, July 27, 1942. Reclassified as small boat, April 15, 1944.

PT 77' Elco

46 Transferred from Squadron 2, July 27, 1942. Reclassified as small boat, April 29, 1944.

47 Transferred from Squadron 2, November 11, 1943. Transferred to MTB Squadrons Training Center, August 7, 1944, for training repair personnel; reclassified as small boat October 14, 1944.

48 Transferred from Squadron 2, July 27, 1942. Transferred to MTB Squadrons Training Center, August 7, 1944, for training repair personnel; reclassified as small boat, October 14, 1944.

59 Transferred from Squadron 2, November 11, 1943. Transferred to MTB Squadrons Training Center, August 7, 1944, for training repair personnel; re-

PT 77' Elco

classified as small boat, October 14, 1944.

60 Transferred from Squadron 2, July 27, 1942. Stricken from Navy Register because of obsolescence, April 21, 1944.

61 Transferred from Squadron 2, July 27, 1942. Reclassified as small boat, February 16, 1944.

The second Squadron 3 was the first squadron to arrive in the Solomons, and fought many strenuous engagements with the Tokyo Express at Guadalcanal. PT's 21, 23, 25, and 26 were stationed at the island of Funafuti, in the Ellice Group, until the middle of 1943. These boats, known as Motor Torpedo Boat Squadron 3, Division 2, were under command of Lt. Jonathan F. Rice, USNR, while on this detached duty.

MOTOR TORPEDO BOAT SQUADRON 4

Commissioned January 13, 1942; decommissioned April 15, 1946.
Squadron Commanders:
Lt. ROLLIN E. WESTHOLM
January 13–February 2, 1942
Lt. Comdr. ALAN R. MONTGOMERY
February 2–May 25, 1942
Lt. Comdr. WILLIAM C. SPECHT
May 25, 1942–February 20, 1943
Lt. Comdr. S. STEPHEN DAUNIS
February 20–September 11, 1943
Lt. Comdr. FRANCIS D. TAPPAAN, USNR
September 11, 1943–March 1, 1944
Lt. CHARLES E. TILDEN, USNR
March 1–July 15, 1944
Comdr. JAMES B. DENNY
July 15–September 27, 1944
Lt. ARTHUR H. BERNDTSON
September 27–October 31, 1944
Lt. Comdr. JACK E. GIBSON
October 31, 1944–June 15, 1945
Lt. Comdr. GLENN R. VAN NESS, USNR
June 15–September 17, 1945
Lt. Comdr. JOHN K. WILLIAMS, USNR
September 17, 1945–April 15, 1946

PT 77' Elco

59 Placed in service March 5, 1942. Transferred to Squadron 2, May 7, 1942.

60 Placed in service February 25, 1942. Transferred to Squadron 2, May 7, 1942.

61 Placed in service February 19, 1942. Transferred to Squadron 2, May 7, 1942.

62 Placed in service February 10, 1942. Transferred to Squadron 5, April 15, 1943.

63 Placed in service February 7, 1942. Transferred to Squadron 5, April 15, 1943.

64 Placed in service January 28, 1942. Transferred to Squadron 5, April 15, 1943.

65 Placed in service January 24, 1942. Transferred to Squadron 5, April 15, 1943.

66 Placed in service January 22, 1942. Transferred to Squadron 8, October 1, 1942.

PT *77′ Elco*

67 Placed in service January 19, 1942. Transferred to Squadron 8, October 1, 1942.

68 Placed in service January 13, 1942. Transferred to Squadron 8, October 1, 1942.

78′ Higgins

71, 72 Placed in service July 21, 1942. Transferred to Squadron 16, January 20, 1943. Transferred from Squadron 17, April 16, 1943. Transferred to Squadron 2(2), March 18, 1944.

78′ Huckins

95 Placed in service July 30, 1943. Placed out of service September 4, 1945.

96 Placed in service August 24, 1943. Placed out of service September 7, 1945.

97 Placed in service August 29, 1943. Placed out of service September 7, 1945.

98, 99, 100, 101, 102 Transferred from Squadron 14, September 17, 1944. Placed out of service January 7, 1946.

80′Elco

139 Placed in service October 13, 1942. Placed out of service January 16, 1946.

140 Placed in service October 10, 1942. Placed out of service January 28, 1946.

141 Placed in service October 10, 1942. Placed out of service January 16, 1946.

78′ Higgins

199 Placed in service January 23, 1943. Transferred to Squadron 2(2), March 18, 1944.

200 Placed in service January 23, 1943. Sunk in collision, February 23, 1944.

295 Transferred from Squadron 16B, December 2, 1943. Placed out of service January 7, 1946.

296 Transferred from Squadron 16B, December 2, 1943. Placed out of service February 1, 1946.

PT *80′ Elco*

314 Transferred from Squadron 5, April 15, 1943. Placed out of service January 16, 1946.

315 Transferred from Squadron 5, April 15, 1943. Placed out of service January 14, 1946.

316 Transferred from Squadron 5, April 15, 1943. Placed out of service January 16, 1946.

317 Transferred from Squadron 5, April 15, 1943. Placed out of service January 28, 1946.

450, 451, 452 Transferred from Squadron 30, March 23, 1944. Placed out of service February 1, 1946.

486 Placed in service December 2, 1943. Placed out of service January 16, 1946.

487 Placed in service January 10, 1944. Placed out of service January 28, 1946.

505 Transferred from Squadron 34, December 29, 1944. Placed out of service February 1, 1946.

545 Placed in service September 8, 1944. Placed out of service February 1, 1946.

557, 558, 559 Transferred from Squadron 29, November 23, 1944. Placed out of service January 28, 1946.

70′ Higgins Hellcat

564 Experimental boat assigned to Squadron 4, November 27, 1944. Placed out of service February 1, 1946.

80′ Elco

613, 616, 619, 620 Transferred from Squadron 42, January 26, 1946. Transferred to Operational Development Force, April 15, 1946.

Squadron 4 was the training squadron, based at the MTB Squadrons Training Center, Melville, R.I. It was the largest squadron, having a peak of 28 boats in service at one time. When the training center was decommissioned early in 1946, Squadron 4 was assigned to the Operational Development Force, and based at Solomons, Md. It was the last squadron to be decommissioned, and its boats, PT's 613, 616, 619, and 620, which remained in serv- ice under the Operational Development Force, were the last World War II PT's in service in the Navy.

MOTOR TORPEDO BOAT SQUADRON 5

Commissioned June 16, 1942; decommissioned February 15, 1945.
Squadron Commanders:
Comdr. HENRY FARROW
June 17, 1942–January 24, 1944
Lt. HENRY J. BRANTINGHAM
January 24–August 5, 1944
Lt. JOHN W. EWELL, USNR
August 5, 1944–February 15, 1945

PT 77' Elco

62 Transferred from Squadron 4, April 15, 1943. Stricken from Navy Register because of obsolesence, January 20, 1945.
63 Transferred from Squadron 4, April 15, 1943. Destroyed by fire in port, June 18, 1944.
64, 65 Transferred from Squadron 4, April 15, 1943. Stricken from Navy Register because of obsolesence, January 20, 1945.

80' Elco

103 Placed in service June 12, 1942. Transferred to Squadron 18, February 15, 1945.
104 Placed in service June 19, 1942. Transferred to Squadron 18, February 15, 1945.
105 Placed in service June 26, 1942. Transferred to Squadron 18, February 15, 1945.
106 Placed in service July 1, 1942. Transferred to Squadron 24, February 15, 1945.
107 Placed in service July 3, 1942. Destroyed by fire in port, June 18, 1944.

PT 80' Elco

108 Placed in service July 7, 1942. Transferred to Squadron 10, February 15, 1945.
109 Placed in service July 10, 1942. Transferred to Squadron 2, September 22, 1942.
110 Placed in service July 14, 1942. Transferred to Squadron 2, September 22, 1942.
111 Placed in service July 16, 1942. Transferred to Squadron 2, September 22, 1942.
112 Placed in service July 18, 1942. Transferred to Squadron 2, September 22, 1942.
113 Placed in service July 23, 1942. Transferred to Squadron 2, September 22, 1942.
114 Placed in service July 25, 1942. Transferred to Squadron 2, September 22, 1942.
314 Placed in service March 11, 1943. Transferred to Squadron 4, April 15, 1943.
315 Placed in service March 15, 1943. Transferred to Squadron 4, April 15, 1943.
316 Placed in service March 18, 1943. Transferred to Squadron 4, April 15, 1943.
317 Placed in service March 19, 1943. Transferred to Squadron 4, April 15, 1943.
318 Placed in service March 23, 1943. Transferred to Squadron 9, February 15, 1945.
319 Placed in service March 26, 1943. Transferred to Squadron 9, February 15, 1945.

Squadron 5 was assigned to Panama Sea Frontier from September 1942 until the spring of 1943, when it was shipped to the Solomons. There its boats were in action at Rendova, Vella Lavella, Treasury, Bougainville, Green, and Emirau. After assignment to the Southwest Pacific area at the end of 1944, the squadron was decommissioned and its boats were distributed to replenish other squadrons which had suffered operational losses.

MOTOR TORPEDO BOAT SQUADRON 6

Commissioned August 4, 1942; decommissioned May 29, 1944.
Squadron Commanders:
Lt. Comdr. CLIFTON B. MADDOX
August 4, 1942–February 1943
Lt. CLARK W. FAULKNER, USNR
February–May 1943
Lt. CRAIG C. SMITH, USNR
May–October 1943
Lt. Comdr. RICHARD E. JOHNSON
October 1943–May 29, 1944

PT 80' Elco
115 Placed in service July 29, 1942. Transferred to Squadron 25, May 29, 1944.
116 Placed in service July 30, 1942. Transferred to Squadron 10, May 29, 1944.
117 Placed in service August 4, 1942. Destroyed by enemy aircraft, August 1, 1943.
118 Placed in service August 6, 1942. Destroyed to prevent capture, September 7, 1943.
119 Placed in service August 8, 1942. Destroyed by fire in port, March 17, 1943.
120 Placed in service August 12, 1942. Transferred to Squadron 8, April 1, 1943.
121 Placed in service August 27, 1942. Transferred to Squadron 8, April 1, 1943.
122 Placed in service August 15, 1942. Transferred to Squadron 8, April 1, 1943.
123 Placed in service August 18, 1942. Destroyed by enemy aircraft, February 1, 1943.

PT 80' Elco
124 Placed in service August 20, 1942. Transferred to Squadron 10, May 29, 1944.
125 Placed in service August 16, 1942. Transferred to Squadron 10, May 29, 1944.
126 Placed in service August 27, 1942. Transferred to Squadron 9, May 29, 1944.
187 Transferred from Squadron 12, May 10, 1943. Transferred to Squadron 9, May 29, 1944.
188, 189 Transferred from Squadron 12, May 10, 1943. Transferred to Squadron 8, May 29, 1944.

Squadron 6 arrived in the South Pacific in time for its boats to participate in some of the last actions with the Tokyo Express at Guadalcanal. Later it had action at Rendova, Vella Lavella, Treasury, Bougainville, Green, and Emirau. After its transfer to the Southwest Pacific in May 1944, the squadron was decommissioned and its boats were distributed to replenish other squadrons which had suffered operational losses. PT's 119–122, with PT's 113 and 114 of Squadron 2, were designated Motor Torpedo Boat Division 17 and were sent to the Southwest Pacific in December 1942. Division 17, under command of Lt. Daniel S. Baughman, was the first PT unit to operate in New Guinea waters. It was absorbed by Squadron 8 on April 1, 1943.

MOTOR TORPEDO BOAT SQUADRON 7

Commissioned September 4, 1942; decommissioned February 15, 1945.
Squadron Commanders:
Lt. ROLLIN E. WESTHOLM
  September 1942
Lt. Comdr. JOHN D. BULKELEY
  October 1942–October 1943
Lt. EDWARD W. ROBERTS, USNR
  October 1943–February 15, 1944
Lt. Comdr. ROBERT LEESON, USNR
  February 15–November 26, 1944
Lt. ROGER H. HALLOWELL, USNR
  November 26, 1944–February 15, 1945

PT 80′ Elco

127 Placed in service September 4, 1942. Transferred to Squadron 12, February 15, 1945.
128 Placed in service September 4, 1942. Transferred to Squadron 21, February 15, 1945.
129 Placed in service September 4, 1942. Transferred to Squadron 8, February 15, 1945.
130 Placed in service September 7, 1942. Transferred to Squadron 8, February 15, 1945.
131 Placed in service September 9, 1942. Transferred to Squadron 21, February 15, 1945.
132 Placed in service September 11, 1942. Transferred to Squadron 21, February 15, 1945.
133 Placed in service September 16, 1942. Destroyed by enemy shore battery, July 15, 1944.

PT 77′ Elco

134 Placed in service September 17, 1942. Transferred to Squadron 25, February 15, 1945.
135 Placed in service September 21, 1942. Destroyed to prevent capture, April 12, 1944.
136 Placed in service September 23, 1942. Destroyed to prevent capture, September 17, 1943.
137 Placed in service September 25, 1942. Transferred to Squadron 33, February 15, 1945.
138 Placed in service September 29, 1942. Transferred to Squadron 33, February 15, 1945.

Squadron 7, assigned to the Southwest Pacific, had action in New Guinea waters at Tufi, Morobe, Kiriwina, Dreger Harbor, and Aitape, and in Philippine waters at San Pedro Bay and at Ormoc. The squadron based for a time at Kana Kopa, New Guinea; Thursday Island, Australia; Fergusson Island, d'Entrecasteaux Group; and Mios Woendi, Dutch New Guinea, but had no action at these bases. PT's 127–132 were on detached duty at Thursday Island from June to August 1943 as Motor Torpedo Boat Division 19, under command of Lt. Comdr. Robert J. Bulkley, Jr., USNR. Squadron 7 was awarded the Navy Unit Commendation for action in the New Guinea area from April 1, 1944, to February 1, 1945.

MOTOR TORPEDO BOAT SQUADRON 8

Commissioned October 10, 1942; decommissioned October 28, 1945.
Squadron Commanders:
Lt. Comdr. BARRY K. ATKINS
  October 10, 1942–November 1943
Lt. ROBERT L. CHILDS, USNR
  November 1943–February 29, 1944

Lt. EDWARD I. FARLEY, USNR
  February 29–August 22, 1944
Lt. ROBERT A. WILLIAMSON, USNR
  August 22, 1944–May 16, 1945
Lt. WILLIAM C. GODFREY
  May 16–October 28, 1945

PT 77' Elco

66 Transferred from Squadron 4, October 1, 1942. Reclassified as small boat, February 23, 1945.

67 Transferred from Squadron 4, October 1, 1942. Destroyed by fire in port, March 17, 1943.

68 Transferred from Squadron 4, October 1, 1942. Destroyed to prevent capture, October 1, 1943.

80' Elco

110 Transferred from Squadron 2, June 1, 1943. Lost in collision, January 26, 1944.

113 Transferred from Squadron 2, April 1, 1943. Damaged by grounding, August 8, 1943; scrapped.

114 Transferred from Squadron 2, April 1, 1943. Placed out of service, stripped and destroyed, October 28, 1945.

120 Transferred from Squadron 6, April 1, 1943. Placed out of service, stripped and destroyed, October 28, 1945.

121 Transferred from Squadron 6, April 1, 1943. Destroyed by Australian aircraft, March 27, 1944.

122 Transferred from Squadron 6, April 1, 1943. Placed out of service, stripped and destroyed, October 28, 1945.

129, 130 Transferred from Squadron 7, February 15, 1945. Placed out of service, stripped and destroyed, October 28, 1945.

142 Placed in service October 10, 1942. Placed out of service, stripped and destroyed, October 28, 1945.

143 Placed in service October 13, 1942. Placed out of service, stripped and destroyed, October 28, 1945.

144 Placed in service October 15, 1942. Transferred to Squadron 2, January, 1943. Transferred from Squadron 2,

PT 80' Elco

June 1, 1943. Placed out of service, stripped and destroyed, October 28, 1945.

145 Placed in service October 17, 1942. Transferred to Squadron 2, January 1943.

146 Placed in service October 20, 1942. Transferred to Squadron 2, January 1943.

147 Placed in service October 23, 1942. Transferred to Squadron 2, January 1943.

148 Placed in service October 27, 1942. Transferred to Squadron 2, January 1943.

149 Placed in service October 29, 1942. Placed out of service, stripped and destroyed, October 28, 1945.

150 Placed in service November 2, 1942. Transferred to Squadron 12, May 10, 1943.

188, 189 Transferred from Squadron 6, May 29, 1944. Placed out of service, stripped and destroyed, October 28, 1945.

Squadron 8, assigned to the Southwest Pacific, had action in New Guinea waters at Tufi, Morobe, Kiriwina, and Aitape; at Rein Bay and Talasea on New Britain, and in Philippine waters at Mindoro, Zamboanga, and Tawi Tawi. The squadron based for a time at Kana Kopa, Dreger Harbor, and Mios Woendi, New Guinea, and at San Pedro Bay in the Philippines, but had no action at these bases.

PT's 139–141 originally were assigned to Squadron 8, but their assignment was changed to Squadron 4 on September 24, 1942, before these boats were placed in service. In exchange, Squadron 8 received PT's 66–68 from Squadron 4.

MOTOR TORPEDO BOAT SQUADRON 9

Commissioned November 10, 1942; decommissioned November 24, 1945.

Squadron Commanders:

Lt. Comdr. ROBERT B. KELLY
November 10, 1942–January 12, 1944

Lt. MICHAEL R. PESSOLANO
January 12–August 1, 1944

Lt. HAMILTON H. WOOD, USNR
August 1, 1944–March 1, 1945

Lt. RICHARD M. MONAHON, USNR
March 1–October 18, 1945

Lt. EDWARD R. BURNS, USNR
October 18–November 24, 1945

PT   80′ Elco

126 Transferred from Squadron 6, May 29, 1944. Placed out of service, stripped and destroyed, November 24, 1945.

151 Placed in service November 4, 1942. Transferred to Squadron 12, May 10, 1943.

152 Placed in service November 6, 1942. Transferred to Squadron 12, May 10, 1943.

153 Placed in service November 10, 1942. Destroyed to prevent capture, July 4, 1943.

154 Placed in service November 13, 1942. Placed out of service, stripped and destroyed, November 24, 1945.

155 Placed in service November 20, 1942. Placed out of service, stripped and destroyed, November 24, 1945.

156 Placed in service November 18, 1942. Placed out of service, stripped and destroyed, November 24, 1945.

PT   80′ Elco

157 Placed in service November 20, 1942. Placed out of service, stripped and destroyed, November 27, 1945.

158 Placed in service November 23, 1942. Destroyed to prevent capture, July 5, 1943.

159 Placed in service November 24, 1942. Placed out of service, stripped and destroyed, November 24, 1945.

160 Placed in service December 7, 1942. Placed out of service, stripped and destroyed, November 27, 1945.

161 Placed in service November 28, 1942. Placed out of service, stripped and destroyed, November 24, 1945.

162 Placed in service December 2, 1942. Placed out of service, stripped and destroyed, November 24, 1945.

187 Transferred from Squadron 6, May 29, 1944. Placed out of service November 24, 1945.

318, 319 Transferred from Squadron 5, February 15, 1945. Placed out of service November 24, 1945.

Squadron 9, assigned to the South Pacific, had action at Rendova, Lever Harbor, Treasury, and Green. Transferred to the Southwest Pacific in May 1944, the squadron had action at Mios Woendi, Dutch New Guinea; Morotai, in the Halmaheras; and at Zamboanga and Tawi Tawi in the Philippines. The squadron also based for a time at Dreger Harbor, New Guinea, and at Samar in the Philippines, but had no action from these bases.

MOTOR TORPEDO BOAT SQUADRON 10

Commissioned December 9, 1942; decommissioned November 11, 1945.

Squadron Commanders:

Lt. Comdr. THOMAS G. WARFIELD
December 9, 1942–February 7, 1944

Lt. Comdr. JACK E. GIBSON
February 7–August 16, 1944

Lt. CHRISTOPHER B. ARMAT, USNR
August 16, 1944–February 26, 1945

Lt. Comdr. FRANCIS H. McADOO, Jr., USNR
February 26–October 14, 1945

Lt. FREDERICK N. GOEHNER, USNR
October 14–November 11, 1945

PT 80' Elco

108 Transferred from Squadron 5, February 15, 1945. Placed out of service, stripped and destroyed, November 11, 1945.

116, 124, 125 Transferred from Squadron 6, May 29, 1944. Placed out of service, stripped and destroyed, November 11, 1945.

163 Placed in service December 4, 1942. Placed out of service, stripped and destroyed, November 11, 1945.

164 Placed in service December 8, 1942. Destroyed by enemy aircraft August 1, 1943.

165 Placed in service December 11, 1942. Lost in transit—tanker torpedoed—May 24, 1943.

166 Placed in service December 22, 1942. Destroyed by U.S. aircraft July 20, 1943.

167 Placed in service December 17, 1942. Placed out of service, stripped and destroyed, November 11, 1945.

168 Placed in service December 22, 1942. Placed out of service, stripped and destroyed, November 11, 1945.

169 Placed in service December 23, 1942. Placed out of service, stripped and destroyed, November 11, 1945.

PT 80' Elco

170 Placed in service December 28, 1942. Placed out of service, stripped and destroyed, November 11, 1945.

171 Placed in service December 30, 1942. Placed out of service, stripped and destroyed, November 11, 1945.

172 Placed in service January 2, 1943. Destroyed to prevent capture, September 7, 1943.

173 Placed in service January 2, 1943. Lost in transit—tanker torpedoed—May 24, 1943.

174 Placed in service January 6, 1943. Placed out of service, stripped and destroyed, November 11, 1945.

Squadron 10, assigned to the South Pacific, had action at Rendova, Vella Lavella, Treasury, Bougainville, and Green. Transferred to the Southwest Pacific in April 1944, the squadron had action at Saidor, New Guinea; Morotai, in the Halmaheras; and at Balikpapan, Borneo. The squadron also based for a time at Mios Woendi, Dutch New Guinea, and at Samar, P.I., but had no action from these bases.

MOTOR TORPEDO BOAT SQUADRON 11

Commissioned January 20, 1943; decommissioned November 11, 1945.

Squadron Commanders:

Lt. Comdr. LeRoy T. Taylor
January 20, 1943–January 22, 1944
Lt. Leonard R. Hardy, USNR
January 22–August 1944
Lt. William S. Humphrey, Jr.
August 1944–January 29, 1945
Lt. John W. Ewell, USNR
January 29–July 1, 1945
Lt. Wendell E. Carroll, USNR
July 1–October 18, 1945

Lt. Robert L. Wessel, USNR
October 18–November 11, 1945

PT 80' Elco

175, 176, 177, 178, 179 Placed in service January 20, 1943. Placed out of service, stripped and destroyed, November 11, 1945.

180 Placed in service January 22, 1943. Placed out of service, stripped and destroyed, November 11, 1945.

181 Placed in service January 26, 1943. Placed out of service, stripped and destroyed, November 11, 1945.

PT 80' Elco

182 Placed in service January 30, 1943. Placed out of service, stripped and destroyed, November 11, 1945.
183 Placed in service February 2, 1943. Placed out of service, stripped and destroyed, November 11, 1945.
184 Placed in service February 4, 1943. Placed out of service, stripped and destroyed, November 11, 1945.
185 Placed in service February 6, 1943. Placed out of service, stripped and destroyed, November 11, 1945.
186 Placed in service February 9, 1943. Placed out of service, stripped and destroyed, November 11, 1945.

Squadron 11, assigned to the South Pacific, had action at Rendova, Vella Lavella, Bougainville, and Emirau. Transferred to the Southwest Pacific in June 1944, the squadron had action at Morotai, in the Halmaheras. It also based for a time at Mios Woendi, Dutch New Guinea, but had no action from that base. PT's 177, 182, 185, and 186, designated as Squadron 11–2, under command of Lt. John H. Stillman, USNR, relieved Division 2 of Squadron 3(2) at Funafuti, in the Ellice Group in July 1943. Squadron 11–2 rejoined the parent squadron at Emirau in May 1944.

MOTOR TORPEDO BOAT SQUADRON 12

Commissioned February 18, 1943; decommissioned October 26, 1945.

Squadron Commanders:

Lt. Comdr. JOHN HARLLEE
February 18, 1943–April 13, 1944
Lt. Comdr. ROBERT J. BULKLEY, Jr., USNR
April 13–August 4, 1944
Lt. WESTON C. PULLEN, Jr., USNR
August 4, 1944–March 7, 1945
Lt. JOHN J. McGLYNN, USNR
March 7–October 26, 1945

PT 80' Elco

127 Transferred from Squadron 7, February 15, 1945. Placed out of service, stripped and destroyed, October 26, 1945.
145 Transferred from Squadron 2, June 1, 1943. Destroyed to prevent capture, January 4, 1944.
146 Transferred from Squadron 2, June 1, 1943. Placed out of service, stripped and destroyed, October 26, 1945.
150 Transferred from Squadron 8, May 10, 1943. Placed out of service, stripped and destroyed, October 26, 1945.

PT 80' Elco

151, 152 Transferred from Squadron 9, May 10, 1943. Placed out of service, stripped and destroyed, October 26, 1945.
187, 188 Placed in service February 18, 1943. Transferred to Squadron 6, May 10, 1943.
189 Placed in service February 19, 1943. Transferred to Squadron 6, May 10, 1943.
190 Placed in service February 19, 1943. Placed out of service October 26, 1945.
191 Placed in service February 24, 1943. Placed out of service October 26, 1945.
192 Placed in service February 25, 1943. Placed out of service, stripped and destroyed, October 26, 1945.
193 Placed in service February 27, 1943. Destroyed to prevent capture, June 25, 1944.
194 Placed in service March 3, 1943. Placed out of service, stripped and destroyed, October 26, 1945.
195 Placed in service March 6, 1943. Placed out of service October 26, 1945.
196 Placed in service May 3, 1943. Placed out of service October 26, 1945.

Squadron 12, assigned to the Southwest Pacific, had action in New Guinea waters at Morobe, Dreger Harbor, Hollandia, and Mios Woendi, and in the Philippines at San Pedro Bay and Ormoc. It also based for a time at Kana Kopa, New Guinea, but had no action from this base. Squadron 12 was awarded the Presidential Unit Citation for action in the New Guinea area from October 1943 to March 1944.

MOTOR TORPEDO BOAT SQUADRON 13

Commissioned September 18, 1942; decommissioned November 23, 1945.

Squadron Commanders:
Comdr. JAMES B. DENNY
September 18, 1942–June 8, 1944
Lt. Comdr. ALVIN W. FARGO, Jr., USNR
June 8, 1944–October 15, 1945
Lt. Comdr. JOHN A. MATZINGER, USNR
October 15–November 23, 1945

PT 78' Higgins

73 Placed in service August 12, 1942. Destroyed to prevent capture, January 15, 1945.

74 Placed in service August 26, 1942. Placed out of service, stripped and destroyed, November 23, 1945.

75 Placed in service August 28, 1942. Placed out of service, stripped and destroyed, November 23, 1945.

76 Placed in service August 31, 1942. Placed out of service, stripped and destroyed, November 23, 1945.

77 Placed in service September 4, 1942. Destroyed by U.S. warships, February 1, 1945.

78 Placed in service September 7, 1942. Placed out of service, stripped and destroyed, November 23, 1945.

PT 78' Higgins

79 Placed in service September 9, 1942. Destroyed by U.S. warships, February 1, 1945.

80 Placed in service September 22, 1942. Placed out of service, stripped and destroyed, November 23, 1945.

81 Placed in service December 7, 1942. Placed out of service, stripped and destroyed, November 23, 1945.

82 Placed in service November 28, 1942. Placed out of service, stripped and destroyed, November 23, 1945.

83 Placed in service December 9, 1942. Placed out of service, stripped and destroyed, November 23, 1945.

84 Placed in service December 7, 1942. Placed out of service, stripped and destroyed, November 23, 1945.

Squadron 13 participated in the Aleutian campaign from March 1943 to May 1944. Transferred to the Southwest Pacific, the squadron had action at Mios Woendi, Dutch New Guinea; Mindoro, P.I., and Brunei Bay, Borneo. It also based for a time at Dreger Harbor, New Guinea, and San Pedro Bay, P.I., but had no action from these bases. As part of Task Unit 70.1.4, Squadron 13 was awarded the Navy Unit Commendation for action at Mindoro from December 15 to 19, 1944.

MOTOR TORPEDO BOAT SQUADRON 14

Commissioned February 17, 1943; decommissioned September 16, 1944.
Squadron Commanders:
Lt. RICHARD E. JOHNSON
February 17, 1943–June 1943

Lt. RICHARD C. MORSE, Jr., USNR
June 1943–April 4, 1944
Lt. HENRY S. TAYLOR, USNR
April 4, 1944–September 16, 1944

PT 78' Huckins

98 Placed in service September 19, 1942. Transferred to Squadron 4, September 17, 1944.

99 Placed in service September 29, 1942. Transferred to Squadron 4, September 17, 1944.

100, 101 Placed in service November 14, 1942. Transferred to Squadron 4, September 17, 1944.

102 Placed in service November 30, 1942. Transferred to Squadron 4, September 17, 1944.

Squadron 14 was assigned to Panama Sea Frontier. It had no action with the enemy. PT's 85–94 and 197 and 198, 78' Higgins boats, were originally assigned to Squadron 14, but were reassigned for transfer under lend-lease to U.S.S.R. before the squadron was commissioned and before any boats were delivered. This reassignment was later modified so that PT's 85–87, 89, and 197 were transferred to U.S.S.R., and PT's 88, 90–94, and 198 were transferred to Britain.

MOTOR TORPEDO BOAT SQUADRON 15

Commissioned January 20, 1943; decommissioned October 17, 1944.

Squadron Commander:

Comdr. STANLEY M. BARNES
January 20, 1943–October 17, 1944

PT 78' Higgins

201 Placed in service January 20, 1943. Transferred under lend-lease to Britain, October 17, 1944.

202 Placed in service January 24, 1943. Destroyed by enemy mine, August 16, 1944.

203 Placed in service January 23, 1943. Transferred under lend-lease to Britain, October 17, 1944.

204 Placed in service January 24, 1943. Transferred under lend-lease to Britain, October 17, 1944.

205 Placed in service January 25, 1943. Transferred under lend-lease to Britain, October 17, 1944.

206, 207 Placed in service February 3, 1943. Transferred under lend-lease to Britain, October 17, 1944.

208 Placed in service February 10, 1943. Transferred under lend-lease to Britain, October 17, 1944.

PT 78' Higgins

209 Placed in service February 9, 1943. Transferred under lend-lease to Britain, October 17, 1944.

210 Placed in service February 10, 1943. Transferred under lend-lease to Britain, October 17, 1944.

211 Placed in service February 11, 1943. Transferred under lend-lease to Britain, October 17, 1944.

212 Placed in service February 12, 1943. Transferred under lend-lease to Britain, October 17, 1944.

213–217 Transferred from Squadron 16, March 13, 1943. Transferred under lend-lease to Britain, October 17, 1944.

218 Transferred from Squadron 16, March 13, 1943. Destroyed by enemy mine, August 16, 1944.

Squadron 15 was the first PT squadron sent to the Mediterranean Theater, where it operated as a unit of the British Coastal Forces. It had action throughout the western Mediterranean, basing at Bizerte and Bone, Africa; Palermo, Sicily; Salerno, Capri, and Leghorn, Italy; Maddalena, Sardinia; Bastia and Calvi, Corsica, and St. Tropez, France.

MOTOR TORPEDO BOAT SQUADRON 16

Commissioned February 26, 1943; decommissioned November 26, 1945.

Squadron commanders:

Lt. Comdr. RUSSELL H. SMITH
February 26, 1943–April 1943
Lt. Comdr. ALMER P. COLVIN
April 1943–December 18, 1944
Lt. JOHN H. STILLMAN, USNR
December 18, 1944–February 1, 1945
Lt. ROBERT J. WEHRLI, USNR
February 1–12, 1945
Lt. PHILIP A. SWART, USNR
February 12–22, 1945
Lt. ROGER H. HALLOWELL, USNR
February 22–October 14, 1945
Lt. JOHN V. McELROY, USNR
October 14–November 26, 1945

PT 78′ Higgins

71, 72 Transferred from Squadron 4, January 20, 1943. Transferred to Squadron 17, March 13, 1943.

213 Placed in service February 16, 1943. Transferred to Squadron 15, March 13, 1943.

214 Placed in service February 18, 1943. Transferred to Squadron 15, March 13, 1943.

215, 216 Placed in service February 26, 1943. Transferred to Squadron 15, March 13, 1943.

217, 218 Placed in service March 5, 1943. Transferred to Squadron 15, March 13, 1943.

219 Placed in service March 5, 1943. Damaged in storm, September 14, 1943; scrapped.

220, 221 Placed in service March 12, 1943. Placed out of service, stripped and destroyed, November 26, 1945.

222–224 Placed in service March 19, 1943. Placed out of service, stripped and destroyed, November 26, 1945.

235 Transferred from Squadron 20, February 10, 1945. Placed out of service,

PT 78′ Higgins

stripped and destroyed, November 26, 1945.

241, 242 Transferred from Squadron 23, February 25, 1945. Placed out of service, stripped and destroyed, November 26, 1945.

295 Placed in service October 15, 1943. Transferred to Squadron 4, December 2, 1943.

296 Placed in service October 18, 1943. Transferred to Squadron 4, December 2, 1943.

297 Placed in service October 20, 1943. Placed out of service, stripped and destroyed, November 26, 1945.

298, 299 Placed in service October 26, 1943. Placed out of service, stripped and destroyed, November 26, 1945.

300 Placed in service October 29, 1943. Destroyed by enemy suicide plane, December 18, 1944.

301 Placed in service November 4, 1943. Damaged by explosion in port, November 7, 1944; scrapped.

Squadron 16 participated in the Aleutian campaign from August 1943 to May 1944. Transferred to the Southwest Pacific, the squadron had action at Mios Woendi, Dutch New Guinea; Mindoro, P.I.; and Brunei Bay, Borneo. It also based for a time at Dreger Harbor, New Guinea, and San Pedro Bay, P.I., but had no action from these bases. As part of Task Unit 70.1.4, Squadron 16 was awarded the Navy Unit Commendation for action at Mindoro from December 15 to 19, 1944.

PT's 295–301, placed in service after the squadron had departed for the Aleutians, were designated as Squadron 16B, which was commissioned as a separate command under Lt. James H. Van Sicklen, USNR. Squadron 16B was placed out of separate commission on May 31, 1944, when it joined the parent squadron in Seattle.

MOTOR TORPEDO BOAT SQUADRON 17

Commissioned March 29, 1943; decommissioned November 19, 1945.

Squadron Commanders:

Lt. Comdr. RUSSELL B. ALLEN
    March 29, 1943–May 1, 1944
Lt. JAMES M. CARNES, USNR
    May 1–June 22, 1944
Lt. RAYMOND R. HARRISON, USNR
    June 22, 1944–August 13, 1945
Lt. JULIAN H. MINSON, USNR
    August 13–October 15, 1945
Lt. JAMES F. HILL, USNR
    October 15–November 19, 1945

PT 78′ Higgins

71, 72 Transferred from Squadron 16, March 13, 1943. Transferred to Squadron 4, April 16, 1943.

225 Placed in service March 29, 1943. Placed out of service, stripped and destroyed, November 19, 1945.

226 Placed in service March 29, 1943. Placed out of service November 19, 1945.

227 Placed in service March 29, 1943. Placed out of service, stripped and destroyed, November 19, 1945.

228, 229 Placed in service March 29, 1943. Placed out of service November 19, 1945.

PT 78′ Higgins

230 Placed in service March 29, 1943. Placed out of service, stripped and destroyed, November 19, 1945.

231, 232 Placed in service March 31, 1943. Placed out of service November 19, 1945.

233 Placed in service April 7, 1943. Placed out of service, stripped and destroyed, November 19, 1945.

234 Placed in service April 14, 1943. Placed out of service November 19, 1945.

Squadron 17, assigned to Hawaiian Sea Frontier, arrived at Pearl Harbor late in 1943. In February 1944, the squadron was shipped to Majuro Atoll, in the Marshalls, where it conducted patrols but had no enemy contacts. The squadron returned to Pearl Harbor in April and was shipped, a few boats at a time, to the Southwest Pacific. Two boats arrived in October 1944, four in December 1944, and four in May 1945. PT's 227 and 230, the first to arrive in the Southwest Pacific, as part of Task Unit 70.1.4, were awarded the Navy Unit Commendation for action at Mindoro, P.I., from December 15 to 19, 1944. As other boats arrived in the area they, too, were sent to Mindoro.

MOTOR TORPEDO BOAT SQUADRON 18

Commissioned March 27, 1943; decommissioned November 1, 1945.

Squadron Commanders:

Lt. Comdr. HENRY M. S. SWIFT, USNR
    March 27, 1943–December 1944
Lt. EDWARD MACAULEY 3d, USNR
    December 1944–June 17, 1945
Lt. Comdr. RICHARD C. MORSE, Jr., USNR
    June 17–October 14, 1945

Lt. RAYMOND S. PATTON, USNR
    October 14–November 1, 1945

PT 80′ Elco

103–105 Transferred from Squadron 5, February 15, 1945. Placed out of service, stripped and destroyed, November 1, 1945.

147 Transferred from Squadron 2, June 1, 1943. Destroyed to prevent capture, November 20, 1943.

PT *80' Elco*

148 Transferred from Squadron 2, June 1, 1943. Placed out of service, stripped and destroyed, November 1, 1945.

362 Placed in service August 15, 1943. Placed out of service, stripped and destroyed, November 1, 1945.

363 Placed in service August 15, 1943. Destroyed by enemy shore batteries, November 25, 1944.

364, 365 Placed in service August 15, 1943. Placed out of service, stripped and destroyed, November 1, 1945.

366 Placed in service August 15, 1943. Placed out of service, November 4, 1945.

367 Placed in service August 15, 1943. Placed out of service, stripped and destroyed, November 1, 1945.

70' Canadian Power Boat

368 Placed in service April 19, 1943. Destroyed to prevent capture, October 11, 1944.

369 Placed in service March 27, 1943. Placed out of service, stripped and destroyed, November 1, 1945.

370 Placed in service April 22, 1943. Placed out of service, stripped and destroyed, November 1, 1945.

PT *70' Canadian Power Boat*

371 Placed in service April 10, 1943. Destroyed to prevent capture, September 19, 1944.

Squadron 18, assigned to the Southwest Pacific, had action at Dreger Harbor, Aitape, Hollandia, Wakde, and Mios Woendi, in New Guinea; at Manus in the Admiralties; and at Morotai in the Halmaheras. It also based for a time at Kana Kopa, New Guinea, and in San Pedro Bay in the Philippines, but had no action from these bases. The squadron originally was planned as a four-boat squadron for service in the Caribbean Sea Frontier. PT's 368–371, 70-foot boats of Scott-Paine design, built by the Canadian Power Boat Co., Montreal, were acquired under reverse lend-lease from the Dutch Government, and were converted by installation of Elco fittings at Fyfe's Shipyard, Glenwood Landing, Long Island, N.Y. The squadron then was reassigned to Southwest Pacific and was augmented by PT's 362–367, 80-foot boats fabricated by Elco and assembled at the Harbor Boat Building Co., Terminal Island, Calif. When completed these boats were identical with the 80-foot Elco model.

MOTOR TORPEDO BOAT SQUADRON 19

Commissioned April 22, 1943; decommissioned May 15, 1944.

Squadron Commanders:

Lt. Comdr. RUSSELL H. SMITH
April 22, 1943–February 14, 1944

Lt. Comdr. GLENN R. VAN NESS, USNR
February 14–May 15, 1944

PT *78' Higgins*

235, 236 Placed in service April 22, 1943. Transferred to Squadron 20, April 19, 1944.

237 Placed in service April 23, 1943. Transferred to Squadron 20, April 19, 1944.

PT *78' Higgins*

238 Placed in service April 22, 1943. Transferred to Squadron 20, April 19, 1944.

239 Placed in service April 30, 1943. Destroyed by fire in port, December 14, 1943.

240 Placed in service April 30, 1943. Transferred to Squadron 20, April 19, 1944.

241 Placed in service May 12, 1943. Transferred to Squadron 23, April 19, 1944.

PT 78′ Higgins

242, 243 Placed in service May 14, 1943.
    Transferred to Squadron 23, April 19,
    1944.
244 Placed in service May 24, 1943.
    Transferred to Squadron 23, April 19,
    1944.

Squadron 19, assigned to South Pacific, had
action at Vella Lavella, Treasury, and
Green. The squadron was decommissioned and its boats were distributed to
replenish other squadrons which had suffered operational losses.

MOTOR TORPEDO BOAT SQUADRON 20

Commissioned June 3, 1943; decommissioned November 24, 1945.

Squadron Commanders:
    Lt. Comdr. GLENN R. VAN NESS, USNR
    June 3, 1943–January 26, 1944
    Lt. ARTHUR H. BERNDTSON
    January 26–July 29, 1944
    Lt. CHARLES R. GILMAN, USNR
    July 29, 1944–January 9, 1945
    Lt. ROBERT C. HARRIS, USNR
    January 9–July 5, 1945.
    Lt. WILLIAM W. STEWART, USNR
    July 5–October 15, 1945
    Lt. EDWARD A. GREEN, Jr., USNR
    October 15–November 24, 1945

PT 78′ Higgins

235 Transferred from Squadron 19, April
    19, 1944. Transferred to Squadron
    16, February 10, 1945.
236–238, 240 Transferred from Squadron
    19, April 19, 1944. Placed out of
    service November 24, 1945.
245 Placed in service May 20, 1943. Placed
    out of service November 24, 1945.
246 Placed in service May 24, 1943.
    Placed out of service, stripped and de-
    stroyed, November 24, 1945.
247 Placed in service May 25, 1943. De-
    stroyed by enemy shore batteries,
    May 5, 1944.

PT 78′ Higgins

248 Placed in service May 26, 1943.
    Placed out of service, stripped and de-
    stroyed, November 24, 1945.
249 Placed in service May 28, 1943.
    Placed out of service November 24,
    1945.
250 Placed in service May 31, 1943.
    Placed out of service November 24,
    1945.
251 Placed in service May 31, 1943. De-
    stroyed by enemy shore batteries, Feb-
    ruary 26, 1944.
252 Placed in service June 14, 1943.
    Placed out of service, stripped and de-
    stroyed, November 24, 1945.
253 Placed in service June 14, 1943.
    Placed out of service November 24,
    1945.
254 Placed in service June 16, 1943.
    Placed out of service November 24,
    1945.

Squadron 20, assigned to the South Pacific,
had action at Treasury and Bougainville.
Transferred to the Southwest Pacific in De-
cember 1944, the squadron saw action off
Palawan, P.I. It also based for a time at
Dreger Harbor, Aitape, and Mios Woendi,
New Guinea, and at San Pedro Bay and
Mindoro in the Philippines, but had no
action from these bases.

MOTOR TORPEDO BOAT SQUADRON 21

Commissioned April 8, 1943; decommissioned November 10, 1945.

Squadron Commanders:

Comdr. SELMAN S. BOWLING
April 8, 1943–January 30, 1944
Lt. PAUL T. RENNELL, USNR
January 30–October 1, 1944
Lt. CARL T. GLEASON
October 1, 1944–March 3, 1945
Lt. Comdr. EDWARD W. ROBERTS, USNR
March 3–October 19, 1945
Lt. HARRY R. HUNT, USNR
October 19–November 10, 1945

PT 80′ Elco

128, 131, 132 Transferred from Squadron 7, February 15, 1945. Placed out of service, stripped and destroyed, November 10, 1945.

320 Placed in service April 8, 1943. Destroyed by enemy aircraft, November 5, 1944.

321 Placed in service April 8, 1943. Destroyed to prevent capture, November 11, 1944.

322 Placed in service April 8, 1943. Destroyed to prevent capture, November 24, 1943.

323 Placed in service April 8, 1943. Destroyed by enemy suicide plane, December 10, 1944.

324 Placed in service April 8, 1943. Placed out of service, stripped and destroyed, November 10, 1945.

PT 80′ Elco

325 Placed in service April 10, 1943. Placed out of service, stripped and destroyed, November 10, 1945.

326 Placed in service April 13, 1943. Placed out of service November 10, 1945.

327 Placed in service April 15, 1943. Placed out of service, stripped and destroyed, November 10, 1945.

328 Placed in service April 17, 1943. Placed out of service November 10, 1945.

329 Placed in service April 21, 1943. Placed out of service, stripped and destroyed, November 10, 1945.

330 Placed in service April 23, 1943. Placed out of service, stripped and destroyed, November 10, 1945.

331 Placed in service April 27, 1943. Placed out of service, stripped and destroyed, November 10, 1945.

Squadron 21, assigned to the Southwest Pacific, had action at Morobe, Dreger Harbor, and Mios Woendi in New Guinea; at Manus in the Admiralties; and at San Pedro Bay and Subic Bay in the Philippines. It also based for a time at Kana Kopa, New Guinea, and at Samar and Basilan Island in the Philippines, but had no action from these bases. Squadron 21 was awarded the Presidential Unit Citation for action in the New Guinea area from October 1943 to March 1944.

MOTOR TORPEDO BOAT SQUADRON 22

Commissioned November 10, 1943; decommissioned November 15, 1945.

Squadron Commander:

Lt. Comdr. RICHARD J. DRESSLING
November 10, 1943–November 15, 1945.

PT 78′ Higgins

302 Placed in service November 9, 1943. Placed out of service October 15, 1945.

303 Placed in service November 29, 1943. Placed out of service November 15, 1945.

PT 78' Higgins

304 Placed in service November 23, 1943. Placed out of service November 15, 1945.

305 Placed in service December 8, 1943. Placed out of service November 15, 1945.

306 Placed in service December 3, 1943. Placed out of service November 15, 1945.

307 Placed in service December 2, 1943. Placed out of service October 15, 1945.

308 Placed in service January 24, 1944. Placed out of service November 15, 1945.

309 Placed in service January 26, 1944. Placed out of service November 15, 1945.

310 Placed in service January 27, 1944. Placed out of service November 15, 1945.

311 Placed in service January 25, 1944. Destroyed by enemy mine, November 18, 1944.

312 Placed in service January 29, 1944. Placed out of service November 15, 1945.

PT 78' Higgins

313 Placed in service January 31, 1944. Placed out of service November 15, 1945.

Squadron 22, assigned to the Mediterranean, based at Bastia, Corsica, and St. Tropez, France, and had action along the northwest coast of Italy and southern coast of France, operating under the British Coastal Forces. After the end of the Mediterranean campaign in April 1945, the squadron was shipped back to the United States for reconditioning and reassignment to the Pacific, but the war ended while the squadron was still in New York.

It will be observed that Squadron 22 was commissioned after and has higher boat numbers than the next higher numbered Higgins unit, Squadron 23. Originally PT's 265–276 were assigned to Squadron 22, but before the squadron was commissioned or any boats were delivered, these boats were reassigned for transfer under lend-lease to U.S.S.R.

MOTOR TORPEDO BOAT SQUADRON 23

Commissioned June 28, 1943; decommissioned November 26, 1945.

Squadron Commanders:

Lt. Comdr. RONALD K. IRVING
June 28, 1943–May 1944
Lt. ALAN W. FERRON, USNR
May 1944–January 5, 1945
Lt. JAMES H. VAN SICKLEN, USNR
January 5–June 20, 1945
Lt. WILLIAM E. STEDMAN, USNR
June 20–October 14, 1945
Lt. DONALD F. GALLOWAY, USNR
October 14–November 26, 1945

PT 78' Higgins

241, 242 Transferred from Squadron 19, April 19, 1944. Transferred to Squadron 16, February 25, 1945.

PT 78' Higgins

243, 244 Transferred from Squadron 19, April 19, 1944. Placed out of service, stripped and destroyed, November 26, 1945.

277 Placed in service July 8, 1943. Placed out of service, stripped and destroyed, November 26, 1945.

278 Placed in service July 9, 1943. Placed out of service November 26, 1945.

279 Placed in service June 28, 1943. Lost in collision, February 12, 1944.

280 Placed in service June 28, 1943. Placed out of service, stripped and destroyed, November 26, 1945.

281 Placed in service July 8, 1943. Placed out of service, stripped and destroyed, November 26, 1945.

PT *78′ Higgins*

282 Placed in service July 12, 1943. Placed out of service, stripped and destroyed, November 26, 1945.

283 Placed in service July 12, 1943. Destroyed by enemy shorefire or U.S. warship, March 17, 1944.

284 Placed in service July 21, 1943. Placed out of service, stripped and destroyed, November 26, 1945.

285 Placed in service July 16, 1943. Placed out of service, stripped and destroyed, November 26, 1945.

286 Placed in service August 4, 1943. Placed out of service, stripped and destroyed, November 26, 1945.

PT *78′ Higgins*

287 Placed in service July 22, 1943. Placed out of service, stripped and destroyed, November 26, 1945.

288 Placed in service July 24, 1943. Placed out of service, stripped and destroyed, November 26, 1945.

Squadron 23, assigned to the South Pacific, had action at Bougainville and Green. Transferred to the Southwest Pacific in December 1944, the squadron had action at Palawan, in the Philippines. It also based for a time at Mios Woendi, New Guinea, and at Mindoro, P.I., but had no action from these bases.

MOTOR TORPEDO BOAT SQUADRON 24

Commissioned May 10, 1943; decommissioned November 6, 1945.
Squadron Commanders:
Lt. Comdr. N. BURT DAVIS
May 10, 1943–November 14, 1944
Lt. STANLEY C. THOMAS, USNR
November 14, 1944–January 25, 1945
Lt. Comdr. EDGAR D. HOGLAND, USNR
January 25–October 14, 1945
Lt. JOSEPH K. ROBERTS, USNR
October 14–November 6, 1945

PT *80′ Elco*

106 Transferred from Squadron 5, February 15, 1945. Placed out of service, stripped and destroyed, November 6, 1945.

332–335 Placed in service May 10, 1943. Placed out of service November 6, 1945.

336 Placed in service May 12, 1943. Placed out of service November 6, 1945.

337 Placed in service May 14, 1943. Destroyed by enemy shore batteries, March 7, 1944.

338 Placed in service May 18, 1943. Damaged by grounding and destroyed, January 31, 1945.

PT *80′ Elco*

339 Placed in service May 22, 1943. Destroyed to prevent capture, May 27, 1944.

340 Placed in service May 25, 1943. Placed out of service November 6, 1945.

341 Placed in service May 28, 1943. Placed out of service November 6, 1945.

342 Placed in service May 31, 1943. Placed out of service November 6, 1945.

343 Placed in service June 1, 1943. Placed out of service November 6, 1945.

Squadron 24, assigned to the Southwest Pacific, had action at Dreger Harbor, Saidor, and Amsterdam Island in New Guinea, and at Mindoro, Zamboanga, Polloc Harbor, Sarangani Bay, and Davao Gulf in the Philippines. It also based for a time at Kana Kopa and Mios Woendi, New Guinea, and at San Pedro Bay and Basilan Island in the Philippines, but had no action from these bases.

MOTOR TORPEDO BOAT SQUADRON 25

Commissioned June 17, 1943; decommissioned November 9, 1945.

Squadron Commanders:

Lt. DANIEL S. BAUGHMAN, Jr.
June 17–November 25, 1943

Lt. JAMES R. THOMPSON, USNR
November 25, 1943–June 8, 1944

Lt. Comdr. RICHARD E. JOHNSON
June 8–August 23, 1944

Lt. WENDELL E. CARROLL, USNR
August 23–December 7, 1944

Lt. Comdr. THEODORE R. STANSBURY, USNR
December 7, 1944–October 16, 1945

Lt. FREDERICK A. STEVENS, Jr., USNR
October 16–November 9, 1945

PT 80' Elco

115 Transferred from Squadron 6, May 29, 1944. Placed out of service, stripped and destroyed, November 9, 1945.

134 Transferred from Squadron 7, February 15, 1945. Placed out of service, stripped and destroyed, November 9, 1945.

344 Placed in service June 17, 1943. Placed out of service November 9, 1945.

345 Placed in service June 17, 1943. Placed out of service, stripped and destroyed, November 9, 1945.

346, 347 Placed in service June 17, 1943. Destroyed by U.S. aircraft, April 29, 1944.

PT 80' Elco

348 Placed in service June 17, 1943. Placed out of service November 9, 1945.

349 Placed in service June 18, 1943. Placed out of service November 9, 1945.

350 Placed in service June 22, 1943. Placed out of service, stripped and destroyed, November 9, 1945.

351 Placed in service June 25, 1943. Placed out of service, stripped and destroyed, November 9, 1945.

352 Placed in service June 28, 1943. Placed out of service, stripped and destroyed, November 9, 1945.

353 Placed in service July 2, 1943. Destroyed by Australian aircraft, March 27, 1944.

354 Placed in service July 6, 1943. Placed out of service November 9, 1945.

355 Placed in service July 8, 1943. Placed out of service November 9, 1945.

Squadron 25, assigned to the Southwest Pacific, had action at Dreger Harbor, Mios Woendi, and Amsterdam Island in New Guinea; Rein Bay and Talasea in New Britain; Mindoro and Ormoc in the Philippines; and Morotai in the Halmaheras. It also based for a time at Kana Kopa, New Guinea, and San Pedro Bay in the Philippines, but had no action from these bases.

MOTOR TORPEDO BOAT SQUADRON 26

Commissioned March 3, 1943; decommissioned December 3, 1945.

Squadron Commanders:

Lt. ROBERT LEESON, USNR
March 3–May 1, 1943

Lt. ANTHONY B. AKERS, USNR
May 1–December 23, 1943

Lt. Comdr. LESTER H. GAMBLE
December 23, 1943–December 3, 1945

PT 78' Huckins

255 Placed in service February 25, 1943. Placed out of service December 3, 1945.

PT 78' Huckins

256 Placed in service February 26, 1943. Placed out of service December 3, 1945.

257 Placed in service March 29, 1943. Placed out of service December 3, 1945.

258 Placed in service March 30, 1943. Placed out of service December 3, 1945.

259 Placed in service May 25, 1943. Placed out of service December 3, 1945.

260 Placed in service May 27, 1943. Placed out of service December 3, 1945.

PT 78' Huckins

261 Placed in service June 30, 1943. Placed out of service December 3, 1945.

262 Placed in service July 7, 1943. Placed out of service December 3, 1945.

263 Placed in service July 31, 1943. Placed out of service December 3, 1945.

264 Placed in service September 7, 1943. Placed out of service December 3, 1945.

Squadron 26 was assigned to the Hawaiian Sea Frontier. It had no action with the enemy.

MOTOR TORPEDO BOAT SQUADRON 27

Commissioned July 23, 1943; decommissioned October 19, 1945.

Squadron Commanders:

Comdr. CLINTON McKELLAR, Jr.
July 23, 1943–June 28, 1944

Lt. Comdr. JOHN S. BONTE, USNR
June 28–November 23, 1944

Lt. Comdr. HENRY S. TAYLOR, USNR
November 23, 1944–October 19, 1945

PT 80' Elco

356, 357 Placed in service July 22, 1943. Placed out of service October 19, 1945.

358 Placed in service July 23, 1943. Placed out of service October 19, 1945.

359, 360 Placed in service July 22, 1943. Placed out of service October 19, 1945.

361 Placed in service July 27, 1943. Placed out of service October 19, 1945.

372 Placed in service August 3, 1943. Placed out of service October 19, 1945.

PT 80' Elco

373 Placed in service August 5, 1943. Placed out of service October 19, 1945.

374 Placed in service August 6, 1943. Placed out of service October 19, 1945.

375 Placed in service August 10, 1943. Placed out of service October 19, 1945.

376 Placed in service August 12, 1943. Placed out of service October 19, 1945.

377 Placed in service August 14, 1943. Placed out of service October 19, 1945.

Squadron 27, assigned to the South Pacific, had action at Treasury and Green. Assigned temporarily to the Third Fleet, the squadron was based at Palau, in the Marianas, from October to December 1944, when it was transferred to the Southwest Pacific. There it had action at San Pedro Bay and Subic Bay in the Philippines, and Balikpapan in Borneo.

MOTOR TORPEDO BOAT SQUADRON 28

Commissioned August 30, 1943; decommissioned October 21, 1945.

Squadron Commanders:

Lt. Comdr. GEORGE A. MATTESON, Jr., USNR
August 30, 1943–May 25, 1945
Lt. DONALD M. CRAIG, USNR
May 25–October 21, 1945

PT 80' Elco

378–382 Placed in service August 30, 1943. Placed out of service October 21, 1945.

383 Placed in service September 1, 1943. Placed out of service October 21, 1945.

546 Placed in service September 3, 1943. Placed out of service October 21, 1945.

547 Placed in service October 4, 1943. Placed out of service October 21, 1945.

PT 80' Elco

548 Placed in service September 7, 1943. Placed out of service October 21, 1945.

549 Placed in service September 10, 1943. Placed out of service October 21, 1945.

550 Placed in service September 14, 1943. Placed out of service October 21, 1945.

551 Placed in service September 16, 1943. Placed out of service October 21, 1945.

Squadron 28, assigned to the South Pacific, had action at Treasury and Green. Transferred to the Southwest Pacific in October 1944, it had action at Lingayen Gulf in the Philippines. It also based for a time at Mios Woendi in New Guinea and at San Pedro Bay in the Philippines, but had no action from these bases.

MOTOR TORPEDO BOAT SQUADRON 29

Commissioned October 22, 1943; decommissioned November 23, 1944.

Squadron Commander:

Comdr. S. STEPHEN DAUNIS
October 22, 1943–November 23, 1944

PT 80' Elco

552 Placed in service October 22, 1943. Transferred under lend-lease to U.S.S.R., April 7, 1945.

553 Placed in service October 22, 1943. Transferred under lend-lease to U.S.S.R., April 12, 1945.

554 Placed in service October 22, 1943. Transferred under lend-lease to U.S.S.R., May 8, 1945.

555 Placed in service October 26, 1943. Destroyed by enemy mine, August 24, 1944.

556 Placed in service October 28, 1943. Transferred under lend-lease to U.S.S.R. April 12, 1945.

557 Placed in service October 30, 1943. Transferred to Squadron 4, November 23, 1944.

PT 80' Elco

558 Placed in service November 2, 1943. Transferred to Squadron 4, November 23, 1944.

559 Placed in service November 4, 1943. Transferred to Squadron 4, November 23, 1944.

560 Placed in service November 6, 1943. Transferred under lend-lease to U.S.S.R., May 8, 1945.

561 Placed in service November 9, 1943. Transferred under lend-lease to U.S.S.R., April 12, 1945.

562 Placed in service November 11, 1943. Transferred under lend-lease to U.S.S.R., April 7, 1945.

563 Placed in service November 22, 1943. Transferred under lend-lease to U.S.S.R., April 12, 1945.

Squadron 29, assigned to the Mediterranean, based at Calvi, Corsica, and Leghorn, Italy, and had action along the northwest coast of Italy and southern coast of France, operating under the British Coastal Forces.

MOTOR TORPEDO BOAT SQUADRON 30

Commissioned February 15, 1944; decommissioned November 15, 1945.
Squadron Commanders:
Lt. Comdr. ROBERT L. SEARLES, USNR
February 15, 1944–October 1945
Lt. Comdr LAWRENCE F. JONES, USNR
October–November 15, 1945

PT 78' Higgins

450–452 Placed in service February 15, 1944. Transferred to Squadron 4, March 23, 1944.
453 Placed in service March 14, 1944. Transferred to Squadron 31, May 11, 1944.
454, 455 Placed in service February 15, 1944. Transferred to Squadron 31, May 11, 1944.
456 Placed in service March 11, 1944. Placed out of service November 15, 1945.
457 Placed in service March 15, 1944. Placed out of service November 15, 1945.

PT 78' Higgins

458 Placed in service March 18, 1944. Placed out of service November 15, 1945.
459 Placed in service March 23, 1944. Placed out of service November 15, 1945.
460 Placed in service March 27, 1944. Placed out of service November 15, 1945.
461 Placed in service March 28, 1944. Placed out of service November 15, 1945.

Squadron 30 had action in the English Channel area during the period June 1944 to June 1945. It was then returned to the United States for reconditioning and reassignment to the Pacific, but the war ended while the squadron was still in New York.

MOTOR TORPEDO BOAT SQUADRON 31

Commissioned April 5, 1944; decommissioned December 17, 1945.

Squadron Commanders:

Lt. JOHN M. SEARLES, USNR
April 5, 1944–October 1945
Lt. Comdr. FRANK B. GASS, USNR
October–December 17, 1945

PT 78' Higgins

453–455 Transferred from Squadron 30, May 11, 1944. Placed out of service December 17, 1945.
462 Placed in service March 29, 1944. Placed out of service December 17, 1945.
463 Placed in service April 1, 1944. Placed out of service December 17, 1945.

PT 78' Higgins

464 Placed in service April 5, 1944. Placed out of service December 17, 1945.
465 Placed in service April 13, 1944. Placed out of service December 17, 1945.
466 Placed in service April 17, 1944. Placed out of service December 17, 1945.
467 Placed in service April 20, 1944. Placed out of service December 17, 1945.
468 Placed in service April 24, 1944. Placed out of service December 17, 1945.
469 Placed in service April 28, 1944. Placed out of service December 17, 1945.

PT 78′ Higgins

470 Placed in service April 29, 1944. Placed out of service December 17, 1945.

471 Placed in service May 5, 1944. Placed out of service December 17, 1945.

472 Placed in service May 11, 1944. Placed out of service December 17, 1945.

473 Placed in service May 16, 1944. Placed out of service December 17, 1945.

Squadron 31, assigned to Pacific Fleet, had action at Treasury Island in the Solomons during October and November 1944; at Palau, in the Marianas, during the period December 1944 to February 1945, and at Okinawa during the period June to August 1945. The squadron also based for a time in San Pedro Bay, in the Philippines, but had no action from this base.

MOTOR TORPEDO BOAT SQUADRON 32

Commissioned June 10, 1944; decommissioned December 18, 1945.

Squadron Commanders:

Lt. Comdr. ROBERT C. WARK, USNR
June 10, 1944–October 13, 1945

Lt. JAMES E. COLEMAN, USNR
October 13–December 18, 1945

PT 78′ Higgins

474 Placed in service June 9, 1944. Placed out of service, stripped and destroyed, November 2, 1945.

475 Placed in service June 15, 1944. Placed out of service December 18, 1945.

476 Placed in service June 16, 1944. Placed out of service December 18, 1945.

477 Placed in service July 1, 1944. Placed out of service, stripped and destroyed, November 2, 1945.

478 Placed in service June 28, 1944. Placed out of service December 18, 1945.

479 Placed in service July 11, 1944. Placed out of service December 18, 1945.

PT 78′ Higgins

480 Placed in service July 15, 1944. Placed out of service December 18, 1945.

481 Placed in service July 22, 1944. Placed out of service December 18, 1945.

482 Placed in service August 3, 1944. Placed out of service December 18, 1945.

483 Placed in service August 12, 1944. Placed out of service December 18, 1945.

484 Placed in service August 30, 1944. Placed out of service December 18, 1945.

485 Placed in service August 29, 1944. Placed out of service December 18, 1945.

Squadron 32, assigned to Pacific Fleet, had action at Treasury Island in the Solomons during the period December 1944 to February 1945. The squadron based at Espiritu Santo, New Hebrides, from February to August 1945, and at Okinawa from September to December 1945, but had no action with the enemy while at these bases.

MOTOR TORPEDO BOAT SQUADRON 33

Commissioned December 2, 1943; decommissioned October 24, 1945.

Squadron Commanders:

Lt. A. MURRAY PRESTON, USNR
December 2, 1943–May 5, 1945
Lt. Comdr. EDWIN A. DuBOSE, USNR
May 5–October 24, 1945

PT 80' Elco

137, 138 Transferred from Squadron 7, February 15, 1945. Placed out of service, stripped and destroyed, October 24, 1945.

488–492 Placed in service December 2, 1943. Placed out of service October 24, 1945.

493 Placed in service December 6, 1943. Destroyed by enemy warships, October 25, 1944.

PT 80' Elco

494 Placed in service December 9, 1943. Placed out of service October 24, 1945.

495 Placed in service December 13, 1943. Placed out of service October 24, 1945.

496 Placed in service December 14, 1943. Placed out of service October 24, 1945.

497 Placed in service December 18, 1943. Placed out of service October 24, 1945.

Squadron 33, assigned to the Southwest Pacific, had action at Aitape, New Guinea; Morotai in the Halmaheras; and San Pedro Bay and Panay in the Philippines. It also based for a time at Dreger Harbor and Mios Woendi, New Guinea, but had no action from these bases. PT's 486 and 487 originally were assigned to Squadron 33, but were reassigned to Squadron 4, December 2, 1943.

MOTOR TORPEDO BOAT SQUADRON 34

Commissioned December 31, 1943; decommissioned March 9, 1945.

Squadron Commanders:

Lt. ALLEN H. HARRIS, USNR
December 31, 1943–July 16, 1944
Lt. HERBERT J. SHERERTZ, USNR
July 16, 1944–March 9, 1945

PT 80' Elco

498 Placed in service December 31, 1943. Transferred under lend-lease to U.S.S.R., March 4, 1945.

499, 500 Placed in service December 31, 1943. Transferred under lend-lease to U.S.S.R., December 30, 1944.

501, 502 Placed in service December 31, 1943. Transferred under lend-lease to U.S.S.R., January 31, 1945.

503 Placed in service January 4, 1944. Transferred under lend-lease to U.S.S.R., December 30, 1944.

PT 80' Elco

504 Placed in service January 11, 1944. Transferred under lend-lease to U.S.S.R., December 30, 1944.

505 Placed in service January 13, 1944. Transferred to Squadron 4, December 29, 1944.

506 Placed in service January 15, 1944. Transferred under lend-lease to U.S.S.R., January 31, 1945.

507 Placed in service January 18, 1944. Transferred under lend-lease to U.S.S.R., March 4, 1945.

508 Placed in service January 21, 1944. Transferred under lend-lease to U.S.S.R., January 31, 1945.

509 Placed in service January 25, 1944. Destroyed by enemy warships, August 9, 1944.

Squadron 34 had action in the English Channel area from June 1944 to October 1944, when orders were received to prepare the boats for delivery to U.S.S.R.

MOTOR TORPEDO BOAT SQUADRON 35

Commissioned February 15, 1944; decommissioned April 10, 1945.
Squadron Commanders:
  Lt. Comdr. RICHARD DAVIS, Jr.
  February 15–June 11, 1944
  Lt. Comdr. ARTHUR N. BARNES, USNR
  June 11, 1944–April 10, 1945

PT 80' Elco

510–513 Placed in service February 15, 1944. Transferred under lend-lease to U.S.S.R., December 30, 1944.

514 Placed in service February 15, 1944. Transferred under lend-lease to U.S.S.R., March 4, 1945.

515 Placed in service February 17, 1944. Transferred under lend-lease to U.S.S.R., March 4, 1945.

516 Placed in service February 24, 1944. Transferred under lend-lease to U.S.S.R., April 7, 1945.

PT 80' Elco

517 Placed in service February 25, 1944. Transferred under lend-lease to U.S.S.R., April 7, 1945.

518 Placed in service February 29, 1944. Transferred under lend-lease to U.S.S.R., April 7, 1945.

519 Placed in service March 1, 1944. Transferred under lend-lease to U.S.S.R., April 7, 1945.

520 Placed in service March 7, 1944. Transferred under lend-lease to U.S.S.R., April 7, 1945.

521 Placed in service March 11, 1944. Transferred under lend-lease to U.S.S.R., April 7, 1945.

Squadron 35 had action in the English Channel area from June to November 1944, when orders were received to prepare the boats for delivery to U.S.S.R.

MOTOR TORPEDO BOAT SQUADRON 36

Commissioned April 3, 1944; decommissioned October 29, 1945.
Squadron Commanders:
  Lt. Comdr. FRANCIS D. TAPPAAN, USNR
  April 3–December 1944
  Lt. JOHN W. MORRISON, Jr., USNR
  December 1944–August 15, 1945
  Lt. RALPH O. AMSDEN, Jr., USNR
  August 15–October 29, 1945

PT 80' Elco

522–525 Placed in service April 3, 1944. Placed out of service October 29, 1945.

526 Placed in service April 5, 1944. Placed out of service October 29, 1945.

527 Placed in service April 11, 1944. Placed out of service October 29, 1945.

528 Placed in service April 17, 1944. Placed out of service October 29, 1945.

PT 80' Elco

529 Placed in service April 22, 1944. Placed out of service October 29, 1945.

530 Placed in service April 27, 1944. Placed out of service October 29, 1945.

531 Placed in service May 4, 1944. Placed out of service October 29, 1945.

532 Placed in service May 11, 1944. Placed out of service October 29, 1945.

Squadron 36, assigned to the Southwest Pacific, had action at Mios Woendi, New Guinea; at San Pedro Bay, Lingayen Gulf, and Tawi Tawi in the Philippines; and at Tarakan, Borneo. PT 533 originally was assigned to Squadron 36, but was reassigned to Squadron 37 before it was placed in service.

MOTOR TORPEDO BOAT SQUADRON 37

Commissioned June 5, 1944; decommissioned December 7, 1945.
Squadron Commanders:
  Lt. Comdr. CLARK W. FAULKNER, USNR
    June 5, 1944–October 1945
  Lt. JAMES J. CROSS, Jr., USNR
    October–December 7, 1945

PT 80' Elco

533 Placed in service May 17, 1944. Placed out of service December 7, 1945.

534–536 Placed in service June 5, 1944. Placed out of service December 7, 1945.

537 Placed in service June 9, 1944. Placed out of service December 7, 1945.

538 Placed in service June 15, 1944. Placed out of service December 7, 1945.

539 Placed in service June 21, 1944. Placed out of service December 7, 1945.

PT 80' Elco

540 Placed in service June 28, 1944. Placed out of service December 7, 1945.

541 Placed in service July 5, 1944. Placed out of service December 7, 1945.

542 Placed in service July 10, 1944. Placed out of service December 7, 1945.

543 Placed in service July 15, 1944. Placed out of service December 7, 1945.

544 Placed in service July 21, 1944. Placed out of service December 7, 1945.

Squadron 37, assigned to Pacific Fleet, had action at Treasury Island in the Solomons from November 1944 to February 1945. The squadron based at Espiritu Santo, New Hebrides, from February to July 1945, and at Okinawa from August to November 1945, but had no action with the enemy while at these bases. PT 545 originally was assigned to Squadron 37, but was reassigned to Squadron 4 before it was placed in service.

MOTOR TORPEDO BOAT SQUADRON 38

Commissioned December 20, 1944; decommissioned October 24, 1945.
Squadron Commander:
  Lt. Comdr. CHARLES A. MILLS, Jr., USNR
    December 20, 1944–October 24, 1945

PT 80' Elco

565 Placed in service December 8, 1944. Placed out of service October 24, 1945.

566 Placed in service December 14, 1944. Placed out of service October 24, 1945.

567 Placed in service December 17, 1944. Placed out of service October 24, 1945.

568 Placed in service December 19, 1944. Placed out of service October 24, 1945.

569 Placed in service December 23, 1944. Placed out of service October 24, 1945.

PT 80' Elco

570 Placed in service December 30, 1944. Placed out of service October 24, 1945.

571 Placed in service January 14, 1945. Placed out of service October 24, 1945.

572 Placed in service January 16, 1945. Placed out of service October 24, 1945.

573 Placed in service January 23, 1945. Placed out of service October 24, 1945.

574 Placed in service February 7, 1945. Placed out of service October 24, 1945.

575 Placed in service February 7, 1945. Transferred to Squadron 39, September 28, 1945.

576 Placed in service February 12, 1945. Transferred to Squadron 39, September 28, 1945.

Squadron 38, assigned to the Southwest Pacific, arrived at Samar, P.I., in May, June, and July, 1945. The squadron based there and at Basilan Island, P.I., but had no action except for some strafing of shore installations in Borneo early in August 1945.

MOTOR TORPEDO BOAT SQUADRON 39

Commissioned March 6, 1945; decommissioned December 24, 1945.
Squadron Commanders:
    Lt. RUSSELL E. HAMACHEK, USNR
        March 6–September 1945
    Lt. CHARLES A. BERNIER, Jr., USNR
        September–December 24, 1945

PT 80' Elco
575, 576 Transferred from Squadron 38, September 28, 1945. Placed out of service December 24, 1945.
577 Placed in service February 21, 1945. Placed out of service December 24, 1945.
578 Placed in service February 24, 1945. Placed out of service December 24, 1945.
579 Placed in service March 2, 1945. Placed out of service December 24, 1945.
580 Placed in service March 6, 1945. Placed out of service December 24, 1945.
581 Placed in service March 8, 1945. Placed out of service December 24, 1945.

PT 80' Elco
582 Placed in service March 13, 1945. Placed out of service December 24, 1945.
583 Placed in service March 20, 1945. Placed out of service December 24, 1945.
584 Placed in service March 22, 1945. Placed out of service December 24, 1945.
585 Placed in service March 28, 1945. Placed out of service December 24, 1945.
586 Placed in service March 30, 1945. Placed out of service December 24, 1945.
587 Placed in service April 4, 1945. Placed out of service December 24, 1945.
588 Placed in service April 10, 1945. Placed out of service December 24, 1945.

Squadron 39, assigned to Pacific Fleet, arrived at Samar, P.I., in July 1945, and was there at the cessation of hostilities. It had no action with the enemy.

MOTOR TORPEDO BOAT SQUADRON 40

Commissioned April 26, 1945; decommissioned December 21, 1945.

Squadron Commander:
    Lt. Comdr. GEORGE E. COX, Jr., USNR
        April 26–December 21, 1945

PT 80' Elco
589 Placed in service April 13, 1945. Placed out of service December 21, 1945.

PT 80' Elco
590 Placed in service April 16, 1945. Placed out of service December 21, 1945.
591 Placed in service April 19, 1945. Placed out of service December 21, 1945.
592 Placed in service April 21, 1945. Placed out of service December 21, 1945.

PT 8o′ Elco

593 Placed in service April 25, 1945. Placed out of service December 21, 1945.

594 Placed in service April 28, 1945. Placed out of service December 21, 1945.

595 Placed in service May 4, 1945. Placed out of service December 21, 1945.

596 Placed in service May 10, 1945. Placed out of service December 21, 1945.

597 Placed in service May 16, 1945. Placed out of service December 21, 1945.

PT 8o′ Elco

598 Placed in service May 21, 1945. Placed out of service December 21, 1945.

599 Placed in service May 25, 1945. Placed out of service December 21, 1945.

600 Placed in service May 31, 1945. Placed out of service December 21, 1945.

Squadron 40, assigned to Pacific Fleet, arrived at Samar, P.I., in the summer of 1945, but had no action with the enemy prior to the cessation of hostilities.

MOTOR TORPEDO BOAT SQUADRON 41

Commissioned June 21, 1945; decommissioned February 6, 1946.
Squadron Commander:
   Lt. Comdr. BRUCE P. VAN BUSKIRK, USNR
   June 21, 1945–February 6, 1946

PT 8o′ Elco

601 Placed in service June 5, 1945. Placed out of service February 1, 1946.

602 Placed in service June 8, 1945. Placed out of service January 30, 1946.

603 Placed in service June 28, 1945. Placed out of service January 30, 1946.

604 Placed in service June 13, 1945. Placed out of service January 30, 1946.

605 Placed in service June 18, 1945. Placed out of service January 30, 1946.

606 Placed in service June 23, 1945. Placed out of service January 30, 1946.

PT 8o′ Elco

607 Placed in service July 4, 1945. Placed out of service January 30, 1946.

608 Placed in service July 14, 1945. Placed out of service January 30, 1946.

609 Placed in service July 9, 1945. Placed out of service February 1, 1946.

610 Placed in service July 19, 1945. Placed out of service January 30, 1946.

611 Placed in service July 25, 1945. Placed out of service February 1, 1946.

612 Placed in service July 31, 1945. Placed out of service February 1, 1946.

Squadron 41 had completed its fitting out and was having shakedown at Miami at the time of the cessation of hostilities in August 1945. Although assigned to the Pacific Fleet, it was never shipped to the Pacific.

MOTOR TORPEDO BOAT SQUADRON 42

Commissioned September 17, 1945; decommissioned February 8, 1946.
Squadron Commander:
   Lt. Comdr. JAMES A. DANVER, USNR
   September 17, 1945–February 8, 1946

PT 8o′ Elco

613 Placed in service August 10, 1945. Transferred to Squadron 4, January 26, 1946.

PT 8o′ Elco

614 Placed in service August 14, 1945. Placed out of service January 28, 1946.

615 Placed in service September 5, 1945. Placed out of service January 28, 1946.

616 Placed in service September 11, 1945. Transferred to Squadron 4, January 26, 1946.

PT *80' Elco*

617 Placed in service September 21, 1945.
Placed out of service January 28, 1946.

618 Placed in service September 24, 1945.
Placed out of service February 4, 1946.

619 Placed in service October 1, 1945.
Transferred to Squadron 4, January
26, 1946.

620 Placed in service October 5, 1945.
Transferred to Squadron 4, January
26, 1946.

621 Placed in service October 12, 1945.
Placed out of service January 28, 1946.

PT *80' Elco*

622 Placed in service October 20, 1945.
Placed out of service January 28, 1946.

Squadron 42 was the only squadron commissioned after the cessation of hostilities. Although assigned to the Pacific Fleet, it was never shipped to the Pacific. PT's 623 and 624 originally were assigned to Squadron 42, but their construction was halted on October 1, 1945, and they were never completed.

MOTOR TORPEDO BOAT SQUADRON 43

Commissioned December 12, 1944; decommissioned March 16, 1945.

Squadron Commander:

Lt. RICHARD C. MORSE, Jr., USNR
December 12, 1944–March 16, 1945

PT *78' Higgins*

625 Placed in service December 8, 1944.
Transferred under lend-lease to
U.S.S.R., May 22, 1945.

626 Placed in service December 19, 1944.
Transferred under lend-lease to
U.S.S.R., May 22, 1945.

627 Placed in service January 8, 1945.
Transferred under lend-lease to
U.S.S.R., May 22, 1945.

628 Placed in service January 17, 1945.
Transferred under lend-lease to
U.S.S.R., May 22, 1945.

PT *78' Higgins*

629 Placed in service January 30, 1945.
Transferred under lend-lease to
U.S.S.R., June 8, 1945.

630 Placed in service February 9, 1945.
Transferred under lend-lease to
U.S.S.R., June 8, 1945.

631 Placed in service February 21, 1945.
Transferred under lend-lease to
U.S.S.R., June 8, 1945.

632, 633 Placed in service March 16, 1945.
Transferred under lend-lease to
U.S.S.R., June 8, 1945.

Squadron 43, assigned to Pacific Fleet, was decommissioned so that its boats might be transferred to U.S.S.R. PT's 634–636 were also originally assigned to the squadron, but had not been placed in service at the time of decommissioning.

MOTOR TORPEDO BOAT SQUADRON 44

PT's 637–648 (78' Higgins) originally were assigned to Squadron 44, but in April 1945 these boats were reassigned, before any had been placed in service, for transfer under lend-lease to U.S.S.R. PT's 761–772 (80' Elco) were then assigned to Squadron 44, but the contract for their construction was canceled on August 27, 1945. Squadron 44 was never commissioned.

MOTOR TORPEDO BOAT SQUADRON 45

PT's 649–660 (78′ Higgins) originally were assigned to Squadron 45, but in April 1945 these boats were reassigned, before any had been placed in service, for transfer under lend-lease to U.S.S.R. PT's 773–784 (80′ Elco) were then assigned to Squadron 45, but the contract for their construction was canceled on August 27, 1945. Squadron 45 was never commissioned.

MOTOR BOAT SUBMARINE CHASER SQUADRON 1

Commissioned February 20, 1941; decommissioned July 17, 1941.

Squadron Commander:

Lt. (jg.) JOHN D. BULKELEY
February 20–July 17, 1941

PTC 70′ Elco

1 Placed in service March 6, 1941. Transferred under lend-lease to Britain, July 15, 1941.

2 Placed in service March 1941. Transferred under lend-lease to Britain, July 15, 1941.

3 Placed in service March 3, 1941. Transferred under lend-lease to Britain, July 15, 1941.

4 Placed in service March 11, 1941. Transferred under lend-lease to Britain, July 15, 1941.

PTC 70′ Elco

5, 6 Placed in service March 6, 1941. Transferred under lend-lease to Britain, April 4, 1941.

7, 8 Placed in service March 12, 1941. Transferred under lend-lease to Britain, April 4, 1941.

9 Placed in service March 9, 1941. Transferred under lend-lease to Britain, April 4, 1941.

10–12 Placed in service March 1941. Transferred under lend-lease to Britain, April 4, 1941.

Motor Boat Submarine Chaser Squadron 1 was abandoned because of failure to develop satisfactory sound gear to enable the boats to locate submarines. The British converted the boats to motor gunboats, designating them as MGB's 82–93.

PT'S NOT PLACED IN SQUADRON SERVICE

PT

1, 2 (58′, built by Miami Shipbuilding Co.) Originally assigned to Squadron 1. Never placed in squadron service but reclassified as small boats on December 24, 1941.

6 The original PT 6, an 81′ boat of Sparkman & Stephens design, built by Higgins, was sold to Finland in 1940. The second PT 6, an 81′ boat designed and built by Higgins, was placed in service in Squadron 1.

49–58 (77′ Elco.) Built as BPT's (British PT's) 1–10 and transferred under

PT

lend-lease to Britain in February and March 1942. Their British designations were MTB's 307–316.

69 (72′ Huckins experimental model.) Not placed in service at a PT; reclassified as a district patrol vessel, YP 106, September 24, 1942.

70 (76′ Higgins experimental boat.) Not placed in service as a PT; reclassified as district patrol vessel, YP 107, September 24, 1942.

85–94 (78′ Higgins.) Built as RPT's (Russian PT's) 1–10. PT's 85–87, 89, transferred under lend-lease to U.S.S.R. February 15, 1943. PT's 88, 90–94, transferred under lend-lease to Britain in April 1943. Their British designations were MTB's 419–424.

197 (78′ Higgins.) Built as RPT 11. Transferred under lend-lease to U.S.S.R., February 15, 1943.

198 (78′ Higgins.) Transferred under lend-lease to Britain in April 1943.

265–276 (78′ Higgins.) Transferred under lend-lease to U.S.S.R. in November 1943.

289–294 (78′ Higgins.) Transferred under lend-lease to U.S.S.R. in December 1943.

384–399 (70′ Vosper.) Built by R. Jacob, City Island, N.Y. Transferred under lend-lease to Britain, May–October 1944. Their British designations were MTB's 396–411.

400–429 (70′ Vosper.) Built by Annapolis Yacht Yard, Annapolis, Md. Transferred under lend-lease to U.S.S.R., January–October 1944.

430–449 (70′ Vosper.) Built by Herreshoff, Bristol, R.I. Transferred under lend-lease to U.S.S.R., February–October 1944.

623–624 (80′ Elco.) Construction halted October 1, 1945; contract canceled.

634–656 (78′ Higgins.) Transferred under lend-lease to U.S.S.R., June–August 1945.

657–660 (78′ Higgins.) Built for lend-lease transfer to U.S.S.R., but not transferred prior to cessation of hostilities. Stricken from Navy Register November 28, 1945.

661–692 (70′ Vosper.) Built by Annapolis Yacht Yard, Annapolis, Md. Transferred under lend-lease to U.S.S.R., November 1944–May 1945.

693–728 (70′ Vosper.) Built by Annapolis Yacht Yard, Annapolis, Md., for lend-lease transfer to U.S.S.R., but not transferred prior to cessation of hostili-

ties. Stricken from Navy Register November 28, 1945.

729–730 (70′ Vosper.) Built by Annapolis Yacht Yard, Annapolis, Md., for lend-lease transfer to U.S.S.R., but not transferred prior to cessation of hostilities. Reclassified as small boats November 23, 1945.

731–760 (80′ Elco.) Transferred under lend-lease to U.S.S.R., October 1944–February 1945. All except PT 731 were shipped in "knocked down" condition for assembly in Russia.

761–790 (80′ Elco.) Contract for construction canceled August 27, 1945.

791–794 (78′ Higgins.) Stricken from Navy Register November 28, 1945.

795–796 (78′ Higgins.) Reclassified as small boats November 23, 1945.

797–802 (78′ Higgins.) Contract for construction canceled October 1, 1945.

803–808 (78′ Higgins.) Contract for construction canceled August 27, 1945.

*BPT**

21–28 (70′ Vosper.) Built by Annapolis Yacht Yard, Annapolis, Md. Transferred under lend-lease to Britain, November 1942–March 1943. Their British designations were MTB's 275–282.

29–36 (70′ Vosper.) Built by Herreshoff, Bristol, R.I. Transferred under lend-lease to Britain, March–June 1943. Their British designations were MTB's 287–294.

37–42 (70′ Vosper.) Built by R. Jacob, City Island, N.Y. Transferred under lend-lease to Britain, February–April 1943. Their British designations were MTB's 295–300.

43–48 (70′ Vosper.) Built by Harbor Boat Building Co., Terminal Island, Calif. Transferred under lend-lease

---

*Unlike BPT's (British PT's) 1–20, which were also designated as PT's 49–68, these BPT's had no corresponding PT designation.

to Britain, February–March 1943. Their British designations were MTB's 301–306.

49–52 (70′ Vosper.) Built by Annapolis Yacht Yard, Annapolis, Md. Transferred under lend-lease to Britain, April 1943. Their British designations were MTB's 283–286.

53–60 (70′ Vosper.) Built by Annapolis

Yacht Yard, Annapolis, Md. Transferred under lend-lease to U.S.S.R., February 1944.

61–68 (70′ Vosper.) Built by Annapolis Yacht Yard, Annapolis, Md. Transferred under lend-lease to Britain, October–December 1943. Their British designations were MTB's 371–378.

APPENDIX B

PT Losses

22 Damaged in storm and later scrapped, Dora Harbor, Alaska, January 12, 1943.

28 Wrecked in storm, Dora Harbor, Alaska, January 12, 1943.

31 Grounded in enemy waters and destroyed to prevent capture, Subic Bay, Luzon, P.I., January 20, 1942.

32 Destroyed to prevent capture, Tagauayan Island, P.I., March 13, 1942.

33 Grounded in enemy waters on December 15, 1941 and destroyed to prevent capture, near Cape Santiago, Luzon, P.I., December 26, 1941.

34 Destroyed by enemy aircraft (strafing attack), Cauit Island, Cebu, P.I., April 9, 1942.

35 Destroyed to prevent capture, Cebu, P.I., April 12, 1942.

37 Destroyed by enemy warships, off Guadalcanal, February 1, 1943.

41 Destroyed to prevent capture, near Lake Lanao, Mindanao, April 15, 1942.

43 Damaged by enemy warships, beached and destroyed to prevent capture, Guadalcanal, January 11, 1943.

44 Destroyed by enemy warships, off Guadalcanal, December 12, 1942.

63 Destroyed by fire in port, Hamburg Bay, Emirau Island, June 18, 1944.

67 Destroyed by fire in port, Tufi, New Guinea, March 17, 1943.

68 Grounded in enemy waters and destroyed to prevent capture, near Vincke Point, New Guinea, October 1, 1943.

73 Grounded in enemy waters and destroyed to prevent capture, Baliquias Bay, Mindoro, P.I., January 15, 1945.

77 Destroyed by U.S. warships, mistaken identification, near Talin Point, Luzon, P.I., February 1, 1945.

79 Destroyed by U.S. warships, mistaken identification, near Talin Point, Luzon, P.I., February 1, 1945.

107 Destroyed by fire in port, Hamburg Bay, Emirau Island, June 18, 1944.

109 Destroyed when rammed by enemy warship, off Kolombangara Island (Blackett Strait), August 2, 1943.

110 Lost in collision, Ablingi Harbor, New Britain, January 26, 1944.

111 Destroyed by enemy warships, off Guadalcanal, February 1, 1943.

112 Destroyed by enemy warships, off Guadalcanal, January 11, 1943.

113 Destroyed as result of grounding, not in enemy waters, Veale Reef, near Tufi, New Guinea, August 8, 1943.

117 Destroyed by enemy aircraft (bombing), Rendova Harbor, August 1, 1943.

118 Grounded in enemy waters and destroyed to prevent capture, off Vella Lavella, September 7, 1943.

119 Destroyed by fire in port, Tufi, New Guinea, March 17, 1943.

121 Destroyed by Australian aircraft, mistaken identification, Bangula Bay, New Britain, March 27, 1944.

123 Destroyed by enemy aircraft (bombing), off Guadalcanal, February 1, 1943.

PT

133 Destroyed by enemy shore batteries, near Cape Pus, New Guinea, July 15, 1944.

135 Grounded in enemy waters and destroyed to prevent capture, near Crater Point, New Britain, April 12, 1944.

136 Grounded in enemy waters and destroyed to prevent capture, Malai Island, Vitiaz Strait, New Guinea, September 17, 1943.

145 Grounded in enemy waters and destroyed to prevent capture, Mindiri, New Guinea, January 4, 1944.

147 Grounded in enemy waters and destroyed to prevent capture, Teliata Point, New Guinea, November 20, 1943.

153 Grounded in enemy waters and destroyed to prevent capture, near Munda Point, New Georgia, July 4, 1943.

158 Grounded in enemy waters and destroyed to prevent capture, near Munda Point, New Georgia, July 5, 1943.

164 Destroyed by enemy aircraft (bombing), Rendova Harbor, August 1, 1943.

165 Lost in transit, tanker torpedoed, 100 miles south of Noumea, New Caledonia, May 24, 1943.

166 Destroyed by U.S. aircraft, mistaken identification, off New Georgia, July 20, 1943.

172 Grounded in enemy waters and destroyed to prevent capture, off Vella Lavella, September 7, 1943.

173 Lost in transit, tanker torpedoed, 100 miles south of Noumea, New Caledonia, May 24, 1943.

193 Grounded in enemy waters and destroyed to prevent capture, Noemfoor Island, New Guinea, June 25, 1944.

200 Lost after collision off Newport, R.I., February 22, 1944. Sank February 23, 1944.

PT

202 Destroyed by enemy mine, off Point Aygulf, France, Mediterranean, August 16, 1944.

218 Destroyed by enemy mine, off Point Aygulf, France, Mediterranean, August 16, 1944.

219 Damaged in storm and scrapped, near Attu, Aleutian Islands, September 14, 1943.

239 Destroyed by fire in port, Lambu Lambu, Vella Lavella, December 14, 1943.

247 Destroyed by enemy shore batteries, off Bougainville, May 5, 1944.

251 Destroyed by enemy shore batteries, off Bougainville, February 26, 1944.

279 Lost in collision, off Bougainville, February 12, 1944.

283 Damaged by enemy shorefire or wild shot from U.S. warship on March 18, 1944, and sank off Bougainville, March 19, 1944.

300 Destroyed by enemy aircraft (suicide attack), Mindoro, P.I., December 18, 1944.

301 Damaged by explosion in port and scrapped, Mios Woendi, New Guinea, November 7, 1944.

311 Destroyed by enemy mine, Ligurian Sea, Mediterranean, November 18, 1944.

320 Destroyed by enemy aircraft (bombing), Leyte Gulf, P.I., November 5, 1944.

321 Grounded in enemy waters and destroyed to prevent capture, San Isidro Bay, Leyte, P.I., November 11, 1944.

322 Grounded in enemy waters and destroyed to prevent capture, near Hardenberg Point, New Guinea, November 24, 1943.

323 Destroyed by enemy aircraft (suicide attack), Leyte Gulf, P.I., December 10, 1944.

337 Destroyed by enemy shore batteries, Hansa Bay, New Guinea, March 7, 1944.

PT

338 Grounded on January 27, 1945, and later destroyed as result of grounding, not in enemy waters, Semirara Island, P.I., January 31, 1945.

339 Grounded in enemy waters and destroyed to prevent capture, near Pur Pur, New Guinea, May 27, 1944.

346 Destroyed by U.S. aircraft, mistaken identification, near Cape Pomas, New Britain, April 29, 1944.

347 Destroyed by U.S. aircraft, mistaken identification, near Cape Pomas, New Britain, April 29, 1944.

353 Destroyed by Australian aircraft, mistaken identification, Bangula Bay, New Britain, March 27, 1944.

363 Destroyed by enemy shore batteries, Knoe Bay, Halmahera, N.E.I., November 25, 1944.

368 Grounded in enemy waters and destroyed to prevent capture, near Cape Salimoeli, Halmahera, N.E.I., October 11, 1944.

371 Grounded in enemy waters and destroyed to prevent capture, near Tagalasa, Halmahera, N.E.I., September 19, 1944.

493 Destroyed by enemy warships, Surigao Strait, P.I., October 25, 1944.

509 Destroyed by ramming enemy warship, English Channel, August 9, 1944.

555 Damaged by enemy mine, off Cape Couronne, Mediterranean, August 24, 1944, and sunk by U.S. gunfire on September 8, 1944.

RECAPITULATION

Destroyed by enemy surface ships . .   7
  By gunfire: PT's 37, 44, 111, 112, 493.
  Rammed by enemy ship: PT 109.
  Rammed enemy ship: PT 509.
Destroyed by enemy aircraft   7

By strafing: PT 34.
By bombing: PT's 117, 123, 164, 320.
By suicide attack: PT's 300, 323.
Destroyed by enemy shore batteries .   5
  PT's 133, 247, 251, 337, 363.
Destroyed by mines   4
  PT's 202, 218, 311, 555.
Damaged by enemy surface ships: beached and destroyed to prevent capture   1
  PT 43.
Lost in transit; transporting ship sunk   2
  PT's 165, 173.
Grounded in enemy waters and destroyed to prevent capture   18
  PT's 31, 33, 68, 73, 118, 135, 136, 145, 147, 153, 158, 172, 193, 321, 322, 339, 368, 371.
Destroyed to prevent capture   3
  PT's 32, 35, 41.
Destroyed by U.S. or Allied aircraft, mistaken identification   5
  By U.S. aircraft: PT's 166, 346, 347.
  By Australian aircraft: PT's 121, 353.
Destroyed by U.S. surface vessels . .   2
  Through mistaken identification: PT's 77, 79.
Destroyed by enemy shorefire or wild shot from U.S. warship . .   1
  PT 283.
Destroyed as result of storms or grounding not in enemy waters   5
  PT's 22, 28, 113, 219, 338.
Destroyed by fire or explosion in port   6
  PT's 63, 67, 107, 119, 239, 301.
Lost in collision   3
  PT's 110, 200, 279.

Total   69

APPENDIX C

Awards and Citations

I. UNIT CITATIONS

PRESIDENTIAL UNIT CITATION

MOTOR TORPEDO BOAT SQUADRONS 12 AND 21

For outstanding performance during the Huon Peninsula Campaign against enemy Japanese forces from October 1943 to March 1944. Highly vulnerable to damage from treacherous reefs and grounding during close inshore patrols, Motor Torpedo Boat Squadrons Twelve and Twenty-one spearheaded a determined waterborne attack on the enemy, boldly penetrating hostile waters and disrupting barge traffic vital to the maintenance of Japanese strongholds in the New Guinea area. Dauntlessly exchanging gunfire with heavily armored gunboats and barges, airplanes and shore emplacements, the boats of Squadrons Twelve and Twenty-One have successfully diverted hostile artillery fire to themselves in protection of Allied Land Forces; they have steadily destroyed the enemy's ships carrying troops, food and combat supplies; they have captured Japanese personnel, landed in hostile territory and effected air and sea rescue missions. Tenacious and indomitable in the face of superior firepower and despite frequent damage to boats and casualties among personnel, the officers and men of Squadrons Twelve and Twenty-One have fought gallantly and served with distinction in crushing enemy resistance in this strategically important area.

MOTOR TORPEDO BOAT SQUADRON 3 and USS JAMESTOWN are included in the award of the Presidential Unit Citation to the First Marine Division, Reinforced, with the following citation:

The officers and enlisted men of the First Marine Division, Reinforced, from August 7 to December 9, 1942, demonstrated outstanding gallantry and determination in successfully executing forced landing assaults against a number of strongly defended Japanese positions on Tulagi, Gavutu, Tanambogo, Florida, and Guadalcanal, British Solomon Islands, completely routing all the enemy forces and seizing a most valuable base and airfield within the enemy zone of operations in the South Pacific Ocean. During the above period, this Reinforced Division not only held their important strategic positions despite determined and repeated Japanese naval, air and land attacks, but by a series of offensive operations against strong enemy resistance drove the Japanese from the proximity of the airfield and inflicted great losses on them by land and air attacks. The courage and determination displayed in these operations were of an inspiring order.

ARMY DISTINGUISHED UNIT CITATION

MOTOR TORPEDO BOAT SQUADRON 3 was awarded the Army Distinguished Unit Citation by the following General Order:

War Department General Orders No. 22

Washington 25, D.C., 30 April 1942 Citation of Units of Both Military and Naval Forces of the United States and Philippine Governments.

As authorized by Executive Order No. 9075 (sec. II, Bull. 11, W.D., 1942), a citation in the name of the President of the United States, as public evidence of deserved honor and distinction, is awarded to all units of both military and naval forces of the United States and Philippine Governments engaged in the defense of the Philippines since December 7, 1941.

By order of the Secretary of War:

G. C. MARSHALL,
Chief of Staff.

NAVY UNIT COMMENDATION

MOTOR TORPEDO BOAT SQUADRON 7

For outstanding heroism in action against enemy Japanese shipping in the New Guinea Area from April 1, 1944, to February 1, 1945. Going in night after night under the heavy fire of fixed and mobile shore guns commanding Japanese barge routes, Motor Torpedo Boat Squadron Seven struck fierce blows at the enemy's life line of supply. In dangerously close proximity to hostile beaches, these stouthearted craft coordinated closely with our night fighters in relentless and vigilant patrols of enemy shipping lanes to destroy shore installations and moving waterborne targets; they spearheaded the torpedo boat drive against 50,000 trapped Japanese threatening our beachhead at Aitape and aided in disrupting enemy water transport facilities; they rocketed and strafed hostile troop concentrations; and they braved heavy fire to rescue our pilots downed deep in hostile territory. Manned by courageous and aggressive officers and men, Motor Torpedo Boat Squadron Seven carried on its gallant and unceasing fight against the enemy despite severe operational handicaps and ship and personnel casualties contributing essentially to the rout of Japanese forces from the Southwest Pacific Area.

TASK UNIT 70.1.4, comprising MOTOR TORPEDO BOAT SQUADRONS 13 and 16, plus PT's 227 AND 230 OF MOTOR TORPEDO BOAT SQUADRON 17, and the task unit commander and his staff:

For outstanding heroism in action against enemy Japanese forces during operations at Mindoro, Philippine Islands, from December 15 to 19, 1944. As the only Naval force present following the retirement of the invasion convoys, this Task Unit served as the major obstruction to enemy counter-landings from near-by Luzon, Panay and Palawan and bore the brunt of concentrated hostile air attacks throughout a 5-day period. Providing the only antiaircraft protection available for personnel ashore engaged in the establishment of a motor torpedo boat operating and repair base, the gallant officers and men who commanded and staffed the Task Unit and who manned the boats maintained the vigilant watch by night and stood out in the open waters close to base by day to fight off repeated Japanese bombing, strafing and suicide attacks, expending in three days the ammunition which had been expected to last approximately three weeks in the destruction or damaging of a large percentage of the attacking planes. Their invaluable service in support of the expeditious completion of operations ashore vital to the furtherance of the Mindoro Campaign reflects the highest credit upon the United States Naval Service.

PT ADVANCE BASE CONSTRUCTION DETACHMENT, 113TH NAVAL CONSTRUCTION BATTALION

For extremely meritorious service in support of combat operations against enemy Japanese forces at Mios Woendi, Amsterdam Island, Morotai, Leyte Gulf, Mindoro, Zamboanga and Balikpapan, from April 1944 to July 1945. Determined to accomplish its vital tasks in the shortest possible time despite adverse weather, air raids and recurrent enemy attacks, this detachment went ashore within several days of initial assault landings to construct advance motor torpedo boat operating and repair bases at each of these seven invasion points. Although subjected to repeated air raids as well as two typhoons at Leyte Gulf, the unit's gallant officers and men unloaded 800 tons of equipment in 24 hours and, ordered to another location, reloaded and expeditiously discharged the equipment at the new site. Undaunted by 30 enemy bombing, strafing and suicide aerial attacks during the first 5 days at Mindoro, the detachment had base facilities supporting PT operations on the second day ashore and subsequently salvaged provisions from partially submerged ships to replenish depleted stocks ashore, at the same time performing most of the salvage work on two seriously damaged vessels. With one-third of their equipment destroyed by enemy mortar and 75-mm. shells at Zamboanga, this unit's resolute personnel braved continuing fire to move the remainder to a more secure location and later ingeniously improvised and salvaged substitute materials to complete the base's construction. Their unfailing cooperation and invaluable service in support of motor torpedo boat operations were vital factors in the blockade and destruction of Japanese shipping in the Southwest Pacific Area.

PT 375: Included in the award of the Navy Unit Commendation to the Ship Salvage Fire-Fighting and Rescue Unit, Service Force, Seventh Fleet, with the following citation:

For distinguished and extremely meritorious service in support of military operations throughout the Philippine campaign. Accompanying the preliminary bombardment groups and working under continuous enemy attack throughout the assault phase of nine major landings, the Ship Salvage Fire-Fighting and Rescue Unit, Service Force, Seventh Fleet, fought and extinguished 10 major fires, completed emergency battle damage repairs on 69 vessels including combat fleet units, refloated and salvaged 146 badly damaged ships, towed 13 major vessels to safety, and recovered one sunken submarine under heavy mortar fire. In 3 months, the Unit completed the emergency clearing of Manila Harbor, opening the port fully to Allied use. During the operation, over 350 vessels of all sizes were raised, removed or disposed of along with large quantities of enemy underwater ordnance. The teamwork, professional skill and unselfish devotion to duty of the entire Unit resulted in accomplishment beyond the highest expectations and contributed immeasurably to the successful liberation of the Philippine Islands.

II. INDIVIDUAL AWARDS

MEDAL OF HONOR

BULKELEY, Lieutenant JOHN D.

For extraordinary heroism, distinguished service and conspicuous gallantry above and beyond the call of duty, as Commander of Motor Torpedo Boat Squadron Three, in Philippine waters during the period December 7, 1941, to April 10, 1942. The remarkable achievement of Lieutenant Bulkeley's command in damaging or destroying a notable number of Japanese enemy planes, surface combatant and merchant ships, and in dispersing landing parties and land based enemy forces during the 4 months and 8 days of operation without benefit of repairs, overhaul or maintenance facilities for his Squadron, is believed to be without precedent in this type of warfare. His dynamic forcefulness and daring in offensive action, his brilliantly planned and skillfully executed attacks, supplemented by an unique resourcefulness and ingenuity, characterize him as an outstanding leader of men and a gallant and intrepid seaman. These qualities coupled with a complete disregard for his own personal safety reflect great credit upon him and the Naval Service.

PRESTON, Lieutenant Commander A. MURRAY, USNR

For conspicuous gallantry and intrepidity at the risk of his life above and beyond the call of duty as Commander Motor Torpedo Boat Squadron Thirty-three while effecting the rescue of a Navy Pilot shot down in Wasile Bay, Halmahera Island, less than 200 yards from a strongly defended Japanese dock and supply area, September 16, 1944. Volunteering for a perilous mission unsuccessfully attempted by the pilot's squadron mates and a PBY plane, Lieutenant Commander (then Lieutenant) Preston led PT 489 and PT 363 through 60 miles of restricted, heavily mined waters. Twice turned back while running the gantlet of fire from powerful coastal defense guns guarding the 11-mile strait at the entrance to the bay, he was again turned back by furious fire in the immediate area of the downed airman. Aided by an aircraft smoke screen, he finally succeeded in reaching his objective and, under vicious fire delivered at 150-yard range, took the pilot aboard and cleared the area, sinking a small hostile cargo vessel with 40-mm. fire during retirement. Increasingly vulnerable when covering aircraft were forced to leave because of insufficient fuel, Lieutenant Commander Preston raced PT Boats 489 and 363 at high speed for 20 minutes through shell-splashed water and across minefields to safety. Under continuous fire for 2½ hours, Lieutenant Commander Preston successfully achieved a mission considered suicidal in its tremendous hazards and brought his boats through without personnel casualties and with but superficial damage from shrapnel. His exceptional daring and great personal valor enhance the finest traditions of the United States Naval Service.

NAVY CROSS

ASCHENBACH, Lieutenant (jg.) JULIUS O., USNR

For distinguishing himself by extraordinary heroism in an action against the enemy on the night of 13 May 1944. At this time, he was Officer in Tactical Command of Motor Torpedo Boats 138 and 133. Four Japanese barges were sighted near Dagua, New Guinea, close in against the beach. As his boat prepared to make a run on the barges, the enemy opened up with heavy and accurate fire from the barges off shore, other barges on the beach, and from 20-mm., 37-mm., and 40-mm. shore batteries located behind the barges. Despite this fire, which killed one man and wounded another, and holed the boats in numerous places, he closed his boat to within 150 yards of the barges and 200 yards of the beach. Fire from his boats sank three of the barges. After the run, it appeared that the engines of the following boat had failed, and that it would be left exposed and helpless to enemy fire. Despite an uncontrolled engine room fire, with aggressiveness and daring he started in again toward the batteries that were still threatening his life and the existence of his boat with their accurate fire. He took these batteries under fire, and only when he saw that the other boat was underway, did he withdraw. His skill, calmness, and fearlessness were an inspiration to his men. His actions were in keeping with the highest traditions of the Navy of the United States.

BARNES, Lieut. Comdr. STANLEY M.

For extraordinary heroism in action as Commander Motor Torpedo Boat Squadron 15 during the Tunisian and Sicilian Campaigns.

Lieutenant Commander Barnes ably administered, trained and courageously operated his squadron during the enemy's evacuation of Tunisia, and the preparatory phase, assault and final operations leading to the occupation of the Island of Sicily. PT boats of this squadron executed patrol and reconnaissance missions which were of inestimable value to our own forces.

They also carried out many daring and damaging raids on shipping, seriously disrupting enemy sea communications. On many of these occasions, the task group was personally commanded by Lieutenant Commander Barnes whose skillful and fearless leadership was responsible for the outstanding success attained. Between 1 and 20 August 1943 he directed offensive sweeps along the North Coast of Sicily which culminated in the capture of the Eolie Islands and stoppage of enemy seaborne traffic thereby contributing materially to the rapid success of the Seventh Army towards Messina.

The exceptional bravery, aggressive leadership, and outstanding devotion to duty displayed by Lieutenant Commander Barnes were in keeping with the highest traditions of the Naval Service.

BLOOM, VICTOR A., Motor Machinist Mate First Class, USNR

For extraordinary heroism and devotion to duty in action against the enemy. From September through December 1943, he was senior engineer of PT 191, during which time he participated actively in more than 30 combat patrols against Japanese barge traffic along the north coast of New Guinea and the west coast of New Britain. On these patrols his boat sank or destroyed ten barges loaded with troops and supplies, two ketches, one lugger, one picket boat and two enemy aircraft, frequently in the face of bitter resistance from the enemy craft and larger calibre shore guns. On three of these occasions his boat was hit by enemy fire. On the morning of December 27, 1943, while effecting a daylight reconnaissance of the coast of New Britain northwest of Arawe, his boat and PT 190 were attacked by 30 to 40 Japanese dive bombers and fighter planes. During the engage-

ment, which lasted 45 minutes, all three of the engines on his boat were hit and damaged. Displaying exemplary coolness and gallantry and in disregard of personal safety he remained at his post although the engine room was filled with fumes from leaking gas and sprayed with hot water from damaged water jackets. With extraordinary skill and presence of mind he maintained all engines in an operative condition through the entire action. Perceiving that the gas tanks were hit and leaking he took immediate and successful action to prevent potential fire by shutting off the tank compartment and blanketing it with carbon dioxide. In the course of the action and in addition to his duties as engineer he administered first aid to two injured members of the crew. His actions were in keeping with the highest traditions of the Navy of the United States.

BOYD, Lieutenant (jg.) HERSHEL F., USNR

For extraordinary heroism as Boat Captain of Torpedo Boat 363 in action against enemy Japanese forces during the rescue of a Navy Fighter Pilot shot down in Wasile Bay, Halmahera Island. On the afternoon of September 16, 1944, after attempts at rescue by airplane had been turned back by hostile anti-aircraft fire, Lieutenant, Junior Grade, Boyd unhesitatingly volunteered to aid in this hazardous mission. Although the two participating Torpedo Boats were twice driven back by intense fire from numerous coast defense guns lining an 11-mile strait at the entrance of the passage, they finally succeeded in reaching their objective and in locating the pilot. Cool and courageous despite fierce Japanese fire which harassed the Torpedo Boat crews throughout the 2½-hour operation, Lieutenant, Junior Grade, Boyd rendered gallant service during one of the most perilous rescues in the Southwest Pacific area. His conduct reflects the highest credit upon himself and the United States Naval Service.

BRUNELLE, ALBERT W., Motor Machinist Mate First Class, USNR

For distinguishing himself by extraordinary heroism in the line of his profession as a member of the crew of PT 493 when it attacked a Japanese destroyer in Surigao Strait, Philippine Islands, on October 25, 1944. During his ship's retirement from the attack, Brunelle was on watch in the engine room when Japanese 4.7-inch shells twice passed through his compartment. Many items of machinery were wrecked, including the auxiliary generator, and a large hole was blown in the side of his ship below the water line. In utter disregard for his own personal safety, he took off his own life jacket and stuffed it into the hole in an attempt to stop the inrushing water. He made emergency repairs upon the machinery which enabled the boat, though apparently in a helpless condition, to maintain its course and escape from the enemy. His magnificent efforts, under the severest of conditions, undoubtedly saved the lives of those on board who survived the enemy shelling. His conduct was an inspiration to all hands and in accordance with the highest traditions of the Navy of the United States.

BULKELEY, Lieutenant JOHN D.

For extraordinary heroism as Commanding Officer Motor Torpedo Boat Number 34 in connection with military operations against the Japanese enemy forces in the Philippine Area. Despite machine gun fire, Lieutenant Bulkeley searched Binanga Bay, Luzon, P.I., for an enemy ship reported therein, located and sank the unidentified 5,000-ton enemy ship with torpedoes without serious damage to his ship or casualty to his crew.

BURK, Lieutenant (jg.) JOSEPH W., USNR

For extraordinary heroism and intrepidity in action against the enemy. During the period November 1943 through January 1944, he made 21 combat patrols, courageously and aggressively pursuing Japanese barges along the north coast of New Guinea and the west coast of New Britain. He has participated in the destruction of 26 enemy barges, time and again in the face of heavy and accurate fire from shore emplacements. He has been bombed by enemy aircraft and sustained a direct hit on his boat by an enemy 3-inch shell. On January 8, 1944, in company with Motor Torpedo Boat 323, while engaged in attacking 10 enemy barges, fire from heavy shore batteries was encountered. As Officer-in-Tactical-Command, he left the barges and proceeded under the shore batteries, silenced them, and returned to press home the attack on the barges, completely destroying them. Two nights later in company with PT's 326 and 327, he successfully attacked and sank four heavily troop laden barges. 160 enemy troops are estimated to have been killed in this action which was bitterly resisted by the enemy, and one prisoner of war was taken. He has on two occasions successfully carried out secret missions far behind the enemy lines. His actions were in keeping with the highest traditions of the Navy of the United States.

CONNOLLY, Ensign BARTHOLOMEW J., III

For distinguished service in the line of his profession while in command of Motor Torpedo Boat PT 115 which engaged a force of Japanese cruisers and destroyers off the Guadalcanal coast on the night of January 14–15, 1943. Ensign Connolly by his skill and daring made a direct torpedo hit on one enemy destroyer from close range sinking or seriously damaging it thereby.

On the night of February 1–2, 1943, Ensign Connolly in command of PT 115 in company with PT 59 and PT 37 engaged a similar Japanese force. The group found themselves surrounded by 12 enemy destroyers. Ensign Connolly with great determination and daring closed one of them to within 500 yards scoring two torpedo hits. He fired his two remaining torpedoes at another ship with unobserved results and made good his escape through a rain of enemy shells with no casualties.

Cox, Ensign GEORGE E., USNR

For extraordinary heroism and courageous devotion to duty as Commanding Officer of the U.S.S. PT 41 when that vessel together with the U.S.S. PT 34 made an effective torpedo attack on a Japanese *Kuma*-class light cruiser screened by four enemy destroyers. Despite heavy shell fire opposition and having expended all his torpedoes, Ensign Cox attacked with machine gun fire on the disengaged side of the cruiser thereby drawing the hostile fire from the PT 34. His actions in thus heroically exposing his position to aid materially in the attack of the accompanying MTB, were in keeping with the highest traditions of the Naval Service.

CRAIG, Lieutenant DONALD M., USNR

For extraordinary heroism in action as Commander of a division of Motor Torpedo Boats engaged in operations against the enemy convoys off the west coast of Italy and the south coast of France in June and July 1944.

Lieutenant Craig led his group on six missions against enemy convoys attempting to maintain supply lines to Axis Armies in Northern Italy. He skillfully and with the utmost courage and determination disposed his forces on these operations to seek out the enemy and intercept and destroy his shipping. On all occasions he patrolled well within enemy coastal waters and conducted his attacks with great daring and effectiveness with minimum damage to his own forces. In the final success of these operations, he accounted for the sinking of one corvette, one coaster and three F-lighters and the severe damaging of one small ammunition ship, two MAS boats and one or more F-lighters, thereby seriously cutting off enemy reinforcements of supplies and other essential materials to the front lines.

The exceptional heroism, intrepidity, and outstanding devotion to duty displayed by Lieutenant Craig were in keeping with the highest traditions of the Naval Service.

DAY, CHARLES D., Motor Machinist Mate First Class, USNR

For distinguishing himself by gallantry and intrepidity in actions against the enemy. He volunteered to accompany two boats to assist in the rescue of a Navy fighter pilot shot down in Wasile Bay. A long narrow approach closely guarded by enemy guns reportedly mined added to the danger. After attempts at rescue by airplane had been turned back by antiaircraft fire, on the third attempt his boat succeeded in gaining entrance and located the pilot. When it became apparent that the flier was too severely injured to help himself, Day unhesitatingly dived overboard and got the wounded flier aboard. His boats were under intense fire for 2½ hours. His actions contributed to the success of one of the most dangerous and thrilling rescues in the Southwest Pacific area. His conduct was in accordance with the highest traditions of the Navy of the Untied States.

DuBose, Lieutenant EDWIN A., USNR

For extraordinary heroism in action as Commander of a Division of Motor Torpedo Boats engaged in operations against enemy coastal traffic off the west coast of Italy in March and April 1944.

Lieutenant DuBose in cooperation with British Coastal Forces led his units on several night missions against enemy convoys attempting to maintain supply lines to axis armies in the Rome, Italy area. He skillfully and with the utmost courage and determination disposed his forces on these operations to seek out the enemy and screen the main attack group from destroyer and E–boat attack. These tasks he accomplished with complete success, enabling the main force to destroy several convoys carrying vital war materials to the front lines. On all occasions he attacked with great daring and drove off all hostile forces which threatened the main body, escaping with minimum damage to himself. In the final success of the operations, he was in large measure responsible for the decisiveness of the action which resulted in the sinking of 15 F-lighters, one corvette, a tug, and the severe damaging of two destroyers.

The exceptional heroism, intrepidity, and outstanding devotion to duty displayed by Lieutenant DuBose were in keeping with the highest traditions of the Naval Service.

FAULKNER, Lieutenant CLARK W., USNR

For distinguished service in the line of his profession while in command of Motor Torpedo Boat PT 40 which together with PT 43 and PT 112 engaged a force of enemy destroyers off the Guadalcanal coast on the night of January 10/11, 1943. The group attacked three destroyers only a few hundred yards off the enemy occupied coast during which time Lieutenant Faulkner made a daring and determined approach in to 500 yards before firing his torpedoes which scored two hits probably sinking the ship. Lieutenant Faulkner made good his escape without casualties through a hail of shellfire which sank the other two motor torpedo boats.

On the night of February 1/2, 1943, Lieutenant Faulkner in command of PT 124, engaged one of a group of 19 enemy destroyers in the same Guadalcanal area and with great skill scored two torpedo hits from a distance of 1,000 yards causing the destroyer to burst into flame and burn for over 3 hours.

GAMBLE, Lieutenant LESTER H., USNR

For distinguished service in the line of his profession while in command of Motor Torpedo Boat PT 45 which engaged Japanese destroyer forces off the Guadalcanal coast on the nights of December 11/12, 1942, January 2/3, 1943, and January 14/15, 1943. Lieutenant Gamble with great skill and daring made such success-

ful attacks as to obtain two torpedo hits on one destroyer the first night, one torpedo hit on each of two destroyers on the second night and one torpedo hit on a destroyer on the last night. The attacks on the last two dates were pressed home against bombing and strafing by enemy aircraft.

KELLY, Lieutenant ROBERT B.

Lieutenant Kelly as Commanding Officer U.S.S. PT 34 on the night of April 8/9, 1942, while illuminated, made joint attack with PT 41 on a Japanese *Kuma* class light cruiser screened by four enemy destroyers, under extremely heavy shell fire from her main and secondary batteries and closed to within 300 yards where he struck her with two torpedoes in her engine rooms, which resulted in final sinking. Again in the morning of April 9, 1942, when attacked by four enemy dive bombers in a narrow channel of Cebu Harbor, Lieutenant Kelly though having a hole blown in his boat 6 feet across, and three of his guns out of action, skillfully maneuvered his boat and avoided direct hits on his boat. He fought back with his remaining guns until five of his crew of six were killed or wounded and then when all guns were out of action, be beached his boat to save the wounded. He directed the removal of the wounded and dead from his vessel under continual strafing from the enemy to a place of safety.

KOVAR, Lieutenant ISADORE M., USNR

For extraordinary heroism as Commanding Officer of PT 137 during action against enemy Japanese forces off Panaon Island, Philippine Islands, during the Battle of Surigao Strait, the night of October 24–25, 1944. On patrol at Binit Point at the entrance to Surigao Strait when a strong Task Force of the Japanese Fleet entered the Strait, Lieutenant (then Lieutenant, Junior Grade) Kovar boldly approached the enemy destroyer *Abukuma,* sighted visually and proceeding southward at slow speed. Closing the range to 700 yards, he launched a skillful torpedo attack and scored a hit which left the target seriously crippled and an easy prey for our air forces to sink on the following day. Immediately illuminated by hostile star shells, Lieutenant Kovar commenced evasive withdrawal action and, by his expert conning of the boat and his cool maneuvering in the face of grave danger, enabled the PT 137 to escape. His courage, skill and devotion to duty were in keeping with the highest traditions of the United States Naval Service.

PAYNTER, Lieutenant (jg.) WILLIAM K., USNR

For distinguishing himself by extraordinary heroism in operations against the enemy. While serving as Commanding Officer of his ship which was engaged with another in a patrol of enemy-held waters in the Southwest Pacific Area he closed the beach to make a firing run on an enemy vessel. The other ship suffered a disabling hit which left her lying dead in the water directly in front of enemy batteries. Without hesitation, and with complete disregard for his own life, he took his vessel between the active shore batteries and his sister ship, and made runs on the batteries in an effort to silence the guns and enable the crippled vessel to effect repairs. When requested to come alongside and take them in tow, he smartly brought his ship around and made preparations for towing. At this moment the Commanding Officer of his sister ship requested that personnel be evacuated from his vessel and gave the command to abandon ship. He successfully evacuated all but one man of the entire crew, many of whom were wounded. The intensity and accuracy of enemy fire throughout the entire action was such that several men on board his own ship were also wounded. His courage, cool judgment, and decisive action enabled an otherwise helpless crew to be saved. His actions were in keeping with the highest traditions of the Navy of the United States.

SEAMAN, Lieutenant DONALD F., USNR

For extraordinary heroism as a Member of a Volunteer Motor Torpedo Boat Crew in action against enemy Japanese forces during the rescue of a Navy Fighter Pilot shot down in Wasile Bay, Halmahera Island. On the afternoon of September 16, 1944, after attempts at rescue by airplane had been turned back by hostile antiaircraft fire, Lieutenant Seaman requested permission to take part in a rescue by surface craft. Although the Torpedo Boats were twice driven back by intense fire from numerous coastal defense guns lining an 11-mile strait at the entrance of the passage, they finally succeeded in reaching the pilot. When it became apparent that the flier was injured too severely to help himself, Lieutenant Seaman quickly dived into the shell-splashed water and assisted him aboard. By his courage, daring and aggressiveness while subjected to fierce concentrations of Japanese fire for 2½ hours during the operation, Lieutenant Seaman was directly instrumental in effecting one of the most perilous rescues in the Southwest Pacific area. His gallant conduct throughout reflects the highest credit upon himself and the United States Naval Service.

SEARLES, Lieutenant (jg.) JOHN M., USNR

For vigorous, determined and daring action, in command of PT 59, on the night of December 9, 1942. On sighting a Japanese submarine and landing barge off Kamimbo Bay, Guadalcanal, B.S.I., he promptly attacked the submarine by firing two torpedoes at 400 yards range; one hit causing a tremendous detonation and a 250-foot column of water; then nothing was left of the submarine except oil which came up profusely for the ensuing 1½ hours. The landing barge was strafed, boarded, and found empty of personnel. By his exemplary leadership and extraordinary heroism, an enemy submarine was destroyed before it could accomplish an important rendezvous with shore.

TATRO, Lieutenant Commander WILFRED B., Jr., USNR

For extraordinary heroism as Boat Captain of a Torpedo Boat in action against enemy Japanese forces during the rescue of a Navy Fighter Pilot shot down in Wasile Bay, Halmahera Island. On the afternoon of September 16, 1944, after attempts at rescue by airplane had been turned back by hostile antiaircraft fire, Lieutenant Commander (then Lieutenant) Tatro requested permission to take part in a rescue by surface craft. Although the Torpedo Boats were twice driven back by intense fire from numerous coastal defense guns lining an 11-mile strait at the entrance of the passage, he finally succeeded in guiding his boat through the narrow approaches to the bay, braving intense concentrations of Japanese fire for 2½ hours until the stranded airman was rescued on the third attempt. Lieutenant Commander Tatro's courage, daring and aggressiveness during this perilous operation reflect the highest credit upon himself and the United States Naval Service.

WALKER, DANIEL V., Seaman Second Class, USNR

For extraordinary heroism and devotion to duty in action against the enemy, on October 15, 1943, while he was bow gunner on Motor Torpedo Boat 133 during an engagement in which his vessel and Motor Torpedo Boat 191 attacked and destroyed four troop-laden enemy landing craft. All guns on his vessel having ceased fire due to stoppages or lack of ammunition, he left a place of comparative safety and proceeded to a forecastle gun which was jammed, but which had ammunition available. On the way he was knocked down by a bullet striking his chest. Nevertheless, he continued on his hands and knees, removed the am-

munition, crawled to his own gun and reopened fire on the enemy. He continued firing until struck in the arm by another bullet. As a result of his resolute action, the enemy fire slackened, and Motor Torpedo Boat 191 was able to close in and destroy the enemy craft. His actions and conduct were in keeping with the highest traditions of the United States Navy.

WALKER, FRANK C., Gunners Mate First Class, USNR

For extraordinary gallantry and intrepidity in action above and beyond the call of duty while serving as gunner on Motor Torpedo Boat 363. On the night of January 7, 1944, off the north coast of New Guinea, his boat engaged and, against bitter resistance, sank five enemy barges. Although mortally wounded in the opening moments of the engagement he remained at his station and continued to fire his machine gun with great effectiveness into the enemy barges throughout the greater part of the engagement until he collapsed to the deck. After the action Walker, although suffering great pain, asked, "Did we get them? How did my guns fire?" His last words before losing consciousness were to his immediate subordinate, "Get those guns cleaned up, Son." So long as consciousness remained his only thoughts were of his duty in the service of his country, for which he gave his life.

His actions were in keeping with the highest traditions of the United States Navy.

DISTINGUISHED SERVICE MEDAL

BOWLING, Captain SELMAN S.

For exceptionally meritorious service to the Government of the United States in a duty of great responsibility as Commander, Motor Torpedo Boat Squadrons, Seventh Fleet, during action against enemy Japanese forces from Wakde through and including the Philippine Islands and Borneo Areas, from February 1944 to August 25, 1945. An inspiring and dynamic leader, highly skilled in the comprehensive planning and coordination of supporting operations launched by his units against a fanatic, determined enemy, Captain Bowling consistently operated in uncharted waters and under extremely difficult conditions, expertly deploying and directing his command in advance strikes to disrupt vital hostile communications, intercept enemy supplies and reenforcements, carry out liaison missions with friendly guerrilla scouts and parties and perform extensive escort and reconnaissance duties. In a fierce engagement with powerful elements of the Japanese Fleet during the Battle of Surigao Straits on October 24 and 25, 1944, his intrepid force spearheaded the main attack with a daringly executed torpedo assault to inflict extensive damage and destruction on hostile shipping which contributed to the memorable success of this decisive action. Captain Bowling's superb professional ability, sound judgment and bold combat tactics, maintained in the face of tremendous odds, were essential factors in the sustained drive toward the conquest of vital hostile strongholds in the Southwest Pacific Area and his dauntless perseverance and valiant devotion to duty throughout reflects the highest credit upon himself, his gallant officers and men and the United States Naval Service.

DISTINGUISHED SERVICE CROSS (ARMY) WITH OAK LEAF CLUSTER IN LIEU OF SECOND DISTINGUISHED SERVICE CROSS

BULKELEY, Lt. JOHN D.

DISTINGUISHED SERVICE CROSS (ARMY)

COX, Ens. GEORGE E., Jr., USNR.
KELLY, Lt. ROBERT B.

DISTINGUISHED SERVICE MEDAL (ARMY)

CALVERT, Capt. ALLEN P.

SILVER STAR WITH GOLD STAR OR OAK LEAF CLUSTER IN LIEU OF SECOND SILVER STAR

AKERS, Ens. ANTHONY B., USNR.
BALOG, JOHN X., CPhM.
BAUGHMAN, Lt. DANIEL S., Jr.
BRANTINGHAM, Lt. HENRY J.
BRUNO, Lt. (jg.) THEODORE F., USNR.
COX, Lt. GEORGE E., Jr., USNR.
GIACCANI, FLOYD R., Bkr2c.
GLOVER, DeWITT L., CQM.
GOODMAN, DAVID, RM2c.
HAINES, Lt. MELVIN W., USNR.
HALLOWELL, Lt. ROGER H., USNR.
HANCOCK, MORRIS W., CMM.
HARRIS, DAVID W., TM2c.
HOULIHAN, JOHN L., TM1c.
HUNTER, VELT F., CMM.
KELLY, Lt. ROBERT B.
LAWLESS, JOHN, MM1c.
LICODO, BENJAMIN, St3c.
LIGHT, JAMES D., CTM.
McELFRESH, Lt. JOHN M., USNR.
MARTINO, JOHN, CTM.
O'BRIEN, Lt. RICHARD H.
REED, Lt. GILBERT L., USNR.
REYNOLDS, WILLARD J., CCStd.
RICHARDSON, CARL C., CMM.
RICHARDSON, Ens. ILIFF D., USNR.
ROSS, ALBERT P., QM1c.
SHEPARD, GEORGE W., Jr., MM1c.
SWART, Lt. PHILIP A., USNR.
TUGGLE, JOHN L., MM1c.
WILLEVER, STEWART, Jr., RM2c.

SILVER STAR

AGNEW, JACK W., GM2c, USNR.
AIKEN, PETER S., GM1c.
AMME, Lt. (jg.) ROBERT G.
ANDERSON, Lt. (jg.) LEO A., Jr., USNR.

ANSTEATT, JOHN, MoMM1c, USNR.
ARANN, SOL, MoMM2c, USNR.
ARBUCKLE, Lt. ERNEST C., USNR.
ARTERBERRY, WINFORD L., MoMM3c, USNR.
ATKINS, Cdr. BARRY K.
AZARIGIAN, Ens. Gregory J., USNR.
BAGBY, LEE A., QM1c.
BAILEY, GRANT R., MoMM2c.
BANNARD, Ens. WILLIAM N., USNR.
BARRETT, ALFRED N., TM2c, USNR.
BARTLETT, GEORGE F., F1c.
BATTLE, Ens. WILLIAM C., USNR.
BAYLIS, Lt. JOHN S., Jr., USNR.
BECKMAN, Lt. (jg.) JOSEPH C., Jr., USNR.
BECKNER, CHARLES C., PhM3c.
BERGIN, Lt. EDWARD R., Jr.
BERNDTSON, Lt. ARTHUR H.
BERNIE, EDWARD L., MoMM2c.
BETTY, RICHARD E., MoMM1c, USNR.
BIELE, ROBERT L., GM3c, USNR.
BLACK, Lt. CHARLES A., USNR.
BONTE, Lt. Cdr. JOHN S., USNR.
BOUDOLF, JOSEPH L., GM1c.
BOWLING, Lt. Cdr. SELMAN S.
BOWMAN, JACK M., GM2c, USNR.
BRADFORD, RICHARD H., TM2c, USNR.
BRADY, Ens. GERVIS S., USNR.
BRETTELL, Ens. ROBERT A., USNR.
BULIK, JOHN, MoMM2c, USNR.
BULKELEY, Lt. JOHN D.
BURK, Lt. JOSEPH W., USNR.
BURKE, Lt. (jg.) BYRON K., USNR.
BURNETT, ROBERT B., TM2c.
BURSAW, Lt. WILLIAM J., USNR.
CABOT, Lt. (jg.) OLIVER H. P., USNR.
CADY, Lt. (jg.) JOHN A., USNR.
CALHOUN, Ens. FRED, USNR.
CANNON, JAMES G. Jr., GM1c, USNR.
CAPPAERT, Lt. (jg.) FRANCIS L., USNR.
CAREY, Lt. (jg.) JOHN L., USNR.
CHALKER, JOSEPH C., MM2c.
CLAGETT, Lt. (jg.) FENDALL M., USNR.
CLARK, JESSE N., BM1c.
CLIFFORD, Lt. (jg.) EUGENE S. A., USNR.
CLIFT, JOHN W., Jr., CY(AA).
COBB, NED M., S1c.
CONN, LEROY G., MM2c.

COOKMAN, Lt. GEORGE E., USNR.
COOLIDGE, Lt. JOHN K., USNR.
COPP, Lt. (jg.) BELTON A., USNR.
CRAIG, CLAYTON A., MoMM1c.
CRESSEY, Lt. (jg.) JAMES T.
CRIMMINS, Lt. (jg.) BERNARD A., USNR.
CROUCH, HAROLD C., MM2c.
DAVIS, Lt. Cdr. N. BURT, Jr.
DAVIS, Lt. (jg.) NELSON, USNR
DEAN, Lt. (jg.) FRANK H., Jr.
DEAN, ORR L., TM2c, USNR.
DeLONG, Lt. EDWARD G.
DENNIS, Ens. HARRY, USNR.
DEVRIES, MARVIN H., TM1c.
DU BOSE, Lt. EDWIN A., USNR.
DUNLAP, Lt. (jg.) RICHARD H., USNR.
EBERSBERGER, GEORGE W., Jr., MoMM1c, USNR.
EICHELBERGER, PAUL E., MM1c.
ELLICOTT, Lt. (jg.) JOSEPH R., USNR.
EMMONS, Lt. (jg.) JAMES W., USNR.
EUBANK, JOSEPH B., S1c, USNR.
EVERETT, Lt. (jg.) CLAYTON F., USNR.
EWING, Lt. (jg.) RUMSEY, USNR.
FARLEY, Lt. EDWARD I., USNR.
FARROW, Cdr. HENRY.
FIDLER, Lt. (jg.) PAUL F., USNR.
FITZPATRICK, Lt. (jg.) JOSEPH J., USNR.
FORAN, Ens. JAMES F., USNR.
FOWX, CHARLES R., MoMM2c, USNR.
FRANKLIN, MORRIS N., MoMM3c, USNR.
FREELAND, Lt. FRANK, USNR.
FRIED, JAY V., GM3c, USNR.
FRIEDMAN, DAVID L., S1c, USNR.
GADD, Lt. (jg.) PETER R., USNR.
GAISER, CLINTON E., TM3c.
GALLAGHER, Lt. (jg.) WESLEY J. H., USNR.
GAMBLE, Lt. (jg.) LESTER H., USNR.
GAMMONS, WARREN R., Cox, USNR.
GIBSON, Lt. Cdr. JACK E.
GIBSON, RENTON T., RM2c, USNR.
GIGAC, JOSEPH, TM2c, USNR.
GIUSTO, SALVATORE, MoMM1c, USNR.
GREEN, Lt. LAURENCE B.
GREENE, Ens. JAMES B., USNR.
GREGG, Ens. HERBERT A., USNR.
GRIFFIN, Ens. WILLIAM F., USNR.

GRIZZARD, HERBERT W., MM2c.
GRUNDY, Lt. (jg.) THADDEUS, USNR.
GUYOT, DALE, CMM.
HALL, Lt. (jg.) WILLIAM P., USNR.
HAMACHEK, Lt. RUSSELL E., USNR.
HAMILTON, Lt. (jg.) EDWARD T., USNR.
HAMILTON, Lt. (jg.) RICHARD A., USNR.
HAMILTON, Lt. STUART, USNR.
HARLLEE, Lt. Cdr. JOHN.
HOGLAND, Lt. EDGAR D., USNR.
HOMER, LAWRENCE C., S1c., USNR.
HORVATH, JOSEPH F., Jr., GM2c, USNR.
HOULIHAN, JOHN L., Jr., TM1c.
HULIK, JOHN, MoMM2c, USNR.
HUNT, Ens. ROBERT R., USNR.
JACOBSON, Ens. FRED L. USNR.
JANIEN, Lt. (jg.) CEDRIC J., USNR.
JEWART, PAUL D., SF1c, USNR.
JOHNSON, Ens. CONE H., USNR.
JOHNSON, HAROLD C., QM1c.
JOHNSON, WILLIAM H., S1c.
JONES, Ens. PAUL H., USNR.
KAUFMAN, ALVEY V., MoMM1c, USNR.
KEATH, HARRY G., SC2c.
KEELER, HERBERT W., EM3c, USNR.
KERNICKY, FRANK S., GM3c, USNR.
KIRCHER, Lt. ROBERT E., USNR.
KNIGHT, Lt. (jg.) HERBERT P., USNR.
KOENIG, Lt. (jg.) ROBERT J., USNR.
KONKO, WILLIAM F., RM3c.
KOZYRA, WALTER A., S2c, USNR.
KREMER, Lt. Cdr. JOHN, Jr., USNR.
KRONMAN, WALFORD J., MoMM2c, USNR.
KURATNICK, Lt. (jg.) MICHAEL A., USNR.
LANGLOIS, DONALD L., SC2c, USNR.
LANGSTON, CLEM L., Cox.
LAPPIN, DONALD L., MoMM2c, USNR.
LEE, WILFRED J., RM3c, USNR.
LEESON, Ens. A. DIX, USNR.
LEESON, Lt. Cdr. ROBERT, USNR
LEGG, JOHN D., CQM.
LERNER, Lt. HAROLD B., USNR.
LEWIS, JOHN H., MM1c.
LEWIS, Lt. (jg.) STUART A., USNR.
LIEBENOW, Lt. (jg.) WILLIAM F., Jr., USNR.
LILLIS, Lt. (jg.) PAUL B., USNR.
LISCHIN, RICHARD H., S2c, USNR.

LIVINGSTON, Lt. STANLEY, USNR.
LONG, Lt. (jg.) ORRIN, USNR.
LYNCH, Ens. ROBERT F., Jr., USNR.
McADOO, Lt. FRANCIS H., Jr., USNR.
McCAFFERTY, Ens. JAMES R., USNR.
McCARTHY, JOHN F., MoMM2c.
McELROY, Lt. (jg.) JOHN E., USNR.
McEVOY, JAMES A., MM2c.
MACAULEY, Lt. EDWARD, III, USNR.
MACKEY, THEODORE, CMoMM, USNR.
MACDONALD, Lt. (jg.) TORBERT H., USNR.
MACMILLAN, THOMAS S., RM2c, USNR.
MALCOLM, Lt. IAN D., USNR.
McNAMARA, Lt. (jg.) EDMUND L., USNR.
MARSHALL, Lt. STANMORE B., USNR.
MASCHKE, Lt. (jg.) ARTHUR W., USNR.
MASIAS, RAYMOND P., GM3c, USNR.
MASTERS, JOHN J., Jr., CMoMM.
MEROWITZ, HAROLD, BM2c.
MILLER, Lt. (jg.) JAMES E., USNR.
MISLICKY, Lt. ROMAN G.
MOLLOY, Lt. (jg.) KENNETH D., USNR.
MONTGOMERY, Lt. Cdr. ALAN R.
MURDOCH, ARTHUR J., GM2c, USNR.
MURRAY, Ens. BOND, USNR.
MURRAY, Lt. CLARKE L., USNR.
MYERS, JOSEPH N., QM3c, USNR.
NAGLE, Lt. ROBERT E., USNR.
NAPOLILLO, FRANCIS J., Jr., SC1c.
NEHER, DELBERT G., F1c, USNR.
NELSON, CLARENCE L., MoMM1c, USNR.
NEWKIRK, WARREN K., GM3c, USNR.
NIKOLORIC, Lt. (jg.) LEONARD A., USNR.
NOEL, OTIS F., QM1c.
O'BRION, Lt. (jg.) RICHARD F., USNR.
OFFRET, ELWOOD H., CMM.
O'NEILL, RICHARD J., S1c, USNR.
OSBORNE, CLETUS E., GM2c, USNR.
OWEN, PAUL A., CMM.
PANNELL, Ens. ERNEST W., USNR.
PARRISH, BENJAMIN F., GM1c.
PELLINAT, CHARLES A., S1c.
PEPPO, MALCOLM A., MoMM3c, USNR.
PERCY, Lt. (jg.) BILLUPS P., USN.
PESSOLANO, Lt. MICHAEL R.
PETERSON, ARTHUR G., TM3c.
PIERSON, ERNEST E., BM2c.
POSEY, WILLIAM H., SC1c.

Post, Horace C., CRM.
Potter, Lt. Philip A., Jr., USNR.
Pressly, Lt. (jg.) Francis Y., USNR.
Preston, Lt. A. Murray, USNR.
Punches, Lt. (jg.) Herbert W., USNR.
Ray, Capt. Herbert J.
Read, Lt. Robert R., USNR.
Reade, Lt. Robert B., USNR.
Regan, Richard A., CMM.
Richard, Norman O., TM2c, USNR.
Richards, Lt. (jg.) Ralph L., USNR.
Riggsby, Lewis H., TM2c, USNR.
Robertson, Lt. (jg.) William H., USNR.
Robinson, Lt. Hugh M.
Rogers, Harold E., GM2c.
Rogers, Patrick M., RM2c.
Rooke, Henry C., SC2c.
Roth, Lt. (jg.) Robert, USNR.
Ruff, Lt. (jg.) John, USNR.
Saganiec, Stanley A., SC2c, USNR.
Schneider, Lt. (jg.) Robert E., USNR.
Schnieders, Lt. (jg.) Oliver J., USNR.
Schumacher, Lt. (jg.) Vincent E.
Searles, Lt. Robert L., USNR.
Sellars, William G., GM3c, USNR.
Sewell, Allen R., SC3c, USNR.
Shambora, John, BM1c.
Shaw, James J., Jr., MoMM2c, USNR.
Shearer, Lt. Robert D., USNR.
Silvestri, Joseph H., MoMM2c USNR.
Sims, Watson S., RM2c.
Sinclair, Lt. (jg.) Thomas L., Jr., USNR.
Smith, Lt. Craig C., USNR.
Smith, Lt. (jg.) Elmer J., USNR.
Snowball, Lt. (jg.) Alfred A., USNR.
Stanley, Robert W., QM2c, USNR.
Stayonovich, Emil P., TM2c.
Stedman, Lt. William E., USNR.
Stewart, Harry D., SC2c, USNR.
Stewart, Lt. William W., USNR.
Stoddard, Lt. Eben, USNR.
Stone, Elmer, MoMM1c, USNR.
Stoneburner, Lt. Seabury D., USNR.
Storms, Lt. John W., USNR.
Stroud, Densil C., CCStd.
Stutsman, Lt. (jg.) Lawrence M., USNR.
Tankenoff, Morton A., RM2c, USNR.

Tappaan, Lt. Cdr. Francis D., USNR.
Taylor, Lt. (jg.) Cyrus R., USNR.
Taylor, Lt. Henry S., USNR.
Taylor, Lt. Cdr. LeRoy T.
Thode, Lt. (jg.) Edward W., USNR.
Tripp, Harry P., RM3c.
Tropea, Joseph C., GM3c, USNR.
Turnbull, Lt. (jg.) Raymond C., USNR.
Tyler, Robert C., Cox.
Van Buskirk, Lt. Bruce P., USNR.
Vanderbilt, Lt. (jg.) Alfred G., USNR.
Wakelin, Lt. (jg.) Edmund F., USNR.
Walbridge, Lt. (jg.) George O. II, USNR.
Warfield, Cdr. Thomas G.
Waters, Lt. (jg.) Robert E., USNR.
Wehrli, Lt. Robert J., USNR.
Wells, Lt. Alexander W., USNR.
Werner, Lt. (jg.) Robert L., USNR.
Westholm, Lt. Cdr. Rollin E.
Wilcox, Walter F., QM3c, USNR.
Williams, Lt. John B., USNR.
Winget, George W., MM2c.
Wood, Lt. Hamilton H., USNR.
Wood, Lt. (jg.) Leighton C., USNR.
Yando, Stephen, MM1c.
Zolper, Ira G., GM3c, USNR.

LEGION OF MERIT (DEGREE OF OFFICER)

Howitt, Lt. Eric M., RANVR.

LEGION OF MERIT WITH GOLD STAR IN LIEU OF SECOND LEGION OF MERIT

Mumma, Cdr. Morton C., Jr.
Mutty, Lt. Cdr. John B.

LEGION OF MERIT

Allan, Cdr. Robert A., RNVR.
Austin, Lt. J. Paul, USNR.

BARNES, Cdr. STANLEY M.

BERNIE, EDWARD L., MoMM2c.

BOWLING, Cdr. SELMAN S.

BULKELEY, Cdr. JOHN D.

BULKLEY, Lt. Cdr. ROBERT J., Jr., USNR.

DAUNIS, Lt. Cdr. S. STEPHEN.

DAVIS, Lt. Cdr. N. BURT, Jr.

DRESSLING, Lt. Cdr. RICHARD J.

FARLEY, Lt. EDWARD I., USNR.

HARLLEE, Cdr. JOHN.

HOLROYD, Cdr. WALTER W., USNR.

LEESON, Lt. Cdr. ROBERT, USNR.

McKEAN, Lt. JOHN F., USNR.

MORAN, Commo. EDWARD J.

NEFF, CHARLES G., MoMM1c, USNR.

OSBORNE, CLETUS E., GM2c, USNR.

OWEN, Lt. (jg.) DWIGHT, USNR.

PULLEN, Lt. WESTON C., Jr., USNR.

RENNELL, Lt. PAUL T., USNR.

SMITH, Lt. Cdr. RUSSELL H.

SPECHT, Cdr. WILLIAM C.

SWIFT, Lt. Cdr. HENRY M. S., USNR.

TAPPAAN, Lt. Cdr. FRANCIS D., USNR.

THROSBY, Maj. JAMES T., AIF.

VANDERBILT, Lt. GEORGE, USNR.

WALSH, Cdr. DAVID J., USNR.

WIGGERS, Lt. (jg) LOWE H. (MC), USNR.

NAVY AND MARINE CORPS MEDAL

AMATEIS, HAROLD L., RM2c, USNR.

BENNETT, HARRY R., MoMM2c, USNR.

BLANKENSHIP, WILLIAM J., F1c, USNR.

CATHEY, OTTIS K., TM2c, USNR.

CAYER, PAUL E., S1c, USNR.

CLAGETT, Lt. FENDALL M., USNR.

CLOUGHERTY, FRANCIS E., MoMM3c, USNR.

COLEMAN, RALPH F., MoMM2c, USNR.

CONNOR, HAROLD W., SC1c, USNR.

COX, ROBERT M., MoMM3c.

CURTIN, Lt. (jg.) EDWARD D., (MC) USNR.

DASILVA, ADELINO J., RM2c, USNR.

DAVIS, Lt. Cdr. N. BURT, Jr.

DWYER, GEORGE A., QM2c, USNR.

EBRIGHT, RICHARD C., GM3c, USNR.

ELSASS, MERLE C., TM2c.

FOEHNER, GEORGE A., RM2c, USNR.

FOLEY, HAROLD W., GM2c, USNR.

GLENN, Ens. SPENCER S., USNR.

GUCKERT, Ens. GEORGE H., USNR.

GULLO, CARMINE R., S1c, USNR.

HABIG, Ens. LEONARD P., USNR.

HALL, Lt. CROWELL C., USNR.

HEMPHILL, HOWARD H., MoMM1c, USNR.

HUNNICUTT, RICHARD L., RM2c, USNR.

KALINOWSKI, EDMUND I., MoMM2c, USNR.

KENNEDY, Lt. JOHN F., USNR.

KHIER, JOHN, F1c, USNR.

LARSEN, WILBUR B., MoMM1c, USNR.

LARSON, VICTOR H., QM3c, USNR.

LOGGINS, LAMAR H., MoMM2c.

LOIZEAUX, PAUL J., TM3c, USNR.

LONG, WALTER L., Cox.

McVEY, C. W., Jr., GM3c, USNR.

MAIZE, JOSEPH F., MoMM1c, USNR.

MEDYNSKI, KORNELLO, GM2c, USNR.

MILLER, EDWARD St. C., BM2c.

MILLS, Ens. WILLIAM J., USNR.

MITCHELL, JOHN J., RM2c.

MITSCHA, MAX E., QM3c, USNR.

MOEN, WILLIAM C. MoMM1c, USNR.

MOORE, ALFRED B., MoMM3c, USNR.

MORROW, LEROY C., BM1c, USNR.

MURRAY, Lt. (jg.) HOWARD L., USNR.

OLSEN, RICHARD A., TM2c, USNR.

PRESSLY, Lt. (jg.) FRANCIS Y., USNR.

ROME, Lt. RUSSEL W., USNR.

ROMERO, ELISANDRO, SC2c, USNR.

ROSS, Ens. GEORGE H. R., USNR.

ROZUMALSKI, RICHARD C., MoMM2c, USNR.

SABELLO, CYRIL A., S1c, USNR.

SANDERS, Lt. CECIL C., USNR.

SECREST, Ens. RICHARD B., USNR.

SIMPSON, Lt. RICHARD C., USNR.

STILLMAN, Lt. JOHN H., USNR.

SUMSTAD, ARNOLD, GM2c.

THOM, Ens. LEONARD J., USNR.

WESTHEIDER, HENRY W., MoMM2c, USNR.

BRONZE STAR WITH GOLD STAR IN LIEU OF SECOND BRONZE STAR

BURK, Lt. JOSEPH W., USNR.
GRIFFIN, Lt. (jg.) HARRY E., USNR.
IRVING, Lt. Cdr. RONALD K.
MONTZ, Lt. (jg.) KERMIT W., USNR.
RAYMOND, Lt. JONATHAN S., Jr., USNR.
STRONG, Cdr. PAUL, USNR.
VAN NESS, Cdr. GLENN R., USNR.

BRONZE STAR

ADAMS, RONALD B., GM3c, USNR.
ALBERT, MIKE, MoMM1c, USNR.
ALEXANDER, Lt. Cdr. DAVID M., USNR.
ALLISON, HENRY C., RT1c, USNR.
ALVERSON, HOWARD E., CQM, USNR.
ANDERSON, Ens. LLOYD, USNR.
ANDERSON, Ens. REX L., USNR.
ANDREWS, GILBERT E., GM3c, USNR.
ANGUS, JOHN M., MoMM3c, USNR.
ATKINSON, Lt. ARTHUR K., Jr., USNR.
AYERS, MARION, GM1c.
BAKER, RAYMOND J., TM2c, USNR.
BAKER, SEBOE, S1c, USNR.
BARKER, GERALD L., CTM.
BARNES, Lt. ARTHUR N., USNR.
BARNES, Ens. WILLIAM, III, USNR.
BARRY, WILLIAM A., GM1c, USNR.
BARSH, RICHARD A., RM1c, USNR.
BASS, ROBERT E., CAerM.
BEASLEY, Lt. (jg.) ROBERT H., Jr., USNR.
BECK, GEORGE R., Bkr2c, USNR.
BECK, WALTER J., TM1c, USNR.
BENNETT, Lt. (jg.) HARRISON L., USNR.
BERLIN, Ens. THEODORE, USNR.
BERNDTSON, Lt. ARTHUR H.
BETZ, HERBERT H., QM2c, USNR.
BLACK, ROBERT A., RM1c, USNR.
BLAKELY, ROBERT P., MoMM1c.
BLANCHARD, Lt. (jg.) OSCAR C., USNR.
BLANDFORD, Ens. MASON H., USNR.
BLISS, Lt. Cdr. HARRY F., Jr., USNR.
BOEBEL, Lt. ROBERT T., USNR.
BOLDT, WILLIAM E., GM2c, USNR.
BONNIOL, LOUIS E., MoMM1c, USNR.

BOOTH, ARTHUR W., CQM.
BOWMAN, Lt. HENRY W., USNR.
BOYLE, Lt. (jg.) HOWARD H., Jr., USNR.
BRIGGS, HARLEY D., TM2c, USNR.
BROGAN, JOSEPH E., MoMM3c.
BROWN, Ens. EARLE P., USNR.
BROWN, MORGAN E., GM1c.
BRUETT, Ens. JAMES M., USNR.
BUBA, EDWIN C., RdM2c, USNR.
BUCK, GORDON V., GM2c.
BUCKOWSKI, ANTHONY J., GM1c.
BURGERS, Lt. (jg.) GEORGE W., USNR.
BURTON, Lt. (jg.) ROBERT H., USNR.
BYETTE, JOHN F., MoMM1c, USNR.
CALHOUN, Lt. (jg.) CHARLES D., USNR.
CAMPBELL, WILLIAM A., MoMM2c, USNR.
CARR, Lt. (jg.,) CHARLES C., USNR.
CARTER, Lt. (jg.) WILLIAM R., USNR.
CARUTHERS, DONALD E., MoMM1c, USNR.
CIVINS, MILTON E., SC2c, USNR.
CLAPP, GLENN M., MoMM2c, USNR.
CLIFFORD, Lt. EUGENE S. A., USNR.
CLOUGHERTY, FRANCIS E., MoMM3c, USNR.
COLEMAN, Cdr. DAVID B.
COLEMAN, RALPH F., MoMM2c, USNR.
COMEAU, THOMAS W., MoMM1c.
CONNOR, HAROLD W., SC1c, USNR.
CONRAD, LEWIS R., GM1c.
CONWAY, Lt. WILLIAM R., USNR.
COOK, EDWIN D., EM2c.
COOPER, FRANCIS O., TM2c, USNR.
COSTELLO, Lt. (jg.) JAMES W., USNR.
COSTIGAN, Lt. (jg.) JAMES H., USNR.
COTTOM, KENNETH E., GM2c, USNR.
CRONIN, ROBERT E., TM2c, USNR.
CUNNINGHAM, M. J., GM3c, USNR.
CYR, PATRICK, CM1c.
DALTON, Lt. (jg.) THOMAS W., Jr., USNR.
DANIEL, Lt. JAQUELIN J., USNR.
DEAN, THOMAS H., CMoMM, USNR.
DEEN, Ens. HARVARD F., USNR.
DELIA, MASSINO B., Cox, USNR.
DEMPSTER, JAMES F., RM3c, USNR.
DENISON, CHARLES F., TM2c, USNR.
DENNIS, Ens. JOHN A., USNR.
DIVER, Lt. (jg.) WILLIAM S., USNR.

DONOHUE, Lt. CARROL J., USNR.
DOWDELL, WILLIAM T., MoMM1c.
DUGAN, HARRY W., CQM.
DUMAS, Ens. HARRELL F., USNR.
EASON, Ens. FREDERICK J., USNR.
EASTHAM, Lt. (jg.) JOHN M., USNR.
EASTWOOD, HERMAN G., Jr., QM3c, USNR.
EDDINS, Lt. (jg.) JOSEPH A., USNR.
EDMONDS, GEORGE E., MoMM2c, USNR.
ELLICOTT, Lt. (jg.) JOSEPH R., USNR.
ELLIS, Lt. LONG, USNR.
ENGLAND, Lt. JONATHAN S., USNR.
EPPERLY, Lt. RAY S.
EVANS, Lt. (jg.) LUTHER C., USNR.
EWELL, Lt. Cdr. JOHN W., USNR.
EWING, Lt. ROBERT S., USNR.
FALVEY, Lt. (jg.) THOMAS E., USNR.
FAY, Ens. PAUL B., USNR.
FERNELIUS, Lt. BYRNE C., USNR.
FERRON, Lt. ALAN W., USNR.
FINAN, Lt. (jg.) WILLIAM D., USNR.
FISLER, WILLIAM F., MoMM2c, USNR.
FONVIELLE, Lt. (jg.) WAYNE A., USNR.
FORGE, HARRY E., MoMM1c, USNR.
FOWLER, Lt. (jg.) GEORGE E., USNR.
FRANCE, LEWIS H., Jr., QM1c, USNR.
FRANKLIN, WAYNE, Jr., MoMM2c, USNR.
GAGLIARDI, JOHN J., CQM.
GARTH, Lt. (jg.) HARLAND L., USNR.
GASS, Lt. Cdr. FRANK B., USNR.
GESSLER, JAMES A., RM1c.
GIANCOLA, DANNY A., GM3c, USNR.
GILBERT, RAYMOND H., BM1c.
GILLIES, Lt. JAMES P., Jr. (SC), USNR.
GLEASON, Lt. CARL T.
GODDARD, BILLIE J., TM1c, USNR.
GOHIER, WILLIAM A., GM2c, USNR.
GORRY, WALTER F., RM2c, USNR.
GRAVES, RAYMOND J., CMoMM.
GREENE, Lt. JAMES B., USNR.
GRIFFITH, WARREN R., QM1c, USNR.
GRONDAHL, ROY S., SC1c, USNR.
GROSSMAN, JOSEPH F., MoMM2c, USNR.
HAAVIND, RAYMOND, CQM.
HALL, Lt. (jg.) THOMAS C., USNR.
HANDLAN, Lt. JOSEPH M., USNR.
HANLEY, JOHN M., RM2c, USNR.
HANLEY, THOMAS M., RM2c, USNR.

HANLY, Lt. Cdr. JOHN H., USNR.
HARDY, Lt. LEONARD R., USNR.
HARING, PAUL T., Jr., MoMM1c, USNR.
HARRIS, Lt. ALLEN H., USNR.
HARRIS, Ens. WALTER J.
HASTINGS, Lt. (jg.) CHARLES A., USNR.
HAUGEN, Ens. EDWARD S., USNR.
HAWRYS, WALTER J., GM3c, USNR.
HAYDE, Ens. THOMAS J., USNR.
HELME, Lt. (jg.) WILLIAM B., USNR.
HENNING, JOHN L., QM1c, USNR.
HENRY, Lt. (jg.) DONALD W., USNR.
HEYL, PAUL A., MoMM2c, USNR.
HICKMAN, Lt. NORMAN G., USNR.
HIEHLE, Lt. FORBES R., USNR.
HIGGINS, Lt. (jg.) JAMES C., USNR.
HILL, ROY F., GM3c, USNR.
HINDS, Lt. (jg.) JACKSON C., (SC), USNR.
HOCHBERG, Ens. RAYMOND A., USNR.
HOGLAND, Lt. EDGAR D., USNR.
HOLLENBECK, GLEN R., CPhM.
HORN, ALBERT H., TM2c, USNR.
HOWE, WILLIAM E., GM2c, USNR.
HUDACEK, Lt. (jg.) STEVE L., USNR.
HURSH, Lt. (jg.) ROBERT M., USNR.
HUSSEY, JAMES G., GM1c, USNR.
JOHNSON, Lt. (jg.) BEVERLY V., USNR.
JOHNSON, Ens. DUDLEY J., USNR.
JOHNSON, MARVIN H., QM1c, USNR.
JORGENSEN, Lt. (jg.) WALTER A., USNR.
JULIANA, Chief Mach. JOHN.
KARPPINEN, EINO A., MoMM2c, USNR.
KASARDA, STEPHEN, TM2c, USNR.
KATONA, GEORGE, PhM1c, USNR.
KAUL, Ens. FREDERIC H., USNR.
KEITH, CLEATUS M., MoMM3c, USNR.
KELLEY, FRANK W., CTM, USNR.
KELLEY, Lt. (jg.) LAWRENCE J., USNR.
KENT, Lt. (jg.) BYRON F., USNR.
KENT, Ens. WILLIAM H., USNR.
KERESEY, Lt. (jg.) RICHARD E., USNR.
KERNICK, EDWARD B., MoMM2c, USNR.
KIRK, DANIEL E., RM3c, USNR.
KIRK, EARL E., GM2c, USNR.
KISE, Lt. WILLIAM D., USNR.
KLINKEWICZ, PAUL, GM3c, USNR.
KLOPMAN, Ens. WILLIAM A., USNR.
KOSKI, Ens. EMIL T., USNR.

KRAWCEYNSKI, EDWIN C., MoMM2c, USNR.

KRUSE, Ens. EDWARD H., Jr., USNR.

KUNZEL, Lt. HERBERT, USNR.

LA CERTE, RAOUL K., TM2c, USNR.

LAMBROS, Lt. JOHN J., USNR.

LARIMER, Lt. DONALD R., USNR.

LARISCY, Machinist THEODORE.

LARKIN, DONALD R., GM3c, USNR.

LAWRENCE, GILBERT H., GM1c, USNR.

LEARY, Lt. (jg.) LEO H., Jr., USNR.

LEE, Ens. NIXON, Jr., USNR.

LEGG, KENNETH, CRM.

LEWIS, Lt. (jg.) DEAN J., USNR.

LEWIS, Lt. (jg.) RAYMOND T., USNR.

LEWIS, Lt. WILLIAM, USNR.

LEYRER, Lt. (jg.) HAROLD J., USNR.

LIDSTER, Lt. ALAN Y., USNR.

LIEBENOW, Lt. WILLIAM F., Jr., USNR.

LOVVORN, Lt. (jg.) T. J., USNR.

LOWELL, RAYMOND H., MoMM1c.

LUCAS, EDWARD P., MoMM2c, USNR.

LYON, Lt. (jg.) JUDSON S., USNR.

McINERNEY, Lt. (jg.) FRANCIS W., USNR.

McKEAN, Lt. JOHN F., USNR.

McKINNIES, JOHN W., CMoMM.

McLEES, GERARD J., TM1c, USNR.

MACHOLTZ, RAYMOND F., MoMM2c, USNR

MacLEAN, Lt. (jg.) ALEXANDER W., USNR

MacSWAN, Lt. (jg.) ELLIOT B., USNR.

MAHONEY, TERENCE W., RM1c.

MAKINEW, GEORGE A., CQM.

MANSFIELD, LAWRENCE R., MoMM1c, USNR.

MATTESON, Cdr. GEORGE A., Jr., USNR.

MAUL, Lt. (jg.) WILLIAM J. Jr., USNR.

MESSIER, ALFRED A., RM3c, USNR.

MICHAEL, WALTER R., QM2c, USNR.

MILFORD, Lt. (jg.) ROBERT S., USNR.

MILLER, Lt. (jg.) GEORGE C., USNR.

MILNE, JOHN, TM3c, USNR.

MINNICK, ROBERT B., Y2c, USNR.

MINOR, LLOYD V., BM1c.

MOFFETT, WILLIAM R., MoMM2c, USNR.

MONAGHAN, Lt. (jg.) AALTON D., USNR.

MORSHEAD, FRANK T., Jr., CPhM, USNR.

MOWRY, HUGH R., TM3c, USNR.

MULLER, Ens. ROBERT H., USNR.

MUNN, Ens. JOHN M., USNR.

MYERS, Lt. (jg.) ERNEST C., USNR.

NAGY, LEWIS J., S1c, USNR.

NASH, Ens. LAWRENCE, USNR.

NETTERSTROM, Lt. RALPH W., USNR.

NEWTON, Lt. (jg.) EMERY M., Jr., USNR.

NORTH, Lt. (jg.) RICHARD M., USNR.

NOVAK, JOHN A., CTM.

O'BRYANT, ARCHIE G., CEM, USNR.

OLDS, Lt. DAVID M., USNR.

OLIVER, GEORGE W., GM2c, USNR.

OLSON, Lt. (jg.) ELMER H., USNR.

OLTON, Lt. FRANK H., USNR.

ORR, JOHN, CMoMM.

OSCHNER, EARL F., CMoMM.

OSTROSKY, DANIEL M., SC2c, USNR.

PAGACZ, FRANK J., MoMM1c, USNR.

PAGE, HERMAN L., TM3c, USNR.

PAGE, Lt. (jg.) ROBERT G., USNR.

PAQUETTE, WILLIAM L., TM3c, USNR.

PATERRA, MARIANO, QM2c, USNR.

PAYNE, Lt. (jg.) DAVID M., USNR.

PERMENTER, J. W., GM3c, USNR.

PHELPS, CHARLES S., MoMM1c, USNR.

PINKLEY, Ens. CLARENCE L., USNR.

PIPPIN, HUGH H., CTM.

POITEVENT, Lt. (jg.) EADS, Jr., USNR.

POLK, Ens. EDWIN W., USNR.

POPE, Lt. EDWARD J., Jr., USNR.

POPE, Lt. RALPH L., Jr., USNR.

POWELL, Lt. (jg.) WALTER E., USNR.

RANDALL, JOHN C., MoMM1c, USNR.

READ, Lt. ROBERT R., USNR.

READE, Lt. ROBERT B., USNR.

REEKS, Ens. EMMETTE H., USNR.

RENERS, WILLIAM H., BM2c, USNR.

REYNOLDS, CONRAD L., CGM, USNR.

RHODE, Lt. (jg.) DONALD A., USNR.

ROBERTS, Lt. EDWARD W., USNR.

ROBERTS, Lt. (jg.) JOSEPH K., USNR.

ROBERTSON, Lt. (jg.) WILLIAM H., USNR.

ROGERS, JAMES B., CGM, USNR.

ROMANSKI, EDWARD W., RT1c, USNR.

ROTH, RUDOLPH G., CEM, USNR.

SAIGER, WALTER C., MoMM1c, USNR.

SAUER, Lt. (jg.) DAVID C., USNR.

SAWIN, Lt. PHILIP Q., USNR.

SCHAFFNER, Ens. WILLIAM D., USNR.

SCHOENBACH, JOSEPH J., CM1c.
SEAMAN, Lt. DONALD F., USNR.
SEEVERS, MARVIN H., MoMM1c, USNR.
SELLS, Lt. WILLIAM C.
SEMBOWER, Lt. JOHN H., USNR.
SEVER, Ens. JOHN W., USNR.
SHAFER, Lt. RAYMOND P., USNR.
SHAPLEIGH, Ens. ROBERT P., USNR.
SHEEHAN, EDWARD F., GM3c, USNR.
SHERERTZ, Lt. Cdr. HERBERT J., USNR.
SHERWOOD, Lt. (jg.) HAROLD B., Jr., USNR.
SHIRLEY, ROLAND H., TM1c, USNR.
SIMONET, ALEXANDER S., S1c.
SMITH, LOUIS, CM1c, USNR.
SMITH, Lt. (jg.) LOUIS E., USNR.
SMITH, MARION C., Jr., RM2c, USNR.
SMITH, Lt. (jg.) RICHARD K., USNR.
SMYTH, CHARLES W., TM3c, USNR.
SNELLING, Lt. WILLIAM M., USNR.
SNYDER, ROBERT J., GM2c, USNR.
SORIANO, JOHN G., GM2c, USNR.
SPARACO, Lt. (jg.) CHARLES W., USNR.
SPARKMAN, Lt. RAYMOND D., USNR.
SPENCER, Lt. (jg.) CHARLES D., III, USNR.
STANLEY, ROBERT W., QM2c, USNR.
STARKEY, GEORGE M., CRT, USNR.
STEELE, Lt. ROLAND B., USNR.
STEPHEN, JAMES J., MoMM1c, USNR.
STEWARD, WILBUR P., CQM, USNR.
STEWART, RAYMOND L., QM1c, USNR.
STILES, GALE M., MoMM2c, USNR.
SUK, STANLEY A., MoMM2c, USNR.
SULLIVAN, CHARLES E., TM2c, USNR.
SUTTENFIELD, Ens. WILLIAM H., Jr., USNR
TAFT, Lt. (jg.) ROBERT S., USNR.
TALLEY, LEROY F., MoMM2c, USNR.
TARRANT, Lt. WILLIAM T., Jr., USNR.
TAYLOR, Lt. HENRY S., USNR.
TAYLOR, HUGH A., GM2c, USNR.
TENNANT, Lt. (jg.) JOHN R., USNR.
TESCH, Ens. RICHARD W., USNR.
THOMAS, Ens. LOUIS E., USNR.
THOMPSON, Lt. JAMES R., USNR.
THRONSON, Lt. (jg.) HARLEY A., USNR.
TODD, Acting Pay Clerk CARL E.
TOON, Lt. MALCOLM, USNR.
TOUSSAINT, RAYMOND S., MoMM2c, USNR
TREVISANO, COSMO, GM2c, USNR.

TRUEBLOOD, Lt. (jg.) ALVA C. (MC) USNR.
TRYBULSKI, FLORIAN J., F1c.
TURNER, EDMUND H., TM2c, USNR.
TURNER, THURSTON D., S2c, USNR.
TWADELL, Lt. CHARLES E., Jr., USNR.
VAN SICKLEN, Lt. JAMES H., USNR.
VITRULS, GEORGE, GM3c, USNR.
WAGNER, Ens. JOHN H., USNR.
WAGNER, LEMUAL H., CMoMM, USNR.
WAKELIN, Ens. EDMUND F., USNR.
WALKER, Lt. (jg.) WESLEY M., USNR.
WALL, WARREN G., MoMM2c, USNR.
WALLACE, Lt. (jg.) LAWRENCE A., USNR.
WALSH, GEORGE T., SC2c, USNR.
WARNER, PAUL R., MoMM2c, USNR.
WARNOCK, Ens. ROBERT B., USNR.
WATTERSON, MELVIN G., MoMM1c, USNR.
WATTS, GEORGE T., GM2c, USNR.
WAUGH, Lt. (jg.) ROGERS V., USNR.
WEAVER, PAUL, CMoMM.
WEIMER, PAUL H., EM1c.
WELKER, EARL R., CMoMM, USNR.
WENNDT, SYLVAN A., GM2c, USNR.
WESSEL, Lt. Cdr. ROBERT L., USNR.
WEST, Ens. WILLIAM P., USNR.
WETHERELL, Lt. (jg.) WELLS S., USNR.
WHORTON, Lt. (jg.) CALVIN R., USNR.
WILLIAMS, Lt. ARTHUR P., USNR.
WILLIAMS, HENRY K., Jr., GM1c, USNR.
WILLIAMS, JENNINGS B., MoMM2c, USNR.
WILLOUGHBY, RUSSELL S., MoMM2c, USNR.
WOJNAR, JOSEPH, Jr., MoMM1c, USNR.
WOOD, DEANE M., GM1c, USNR.
WOOLSTONCROFT, MARK H., MoMM2c, USNR.
YEAGER, HAROLD C., S1c, USNR.
YOUNG, Lt. (jg.) ALBERT A., USNR.
ZAGROCKI, JOSEPH A., TM2c, USNR.

COMMENDATION RIBBON WITH GOLD STAR IN LIEU OF SECOND COMMENDATION RIBBON

COOK, Lt. (jg.) JOHN E., USNR.
EWELL, Lt. JOHN W., USNR.
JONES, Lt. Cdr. LAWRENCE F., USNR.

COMMENDATION RIBBON

ANGUS, Machinist ROBERT B., USNR.
ARMSTRONG, CHARLES R., GM1c.
BAKER, Lt. Cdr. ALFRED T. III, USNR.
BAKURA, Lt. (jg.) JOSEPH, USNR.
BALOG, JOHN X., CPhM.
BANKS, HOMER, MoMM1c, USNR.
BATES, ALBERT G., MoMM2c, USNR.
BELL, JOHNNIE F., GM2c, USNR.
BOERWINKLE, Lt. (jg.) JAMES J., USNR.
BOGIE, EDWARD P., MoMM2c, USNR.
BOLING, WAYNE E., MoMM2c.
BONTE, Lt. Cdr. JOHN S., USNR.
BRETTELL, Ens. ROBERT A., USNR.
BRODERICK, Lt. DANIEL T., Jr., USNR.
BROUILLETTE, Lt. JOSEPH P. E.
BRUCE, EDWARD L., TM2c, USNR.
CALLIHAN, LESLIE E., F1c, USNR.
CAMERON, Lt. WILLIAM B., USNR.
CANNON, Lt. (jg.) ROBERT L., USNR.
CARTER, Lt. (jg.) WILLIAM R., USNR.
CASEY, L. A., CMM.
CHAMPE, Lt. (jg.) ROBERT E., USNR.
CHILDS, Lt. EARLE B.
CLARK, ALBERT C., GM2c, USNR.
CONLEY, FRANK G., RdM3c, USNR.
COX, Lt. F. GARDNER, Jr., USNR.
CRAWFORD, JACK, RM2c, USNR.
DAVIDSON, Lt. ROBERT L. D., USNR.
DAY, JOHN R., GM3c, USNR.
DEVOL, Lt. NORMAN, USNR.
EDWARDS, L., MoMM2c.
ELDREDGE, Lt. (jg.) WILLIAM K., USNR.
ERICKSON, ALBERT F., TM2c, USNR.
FERRON, Lt. ALAN W., USNR.
FOLK, NORMAN E., QM3c, USNR.
FONTAINE, STUART J., RM1c, USNR.
FRANCK, Lt. JACK V., USNR.
FRY, Chief Carpenter JOE B., USNR.
FULLER, JOHN W., RdM2c, USNR.
GALE, HOWARD D., QM3c, USNR.
GALLAGHER, Lt. (jg.) WESLEY J. H., USNR.
GARRETT, EARL M., BM2c, USNR.
GASS, Lt. Cdr. FRANK B., USNR.
GERTH, HAROLD F., MoMM1c, USNR.
GORMAN, ROBERT J., QM2c, USNR.
GORSUCH, Lt. HARRY R., USNR.

GRAVE, O. S., S1c.
GUYOT, DALE, CMM(AA).
HARRIS, Lt. (jg.) EDWIN F., USNR.
HARRIS, E. R. SC1c.
HART, THOMAS, B. GM1c, USNR.
HAWKES, PHILIP K., CRM.
HAYDEN, RUSSELL L., Jr., SM1c, USNR.
HAYES, Lt. OLIVER W., USNR.
HILL, ROBERT J., QM2c, USNR.
HIRSCH, MARVIN K., SF2c, USNR.
HOULIHAN, JOHN L., Jr., TM1c.
INGVALDSON, Lt. (jg.) WELDEN S., USNR.
JANSEN, Ens. LEONARD L., USNR.
JENKINS, Lt. HARRY M., USNR.
JOCHIMS, E. H., S1c.
JOHNSON, R. T., EM2c.
JOHNSON, ROBERT W., GM3c, USNR.
KELLER, Lt. (jg.) CHARLES P., USNR.
KUHN, Lt. JAMES C. Jr., USNR.
LABRUM, Lt. (jg.) WILLARD D., USNR.
LAWRENCE, WILLIAM J., CPhM, USNR.
LERNER, Lt. (jg.) HAROLD B., USNR.
LITTON, Lt. (jg.) JACKSON D., USNR.
LOYD, JOSEPH, Jr., GM3c, USNR.
LUSK, Lt. (jg.) ALBERT FINLEY, USNR.
McCLAIN, Lt. (jg.) CLINTON, USNR.
McLEOD, Lt. (jg.) ROBERT D., USNR.
MARSHALL, Lt. (jg.) STANMORE B., USNR.
MEUS, JOSEPH F., RdM3c, USNR.
MITCHELL, Lt. (jg.) SAMUEL W., USNR.
MORRISON, Lt. DAVID J., USNR.
NICHOLSON, JOHN M., MM1c, USNR.
NORWOOD, ALFRED R., CTM.
NUGENT, Lt. (jg.) HAROLD J., USNR.
OSWALD, Lt. (jg.) JOHN W., USNR.
PALMER, Lt. (jg.) LOWELL M., III, USNR.
PATTERSON, Lt. (jg.) GEORGE E., USNR.
PERESICH, Lt. GILES H., USNR.
PETIPREN, Machinist GEORGE L., USNR.
POLLARD, Lt. (jg.), RAY, USNR.
RATCHFORD, FRED T., CPhM, USNR.
REYNOLDS, Lt. (jg.) BENJAMIN R., Jr., USNR.
RITCHEY, J. M., MoMM2c.
SANDERS, Lt. CECIL C., USNR.
SERMERSHEIM, Machinist, DENNY M., USNR.
SHARPLES, C. T., QM2c.

SHINSTROM, Lt. (jg.) FRANK R., USNR.
SMITH, C. G., MM2c.
SMITH, Lt. (jg.) HAMLIN D., USNR.
SPOFFORD, ROBERT N., Jr., TM3c, USNR.
STEINSON, Lt. (jg) JOHN A., Jr., USNR.
STEWART, Lt. (jg.) JAMES M., USNR.
STILLMAN, Lt. GUY, USNR.
STONEY, Lt. (jg.) LAWRENCE O., USNR.
SZCZECH, ALEXANDER J., GM2c, USNR.
TAPPAAN, Lt. Cdr. FRANCIS D., USNR.
TAYLOR, Lt. Cdr. LeRoy T.
TILDEN, Lt. CHARLES E., USNR.
TIMCHISZIN, MYRON W., TM2c.
TODD, Acting Pay Clerk CARL E.
TORRANCE, Lt. (jg.) JOHN M., USNR.
TREMBLAY, HENRY M., CM1c, USNR.
TRESCH, Lt. (jg.) ROBERT E., USNR.
TULLOCH, Lt. (jg.) PAGE H., USNR.
VENCHE, C., SC3c.
WARFIELD, Cdr. THOMAS G.
WELLS, Ens. ALEXANDER W., USNR.
WHALEN, Radio Electrician KENNETH H., USNR.
WHITE, Lt. CHARLES R., Jr., USNR.
WITTEBORT, Lt. ROBERT J., USNR.

DISTINGUISHED CONDUCT STAR (PHILIPPINE)

BULKELEY, Lt. JOHN D.
COX, Ens. GEORGE E., Jr., USNR.
HOULIHAN, JOHN L., Jr., TM1c.
LIGHT, JAMES D., CTM.

DISTINGUISHED SERVICE CROSS (BRITISH)

BARNES, Cdr. STANLEY M.
BOEBEL, Ens. ROBERT T., USNR.
DuBOSE, Lt. EDWIN A., USNR.
GRUNDY, Lt. (jg.) THADDEUS, USNR.
HICKMAN, Ens. NORMAN G., USNR.
OSWALD, Lt. (jg.) JOHN W., USNR.

DISTINGUISHED SERVICE MEDAL (BRITISH)

FITZGERALD, WILLIAM E., GM1c, USNR.
GRAY, GERALD M., QM2c, USNR.

APPENDIX D

Casualties

KILLED IN ACTION

ADELMAN, Ens. WILLIAM I., USNR.
ADLER, DONALD, S1c, USNR.
ALBERT, RAYMOND, S1c, USNR.
ALBRIGHT, ELMER F., MoMM2c, USNR.
AMOS, JOSEPH G., RM3c, USNR.
ANDREWS, HARRY E., GM3c, USNR.
ARCHIBALD, ROBERT J., S1c, USNR.
AUSLEY, WILLIAM S., GM3c, USNR.
AVANT, EDWIN H., MoMM1c, USNR.
BADGER, Lt. (jg.) SAMUEL E., Jr., USNR.
BALES, Ens. BRUCE S., USNR.
BALL, JOHN W., QM2c, USNR.
BALLOUGH, RUDOLPH, MM1c.
BANFIELD, JEROME C., S1c, USNR.
BANGERT, RALPH W., RdM3c, USNR.
BARRY, JOSEPH M., RdM2c, USNR.
BARTELL, FREDERICK O., GM1c.
BASSO, ALBERT J., S1c, USNR.
BATCHELOR, CLIFFORD, GM2c.
BEAULIEU, RICHARD J., S1c, USNR.
BEAUREGARD, VALMORE W., F1c, USNR.
BECKETT, ARNOLD F., TM2c, USNR.
BEER, GEORGE J., MoMM1c, USNR.
BELL, JACK O., SC2c.
BENDL, LEWIS J., S2c, USNR.
BENEKE, Ens. JAMES R., USNR.
BENNETT, JAMES G., QM3c, USNR.
BERRA, VINCENT A., QM3c, USNR.
BETZ, HERBERT H., QM2c, USNR.
BLAIR, DONALD F., S2c, USNR.
BLASZKOWSKI, ADOLPH M., WT3c, USNR.
BOONE, ALBERT E., GM3c, USNR.
BOUGERE, LOUIS C., MoMM2c, USNR.
BOWERS, JOHN R., MoMM2c, USNR.
BRADISH, CARROLL E., EM3c, USNR.
BREEN, DANIEL R., RM3c, USNR.

BRENDLINGER, RALPH E., MM1c.
BRICKER, DARREL A., RdM3c, USNR.
BRIGHTMAN, Machinist WILLIAM C.
BRINE, WILLIAM E., S1c.
BROWN, JAMES T., CTM.
BROWN, JOHN J., CGM.
BRUMM, BOYD W., GM3c, USNR.
BRUN, ROLAND J., TM3c.
BRUNNER, JOSEPH M., MM1c.
BUCAR, JOSEPH S., MoMM2c, USNR.
BURK, Lt. (jg.) JAMES R., USNR.
BURNS, FRANK N., MM3c, USNR.
CAMPBELL, JOHN L., F1c, USNR.
CANTERBURY, MORGAN J., TM2c, USNR.
CARPENTER, ROBERT A., RM2c, USNR.
CARPENTER, WILLIAM B., GM3c.
CARY, Lt. (jg.) DeWAYNE E., USNR.
CHALKER, JOSEPH C., MM2c.
CHESTER, Ens. JOHN D., USNR.
CHRISTIANSEN, CHARLES W., MoMM2c, USNR.
CILUFFO, DOMENIC J., MoMM1c.
CLAYTON, ALONZO L., RM2c, USNR.
CLEARY, CORNELIUS C., Y1c, USNR.
COATSWORTH, JOHN T., F1c.
COOK, Ens. FRANK E., USNR.
COOK, WILLIAM E., MM1c.
COOKMAN, Lt. GEORGE E., USNR.
COOPER, MARCUS W., MoMM1c, USNR.
CORTESE, ANGELO R., GM3c, USNR.
COTTOM, KENNETH E., GM2c, USNR.
COWLES, DONALD H., MoMM1c, USNR.
CREAD, WALTER I., F2c, USNR.
CREELMAN, Lt. (jg.) BRENTON W., USNR.
CRIST, Lt. HARRY M., USNR.
CROWE, WILLARD A., QM1c.

Curran, William J., Y2c, USNR.
Curtin, Lt. (jg.) Edward D., (MC) USNR.
Curtis, Robert H., RM2c.
Cuthriell, Norman F., Jr., F1c, USNR.
Dabakis, James J., TM2c, USNR.
Daley, Lt. (jg.) John F., USNR.
Daley, William Jr., MoMM1c, USNR.
Davison, James H., S1c, USNR.
Dean, William R., QM3c.
DeLong, Lt. Edward G.
Devaney, Thomas F., SC3c, USNR.
Dhonau, Harvey H., QM2c, USNR.
Donnell, Ens. John G., USNR.
Duckworth, Ens. John C., Jr., USNR.
Dudas, William L., MoMM2c, USNR.
Dunleavy, John J., GM2c, USNR.
Dunner, John H., Cox, USNR.
Eichelberger, Paul E., MM1c.
Emmons, George D., Jr., GM2c, USNR.
Ennis, Charles E., Jr., RM3c, USNR.
Eno, William E., EM1c, USNR.
Farnese, Joseph M., F1c, USNR.
Ferchen, Richard H., RM2c, USNR.
Fischer, Raymond B., CCM, USNR.
Fiume, Samuel F., SC3c, USNR.
Foley, Raeburn J., S1c, USNR.
Foster, Albert P., S2c, USNR.
Francesca, Albert J., SC2c, USNR.
Fravel, Marcus L., F1c, USNR.
Freeland, Lt. Frank, USNR.
Fried, Jay V., GM3c, USNR.
Friedman, David L., QM3c, USNR.
Fries, Robert W., MM3c.
Frudenfeld, Monte N., S1c, USNR.
Fucili, Evo A., MoMM3c, USNR.
Gaffney, William E., Jr., PhM2c, USNR.
Gallo, Anthony F., S1c, USNR.
Ganz, Edward W., SC2c, USNR.
Giaccani, Floyd R., Bkr2c.
Giddens, Roy A., MM1c.
Gleason, Lawrence M., MoMM2c, USNR.
Goolsby, Montie W., Jr., F1c.
Gormley, John J., S1c, USNR.
Gray, Elmer M., F1c, USNR.
Greenhalge, William J., S2c, USNR.
Gregory, Allen B., Jr., QM2c, USNR.
Griebel, Lt. (jg.) Russell J., USNR.

Griffith, Glen G., CMoMM.
Grizzard, Herbert N., MM1c.
Gross, Philip S., QM2c, USNR.
Guest, Harold R., TM2c, USNR.
Harris, David W., TM2c.
Hartz, George D., TM2c, USNR.
Harvey, Malcolm L., SF1c, USNR.
Haughian, Lt. (jg.) Michael A., USNR.
Hawkins, Benton F., MoMM2c, USNR.
Hayes, Electrician Charles R., USNR.
Haywood, Ens. Alfred W. Jr., USNR.
Heaton, Ben A., Jr., MoMM2c, USNR.
Hill, Warren J., TM3c, USNR.
Hirsch, Willard E., S1c, USNR.
Hix, Lt. (jg.) Sidney D., USNR.
Hogan, Lt. (jg.) George W. M., Jr., USNR.
Holland, Patrick, TM2c.
Holloway, Earnest T., S1c, USNR.
Hooper, Elvin E., GM3c.
Horan, Charles E., S2c.
Hornbrook, Ens. Philip R., Jr., USNR.
Horsfield, Richard E., MoMM2c, USNR.
Hubbard, Lewis B., MoMM1c, USNR.
Humrich, Clark L., MM3c, USNR.
Hyde, Ens. Robert W., USNR.
Jackson, Clifford D., MoMM2c, USNR.
Janusz, Stanley J., GM3c, USNR.
Johnson, Herbert W., S2c, USNR.
Jolley, Cerell C., MoMM2c, USNR.
Juneau, Raymond T., S1c, USNR.
Kaasinen, Wilho A., RM2c, USNR.
Keefe, Joseph F., TM3c, USNR.
Kelly, Ens. James J., USNR.
Kent, Ens. William H., USNR.
Kiene, Charles B., F1c, USNR.
King, Lloyd O., S1c.
Kirk, George E., SF2c, USNR.
Kirksey, Andrew J., TM2c, USNR.
Klann, Ralph F., MoMM2c, USNR.
Klesh, Joseph E., MoMM1c, USNR.
Koerner, Woodrow H., MoMM2c.
Kornak, Charles A., GM3c, USNR.
Kossman, Lawrence C., S1c.
Koury, Sam R., RM1c, USNR.
Krenzar, Albin J., S1c, USNR.
Kyriss, Jack, S1c.
Laker, Andrew V., SC3c, USNR.

LAMPI, WILLIAM A., S1c.
LANE, Lt. (jg.) J. FRANKLIN, Jr., USNR.
LEE, Ens. NIXON, Jr., USNR.
LEEDS, HARRY R., SC3c, USNR.
LENGLING, RAYMOND R., S2c.
LEONARD, LOYD W., S1c.
LIGHT, JAMES D., CTM.
LINDBERG, RAY F., MoMM2c, USNR.
LINDSAY, WILLARD G., S1c, USNR.
LINE, KENNETH R., SC2c, USNR.
LOSSIN, MARVIN W., MoMM2c, USNR.
McCARLEY, TURNER E., MM1c.
McCORMACK, CHARLES T., S2c, USNR.
McDONALD, JAMES J., S2c, USNR.
McKINNEY, RUSSELL H., Jr., F1c, USNR.
McKINNEY, WILLIAM J., S2c, USNR.
McLAUGHLIN, Lt. (jg.) JOSEPH D., USNR.
McMULLAN, JOHN L., SC2c, USNR.
MALONE, WILLIAM V., MoMM2c, USNR.
MANLEY, VERNON A., GM3c, USNR.
MARNEY, HAROLD W., MoMM2c.
MARSH, ROBERT E., MM1c.
MASTERS, JOHN J., Jr., CMoMM.
MATHES, Lt. (jg.) JAMES M., Jr., USNR.
MERCER, LAWRENCE D., MoMM2c.
MIDGETT, CHARLES F., Jr., MoMM3c, USNR.
MILLS, ROBERT W., SC2c, USNR.
MITCHELL, Lt. FRANK K., Jr., USNR.
MOORE, WALTER A., RM1c.
MOORMAN, Ens. Madison K., USNR.
MORRONE, UGO A., S2c, USNR.
MUNOZ, LOUIS L., S2c.
MURRAY, Ens. BOND, USNR.
MURRAY, Lt. (jg.) HOWARD L., USNR.
MUSE, CLYDE J., GM3c, USNR.
MYSLIWIEC, JOHN L., GM2c, USNR.
NANNEY, ROBERT M., CQM.
OWSIANNY, WALTER, MM2c.
PACE, ROBERT J., S1c, USNR.
PACEL, JOSEPH P., MoMM2c, USNR.
PARIS, MANLEY L., F1c.
PASTERIK, Ens. LADISLAV T., USNR.
PAUL, BERTIS I., MoMM1c.
PAVLIS, Lt. (jg.) JOHN K., USNR.
PETRULAVAGE, GEORGE, S1c, USNR.
PIERSON, ERNEST E., BM2c.
PINKLEY, Ens. CLARENCE L., USNR.

PLANT, Ens. WILLIAM H., USNR.
POSEY, WILLIAM H., SC1c.
PRZYBYS, RICHARD, MoMM3c.
RAKOWSKI, EDWARD A., RM3c., USNR.
RAMSDELL, ARTHUR C., TM3c, USNR.
RAUCH, ROBERT W., MoMM2c, USNR.
RAYL, NORMAN H., SC2c, USNR.
RAYMOND, Lt. JONATHAN S., Jr., USNR.
REGAN, Machinist RICHARD A.
REILLY, RAYMOND R., TM2c., USNR.
REYNOLDS, TONY S., RM2c, USNR.
REYNOLDS, WILLARD J., CCStd.
RICCI, ALFRED A., GM3c, USNR.
RICE, GLEN C., S1c, USNR.
RIEDL, JOHN J., SC3c, USNR.
RIHN, BURNELL V., TM1c.
ROBISON, CLARK L., S1c, USNR.
RODGERS, ERNEST E., Jr., RM1c.
ROMEOS, RAYMOND A., BM2c, USNR.
ROSS, THOMAS M., GM1c.
ROTHENBERG, LEIGH, Jr., TM3c.
ROULEAU, RAYMOND A., MoMM2c, USNR.
SABELLO, CYRIL A., S1c, USNR.
SAGANIEC, STANLEY A., SC2c, USNR.
SALIBA, GEORGE, SC3c, USNR.
SAMMARTINO, VITO A., F1c.
SAUL, Lt. (jg.) ROBERT M., USNR.
SAUL, WILLIAM K., SC2c, USNR.
SCHAFFROTH, RUDOLPH W., TM2c, USNR.
SCHARMUCK, DAVID A., GM3c, USNR.
SCHMIDT, EDGAR L., TM2c, USNR.
SCHWERDT, ARTHUR J., QM1c, USNR.
SCRANTON, LEROY W., Jr., MM3c, USNR.
SENESE, ALFRED O., S1c, USNR.
SHAFFER, Lt. (jg.) PAUL F., USNR.
SHAW, JAMES J., Jr., MoMM2c, USNR.
SHERMAN, Ens. REX A., USNR.
SHRIBMAN, Lt. (jg.) PHILIP A., USNR.
SILEO, LEONARD, MoMM2c.
SIPPIN, VICTOR, MoMM2c.
SMITH, Boatswain EDWARD.
SMITH, JOHN C., Jr., S1c, USNR.
SORENSON, MILTON C., GM3c, USNR.
SPARROW, NORMAN R., MoMM1c.
SPASEFF, PAUL P., RM2c, USNR.
SPEER, WILLIAM J., TM2c.
SPICHER, PAUL L., RM3c, USNR.
STADLER, Lt. (jg.) HERBERT, USNR.

STAMBAUGH, WILLIAM A., CY.
STANLEY, JAMES D., M3c, USNR.
STAPLES, Ens. PARKER W., USNR.
STEARNS, FLOYD M., CEM, USNR.
STILLMAN, Lt. JOHN H., USNR.
STOCKWELL, DONALD L., S1c, USNR.
STONE, ALLEN R., Cox.
STUCKEY, VESPER D. Sr., StM1c, USNR.
SUTHERLAND, GEORGE D., MoMM2c.
SUTTON, JOHN T., QM3c, USNR.
TATAREK, ANTHONY P., SC1c.
TAYLOR, Lt. (jg.) CYRUS R., USNR.
TAYLOR, WILLIAM W., SK3c.
THALE, EDWARD C., QM2c, USNR.
THOMAS, DEWEY C., MoMM1c, USNR.
THOMPSON, FERREE E., Jr., S1c, USNR.
THOMPSON, JOHN, S1c, USNR.
TIGNER, GERALD R., MoMM2c, USNR.
TODD, MERWIN K., GM2c, USNR.
TREVISANO, COSMO, GM2c, USNR.
TURNBULL, WILLIAM C., Jr., SK3c, USNR.
VINING, THOMAS R., Jr., RM3c, USNR.
WACHSMUTH, JACK H., Jr., M2c, USNR.
WACKLER, RUSSELL J., RM2c.

WAJERT, FRANK J., S1c, USNR.
WALKER, Lt. (jg.) DANIEL T., USNR.
WALKER, FRANK C., GM1c, USNR.
WALKINGTON, KEITH L., S1c, USNR.
WALLACE, JOSEPH T., TM3c, USNR.
WALTERS, LEONARD F., F1c, USNR.
WALTERS, WILLIAM N., S1c, USNR.
WALZHAUER, ALLEN F., GM3c, USNR.
WATSON, WARREN R., F1c, USNR.
WEBB, GEORGE T., MoMM1c, USNR.
WEBER, NEVIL T., Jr., MoMM3c, USNR.
WICKS, LESLIE W., S1c, USNR.
WIDSTRAND, ROY P., F1c, USNR.
WILKERSON, WILLIAM R., MoMM2c, USNR.
WILLETT, CHARLES A., MM3c.
WILLIAMS, THOMAS C., Jr., SK2c.
WINGFIELD, RICHARD H., S2c, USNR.
WISNIEWSKI, STANLEY, QM3c, USNR.
WYPICK, WALTER P., GM3c, USNR.
YENSAN, ROBERT E., SF3c.
YOUNGS, WILLIAM H., QM3c, USNR.
ZIETHEN, Ens. FREDERICK A., USNR.

WOUNDED

ACKERLE, PAUL, MoMM3c, USNR.
ADAMS, EDWARD F., GM2c, USNR.
ADAMS, MARION G., SC3c, USNR.
ADAMS, RONALD B., GM2c, USNR.
ADLER, FRED, F1c, USNR.
AGNEW, JACK W., GM2c, USNR.
ALBERTSON, WILLIAM F., F1c, USNR.
ALEXANDER, HARRY R., SC3c, USNR.
ALEXANDER, JOHN E., RT2c, USNR.
ALKIRE, JAMES P., MoMM2c, USNR.
ALLEN, Ens. MILTON R., USNR.
AMATEIS, HAROLD L., RM2c, USNR.
ANDERSON, Lt. RAYMOND B., Jr., USNR.
ANDERSON, REUBEN M., S2c.
ANDREWS, DARWIN D., SC3c, USNR.
APOSTLE, JOHN, GM3c, USNR.
ARBUCKLE, Lt. ERNEST C., USNR.
ARCHER, ROBERT, QM3c, USNR.
ARTERBERRY, WINFORD L., MoMM2c, USNR.

ASHWORTH, JOHN C., MoMM1c, USNR.
ASKEW, RUEBEN S., CTM.
ATHERTON, WILLIAM R., GM3c, USNR.
ATZEN, HERBERT H., MoMM3c, USNR.
BADGER, Lt. (jg.) PHILIP O., Jr., USNR.
BAER, EDWARD L., S2c, USNR.
BAGGETT, RICHARD C., MM2c.
BAILEY, MELVIN L., RdM3c, USNR.
BAKER, HAROLD R., MoMM1c, USNR.
BAKKEN, ALDON H., S1c, USNR.
BALSLEY, Lt. (jg.) GERALD E., USNR.
BARNES, FRANK TAYLOR, QM2c, USNR.
BARNETT, WILLIAM C., QM2c, USNR.
BARR, ROBERT J. C., EM3c.
BATHEL, HAROLD W., GM2c, USNR.
BAZEMORE, JACOB L., MoMM2c, USNR.
BELL, MERTON A., QM1c.
BENNETT, GILLIS D., Jr., TM3c, USNR.
BENNETT, LAWRENCE S., QM2c, USNR.
BENNETT, THOMAS L., TM1c, USNR.

BENSON, Lt. (jg.) PAUL R., USNR.
BERTON, WILLIAM P., MoMM2c, USNR.
BETTINA, FRANK, EM1c, USNR.
BETTY, RICHARD E., MoMM1c, USNR.
BIELE, ROBERT L., GM3c, USNR.
BIGGINS, ROBERT A., Y2c, USNR.
BLACK, DANIEL J., RM3c, USNR.
BLACK, ELMER J., MoMM3c, USNR.
BLAZER, HAROLD L., RdM3c, USNR.
BLISS, CHESTER M., RM2c, USNR.
BOGUCKI, THADDEUS F., MoMM2c, USNR.
BOHAN, WILLIAM M., GM2c, USNR.
BOKOR, SPENCER, GM3c, USNR.
BONNIOL, LOUIS E., MoMM1c, USNR.
BOUCHER, HARRY M., MoMM2c, USNR.
BOWERS, EDWIN S., MoMM1c, USNR.
BRACKNEY, DONALD J., MoMM2c, USNR.
BROOKS, CLINTON J., MM3c, USNR.
BROOKS, JOSHUA H., GM3c, USNR.
BROSNAHAN, DANIEL B., Jr., S1c.
BROUSSARD, Uolz F., CY, USNR.
BROWN, DONALD A., S1c, USNR.
BROWN, HAROLD F., SC2c, USNR.
BROWN, Lt. (jg.) RICHARD W., USNR.
BRUETT, Ens. JAMES M., USNR.
BRUNETTE, JAMES J., MoMM2c, USNR.
BULGER, GERALD J., S1c, USNR.
BULKELEY, Lt. JOHN D.
BULLIS, ROBERT E., S1c, USNR.
BURKE, JOSEPH J., EM2c.
BUTDORF, CLIFFORD J., MoMM3c, USNR.
CABAY, EMIL E., F1c, USNR.
CACY, PAUL E., RM2c, USNR.
CALHOUN, Lt. (jg.) FRED, USNR.
CAMERON, MURRAY D., RM3c, USNR.
CANNON, JAMES G., Jr., QM2c, USNR.
CARLSEN, Lt. (jg.) FRANK P., Jr., USNR.
CARLSON, HARRY R., Jr., TM2c.
CARLSON, ROBERT C., TM1c, USNR.
CARLSON, ROY G., Cox.
CARRAS, HARRY L., GM3c, USNR.
CARROLL, VINCENT T., GM3c.
CARTER, Ens. ROBERT E., USNR.
CARTER, Ens. STUART R., USNR.
CHAFFEE, EDWIN E., S1c.
CHANDLER, Ens. BARRON W., USNR.
CHEEK, JAMES H., PhM2c, USNR.
CHILDS, Lt. EARLE B.

CHOCK, RAYMOND E., GM3c.
CHOLIPSKI, ROBERT, TM3c, USNR.
CHRISTLY, GEORGE N., S1c, USNR.
CIPOLLETTI, ALFRED F., MoMM2c, USNR.
CLAGETT, Lt. JOHN H.
CLARKE, Ens. DONALD M., USNR.
COFFEY, DONALD A., SC1c, USNR.
COHEN, MELVIN L., MoMM2c, USNR.
COKRLIC, BOGDON, MoMM2c, USNR.
COLE, MELVIN, CMM.
COLE, WILLIAM A., SC2c, USNR.
COLVIN, Lt. Cdr. ALMER P.
CONNOR, HAROLD W., SC2c, USNR.
CONRAD, LEWIS R., GM2c.
CONRADY, HAROLD P., TM3c, USNR.
CONSTANTINE, JAMES, Jr., QM2c, USNR.
COOPER, FRANCIS O., TM3c, USNR.
COOPER, LEO C., MoMM2c.
COTTEN, A. J., MoMM2c, USNR.
COVINGTON, HENRY R., Jr., MoMM1c, USNR.
COYLE, ARTHUR P., SC1c, USNR.
CRAIG, CLAYTON A., MoMM2c.
CRANFORD, HAYWARD T., F1c, USNR.
CRARY, DAVID W., S1c, USNR.
CROSS, LESLIE M., TM3c, USNR.
CROSS, RICHARD H., MoMM1c, USNR.
CROSS, Ens. WALTER D., Jr., USNR.
CRUDEN, EARL M., Jr., F2c, USNR.
CUMMINGS, Ens. LESLIE L., USNR.
CUNNINGHAM, JOHN T., S1c.
CURY, THEODORE, S1c, USNR.
CUSACK, JOHN, Jr., SC2c, USNR.
CYSON, STANLEY J., RM2c, USNR.
DANIELS, SAM W., TM3c, USNR.
DAVIS, JOSEPH N., S1c, USNR.
DAVIS, Lt. Cdr. N. BURT.
DEAN, THOMAS H., CMoMM, USNR.
DeCAMP, ROBERT W., QM2c, USNR.
DELEY, CYRIL M., MM3c, USNR.
DENNIS, HARRY, RT1c, USNR.
DEPONS, CELESTIN S., SC2c, USNR.
DeSAUTELS, DONALD J., F1c, USNR.
DeWEESE, SHELTON, CTM, USNR.
DICK, FRED G., MoMM3c, USNR.
DIVOLL, Ens. NATT L., Jr., USNR.
DIXON, FRENCH G., TM3c, USNR.
DOBBINS, HUBERT, S2c, USNR.

DODWELL, ORVILL B., QM2c, USNR.
DOLLAR, CLAUDE RUSSELL, TM2c.
DOROHOVICH, CHARLES, GM2c, USNR.
DOUCET, PERCY J., S2c, USNR.
DRAWDY, LEON E., F1c, USNR.
DRIGGERS, WILLIAM L., CEM.
DRINKWATER, JOHN F., F1c.
DUNLAP, Lt. (jg.) RICHARD H., USNR.
DUPUIS, JEROME E., MoMM2c, USNR.
DUTCHER, ARTHUR E., GM2c, USNR.
DWINELL, HARLEY J., F1c, USNR.
DZIERZAK, EDWARD J., GM3c, USNR.
EANNELLI, RALPH L., TM1c.
EDDINS, Lt. (jg.) JOSEPH A., USNR.
EICK, WILLIAM J., F1c, USNR.
ELLIS, Lt. (jg.) LONG, USNR.
ELLIS, LESTER P., QM2c, USNR.
ENGLISH, LYLE L., MoMM1c.
EPTING, EDWARD E., GM2c, USNR.
ESPENSON, DONALD C., RdM3c, USNR.
EWING, Ens. RUMSEY, USNR.
FAHEY, BARTHOLOMEW L., CBM.
FARRELL, WARREN J., RT3c, USNR.
FASO, CARMINE, RdM3c, USNR.
FAUCHER, CHARLES O., RdM3c, USNR.
FIDLER, Lt. (jg.) PAUL F., USNR.
FINGER, ROBERT L., RM2c, USNR.
FINN, WILLIAM R., RM3c, USNR.
FISHER, DONALD E., RM2c, USNR.
FIVEASH, CLYDE B., GM1c.
FORNEY, VERNON W., RM2c, USNR.
FRANKS, JOHN C., BM1c, USNR.
FRICK, MARK R., RM2c, USNR.
FULLER, WILLIAM I., TM2c, USNR.
FULLERTON, CECIL C., TM1c.
GALIMORE, ED M., S1c, USNR.
GALLOWAY, CHARLES M., S1c, USNR.
GARIEPY, MAURICE A., CM2c.
GAYNOR, ROBERT A., MM2c, USNR.
GEESAMAN, LESTER E., GM3c.
GENARO, OTTO, S2c, USNR.
GENT, FREDERICK W., MoMM3c, USNR.
GERAGHTY, JOSEPH P., TM2c, USNR.
GEROULO, THOMAS F., Jr., S1c, USNR.
GIGAC, JOSEPH, TM2c.
GILLIES, KENNETH H., S1c.
GLASCO, CECIL E., SC3c, USNR.
GLEN, WALLACE M., MoMM2c, USNR.

GLOWACKI, STEVE S., S1c, USNR.
GLUSKO, NICHOLAS, QM2c, USNR.
GOODNOFF, SOLOMON, RdM3c, USNR.
GORDON, JOHN E., GM3c, USNR.
GORMAN, ROBERT J., QM2c, USNR.
GRAFF, WILLIAM J., S2c, USNR.
GREEN, Ens. HOWARD I., USNR.
GREEN, Lt. LAURENCE B.
GREENE, EDWARD M., TM3c, USNR.
GREENWELL, CLAUDE, Jr., MoMM2c,
  USNR.
GRENDZINSKI, JOHN J., GM2c, USNR.
GRIFFIN, OWEN P., S1c, USNR.
GROSSMAN, JOSEPH F., MoMM2c, USNR.
GUCKERT, Ens. GEORGE H., USNR.
GUERTIN, DONALD N., GM3c, USNR.
GUINN, Ens. HARRY E., USNR.
HABIG, Ens. LEONARD P., USNR.
HALL, CLIFTON W., QM3c, USNR.
HALL, Lt. CROWELL C., USNR.
HALL, DALLAS E., S1c, USNR.
HALL, JOHN R., F1c, USNR.
HALL, Lt. (jg.) THOMAS C., USNR.
HALL, Lt. (jg.) WILLIAM P., USNR.
HAMILTON, HARRY R., QM2c, USNR.
HAMILTON, Lt. (jg.) RICHARD A., USNR.
HAMILTON, Lt. STUART, USNR.
HAMMOND, JAMES M., CRM.
HANLY, Lt. Cdr. JOHN H., USNR.
HARKNESS, HULON A., S1c, USNR.
HARRIS, CHARLES A., GM2c.
HARRIS, OWEN V., S1c, USNR.
HARVEY, WAYNE G., QM3c, USNR.
HATFIELD, CHARLES H., S2c, USNR.
HEATTER, Lt. (jg.) BASIL, USNR.
HEENAN, LEO J., Jr., GM2c.
HELME, Lt. (jg.) WILLIAM B., USNR.
HENNING, JOHN L., QM2c, USNR.
HENRY, Lt. (jg.) DONALD W., USNR.
HILL, RAYMOND C., SC2c, USNR.
HILLIARD, Ens. HARRY T., USNR.
HIRSCH, MALCOLM L., S1c, USNR.
HOLT, LOUIS A., QM2c, USNR.
HONSTEAD, JAMES M., F1c, USNR.
HOPKINS, JIMMY D., MoMM3c, USNR.
HOPKINS, ROBERT E., S1c, USNR.
HOUCK, GLENN R., RM2c, USNR.
HOUSEL, CLIFFORD B., MoMM2c, USNR.

HOUSTON, JESSE, SM1C, USNR.
HOWELL, HAYDEN B., JR., S1C, USNR.
HOWITT, Lt. ERIC M., RANVR.
HUGGINS, CYRUS F., MoMM1C, USNR.
HUNSUCKER, FRANK E., JR., TM3C, USNR.
HUNT, ALBERT, S2C, USNR.
HUNTER, VELT F., CMM.
INGLE, HARRY A., S1C, USNR.
IRVING, Lt. Cdr. RONALD K.
JACOBS, Ens. EDMUND F., USNR.
JARVIS, WILLIAM L., QM1C.
JENKINS, Lt. (jg.) RAYMOND L., USNR.
JENTER, ELDON C., MM1C.
JOHNSON, Ens. DAVID A., USNR.
JOHNSON, EDWARD C., GM2C, USNR.
JOHNSON, ROBERT W., GM3C, USNR.
JOHNSTON, WILLIAM, MoMM2C.
JONES, Ens. PAUL H., USNR.
JONES, Lt. (jg.) SHELDON C., USNR.
JUMP, CHARLES W., F1C, USNR.
JUNE, GEORGE C., QM3C, USNR.
KALINOWSKI, EDMUND I., MoMM2C, USNR.
KELLY, FRANCIS H., MoMM2C, USNR.
KELLY, THOMAS H., QM2C.
KENNEDY, Lt. DOUGLAS S., USNR.
KERZNER, NICHOLAS A., S1C, USNR.
KESSELL, LEWIS, CM3C, USNR.
KESTER, WILLIAM J., S1C, USNR.
KEYS, FRANCIS D., GM2C, USNR.
KILPATRICK, JAMES W., S1C, USNR.
KINGCAID, MELVIN L., SF2C, USNR.
KINLAW, GORDON B., QM1C.
KIRK, DANIEL E., RM2C, USNR.
KIRK, EARL E., GM3C, USNR.
KIRK, JOSEPH L., MoMM1C, USNR.
KLEINKE, KERMIT W., S1C, USNR.
KNAPP, KAY D., F1C, USNR.
KNOWLES, DAVID W., S1C, USNR.
KOFILE, FRANK, MoMM2C
KOLB, DOUGLAS F., MoMM2C, USNR.
KOONS, CHARLES W., F1C, USNR.
KORT, EDWIN R., F1C, USNR.
KOWAL, MAURICE L., GM3C, USNR.
KRESHA, JOHN G., MoMM1C, USNR.
KUDLA, MATTHEW I., MoMM2C, USNR.
KUHN, WILLIAM A., QM2C, USNR.
KUIKEN, ROBERT, MoMM2C, USNR.

KUPFERER, PAUL L., MoMM3C., USNR.
LAFARNARA, PASQUALE, SC2C, USNR.
LAFORTUNE, ARTHUR, GM2C, USNR.
LAMBROS, Ens. JOHN J., USNR.
LANG, ALAN L., QM3C, USNR.
LARSON, VICTOR H., QM3C, USNR.
LAUTERBACH, Lt. FRED A., JR., USNR.
LAW, LAWRENCE J., S1C., USNR.
LAWLOR, EDWARD T., SC1C, USNR.
LAWRENCE, RAYMOND F., S1C.
LEE, J. W., F1C, USNR.
LEWIS, DONALD K., SC3C, USNR.
LILLIS, Lt. (jg.) PAUL B., USNR.
LITTLE, PHILIP E., S1C, USNR.
LLOYD, FRED B., GM3C, USNR.
LOIZEAUX, PAUL J., TM3C, USNR.
LONG, EUGENE P., RT2C, USNR.
LONNQVIST, JOUKO O., RM2C, USNR.
LOWE, RICHARD F., TM3C, USNR.
LUCKNER, CLINTON T., S1C, USNR.
LYNCH, ROBERT P., GM3C, USNR.
McCARRON, FELIX J, MoMM3C.
McCARTY, PAUL C., SC3C, USNR.
McCLINTOCK, JAMES K., QM3C, USNR.
McCOLGAN, ARTHUR G., S2C.
McDONALD, JOSEPH J., GM3C, USNR.
McKEAN, Lt. JOHN F., USNR.
McKENNA, JOSEPH V., GM3C, USNR.
McLAUGHLIN, ROBERT L., GM1C.
McMAHON, PATRICK H., MoMM2C, USNR.
MacKENZIE, HOWARD G., SM1C, USNR.
MacLEMALE, HARRY A., JR., GM3C, USNR.
MacMILLAN, THOMAS S., RM2C, USNR.
MAGUIRE, JOHN E., RM2C, USNR.
MAHONEY, CHARLES F., TM2C, USNR.
MAKOWSKI, STANLEY J., SC3C, USNR.
MALAK, DONALD J., MoMM3C, USNR.
MALONE, RUFUS E., JR., S1C, USNR.
MANCO, HAROLD V., F1C, USNR.
MARAGOS, JAMES K., SC1C, USNR.
MARCHANT, LAMONT D., M1C, USNR.
MARKS, HAROLD E., JR., GM1C.
MARTELL, GEORGE M., S2C, USNR.
MARTIN, ELMER E., TM2C, USNR.
MARTINDALE, EDGAR E., S2C, USNR.
MARTINEZ, SEFRO, JR., SC2C, USNR.
MARTINO, JOHN, CTM.
MASIAS, RAYMOND P., GM3C, USNR.

MASSE, ROLAND O., GM3c, USNR.
MAUER, EDMAN E., QM3c.
MAY, FORREST L., GM2c, USNR.
MECCA, FRANK, TM2c, USNR.
MELTON, BRENFORD B., MoMM2c, USNR.
MERMELSTEIN, BERNARD, F2c.
MESSIER, ALFRED A., RM3c, USNR.
MILFORD, Ens. ROBERT S., USNR.
MILLARD, FREDERICK P., MoMM3c, USNR.
MILLS, WARREN D., MoMM3c, USNR.
MILLS, Ens. WILLIAM J., USNR.
MIXSON, CLIFFORD M., MoMM1c.
MOELLER, Lt. (jg.) RALPH H., USNR.
MONETTE, LESTER W., S1c, USNR.
MOONEY, CHARLES F., F1c, USNR.
MOREHOUSE, DONALD C., QM3c, USNR.
MORIN, ROBERT L., SC3c, USNR.
MOZINGO, RUSSELL N., SC3c, USNR.
MULLER, Ens. ROBERT H., USNR.
MURNICK, JOSEPH, MoMM3c, USNR.
MYERS, FRANCIS E., TM2c.
MYERS, JOSEPH N., QM2c, USNR.
NADEAU, NORMAN A., GM2c, USNR.
NELSON, EDWIN N., TM2c.
NELSON, RAYMOND J., TM2c.
NELSON, ROBERT W., RM2c, USNR.
NEWLAND, RICHARD D., RM3c, USNR.
NICHOLSON, JOHN M., MM1c, USNR.
NIEMEYER, ROBERT H., Jr., TM3c, USNR.
NORMAND, Lt. (jg.) JOSEPH R., USNR.
NORTON, RALPH D., S1c.
NOUSE, JACK E., RM3c, USNR.
NOVAKOSKI, ALBIN W., MoMM2c, USNR.
NUGENT, ALBERT R., S1c.
NUSSMAN, EVERETT V., TM2c, USNR.
O'CONNELL, HENRY P., GM2c, USNR.
O'DONNELL, EMMET W., MoMM1c, USNR.
O'HERN, JOHN C., QM3c, USNR.
OLSON, WILLIAM W., MoMM2c, USNR.
OLTON, Lt. FRANK H., USNR.
ORR, HERBERT J., RdM3c, USNR.
OSHANN, ROBERT F., MoMM3c, USNR.
OSTERHOLT, THOMAS E. J., MoMM3c, USNR.
OSTROSKY, DANIEL M., SC2c, USNR
OWOCKI, HENRY S., GM3c.
PAGE, JOHN L., RdM3c, USNR.

PALUBICKI, ARTHUR A., RM2c, USNR.
PAQUETTE, ROBERT F., S2c, USNR.
PARAZINSKI, ROBERT J., MoMM3c, USNR.
PARDUE, WILLIAM O., S1c, USNR.
PARKER, KENNETH E., S1c, USNR.
PARKS, Lt. (jg.) ALEXANDER E., USNR.
PASCHAL, DEWITT F., RM2c, USNR.
PATCHETT, WILLIAM L., MoMM3c, USNR.
PATTERSON, Lt. (jg.) GEORGE E., Jr., USNR.
PATTERSON, ISHMEAL L., CM2c, USNR.
PAUL, WILLIAM E., RM3c, USNR.
PAWLOSKI, WILLIAM S., TM1c, USNR.
PAXTON, LEWIS A., MoMM3c, USNR.
PAYNE, Lt. (jg.) DAVID M., USNR.
PELLE, STEPHEN A., S1c, USNR.
PEPPELL, PAUL B., MoMM2c, USNR.
PERRON, HENRY P., GM2c, USNR.
PETERSON, ARTHUR G., TM3c.
PETITT, WILLIAM H., S1c.
PFISTER, ROBERT S., ARM2c.
PIERCE, JACK R., QM3c, USNR.
PIPPIN, RAMON B., MoMM1c.
PIRTLE, WAYNE J., RM1c.
PITTS, RAYMOND H., GM3c.
PLUTZNER, FRANK F., QM1c, USNR.
POLK, DAVID T., QM2c.
POLK, Ens. EDWIN W., USNR.
POLSON, HECTOR G., Cox, USNR.
POUR, CHARLES P., GM2c, USNR.
POWELL, JOHN A., S2c, USNR.
PRICE, LEONARD A., S1c.
RAAB, GEORGE W., GM2c, USNR.
RACKAM, MILTON, MoMM3c, USNR.
RAIA, PAUL J., F1c, USNR.
RAMM, JOSEPH J., RM1c.
RAYMOND, WALTER E., GM3c, USNR.
REILLY, WILLIAM F., GM3c, USNR.
RENARD, ROLAND J., GM3c, USNR.
RENNELL, Lt. PAUL T., USNR.
REQUA, Lt. (jg.) PATRICK A., USNR.
REYNOLDS, WILLIAM G., GM3c, USNR.
RICHARD, ROLAND P., S1c, USNR.
RICHARDS, GARLAN D., S1c, USNR.
RICKETTS, CHAUNCEY J., Jr., TM3c, USNR.
RITCHIE, DANIEL E., BM2c, USNR.
RIZEN, GEORGE E., GM3c, USNR.
ROBERTS, CLARK G., CQM.
ROBERTSON, JOSEPH, S1c, USNR.

Robinson, Joseph T., TM3c.
Robinson, Lawrence D., SC2c.
Roby, James T., S2c, USNR.
Rodriguez, Florencio L., RM1c, USNR.
Rollberg, Raymond A., MoMM2c, USNR.
Rorick, Jimmie H., MoMM2c, USNR.
Rorick, William J., QM3c, USNR.
Ross, Albert P., QM1c.
Rowe, James W., S2c, USNR.
Rudolph, James A., MoMM3c, USNR.
Rupp, William R., MoMM2c, USNR.
Ryan, Robert W., S1c, USNR.
Sabene, Victor, SC3c, USNR.
Salerno, Ralph F., RM3c, USNR.
Salerno, Samuel J., S2c, USNR.
Sanborn, John W., S1c, USNR.
Sand, Norman L., MoMM2c, USNR.
Sanders, Robert A., S1c, USCGR.
Schaffner, Ens. William D., USNR.
Schofield, Richard B., QM1c, USNR.
Scholljegerdes, Walter L., S1c.
Sciutto, August, MoMM2c.
Secor, James R., F1c, USNR.
Secrest, Ens. Richard B., USNR.
Sellars, William G., S1c, USNR.
Seydel, Jack D., S1c.
Sharp, Joseph E., GM3c, USNR.
Sheehan, Edward F., GM3c, USNR.
Silveira, Harvey J., GM3c, USNR.
Simmons, Joseph, Jr., S1c, USNR.
Sintich, George F., MoMM3c, USNR.
Slickers, Ens. Allen, USNR.
Smith, Lt. (jg.) Elmer J., USNR.
Smith, Lt. (jg.) Hamlin D., USNR.
Smith, John F., S1c, USNR.
Smith, Park J., QM2c, USNR.
Smith, Robert, MoMM2c, USNR.
Smith, Sam, StM1c, USNR.
Smith, Stanley A., SC2c, USNR.
Smith, Willard B., GM3c, USNR.
Snoots, Harry F., Jr., F1c, USNR.
Sowers, Robert W., TM1c.
Sparaco, Lt. (jg.) Charles W., USNR.
Spencer, Royston M., RM2c, USNR.
Spurdle, Montague O., MoMM1c, USNR.
Stanich, George, S1c, USNR.
Starita, Joseph R., RM2c, USNR.
Starkey, Orville D., SC1c, USNR.

Stellman, Vincent M., S1c, USNR.
Stevens, John T., S1c, USNR.
Steward, Wilbur P., QM1c, USNR.
Stolwich, Frank S., MoMM3c, USNR.
Stovall, William L., CTM.
Strokus, Joseph M., Jr., S1c, USNR.
Sunderhauf, Ralph A., MoMM2c, USNR.
Surber, Gordon E., TM2c, USNR.
Tall, Elbert W., RM2c, USNR.
Talley, LeRoy F., MoMM3c, USNR.
Tappaan, Lt. Cdr. Francis D., USNR.
Taulman, Carl J., S1c, USNR.
Taylor, Ens. Strawn W., USNR.
Thomas, Ens. Louis E., Jr., USNR.
Thompson, Lt. James R., USNR.
Thurman, Denver L., MoMM2c, USNR.
Tollefsrud, Selvin H., GM3c, USNR.
Torres, Anthony, Cox, USNR.
Trafton, Ward E., MoMM2c.
Tripp, Arnold D., QM2c, USNR.
Turner, James J., III, QM2c, USNR.
Tweedy, Roger W., TM3c, USNR.
Underwood, Harry H., SC3c, USNR.
Vachlon, Albert J., BM2c, USNR.
Valenzio, Vibo V., CPhoM, USNR.
Vanleuven, James E., S1c, USNR.
Viger, Francis F., Jr., MoMM2c, USNR.
Vrbka, Raymond L., S2c, USNR.
Walbridge, Lt. George O. II, USNR.
Walker, Daniel V., S2c, USNR.
Walker, Floyd W., MoMM2c, USNR.
Walker, Horace A., RM1c.
Walsh, George T., SC2c, USNR.
Walter, Robert C., MoMM2c, USNR.
Walters, Frank W., S1c, USNR.
Walton, Robert D., F1c, USNR.
Wasalesky, Charles J., GM1c, USNR.
Watson, Harold E., QM2c, USNR.
Watts, Neill L., TM3c, USNR.
Weber, Henry C., MoMM2c, USNR.
Welch, Cortlandt A., EM3c.
Welch, Myles J., S1c, USNR.
Welsh, Joseph G., TM2c.
Westenberg, Arthur J., GM2c, USNR.
Westmoreland, Thomas F., SC3c, USNR.
Wheelbarger, Frank W., S1c, USNR.
White, John M., TM3c, USNR.
Whitmore, Paul E., RM2c, USNR.

WILBUR, RAYMOND L., S2c, USNR.
WILCOX, WALTER F., QM2c, USNR.
WILDE, Ens. GUSTAV W., USNR.
WILLIAMS, Boatswain DAVID R.
WILLIAMS, PHEOFLESS, StM1c, USNR.
WILLIAMS, Lt. (jg.) ROBERT J.
WILLIAMS, WILLIAM R., GM2c, USNR.
WILSON, JOHN A., S2c, USNR.
WINTER, LLOYD T., GM2c.
WISDOM, VERLE J., Y2c, USNR.

WOLOCKOWICZ, WILLIAM B., MoMM3c, USNR.
WOOD, CALVIN N., TM3c, USNR.
WOOD, DEANE R., CM2c, USNR.
YANCEY, CARLTON L., S2c, USNR.
YOUNG, HOWARD J., SF2c, USNR.
YUHAS, JOSEPH, S2c, USNR.
ZINK, ELLSWORTH S., TM1c, USNR.
ZOLPER, IRA G., GM3c, USNR.

A Note on Sources

A. GENERAL DISCUSSION

The key sources used by the author and the Naval History Division in the preparation and checking of this book were the action reports, war diaries, and other official records submitted by PT units and personnel, together with certain captured German and Japanese records. This material is in the possession of the Naval History Division and is listed in detail in Part B of this note.

In addition to these primary materials, various secondary sources have been used either in the original preparation of the manuscript or in the revisions that were made in 1962. The most important of these books are described below. The author also relied to some extent on correspondence and personal conversations with many of the participants in the actions, particularly for background details not available in the official reports.

For the general course of the war, the indispensable source is Samuel E. Morison's 15-volume *History of United States Naval Operations in World War II* (Boston: Little Brown and Co., 1946–61). In addition, the Navy Department publication *United States Naval Chronology, World War II* (Washington: Government Printing Office, 1955) is of great value.

Relatively few books have been written exclusively on PT boat operations and of those that have appeared few have historical merit. Probably the best books have been written on the loss of President Kennedy's PT-109, including Robert Dono-

van's carefully researched *PT-109* (New York: McGraw Hill, 1961), Chandler Whipple's *Lt. John F. Kennedy—Expendable* (New York: Universal Publishing Corp., 1962), and Richard Tregaskis's *John F. Kennedy: War Hero* (New York: Dell Publishing Co., 1962). This incident was also the subject of an excellent article by John Hersey, "Survival," in the *New Yorker* of 17 June 1944. Edward I. Farley's *PT Patrol* (New York: Exposition Press, 1957) is a colorful book primarily relating the author's own experience as a PT boat officer in the Pacific. W. L. White's *They Were Expendable* (New York: Harcourt, Brace, 1942) is an over-dramatic account of the first Philippine campaign, but one which is still of limited use. An excellent account of British PT operations is contained in Peter Scott's *The Battle of the Narrow Seas* (London: Country Life Limited, 1945). The British boats often operated in conjunction with our PT's.

For the technical development of the PT boat, the best source is an unpublished manuscript in the possession of the Naval History Division, *An Administrative History of PT's in World War II*, prepared by Frank A. Tredinnick, Jr., and Harrison L. Bennett. This manuscript also provides valuable data on the training of PT boat personnel and other administrative matters. Two articles by S. A. Peters, who was personally involved in PT design matters, are also of great value in tracing the technical development of the boats: "The PT Boat" (*Bureau of Ships Journal*, August 1953, pp. 2–8) and "The Motor Torpedo Boat" (*Ordnance*, May–June 1954, pp. 943–946).

There are two basic sources listing Japanese ship losses due to U.S. action: Joint Army-Navy Assessment Committee, *Japanese Naval and Merchant Shipping Losses During World War II by All Causes* (Washington: Government Printing Office, 1947); and General Headquarters, Far East Command, *The Imperial Japanese Navy in World War II* (Tokyo: Far East Command, 1952). An official publication of the Office of the Chief of Naval Operations, *German, Japanese, and Italian Submarine Losses* (Washington: Chief of Naval Operations, 1946) is of value on this subject. Specific claims in all of these sources can be and have been questioned, but together they represent the best information available in print on Axis naval losses.

B. SPECIFIC CITATIONS

Part I. Into Action—Pearl Harbor and the Philippines

1. *The Lineup:* Navy Department, *Navy Directory*, 1941–42 (Washington: Government Printing Office, 1941–42); Navy Department, *Ships Data U.S. Naval Vessels*, 1941–49 (Washington: Government Printing Office, 1941–49); 16th Naval District war diary.
2. *"They Look Like Japs":* MTB Squadron 1 action report of 12 December 1941; *Ramapo* action report of 11 December 1941.
3. *Manila Bay:* 16th Naval District war diary; MTB Squadron 3 action report of 21 May 1942.
4. *The Fleet Withdraws:* 16th Naval District war diary; Narrative of Rear Adm. F. W. Rockwell, 1 August 1942; S. E. Morison, *The Rising Sun in the Pacific*, (Boston: Little, Brown, 1948) pp. 164–83.
5. *SS* Corregidor: MTB Squadron 3 action report of 21 May 1942.
6. *"Motor Torpedo Boats are Rapidly Deteriorating":* 16th Naval District war diary; MTB Squadron 3 action report of 21 May 1942.
7. *Visit to Binanga:* MTB Squadron 3 action report of 20 January 1942.
8. *End of the 31:* PT 31 action report of 23 January 1942.
9. *Gunnery Actions:* PT 41 action report of 18 February 1942; MTB Squadron 3 action report of 1 March 1942.
10. *Return to Subic:* MTB Squadron 3 action report of 26 January 1942.
11. *32 in Action:* MTB Division 9 action report of 3 February 1942.
12. *Subic Again:* MTB Squadron 3 action report of 17 February 1942.
13. *The General Departs:* Narrative of Rear Adm. F. W. Rockwell, 1 August 1942; 16th Naval District operation order of 10 March 1942.
14. *The 32:* PT 32 action report of 15 March 1942.
15. *President Quezon:* Joint Narrative of Ens. D. L. Glover, Chief E. H. Offret, and Chief F. J. Napollilo, 10 February 1944; Narrative of Warrant Electrician W. F. Konko, 16 February 1945; W. L. White, *They Were Expendable* (New York: Harcourt, Brace and Co., 1942), pp. 149–153.
16. *Engagement Off Cebu:* MTB Squadron 3 action report of 12 April 1942; Lt. Comdr. R. B. Kelly, personal letter to the author, 10 April 1946; White, *They Were Expendable*, pp. 161–171.
17. *"We Could No Longer Fight":* Lt. Comdr. R. B. Kelly, personal letter to the author, 10 April 1946.
18. *And Then There Were None:* MTB Squadron 3 action report of 21 May 1942.
19. *End of the Squadron:* MTB Squadron 3 action report of 21 May 1942; Narrative of Lt. Iliff D. Richardson, USNR, 3 January 1945.
20. *"Two Hundred Boats if Possible":* MTB Squadron 3 letter to Chief of Naval Operations, 21 May 1942.

Part II. DEVELOPMENT—A NEW TYPE EMERGES

1. *What is a PT?* Navy Department, *Ships Data U.S. Naval Vessels,* 1941–49 (Washington: Government Printing Office, 1941–49); Frank A. Tredinnick, Jr., and Harrison L. Bennett, *An Administrative History of PT's in World War II;* S. A. Peters, "The PT Boat" (*Bureau of Ships Journal,* August 1953, pp. 2–8); S. A. Peters, "The Motor Torpedo Boat," (*Ordnance,* May–June 1954, pp. 943–946).
2. *Ancient History:* Tredinnick and Bennett, *op. cit.* Records of the General Board of the Navy (file 420–14).
3. *World War I and After:* Tredinnick and Bennett, *op. cit.;* Records of the General Board of the Navy (file 420–14).
4. *Scott-Paine and Vosper:* Tredinnick and Bennett, *op. cit.;* Records of the General Board of the Navy (files 407 and 420–14).
5. *Renewed Interest:* Tredinnick and Bennett, *op. cit.;* Records of the General Board of the Navy (files 420–14 and 407); *U.S. Statutes at Large,* Vol. 52.
6. *The Design Contest:* Tredinnick and Bennett, *op. cit.*
7. *PT 9: Ibid.*
8. *The Elco Contract:* S. A. Peters, "The PT Boat" (*Bureau of Ships Journal,* August 1953, pp. 2–8); S. A. Peters, "The Motor Torpedo Boat," (*Ordnance,* May–June 1954, pp. 943–46); Comdr. Robert B. Carney letter to Secretary of the Navy, 2 November 1939 (in Records of the General Board of the Navy, file 420–14).
9. *The Squadrons:* Navy Department, *Navy Directory,* 1940–41; Navy Department, *Ships Data U.S. Naval Vessels,* 1939–41; S. A. Peters, "The PT Boat".
10. *The 77-foot Boat:* Records of the General Board of the Navy (file 420–14).

11. *Southern Waters and Lend Lease:* S. A. Peters, "The PT Boat"; S. A. Peters, "The Motor Torpedo Boat".
12. *PTC's:* Navy Department, *Navy Directory,* 1941; Navy Department, *Ships Data Book U.S. Naval Vessels, 1949.*
13. *The Plywood Derbies:* U.S. Navy Board of Inspection and Survey, "Report of Comparative Service Tests of Motor Torpedo Boats," 14 August 1941 (in Records of the General Board, file 420–14).
14. *Standardization:* Tredinnick and Bennett, *op. cit.*
15. *Reshuffling the Squadrons: Ibid.*
16. *The Training Center: Ibid.*
17. *Taboga: Ibid.*
18. *Shakedown: Ibid.*
19. *Commissioning Details: Ibid.*
20. *Ferrying Command: Ibid.*
21. *Tenders: Ibid;* Capt. F. A. Munroe, "Munroe's Story or How To Be Happy Through Tending PT's".
22. *Bases:* Tredinnick and Bennett, *op. cit.;* Office of the Chief of Naval Operations, *Catalogue of Advanced Base Functional Components,* 1 November 1944.
23. *Hellcat and Elcoplane:* Tredinnick and Bennett, *op. cit.*

Part III. GUADALCANAL AND BEYOND— THE SOLOMONS CAMPAIGN

1. *Midway: Between Two Campaigns:* MTB Squadron 1 action report of 9 June 1942; Marine Air Group 22 action report of 7 June 1942.
2. *To the South Pacific:* MTB Flotilla 1 action report of 7 March 1943.
3. *The Struggle for Guadalcanal: Ibid.;* S. E. Morison, *The Struggle for Guadalcanal* (Boston: Little, Brown, 1949), *passim.*
4. *Meeting the Tokyo Express:* MTB Flotilla 1 action report of 7 March 1943; Joint narrative of Chief John D. Legg, Chief Arthur Stuffert, Chief Charles Tufts, 9 April 1943.

5. *The Battle of Guadalcanal:* MTB Flotilla 1 action report of 7 March 1943; Morison, *The Struggle for Guadalcanal,* pp. 225–87.
6. *After Tassafaronga:* MTB Squadron 2 action report of 9 December 1942; MTB Flotilla 1 action report of 7 March 1943; Morison, *The Struggle for Guadalcanal,* pp. 337–39; MTB Flotilla and Base Tulagi action reports of 13, 15, and 16 January 1943; Anti-Submarine Incident Folder, 2998.
7. *Evacuation:* Morison, *The Struggle for Guadalcanal,* pp. 366–71; MTB Flotilla 1 action report of 2 February 1943.
8. *A Lull in Operations:* MTB Flotilla 1 action report of 6 March 1943; *Niagara* action report of 8 April 1943.
9. *Loss of Niagara: Niagara* action report of 25 May 1943.
10. *The Stanvac Manila:* MTB Squadron 10 action report of 25 June 1943.
11. *The McCawley: McCawley* action report of 4 July 1943; S. E. Morison, *Breaking the Bismarcks Barrier,* (Boston: Little, Brown, 1950) pp. 146–51; Mine Squadron 2 action report of 10 July 1943; Mine Squadron 2 war diary.
12. *Transition:* Morison, *Breaking the Bismarcks Barrier, passim.*
13. *First Action at Rendova:* Office of Naval Intelligence, "Operations in the New Georgia Area," 1944.
14. *Costly Errors:* MTB's Rendova, action report of 18 July 1943; Marine Fighting Squadron 122, action report of 20 July 1943.
15. *They Didn't Pass the Word:* MTB's Rendova action report of 5 August 1943.
16. *The 109:* Intelligence Officers Memorandum to MTB Flotilla 1, 22 August 1943.
17. *Barge Hunting:* Commander South Pacific Force action reports of 23 October and 23 August 1943; Commander in Chief Pacific action report of 23 November 1943; Joint Intelligence Center, Pacific Ocean Area, Captured Japanese

document item 5782–A; MTB Squadron 9, Summary of Operations, 11 December 1943; MTB's South Pacific Force, "Mosquito Bites," 1 February and 1 June 1944; MTB Squadrons Pacific Fleet, "Information and Tactical Bulletin," January 1944; MTB Squadrons Seventh Fleet, "Information Bulletin," 1 March and 21 October 1944; MTB's Rendova action report of 7 September 1943.
18. *Vella Lavella:* Commander South Pacific Force action report of 22 August 1943; Commander in Chief Pacific action report of 23 November 1943, MTB's Rendova action reports of 25 and 26 September 1943; Morison, *Breaking the Bismarcks Barrier,* pp. 227–28.
19. *Daylight Strikes:* Commander in Chief Pacific action report of 23 November 1943; MTB's Rendova action report of 15 September 1943.
20. *End of the New Georgia Campaign:* MTB Flotilla 1, "Mosquito Bites," 15 November 1943 and 1 February 1944; *Chevalier* action report of 15 October 1943; MTB's Rendova action report of 8 October 1943; MTB's Lever Harbor action report of 30 September 1943; MTB Squadron 19 action report of 16 December 1943; Morison, *Breaking the Bismarcks Barrier,* pp. 241–43.
21. *Treasury and Bougainville:* Morison, *Breaking the Bismarcks Barrier, passim;* MTB's Lambu-Lambu action reports of 23 and 29 October 1943; MTB Squadron 9, "Factual History," 12 October 1945; MTB Squadron 6, war diary; MTB's South Pacific Force. "Mosquito Bites," 1 January 1944.
22. *A Brush with Torpedo Bombers:* MTB Flotilla 1 action report of 14 November 1943; MTB Flotilla 1, "Mosquito Bites," 15 November 1943.
23. *Destroyers Again:* MTB's Bougainville action reports of 8 and 25 November 1943; *Hudson* action report of 9

November 1943; *Anthony* action report of 15 November 1943.

24. *Shore Batteries:* MTB's Treasury Island action reports of 14 November 1943 and 8 January 1944.

25. *To Green Island:* MTB's South Pacific Force, "Mosquito Bites," 1 February, 1 March, and 1 May 1944; MTB Squadron 6 war diary; MTB Squadron 9 war diary; Morison, *Breaking the Bismarcks Barrier*, p. 413.

26. *Collision:* MTB Squadron 23 war diary.

27. *Action in Empress Augusta Bay:* MTBs' Bougainville action report of 26 February 1944.

28. *Rabaul:* MTBs' Green Island action report of 1 March 1944; Task Unit 36.4.1 action report of 1 March 1944; MTB Squadron 11 war diary; MTB's South Pacific Force, "Mosquito Bites," 1 April 1944.

29. *March and April 1944:* MTB's Seventh Fleet, "Information Bulletin," 1 June 1944; MTB's Bougainville action report of 18 March 1944; MTB's Emirau action reports of 28 March, 9, 25, and 29 April 1944; MTB's Green Island action report of 29 March 1944; *Franks* action report of 25 March 1944; *Haggard* action report of 24 March 1944; MTB's South Pacific Force, "Mosquito Bites," 1 May 1944.

30. *The Rugged Life:* Article by Comdr. LeRoy T. Taylor in MTB's Pacific Fleet, "Mosquito Bites," 1 July 1944.

31. *Task Group 30.3:* MTB's South Pacific Force war diary; MTB's Pacific Fleet, "Mosquito Bites," 1 May 1944; Task Group 30.3 action report of 23 June 1944; MTB Squadrons 5, 6, 9, 10, 11, 27, and 28, war diaries.

32. *A Trap:* MTBs' Treasury action report of 6 May 1944.

33. *Task Group 70.8:* Commander South Pacific war diary; MTB's Pacific Fleet, "Mosquito Bites," 1 July 1944; Task Group 70.8 action report of 2 July

1944; Commander Naval Forces Northern Solomons war diary; MTB Squadrons 27 and 28, war diary; MTB Squadrons Pacific war diary; Task Group 70.8 action report of 2 July 1944.

Part IV. SOUTHWEST PACIFIC—CONQUEST OF NEW GUINEA

1. *To the Buna Campaign:* Morison, *Breaking the Bismarcks Barrier*, pp. 27–52.

2. *The Cruise of the* HILO: Capt. F. A. Munroe, "Munroe's Story or How to be Happy through Tending PT's"; Defense Force Funafuti action report of 15 November 1942; Narrative of Lt. E. M. Gordon, 13 January 1944.

3. *Tufi:* Capt. F. A. Munroe, "Munroe's Story or How to be Happy through Tending PT's"; PT 122 action report of 25 December 1942; Task Group 50.1 action reports of 22 January 1943.

4. *Task Group 70.1:* Morison, *Breaking the Bismarcks Barrier*, p. 53; Capt. F. A. Munroe, "Munroe's Story or How to be Happy through Tending PT's"; History of Service Force, Seventh Fleet.

5. *Battle of the Bismarck Sea:* South Pacific Force Intelligence Division, "Report on Destruction of the Lae Convoy," undated; MTB Squadron 8 action report of 4 March 1943; Morison, *Breaking the Bismarcks Barrier*, pp. 54–65; Task Group 70.1 action report of 17 April 1943.

6. *Some Barges and a Fire:* Task Group 70.1 action report of 30 March 1943; MTB's Seventh Fleet war diary.

7. *Douglas Harbor and Morobe:* MTB's Seventh Fleet war diary.

8. *Thursday Island: Ibid;* Morison, *Breaking the Bismarcks Barrier*, pp. 116–117; MTB Squadron 7 war diary.

9. *Kiriwina, Woodlark and Nassau Bay: Ibid.,* pp. 132–37; Task Group 70.1 war diary; Task Group 70.1, intelligence report, 11 July 1943; Morison, *Breaking the Bismarcks Barrier*, pp. 136–37.

10. *Actions in Huon Gulf:* Task Group 70.1 action report of 15 May 1943; MTB's Seventh Fleet, "Information Bulletin", January 1944; MTB Squadron 8 action report of 30 July 1943; MTB's Seventh Fleet war diary; MTB's Seventh Fleet action report of 14 and 27 September 1943; Task Group 70.1 action report of 6 September 1943; Allied Translator and Interpreter Section, Bulletin 548, p. 5.

11. *Lae, Salamaua, and Finschhafen:* Destroyer Squadron 5 war diary; MTB's Seventh Fleet war diary; Task Group 70.1 action report of 3 October 1943.

12. *Morobe: October and November:* MTB's Seventh Fleet war diary; MTB's Seventh Fleet, "Information Bulletin," 1 March 1944; MTB Squadron 8 action reports of 4 and 30 October 1943; MTB Squadron 12 action report of 11 November 1943; MTB Squadron 21 action reports of 23 November and 13 December 1943.

13. *A Letter from General Berryman:* MTB Squadron 12, letter of 1 February 1944, enclosure B.

14. *Tenders, Staff, and Logistics:* Capt. F. A. Munroe, "Munroe's Story or How to be Happy through Tending PT"s"; *Portunus* war diary; Task Group 70.1 war diary; MTB's Seventh Fleet, "Information Bulletin", 1 March 1944 and 15 August 1944.

15. *Kiriwina:* Task Group 70.1 war diary; MTB's Seventh Fleet action report of 18 March 1944; MTB's Seventh Fleet war diary.

16. *Dreger Harbor:* MTB's Seventh Fleet war diary; *Portunus* war diary; LST 201 war diary; MTB's Seventh Fleet, "Information Bulletin," 1 March 1944.

17. *Action on a Reef:* MTB Squadron 18 action report of 27 January 1944.

18. *A Submersible:* MTB Squadron 12 action report of 27 January 1944.

19. *Planes at Arawe:* MTB Squadron 21 action report of 27 December 1943;

MTB Squadron 18 action report of 27 December 1943.

20. *Actions Along the New Guinea Coast:* MTB Squadron 12 action report of 6 January 1944; PT 324 action report of 8 January 1944; MTB's Seventh Fleet action report of 16 March 1944; PT 320 action report of 9 January 1944.

21. *Expansion:* MTB's Seventh Fleet, "Information Bulletin," 1 June 1944; MTB's Seventh Fleet war diary.

22. *Destruction in Hansa Bay:* PT 335 action report of 6 March 1944; PT 338 action report of 7 March 1944; MTB Squadron 24 action report of 12 March 1944; MTB Squadron 18 action report of 8 May 1944.

23. *The Admiralties:* Morison, *Breaking the Bismarcks Barrier*, pp. 432–48; MTB's Seventh Fleet action reports of 19 March, 10 April, 19 April, and 27 May 1944; MTB Squadron 18 war diary; PT 323 action report of 11 March 1944; MTB Squadron 21 action reports of 13 and 24 March 1944; MTB Squadrons 18 and 21 war diaries; MTB Squadron 18 action reports of 15 March, 16 March, and 10 April 1944; PT 363 action report of 12 March 1944; *Oyster Bay* war diary; MTB's Seventh Fleet, "Information Bulletin," 1 June 1944.

24. *Rein Bay and Talasea:* MTB's Seventh Fleet action report of 10 April 1944; MTB's Seventh Fleet war diary; MTB Squadron 25 action reports of 25 April and 11 May 1944; MTB's Seventh Fleet, "Information Bulletin," 1 June 1944; MTB Squadron 8 action report of 19 April 1944; MTB Squadron 25 war diary; MTB's South Pacific Force, "Investigation of an incident involving PT Boats and Aircraft on 28 April 1944," 10 June 1944.

25. *New Britain: South Coast:* MTB's Seventh Fleet, "Information Bulletin," 1 June 1944; PT 146 action report of 17 March 1944; PT 192 action report

of 19 March 1944; PT 150 action report of 19 March 1944; MTB Squadron 7 action reports of 15 April 1944; PT 193 action report of 13 March 1944; PT 196 action report of 13 March 1944.

26. *Saidor:* MTB's Seventh Fleet, "Information Bulletin," 1 June and 15 August 1944; MTB Squadrons 10 and 24 war diaries; PT 339 action report of 3 April 1944; PT 441 action report of 3 April 1944; PT 334 action report of 5 April 1944; PT 340 action report of 5 April 1944; PT 336 action report of 9 April 1944; PT 341 action report of 9 April 1944; PT 337 action report of 8 March 1944; PT 339 action report of 28 May 1944; MTB's Saidor, "Weekly Intelligence Summary," May–June 1944; Destroyer Squadron 24 action report of 13 April 1944; MTB Squadron 24 war diary.

27. *Aitape:* Task Force 77 action report of 6 May 1944; *Oyster Bay* war diary; MTB Squadron 18 action report of 29 April 1944; MTB's Seventh Fleet, "Information Bulletin," 1 June and 15 August 1944; MTB's Aitape, "Weekly Intelligence Report," May 1944; MTB's Seventh Fleet action report of 29 June 1944; PT 129 action report of 4 May 1944; PT 133 action report of 16 July 1944; PT 128 and PT 133 action report of 16 July 1944; PT 130 action report of 27 June 1944; PT 132 action report of 27 June 1944; PT 134 action report of 4 July 1944; PT 189 action report of 3 July 1944; PT 128 action report of 4 June 1944; PT 144 action report of 20 July 1944; PT 149 action report of 20 July 1944; Destroyer Division 48 action report of 14 May 1944; Task Group 75.5.1 action report of 24 June 1944; MTB Squadron 33 war diary; MTB's Seventh Fleet war diary; Destroyer Division 4 action report of 3 September 1944.

28. *Mios Woendi:* MTB Squadron 18, "Weekly Report of Operations," 8 May 1944; MTB's Seventh Fleet, "Information Bulletin," 1 June and 15 August 1944; MTB Base Mios Woendi action report of 24 June 1944; MTB Squadron 18 action report of 12 June 1944; MTB's Seventh Fleet war diary; *Hilo* war diary.

29. *Operations in Geelvinck Bay:* MTB Squadron 21 action reports of 13 June and 12 September 1944; *Kalk* action report of 21 June 1944; MTB's Mios Woendi, "Weekly Intelligence Report," 12–19 June 1944; MTB's Seventh Fleet, "Information Bulletin," 15 August 1944; MTB Squadron 18 war diary; PT 161 action report of 22 June 1944; PT 320 action report of 22 June 1944; PT 193 action report of 25 June 1944; PT 331 action report of 24 July 1944; PT 160 action report of 7 July 1944; PT 320 action report of 16 July 1944; PT 329 action report of 16 July 1944; PT 161 action report of 8 July 1944.

30. *Amsterdam Island:* MTB's Seventh Fleet war diary; MTB's Seventh Fleet, "Information Bulletin," 21 October 1944; MTB's Amsterdam, weekly reports, August–October 1944.

31. *End of the New Guinea Campaign:* MTB's Seventh Fleet, "Information Bulletin," 15 August, 21 October, and 30 December 1944; PT 326 action report of 11 August 1944; PT 325 action report of 17 August 1944; PT 155 action report of 18 August 1944; PT 156 action report of 18 August 1944; PT 326 action report of 19 August 1944; PT 191 action report of 7 September 1944; PT 323 action report of 19 August 1944; PT 329 action report of 19 August 1944; MTB's Seventh Fleet war diary.

Part V. The Aleutians—A Battle Against Weather

1. *A Race for Islands:* S. E. Morison, *Coral Sea, Midway and Submarine Actions* (Boston: Little, Brown, 1949), pp. 160–

84; S. E. Morison, *Aleutians, Gilberts and Marshalls* (Boston: Little, Brown, 1951), pp. 3–19.

2. *MTB Division 1:* MTB Division 1 war diary; MTB Division 1 action report of 15 January 1943.

3. *Squadron 13:* James A. Danver, "Early History of Motor Torpedo Boat Squadron Thirteen"; MTB Squadron 16 war diary; MTB Squadron 16 action report of 21 September 1943; MTB Squadron 13 war diary.

Part VI. THE MEDITERRANEAN—TORPEDO WAR

1. *Squadron 15:* MTB Squadron 15 war diary.

2. *North Africa: Ibid.;* German Naval Staff, Operations Division, war diary; MTB Squadron 15 action report of 23 November 1943; MTB Squadron 15, "Arabian Nights in the Mediterranean: A PT Odyssey".

3. *Bizerte: Ibid.;* MTB Squadron 15 war diary; MTB Squadron 15 action reports of 11 June, 30 June, and 23 November 1943.

4. *Sicilian Invasion:* S. E. Morison, *Sicily, Salerno, Anzio* (Boston: Little, Brown, 1954), p. 28, p. 78; MTB Squadron 15 action report of 23 November 1943.

5. *Palermo: Ibid.;* MTB Squadron 15 war diary; Morison, *Sicily, Salerno, Anzio,* pp. 189–90; MTB Squadron 15 mission report no. 34, 29 July 1943; MTB Squadron 15, "Arabian Nights in the Mediterranean".

6. *Invasion of Italy:* MTB Squadron 15 action report of 23 November 1943; Western Naval Task Force (Eighth Fleet) action report of 11 January 1945.

7. *Maddalena and Bastia:* MTB Squadron 15 war diary; German Naval Staff, Operations Division, war diary; MTB Squadron 15, "Arabian Nights in the Mediterranean"; MTB Squadron 15 action report of 23 November 1943.

8. *Winter Operations:* MTB Squadron 15 war diary; MTB Squadron 15, "Arabian Nights in the Mediterranean."

9. *Collision with a Minesweeper:* German Naval Staff, Operations Division, war diary; MTB Squadron 15 action report of 8 December 1943.

10. *Anzio: Sway* action report of 4 March 1944; MTB Squadron 15 war diary.

11. *TB Destroyers: Ibid.;* MTB Squadron 15 action report of 6 January 1944; German Naval Staff, Operations Division, war diary; MTB Squadron 15 action report of 7 March 1944.

12. *Fun with Rockets: Ibid.;* German Naval Staff, Operations Division, war diary.

13. *Operation Gun:* Captain Coastal Forces Mediterranean action report of 8 March 1944; Senior Officer Inshore Squadron action report of 29 March 1944; German Naval Staff, Operations Division, war diary; MTB Squadron 15 action report of 14 April 1944.

14. *Expansion:* MTB Squadron 15 action report of 3 July 1944; MTB Squadron 15 war diary; MTB's Eighth Fleet war diary.

15. *Corvettes and Destroyers:* MTB's Eighth Fleet action report of 3 July 1944; German Naval Staff, Operations Division, war diary; MTB Squadron 22 action report of 12 June 1944; MTB's Eighth Fleet, "Detailed Interrogation Report of Survivors of German Torpedo Boat 24," 8 April 1945; MTB Squadron 29 action report of 21 June 1944.

16. *Elba:* MTB's Eighth Fleet action report of 26 July 1944; Harold J. Nugent, personal letter to the author, 17 August 1946; MTB Squadron 15 action reports of 25 July and 1 August 1944; MTB's Eighth Fleet war diary; German Naval Staff, Operations Division, war diary.

17. *Capture of an MAS:* MTB Squadron 22 action report of 2 July 1944; Ger-

man Naval Staff, Operations Division, war diary.

18. *The Thunderbolt:* MTB Squadron 29 action reports of 18 and 19 July 1944.

19. *Southern France:* MTB's Eighth Fleet action report of 7 October 1944.

20. *The Advance Landings:* Task Force 86 action report of 21 October 1944; Eighth Fleet action report of 29 November 1944.

21. *Diversionary Operations:* Task Group 80.4 action report of 4 September 1944; *Endicott* action report of 23 August 1944.

22. *Mines:* MTB Squadron 15 action report of 6 September 1944.

23. *Porquerolles:* Cruiser Division 8 action report of 21 October 1944.

24. *The Gulf of Fos: Ibid.;* MTB Squadron 29 action report of 10 October 1944.

25. *Explosive Boats and Human Torpedoes: Catoctin* action report of 30 October 1944; MTB's Eighth Fleet action report of 7 October 1944; MTB's Eighth Fleet war diary.

26. *Last Days at Bastia:* MTB Squadron 29 action reports of 20, 21, and 24 September 1944; German Naval Staff, Operations Division, war diary; MTB Squadron 15 action report of 23 November 1943.

27. *Leghorn:* MTB's Eighth Fleet war diary; Senior Officer Inshore Squadron, "Report of Proceedings," 4 April 1945; German Naval Staff, Operations Division, war diary; MTB Squadron 22 action reports of 1, 18, 20 December 1944 and 10 March 1945; Eighth Fleet, "Detailed Interrogation Report of Survivors of German Torpedo Boat 24," 8 April 1945.

28. *Torpedoing the Harbors:* MTB's Eighth Fleet action report of 4 May 1945.

29. *The Last Patrols:* MTB's Eighth Fleet war diary; MTB Squadron 22 action report of 24 April 1945; Naval Forces Northwest Africa action report of 29 June 1945.

Part VII. THE ENGLISH CHANNEL—D-DAY AND AFTER

1. *D–Day and the Mason Line:* MTB Squadron 2 war diary; A. H. Harris, "U.S.N. Motor Torpedo Boat Activities in the English Channel Area"; S. E. Morison, *The Invasion of France and Germany* (Boston: Little, Brown, 1957), *passim;* Task Unit 124.4.4 action report of 14 July 1944; Narrative of Comdr. John D. Bulkeley, 4 July 1944; MTB Squadron 34 action report of 13 July 1944; MTB Squadron 34 war diary; Task Unit 122.4 action report, no date (serial 0067); MTB Squadron 35 action report of 8 July 1944.

2. *The Channel Islands:* MTB Squadron 34 action reports of 15 and 25 August and 12 September 1944; German Naval Staff, Operations Division, war diary; Personal interview by the author with John L. Page, RdM2c, USNR, 2 April 1946; Harris, "U.S.N. Motor Torpedo Boat Activities in the English Channel Area".

3. *The Eastern Flank:* MTB Squadron 35 action reports of 9, 11, 29, and 31 August 1944; MTB Squadron 30 action report of 17 August 1944; German Naval Staff, Operations Division, war diary.

4. *End of the Campaign:* MTB Squadron 2 war diary; Harris, "U.S.N. Motor Torpedo Boat Activities in the English Channel Area"; MTB Squadrons 34 and 35, war diaries; German Naval Staff, Operations Division, war diary.

Part VIII. SOUTHWEST PACIFIC—RETURN TO THE PHILIPPINES

1. *Morotai:* S. E. Morison, *Leyte* (Boston: Little, Brown, 1958), pp. 19–29.

2. *Rescue in Wasile Bay:* MTB Squadron 33 action report of 17 September 1944;

Carrier Division 22 action report of 10 October 1944.

3. *Losses:* PT 368 action report of 12 October 1944; PT 362 action report of 26 November 1944.

4. *Containing and Harassing:* MTB Squadrons 9, 10, 11, 18, 33 war diaries; MTB's Seventh Fleet, "Information Bulletin," 30 December 1944 and 25 April 1945; MTB's Seventh Fleet, Weekly Intelligence Reports.

5. *Battle of Surigao Strait:* Morison, *Leyte, passim;* MTB's Seventh Fleet war diary; Seventh Fleet action report of 31 January 1945; Cruiser Division 4 action report of 2 November 1944; Fleet Admiral Ernest J. King, *U.S. Navy at War* (Washington: Navy Department, 1946), pp. 121–22; U.S. Strategic Bombing Survey, *Interrogations of Japanese Officials* (Washington: Government Printing Office, 1947), Vol. I, p. 240; MTB's Seventh Fleet action report of 1 December 1944 (enclosing individual boat reports); U.S. Naval War College, *The Battle for Leyte Gulf: Strategical and Tactical Analysis;* MTB Squadron 36 action report of 24 November 1944; Commander in Chief, Pacific, "Operations in Pacific Ocean Area," October 1944.

6. *Air Attacks:* Morison, *Leyte,* pp. 344–60; MTB's Seventh Fleet, "Information Bulletin," 30 December 1944; *Wachapreague* action report of 29 December 1944; *Willoughby* action report of 18 November 1944; PT 134 action report of 26 October 1944; PT 132 action report of 28 October 1944; PT 523 action report of 28 October 1944; *Oyster Bay* action report of 11 December 1944; *Oyster Bay* war diary; MTB Squadron 21 action report of 18 November 1944; MTB Squadron 33 action report of 5 January 1945; PT 494 action report of 8 December 1944; PT 323 action report of 18 December 1944; PT 327

action report of 18 December 1944; PT 532 action report of 11 December 1944.

7. *Leyte and Cebu:* PT 524 action report of 11 November 1944; PT 525 action report of 11 November 1944; PT 492 action report of 11 November 1944; PT 497 action report of 11 November 1944; MTB Squadron 21 action report of 18 November 1944; MTB's Leyte, "Weekly Intelligence Report," 12–19 November 1944; MTB Squadron 7 action report of 8 December 1944; PT 490 action report of 18 December 1944; PT 492 action report of 18 December 1944; Morison, *Leyte, passim;* MTB Squadrons 7, 12, and 25 war diaries; MTB Squadron 33 action report of 18 December 1944; PT 134 action report of 25 March 1945; PT 348 action report of 25 March 1945; MTB's Ormoc, "Weekly Intelligence Reports," March–May 1945; Eighth U.S. Army, "Report of Leyte-Samar-Visayan Operations," no date.

8. *First Days at Mindoro:* Task Unit 78.2.12 action report of 25 December 1944; PT 230 action report of 1 February 1945; PT 77 action report of 6 February 1945; PT 223 action report of 1 February 1945; PT 298 action report of 1 February 1945; PT 297 action report of 24 December 1944; PT 224 report of 24 December 1944; PT 300 action report of 26 December 1944; MTB's Mindoro, "Weekly Intelligence Reports," December 1944.

9. *A Japanese Task Force:* MTB's Seventh Fleet action report of 1 March 1945; MTB's Mindoro, "Weekly Intelligence Reports," December 1944.

10. *Mindoro Convoy:* MTB's Seventh Fleet war diary; Task Group 77.11 action reports of 4, 14, and 20 January and 12 February 1945; MTB's Mindoro, "Weekly Intelligence Reports," December 1944; MTB Squadron 13

war diary; Task Group 70.1 war diary.

11. *Task Group 77.11:* Task Group 77.11 action reports of 14 and 20 January 1945 and 6 and 12 February 1945; Task Group 70.1 war diary; PT 188 action report of 28 January 1945; PT 149 action report of 28 January 1945; PT 338 action report of 2 February 1945.

12. *Mindoro Patrols:* MTB's Seventh Fleet, "Information Bulletin," 25 April 1945; PT 220 action report of 10 February 1945; PT 223 action report of 10 February 1945; MTB's Mindoro, "Weekly Intelligence Reports," January–February 1945; MTB's Seventh Fleet action reports of 16 February, 2 March, and 10 April 1945; PT 73 action report of 31 January 1945.

13. *Bases and Logistics:* MTB's Seventh Fleet, "Information Bulletin," 20 February 1945; MTB's Seventh Fleet war diary.

14. *Lingayen Gulf:* MTB's Seventh Fleet, "Information Bulletin," 20 February and 25 April 1945; MTB's Lingayen, "Weekly Intelligence Reports," January–June 1945; MTB Squadrons Seventh Fleet action reports of 7 April and 13 July 1945; MTB Squadron 28 war diary.

15. *Return to Manila Bay:* Task Group 78.3 action report of 4 March 1945; MTB's Seventh Fleet action report of 14 April 1945; MTB's Seventh Fleet, "Information Bulletin," 25 April 1945; MTB's Subic, "Weekly Intelligence Reports", February–March 1945; MTB Squadron 27 war diary.

16. *Palawan:* MTB's Seventh Fleet, 25 April 1945; MTB's Palawan, "Weekly Intelligence Reports," March–April 1945; MTB's Seventh Fleet, "Information Bulletin," 25 April 1945.

17. *Zamboanga:* Oyster Bay war diary; Task Group 78.1 action report of 26 March 1945; MTB's Seventh Fleet action reports of 2 and 31 May and 5

August 1945; MTB's Seventh Fleet, "Information Bulletin," 15 April 1945; *Pocomoke* war diary; PT 122 action report of 29 April 1945; PT 189 action report of 29 April 1945; MTB's Zamboanga, "Weekly Intelligence Reports," April–May 1945.

18. *Panay:* Eighth Army action report for the period 24 March–16 June 1945, no date; MTB's Seventh Fleet, "Information Bulletin," 25 April and 25 June 1945; MTB Squadron 33 war diary; *Portunus* war diary.

19. *East to Davao:* MTB's Seventh Fleet, "Information Bulletin," 25 June and 10 September 1945; MTB's Polloc, "Weekly Intelligence Report," April–May 1945; *Oyster Bay* war diary; MTB's Seventh Fleet action reports of 16 June and 5 August 1945; Task Unit 70.1.14 action report of 20 May 1945; PT 335 action report of 20 May 1945; PT 343 action reports of 20 May 1945; PT 106 action reports of 20 May 1945; PT 341 action report of 20 May 1945; PT 336 action report of 20 May 1945; PT 334 action report of 20 May 1945; PT 332 action report of 20 May 1945; PT 106 action report of 20 May 1945; MTB Squadron 24 war diary; Task Group 78.2 action report of 22 May 1945.

20. *Tarakan:* MTB's Tarakan, "Weekly Intelligence Reports," May–August 1945; MTB's Seventh Fleet action reports of 5 May and 5 August 1945; MTB's Seventh Fleet, "Information Bulletin," 25 June and 10 September 1945; Task Group 78.1 action report of 5 May 1945; Task Group 74.3 action report of 17 May 1945; PT 523 action report of 1 May 1945; PT 532 action report of 1 May 1945; PT 532 action report of 9 May 1945; PT 528 action report of 9 May 1945.

21. *Tawi Tawi:* MTB's Seventh Fleet action reports of 5, 14, 21, and 27 August

1945; MTB's Seventh Fleet, "Information Bulletin," 25 June and 10 September 1945; MTB Squadrons 8 and 9 war diaries; *Oyster Bay* war diary; MTB Squadron 9 action report of 2 June 1945; PT 130 action report of 30 May 1945; PT 144 action report of 30 May 1945; PT 160 action report of 8 July 1945; PT 187 action report of 8 July 1945.

22. *Brunei Bay:* Task Group 78.1 action report of 19 June 1945; MTB's Brunei Bay, "Weekly Intelligence Reports," June–August 1945; MTB's Seventh Fleet action reports of 10 and 27 August 1945.

23. *Balikpapan:* MTB's Seventh Fleet, "Information Bulletin," 25 September 1945; MTB's Seventh Fleet war diary; PT 359 action report of 30 July 1945; PT 373 action report of 28 July 1945; MTB's Seventh Fleet action reports of 22 and 27 August 1945; MTB's Balikpapan, "Weekly Intelligence Reports," July–August 1945.

24. *MTBRonsPac:* MTB's Seventh Fleet, "Information Bulletin," 25 September 1945; MTB's Pacific war diary; MTB Squadron 31 war diary; MTB's Seventh Fleet war diary.

25. *Surrender:* MTB's Philippine Sea Frontier action report of 10 October 1945; MTB's Morotai, "Weekly Intelligence Report," August 1945; MTB's Seventh Fleet action report of 27 August 1945; MTB Squadron 33 war diary; MTB's Philippine Sea Frontier, "Information Bulletin," 10 September 1945.

26. *The End and the Beginning:* MTB's Seventh Fleet, "Information Bulletin," 21 October 1944.

Index

Ranks and ratings are the highest mentioned in the text. As elsewhere in this volume, they are USN unless otherwise noted (asterisk indicates USNR), but flag and general officer grades are telescoped to "Adm." or "Gen." for compression; only ship names are italicized. Page references in italics are to photos.

Index **561**

The Naval Institute Press is the book-publishing arm of the U.S. Naval Institute, a private, nonprofit, membership society for sea service professionals and others who share an interest in naval and maritime affairs. Established in 1873 at the U.S. Naval Academy in Annapolis, Maryland, where its offices remain today, the Naval Institute has members worldwide.

Members of the Naval Institute support the education programs of the society and receive the influential monthly magazine Proceedings and discounts on fine nautical prints and on ship and aircraft photos. They also have access to the transcripts of the Institute's Oral History Program and get discounted admission to any of the Institute-sponsored seminars offered around the country.

The Naval Institute also publishes Naval History magazine. This colorful bimonthly is filled with entertaining and thought-provoking articles, first-person reminiscences, and dramatic art and photography. Members receive a discount on Naval History subscriptions.

The Naval Institute's book-publishing program, begun in 1898 with basic guides to naval practices, has broadened its scope to include books of more general interest. Now the Naval Institute Press publishes about one hundred titles each year, ranging from how-to books on boating and navigation to battle histories, biographies, ship and aircraft guides, and novels. Institute members receive significant discounts on the Press's more than eight hundred books in print.

Full-time students are eligible for special half-price membership rates. Life memberships are also available.

For a free catalog describing Naval Institute Press books currently available, and for further information about subscribing to Naval History magazine or about joining the U.S. Naval Institute, please write to:

Membership Department
U.S. Naval Institute
291 Wood Road
Annapolis, MD 21402-5034
Telephone: (800) 233-8764
Fax: (410) 269-7940
Web address: www.navalinstitute.org